THE
CAMBRIDGE HISTORY
OF THE BIBLE

THE WEST FROM
THE REFORMATION TO
THE PRESENT DAY

THE CAMBRIDGE HISTORY OF THE BIBLE

THE WEST FROM THE REFORMATION TO THE PRESENT DAY

EDITED BY

S. L. GREENSLADE, F.B.A.

Regius Professor of Ecclesiastical History in the University of Oxford

CAMBRIDGE

AT THE UNIVERSITY PRESS

Published by the Syndics of the Cambridge University Press
The Pitt Building, Trumpington Street, Cambridge CB2 IRP
Bentley House, 200 Euston Road, London NWI 2DB
32 East 57th Street, New York, NY 10022, USA
296 Beaconsfield Parade, Middle Park, Melbourne 3206, Australia

Library of Congress catalogue card number: 63-24435

hard covers ISBN: 0 521 04254 2
paperback ISBN: 0 521 29016 3

First published 1963
First paperback edition 1975
Reprinted 1976

First printed in Great Britain
at the University Printing House, Cambridge
Reprinted in the United States of America
bv Vail-Ballou Press Inc., Binghamton, New York

CONTENTS

PREFACE

The idea of a Cambridge History of the Bible originated within the University Press and was considered, approved and benevolently assisted through its early stages by a committee consisting of Professors M. D. Knowles and Norman Sykes. It was at first intended that the History should appear in two volumes, divided chronologically at the Reformation; and Dr G. W. H. Lampe, then Professor of Theology in the University of Birmingham, and Dr S. L. Greenslade, then Professor of Divinity in the University of Durham, were invited to edit them. In the event, the plan has been extended. The two volumes originally planned will deal with the history of the Bible in the West only, that is, in western Europe and America. A history of the Bible in English, more ample than any recent one, is envisaged, and further volumes may take up other aspects of the story or cover other areas.

The term 'history of the Bible' is used in a limited sense. These two volumes do not include the composition of the individual books, nor the historical and religious background and content of the Bible itself. They are neither a history nor a summary of Christian doctrine, though considerable attention is paid to theories of biblical authority and inspiration and to principles and methods of exegesis. Nor are they a systematic history of biblical scholarship (a subject which deserves separate treatment), though aspects of it are discussed at some length. To put it more positively, we have tried to give in the first two volumes an account of the text and versions of the Bible used in the West, of its multiplication in manuscript and print, and its circulation; of attitudes towards its authority and exegesis; and of its place in the life of the western Church. And, with much reserve, something has been said of the impact of the Bible upon the world. It is believed that the present volume will be found to be reasonably self-sufficient. It will be followed by that edited by Professor Lampe, which covers the period from the Fathers to the Renaissance.

Though the volumes are substantial, they cannot include everything. Selection and proportion have been difficult, in view of the need to take into account the major interests of English-speaking readers. The present editor sympathizes with those of his contributors who would have liked more space, and is grateful for their self-restraint.

The select bibliographies are intended simply to direct attention to the principal works on each subject and to indicate where it may be more fully studied.

Thanks are due, and are offered, to a great many scholars who have generously assisted the contributors. It is not possible to name them all, but we cannot omit to record our deep regret at the death of Norman Sykes so soon after he had left Cambridge to become Dean of Winchester. This volume contains one of his last writings.

S. L. G.

OXFORD
January 1963

CHAPTER I

THE BIBLE IN THE REFORMATION

'SOLA SCRIPTURA'

The reformers dethroned the pope and enthroned the Bible. This is the common assertion; but when so stated it is not valid, because a book cannot replace a man. A book has to be interpreted. This was the main reason why authority had come to be ascribed to the pope in faith and morals. Catholics argued that if there were no infallible interpreter, there could be no infallible revelation. Scripture at many points is not clear, and when a difference of opinion arises as to the meaning, unless there be some authoritative way of knowing which is right, the inevitable result will be uncertainty. If then God desired to make a revelation of himself in Jesus Christ, and the record of that revelation is a document in some respects obscure, God must have ensured the revealing quality of the revelation by establishing an inerrant interpreter, who is able to declare the truth partly because he is the custodian of the tradition and partly because he is guarded from error by the Holy Spirit. This role was assigned by God to the bishop of the church of Rome, founded by the two martyr apostles, Peter and Paul. Her bishop is the successor of Peter to whom were given the keys of the kingdom of heaven.

Such claims Luther roundly denied. In his *Address to the Nobility of the German Nation*, in the summer of 1520, the reformer prayed that he might be given the trumpet of Joshua with which to tumble down the three walls of the modern Jericho. The second of these walls was the claim that the popes

> alone are the lords of Scripture, though by their lives they have learned nothing about it....With shameless words they conjure up the assertion that the pope cannot err in the faith, be he good or bad, and for this they adduce not a single letter [of Scripture]....Since they assert that the Holy Ghost has not deserted them however ignorant and bad they may be, they venture to decree just what they please. But if this be so, what need or use is there for holy Scripture? Why not burn it all, and content ourselves with

these unlearned lords at Rome, who have the Holy Ghost within them, though in truth the Holy Ghost can dwell only in a godly heart...? They must admit that there are many among us, godly Christians, who have the true faith, spirit, understanding, word and mind of Christ, and why then should one reject their word and understanding and follow the pope who has neither faith nor spirit?...Since we are all priests and all have one faith, one gospel and one sacrament, why then should we not have the authority to test and determine what is right or not right in the faith? The word of Paul stands fast, I Corinthians ii, 'A spiritual man judges all things and is judged of none'....Abraham had to listen to Sarah who was more subject to him than we are to anyone on earth, and Balaam's ass was wiser than the prophet himself. If then God could speak through an ass against a prophet, why can he not speak through a godly man against the pope?[1]

Luther here asserted both that the Scripture is the ultimate recourse, and that the pope is not the sole interpreter. Luther was not entirely original at this point, though he gave a sharper edge to positions previously taken. William of Occam had already said that to be saved a Christian is not called upon to believe that which is not contained in Scripture or to be derived from Scripture by manifest and inescapable logic. At the same time Occam was no drastic insurgent. His divorce of theology and philosophy left him without a rational undergirding of the faith, and threw him back upon the authority of the Church. For that reason, he declared himself ready to submit his judgment to hers, should anything in his book be deemed repugnant to received teachings.

Again, the conciliarists appealed to the Bible against the pope. One of them in particular, Nicolo de Tudeschi, known as Panormitanus, made the statement, very congenial to Luther's spirit, that 'in matters touching the faith, the word of a single private person is to be preferred to that of a pope if that person is moved by sounder arguments from the Old Testament and the New Testament'.[2] This saying was so often quoted by Luther, and sometimes without the source, that it came to be attributed to him; but it did not express his full mind, which went far beyond that of the conciliarists, who were concerned to diminish the authority of the pope in order to exalt the authority of councils. And anyone who impugned this authority might be sent to the stake: witness the execution of John Hus with the entire approval of that great

[1] Bonn edition 1, 870–2, Weimar ed. 6, 411–12 (abbreviation hereafter W).

[2] *Abbatis Panormitani Commentaria* (Venice, 1571), Tom. 1, 142. Compare my article 'Probleme der Lutherbiographie', in *Lutherforschung Heute* (1958), p. 27.

conciliarist, Cardinal D'Ailly. Luther found himself driven to challenge the authority not only of the pope but also of councils as interpreters of Scripture.

The stages by which Luther reached this conclusion may be briefly reviewed. In his early period he was influenced by the mystics, who held that the way of salvation is the way of humility and humiliation. God grants his grace only to the humble. Humility does not earn his grace. Humility cannot be a good work. If it made any pretence to be a good work, it would not be humility. But only to the humble can God grant his grace, only to those who make no claim, who accept humiliation. To be saved, one must first be damned.[1] This position demolished the entire concept of merit and excluded the possibility of superfluous credits accumulated in the treasury of the merits of the saints, transferable by the pope to others, even to those in purgatory. The entire theory of indulgences was thus undercut. This attack on the very concept of merit constituted the heresy in Luther's ninety-five theses. When in consequence the Master of the Sacred Palace, on the pope's behalf, declared Luther to be a heretic on the ground that the Church consists representatively in the cardinals and virtually in the pope, and that he who dissents from what the Church actually does is a heretic, Luther retorted that the Church consists representatively in a council and virtually in Christ. The pope may err, so too may councils. The only authority is to be found in the canonical Scriptures. This was in August 1518. In that same year Luther was examined at Augsburg by Cardinal Cajetan who confronted him with the bull *Unigenitus* of Pope Clement VI in which the doctrine of the treasury of the superfluous merits of the saints was set forth. Luther was driven to reject the authority of this bull and thereby, of course, to impugn the authority of its author. 'The new adulators in our day', said Luther, 'have put the pope above a council. They make everything depend upon one man, the pope. There are those who put the pope above Scripture and say that he cannot err. In that case, the Scripture perishes and nothing is left in the Church but the word of man.' The question came up again at the Leipzig debate in 1519 when John Eck told Luther that his teaching betrayed the Bohemian virus, in his reliance 'more on sacred Scripture than on the supreme pontiffs, councils, doctors and

[1] On these themes in Luther's early theology compare Ernst Bizer, *Fides ex Auditu* (1958).

universities...inasmuch as the Holy Spirit does not desert the Church'. Luther replied that he did not disdain the opinions of the most illustrious Fathers, but that clear Scripture is to be preferred. The authority of Scripture is beyond all human capacity, 'councils can err, have erred, and may not institute new articles of faith'.[1] Finally at Worms Luther asserted that unless refuted by Scripture and manifest reason, he would not recant.

The principle of *sola scriptura* had thus come to be affirmed. Nothing as to the faith can be asserted which contradicts or goes beyond Scripture. The Bible is not to be, as it had not been, infallibly interpreted by popes and councils. The true sense has even sometimes been better grasped by godly, though unlearned, laymen.

This position was basic for all the Protestants. Zwingli took his stand on this ground at the first Zurich disputation in 1523 before the city council. The delegates of the bishop of Constance protested that such an assembly could not judge of doctrine and change ancient custom. This only a general council could do. A village like Zurich could not legislate for Christendom. What would Spain, Italy and France and the northern lands have to say on the subject? The universities must be consulted, Paris, Cologne, Louvain. Zwingli facetiously interjected, 'Erfurt and Wittenberg'. Then, when the laughter subsided, he turned to a serious refutation. The present assembly, he declared, was perfectly competent to judge of doctrine and usage, because an infallible judge lay on the table in Hebrew, Greek and Latin, namely Holy Writ. And there were those present quite as conversant in these languages as any at the universities named. Here, the humanist Zwingli assumed that the understanding of Scripture required philological competence. Yet he went on, after the manner of Luther, to say that the assembly contained also Christian hearts who through the spirit of God could tell which side rightly and which side wrongly interpreted Scripture.[2]

Confronted with the charge of innovation, Zwingli replied that he was teaching nothing but that which was fifteen hundred and twenty-two years old. 'We shall test everything', he affirmed, 'by the touch-

[1] W, 1, 2, 391–2. W, 2, 282. *Ibid.* 309, line 34. *Ibid.* 303, lines 16–21.

[2] Zwingli, *Sämtliche Werke*, 1, 479–569 (abbreviation hereafter Z). English translation in S. M. Jackson, *Selections from Zwingli* (1901), pp. 49–57.

stone of the Gospel and the fire of Paul.' The Catholics retorted that the Church must be the lord of Scripture because the Church made the Scripture, inasmuch as the Church determined what books should be included in the canon of Scripture. Zwingli replied that the Gospel did not owe its existence to the sanction of the Fathers. The Gospel of Christ is 'the power of God unto salvation to everyone that believeth'. To say that this Gospel derives its sanction from an assembly of men is blasphemy. The Church did not create the Gospel. The Church merely decided that some books did not proclaim the Gospel, precisely as the reformers themselves were removing corruption.[1]

Calvin had to wrestle with the same objections, which in the meantime had been fully formulated and published by Catholic opponents. 'If the Church had not given its approval,' he demanded, 'would there never have been the doctrine without which the Church would never have existed?' If it be asked how we may know that this doctrine is from God unless we have recourse to a decree of the Church, this is like asking, 'How do we know light from darkness, black from white, bitter from sweet?'[2] One notes that Luther appealed to the Spirit to validate and interpret Scripture. Zwingli added philology, and Calvin adduced plain common sense.

Of all the parties in the Reformation, the Anabaptists were the most scriptural. They were the ones who formulated and adhered to the principle often attributed to Zwingli, that only that which is expressly allowed in the Bible is permissible. The vicar of Constance attempted to pin Zwingli down on this point, and asked him whether he would admit only that which was written in the Gospel. In that case, how could he subscribe to the Apostles' Creed and how could he retain the word *homoousios* in the Nicene Creed?[3] Zwingli's reply was evasive, but that of Conrad Grebel, the Anabaptist, was not, for he said, 'What we are not told to do in clear words and examples [in Scripture] we are to consider forbidden as if it were written "thou shalt not".'[4]

The Thirty-nine Articles of the Church of England include one article 'Of the Sufficiency of the holy Scriptures for salvation'.

[1] *Architeles*, art. LX. Z, I, 319; art. XXXVI. Z, I, 293–4. English translation, *The Latin Works...of Huldreich Zwingli*, ed. S. M. Jackson, vol. I (1912), pp. 250, 280.

[2] *Instit.* I, vii, 1–2.

[3] Z, I, 553 footnote. *Selections*, ed. S. M. Jackson, p. 98.

[4] Harold Bender, *Conrad Grebel* (1950), p. 277, note 89, citing *Epistel*, p. 94.

'Holy Scripture containeth all things necessary to salvation: so that whatsoever is not read therein, nor may be proved thereby, is not to be required of any man, that it should be believed as an article of the Faith, or be thought requisite or necessary to salvation.'

THE CANON OF SCRIPTURE

But if the Scripture were the authority, what then was the Scripture? That question might seem long ago to have been settled because the canon, both of the Old Testament and of the New, had been fixed since the days of the early Church. But if, as the reformers said, the Gospel was prior to the canon and only those books should be received which proclaimed the Gospel, might not the canon be re-examined? Many strictures were actually passed upon the books of the Old Testament and even of the New, both by humanists and reformers. And the outcome might have been a reduction of the canon, but this did not occur. Conceivably the rise of the radicals who disparaged the entire written Word made its defenders more rigid.

Erasmus threw out a disquieting remark in the course of his controversy with Luther over the freedom of the will. In favour of this doctrine Erasmus cited a passage from Sirach in the Apocrypha of the Old Testament. 'I think no one should detract from the authority of this book because Saint Jerome indicated that it did not belong to the Hebrew canon, since the Christians received it into their canon, and I cannot see why the Hebrews excluded it when they included the Parables of Solomon [presumably Ecclesiastes rather than Proverbs] and the amatory Canticles.'[1] The point of Erasmus was to defend Sirach rather than to reject Ecclesiastes and the Song of Songs. But another, reading his words, might have been disposed to take the other alternative.

Luther did not. He answered that though he might exclude Sirach, for the moment he would accept it rather than become involved in a controversy with regard to the canon of the Old Testament 'which you, Erasmus, gnaw and ridicule'. But on other occasions Luther behaved as if he were minded to open a controversy on the canon not only of the Old Testament but also of the New. 'I so hate Esther and

[1] *De Libero Arbitrio*, ed. J. von Walter, *Quellenschriften zur Geschichte des Protestantismus*, VIII (1935), IIa I, pp. 19–20.

II Maccabees that I wish they did not exist. There is too much Judaism in them and not a little heathenism.'[1] II Maccabees was not a great problem, because it belonged to the Apocrypha of the Old Testament which Luther placed in a lower category as suitable for edification but not for disputation. He had good reason to exclude this particular book from disputation because it contains the text on which the Catholics base the doctrine of purgatory (xii. 40–6); but Esther belongs to the canon.

Even more serious was the disparagement of books in the New Testament. Luther's caustic remark about the Epistle of James is notorious: he characterized it as an 'epistle of straw'. As for Revelation, in 1522 he declared that he could not regard it as prophetic or apostolic or even as the work of the Holy Ghost because so replete with visions and images. The worst was that in this book Christ was neither taught nor known. Luther would not impose his own opinion upon others, but for himself his spirit could not find its way into this book.[2]

Yet despite these strictures he did not exclude any of these books from the canon. Whether they were actually written by apostles was to him of no consequence. The whole question of authorship was indifferent. Carlstadt had impugned the Mosaic authorship of the Pentateuch on the ground that Moses could not have written the account of his own death.[3] Luther agreed that this portion must have been appended by another hand, but accepted Moses as the author up to that point. The question, however, was for him entirely immaterial. Luther could not regard Revelation as apostolic or Hebrews as Pauline, but dislodged neither from the canon. The test was whether a book proclaimed Christ. 'That which does not preach Christ is not apostolic, though it be the work of Peter or Paul and conversely that which does teach Christ is apostolic even though it be written by Judas, Annas, Pilate, Herod.'[4]

By this token, however, he should have left out Esther and also Revelation if his statement about it were correct; and James too might well have gone. But they were all retained. The reason in the case of

[1] W, 18, 666, lines 18–22; *Tischreden* (TR), 1, no. 475, p. 208.

[2] Erlangen edition (abbreviation hereafter EA), 63, 115, 169. The Erlangen edition is at this point more convenient for speedy reference because all of the prefaces are collected in a single volume, whereas in the Weimar edition they are attached to the successive editions to which they refer.

[3] Herman Barge, *Andreas Bodenstein von Karlstadt*, 2 vols. (1905), 1, 193.

[4] EA, 63, 156f.

Esther may have been sheer conservatism. In the case of the other two Luther was able to discover words of palliation. 'James', he would concede, 'was a good man who jotted down some remarks made by the disciples of the Apostles. His book is not to be forbidden, because it does contain some good sayings.'[1] The castigation of Revelation cited above is from the preface to the New Testament in 1522. In 1545 it was superseded by another preface which contrived to find in the book a condemnation of Thomas Müntzer and summed up the message of Revelation as this: 'That Christ is with his Saints to the end of the world despite plagues, beasts, and evil angels.'[2] The canon, then, was to be retained.

An actual attack occurred at Geneva in Calvin's circle where Sebastian Castellio, an Erasmian in the courts of the Lord, was denied ordination to the ministry on the ground among others that he rejected the inspiration of the Song of Songs. The ministers of Geneva including Calvin gave this account of the incident:

Castellio said that it was a lascivious and obscene poem in which Solomon described his indecent amours. We told him first that he should not be so rash as to despise the perpetual consensus of the Church universal. There was no book of doubtful authenticity which had not been debated, and those books which we now receive without question were at first disputed. But this book has never been openly rejected by anyone. We told him also that he should not trust so to his own judgment, especially when he advanced nothing which had not been obvious to every one before he was born. As for the book we contended that it was an epithalamium not unlike Psalm 45. The only difference is that the one gives briefly what the other develops in detail. The Psalm of Solomon sings the beauty and adornment of the bride, so that the substance is the same. The difference is merely a matter of style.

When this did not weigh with him we considered what we should do. We were all agreed that it would be dangerous and would set a bad example if he were admitted to the ministry on this condition. To begin with, good people would be not a little offended if they heard that we had ordained a minister who openly rejected and condemned a book accepted as Scripture by all the churches. Further the door would be open to adversaries and detractors who seek to defame the Gospel and disrupt this church. Finally we should be without an answer for the future to any one who wanted to repudiate Ecclesiastes or Proverbs or any other book, unless we wanted to debate whether or no the book were worthy of the Holy Spirit.

[1] EA, 63, 157. [2] *Ibid.* pp. 161 and 168.

That no one may suppose that there was any other reason for Sebastian's leaving we wish to attest wherever he goes that he gave up his position as schoolmaster of his own free will. He has so conducted himself that we deem him worthy of the ministry. He has been rejected not because of any blemish in his character, nor because of failure to accept the fundamentals, but simply for this reason which we have mentioned. The ministers of the church at Geneva. Signed in the name and by the mandate of all, John Calvin.[1]

Yet when Castellio translated the Bible both into Latin and into French, the Song of Songs was not left out. The canon stood.

As for the Old Testament Apocrypha, though retained at a lower level, certain portions were very highly esteemed and none more so than the smallest of all its books, the Prayer of Manasses, because it is so filled with the spirit of contrition. The following portion well exhibits its spirit and shows why Luther and the reformers should have esteemed it so highly. The prayer celebrates the majesty and mercy of God and continues:

Surely thou, O Lord, the God of the just, hast not appointed repentance for the just, for Abraham and Isaac and Jacob who have not sinned against thee; but thou hast appointed repentance for me a sinner: for I have sinned above the number of the sand of the sea. My transgressions are multiplied, O Lord, they are multiplied, and I am not worthy to look at or see the height of heaven, for the multitude of my iniquities, being bowed down by many iron bonds, so that I cannot uplift my head, and there is no release for me, because I have provoked thy anger, and have done evil before thee, not doing thy will, nor keeping thy commandments, but setting up abominations and multiplying offences. And now I bend the knee of my heart, beseeching thy goodness: I have sinned, Lord, I have sinned, and I acknowledge my transgressions: but I pray and beseech thee, release me, Lord, release me, and destroy me not with my transgressions; keep not evils for me in anger for ever, nor condemn me to the lowest parts of the earth: because thou art God, the God of the repenting; and in me thou wilt shew all thy benevolence, for that me unworthy thou wilt save, according to thy great mercy: and I will praise thee continually all the days of my life: for all the host of the heavens sings to thee, and thine is the glory for ever and ever. Amen.

Significantly a woodcut by Holbein portrayed on one side the indulgence traffic and on the other three sinners who because of their penitence were acceptable to God, and one of these was King Manasses.

[1] *Cal. Op.* XI, 674–6 (= *Corpus Reformatorum* 39). See p. 72 below.

THE TEXT OF SCRIPTURE

With the canon settled, next came the question of the text. Reuchlin had shown the necessity in the case of the Old Testament of going behind the Vulgate to the Hebrew, and Lorenzo Valla and Erasmus had insisted in the case of the New Testament that one must have recourse to the Greek. Erasmus cannot be considered a great textual critic. He used only a few manuscripts for his edition of the Greek New Testament, and did not correctly evaluate those employed. But his contribution is not to be minimized, for it was he who first made universally accessible any text whatsoever of the New Testament in the original tongue. The first edition came from the press of Froben in 1516. Cardinal Ximenes rendered the same service for the Old Testament in the Complutensian Polyglot published in 1522, though it had been printed earlier by the Jews. These publications disclosed discrepancies from the Vulgate, in some instances not because the original had been misunderstood but because the same text had not been employed. Nigri made the preposterous proposal that the Jews had falsified the text of the Hebrew in order to eliminate references to Christ.[1] He did little more thereby than to call attention to the problem.

In the case of the New Testament Erasmus shocked contemporaries by omitting the famous proof text for the Trinity in I John v. 7 where the genuine text reads: 'There are three that witness, the Spirit, the water, and the blood, and these three are at one.' The spurious addition amplifies thus, 'There are three that witness on earth, the Spirit, the water, and the blood, and these three are one in Christ Jesus, and there are three that give testimony in heaven, the Father, the Word, and the Spirit'. Erasmus could not find this form in any Greek manuscript, and therefore omitted it. Such was the outcry that he rashly promised to insert the reference to the heavenly witnesses could it be found in any Greek manuscript. One was discovered at Dublin, late and worthless. Erasmus, having sworn to deliver the head of John the Baptist, made the insertion in his second edition in 1519. Happily Luther in his translation did not follow him at this point. But others did, including the King James Version. As late as 1897 the Sacred Congregation of the Holy Office, with the endorsement of Pope Leo XIII, declared the passage to be authentic. Forty years later this decision was

[1] W. Schwarz, *Principles and Problems of Biblical Translation* (1955), pp. 63–4.

reversed.[1] In general it may be said that the sixteenth century became aware of textual problems but made no great stride toward their solution.

Greater gains were made in the area of exegesis. Translation was itself exegesis. And although a detailed account of the translations belongs to another chapter, a word on this score cannot be omitted here. The translator has a twofold task. He must find the best expression to render the sense of the original, but first of all he must determine what was the sense of the original. To do so he will have to be a philologist, an historian and a theologian. There were certain translations in the age of the Reformation deemed highly 'offensive to pious ears'. More complained of Tyndale that he turned 'charity' into 'love', 'church' into 'congregation', and 'priest' into 'senior'. The question here was what the early Church really meant by *agape*, *ecclesia*, and *presbyteros*. The reformers were seeking to divest themselves of the accretions of the ages and projected themselves into the period of the New Testament, that by steeping themselves in its thought world they might recover the genuine meaning of words.

The same problem arose even if one were not translating into a modern vernacular but only into Latin. In this case the divergence from the Vulgate was even more glaring. Erasmus ruffled contemporaries when he rendered *logos* in the prologue of John not by the traditional *verbum* but by *sermo*. The difference in meaning is not great. Both have reference to verbal expression, but *verbum* through usage carries all of the overtones of consubstantiality with the Father, and he who substituted *sermo* might plausibly be suspected of entertaining a lower view of Christ's person.

Even more of an affront was the rendering of *metanoeite* in Matt. iv. 17. The Vulgate had *poenitentiam agite*, which might be taken to mean *do penance*. Erasmus rendered it *resipiscite* which means *be penitent*. With what avidity Luther laid hold of this translation to bolster his critique of the penitential system of the Church!

[1] Preserved Smith, *Erasmus* (1923), pp. 165–6 and Edmund Sinott, *Two Ways to Truth* (1953), p. 161. See also ch. II, pp. 59–61; ch. VI, pp. 203, 233 below.

THE INSPIRATION OF SCRIPTURE

The principle of *sola scriptura* was established. The canon stood, the text was generally accepted, translation produced debates but no serious ruptures. The Protestants rejected any tradition of the Church not deemed consonant with Scripture. And some went further and rejected whatever was not enjoined in Scripture. But by what right? The Scripture was called the Word of God. In what sense was it the Word of God? The Scripture was said to be inspired. How far inspired? In every letter? Were there or were there not levels in Scripture? Were all portions equally to be received? Such were the questions which engaged the reformers as to the meaning and scope of the inspiration of the Scriptures.

The main reformers believed in the verbal inspiration of the Scriptures, though for them the phrase did not carry its modern connotations. Luther affirmed that 'the Bible is the Holy Spirit's own peculiar book, writing and word'. 'God is in every syllable.' 'No iota is in vain.' 'One should tremble before a letter of the Bible more than before the whole world.' Everything in the Bible is to be believed because the book constitutes a whole, 'And he who does not believe one statement cannot believe anything'.[1] For Calvin, the biblical writers were 'the secretaries of the Holy Ghost, *authentici amanuenses, notaires authentiques*'. The Holy Spirit dictated to them; the Holy Ghost determined that the 119th Psalm should be set up alphabetically, and that the cry of Christ *Eli, Eli, lama sabachthani* should have been left in Aramaic without translation. Calvin could speak of the style of the Holy Ghost. To be sure the writers were not mere speaking-tubes like Balaam's ass, and they do exhibit different styles of their own. Yet all of Scripture is to be received as if God were speaking.[2]

Nevertheless, inspiration did not insure inerrancy in all details. Luther recognized mistakes and inconsistencies in Scripture and treated them with lofty indifference because they did not touch the heart of the Gospel. 'The Holy Ghost', said he, 'has an eye only to the substance and is not bound by words.' Luther recognized that Matt. xxvii. 9

[1] W, 1, 648. W, 54, 474. TR, no. 1983. W, 5, 184, line 32. W, 26, 450. W, 56, 249, lines 19–21.

[2] Many passages are collected by Werner Krusche, *Das Wirken des Heiligen Geistes nach Calvin* (1957), pp. 162–74. For *amanuenses* see *Institutes*, IV, viii, 9.

mistakenly cited Jeremiah for Zechariah. 'But such points do not bother me particularly.' He did not know why the Holy Ghost had permitted Matthew and Luke to give unharmonized accounts of the birth stories, but the fact was indisputable. Equally serious was the discrepancy between Matthew who had Jesus enter Jerusalem after the triumphal entry at the end of his ministry and John who placed the entry directly after the baptism at the beginning. 'These are questions that I am not going to try to settle. Some people are so hairsplitting and meticulous that they want to have everything absolutely precise. But if we have the right understanding of Scripture and hold to the true article of our faith that Jesus Christ, God's Son, died and suffered for us, it won't matter much if we cannot answer all the questions put to us.' Stephen's speech in Acts does not accord with the account in Genesis. In this case Luther said that Moses was to be preferred because Stephen was dependent on him. Moses was an historian. Stephen was not punctilious as to the circumstances.

Calvin went into this point more fully. The discrepancy is that in Gen. xlvi. 27 the family of Jacob that went down into Egypt numbered seventy, whereas in Acts vii. 14 the number is given as seventy-five. The mistake goes back to the Septuagint translation. Calvin tried to save Luke by assuming that he was aware of the error and deliberately accommodated himself to the people who would have been disturbed by any divergence from the familiar Greek translation. In that case the Holy Ghost practised deliberate pedagogical inaccuracy. But Calvin like Luther was quite ready to recognize manifest error in the New Testament, in a citation from the Old Testament and in matters of chronology. He would not hold the Holy Ghost responsible for every *dagesh forte*. And the position of the two reformers was well expressed by Luther who recognized that John's Gospel was confused as to the localities where Peter denied Christ, but no one would go to heaven or to hell for believing that all three took place in the house of Caiaphas.

There were those among the reformers who did expend incredible ingenuity on efforts at harmonization. The most outstanding was Andreas Osiander in his *Harmonia Evangelica* (Paris, 1545). The simplest way to achieve a reconciliation between contradictory accounts of the same event is to have the event occur in as many forms and on as many occasions as may be needful to validate all the versions. Osiander posited that Christ must have twice been crowned with thorns and clad in purple, and that Peter must have warmed himself four times. The point was not to emphasize the cold but to accommodate all of the recitals. Luther scorned all such devices.[1] Again, what did it matter whether Christ cleansed the temple once or twice? Luther's point was not so much that harmonization is impossible as that rigorous consistency is so inconsequential as to be unworthy of such effort.

Castellio, the Protestant Erasmian, was more concerned to insist on the impossibility, whatever might be the consequences. He drew out the absurdity in Osiander's method by pointing out to him that since there are four accounts of Peter's denial and four accounts of the prediction of the denial and since the fulfilment must be assumed to have corresponded perfectly to the prediction, therefore to account for all of the verbal differences one would have to assume eight denials. For himself Castellio affirmed that the inconsistencies did not negate the inspiration, but if they did he could not deny the inconsistencies.[2] No one else was quite so blunt, but Luther and Calvin certainly did not deny the discrepancies.

Not only did verbal inspiration not insure inerrancy, it did not even guarantee impeccability. According to Luther the Holy Ghost caused Jacob to deceive Laban. 'Even though this was deceit and falsehood, nevertheless Jacob did it under divine authority...when God commands his saints and faithful men to do anything, without any doubt that deed is right and holy.' Here was the problem of the immoralities of the patriarchs which had long since troubled the Church. If the Holy Ghost was responsible for everything recorded in Scripture without a hint of disapproval, what then should one think of the theft of the Israelites from the Egyptians, the polygamy of the patriarchs, the suicide of Samson, the tyrannicide of Judith, and so on? There were in general three answers. The one was allegory, which denuded the recital completely of its historical meaning. Origen for example held that the Holy Ghost would never have permitted the recording of the Old Testament wars had the reference not been really to conflict with our vices. A second method was that of natural law, in which case some

[1] TR, no. 4567. W, 23, 642. W, 49, 186–90. W, 46, 726, line 11. W, 42, 459–60. Passages collected in Krusche, *op. cit.* p. 180. W, 28, 269. W, 17, 2, 39, lines 29–30. W, 40, 1, 420 and 458. W, 46, 725–38.

[2] 'De Arte Dubitandi', ed. E. Feist (Hirsch), in 'Per la Storia degli Eretici Italiani', *Reale Accademia d'Italia, Studi e Documenti*, VII (1937), 340–2.

extenuating circumstance would be discovered which would bring apparent immorality into accord with universal moral principles, even though at variance with the normal code. The third way was to say that the Old Testament worthies had received a special command from God whose will is necessarily right whatever he commands. As for contemporary ethics, allegory would entirely eliminate the problem. The way of natural law makes the behaviour reputable in the present provided the same extenuating circumstances recur. The way of a special divine command likewise renders the act capable of imitation provided the command recurs. The normal assumption among the Reformers was that God now spoke only through Scripture and consequently the eccentricities and immoralities of the patriarchs were not to be revived. Such was Luther's position, as the following passages illustrate:

If any one wishes to imitate Noah and get drunk, he deserves to go to hell. So Paul swore, but it is not permitted to me.

Samson was called upon by God to plague the Philistines so as to save the children of Israel....But no one will follow this example, be he a true Christian and full of the Spirit....First you must be like Samson; then you may do as Samson.

The Spirit can and does produce works which seem to be contrary to all of God's commands, but they are only against the commands of the second table, which have reference to one's neighbour, and are in accord with the first three commands in the first table, which refer to God. You must first be a Peter, Paul, Jacob, David, and Elias. Then in God's name you may well curse with highest merit before God.

As for the fact that the Jews smashed altars and idols, they had in that time a special command of God for that work, which we in this time do not have. As for Abraham sacrificing his son, he had a special command of God for it.[1]

Calvin pursued the same method, and repudiated tyrannicide, explaining the examples of Moses and Othniel as due to a 'legitimate calling of God', with which they were 'armed from heaven'. Sometimes, however, Calvin adduced extenuating circumstances. For the practice of polygamy Abraham had a special reason which is not valid today, in that it was needful for him to raise up seed for the fulfilment of the promise. Similarly, Jacob was justified in using the handmaids

[1] W, 43, 694. W, 11, 205, line 8. W, 11, 261, lines 16f. W, 17, 2, 32–60. W, 15, 220.

at the instance of his wives, but the taking of Rachel is inexcusable, for this was an indulgence of the flesh.[1]

Some, however, held that the day of special revelations was not closed. This view came to light among the Anabaptists at Münster. Their leader, Bernhard Rothmann, relates that 'we laid off our arms and weapons and prepared us for the slaughter', until God 'through a spiritual revelation' showed us that 'now is the time of the restitution of all things', and that 'we and all true Christians in this time may not only ward off the force of the godless with the sword, but also because he has placed the sword in the hands of his people to avenge all unrighteousness'.[2]

But if inspiration did not mean inerrancy or impeccability neither could it mean uniformity in quality and authority. Certainly an inaccuracy, however trivial, could not have the weight of the unassailable affirmations, and the deviations from morality however explicable could not rank with the Beatitudes. There must be levels in Scripture, not only for these reasons but because the Old Testament cannot rank with the New, not even for those Reformers who like Luther, Zwingli, Calvin, and Cranmer regarded the Old Testament as a Christian book in which the pre-existent Christ was speaking through the mouths of Moses and of David. Yet this Christ in the Old Testament was veiled, and the New Testament was the book of disclosure. The Old Testament was indeed highly esteemed. Luther loved it and devoted actually more time to the exposition of the Old Testament than of the New. On three books of the New Testament he wrote commentaries, Romans, Galatians, and Hebrews, but on five of the Old Testament: Genesis, Psalms, Isaiah, Habakkuk, and Jonah, with lesser treatments of many more. His expositions of the Old Testament books occupy much more space, no doubt in part because the books themselves are more compendious. Yet not without justice has Luther been called an expositor of the Old Testament.[3] And as for Calvin, he was a syste-

[1] *Instit.* IV, XX. *Cal. Op.* X, 258–9. See also ch. IV, p. 146 below.

[2] 'Restitution', *Neudrucke deutscher Literaturwerke*, nos. 77 and 78, pp. 107 and 110. Rothmann says that they were taught 'durch geistlike apenbaringe'. The above passages are taken from my article 'The Immoralities of the Patriarchs according to the Exegesis of the late Middle Ages and of the Reformation', *Harvard Theological Review*, XXIII, I (Jan. 1930), 39–49.

[3] Heinrich Bornkamm, *Luther und das Alte Testament* (1948), illuminating at many points.

matic commentator on the whole Bible, and the Old Testament by reason of its bulk received greater attention. Among the Reformed Churches the Old Testament loomed larger also because it served to provide a framework for the constitution of a Holy Commonwealth. This it could never do for Luther, because he did not believe in the possibility of a Holy Commonwealth.

The Anabaptists exhibited great diversity as to the Old Testament. The Münsterite Bernhard Rothmann said that the core of Scripture, that which may properly be called God's Word, is Moses and the Prophets. But this he said only because of the word of Christ, 'If they hear not Moses and the prophets, neither will they be persuaded though one rose from the dead'.[1] Others among the Anabaptists disparaged Moses on the ground that his covenant was superseded by the new covenant and his law by the new law of the Sermon on the Mount. Naturally all of the pacifist advocates of religious liberty rejected the wars of the Old Testament and would not suffer the frightful treatment recommended for apostates in Deuteronomy xiii to be applied to Christian heretics. Such a view led, however, only to discrimination in the use of the Old Testament. That great champion of liberty Sebastian Castellio wished only that 'the persecutors would select the finer portions of Moses, those which better accord with the mercy of Christ. If only they would imitate the Moses who, though the children of Israel wished to stone him, nevertheless appeased the anger of the Lord against them and desired to be blotted out of the Book of Life rather than that they should perish'.[2] By all Christians the Old Testament had to be received with greater qualification than the New.

An ancient problem, and for Luther a particular problem, was that of the law. The Apostle Paul had said that the law was a schoolmaster to lead us to Christ, but having done so could be dismissed. Yet the book of Deuteronomy pronounced an everlasting curse on any who did not observe the law. Marcion went beyond Paul and rejected not only the law but the book which contained the law. The Church was more discriminating and commonly made a distinction between the ceremonial law which was abrogated and moral law which was binding.

[1] Luke xv. 31. *Von Verborgenheit der Schrift*, ed. G. W. H. Hochhuth (1857), pp. 7 and 15–16. Cf. *Restitution*, pp. 18–21.

[2] *De Haereticis Coercendis*, ed. Van der Woude (Geneva, 1954), p. 144. English translation in R. H. Bainton, *Castellio Concerning Heretics* (1935), p. 230.

This solution could not satisfy Luther, because for him law as law, as a device for satisfying God, could work only damnation since no man can fulfil it. One would think that this view might have led him to reject alike the law and the Old Testament, but not so, because through the Holy Spirit the law can become the Gospel and without the Spirit the Gospel can become the law. And if the Sermon on the Mount be treated as law, it is even more devastating than are the Ten Commandments.

Yet there is no escaping the fact that the Old Testament does contain law, promulgated as law and enjoined to be kept with rewards and punishments attached. Luther handled the problem by making a distinction within the law between that which is of universal validity as an expression of the law of nature such as the commands, Thou shalt not kill, Thou shalt not commit adultery, and the like. The other portion he called the *Jüdisches Sachsenspiegel.* He meant that as the *Sachsenspiegel* was the local law of the Germans, so the Pentateuch and even the Ten Commandments contained portions which were specifically directed to the Jews and only to the Jews. 'I am the Lord thy God who brought thee up out of the land of Egypt.' God did not bring the Germans up out of the land of Egypt. Consequently, this could not be meant for them. The command as to the Sabbath has two aspects. As an injunction to rest one day out of the week it is of universal validity, but as a command to observe Saturday it was directed only to the Jews.

Curiously Luther omitted from the Ten Commandments the one against graven images partly on the ground that it was meant only for the Jews. In consequence Luther's list of the commandments ran in part as follows: (1) Thou shalt have no other gods before me. (2) Thou shalt not take the name of the Lord in vain. (3) Remember the Sabbath day. (4) Honour thy father and thy mother. But Calvin did not admit the validity of Luther's distinction at this point. Consequently his list read: (1) Thou shalt have no other gods. (2) Thou shalt not make unto thee any graven image. (3) Thou shalt not take the name.... (4) Remember the Sabbath day, etc. This is why in Germany the fourth commandment is the one which enjoins obedience to parents and, in Luther's exposition, to all those in authority, including magistrates. But in the Reformed lands the fourth commandment refers to the Sabbath. In England, for example, Nicolas Bownd introduced

Sabbatarianism into Puritan England by his book, *The Eternal Sanctity of the Fourth Commandment.* Luther compensated for his omission of the second on images by making two commandments out of the tenth. For him the ninth forbade coveting the neighbour's house, and the tenth, coveting his wife, etc.[1]

Some of the law then is not binding. But law in so far as it is universally applicable does have a role in the Christian religion. Three uses were assigned to the law. The first was theological. The function of the law is to confront man with a standard which convicts him of sin and induces contrition, humility, and dependence because he is made aware of his failure and inability to fulfil the commands. The second use is in civil and political administration, where obviously law cannot be discarded. The third is for moral guidance. Calvin recognized this use very explicitly, for, said he, 'Though one desire with all his heart to serve the Lord, yet he must give diligence to explore more precisely the *mores* of the Lord that he may conform himself thereto'.[2] Whether Luther recognized at all this third use of the law is debated. He was so much of an antilegalist, so insistent that morality is the spontaneous behaviour of him who is a new creature overflowing with gratitude to his Redeemer, that no prescriptions of any kind should be necessary. Yet Luther emphatically did not abrogate the Christian code of behaviour and stoutly opposed the Antinomians.

Yet for the law Luther did have a third use, which he denominated not moral but spiritual. As such it cut across the line of the Old Testament and the New.

> The law of the letter [said he] is whatever is written in letters, said in words, conceived in thoughts, the tropological, allegorical, anagogical or whatever other mystical sense. This is the law of works, the old law, the law of Moses, the law of the flesh, the law of sin, the law of wrath, the law of death, damning all things, making us all culprits, increasing concupiscence, killing by so much the more as it is spiritual because the command 'thou shalt not lust' makes many more guilty than the command 'thou shalt not kill'. All of these are carnal and literal when the letter has sway and the spirit is absent.

There is also a distinction between the law and the Gospel, but it does not coincide precisely with the Old Testament and the New

[1] Walter Dress, 'Die Zehn Gebote in Luthers theologischen Denken', *Wissenschaftliche Zeitschrift der Humboldt Universität zu Berlin*, Gesellsch. und sprachwiss. Reihe, Nr. 3, Jr. III (1953–4), pp. 213–18.

[2] *Instit.* II, vii, 12.

because there is law in both and Gospel in both. This distinction alone matters. This is the line that cuts through the whole Bible and determines its scale of values. This is the basis for the distinction between Scripture and the Word of God. His Word is also his work. It is both his self-disclosure and his redemptive act in saving men from sin and death through the death and resurrection of his Son Jesus Christ. By believing that this is so, by humble acceptance of God's proffered grace, by utter abandonment of any claim to merit, we are saved by faith. This is the Gospel. This is the Word of God. This 'Gospel is not what was written by Matthew, Mark, Luke, and John.... It is the word concerning the Son of God.'

This Word of God has to be communicated to us and Scripture is the means. 'Scripture is Christ's spiritual body.' 'We must be shown the place where Christ lies. This is the manger where we may find him even though Joseph and Mary are not there. That is to say, that Christ is swaddled in Scripture; the manger is the preaching in which he lies and is contained, and from which one can take food and fodder... it is only a slight and simple word, but Christ is in it.' Without the manger we should not find the Master. 'For though Christ were given and crucified for us a thousand times it were all vain if the Word of God did not come and hand this present to us and say "this is meant to be yours".' Strictly speaking the Word of God is not at all that which is written. 'The Gospel', said Luther, 'actually is not that which is in books and composed in letters, but rather an oral preaching, a living word, a voice which resounds throughout the earth.' Luther looked nostalgically upon the days of Abraham and Noah when there were no books. 'Now we have books, and we have to be suckled from them.'[1]

The distinction between the Word and Scripture accounts for the apparent contradiction that Luther regarded every iota of Scripture as inspired but nevertheless found in Scripture a graded scale of values. Like straw in the manger, one might say that all Scripture was laid there by the Holy Ghost. Yet the straw is not the baby Jesus.

This principle, though not based on rationalism, introduced a rational criterion by which Scripture might be reduced to order. Christ's saving work is the Gospel, and whatever preaches Christ is the Word of God. There is the touchstone. Therefore, Luther said, 'If our adver-

[1] W, 2, 499–500. W, 56, 169, lines 11f. W, 7, 315, line 24. W, 18, 202–3. W, 27, 154, lines 3–5. W, 14, 180, line 25.

saries cite Scripture against Christ, I will cite Christ against Scripture.' 'If a thousand passages in Scripture are adduced in favour of justification by works....I have the author and the Lord of Scripture.' For that reason Luther could introduce into the preface of his first translation of the New Testament in 1522 a paragraph entitled, 'Which are the true and noblest books of the New Testament?' He answered, 'St John's Gospel and his first epistle, St Paul's epistles, especially Romans, Galatians, and Ephesians, and the first epistle of Peter. In these works you will find little about the deeds and miracles of Christ, but you will find a masterly description of the way in which faith in Christ overcomes sin, death, and hell, and gives life, justification, and blessedness.'[1] Then follows the famous characterization of James as an 'epistle of straw'. The Old Testament likewise had its scale. The books there to be preferred were Genesis, because it told how Abraham was saved by faith, the Psalms because of the penitential mood and the assumption that Christ spoke therein, Habakkuk because it contained the verse 'the just shall live by faith', and Jonah because in the dark asphyxiating belly of the whale he composed a psalm of confidence.

THE EXEGESIS OF SCRIPTURE

The Bible then is an inspired book in every part but not with uniform inspiration. The kernel is encased in a shell, the baby lies in a manger, the Word of God is contained. How, then, shall one know which is which? How is Scripture to be interpreted? The answer of all parties was that the Spirit must give the understanding. This was as true for the Catholics as for the reformers. The pope was guided by the Spirit. Luther objected that this spelled the very height of individualism. The Catholics rejoined that if the Spirit were not concentrated in one man, there would be a welter of private interpretations. Luther replied,

> They complain that each interprets the Scripture according to his own spirit, and they would assign to one man, the Roman Pontiff, surrounded only by unlearned sophists, the exercise of the right of interpreting sacred Scripture by virtue of the sole majesty of his sublimity and power against all intelligence and erudition, thus fabricating the view that the Church, that is the pope, cannot err as to the faith....But Scripture is to be understood only by

[1] Paul Drews, *Disputationen Dr. Martin Luthers*, Th. 49 (1896), p. 12. W, 40, 1, 458, line 8f. EA, 63, 114–15.

that spirit in which Scripture was written, because the Spirit is never to be found more present and lively than in the sacred writings themselves. Putting aside all human books we should steep ourselves in Scripture...we must recognize that Scripture is of itself most certain, simple and open. Scripture is its own interpreter, proving, judging, and illuminating everything....I do not wish to boast that I am more learned than all, but that Scripture alone should reign, nor do I pretend that it is to be interpreted by my spirit or that of other men. But I wish to understand it by its spirit.[1]

Luther here assumed the need both of erudition and of the Spirit, not the private spirit of each man but the spirit in which the Scripture was written. In that case the reader of Scripture must be inspired like the writer. But how will such inspiration come to pass? What form will it take? The answers to these questions depended upon the view taken of God's mode of revelation. There were three main positions on this score among the Reformers. The first was tied to history and looked upon the Spirit as the interpreter of a revelation given once and for all. The second was more rational and therefore more universal because the light of reason which lighteth every man that cometh into the world both explicates the Scriptures and gives also to all men, even beyond the Scriptures, a sufficient knowledge for salvation. The third was ecstatic. The Spirit was an inrushing from God, given in the present as in the past and rendering the ancient revelation basically unnecessary.

The first and the main line among the Reformers took the view that Christianity is a religion of history for which the self-disclosures of God are to be found in events. The supreme event was the incarnation of God in Christ. This took place in time. Christ was born when a decree went out from Augustus Caesar and Christ came to baptism in the fifteenth year of Tiberius. God had never so disclosed himself before and has never so disclosed himself since. God is not equally accessible to all men in all times and in all places. He has chosen special moments of revelation. The Bible is the record of the unique revealing. To be in the spirit in which the Bible was given cannot mean that one stands actually in the position of those to whom the message was first spoken. The message does not come to us independently of them. It was given once and for all, in time, in the past. The Spirit enables us in the present only to understand, not to reduplicate or supplement. This was the position of Luther, Zwingli, Calvin and the Anglicans.

[1] W, 7, 96–8.

But precisely what they meant by being in the spirit of Scripture is not easy to define. Emotional warmth was certainly an ingredient. 'The Word of God', said Luther, 'kindles a fire.' He was reproachful of himself and others who on hearing the message of the angels, 'Behold I bring you good tidings', never feel one spark of joy. 'I hate myself because when I see Christ laid in the manger or in the lap of his mother and hear the angels sing my heart does not leap into flame. With what good reason should we all despise ourselves that we remain so cold when this word is spoken to us, over which all men should dance and leap and burn for joy! We act as though it were a frigid historical fact that does not smite our hearts, as if someone were merely relating that the sultan has a crown of gold.'[1]

Luther steeped himself in Scripture, projected himself into the experiences of biblical personages, thought their thoughts after them, and sometimes with more acuteness of feeling than the record itself relates. How Luther marvelled at Noah who had the courage to believe in God's Word and to build an ark when there was no cloud in the sky! How his neighbours must have mocked him for constructing a sea-going vessel far from the coast! It was all the harder for Noah because he lived so long. Not only while the ark was under construction, but for hundreds of years beforehand he must have endured the taunts of unbelievers. 'If I had seen such men in the camp of the ungodly opposing me I should have thrown down my ministry in sheer desperation. Nobody knows how hard it is for one man to stand out against the consensus of all the other churches and against the judgment of his noblest and choicest friends.' 'To be the only one to be wise is hard.' How Luther suffered with Joseph in the house of Potiphar, with Jonah in the whale, with the virgin Mary when the child Jesus was lost, with the Syrophoenician woman when Christ appeared to have called her a dog, and with the Lord himself as he cried out upon the cross 'My God, My God, why hast thou forsaken me?'

Luther in dealing with the Scriptures became oblivious to time. The experiences of biblical characters were his and his were theirs. That is why one will find references to events of his own day in his commentaries at the most unexpected points. When Carlstadt took a farm in order to support himself as a minister by manual labour Luther flung at him the gibe that, did his office permit, he too would much rather

[1] W, 27, 154, lines 3–5. W, 49, 176–7.

dig dirt than carry the load of a parish. This sally is to be found in the commentary on Genesis where the 'sweat of the brow' is made to cover more than literal perspiration. Again in the course of Luther's lectures on Psalm cxii in the year 1526 when the emperor and the princes at the Diet of Speyer were considering how to suppress the Gospel, Luther illustrated the mind of the Psalmist with the remark, 'These good folk do not suppose that God knows what they are up to. They think he has gone to Calcutta or is having dinner with the Moors.' Another example is afforded by the account of Abraham after he had pleaded in vain for Sodom.

He arose before dawn thinking that perhaps God would not be so hard. Filled both with hope and fear he cast about his eyes. How worried he was as he thought of Lot, just as I am about Melanchthon in Frankfurt! But then what? Abraham looked and saw the smoke arising as the smoke of a furnace. It was without flame, otherwise he would have seen it in the darkness. Just a wisp of smoke arising from ashes! He knew that nothing was left. How anguished Abraham must have been! My Lot? What has happened to him? Is he alive? Are his wife and daughters alive? And Abraham broke into tears. 'And it came to pass when God destroyed those cities, he remembered Abraham and he saved Lot from their midst.' Observe in all the sacred history how side by side lie crosses and liberations, sufferings and consolations, tears and joy.[1]

The treatment of the New Testament was no different. That was why an account of Luther's appearance at the Diet of Worms could take the form of a parody of the gospel account of the trial of Jesus. The men of Luther's circle moved in a perpetual passion play. They were themselves taking the parts of the patriarchs, the prophets, the apostles, and even of the Master. This was essentially what was meant by being in the spirit in which the Scriptures were written.

Such an approach disrupted the traditional mode of exegesis. During the Middle Ages the commentators had endeavoured wherever possible to extract from a passage of Scripture four senses. The literal had reference to what happened; the allegorical made words refer by an unnatural meaning to the Church or to some article of the faith; the tropological dealt with morals and the anagogical with hope. Early in his career Luther abandoned this procedure. He is held in consequence to have made an enormous advance in the art and science of exegesis.

[1] W, 42, 301–2. W, 40, 2, 595. W, 42, 157–8. W, 19, 314–15. W, 43, 92–3.

The advance lay more in the form than the substance, because the Middle Ages agreed that the literal was the primary sense and that allegory was not to be used in disputation. Luther never ceased to use it for edification nor could he reject it utterly, since it had been employed by the Apostle Paul who caused Isaac and Ishmael as sons of the free woman and the slave woman to signify the children of Abraham according to the Spirit and according to the flesh. Since the tropological brings out the implications of a passage for conduct and the anagogical for consolation, they could never be ruled out in preaching. The gain lay primarily in the relinquishment of a wooden schematization, with consequent freedom to roam and soar and indulge in interpretations plastic, fluid, and profound.

One must also not forget that Luther did retain allegory of a sort, though that depends on one's belief with regard to the facts of the case. Following Lefèvre d'Étaples he equated the literal sense with the prophetic, and the prophetic meant not a specific prophecy but the forward reference to Christ implicit in and perhaps hidden beneath the description of some purely contemporary event. This might be called the Christian sense as distinguished from the Jewish sense. The rabbis saw in the Old Testament only a plain historical reference. The Christians saw an anticipation of Christ. Now if, as a matter of fact, the Old Testament is a Christian book, if its writers were actually mouthpieces of the pre-existent Christ, if they did foresee his literal coming in the flesh, if they did regard the events of their own time as foreshadowing that which was to come, then the prophetic sense was really the literal sense. This Luther, like Lefèvre, assumed to be the case. But if the rabbis are right that the Old Testament is a Jewish book, then this mode of interpretation is closely akin to allegory. Certainly Luther regarded the Old Testament as a Christian book, and as we have already noted this was the main reason why he kept it in the canon. And that was why in his exegesis he could find Paul's theology in the Psalms. His conviction affected even his translation which in turn confirmed his conviction, because the word *life* in the Old Testament was rendered as *eternal life*, *mercy* became *grace*, and *the deliverer of Israel* was translated as *the Saviour*.

This raises again the problem of linkage between the Old Testament and the New. One way of bridging the gap was by typology. This is not exactly allegory. In John's Gospel we read, 'As Moses lifted up the serpent in the wilderness, even so must the Son of man be lifted up' (iii. 14). The serpent suspended on a pole in the sight of ancient Israel was a type of Christ upon the cross. According to this mode of exegesis the history of the Old Testament becomes as it were a symphony in which a theme is developed with variations, never with exact repetition, but with recognizable adaptations and perchance antitheses leading up to an ultimate resolution. Even so God anticipated the redemption of the world through his Son by the suffering of Abel at the hands of Cain, the near sacrifice of Isaac, and the trials of Joseph at the hands of his brethren. The resurrection was foreshadowed by Jonah's emergence from the whale. The reference in this case could not have been missed because of the verse in Matthew's Gospel, 'As Jonah was three days and three nights in the belly of the whale, even so shall the Son of man be three days and three nights in the heart of the earth' (xii. 40). These prefigurations were systematized in the late Middle Ages, and the *Biblia Pauperum* carried woodcut triptychs with a New Testament scene in the centre flanked by two from the Old Testament as types of the New. Thus the descent of Jesus into the tomb appeared between the descent of Joseph into the well and of Jonah into the whale.

Some have supposed that Luther rejected not only such crude examples but also this whole philosophy of history because for him Christ himself was present throughout the whole of the Old Testament, so that when God spoke through Moses or the Prophets or the Psalmist, Christ himself was speaking. This may be so, but typology is not necessarily excluded, because in the Old Testament Christ was hidden, God was hidden, the Church was hidden. There was thus need for disclosure. One can hardly say that this disclosure was progressive, but it was continuous and the Old Testament figures were types of Christ, not pre-incarnations. Abel was not Christ, nor Isaac, nor Joseph and Jonah, and their experiences were not identical with his. Isaac as a matter of fact was not sacrificed. But similarities of pattern were discernible. God was operating with the constituents of a great intent anticipated prior to its perfect realization in Christ, just as in the succeeding centuries its essential themes have been continually repeated, for every Abel must have his Cain and every Christ his Caiaphas.[1] This the eye of faith discerns. This the Spirit discloses.

[1] W, 42, 189. Cf. Walther von Loewenich, 'Luthers Theologia Crucis', *Forschungen zur Geschichte und Lehre des Protestantismus*, IX (1940).

Luther was quite clear that this approach would not issue in a multiplicity of interpretations because the Spirit is one. Yet it is instructive for us to see how three men, all sinking themselves experientially into the Scriptures, could find in the same account valid yet variant elements consonant with the faith and experience which they brought to the passage. Take for example the story of Joseph sold into Egypt. Luther's attention focused upon Joseph in prison under false accusation from his master's wife with none to vindicate his good name. How he must have wondered whether he would ever be cleared, whether he would be released, whether he would ever see his father and his brethren again.[1] Calvin centred on God's overruling providence. The brothers of course were incited by diabolical fury and had they been possessed of a grain of humanity they would never have sat down to eat after putting their brother down the well. But unwittingly and unwillingly they were the instruments of providence to their own ultimate salvation.[2] But Castellio, the prophet of religious liberty, fastened upon Reuben's device for saving his brother from murder saying, 'Let us not kill him...shed no blood but cast him into this pit...that he might rid him out of their hands, to deliver him to his father again' (Gen. xxxvii. 21–2). In Castellio's version the speech of Reuben is amplified. 'It is a crime to stain our hands in the blood of a boy and a brother at that. Do not do it; you cannot suggest anything worse for our father... does it seem to you so wicked that a callow lad should dream? What harm is there in dreams?'[3] For the first commentator the point was the anguish of the forsaken, for the second the providence of God, and for the third the iniquity of persecution. All three interpretations are valid. Each writer laid hold of a genuine aspect of the scriptural account. The point here is simply that the experiential approach can itself lead to diversity, though not necessarily to contradiction.

But there were also contradictions in interpretation. The Catholics claimed that this was bound to be the case and that the Spirit would not resolve them. Erasmus taxed Luther and even more his followers with relying too much upon the Spirit. The tract of Erasmus on the *Freedom of the Will* against Luther began precisely with this charge.

The question is not as to the authority of Scripture. I confess that the sole authority of divine Scripture is above all the suffrages of human beings. The

[1] W, 44, 372. [2] *Cal. Op.* XXIII, 482–7 and XXIV, 16–24.
[3] *Dialogi Sacri* (1543).

controversy is not about the Scriptures. Each side accepts and reveres them. The point is as to the interpretation....Am I told that there is no need for an interpreter because the sense of Scripture is perfectly plain? But if it is all so plain why have so many excellent men for so many centuries walked in darkness?...But grant what is indeed true, that the Spirit may reveal to the simple and unlearned person that which is hidden from the wise and prudent...nevertheless if Paul in the early days, when the gift of the Spirit was prevalent, commanded to prove the spirits whether they be of God, how much more is this necessary in our carnal age? Where then shall we discover the Spirit? Through learning? Both sides are scholars. Through the life? Both are sinners....Furthermore the whole chorus of the saints believed in free will. You say: true, but they were men. But I am not comparing men with God, but men with men. I am asked what numbers have to do with the sense of the Spirit and I ask what have handfuls to do with it? You ask what the mitre has to do with the understanding of holy writ and I ask what have the sack and cowl to do with it? You ask how does the knowledge of philosophy contribute to the knowledge of the sacred writing? And I reply, how does ignorance help? You ask what good there is in a council in which no one may have the Spirit and I ask, What in a little conventicle where even more probably no one has the Spirit?...The apostles were not believed unless they worked miracles...not because they proclaimed paradoxes.... I am not speaking against Luther whom I do not know personally and whose writings affect me diversely but about some others I know, who, when a controversy arises about Scripture and we cite the ancient interpreters, retort that these were men. If then we ask, seeing that both sides are men, how we are to know the true interpretation of Scripture they answer that they know by the prompting of the Spirit. But if it be asked why those who worked miracles lacked the Spirit rather than themselves they answer that for some thirteen hundred years there has been no Gospel in the world. If you ask of them a life worthy of the Spirit, they say they are saved by faith and not by works. If you call for miracles, they answer that miracles have ceased, and there is no need for them now because Scripture is so clear. If you respond that at this point Scripture is not clear, since so many good men are in the dark with regard to it, the argument has come back to the point at which it started.[1]

At first blush this complaint that Luther and his party relied too much upon the Spirit may seem strange to one familiar with Erasmus who so frequently quoted the text, 'the letter killeth but the spirit giveth life'. He was very fond of upbraiding those who preferred a bone of the Apostle Paul to his spirit shining through his writings.

[1] *De Libero Arbitrio*, I b3–7, ed. Walther, pp. 14–17.

Pilgrimages, relics, fasts, monastic habits, holy days, crucifixes, all of these are vain without the spirit. And with the spirit they are not wrong, yet superfluous. Erasmus was here using the term spirit in a sense different from that of Luther and his circle. Behind the Erasmian terminology lay the Neoplatonism of the Florentine Academy. For this school, spirit is that which is opposed to the material, to the corporeal in man and the physical in the universe. There are grades of value in the great chain of being. The material is below; the spiritual is above. Man lies between. He is the arbiter of his destiny in that he is capable of sinking to the level of the material or of rising to the realm of spirit. The corporeal is an impediment. Such an interpretation was read into the words of the Apostle Paul when he contrasted flesh and spirit. But flesh for him was all that which resists the Spirit and in the sense of the non-corporeal it can itself be spiritual. This was the view of Luther.

The Erasmian position was to have the most disruptive consequences for traditional Christianity and this particularly when taken over into the Protestant camp. Well did Melanchthon remark, 'The views of Erasmus might have caused greater tumults if Luther had not arisen to arrest them...all of this tragedy about the Lord's Supper started from him'.[1] More even was involved than the Lord's Supper because if the physical be an impediment to piety, then religion should divest itself of all external devices such as images and music. Strictly speaking, the bread and the wine in the Lord's Supper should be discontinued or, if they be used, must be treated only as memorials and symbols. The Erasmian influence led to Protestant iconoclasm at the hands of Carlstadt at Wittenberg and of Zwingli at Zurich. One might say that Erasmus was not the author of this tumult but rather Moses who gave the commandment, 'Thou shalt not make unto thee any graven image'. But Scripture cannot have been the primary reason because there were ways of getting round Scripture. One recalls that Luther omitted this command from his list of the Ten Commandments. He did so partly on the ground that it was directed initially only to the Jews who could not be trusted with images, but also on the ground that if the command were of universal application its meaning was simply that images were not to be worshipped. At this point Luther was certainly not fair to the word, because the commandment does not say that images are not

[1] *Corp. Reform.* I, no. 624, cols. 1083–4.

to be worshipped but that images are not to be made at all. Curiously in this instance Carlstadt, who objected to the images as carnal, appealed against them to the letter of the Scripture, whereas Luther insisted on the spiritualization of the meaning.

The reverse was the case when it came to the Lord's Supper. Here Carlstadt and Zwingli insisted that the words 'This is my body' should be taken spiritually, Zwingli in this instance more strongly than Carlstadt who had the peculiar exegesis that Christ was pointing not to the bread but to his own body. But Zwingli cited the text, 'The letter killeth but the Spirit giveth life'. Luther contended that if these words of institution were not decisive, then there was that other word of Paul, 'The cup of blessing which we bless, is it not the communion of the blood of Christ? The bread which we break, is it not the communion of the body of Christ?' (I Cor. x. 16). 'This', said Luther, 'is the *Donnerschlag*, the thunderclap, to demolish Carlstadt and Zwingli.' Here Luther was the literalist.[1]

With regard to music, Carlstadt found it diverting from religious devotion. Zwingli, though an accomplished musician, would not have music in church. Together with the early Anabaptists he found support in Col. iii. 16, 'Admonishing one another in psalms, and hymns and spiritual songs, singing with grace *in your hearts*', the whole emphasis being upon singing internally in the heart, not audibly with the mouth.[2]

The assumption underlying the attitude in these three instances to images, music, and the physical presence in the sacrament was the Neoplatonic disparagement of the physical. Those who entertained this view of the corporeal inevitably spiritualized everything in the Scriptures which did not comport with their position. Conversely Luther, who esteemed and insisted on all three, found ways to circumvent the command against images.

The Erasmian view of the spiritual is closely akin to the rational, which was mentioned above as the second type in the meaning ascribed to spirit by the reformers. In Neoplatonism the realm of the spiritual is the realm of the *nous*, reason, mind, intelligence. The process of

[1] R. H. Bainton, *Here I Stand, a Life of Martin Luther* (1950), p. 200.

[2] Charles Garside, 'The Literary Evidence for Zwingli's Musicianship', *Archiv für Reformationsgeschichte*, XLVIII, 1 (1957), 56–75. Muralt and Schmidt, *Quellen zur Geschichte der Täufer in der Schweiz*, I (1952), 14. Bender, *Conrad Grebel* (1950), pp. 174–6.

salvation must necessarily be a way of enlightenment. For the Christian the end can never be identification with the cosmic intelligence, but only with the Father of our Lord Jesus Christ. Yet God can be conceived in terms of intelligence and the way to him involves the overcoming not only of the corporeal but also of the erroneous. Yet this view did not lead on the part of Erasmus nor later of the writers of the eighteenth-century Enlightenment to the elaboration of an intricate and closely knit theological system like that of Aquinas or Calvin. The enlightenment consisted in the rejection not only of superstition but also of sophisticated speculation about that which cannot be known. Wisdom consists in the recognition of the limits of reason. All the powers with which man has been endowed are to be used within the sphere assigned to him. Therefore the scholar must bring to bear philological tools and historical criticism to the elucidation of holy Scripture, but there is no use prying into the inscrutable.

Nor is there any need, because God has given us all that we need to know in order to be saved. The Scriptures indeed contain conundrums but in all essentials they are plain. The majesty and the mercy of God, the sanctity and the compassion of Christ—these require no demonstration. At this point Erasmus was profoundly affected by the Brethren of the Common Life whose patron saint was the penitent thief because he was saved with so little theology. But this view carried with it also the possibility—and here the rationalism enters—that even outside of the Scriptures the light that lighteth every man may communicate sufficient knowledge for salvation. By this token the pious heathen may be saved. But in that case the great historic drama of redemption, the revelation once and for all in time, is undercut because God discloses to all men in all times all that they really need to know. In that case Christianity ceases to be essentially a religion of history.

With regard to the salvation of the heathen, Luther and Calvin denied them any hope, but Zwingli would admit them to paradise; not for the same reason, however, as Erasmus. In Zwingli's case the doctrine of election cut athwart the drama of redemption. If God from before the foundation of the world had determined that some should be saved and others damned, what real need was there for the drama of redemption? The doctrine of predestination thus tends from another angle to destroy Christianity as a religion of history, though we must recall that those who espoused it did not permit it to go to such lengths.

One observes that the rationalism of Erasmus was in a sense irrationalism because it looked upon many areas of Christian theology as not amenable to rational understanding. And one is not to speak of Erasmus as a rationalist and Luther as an irrationalist without discrimination. Both were irrationalists with regard to some at least of the doctrines because both were Occamists, and Occam had split apart theology and philosophy so that many of the dogmas, notably that of the Trinity, had simply to be believed. Erasmus held that philosophically speaking the doctrine of the Trinity involves tritheism. Luther on this subject said, 'When now I hear that Christ is of one substance with the Father and yet there is only one God, how can I make that out? It sounds preposterous and is not compatible with reason, nor should it be. When I hear the Word of God speak from above, I believe, though I cannot understand, and do not see how I can get it through my head. I can understand that two and five make seven and no one can prove the contrary. But if God from above says that they make eight, then I must believe against my reason and feeling.'[1]

With regard to Scripture Luther like Erasmus was willing to make use of reason in the case of logical deduction and, when at Worms he declared himself unwilling to recant unless refuted by Scripture and reason, he appeared to give reason a scope alongside of and perhaps independent of Scripture. Yet he would reject nothing in Scripture on rational grounds. With regard to the story of the bears which came out of the wood and ate up the little boys who mocked Elisha's bald head, his comment was that this account would 'certainly appear utterly absurd if it occurred anywhere else and were not supported by the authority of Scripture'. Erasmus also would not have rejected the passage on rational grounds, although almost certainly he would have allegorized the meaning rather than attribute such cruelty to God. One wonders indeed whether even Erasmus would have endorsed the views of a Copernicus any more than Luther who insisted that Joshua commanded the sun to stand still and not the earth.[2]

But Luther's irrationalism was basically of another quality. It was moral even more than intellectual, because man is not good enough to understand what God has done. Consider all that is involved in the word of redemption, that God the Creator and Sustainer of the heavens and the earth gave to man paradise to enjoy with lordship over the

[1] W, 37, 402. [2] W, 4, 639, line 24. TR, no. 4638.

beasts of the field, the fish of the sea, and the birds of the air, and then man in utter ingratitude disobeyed his Creator and Benefactor. What then should be done? Luther knew what he would have done. He would have wiped out the human race with brimstone, but God instead sent his only beloved Son that he should lie in the feed-box of a donkey and die upon a cross, that those that believe in him should not perish but have everlasting life. What man would have done so much for his fellow? One can put oneself into the place of Abraham, but how can one put oneself into the place of God and conceive of acting as he has done? Before the condescension and compassion of God we can only stand stupefied, and the trouble with Erasmus, thought Luther, was that he lacked wonder.

There was also another form of irrationalism for Luther, namely to believe that God has done all this for us when experience indicates the contrary. How do events belie his love when man is afflicted, sawn asunder, drowned or burned for the faith? How then shall one believe in the promises of God? Reason and feeling indicate God's rejection. Then one can be saved only by faith.

This entire point of view is of immense importance for the understanding of Scripture. Erasmus could rely upon universal reason, the light that lighteth every man, because for him the darkness was not so intense. For Luther, the light that lighteth every man would at times leave him in utter blackness. Only in Scripture could he find a light to lighten the Gentiles.

If Luther was thought to rely too much upon the Spirit by the Catholics and notably by Erasmus, he was accused of too little reliance by those within his own camp who may be called spiritualists. This term needs to be saved from those who have pre-empted it to signify communication with departed spirits. The word is needed to describe those whose religion centres on the conversion experience, the new birth in the Spirit, the Pentecostal visitation descending like a tongue of fire. Of such was Thomas Müntzer. 'It is of no use', said he, 'to have swallowed the Bible one hundred thousand times.' To which Luther retorted that he would not listen to Müntzer even though he had swallowed the Holy Ghost, feathers and all, unless he adduced Scripture. Müntzer recorded that Scripture as a book would never convince an unbeliever, who can be overpowered only by the living Word of God. Luther, said he, was a scribe, learned in the sacred writing, addicted to the dead letter, a robber of the Bible, stealing its words without their spirit, 'a Bible gobbler'. 'The scribes say, "God does not speak any more. We are rooted in Scripture. We will not believe a new revelation." What would such people have said to the prophets? Would they have believed them or would they have put them to death?' Only the living word matters, the inward word in the ground of the soul.[1]

This expression, 'the ground of the soul', links Müntzer to the medieval mystics, for whom the way of salvation consisted in the overcoming of the I, and the Me and the My, and all that is of the self, that nothing may impede union with the Godhead. The way is a way of ascents. First must come the mortification of the flesh and all desires. The way of salvation is the way of the cross. Suffering must even be sought. Luther retorted that there is no need to go in search of the cross. It will overtake one soon enough. Müntzer railed at him as 'Dr Comfortable', a stranger to the way of mortification. The dying to self rather than the enlightenment of the mind is the path which issues in *Vergottung*, being made God. Thus far Müntzer spoke the language of the mystics. But then came a leap. Mysticism tends to become less and less concrete as the images fade and God becomes all in all. But for Müntzer the Holy Ghost came as a tongue of fire, disclosing revelations even in dreams and visions, making men prophets as of old. Thus in another way the uniqueness of the ancient revelation, given once and for all, was diminished through the universalism of the Spirit.

Spiritualism in Müntzer's case was combined with predestinarianism because the Spirit is not actually given to all but only to those whom God has chosen, his elect. They are able to recognize each other because the experience of the new birth is definite and distinguishable. To this little company, God has given his kingdom and they are to usher it in with the sword of Gideon. Here Müntzer the spiritualist turned to the carnal weapon. This was one reason why Luther claimed that the radicals turned spirit and flesh, inward and outward, upside down. One may well wonder how Müntzer could end with such concreteness, creatureliness and literalism as he did with regard to eschatology and the coming of the Lord. Similarly, Rothman of the Münsterites protested against any spiritualization of the last day.

Curiously perhaps, spiritualism was combined also with legalism. Müntzer would not have a razor touch his face and one may note that

[1] Brandt, *Thomas Müntzer* (1933), pp. 154, 60, 177, 154.

Carlstadt and Zwingli, those spiritualists of another stripe, also ended in legalism. Carlstadt insisted not that a minister might marry but that he must, and Zwingli introduced prohibitions with regard to images and music. The suggestion has been made that spiritualism must issue in legalism as a psychological necessity because the spirit is too rarefied and some return to the world of sense imposes itself. But one may question the validity of this explanation since Denck and Franck do not fit the formula. Several suggestions by way of explanation may be offered. For those with the Neoplatonist disparagement of the flesh, there must almost of necessity be some rules of touch not, taste not. For those who believe in the possibility of a holy commonwealth, there must be some rules for governance. This would apply particularly to Müntzer, Zwingli, and Calvin. And where should those rules more appropriately be found than in the sacred writings which the reformers were endeavouring to rehabilitate? The idea of the restoration of primitive Christianity inspired all of the reformers, but with Luther the restoration applied more particularly to the theology of Paul. For the Reformed churches, however, and especially the Anabaptists, the restitution applied to the way of life in the New Testament. The Sermon on the Mount became a norm for them particularly because they rejected all connection between the Church and the State. Those who accepted this alliance found in the Old Testament a more fitting pattern for their society. Thus it was for the Calvinists.

Again, if, as for Müntzer, the preparation for receiving the Holy Ghost is the way of mortification, then there must be a strict discipline and this readily codifies itself into rules. For Luther mortification was a fruit of the spirit and bound to no prescribed forms. For him the externals were a matter of indifference. They belonged to the *adiaphora*. The doctrine of the Gospel for him was alone essential. Moreover, his definition of inward and outward was quite different. For him the outward was not the physical, nor the inward the spiritual, because the spiritual might be outward. God is outward in the sense of being beyond man. When the spirit of God enters the heart, it becomes inward. When again it bears fruit in good works, it is then outward.[1] The *foci* for Luther were God, man and the world, not spirit and flesh. These are never separated. God himself is in flesh. The incarnation

[1] H. Bornkamm, 'Äusserer und innerer Mensch bei Luther und den Spiritualisten', *Imago Dei, Festschrift G. Krüger* (1932), pp. 85–109.

literally means being in flesh. God is present in all physical reality, and Christ as God is ubiquitous and does not need to be made present in the elements of the Lord's Supper by any miracle. The minister serves not to put Christ into the bread and wine but only to disclose his presence.[1] Spirit and flesh are not separated in man. Both of them together constitute in him a whole, and this is why the physical may be employed as a means of communication with the divine. Music, images and the elements in the sacraments all have their place. Especially, the Word of God does not dispense with the external, nor communicate itself directly, but only through the Scriptures and the sacraments. One is not to listen to those who pretend to revelations and talk of familiar colloquies with the Most High. One does not chat with the Most High. God is a consuming flame.

Müntzer's pretension to prophetic powers was not confined to himself alone. Among the Münsterites there came to be a crop of Elijahs and Elishas making conflicting claims so that the movement recoiled and found itself driven back to the outward Word as a test. When David Joris appeared among the Anabaptists of Strassburg, demanding abject submission to his imperious pronouncements as the third David and the mouthpiece of the Lord, he was told that his word could not be received unless confirmed by Scripture.[2]

The extravagances of the Spirit-filled called forth criticism from those whose variety of spiritualism was properly mysticism. Hans Denck in his closing years, and especially Sebastian Franck, belong in this category. Curiously, Franck ascribed the most eccentric behaviour of the spiritualists to their reliance on the letter because, of course, they always did find some passage in Scripture by way of justification. His method of dealing with them was to confront them with a contradictory passage of Scripture, just as Christ, when the Devil quoted to him the ninety-first Psalm, did not allegorize but adduced against him other passages from the Bible. Contradictions in the Bible, said Franck, are not hard to find because it is a book of paradoxes, a 'book sealed with seven seals which no man can open unless he has the key of David which is the illumination of the Spirit through the way of the cross'. This alone matters. 'The theology of the world is nothing but an idle

[1] H. Bornkamm, 'Das Sakrament', in *Luthers Geistige Welt* (1953), English translation, *Luther's World of Thought* (1958).

[2] R. H. Bainton, 'David Joris', p. 43.

quibble about Moses' grave...ceremonies and elements, as to whether leavened bread may be consecrated, whether Mary was conceived in sin, whether she may be called the Mother of God, questions which are not necessary for salvation, but are rather detrimental.' Franck could consider such questions so indifferent and irrelevant because for him the essential was the mystic way of union with God. And this is not confined to Christians. There is a spark of the divine in all men and to all, even to those beyond the Christian fold, sufficient divine illumination is given to bring them into the way. The Christian drama of redemption is universalized; the incarnation, the atonement, the crucifixion are not isolated events in history, but continually recurring experiences. Christ is born in me and dies in me. And this may happen in all men because 'So far as human language can describe it, the Word of God is nothing other than an emanation, essence, outpouring, image, picture and appearance of God in all creatures, but especially in all surrendered hearts...illumining and teaching them from the beginning, Adam, Abel, Noah, Lot, Abraham, Job, Trismegistus, Mercury, Plotinus, Cornelius, and all the godly heathen.' 'Wherefore my heart is alien to none. I have my brothers among the Turks, Papists, Jews, and all peoples. Not that they are Turks, Jews, Papists, and Sectaries or will remain so; in the evening they will be called into the vineyard and given the same wage as we. From the East and from the West children of Abraham will be raised up out of the stones and will sit down with him at God's table.'[1] Thus Franck's universalism dissolved the Church.

But this certainly was not the conclusion of the Reformation. The main line was that described first above which kept the spirit and the letter in association, which looked upon the Scriptures as the container of the Word of God, uniquely given at a definite point in the past, to be recovered and appropriated in every generation through the inspiration of the Holy Spirit. Not in dreams and visions, not in direct communications, but in a warming of the heart enabling the hearer or the reader to see, feel, participate, and believe in that which God once spoke by the mouth of Moses, the prophets, the evangelists, and the apostles.

[1] *Das verbüthschiert mit siben Sigeln verschlossen Buch* (1539), Vorrede and f. 412*b*, cf. f. 401*a–b*. *Paradoxa* (1534), nos. 200–3. *Von dem Bam des Wissens*, ff. 164–6*b*. *Das verbüthschiert...*, f. 429.

CHAPTER II

BIBLICAL SCHOLARSHIP: EDITIONS AND COMMENTARIES

BIBLICAL HUMANISM AND ITS RESOURCES

Near the time when Lefèvre issued his version of the Epistles of St Paul with commentaries from the press of Henri Estienne at Paris in 1512, he said to the young Guillaume Farel, 'My son, God will renew the world and you will be a witness of it.' Ten years later, he gave as one ground for this hope that, amid the discovery of new lands and the wider diffusion of the name of Christ, 'the knowledge of languages and especially of Greek and Latin (for it was only later that the study of Hebrew letters was reanimated by Johann Reuchlin), began to return about the time when Constantinople was captured by the enemies of Christ...'. Here is confident enthusiasm for the potent renewal, spiritual and intellectual, to be found in a clearer understanding of Latin, Greek and Hebrew. This is something new and fundamental to the cultural world of the early sixteenth century: it cannot be set down as merely a further stage in the development of humanist studies which had begun in the fourteenth century or earlier. There was a *preparatio evangelica* in the first quarter of the sixteenth century, for it was then, and not before, that there appeared in combination the achievements of the humanist scholar-printers; the fruits of intensive study in the grammar and syntax of the three languages; and the energy provided by the economic development and regional patriotism of the cities where *bonae litterae* flourished—Basle, Wittenberg, Zurich, Paris, Strassburg, Geneva.

Further, it was in this period that was felt the full force of the demand—an insistent demand which was not merely captious or irresponsible—for a well-grounded knowledge of the Bible. It is significant too that this demand was coming not only from a scholarly priest like Lefèvre, but also from the educated laity: from a prince like Frederick, Elector of Saxony, from a great lady like Margaret of

Angoulême, and from a member of the city *bourgeoisie* like the Strassburg diplomatist, Jacob Sturm, representative of so many of similar zeal among the citizens of Augsburg, Basle and elsewhere. An attempt to meet this increasing demand can be seen in the large number of vernacular translations from the Vulgate in Germany and France in the later fifteenth and earlier sixteenth centuries. Lefèvre was not alone when he appealed to 'the sovereign pontiff, kings, princes and noblemen, the peoples of every race, to attach themselves only to Christ and the vivifying Word of God, his holy Gospel'.[1] The desire for the knowledge of Scripture, the place where God speaks to men, was insistent in face of the shortcomings and partial breakdown in the life of the Church at this time. The best minds among those who sought to answer this need, whether Catholics or those who were to become Protestants, were not content to submit scriptural interpretation to the old dialectical machinery of the Schools, and sought instead to benefit from the improved resources derived from the return by humanist scholars *ad fontes*, that is, to the original languages of Scripture. The reliability of the current text of the Vulgate began to be doubted by scholars as long ago as Roger Bacon, and this doubt increased until Erasmus, whose reputation was authoritative, said plainly, 'Jerome emended, but what he emended is now again corrupted'. When scholars demanded an authentic text revised by the study of the original languages, and when devout laymen demanded the means for an intelligent understanding of it, three needs required satisfaction. First, the effort to make available the original texts, and the desire that these might be translated into Latin anew; secondly, the production of a standard text (here the scholar-printers were important, for their skills and learning made standardizing possible); thirdly, the work of commentary, from simple marginal note to extensive theological interpretation. It is the purpose of this chapter to show briefly the ways in which these requirements were met.

The first step was for scholars to master the discipline of grammar in the three languages. Bad style and inferior vocabulary had come to imply not merely dullness but moral obloquy. It was felt that a purified and supple latinity must be the introduction to Hebrew and Greek

[1] Lefèvre's words to Farel are referred to in A.-L. Herminjard, *Correspondance des Réformateurs* (1866), I, 15. The other quotations from Lefèvre are taken from his address to the Christian reader in his *Commentarii Initiatorii in Quatuor Evangelia* (1522).

studies, *bonae litterae* must serve *sacrae litterae*. This emphasis is made plain in the inaugural lecture given by Melanchthon on his appointment, at the age of twenty-one, as professor of Greek at Wittenberg in 1518, where his enthusiasm startled and delighted his audience as he spoke of the vivifying study of Hebrew, Greek and Latin. Both his directness and his aspiration can be seen in these words, 'Now away with so many frigid petty glosses, these harmonizings and "disharmonies" and other hindrances to intelligence, and when we shall have redirected our minds to the sources, we shall begin to taste Christ. His command will become clear to us, and we shall become suffused with that blessed nectar of divine wisdom.'[1]

It was the desired but not always attainable goal of many a humanist of the early sixteenth century to be *trium linguarum gnarus*.[2] Yet this was a laborious task in view of the lack of resources; it was essential to provide colleges to aid the young scholar, and no less essential (though more difficult to fulfil) to find scholars competent to teach in them. Powerful patronage met this need in founding the trilingual colleges. In England, Bishop Fox founded Corpus Christi College, Oxford. In Spain, Cardinal Ximenes established the new university at Alcalá, which soon concentrated its attention on trilingual studies. In France, Francis I provided the *noble et trilingue Académie*, the *Collège des Lecteurs Royaux*, later to be called the *Collège de France*. In Germany, Frederick of Saxony endowed the University of Wittenberg with chairs in the three languages. After considerable opposition a trilingual college was established at Louvain. England lagged some way behind these other centres whose important contributions to biblical studies will be shown later. It was one thing to found a trilingual college but another thing to obtain competent teachers; this was England's chief problem in the field at the time. At the end of the fifteenth century very few humanist scholars had a sound knowledge of Greek. Erasmus gained his mastery of it only by expense of time and money, and by travelling far to find teachers to aid him.

Latin was important because some held it to be essential to have a

[1] Melanchthon, *Corpus Reformatorum*, *Melanchthonis Opera*, eds. Bretschneider and Bindseil (1834–60), XI, 23: 'Facessent iam tot frigidae glossulae, concordantiae, discordantiae, et si quae sunt aliae ingenii remorae. Atque cum animos ad fontes contulerimus, Christum sapere incipiemus, mandatum eius lucidum nobis fiet et nectare illo beato divinae sapientiae perfundemur.'

[2] 'Well acquainted with the three languages', that is, Hebrew, Greek, Latin.

well-articulated latinity so that the Hebrew 'verity' and the Greek of the New Testament could be translated afresh. For others, good latinity was held to be needed to assist the effective emendation of the corruptions which had come into the Vulgate text. Moreover, many a devout scholar believed that purification of Latin style would bring purification and renewal in theology. This renewal of good Latin was effective in Italy as early as 1444 when Valla showed in the very title of his frequently printed book one aspect of what was required, *Elegantiae Latini Sermonis*. A useful grammar, however, did not appear before 1501 when Aldus Manutius, the first of those humanist printers whose aid in trilingual studies was to prove so effective, issued his *Institutiones Grammaticae*. The effort to establish good Latin was now moved northwards, first to England where Linacre prepared his dull but sound work on grammar (this was later translated into Latin by the Scottish humanist Buchanan and became popular abroad), and followed it up with his difficult work on syntax which endured long enough at our universities for Milton to complain of it. Two other Englishmen, Lily and Colet, also urged the virtues of studying syntax. Erasmus praised this English work and then did even better, for, after re-editing the combined English studies, he published in 1528 a book on the right pronunciation of Latin and Greek which showed the concern to avoid treating these as merely dead languages. Men of conservative mind, and less committed to the 'new learning', were disturbed by this; for example, Bishop Gardiner threatened expulsion to any undergraduate at Cambridge who used the new system. Melanchthon in 1526 produced both a Latin grammar and a syntax which show him well on the way to deserving his future fame as the 'Preceptor of Germany'. The next important development was in France where Dolet published his *Commentariorum Linguae Latinae Tomus primus* (1536), *et Tomus Secundus* (1538); and Cordier, who gave the young Calvin his taste for humanist studies, condemned bad latinity in his *De corruptelis sermonis apud Gallos et loquendi Latine ratione libellus* (1530). The pressure of these and other works made eager minds desire a mastery of style capable of expressing delicate shades of meaning, and a linguistic skill which could replace, for these new studies, the technical Latin idiom of scholastic philosophy and theology which, though valid for precision in its own field, was too unyielding and limited for the work of biblical translation and commentary.

The theologians of Paris, Cologne and Louvain, and men of the 'old learning' in general, were suspicious of this 'new learning'. Greek was regarded as the language of the eastern heretics and schismatics; therefore, good work in Greek had to struggle against this traditional disapproval. However, sound foundations for the improved knowledge of Greek owed much to these Latin studies which in turn stimulated the quest for the mastery of Greek style and the extensive grammatical work this required. Here it was unfortunate that western scholars borrowed too readily from the Alexandrian theorists of grammar; for Apollonius Moschopoulos and the rest led many sixteenth-century humanists wandering in a prolific undergrowth of rhetorical figures. Again, when Melanchthon in the lecture already quoted said, 'Homerum habemus in manibus, habemus et Pauli epistolam ad Titum', he must have brought some struggling Wittenberg students near to despair when thus sharply introduced to the full range of diversity in Greek. This underlines too the tendency of that age to come to the study of Greek through the Classics and the Eastern Fathers, with the consequent failure to allow sufficiently for the importance of the Semitic idiom which lay behind the Septuagint and the New Testament. This was not satisfactorily studied until the next century and later. But the humanists' enthusiasm for Greek learning was intense. Nearly forty grammars were published in as many years. Among these appear familiar names. The third book to come from the press of Aldus Manutius was the Greek grammar of Lascaris, 1495, and in his preface these significant words occur, 'There is a multitude of those who yearn to be well-instructed in Greek'. In 1516 Erasmus issued his translation of the Greek grammar of Theodore of Gaza, and Melanchthon published in the year of his professorial inauguration, 1518, an elementary Greek grammar. Later, Budé at Paris made France famous among humanists by his profound but difficult to use *Commentarii Linguae Graecae* of 1520. (This was to draw from Calvin, who was never to lose the humanist's concern for integrity of scholarship, praise for this product of his fellow-countryman's linguistic studies, 'Today Budaeus appropriates for our France the palm of erudition'.) However, Erasmus—in his work on the correct pronunciation of Greek and Latin—had to protest against a general tendency to maintain an old tradition in grammatical nomenclature. The force of his argument was not to be clearly seen until after 1540. Robert Estienne, ever practical as well as scholarly, helped to meet this need for better nomenclature by publishing 'Alphabets' of Greek which gave a clear analysis of the elementary rules of grammar. But the production of dictionaries which took account of these new grammatical resources, and showed the various shades of meaning by quotation and precise definition, was less satisfactory. There was no dictionary of Latin (save the pedestrian one of Calepinus) to complete the humanist achievement until Robert Estienne produced his *Thesaurus Linguae Latinae* in the years 1531–43. It was left to his son Henri to produce the best Greek dictionary of the century, and this not until 1572 when he published at Geneva his *Thesaurus Linguae Graecae.* (An exception must be made here for the *Lexicon Graeco-latinum* printed at Paris in 1530, the long title of which refers to the inclusion of additions and interpretations from all the Greek lexicons of previous decades and from the writings of Budé, Erasmus, Valla, and others less well known. It also contains a brief account by Melanchthon of the Greek names of the months and the calendar. While this dictionary is like the older glossaries, it does contain useful explanations, taken from the authors named, of words like *agape.*) Apart from these, scholars had to be content with the old glossaries which were more word books than dictionaries. Yet this very need made men work to find for themselves, through wide reading and meditation on the use of words, how to compare passage with passage and analyse the shade of meaning a word had in a given context. This resulted in the confidence and intuitive skill, as well as the occasional errors, of the sixteenth-century biblical exegetes who worked without the lexical aids we know today.

The peculiar problem of Hebrew studies was that suspicion of the motive for them was all too readily aroused. A monk of Freiburg (where Reuchlin studied) said plainly in 1521, 'Those who speak this tongue are made Jews'. And Jews themselves discovered that they might suffer if they taught Christians Hebrew, for they could be accused of destroying the faith of their pupils. Towards the end of the fifteenth century northern Italy was the home of Hebrew studies where Jews and Christians found mutual benefits like the partnership of the Christian printer Bomberg with the Jew Jacob b. Chayim at Venice. But the attraction of Christian humanists in Italy to rabbinical studies tended to draw them away from the biblical basis and lose themselves in esoteric study of the Cabala. It was elsewhere—apart from the well-printed Hebrew bibles of Soncino and Bomberg at Brescia and Venice—that Hebrew studies were more fruitful for biblical scholars. For example, as we might expect, Spain, home of brilliant Jewish scholars like the Kimḥis, father and son, and of treasured manuscripts of Hebrew learning, produced the converted Jew Zamora and the Christians Negri and, especially, Nebrija who helped so ably with the first great polyglot Bible, the Complutensian. But the Spanish situation and temperament meant that this work could also have a polemic aim; for example, Negri's scholarship and purpose were limited by his consistently violent anti-Jewish writing. In fact Reuchlin could justify his own estimate of himself as the first important Christian Hebrew scholar of the West. Referring to the dictionary contained in his *De Rudimentis Linguae Hebraicae*, published at Pforzheim in 1506, he said, 'before me among the Latins no one appears to have done this'. This German layman, doctor of law, and professor of Greek and Hebrew, without false modesty set down in the preface of his *De Rudimentis* an account of his work for the world of scholarship in Latin and Greek studies, and complained about the money he had had to pay to learned Jews for instruction. His book consists of a description of the alphabet, a dictionary in two parts, and a brief but adequate grammar of Hebrew. It is a handsome volume, printed so as to be read from the back page forwards, like a Hebrew Bible, in a temporary fashion characteristic of the pedantry of those humanists who published in like manner works on Hebrew grammar. It brought him what he wanted, undying fame as a scholar. The concluding words of his book show the curious combination of biblical piety and classical allusion common to the humanists: '...et pro hoc ergo memento mei deus et parce mihi secundum multitudinem miserationum tuarum. amen', and then 'Exegi monumentum aere perennius'.[1] Not the least part of Reuchlin's achievement was that he influenced princes and humanists to help to establish chairs of Hebrew in the universities of the Empire, and through his pupils, and correspondence on Hebrew studies, raised up scholars to fill them. Yet there was still much to be done, as the disheartened Campensis of Louvain showed when he wrote in a letter to Bomberg in 1528, 'I think that to read Hebrew without points is not to read but to

[1] '...and for this remember me, O God, and spare me according to the multitude of thy mercies [cf. Ps. xxv. 7, li. 1]...I have finished a monument more enduring than brass [Horace, *Odes*, III, 30].'

guess'.[1] Obviously to avoid making guesses the rules of grammar had to be more deeply studied and explained, so that men could learn to point correctly the consonantal text of Hebrew.

The evolving of grammatical theory for Hebrew raised the problem of nomenclature, and this led to the imposition of Latin grammatical forms on the distinctive genius of Hebrew. A problem that immediately arose was, How can the Hebrew article be described since Latin has no article? Even Reuchlin, usually astute and well-informed, included the conjunction 'ש' among the articles. Pellican, a Minorite from Alsace, tells us in his autobiography of his laborious struggle to learn Hebrew self-taught; he writes with the excitement and enthusiasm of a modern scholar trying to decipher Cretan Linear B. Before Reuchlin he issued a small book at Strassburg *De modo legendi et intelligendi Hebraeum* in 1503 or 1504, but compared with Reuchlin's work some two years later this can hardly be called a Hebrew grammar.[2] His later work on Hebrew studies was more effective. There are other names to record, Clénard of Louvain and Pagnini of Lucca, men who unlike Pellican and Capito, who produced a small Hebrew grammar at Basle in 1518, remained Catholics. Pagnini, whose Latin translation of the Hebrew Old Testament was to have a strong influence on the Latin and vernacular versions of the sixteenth century, had the good fortune five years after his death to have his Hebrew grammar of 1546 printed by Robert Estienne; this made it the best presented Hebrew grammar of the time. The preface of Pagnini contained words ominous for conservative minds, 'the translation of Jerome is not uncorrupted'. But the great name in Hebrew studies after Reuchlin was that of Sebastian Münster of Basle. He had had Pellican for master, and dedicated a lifetime to Hebrew studies, producing over forty books which show a capacity for work as prodigious as the range of his subjects. In 1527 he produced the first Aramaic grammar written by a Christian. He made available to Christian scholars through his Latin translations the best work of Elias Levita, the greatest of Jewish grammarians in that

[1] 'Ego legere sine punctis non legere puto sed divinare.' Campensis, prefatory letter to Bomberg in *Ex variis libellis Eliacae*. For further information on the grammatical work of the period see L. Kukenheim, *Contributions à l'histoire de la Grammaire Grecque, Latine, et Hébraïque à l'Époque de la Renaissance* (1951).

[2] Pellican's grammar was printed in Reisch's *Margarita Phylosophica* (1504); but the date of the first edition is probably 1503. See W. Schwarz, *Principles and Problems of Biblical Translation* (1955), p. 66 n. 4.

age. (By the beginning of the sixteenth century Judaism had reached a period of intellectual stagnation leading to one-sided study of the Talmud to the neglect of other learning; therefore Levita had emigrated from Germany to Italy to share in the grammatical study which flourished there, and published his Hebrew grammar at Rome in 1508. His Aramaic dictionary was published by the Christian Fagius at his own Hebrew press at Isny in 1514.) Münster wrote explicitly, 'In the grammatical works written by Christians before Elias had begun his task the true foundation was missing.'[1] By his self-effacing devotion Münster laid this true foundation, and through Levita learned (among many other merits) how to explain the use of the point *dagesh*. Two more Protestant scholars should be mentioned. Fagius of Strassburg—who in his early days as schoolmaster at Isny set up his own Hebrew press mentioned above, and then, after leaving Strassburg, became regius professor of Hebrew for a time at Cambridge—translated into Latin the *Perke Aboth* and, later, the *Targum of Onkelos*. He stated in the preface to this targum that Aramaic was the language of Palestine in the time of Christ and his Apostles, and made clear how useful the targum could be for understanding difficult passages in the Pentateuch. Another Hebraist, of less distinction than Fagius, was Forster of Wittenberg who issued a Hebrew dictionary in 1557. This did not meet the need for a dictionary of Hebrew which could match the Latin and Greek dictionaries of the Estiennes, nor had the similar work of others who preceded him done so. Zamora had provided in the volume of apparatus added to the Complutensian Polyglot a lexicon larger than Reuchlin's and easier to use because it had Latin catchwords in the margins showing the contents of the columns (the Hebrew roots were also given in the margins), and a selection of passages from the Old Testament in Latin to illustrate the meaning of the Hebrew words. Even so this Hebrew dictionary was essentially no more than a glossary, for the effective explanation of various meanings was not provided. Pagnini and Münster had also published dictionaries—Münster's was trilingual. These were more effective but they were not without faults and obscurities. Forster's dictionary showed a significant change of attitude which helps to mark the close of the humanist stage of biblical studies. For in this work rabbinical aid and the imitation of Jewish

[1] In the preface to his Hebrew grammar based on the work of Elias Levita, *Opus Grammaticum consummatum ex variis Elianis libris concinnatum* (Basle, 1556).

methods by Christian scholars were firmly set aside. From now onwards Protestant dogmatic preoccupations increasingly controlled linguistic study; for this is part of the reaction from the intransigence of the decree on Scripture made by the Council of Trent. In the remaining half-century biblical studies will be too often subjected to Catholic and Protestant dogmatic concerns. The eagerness and hope of men like Lefèvre, who early in the century had looked for a world renewed by the humanist study of the three languages and biblically grounded faith in Christ, had declined into rival orthodoxies. Not until the seventeenth century could linguistic and biblical studies find a renewal of energy. For the remarkable achievement of the Antwerp Polyglot of Plantin was a later flowering of the earlier sowing in the Complutensian of which it was—in some ways only—a careful revision. It would not be too great an exaggeration to say that the theological preoccupations and inhibitions among both Catholics and Protestants prevented much real advance in higher or lower criticism until the eighteenth and nineteenth centuries.

What did all this linguistic work in the period reviewed achieve for biblical studies? The world of scholarship was international and yet compact. The *respublica litterarum* was a world of men eager and alert for what could be found at the great book fairs, who in their correspondence with one another saw the Bible as a living force, and related it not merely to dogmatic concerns but also to moral and political behaviour in the changing society of that time. Artists, in illustrating the Bible, adorned the figures of patriarchs, kings and prophets with a contemporary appearance in dress and background. Men found this biblical renewal to be a determinative discovery. Many who had felt themselves to be subject to the mortmain of old scholastic methods, of the run-down machinery of theological debate and administrative emptiness, sought here the means of renewing both Church and society. They found strength in the biblical humanists' conviction that by clarity of expression based upon the quickening spirit of the languages of the prophets and apostles, the Word of the living God would renew the world. This conviction may seem somewhat naïve to us, but in that age it was a potent attraction. The renewal of Hebrew learning had given an impetus to Old Testament study which brought God as the providential ruler of time and men into the forefront of life. Greek studies brought freshness and freedom; to be able to read the

New Testament in its original form seemed to be like discovering the first freshness of a painting which had been overlaid by heavy varnish. A purified latinity provided the translation of Erasmus, the corrected Vulgate of Estienne, and the directness of the biblical commentators. There were weaknesses (for example, the failure to use effectively the Septuagint), but in comparison with the state of biblical learning in 1500 the advances were decisive. Men felt themselves to be delivered from the despairing conclusion of Geiler of Kaisersberg, who at the end of the fifteenth century said that the Scripture was a 'nose of wax' to be turned in any way by the too frequent misuse of the allegorical method of interpretation. The methods of the new scholarship were directed much more to the historical or literal sense. The results of these renewed studies for the various editions of the Hebrew, Greek and Latin Bibles of the sixteenth century will now be examined.

THE HEBREW, GREEK AND LATIN TEXTS OF THE BIBLE

Although Spain was the home of the best Hebrew manuscripts and of Jewish scholars and commentators; and Germany was the home of printing and possessed manuscripts and Jewish scholars who were acquainted with the skills of this technological advance; yet it was in northern Italy that the printing of the Hebrew Bible (including the first complete edition of the text, and the first edition of the rabbinical Bible) was achieved.[1] The scribal schools of Toledo had attained such a standard of accuracy and clarity that Spanish Jews had not felt the need to use the printing press; although recent research has shown that some Hebrew printing was going forward in Spain, for example at Montalban,[2] before the expulsion of the Jews in 1492. But northern Italy had become a centre of Hebrew grammatical study in the late fifteenth century. It has already been shown that Levita came there for that reason, and since the Italian humanists acquired a deep though often ill-informed devotion to the study of Hebrew, including the mysteries of the Cabala, a sympathetic environment was possible for Jewish immigrants, many of whom came from Germany bringing their

[1] C. D. Ginsburg, *Introduction to the Massoretico-critical Edition of the Hebrew Bible* (1897), pp. 770 ff.

[2] Lucien Febvre and H. J. Martin, *L'Apparition du Livre* (1958), p. 406.

codices of German provenance with them. Hebrew printing began in Italy probably before 1475; certainly a consonantal Psalter with Kimḥi's commentary appeared at Bologna in 1477, and in 1482 a Pentateuch with vowel points and accents accompanied by the *Targum of Onkelos* and Rashi's commentary. But it was in the small town of Soncino near Mantua that the first great achievements of Hebrew printing appeared through the efforts of Jews from south Germany. In 1485/6 came the first edition of the Prophetic Books. Here can be seen the beauty and technological accomplishment of this press which established a standard and a name which echoed again in our day. An enthusiastic type-setter in the philosophic work *Iḳḳarim*, 1485, turned a quotation in it of Isaiah ii. 3 to read, 'Out of Zion shall go forth the law, and the word of the Lord from Soncino'.[1] And it was from the Soncino press in 1488 that the whole of the Old Testament, with vowel points and accents but without any commentary, came as a beautifully printed small folio book. Its peculiarities of orthography and other small variations from the Massoretic text are mostly due to printers' errors, but some derive from the scribal traditions of the German manuscripts. The second edition of the Old Testament appeared without place or date being given; it is thought to be a product of the Soncino press working at Naples in 1491–3. The vowel points and accents in this well-printed text are in their proper positions—this had been a technological problem for printers and already a stumbling-block for the clumsy efforts of predecessors. The type shows the Sephardic script which increased the fine appearance of the page and suggests the provenance of the manuscripts used. As in the first edition the Q^{e}rê appear confusingly with the vowel points of the K^{e}thîbh, and the latter are not given in the margins. The text is nearer to the present Massoretic text than was that of the former edition. For the historian of the Reformation this edition has interest because a copy of it is preserved at Zurich inscribed in the handwriting of Pellican who describes it as a gift to himself in 1500, and who states, erroneously, that it was printed at Pesaro in 1494. The Soncino firm transferred to Brescia and issued there in two parts, in 1492 and 1494, the next edition of the Hebrew Bible using codices similar to those of the 1488 edition (the same obscure manner of printing the Q^{e}rê and the K^{e}thîbh was used in this edition also). It was this Brescia edition that Luther used in preparing

[1] *The Jewish Encyclopaedia*, article 'Soncino', XI, 463.

his translation of the Old Testament into German. Perhaps he took comfort for his labours on reading the address of Gershom the Soncinian, the printer, at the end of Deuteronomy, and again at the end of Chronicles, 'Have courage and let us be courageous'!

This vigour in Hebrew printing (for other editions of parts of the Old Testament were also printed) should have increased the flow of editions of the whole or parts of the Hebrew Bible in Italy. But there is an ominous gap from 1494 to 1510, perhaps to be accounted for by the expulsion of the Jews from Spain in 1492, and from Portugal in 1498; the flood of exiles to be supported would take up a good part of the resources of the Italian Jews. But one result of this immigration was that Gershom of Soncino and his colleagues produced—at Pesaro now—a magnificent folio edition of the Former Prophets with the commentary of Isaac Abravanel, the Spanish statesman and scholar who died in his Italian exile. The influence of the Spanish Jews can be seen also in the use of a type representing the Sephardic script, and a scribal tradition almost identical with the Massoretic recension.

Christian biblical scholars had contributed nothing so far to the printing of the Hebrew Old Testament though they were eager to obtain examples of the Jewish printers' work. However, the next stage is marked by the great Complutensian Polyglot of Alcalá, 1514–17. (These are the years during which the work was printed; it was not authorized for publication by the pope until 1520 and not issued until, probably, 1522.) Cardinal Ximenes de Cisneros (d. 1517), regent of Castille and archbishop of Toledo—a centre of Jewish studies already mentioned—had established the trilingual university at Alcalá (Complutum). In view of the labours involved it has been assumed that work upon this trilingual edition of the Scriptures must have been begun about 1502. Together with Nebrija, whose Hebrew studies have been referred to, there were also three converts from Judaism to Catholicism working on the Hebrew text, the foremost of whom was Alfonso de Zamora. Ximenes spent much money in obtaining good manuscripts (according to Le Long 4000 ducats were spent on seven Hebrew manuscripts alone) and manuscripts were borrowed from Venice and the Vatican. In the four volumes of the Old Testament the Vulgate is set in the centre of a page, the Septuagint with an interlinear Latin translation is in the inside column, and the Hebrew text is in the outside column. In the margins are given the Hebrew roots. The *Targum of*

Onkelos is given below the Pentateuch and is accompanied by a Latin translation. The apocryphal or deuterocanonical books[1] accepted in the Church are given in the Septuagint version with the Vulgate printed interlineally (but III Maccabees appears in Greek only). The New Testament of volume five will be considered in its place in the discussion of the editions of the Greek New Testament. Volume six contains a variety of 'aids to study'; Zamora's Hebrew and Aramaic dictionary; an interpretation of the Greek, Hebrew and Aramaic names; and a short Hebrew grammar followed by a Latin index to the dictionary. Volume one has a variety of prefatory material; this includes Jerome's *Preface to the Pentateuch*, the bull of Leo X sanctioning the issue of the work, introductions to the Hebrew and Aramaic dictionary and the Hebrew grammar of volume six, and two statements about the method of studying Scripture.

The most interesting of these documents for our purpose is the Prologue addressed to Leo X, and made by, or written for, Cardinal Ximenes, which contains these words: 'Certainly since there can be no word, no combination of letters, from which there does not arise, and as it were spring forth, the most concealed senses of the heavenly wisdom; and since the most learned interpreter cannot explain more than one of these, it is unavoidable that after translation the Scripture yet remains pregnant and filled with both various and sublime insights which cannot become known from any other sources than from the very fountain of the original language.' Here is the voice of biblical humanism: but from Alcalá this voice also spoke with a sardonic Spanish note. In the Prologue to the Reader describing the arrangement of the columns of the text the editors write: 'We have placed the Latin translation of blessed Jerome as though between the Synagogue and the Eastern Church, placing them like the two thieves one on each side, and Jesus, that is the Roman or Latin Church, between them.' Ginsburg sought to demonstrate that this insistence on the primacy of the Vulgate brought the editors occasionally to accommodate the Hebrew text to conformity with the Vulgate, for example, in Psalm xxii. 17.[2] The editors made obscuring modifications

[1] 'Apocryphal' is the Protestant term: 'deuterocanonical' is the Catholic term. The lists of books differ.

[2] C. D. Ginsburg, *Introduction to the Massoretico-critical Edition of the Hebrew Bible*, p. 925.

in the vowel points and the accents were omitted save for one, Athnach, which was used arbitrarily in a manner contrary to the Massoretic recension. The editors excused themselves on the ground that the accents were used by the Jews only to aid in the chanting of the text. However, Professor Kahle, in his revised edition of his Schweich lectures on the Cairo Geniza, argues that the Complutensian editors were in fact using an ancient manuscript (made prior to the work of the Massoretes) which showed the simplified Babylonian vocalization and the method of placing the Athnach displayed in the Complutensian text. Therefore, he concludes, the Complutensian editors compromised, in the vowel points and accents, between the ancient Babylonian codices and the Tiberian punctuation of the Ben Asher text.[1] But since the Babylonian codex supposed to have been used no longer survives among Ximenes's manuscripts at Madrid, final proof is still wanting.

In the closing years of the printing of the Complutensian Polyglot a Christian printer, Daniel Bomberg ('a countryman of Flanders' as he is called in a Hebrew epigraph), with a Christian Jew as editor, Felix Pratensis, printed, in 1516/17, the first edition of the rabbinical Bible, that is, the Hebrew text of the Old Testament accompanied by the targums and rabbinical commentaries. Here for the first time Samuel and Kings were each divided into separate books in a Hebrew Bible, and a note was added explaining that this division was intended for the use of readers not of Jewish faith. Bomberg and his editor obtained a licence from Leo X forbidding any other printer to produce a Bible with targums and commentaries for ten years from 1515. This is the first printed Bible to have the official Qᵉrê in the margins: the margins also contain many variant readings apart from these. In his preface the claim of Felix Pratensis for the Hebrew Bible that 'on this book the entire superstructure of Christianity rests' contrasts with the view of the Complutensian editors. Almost ten years after Leo's licence expired the second edition of the rabbinical Bible was printed by Bomberg at Venice in 1524/5. This was the greatest step forward yet taken towards obtaining the best text of the Hebrew Bible, for it included the results of the extraordinary labours of the Tunisian refugee, Jacob b. Chayim, on the Massorah. In his introduction to this Bible Chayim tells us that 'God sent a highly distinguished and pious

[1] P. E. Kahle, *The Cairo Geniza* (2nd ed. 1959), pp. 124–9.

Christian Daniel Bomberg to meet me' who showed him his printing-office and said '...I want thee to revise the books which I print, correct the mistakes, purify the style, and examine the works till they are as refined silver and as purified gold'. Having learned the value of the Massorah Bomberg 'did all in his power to send into all the countries in order to search what may be found of the Massorah...nor did he draw back his right hand from producing gold out of his purse to defray the expenses of the books and of the messengers...'. Chayim has this moving conclusion, 'I would not be deterred by the enormous labour, for which cause I did not suffer my eyelids to be closed long, either in the winter or the summer...as my aim and desire was to see the holy work finished'.[1] Not only was the text accurately printed but also this edition settled the standard form of the Massoretic text for future scholarship. For the first time the Q^{e}rê and K^{e}thîbh were properly arranged and received their appropriate marginal mark. Chayim provided also for this edition the marginal variants of the different—and, it should be added, late—manuscripts collated by him.

After these labours of Chayim there was no development in the establishing of the text of the Old Testament. The third rabbinical Bible issued at Venice by Adelkind brothers in 1548 showed variations in the text of the rabbinical commentaries only and not in the biblical text. Before this, interest in the printing of the Hebrew text had developed north of the Alps among the Christian Hebraists who had by now sufficient confidence to undertake this work. Sebastian Münster edited a Hebrew Bible at Basle in 1535 and accompanied it with his own Latin translation. It is strange that Münster's interest in Jewish scholarship did not lead him to adopt the text of Chayim; instead he gave the text of the first rabbinical Bible of Felix Pratensis together with several readings derived from the Brescia Bible.

Two more editions of the Hebrew Bible deserve comment for the beauty of their type and presentation distinctive of the work of the scholar-printers who published them. Robert Estienne printed slowly through the years 1539–44 a Hebrew Old Testament in quarto size in two excellent founts of type (the larger for the text: the smaller for the sparsely provided commentary) but with a number of errors—this no doubt meant that Estienne could not control effectively printing of a

[1] C. D. Ginsburg, *Jacob ben Chajim's Introduction to the Rabbinic Bible* (1865), pp. 2, 34, 39.

language which, compared with his great attainments in Latin and Greek, he understood imperfectly. It is characteristic of him, however, that he chose what he conceived to be the best available text for his press, that of the second rabbinical Bible of Chayim and Bomberg which he follows with only a few variations. He began by printing the Twelve Minor Prophets together with Kimḥi's commentary and some notes by the Parisian Christian Hebraist François Vatable of the *Lecteurs Royaux*. The book of Daniel alone has the marginal Massorah but elsewhere very few sections have the Qᵉrê. The ageing Pellican wrote to Calvin at Geneva in 1543 asking him to obtain for him the later volumes of this edition because the type suited his failing eyesight. There were other editions of the Old Testament in Hebrew including the fourth rabbinical Bible at Venice, and an edition of Bomberg's second rabbinical Bible by Christopher Plantin at Antwerp which was sold largely and profitably among the Barbary Jews. After Robert Estienne, Plantin was the greatest printer of that age and his finest achievement was the Royal Polyglot of Antwerp, an edition made possible by the parsimonius patronage of Philip II of Spain. The first four volumes contain the Old Testament and targums and were printed in the years 1569–72. This Royal Polyglot deliberately reflected that of Cardinal Ximenes and used the Complutensian Hebrew text with only occasional modification by the introduction of readings from the second rabbinical Bible. The editor was the Spaniard Benedictus Arias Montanus, a Benedictine and an orientalist who had studied in his youth at the University of Alcalá. He was assisted in his great labours—which included his checking each sheet as it came from the press—by three professors of Louvain. (The story of the young Magdelaine Plantin reading aloud to Arias Montanus the proofs of the Polyglot in five languages is touching,[1] but her knowledge of Semitic languages can hardly have been deeper than that of the blind Milton's daughters in Latin and Greek. It is surely difficult to accept her responsibility for the final accuracy of the Polyglot in its Hebrew, Aramaic and Syriac texts—even though her real competence in Latin and Greek should be granted.) The Pentateuchal targum was reprinted from the Complutensian edition, but the remaining targums were taken from the second rabbinical Bible although slightly modified by the use of manuscripts at Alcalá. The arrangement of the texts is different from that of the

[1] *Correspondance de Christophe Plantin*, ed. by Max Rooses (1883), II, 175.

Complutensian Polyglot. There are four columns arranged over two pages: the Hebrew, the Vulgate, a literal Latin version of the Septuagint, and then the Septuagint, with the targums and their accompanying Latin translations across the foot of the two pages. The Hebrew text was printed again in volume seven together with a revision of the Latin version of Pagnini, given interlineally. In volume six were provided the Hebrew lexicon of Pagnini revised by the professor of Hebrew at Cologne, a short Hebrew grammar, an Aramaic dictionary and grammar; a Syriac grammar by Masius; a Greek lexicon and a Greek grammar. Volume eight contained various indexes, and elaborate discussions intended for the better understanding of the text, for example, on the partition of Canaan and the vestments of the priests. It also contained lists of variant readings in the several texts prepared by the theologians of Louvain. Finally, the editor Arias Montanus drew up the account of the nature and use of the Massorah which appeared in this volume.

Plantin was offered help towards meeting the great cost of the work by some Protestant princes who were ready to grant him speedier financial aid than that which Philip grudgingly gave. He was also offered help by Protestant scholars like Tremellius who were ready to assist him in his labours, but Plantin said that his oath of fidelity to Philip II (in whose dominions Antwerp lay) prevented him from accepting these aids. Plantin's circumspection was doubly necessary, for it was with difficulty that he quieted the doubts about his orthodoxy which the chancellor Cardinal Granvelle had raised discreetly with him. The Spaniards did well to suspect him, for, though he outwardly conformed and was undetected, he was a faithful member of the secret and proscribed sect of the 'Family of Love' obnoxious to both Catholics and Protestants. Plantin's Polyglot received papal sanction in September 1572, after Arias Montanus had sought it by a visit to Rome. But the result of his 'œuvre de labeur, travail, et fraiz indicibles' was regarded with suspicion by many in the Catholic world, where, as in Protestantism, the eager hope of the earlier biblical humanists had died. The Polyglot was attacked especially by Spanish theologians, at Salamanca and by the Jesuit Mariana; sixteen years of struggle against debt were left to Plantin.

There is a strange lapse of time between the printing of the Hebrew text and the printing of the Old and New Testaments in Greek.

Further, Greek printing did not begin as early as did that of Latin and Hebrew. The demand for printing of works in Greek was probably the result of the turning of Italian humanists from their former zeal and expense in collecting beautifully written Greek manuscripts as works of art to be treasured, to obtaining the more compendious and cheaper products of the press which could be put to ordinary daily use. The only biblical Greek to be printed before the sixteenth century was the Latin and Greek Psalter first issued at Milan in 1481 which also contained the Magnificat and Benedictus. Aldus Manutius also issued before 1498 a diglot (Latin and Greek) Psalter and followed this up in 1504 with six chapters of the Gospel of John.

The first edition of the Septuagint to be printed was that of the Complutensian Polyglot, and the first complete edition of the Greek New Testament was that of Erasmus in 1516 which, though printed later than the Complutensian volume five, the New Testament, was published several years before it. Interest in achieving an accurate text of the Septuagint, together with careful appreciation of its nature and significance, was lacking in the sixteenth century and it received less attention than its importance merited. However, the scholars of that age should not be too severely judged when we recollect that many septuagintal problems are still unresolved. The sixteenth-century scholar tended to view the Septuagint as a version of the Hebrew text which was at many points deliberately corrupted by the Jewish translators, or at best ill translated, and therefore of secondary importance when compared with the Hebrew or Vulgate texts. Nevertheless, it was regarded as having an antiquarian and pious interest since it was the Bible of the early Church. Catholic and Protestant exegetes, while they refer to it in their commentaries, were not prepared to give the attention which modern exegetes would bring to it. Typical of the Protestant view of the Septuagint is that of Luther, who said in his Lectures on Genesis (iv. 7), 'The translators of the Septuagint appear not to have had adequate knowledge to cope with the vastness of the task they had undertaken'. But Zwingli once suggested that exegetes discommended it too much: he was no doubt aware that Augustine had upheld the divine inspiration of the Septuagint (Protestants, nevertheless, could adduce Jerome's aid in insisting that the Hebrew text is alone the 'verity' of the Word of God).

The Complutensian editors of the Septuagint used manuscripts obtained from the Vatican library, the library of St Mark at Venice, and from the private collection of Ximenes. In the dedicatory epistle to Pope Leo X the claim is made that 'the oldest examples out of the apostolic library' were used, but the editors did not have before them codex Vaticanus B which is the best of those to be found in the Vatican library. When the editors were faced occasionally by passages present in the Vulgate but absent from the Greek they filled in these gaps by translation from the Latin. This led Bishop Walton, editor of the greatest of the Polyglot Bibles, that of London 1657, to describe the Complutensian edition of the Septuagint as 'consarcinata'. Since the Complutensian was not issued for some years after it was printed, the Aldine press won the glory of the first publication of the whole Bible in Greek in 1518/19 (the Septuagint was accompanied by the 1516 edition of Erasmus's Greek New Testament). The text of the Aldine edition was established by Andreas Asolanus from manuscripts he used in Cardinal Bessarion's collection in the library of St Mark at Venice: no Latin version accompanied the text. Bishop Walton considered the Aldine edition to be purer than the Complutensian. The Aldine text was reprinted, with a few changes, in a new edition of the whole Bible in Greek at Strassburg in two volumes in 1526/4; the Apocrypha were brought together in a separate section, and the sequence of the biblical books followed that of Luther. Another edition of the Aldine text of the whole Bible in Greek was published at Basle in 1545 (now with the New Testament according to the fifth edition of Erasmus) with a preface by Melanchthon who described the Septuagint version as 'rougher' (*squalidiorem*) than the original, and the translators as not taking sufficient care in the choice of words and sentence structure. He added that it was useful to study the Septuagint because this was the version cited by St Paul and that the apostolic writings can be better understood by the attentive study of this version which was that in the hands of the apostles themselves. His preface ends by being dated on the Feast of the Purification of the Temple and with the wish that God would purify his Church; characteristically implying in the biblical humanist manner that the study of the Greek Bible would serve this desirable end.

The next edition of importance was that of the Antwerp Royal Polyglot of Plantin in 1572, for which Arias Montanus chose the Complutensian text with some readings introduced from the Aldine text. For over half a century there had been no advance in the provision of an adequate text of the Septuagint since the Complutensian edition, and of this Andreas Masius, a scholar whose collation of manuscripts aided the editors of the Sixtine edition, wrote that it would be mere ignorance for anyone to say that it represented the pure text of the Septuagint. A pure text was only achieved by the Sixtine edition of 1587 at Rome which by modern standards is perhaps the only satisfactory achievement in the editing of a biblical text obtained in the sixteenth century, and its editors could rightly claim that by diligent correction it had been restored to its former splendour. This achievement was aided by the discovery made by Cardinal Antonio Carafa and his assistant editors of the codex in the Vatican library known as Vaticanus graecus 1209 (Vatican B), of which they said rightly that 'this codex is by far the best of those extant': their work provided the first edition to be based on an extensive uncial manuscript. They also added a number of variant readings from other manuscripts in which they were aided by the great labours of collation undertaken some years before his death by Andreas Masius, whose considerable acumen as a textual critic led to his posthumously published work on Joshua being placed on the Index in 1574. Cardinal Carafa and his assistants rightly insisted on the value of the Septuagint for the right understanding of the use of Scripture by the Fathers and for the text of the Vulgate; but they do not appear to have grasped the value of the Septuagint for getting behind the Massoretic revision of the Hebrew text. This edition was accompanied by three groups of annotations: alternative readings and scholia from other manuscripts; illustrative references and quotations from the Patristic writings and the old translations; and illustrative references to the other Greek translations, Aquila, Symmachus, and Theodotion. It will be remembered that the first volume of the Complutensian Polyglot to be printed was the fifth which contained the New Testament in Greek. The manuscripts used for this edition by the editors—of whom Stunica the opponent of Erasmus was probably the chief—were late although they call them 'antiquissimos codices'. What these were is not known, for the surviving manuscripts of Ximenes at Madrid do not include the New Testament. But since the printed text represents the script of manuscripts of the tenth century it is possible, but only possible, that the Complutensian text is based on some manuscripts older than those used by Erasmus. The accentuation of the Greek was peculiar: it was justified by the editors on the ground that it formed no part of the genuine text and was absent from older manuscripts; and no 'breathings' were provided (yet the editors gave the normal accentuation to their text of the Septuagint). The *comma Joanneum*, that is, I John v. 7 and 8, was interpolated by translating it from the Vulgate; but in general there is no evidence of an editorial aim to make the Greek conform to the Vulgate text. It is possible, however, that four or five passages in Romans and Galatians show assimilation to the Vulgate.[1] When Erasmus inquired during his controversy with Stunica where the *comma Joanneum* could be found since it was in no Greek manuscript known to himself, Stunica replied with Spanish intransigence that it was well known that the Greek codices were corrupted but that the Vulgate contained the truth itself.

While the printed sheets of the Complutensian edition lay stored from 1514 to 1521/2, when they were bound and published, an edition of the Greek text appeared at Basle edited by Erasmus and printed by Froben. It is probable that Froben had heard of the Complutensian edition, and of the probably protracted delay in its appearance, through trade channels, if not from the gossip of humanist circles, and saw the glory to be gained from publishing the *editio princeps* of the Greek New Testament. He urged Erasmus in a letter of April 1515 to press on with his desultory work on the New Testament, and stated bluntly that if Erasmus did not edit and publish the Greek text then another soon would do so. Erasmus replied with his usual caution—for he foresaw how unpopular this work would be with the men of the 'old learning'—nevertheless he prepared the text after the collation of some readily available manuscripts at Basle, and sent with it to the press a new Latin version which he already had by him, and full annotations many of which he had been working on for some time. The work was done swiftly in a few months and showed plainly the signs of undue haste; his candid admission of this to the reader is frequently quoted, 'praecipitatum verius quam editum'. The book went through Froben's press in six months and was published in March 1516. Erasmus was assisted in the proof-reading by the young scholar Oecolampadius whose Greek learning was to make of him the future reformer of Basle. Because of the haste in which Erasmus and the press worked there are many typographical errors, for example, 501 itacisms have been counted,

[1] C. R. Gregory, *Textkritik des Neuen Testamentes* (1909), p. 927. See also pp. 11 above, 203, 233 below.

and the ghostly name of a non-existent Vulgarius is listed on the title-page with other authorities, whereas the name provided should have been that of Theophylact, archbishop of Bulgaria. Further, while Erasmus suggested that he had consulted many manuscripts, in fact he used few in the preparation of the text he published, and most of these he found in Basle. His only manuscript of Revelation was defective; six verses which he found to be missing from it he translated from the Vulgate into Greek: some words of this Erasmian Greek have oddly survived to our own time. Erasmus also interpolated Acts vii. 5 and 6, by translation from the Vulgate, but he omitted the *comma Joanneum*. Occasionally a reading quoted in his annotations differs from that in his text; this is explicable on the ground that he had prepared his annotations in part some time before he edited the Greek text; nevertheless these readings show the haste of his editorial work. The whole work, like the Complutensian Polyglot, was dedicated to Leo X, that willing target for the aspirations of the early biblical humanists. This edition was soon attacked, particularly because Erasmus had dared to provide his own Latin translation; conservative scholars like Lee, archbishop of York, argued, as men of the 'old learning', that if Erasmus's Greek codices did not contain what was in the Vulgate then they should have done and must be rejected as erroneous. Stunica, though a representative of the 'new learning', attacked Erasmus vigorously at all levels, from the sharp and patriotic rebuke that Erasmus had omitted the 'I' in 'Ισπανία (Erasmus put Σπανία at Romans xv) to more usual, if somewhat obtuse, textual criticism.[1] Erasmus's second edition of 1519 was greatly improved, for the majority of the misprints were removed and he introduced readings from a better codex of the Gospels, Acts and the Pauline Epistles. In the third edition of 1522 he inserted I John v. 7 and 8, having learned that a Dublin manuscript contained it, although there is no doubt that this version of the *comma* is also a translation from the Vulgate: having thus appeased in part his critics he felt he could add to this edition a reply to the 'morosos et indoctos'. The fourth edition of 1527 contains, together with his own Latin version, the Vulgate text as a further attempt to appease the 'morosos', and there are many changes in Revelation derived from the Complutensian text. The fifth edition of

[1] S. P. Tregelles, *An Account of the Printed Text of the Greek New Testament* (1854), p. 23 n.

1536 omitted the Vulgate and included several further textual changes. Froben's initiative gained for the Erasmian text a wider circulation than that of the Complutensian, which was confined to an issue of about six hundred copies, whereas there were about three thousand three hundred copies of the first and second editions of Erasmus; also, the popularity of the Erasmian editions was increased by their being printed in a convenient small folio size more easily handled and less expensive than the Complutensian version.

In 1534 Simon Colines (Colinaeus) the Parisian printer, and step-father of Robert Estienne, published the first attempt to achieve a critical edition of the Greek New Testament. He used the texts of Erasmus (probably that of the third edition) and the Complutensian, but he provided a number of unique readings which may well have had manuscript authority, although it is not known what manuscripts were used by him. Although he omitted I John v. 7 and 8, he made no mention of the sources of his edition of the text, in which there are unique readings, most of which later scholarship has recognized as significant. It is possible that Calvin may have used Colines's text as well as those others by Erasmus and Estienne which were available to him. It has been suggested with reason that if Colines had followed up his own method of collation, and persuaded others to adopt it, a good critical edition of the text of the New Testament would have been made available many decades in advance of its realization: but this version had no influence on later editions. The printers of Basle and Zurich preferred the eminent name of Erasmus to ensure the sale of their convenient editions in which they introduced slight modifications of his text. It was at Paris once again that new depth was given to the appreciation of the importance of textual accuracy by the folio edition of Robert Estienne's Greek Testament in 1550. His first two editions of 1546 and 1549 were in duodecimo size: they have no mention of Erasmus, and claim in the preface to be based on ancient codices; yet the text differs little from the Complutensian and later Erasmian editions. The important change comes with the third edition of 1550 printed in the large beautiful type cut for Estienne by Claude Garamond (this was based on the Hellenic script of the calligrapher of Francis I, the Cretan Angelo Vergecio), for here Robert Estienne provided in the inner margins of the page variant readings from a number of manuscripts collated for this edition by his son Henri. The inner marginal references are to the Complutensian text and to fifteen manuscripts most of which were in Parisian libraries, although some from elsewhere had been collated, including that which Estienne marked β and is better known as the Codex Bezae. In the outer margins references and chapter divisions were provided and also references to passages from the Septuagint quoted in the text. Together with the usual material reproduced by Erasmus, the lives of the Gospel writers and the Eusebian canons, Estienne included St Chrysostom's Prologue to the Pauline Epistles and his Homily 1 on Matthew and also columns of quotations from the Septuagint which were quoted literally or in paraphrase in the New Testament.

The fourth edition was printed as a small portable volume by Estienne in 1551 at Geneva whither he had fled from the intensive pressure of the Sorbonne doctors against him: this edition included Erasmus's Latin version and the Vulgate, and the Greek text was for the first time divided into separate verses. Calvin's successor at Geneva, Théodore de Bèze (Beza), was the editor of the next important edition of the Greek New Testament, which appeared in 1565 (his own Latin version had been printed in 1557) and went through many editions in folio and octavo, accompanied in the larger size by his own Latin version; the Vulgate and full annotations are included. In the preparation of his text Beza made full use of the collations and notes of Henri Estienne which had only partially been incorporated by Henri's father in 1550; he also had before him the version made by Tremellius from the Peshitta New Testament, and manuscripts of his own including the two remarkable uncials $D^{evv\ Acts}$ (Codex Bezae) and D^{paul} (Codex Claromontanus). Estienne's folio volume of 1550 with its accompanying variant readings made this edition of the Greek New Testament the earliest to be published with a critical apparatus, and provided the basis for future work on the text. How far Estienne made effective use of his sources is arguable, but he had shown the value of collating the manuscripts and publishing the results. In spite of this there is little evidence that Beza saw the importance of Estienne's innovation, or of the two ancient manuscripts in his own possession. He made little significant change from the fourth edition of Estienne (which did not have the critical apparatus) and the Complutensian text, both of which he had before him in preparing his own edition. Further, he made little use of the two famous codices in his possession because they differed too frequently from those printed versions; he preferred to choose a reading which agreed with the traditional theological interpretation of the text. While he received in 1581 a remarkably flattering letter of thanks from the University of Cambridge for his gift of the Codex Bezae, which went so far as to describe Beza and Calvin as men whom that university regarded as the most memorable of all writers for their knowledge of Scripture to whom they would prefer no others, yet Beza has been attacked from the early seventeenth century onward for modifying the text to suit his own theological presuppositions. On the contrary his text is conservative, as has been shown, and the criticisms made against him are for his renderings in his Latin version and his annotations; for example, Acts ii. 47 τοὺς σωζομένους is rendered in the note by a proposed alteration of the Greek to read 'those who were to be saved' (were added to the Church): this alteration would accord with Beza's view of election. Simon, and the Englishman John Bois, an anti-Calvinist prebendary of Ely, whom he quotes with approval, should be corrected by the judgment of Bishop Westcott who wrote 'the cases in which Beza has corrected the renderings of former translators are incomparably more numerous than those in which he introduced false readings' (that is, Latin translations of passages in which Beza suggested an emendation of the Greek).[1]

The Greek New Testament in the Royal Polyglot of Plantin was presented in two forms: in the fifth volume it appears with the Syriac and the Latin versions, in the seventh volume it is given with the Latin placed interlineally. It is curious that the two texts of the Greek differ slightly: that of volume five is the Complutensian with variant readings introduced from the third edition of the Estienne text, whereas volume seven gives the Complutensian with a larger number of readings from the Estienne text.

The desire of the biblical humanists had been to arrive at an authentic text of the Hebrew and Greek originals which they believed to have greater authority than the Vulgate since it was taken for granted that this version came later in time than the others. One result of this desire was to rest content with what seemed to be a reasonably authenticated text and inquire no further into textual criticism as a discipline for its own sake. By the mid-sixteenth century men felt that they had arrived at reasonably authoritative versions of the Hebrew and Greek texts of the Old and New Testaments. This accounts for the conservatism of

[1] B. F. Westcott, *History of the English Bible* (3rd ed. 1905), pp. 228–9.

both Beza's edition and that of Plantin's Royal Polyglot. It is not surprising, therefore, that the Elzevir press, printing at Leyden their popular, convenient and cheap editions of standard texts, could include in 1624 a copy of the Greek New Testament and affirm in the preface to the second edition of 1633, 'Textum ergo habes, nunc ab omnibus receptum; in quo nihil immutatum aut corruptum damus'. In creating the phrase *textus receptus* they had confirmed acceptance of the third edition of Estienne and Beza's recension of it as the standard version. Effective awareness of the significance of textual criticism for the ancient versions of the biblical text may be said to begin only with the *Biblia Polyglotta* of Bishop Walton in 1657.

The men of *sacrae litterae*, for whom the publication of the Hebrew and Greek texts of the Bible, according to the improvements shown in the texts by the collation of manuscripts, did not exclude interest in the Scriptures in Latin—the language not only of Churchmen but of all scholars—now undertook the pedagogical task of assisting those whose knowledge of Hebrew and Greek was insufficient by providing them with a literal Latin version. To meet this interest three methods were used; first, the provision of a corrected version of the Vulgate by bringing it closer to the Hebrew and Greek texts established by 1525; secondly, to seek out, as Valla had suggested some time before, the earliest manuscripts of the Vulgate and from these to discover the best form of the text; thirdly, by translating anew into Latin, directly from the Hebrew and Greek, to provide either very literal versions for the assistance of students, or versions of good latinity which would appeal to men of cultivated taste for whom lack of time or interest made Hebrew and Greek unobtainable. The results of this threefold effort will be considered in turn. Cardinal Cajetan in his preface to his commentary on the Psalms, 1530, had argued that the Vulgate was essentially an interpretation of the original Hebrew and Greek and was not a satisfactory substitute for the pure Word of God given in the Hebrew and Greek texts. Moreover, he implied, since the Vulgate text in current use showed a number of errors which had been introduced in the course of time, a new translation of the Bible into Latin could be undertaken, even though this would be an interpretation subject also to errors and inevitably inferior to the original texts. (It is not surprising that, after his death, these views of Cajetan which so closely resembled those of Protestants were repudiated at the Council of Trent, for by this time confessional narrowness had broken up the common ground of the biblical humanists.)[1] Cajetan's own commentaries show his efforts to correct the Vulgate by the original versions written in languages which he imperfectly understood and for which he had taken as assistants men more linguistically capable than himself. At Wittenberg in 1529 the Old Testament from Genesis to II Kings and the New Testament were published according to the Vulgate version corrected by the Hebrew and Greek: this was intended for the use of university students, but it soon was lost sight of because of the numerous errors of the press, including the failure of the printer to print his own name correctly (Schirleitz for Schirlentz). Andreas Osiander at Nürnberg produced a more correctly printed and better version of the Vulgate in 1522 which was reprinted at Cologne in 1527. Pellican in his admirable seven volumes of plain commentary on the whole Bible in 1539 used the Vulgate for the Old Testament corrected by the original Hebrew. But the correction of Jerome by partially rewriting him was an obviously unsatisfactory approach to the problems raised by the Vulgate text.

The second method was that of Robert Estienne who by diligent search for early manuscripts and by constant revision of his work produced eventually a version of the text of Jerome which was better than that of any previously printed edition, and which was attained in spite of the strong opposition of the Sorbonne. This labour of collation was begun in the vigour of his youth and by 1524 he was going through the libraries of Paris 'to select from them the authentic readings, and, supported by their authority, restore what was corrupt, satisfying those scrupulous readers who find it a stumbling-block to see so much as a word altered'. He was pleased to see that the revision he was undertaking was largely corroborated by the text printed in the Complutensian Polyglot, which had been based on the collation of older manuscripts than those used in earlier printed editions. Estienne published in 1528 his first version of the first effective effort to establish a critical edition of the text of Jerome, for not only did he use the best printed editions including the Complutensian, but also he used manuscripts—including one of the Carolingian age—which he had worked through in Parisian libraries. His Bible further differed from others of the time because he omitted much of the traditional introductory

[1] P. Sarpi, *Historia del Concilio Tridentino* (3rd ed. 1656), p. 160.

material from Jerome; he placed Acts after the Gospels and before the Pauline Epistles; provided a new index and interpretation of the Hebrew names; and gave occasionally in the margins alternative renderings derived from the Hebrew. Estienne received the royal privilege by letters patent for these 'collations, indices and interpretations'. He acknowledged, however, that the complaint of his friends that he had nodded somewhat in this first edition was justified, and in a revision issued in 1532 he claimed to have restored the Vulgate to the completeness and correctness in which 'the translator himself wrote it'. Yet he was still not content: he investigated further in the library of the Abbey of St Germain, as well as in provincial libraries, and found three further ancient manuscripts written prior to the tenth century. Thereafter, he produced another revision in 1540 (based on this new labour of collation) which included the printing of the Greek text of the Prayer of Manasses accompanied by a Latin version 'never formerly composed'. He also issued with the revised version the brief statement of his own *Summa totius Sacrae Scripturae* which described what is taught in Scripture on such topics as God, man, sin, Christ, the law, justification, good works, and eternal life, and concluded with the assertion that there is no other foundation but Christ. Estienne also provided code letters in the inner margins to show the sources of the variant readings; and gave the added splendour of finely engraved plates, for several Old Testament subjects, under the guidance of Vatable. In 1545 he issued two octavo volumes which gave in parallel columns the Vulgate version and that of the Zurich Latin Bible—though he did not name the source of the latter text. This edition was accompanied by a considerable number of annotations which he claimed were derived from Vatable's lectures, and which he had already used to a much less degree in his Hebrew Old Testament. He reprinted the folio edition of 1540 magnificently in 1546: it is one of the most remarkable achievements of typographical art combined with scholarship and it makes this Bible the crown of Estienne's achievement in the printing of a Latin text. In 1557 he produced his last and largest edition of the Latin Bible in three folio volumes at Geneva, whither he had fled from the censorship of the theologians of Paris in search of freedom for his work. Volumes one and two contained the Old Testament Vulgate from the edition of 1546 with the Pagnini version revised by Estienne, and a new Latin version of the Apocrypha by the

Frenchman Claudius Baduellus based on the Greek text of the Complutensian Polyglot; and the third volume (dated 1556) provided the first and less satisfactory form of Beza's Latin version of the New Testament, which Estienne had masterfully persuaded Beza to produce at short notice. The three volumes were accompanied by a considerable array of annotations from Vatable and other scholars, and new and larger concordances were added which gave references to the verse numbers which Estienne had provided for the whole Bible.

From the time of the first appearance of this corrected Vulgate Estienne was in trouble with the censorship of the Theological Faculty of the University of Paris; for he was a layman working without their control, and yet he was correcting the received contemporary version of the Vulgate by pointing to allowable variants from earlier sources and adding, later, interpretative notes. His long struggle, fought with shrewd reliance on Francis I who wished to be thought of as the supporter of humanist studies, has been described more than once,[1] best of all by Estienne himself when he wrote from that city of refuge, Geneva, his own account in a Latin work which was the first book to appear from his newly established press there. One example of the censures to which his Bibles were exposed (and which also illustrates the nature of the problem which the biblical humanists had to face) may suffice: Matt. xviii. 17, 'Que sil ne les escoute, di le a l'Eglise'. Annotation: 'L'Eglise, c'est a dire a l'assemblee publique.' Censure: 'Ceste proposition est amoindrie, et fallacieuse, et favorise a l'erreur des Vauldois et des Wiclefistes: et aussi ille derogue a la puissance des prelats de l'Eglise.' To which Estienne writes that he was not producing a commentary, and adds admirably 'la principale grace d'une annotation c'est briefvete'.[2]

Other scholars besides Estienne sought to use ancient manuscripts to arrive at a better version of the Vulgate text. For example, Johannes Benedictus edited for Colines, in 1541, a Vulgate text which he claimed to be emended from errors and restored by the use of earlier and better manuscripts. His achievement was less able than Estienne's but that did not save his version from being entered on the Index. Other Catholic scholars were more fortunate than Benedictus since they were not of Paris but of Louvain. Charles V, who had issued an imperial

[1] E. Armstrong, *Robert Estienne* (1954).

[2] Robert Estienne, *Les Censures des Théologiens de Paris* (1552), p. 72 verso.

edict for the withdrawal from circulation of all Bibles, Latin or vernacular, suspected of heretical tendencies, urged the biblical theologians of Louvain to provide a revised version of the Vulgate. Their response, edited by Hentenius, a Dominican of Louvain, and printed there in 1547, was based on Estienne's edition of 1538–40 to which were added a great many variant readings obtained through the collating of thirty-one manuscripts and the printed texts of Colines and Keyser (the leading printer of Bibles at Antwerp). This version of 1547, and the improved form of it in 1574 made by the editor of Plantin's Polyglot, Arianus Montanus (who collated over sixty manuscripts in Belgian libraries in preparing it), together with the text of the Vulgate printed in Plantin's Polyglot of 1572, formed the recognized Catholic versions of the Vulgate prior to the Sixtine edition at Rome in 1590. For the decree of the Council of Trent made in April 1546 declaring that the Vulgate version alone must be used for public readings, disputations and sermons, without any permissible deviation from this rule, had urged upon Catholics the necessity of having available an uncorrupted and uniformly agreed text. But nothing was achieved at Rome before 1590. It was due to the initiative of Sixtus V who, more successful than his predecessors, reinvigorated a dilatory biblical commission which probably used as the basis of their work the edition of the Louvain Bible issued by Plantin in 1583 with an appendix of many variant readings gathered by Luke of Bruges, and in addition consulted a large number of early manuscripts. Sixtus himself worked through the variant readings, and revised the proofs of the three volumes as they came from the press newly established for printing this edition at the Vatican. This Bible was supported by a minatory bull which forbade any other text to be used under any circumstances whatsoever. This created a most difficult situation for Catholic scholars who privately, and soon in print, began to point out many inaccuracies in the readings of the Sixtine edition. Not least because of the notable attack on it made by Cardinal Bellarmine (who had been a professor at Louvain), Clement VIII in 1592 ordered copies of the Sixtine edition to be withdrawn, if necessary by repurchase.[1] By the end of that year a new and critically better edition appeared, and to avoid the heavy penalties for any deviation from the 1590 version the editors, among whom was Bellarmine, placed the name of Sixtus on the title-page instead of that of Clement: an

[1] X.-M. le Bachelet, *Bellarmin et la Bible Sixto-Clémentine* (1911).

appendix was added containing the Prayer of Manasses and III and IV Esdras which had been omitted in 1590. Unlike the Louvain Bibles and that of Estienne, this recension contained no variant readings: this version was to be final, and the stringency of the papal bulls relating to this Sixto-Clementine edition meant that until the nineteenth century new critical work on the Vulgate text was difficult for Catholics to undertake (see pp. 208–11).

Apart from attempting to revise the Vulgate according to the Hebrew and Greek texts, and the major work of correcting the Vulgate by the collation of manuscripts, there were also entirely new translations into Latin from the Hebrew and Greek. The first of these new translations was that made by the Italian Dominican Santi Pagnini, whose version went through several editions and revisions, and was used by both Catholic and Protestant scholars. His version of the New Testament soon gave way to that of Erasmus and others, but his Old Testament found favour because of its extreme literalness which made it useful for understanding the sense of the Hebrew, however distasteful its barbarous latinity. Erasmus, in defending the right of his own Latin version of the New Testament to exist alongside that of Jerome, had claimed that it was doubtful whether Jerome had translated the whole Vulgate himself because of the inaccuracies to be found in it, and that, while the Septuagint was the received text in Jerome's day, yet Jerome had undertaken a new translation or revision. Pagnini used the same arguments for his own Latin version of the Old Testament. He had obtained the good-will of Leo X at an early stage of his work, and when the translation appeared in 1528 it was accompanied by commending letters, granting privileges, from Leo's successors Adrian VI and Clement VII. After over twenty years of labour—and when Pagnini began about 1500 there was less available to him in Hebrew studies than there was for his successors as translators, the Protestants Münster and Jud—he had given men eager to acquire Hebrew learning the great assistance of his most literal version of the 'Hebrew verity'. For, while his Latin was unidiomatic and harsh, it gave self-taught students the help they needed, especially when this version was printed interlineally with the Hebrew text. Pagnini divided his text into numbered 'verses', but some of these are a paragraph in length; the apocryphal books were given in a separate section; and there was an appendix containing the 'Interpretation of the Hebrew, Aramaic and Greek names'.

There were Catholic and Protestant revisions of the version of Pagnini, for example, in Plantin's Polyglot and in Estienne's later Bible of 1557. Pagnini was criticized by Luther and others for having leaned too much to Jewish scholarship, and for having followed the targums in his rendering of the Hebrew text. Perhaps this and its literalism made it the only Christian Latin version which the Jews seem to have respected. His interpretation of Job xix. 25 at any rate is nearer to that of modern scholarship than to that of either the Vulgate or the English Authorized Version.[1]

Servetus revised Pagnini's version for the printer Hughes de la Porte of Lyons, 1542; it is possible that the emendations derive from those which Pagnini had made by hand in a copy of the edition of 1528. Because of the matter in some of the marginal notes which Servetus had added, this Bible was put on the Index and suppressed—Servetus had entered deeper into his covenant with death.

The hebraist Sebastian Münster of Basle departed from the extreme literalism of Pagnini in his own Latin version of the Old Testament: he left aside the New Testament. While it 'did not depart by a nail's breadth from the Hebrew verity', this version was written in better Latin: it accompanied the Hebrew text of Münster referred to above. It appeared in 1535 in two folio volumes and was reprinted in quarto size in 1539 accompanied by the Complutensian version of the Apocrypha and by Erasmus's Latin New Testament, and then again in its original form in 1546. This version gave an impetus to Old Testament study similar to that which Erasmus had given to the study of the New Testament: in his preface Münster wrote that he expected to be attacked as Erasmus had been before him—and added that he hoped that the printers would be more diligent with this version than the Italian printers of Pagnini's version from which whole lines had been dropped! This suggests not so much that the printing-masters were careless as that they knew how large and profitable a market lay before them and therefore drove their workmen hard. But Froschauer's press did well. This version had a powerful influence among the Swiss reformers, German and French, and it affected many of the renderings of Coverdale's English Bible. Münster's weakness lay in the depth of his respect for rabbinical learning, for he used, as did Pagnini, the targums and

[1] Ego novi redemptorem meum vivum, et novissimo super terram (pulverem) statutum, et postquam pellem meam contriverint hanc: et de carne mea videbo Deum.

rabbinical commentaries in moulding his translation, and paid little attention to the Septuagint or Vulgate. His version would have been better if he had heeded the opinion of other reformers, for example Luther, that one should take grammar from the Jews but not their interpretation of the sense of the Hebrew text. After 1546 this version lost ground before those of other men, including the revisions of Pagnini. The Zurich translation was certainly of better latinity and it was less rabbinical: this, and the later translation of Tremellius, superseded Münster's version but not his annotations, which long continued to hold the respect of scholars and were reprinted in the late seventeenth-century collection of commentaries, the *Critici Sacri*.

The Zurich Latin Bible appeared in 1543, the work of several scholars of whom the chief was Leo Jud who died a year before the work was completed. It included a new translation of the Apocrypha made by Cholinus who had been tutor to Beza at Bourges, and the Latin New Testament of Erasmus revised by the Zurich reformer Gualther. The Latin, unlike that of the preceding versions, reads well and avoids hebraisms and justifies the claim made in its preface that it was brought forth with great learning and industry. It included also a preparatory account by Bullinger which set forth the chief principle of interpretation to be Christ as the 'scope of Scripture'. The editors initiated the device of using square brackets to contain words added to complete the sense. Estienne reprinted the version in 1545 at Paris, as has been shown, without naming its heretical origin. It was nevertheless condemned by the theologians of Paris: but it is a curious irony that the theologians of Salamanca were allowed by the Inquisition to publish in 1584–6 a revised version of Estienne's edition of 1545 with the accompanying Zurich version, apparently in ignorance of its origin and its condemnation by the theologians of Paris.

In contrast to the over-literal method of Pagnini and Münster, and carrying forward the principle of good latinity in translation shown by Jud and his fellow workers, Sebastian Castellio produced single-handed an entirely new translation of the whole Bible and the Apocrypha. This version may be described as perhaps the first example of a 'Bible intended to be read as literature': there are no verse divisions here, and the Latin has an elegance which even Valla would have approved. This Bible first appeared in 1551 at Basle where the brilliant trilingual humanist Castellio found a life of poverty and scholarship, and also an uneasy refuge from which he could attack Calvin and Beza for failing to accept his own liberal theological opinions. It achieved several editions: that of 1554 covered the transition from the Old Testament to the New with long extracts from Josephus given in Latin and printed in italic type. Castellio's desire for elegance could lead him to some inexactness which was sharply attacked by Beza, who had too little competence in Hebrew to justify him, but whose undoubted ability in Greek helped him to show that Castellio had weakened the force of many passages in the New Testament by his zeal for Ciceronian polish. Castellio's failure to express Hebrew idiom can be seen, for example, in his translation of Gen. i. 3, 'jussit Deus ut existeret lux' (Luther had shown many years before the significance of the Hebrew conception of 'Word' as God's action). Castellio's ability to smooth Hebrew into the style of Catullus, when called for, can be seen in his version of the Song of Solomon, wherein he showed also his triumphant rejection of Calvin's uneasy disapproval of regarding this book as a poem celebrating an all too human love.[1] For example, ii. 14, 'Mea columbula in petrae forculis, in cochleae latibulis, ostende mihi tuum vulticulum, fac ut audiam tuam voculam'. Castellio transformed *angelus* into *genius*, *fides* into *confidentia*, *templum* into *fanum*, *ecclesia* into *respublica*, *baptismus* into *lavacrum*. Here was a later flowering of something of the spirit of Valla in this work of a humanist scholar of undoubted ability, whose translation and annotations were to foreshadow the work of Grotius and of the Socinian commentators of the end of the seventeenth century.

The version of the Old Testament and the Apocrypha by Tremellius and Junius published in 1575–9 was the last Latin translation to appear and acquired great fame among Protestants, particularly those of the Reformed Church. Tremellius had had a long religious pilgrimage, before he began his work of translation in 1571. He had come from the ghetto in Ferrara, and, after being converted to Catholicism under Cardinal Pole, moved into Protestantism and eventually to Pole's own country, where he became regius professor of Hebrew at Cambridge, 1549; thence he moved, at the Catholic restoration, to professorships at Heidelberg and Sedan—strongholds of Reformed theology. Junius,

[1] Castellio left Geneva after disagreement with Calvin and the ministers upon certain matters, including his view of the Song of Songs which, it was felt—whether correct or incorrect—was being urged tactlessly and forcefully by Castellio. See p. 8 above.

who came from Bourges, had a less spectacular career as son-in-law to Tremellius, and became eventually professor of theology at Leyden. Later editions of this version were accompanied by either the translation of the Syriac New Testament by Tremellius or the Latin version of the Greek New Testament by Beza, or both. This version turned away from the method of Castellio to the older more literal method of Münster, and sought to convey the Hebrew sense and idiom without sacrificing Latin style ('Hebraici sermonis ordinem, ut per Latinam linguam licuit servavimus...'). The hebraizing of the Latin biblical names, the use of Mosche for Moses, for example, was defended. It is curious that there was no direct information given upon the version of the Hebrew text used for the translation—and this lack is common to most of the Latin versions. Scholars were provided with alternative renderings of the Hebrew in the marginal annotations, but the value of a reading is not argued, it tends to be assumed—again this is common to most of the Latin versions. One peculiarity of the Latin version of Beza's New Testament was the frequent use of demonstrative pronouns, for example, John i. 1, 'In principio erat Sermo ille, et Sermo ille...'. Yet, in spite of Simon's petulant treatment of this version of Tremellius and Beza, it marked an advance beyond Estienne, for it combined the best results of Hebrew and Greek scholarship in its annotations, after due allowance is made for the occasional doctrinal particularity of the Bezan version of Calvinism.

The impact and curious history of the printing of the Syriac version of the New Testament should not be overlooked, therefore some account of the Latin translations of it should be given. When the Syriac (or Peshitta) version first appeared in print in 1555 it caused a great stir: scholars hoped to find here the original of Matthew and Hebrews, and it was even believed that Syriac had been spoken by our Lord himself. The Protestants claimed that the existence of a vernacular text for the ancient Syrian Church disallowed the papal claim for the exclusive use of the Latin Vulgate, which, it was alleged, was of later date than the Syriac. The Catholics countered by showing that the antiquity of the Syriac text was being greatly overrated, and that this version was no longer understood by the laity in contemporary Syria where the vernacular was Arabic. So vigorous were the claims and counter-claims; so devious were the activities in the fifties of the Syrian priest Moses, who claimed to be the agent of the patriarch of the Jacobite

Syrian Church; and so evasive was the attitude of that patriarch to the papacy which was seeking through this link to bring the Jacobite Church into unity with Rome (for the Maronite patriarch was already in communion with Rome), that western scholars, Catholic and Protestant, seem to have exhausted their interest in this version by the seventies.

The preface of the first printed edition of the Syriac New Testament tells vividly how the knowledge of Syriac developed in the West. It began with the appearance of three Maronite clergy at the Fifth Lateran Council, 1512–17. When one of them asked permission to say mass in Syriac, a scholarly priest from Pavia, Ambrogio, was required to examine the Syrian liturgy. This otherwise impossible task was carried out with the help of a Jew who retranslated into Latin the Syrian priest's literal translation of his liturgy into contemporary Arabic. Ambrogio, from this time, sought to master the language. Once again Leo X appears as the patron of biblical learning, for he encouraged Ambrogio to persevere. Type was prepared, based on the Syriac script he had learned, and Ambrogio got ready for the press an edition of the Syriac Psalter, but his papers and the type were lost in the sack of Pavia in 1527 by Francis I who pursued a quite different humanist ideal of glory. Ambrogio was able to achieve in 1539 the printing—with poor workmanship—of small portions of the Syriac New Testament, for example, the Lord's Prayer, in a work providing specimens of various oriental biblical languages. But the determined vigour of a young German Catholic layman, trilingual scholar and diplomatist, Widmanstadt, who had eventually a greater enthusiasm than Ambrogio, made possible the fine printing of the full Syriac version of the New Testament. The aged Ambrogio gave Widmanstadt a Syriac manuscript of the Gospels and urged him to acquire the language sanctified by the lips of Christ himself, and taught him all he could.[1] The German improved his knowledge later with the help of a Maronite bishop, and eventually went to Vienna as Chancellor of Lower Austria. There he was sought out by a Jacobite priest, Moses, who showed him a manuscript of the Syriac New Testament dating from the twelfth century or earlier. With financial help from the emperor, and with Moses to assist him, Widmanstadt prepared to print it. He had the matrices struck in steel and the

[1] The title of this edition includes the words '...Jesu Christo vernacula, Divino ipsius ore consecrata'.

types cast in tin: work which was one of the remarkable achievements of the printer's craft in an age of great typographers. The book appeared in 1555, omitting, in conformity with the Syrian canon, II Peter, II and III John, Jude and Revelation; the *pericope de adultera* and the *comma Joanneum* were also absent; and the text did not have complete vocalization. Widmanstadt, in his preface, gave this moving account of Ambrogio's work and his own effort to bring the knowledge of Syriac to the West, and closed with the hope that the reunion of the Eastern Churches and Rome would now be nearer. There was no Latin translation accompanying this version, for five hundred copies of the edition were set aside for the use of the Jacobite Church (three hundred for the patriarch and two hundred for Moses—but the latter sold these, unknown to Widmanstadt, in Europe and the Levant). The remaining five hundred copies were later redated 1562 and sold in Europe. To aid scholars Widmanstadt published a small Syriac grammar in 1556. By the end of the nineteenth century Nestle could still affirm that Widmanstadt had given a clear presentation of the Syriac version which was still not finally superseded. The next two editions of the Syriac New Testament were those of Tremellius in 1569, and of Masius in the Royal Polyglot of Plantin, and both were based on Widmanstadt. Tremellius used also a manuscript in the library at Heidelberg where he was professor of Hebrew. Since no Syriac type was available to him, and since he wished to make the version more readily intelligible to biblical students, he printed his edition in Hebrew characters; gave it an almost complete vocalization; and provided a literal translation into Latin. The press was that of Henri Estienne at Geneva, who printed this edition in 1569 in folio size with four columns giving the Greek, the Syriac, the Vulgate and the Latin of Tremellius. As has been stated, controversial use was made of the Syriac version: the dedication of this volume to Queen Elizabeth contained the misleading assertion that in the Jacobite Church this version was generally understood. The Catholic reply contrived to combine truth and error in claiming that Syriac was no longer a vernacular language, and that it could have no high antiquity because it agreed with the Greek version against the Vulgate. In the fifth volume of Plantin's Polyglot in 1571 Masius gave a new edition of Widmanstadt's text after collating it with another manuscript which had belonged to the esoteric French orientalist Postel: Boderianus for this edition provided a Latin translation. Masius added in the last volume of the Polyglot, with other grammatical and lexicographical aids, a new Syriac grammar. But it was not until the seventeenth century that effective work was begun on the Syriac version of the New Testament to discover its bearing on variant readings.

ANNOTATIONS AND COMMENTARIES ON THE BIBLE

The history of biblical exegesis is one of the most neglected fields in the history of the Church and its doctrines when compared with the attention given to persons, institutions, confessions, liturgies, and apologetics. It is remarkable that the passionate devotion to biblical studies in the sixteenth century, which involved the commitment of men and whole communities to ways of living based on their interpretation of the Scriptures, has aroused so little interest among historians. The history of biblical exegesis in both Catholicism and Protestantism would provide profounder insights for the understanding of the age of the Reformation than the more usual study of the polemic of attack and counterattack which was largely peripheral to the religious needs and aspirations of the writers of the time. For example, Luther's vigorous reply to Erasmus's challenge on free-will is of less value than what he wrote on this aspect of grace, in commentaries and sermons, where he could sail clear of the treacherous narrows of controversy. With the renewal of biblical theology (and with the study of the history of exegesis which is being renewed in our time) the opportunity has come for a fresh reading of Christian thought and life not only in the Reformation age, but also in the Patristic age and in the high Middle Ages. This work, when accomplished, will change for the better some fixed patterns of interpretation.

A brief introduction to the work of the commentators of the sixteenth century will be appropriate here. The religious problem at the close of the fifteenth century was largely created by the general disintegration of authority, spiritual, doctrinal, and pastoral, into which the Church had slowly declined. Men frustrated by a confused awareness of the situation blamed the papal curia, or the weaknesses which had developed in the religious orders, or episcopal non-residence, or the secular-mindedness of ecclesiastical administrators. But there was one theme on which the greater number of scholars were agreed—both

Catholics and those who, despairing of Catholic methods of reform, became Protestants—namely, that decayed Scholasticism must be thrown off and replaced by the recovery of a better grounded authority in religion, and one which would renew spiritual vitality. In the first half of the sixteenth century men found this authority in that sense of splendid renewal through the study and interpretation of the Scriptures which has been described earlier. In the second half of the century, because of the restored and more narrowly defined ecclesiastical authority established at the Council of Trent, there appeared two entrenched and opposed orthodoxies. These were the restored Catholic scholasticism emphasizing obedience to the authority of the Church of Rome, and the theological response of the Lutheran and Reformed Churches which opposed to this Catholic position the authority of the Bible, defined by renewed Aristotelian logical method and regarded as self-sufficient and self-authenticating. Protestantism, recoiling before the victories of the Counter-Reformation, had to defend itself with the weapons of its adversary. Aristotle, dethroned by Luther, began again to master biblical theology among the followers of the first reformers. The theological readjustments of the decade 1550–60 cut deeply into the biblical studies of the period. Few scholars could enjoy peacefully the fruits won for them by the energies of the men of the thirties: polemists on both sides could turn the careful precision of biblical scholarship into a weapon weighted with the again triumphant syllogism. The consequence for biblical exegesis was the transition from regarding the Scriptures as containing the living Word of God to regarding, increasingly, all the enumerated books of a defined canon of Scripture as expressing in their very words the Word of God.

These are general statements and they need to be qualified by the reminder that some writers provided the grammatical exposition of the text, without emphasizing what the theologians believed to be the analogy of faith, or the tradition of the Church, by which the Scriptures should be interpreted. This line of development can be seen moving on from Valla through the German disciple of Melanchthon, Camerarius (who, in his work on the Gospels in 1572, praised Valla and said he wished to avoid contention and examine only the meanings of words), and onward to the seventeenth-century Dutch layman, Grotius. But the main body of exegetical work was not undertaken by these men who concerned themselves with the grammatical meaning of Scripture occasionally graced by examples of morals or piety; it was undertaken rather by the men who combined linguistic exactness with theological interpretation. These exegetes sought to expound the spiritual sense in close association with the literal or grammatical sense. Unfortunately, the Council of Trent sharply raised the issue, by what criteria could this spiritual sense be determined? If the spiritual sense was to be determined by the grammatical meaning, then the freedom of the Word of God (as Protestants would say), or the tradition of the Church (as Catholics would say), would be endangered by being bound to the pedagogy of grammarians. If the analogy of faith was to be the key to unlock the Scriptures then the danger appeared of placing the Word of God under the arbitrament of dogmatic theology. If the internal testimony of the Holy Spirit gave an assured understanding of the Scriptures, then came the difficulty of knowing within what community of Christians the Holy Spirit was speaking most clearly. These roads of argument led to a retreat from the authority of the living Word of God in the Bible (as it had been known, for example, to Luther) into four extreme positions. The Church of Rome affirmed that the hierarchy had been endowed with the sevenfold charisms of the Holy Spirit, and therefore the hierarchy alone had the right to guard the interpretation of the Scriptures made by exegetes and theologians. This could lead to the vitality of Catholic exegesis declining into the orthodox allegories and prolix moralizing of the commentaries of Cornelius a Lapide (d. 1637). Protestant orthodoxy, especially in seventeenth-century Lutheran scholasticism, could reach the state of the theological faculty of Wittenberg which denounced the blasphemous presumption of Beza for having written that the Greek of the New Testament contained solecisms and barbarisms. The addiction of the Socinians to the grammatical sense, interpreted in accordance with the light of nature, could lead to rationalistic disintegration of the unity and authority of the Word of God. The Anabaptists believed that since 'the letter kills' therefore the 'inner Word', or illumination by the Spirit, alone was significant. This could lead, through their spiritual heirs in some English seventeenth-century nonconformist groups, to an individualistic and pietistic use of Scripture, which, though it could rise to the imaginative splendour of Bunyan, was certainly far removed, as was the practice of the other three extreme positions, from the exegetical and grammatical discipline of the men of the *respublica litterarum* prior to 1562.

These earlier exegetes were faced by the twofold problem set for them by the methods of medieval exegesis and by the impact of Italian humanism with its concern for grammatical precision and textual criticism. They answered it by greatly modifying the medieval practice (there was, of course, no severance from the past save among the Anabaptists and Socinians) and adapting it to the principles of the Italian method, that is, they emphasized the literal, historical, grammatical sense, and found in Christ that spiritual sense which quickened the other into becoming the life-giving Word of God.

> Litera gesta docet: quid credas, Allegoria:
> Moralis, quid agas: quo tendas, Anagogia.

Here were the essential themes of medieval exegesis. An example of this can be seen in the interpretation of the name Jerusalem. Literally (or historically) it is the bloody city; allegorically (or figuratively) it is the Church militant; tropologically (or morally) it represents the faithful soul whose conscience is at peace; anagogically (or, as we might say, eschatologically) it is the Church triumphant.[1] Nicholas of Lyra (d. 1349), the greatest of the medieval exegetes, and a writer whose work was admired and used by Luther, had protested in the Second Prologue to his commentaries in his *Biblia Sacra cum Glossa Ordinaria* that 'the literal sense is nearly suffocated among so many mystical expositions'. But in this judgment he was unusual, and a century later Paul of Burgos in an additional preface to the same work sharply repudiated Lyra's too great concern with the literal sense. As we have seen, the resulting methods of biblical interpretation by the end of the fifteenth century were described by Geiler of Kaisersberg as making of the Bible a nose of wax.

It was the lucid critical mind of the Italian humanist, Lorenzo Valla, who first broke out of what Erasmus described as 'those impure marshes' of the allegorists and scholastics in the annotations on the New Testament which he left unpublished at his death in 1465. When Erasmus found a copy of this manuscript half a century later in a monastic library near Brussels, he also found corroboration of much of what he was working out for himself in his own study of the Greek

[1] S. Berger, *La Bible au seizième siècle* (1879), p. 26.

New Testament. It is possible that his publication of Valla's annotations in 1505 at Paris was not only due to a scholar's pleasure in making available such distinguished work, but also to his wish to open a breach through which he could thrust himself. (Erasmus, unlike his less devious contemporaries, had an elaborate strategy for his literary production which ably assisted his fame as a man of letters as well as making it difficult for censorious churchmen to attack him.) Valla's notes on the Vulgate text, which show that he used at least three Greek manuscripts, are concerned with brief grammatical analysis and avoid theological interpretation. Valla underlined weaknesses in the Vulgate version; he frequently expressed contempt for scholastics who wrote on the New Testament without regard for the original Greek; and he made the point that theologians must work from the grammatical sense for the meaning of the text. Erasmus praised 'the admirable wisdom [*mira sagacitate*] with which he sifted the New Testament even though he was a grammarian' (*homo rhetoricus*, that is, not a theologian).[1] Valla's notes were of such precision that they attained to that Pantheon of exegetes the *Critici Sacri* of the late seventeenth century. Different in kind and quality was the work of the Picard Jacques Lefèvre d'Étaples (Faber Stapulensis) who, after travelling in Italy where he caught the passion for Greek learning and a less desirable platonizing mysticism, produced his *Psalterium Quincuplex* (1505), and his commentaries on the Latin text of the Pauline Epistles (1513), and of the Gospels (1522). His passionate devotion to the renewal of Church and society by the Word of God has already been shown. While this was not matched by his scholarship, in which he was inferior to Erasmus, yet he stirred men to discipleship not only in France, where he was the leading scholar of the 'Évangéliques', but also in the humanist cities of Switzerland, and his letters show how many of the biblical humanists were in touch with him. His method in his commentaries was to give a paraphrased exposition, and then add to this brief notes showing by illustration the meaning of the Greek. In the preface to his commentary on the Gospels he wrote, 'The Word of God suffices. It is the only rule and guide of eternal life', and in his exposition of Romans ix, in the commentary on the Pauline Epistles of 1513, he came near to what Luther was soon about to proclaim on justification by faith. These were bold utterances. Erasmus, with characteristic diplomacy, for he him-

[1] Erasmus, *In Novum Testamentum Annotationes* (1535), Acts xxii. 9.

self attacked scholastic writers in his own annotations, wrote that he would have preferred Lefèvre to speak more civilly of those pillars of the Church.[1] And while Erasmus could approve of Lefèvre's 'most ardent study for restoring good letters', yet he could firmly reject some of his more arbitrary interpretations and his defective grammatical knowledge. That Lefèvre could include with the Pauline writings the *Epistle to the Laodiceans* and the spurious letters of Seneca to Paul, and support this by the unsatisfactory critical judgment that he had found *Laodiceans* accompanying the Pauline corpus in libraries at Padua, Cologne and Paris, shows how much inferior he was to Erasmus. But it was no doubt his 'lutheranizing' rather than his lack of critical acumen which caused his commentary on Paul to be placed on the Index.

Lefèvre had tried to do with enthusiasm but insufficient grounding what Valla had ignored: he had tried to relate the study of the literal meaning of the text, by reference to the Greek original, with the spiritual meaning, that is, Christ himself speaking through the writings of the apostles. This twofold work of interpretation was done by Erasmus with much greater judgment, with profounder learning, and with a more lucid and beguiling latinity. In the annotations which accompanied his edition of the Greek text from 1516 he not only showed the inadequacy of the Vulgate translation by printing his own Latin version beside the Greek text, but he could also write, in one of several criticisms, of 'an inexcusable error in the text of the Vulgate'. Like Valla, to whom he often referred, he gave concise interpretation of the meaning of the Greek almost verse by verse; the humanists could feel at home from the first when at Matt. i. 19 Martial, Petronius and Seneca are given the sanction of quotation; and on occasion up to two pages could be given to the spiritual application of a passage by that mellow 'philosophy of Christ' with which Erasmus tempered evangelical zeal. Erasmus emphasized neither justifying faith nor the immediacy of a Hebraically conceived Word of God; and for the doctrine of grace he leaned to Chrysostom rather than to Augustine—it was Lefèvre who in some ways foreshadowed Luther and not Erasmus. But he was at one with Luther and others of the earlier generation of exegetes in asserting (on Matt. ii. 6) that while errors may occur in the transmission of the text and the apostle seems to stumble, yet we should not be disturbed,

[1] Erasmus, *In Novum Testamentum Annotationes*. Heb. ii. 7.

for Christ alone has spoken the truth and he delivers from all error. Erasmus wrote elsewhere on homiletic method in his *Ecclesiastes* and on theological method in his *Ratio seu Methodus*: in the former he could reply to those who wished Scripture to be kept confined to the safe hands of theologians, 'the Spirit teaches, not Aristotle; grace not reasoning; inspiration not the syllogism'.[1] Yet for all his lucidity Erasmus could be confused about the use of allegory in interpreting Scripture, and tried to provide rules for the use of the mystical sense: his admiration for Origen influenced him here. The compiler of the humanists' 'dictionary of quotations', the *Adagia*, who searched for the hidden mysteries in men's proverbs, could be turned to allegorizing speculations. These, however, did not appear in his annotations on the New Testament, where he urged that real knowledge of Scripture cannot derive from mere respect for the Fathers, nor from the old laborious compilations (*consarcinatis glossematis*, II Cor. xi. 23) on the different senses of Scripture.

Erasmus had, therefore, clearly established that there were two principles fundamental to sound biblical exegesis; those who followed after him could not return again to allegorizing. These principles were, that the grammatical sense must be interpreted by the highest linguistic skills, and that the spiritual sense, the divine truth in Christ, must be expounded in close relationship to this grammatical sense. These principles can be seen plainly, if with varying emphasis, in the annotated Bibles (or parts of the Bible) which were published between 1535 and 1575. Sebastian Münster provided for his edition of the Bible of 1535 extensive notes which display effectively his knowledge of the rabbinical commentators—his first comment consists of a quotation from the rabbis accompanied by his own refutation. Estienne and others after him printed that collation of students' lecture notes which appears under the name of Vatable of the *Lecteurs Royaux* of Paris: the form of these comments shows this stenographic origin in their terse brevity. Fagius produced three different volumes in the forties which provided notes on the Pentateuch, or parts of it, displaying rabbinical learning as well as sound exegetical judgment. It was no doubt the fame he acquired by this work which brought him, through Cranmer's invitation, to the regius chair of Hebrew at Cambridge. The Latin Zurich Bible of 1542 was accompanied by explanatory prefaces and brief notes

[1] Erasmus, *Enarratio Primi Psalmi*, *Opera Omnia* (1703–6), v, 183.

marked by directness and practical simplicity. But it was Castellio, in the annotations he gave to his Latin version of 1551, who showed more plainly than his predecessors the application of the Erasmian principles. His comments have less weight of learning than those of Münster: they are lucid, relevant and attractive in style; but they also show less concern about the nature of the spiritual sense which had worried Erasmus in his *Ecclesiastes*. In addressing his readers Castellio wrote that the Spirit of God dictated the matter and teaches from it, but that he did not have this Spirit which is not subject to human arts and devices, and that therefore he confined himself to elucidating what the words plainly state. This modesty annoyed Beza who saw here a cloak for heterodoxy and attacked Castellio's interpretations as 'ambiguas, violentas, absurdas, ineptas' in his own annotated New Testament. Castellio had written at Romans ix a long note on predestination deliberately repudiating Genevan orthodoxy on this head, and asserted that 'no one is compelled: faith is free'. To Beza this was both true and irrelevant: for him Castellio was doing less than justice to Paul. Castellio's concluding comment on the description of the Ark of Noah in his first edition deserves commendation; avoiding rabbinical allusions and pedantic theories he wrote 'I do not understand this subject', but, alas, in his final edition he could not resist a brief explanation of the construction of the Ark. Beza's annotations to his Greek and Latin New Testament showed great erudition and carried further the tentative suggestions of Erasmus about the critical use of variant readings in the manuscripts—although he was afraid to follow up the implications of the readings which alarmed him in Codex D. His grammatical competence in Greek combined with theological insight gave greater value to his annotations than had been attained by any previous scholar. But his theological interpretation was occasionally too particular, notably on the doctrines of election and predestination. Selections from Beza's notes also appeared with his Latin version in the Bible prepared by Tremellius and Junius in 1575, and accompanied by their own annotations. These were frequently terse but unattractive in style; they showed wide learning and narrow judgments; and because of their provenance and practical brevity obtained a wide circulation among ministers of the Reformed Churches and English Puritans.

Before we turn from the annotators to the writers of full-scale commentaries on separate books of the Bible, an early biblical humanist deserves to be rescued from oblivion, Pellican of Zurich. He issued seven volumes of paraphrastic commentary which interlaced the text of almost the whole Vulgate version corrected by himself. His prefaces and commentary were clear and practical and this work was attractively presented by Froschauer's press: but other names from Basle and Zurich drew more attention. These were Oecolampadius who had helped Erasmus to see his New Testament through the press at Basle; Zwingli the militant Antistes of Zurich; and his more scholarly successor Bullinger. The men of the small city republics of Basle and Zurich believed that their independence must be maintained not only by the rejection of the Empire but also of the papal power which was associated with it. Victory over the emperors had been won by their fathers: the combination of the humanist spirit with the civic energies of the guilds and merchants brought the overthrow of hierarchical control, and the vigorous transformation of the Church according to the modified Erasmian interpretation of Scripture characteristic of Zwinglianism. Since the papal ecclesiastical system was grounded in a particular view of man's free-will and involved the doctrine of merit, then the Erasmian 'philosophy of Christ', also based on free-will and merit, had to be repudiated by his Swiss disciples—but his exegetical method was maintained, reinforced by justifying faith. Oecolampadius, who had worked for Erasmus at Froben's press in Basle, had been—like his friend Pellican—a pupil of Reuchlin, and was, therefore, a good Hebraist who knew how to use the targums and Kimḥi. He wrote compact commentaries on Genesis and the Prophets and on parts of the New Testament, in which can be seen the Erasmian emphasis on the grammatical sense and on the relation of secular learning to 'the scope of piety'.[1] He added to this something more significant for the future which can be seen, for example, in his commentary on Daniel (1530). This was prefaced by an *Epistola Apologetica ad Ecclesiam Catholicam* in which he wrote that where Christ's Word is not heard and discipline not maintained there is an *ecclesia decrepita*, and gave those notes of the Church which were to be characteristic of the Swiss Reformation, including the Zwinglian doctrine of the Lord's Supper and the necessity of the discipline of manners. Grynaeus (to whom Calvin admiringly addressed the preface of his first commentary in 1539), like Capito who left for Strassburg to assist Bucer, wrote at Basle with similar methods.

[1] Oecolampadius, *In Danielem Prophetam*, I, 4.

Zwingli of Zurich, who died in the same year as Oecolampadius, 1531, had little time from statesmanship, controversy and pastoral care to produce commentaries: most of his biblical exposition was essentially homiletic. In his student days he acquired a deep devotion to Erasmian humanism, an influence which never left him. This shows in his discussion of biblical phrases through the analysis of rhetorical figures, and in his going straight to the public exposition of Matthew's Gospel, at the opening of the Zurich Reformation, rather than to Paul. His Hebrew learning was thin, although he wrote on Isaiah and Jeremiah and could see the Hebraic background to the *logos* in John i. Unlike Luther, he made no distinction between law and Gospel; for Zwingli the law was a mirror of God's will and was fulfilled in the Gospel. For him the Epistle of James contained no problem. Bullinger, the successor to Zwingli as Antistes of Zurich, was the most thorough of these Swiss commentators. He wrote on the whole New Testament and on Jeremiah. The interest of these Swiss Reformers of city republics in emphasizing Jeremiah, with its doctrine of God's covenant with his people, and the Gospels which contained the new law of love in Christ, is characteristic. The discipline of manners in association with 'evangelical doctrine' can be seen in the purposeful digressions on these themes which Bullinger interpolated with exposition of the text—in this he was typical of the new generation of commentators.

Erasmus, seeking the original fountain of Scripture, resembles Petrarch sonnet-making before the Fountain of Vaucluse when compared with Luther's search for the meaning of the Bible, a search for biblical theology which led to something like the fertilizing inundation of the Nile. Erasmus and Luther sought different things, and the shock of Luther's successful discovery of the authoritative and immediate Word of God speaking out of Scripture transformed biblical exegesis for two generations. Luther did not seek for critical canons like the humanists: he regarded these as another attempt by men to bind the free Word of God. Luther was new, more so than Erasmus or Zwingli or his other contemporaries; and his insights remain fresh, fruitful and stimulating today—in part because he refused to be a systematic exegete tied by the Erasmian rules of exegesis. Since the reign of Elizabeth his best-known work in English has been described as a commentary on Galatians: but it is not a formal commentary, it consists of a stenographic record, later overseen by Luther, of his extempore lectures from notes. All his well-known works of biblical exposition, the lectures on Genesis, the sermons on John, and the Psalms, and the rest, have this same origin. His fundamental principle of interpretation was theological. Increasingly, from the date of his appointment as professor of biblical exegesis at Wittenberg in 1512 up to his breakthrough by 1521, he wrestled with the problem of how man can become righteous before God. What he described as his 'discovery of mercy', was his grasp of the fact that the heart of scriptural teaching is that justification from sin before God lies in faith which is an existential personal relationship grounded in God's initiative of grace towards men. This he derived from both experience and its objective correlate in the Word of God in Scripture. Luther himself gave some account of the development of his transforming experience, and it has been the subject of thorough scholarly analysis in the last forty years. The law is both God's demand upon men and judgment because of their inability to fulfil them: the Gospel is deliverance, through the person and work of Christ, from the law and its judgment. Only within the freedom of justifying faith in Christ can the works of love be performed. All views of Luther's theology which seek to derive it, for example, from Augustinianism, or Nominalism, or the mysticism of the Rhineland, fail to meet Luther's insistence that it was through the living Word of God—which is God's speech, his action, the Word made flesh in Christ, and therefore forgiveness of sins—out of the Scriptures that he found these verities. For Luther the Gospel of John, the Epistles of Paul, and I Peter are the very marrow of the New Testament. Further, Genesis, for example, consists of illustrations of faith and unbelief and therefore has much of the Gospel in it. For Luther the Old Testament is the swaddling-clothes of Christ. 'The Gospel is the key to unlock the Old Testament.' Since Luther placed Christ at the heart of Scripture he could be critical of the Bible as a book in a manner which would have scandalized later Lutherans: the chapters of Isaiah are out of order; James is 'a good book but it is not an apostolic book';[1] Revelation is neither apostolic nor prophetic and resembles the dreams of the Abbot Joachim; the Book of Kings is a Jewish calendar; it does no harm to say that the Pentateuch could not have been written by Moses; Paul did not write Hebrews and perhaps Apollos did. For Luther canonicity depended on the Gospel not on chronology. But he insisted

[1] *Works of Martin Luther* (Philadelphia ed. 1932), VI, 477.

that the historical sense was the basis for exegesis; for 'the historical sense teaches, consoles, confirms'. When he used allegory it was for illustration: it was not a principle. Where parts of Scripture are obscure they can be illumined by other passages, but the experience of faith is necessary: to rationalize texts is to lose their meaning.

Luther had many ardent disciples but none of them could match his creative powers and exegetical tact—Bugenhagen, Cruciger, Jonas were epigoni, and even Brenz could not compare with Luther, although he followed a more systematic method. Melanchthon produced little of value in Old Testament exegesis; his humanism helped him to adorn his *scholia* on Proverbs and Ecclesiastes with classical allusions, and he could allegorize the account of 'day' and 'night' in Genesis i into symbols of death and resurrection. Out of his exegesis of Romans grew his famous *Loci Communes*: while this indicates his exegetical purpose, yet it belongs rather to the history of doctrine. Melanchthon's attempt to unite Erasmian methods with Lutheran insights brought forward a fierce controversy in the fifties. Flacius Illyricus denounced Melanchthon for turning aside from Luther's purpose, and, himself a man of the Tridentine generation, put the Scriptures again under a formalized pattern of interpretation and hermeneutic theory in his *Clavis Scripturae Sanctae* (1562). This marks the beginning of that Lutheran scholasticism which in the next sixty years, through Chemnitz and his successors, produced a dry and over-formulated orthodoxy.

One of this group of Lutherans was the persistent allegorizer Hunnius, who vigorously attacked Calvin in his *Calvinus Judaizans* (1595) for opening the way to Judaism and Arianism because of the impious manner in which he had corrupted the interpretation of Scripture. For example, Calvin in his comment on Gen. i. 1 had dared to say that *elohim*, though a plural, did not refer to the Persons of the Holy Trinity: '[this interpretation] seems to me to have little solidity... readers should be warned against violent glosses'. (In quoting this, Hunnius was horrified into capitals for MIHI and VIOLENTIS. Moreover, it is significant of the difference between Calvin and later 'Calvinists' that the nineteenth-century English translator of Calvin's commentary on Genesis added a footnote to this comment of Calvin to explain away its forthrightness.) But the quotation from Calvin is typical of his exegetical method: he wanted to set forth the plain sensible meaning of a passage; he wished to establish what the biblical words mean in their context. He sought more frequently than most men of his age to interpret the writings of the Old Testament according to the circumstances and purposes of their own day, even though he always felt the gravitational pull of the needs of the analogy of faith. And the fact that he neither commented, nor preached, on certain books of the Bible should not be dismissed as accidental. In his expositions Calvin showed his method plainly, he did not conceal matters from his readers; he led them openly, from evidence he had adduced, to his interpretations. Calvin has been criticized for avoiding allegory only by falling into typology, but while for him 'Christ is the end of the law', yet in fact his use of typology is comparatively sparing—so sparing indeed, in comparison with others of that time, that Hunnius indignantly attacked him on this ground. The other characteristic of Calvin was what he himself called 'perspicuous brevity' in his letter to Grynaeus of Basle which prefaced his own commentary on Romans (1540), and which gives a succinct account of Calvin's views on some contemporary exegetes and on exegesis—the aim should be that plainness which avoids prolixity. Calvin was never diffuse and avoided the mere display of learning; he toiled after clear instruction in the interpretation of the text and edification from it. He wrote on the following: Genesis, a harmony of the four remaining books of the Pentateuch, Joshua, Psalms, the Major and Minor Prophets, and all of the New Testament save for II and III John and Revelation. Not all of these were formal commentaries: some were stenographic reports of his biblical lectures in the Academy of Geneva, later overseen and revised by himself (for example, the *Praelectiones in librum prophetiarum Danielis*). After his death in 1564 appeared collections of his sermons on Deuteronomy, Job and I Samuel, which had been taken down by hearers who found in them matter almost as useful as his commentaries. Unlike Luther, Calvin accepted almost without qualification the canon of Scripture to which Protestants are now accustomed; his silence on the books which he omitted from exegetical comment or sermon is notable, but he occasionally quotes from them in his formal theological writings. Yet, while he gave good grounds for doubting the Pauline authorship of Hebrews and the Petrine origin of II Peter, he was little concerned with critical questions on the canon, or on 'higher' or 'lower' criticism. What is often described as 'fundamentalist literalism'—the infallible divine inspiration of the words, and even the letters, of Scripture—was not an interest of the first reformers: this was a question, posed in various ways, which beset their followers and some post-Tridentine Catholics. For Calvin the Scriptures were self-sufficient through the authenticating power of the Holy Spirit, since for him Word and Spirit witness to each other.

Calvin's resources as an exegete made him superior to all his contemporaries if we allow his purposes in exegesis to be sufficient. He was competent in Hebrew without being a distinguished Hebraist: he had studied at Paris and at Basle under Münster whose Hebrew Old Testament appeared during Calvin's stay there. His Greek was also effective for his purpose: he can often quote the Septuagint to justify his reading of a Hebrew word or phrase. He gave his own Latin translation of the passage he expounded, frequently suggesting variant translations to bring out the force of a word. Calvin was an *homme trilingue*, a worthy representative of French biblical humanism. He could make mistakes in his Hebrew readings, but he often did so in good company.[1] However, he kept his balance as an exegete by insisting on looking at a word in its context. Something of Calvin's manner and method can be seen in the following quotations. In his comment on Joel i. 1 he wrote: 'As to the verb הָיָה *hayah* [Vulg.: *factum est*] there is no ground for philosophizing so acutely as does Jerome on, How was the Word made? For he was afraid lest it should be said that Christ was made, since He is the Word [*verbum*] of the Lord. These are the most puerile trifles...for the Prophet here says plainly that the Word [*sermo*] of the Lord was directed to him, that is, that the Lord used him as his agent to the whole people.' Again, on Rom. viii. 3, 'The particle ἐν ᾧ Erasmus has rendered "ex parte qua", [in that part in which]; but because I consider it to be causal, it is better to translate it "*eo quod*" [because]. Although such a manner of speaking perhaps does not occur among sound authors in the Greek language, yet, because the apostles everywhere take over Hebrew diction, this interpretation should not be thought harsh.' (Commentators are still divided on this point.) Calvin's background of humanism gave him illustrative quotations from the Greek and Latin Fathers, as well as from Plutarch and Plato, Cicero and Quintilian, and others: and his contemporaries are not forgotten, for example, Budé, Bucer

[1] J. Baumgartner, *Calvin Hébraïsant et interprète de l'Ancien Testament* (1881), p. 50.

and Melanchthon. However, these references are given sparingly, and not for ostentation but rather for usefulness.

In his preface to his commentary on the Psalms Calvin gave high praise to the commentary on them by Martin Bucer, that nursing-father of religious refugees at Strassburg among whom Calvin had been one. Yet Calvin could also write of Bucer's works to Grynaeus, in prefacing his commentary on Romans, as being too full, although sound and useful. Both judgments are correct. Bucer was, like Melanchthon on Romans, given to doctrinal and moral digressions in his commentaries, particularly those on the Gospels and Romans. These digressions, for example, in his *In sacra quatuor Evangelia, Enarrationes perpetuae* (1536), on such subjects as the Lord's Supper, the Magistrate, Wages, Anabaptism, while they are sound and useful, yet they distract the reader's attention. Estienne thought so highly of Bucer's commentaries that he graced some of them before his death with the typographical splendour of his press at Geneva. And Bucer's appeal to 'holy antiquity' and 'the agreement of the ages' in his address to Bishop Fox of Hereford set before his commentary on the Gospels, together with his great patristic learning, must have endeared him to Archbishop Cranmer who was delighted that he could persuade him to a regius chair at Cambridge in 1549. Bucer had no passion for philological ingenuity (although he can use the translation *Autophyes* for the name of God in the Psalter), nor for textual criticism; his purpose was religious edification based on a sufficient elucidation of the text.

The Florentine, Peter Martyr (Pietro Martire Vermigli), an Augustinian and Visitor-General of his Order in Italy (who had among his pupils the converted Jew Tremellius, who followed his master into Protestantism), after wide reading in the Fathers and the new biblical learning, left Italy for a distinguished professorial career at Strassburg, Oxford, and Zurich, where he succeeded Pellican. His commentaries on Samuel, Kings, Judges, Corinthians and Romans resemble in method and interests those of Bucer in their concern for edification, their patristic learning, and their set discussions of doctrinal, moral, and social themes. He claimed, reasonably, in his preface to Corinthians, that he did not set aside on polemic grounds anything which is agreeable to the Word of God.

But Beza at Geneva was, unlike Martyr, willing to associate the exposition of the New Testament with polemic argument, as we have seen already. Beza's Geneva was to become the stronghold of an ecclesiastical particularism like the Wittenberg of Lutheran scholasticism. Beza's annotations on the whole New Testament, in spite of the excellent Greek manuscripts before him, showed too little concern for textual criticism. He turned away from Calvin's arguments against the Pauline authorship of Hebrews and the Petrine authorship of II Peter, and he even published a number of sermons on the Song of Songs with the usual allegorizing. In these as in other ways, he gained the discipleship of English Puritans who, it is too little realized, were more Bezanists than Calvinists.

Musculus of Berne produced several extensive commentaries which were unique in their method, differentiating his work from all other commentaries of his time. He wrote very fully on Genesis, Psalms, Isaiah, Matthew, John, and the Pauline Epistles, in a threefold method—first he gave the textual meaning in translation or paraphrase; next, he gave a thorough discussion of the grammatical and historical sense in which he showed excellent exegetical tact; and, finally, he provided 'questions' or 'observations', that is, doctrinal and practical conclusions. Thus he avoided the diffuseness of Bucer, and made plain to his readers, by the sub-titles of his divisions, where to find what they wanted.

The Catholic commentators of the period must be mentioned here, for their work, especially after the Council of Trent, represented the Catholic response to Protestant methods in biblical scholarship by an impressive use of certain of the tools which the Protestants had made effective. Catholic scholarship from the time of Cardinal Cajetan onward was faced by the twofold problem of how to avoid the appearance of accepting the Protestant appeal to the Hebrew and Greek texts of the Bible according to a different view of the analogy of faith, and how to discover a clear definition of what was meant by the requirements of the Council of Trent upon 'the sense in which Holy Mother Church has held and holds the interpretation of Scripture' and 'the unanimous consent of the Fathers'.[1] However, it is interesting to notice that some Catholic scholars interpreted this decree as allowing them a greater freedom in textual criticism, where faith and morals were not at stake, than many Protestants could allow. But the greater freedom of the Catholic scholars should not be exaggerated. For example, Cardinal

[1] The Fourth Session of the Council of Trent, 8 April 1546: the Decree concerning the Canonical Scriptures.

Cajetan, a Dominican, appealed in his commentaries, written before the Council of Trent, to the literal and grammatical sense of Scripture, since Protestant heresy could only be confuted adequately on the ground it had chosen for itself; but he was vigorously attacked by a fellow Dominican, Catharinus, who could say, with much else, that Cajetan argued like Julian the Apostate since he had raised doubts about the canonicity of Hebrews. Further, the tentative work in textual criticism undertaken by Cardinals Sadoleto and Contarini, and later by Cardinal Bellarmine, could be denigrated by Catholics for its 'Protestantizing'. And the layman Masius and the Portuguese Dominican Oleaster who raised questions of higher criticism—Masius, in his commentary on Joshua, had shown the difficulties in assuming the Mosaic authorship of the Pentateuch—found their books placed on the Index. However, men like the Italian Benedictine Isidore Clarius, before Trent, could use the method of linguistic precision found in the exegesis of Erasmus while avoiding his hermeneutic interpretation. This method was also that of Lucas of Bruges, and of the Jesuits Maldonatus, Sa, Sanchez, and the Dominican Foreirius (whose excellent commentary on Isaiah long remained, like that of Maldonatus on the Gospels, a standard work) and attained its climax with Cardinal Bellarmine who combined controversial brilliance with sound biblical scholarship. After Bellarmine came the Jesuit Cornelius a Lapide whose commentaries, already mentioned as examples of prolixity, show plainly that decline noted sharply by the Catholic Simon as due to 'la méthode des Théologiens Scholastiques qui se copient les uns les autres sans consulter les Auteurs dans leur source'.[1]

It should not be forgotten that there were many others, Protestant and Catholic, who wrote commentaries on the Scriptures besides those who have been named here: Frenchmen, Swiss, Germans, Spaniards, and men of the Low Countries, all were affected in varying ways by the work initiated by the trilingual studies of biblical humanism. It is significant that no English names appear. Almost no grammar, lexicon or commentary by an English scholar won a European reputation before the seventeenth century. The reason for this should be obvious. Trilingual studies at Oxford and Cambridge, in comparison with the

[1] Richard Simon, *Histoire Critique des Principaux Commentateurs du Nouveau Testament* (1693), p. 661. For Catholic commentaries see further pp. 213–17 and for Simon, pp. 193–5, 218–21 below.

continental achievement, were almost stillborn, and the energies of English scholars were absorbed in the intense controversial and political struggle between Catholic and Protestant. The appearance of Bucer, Fagius, Tremellius and Martyr in our universities was brief, but they had laid solid foundations for biblical studies. It is characteristic of the English situation that as late as the end of the sixteenth century Hooker, who was a specialist in Hebrew, achieved his great renown for his work as an apologist and philosopher. But by the mid-seventeenth century the position had changed. While Europe was sunk in religious wars and the stalemate induced by the refutation by Catholics and Protestants of each other's scholastic positions, England fulfilled the work begun at Alcalá and Basle, Paris and Louvain, in the noblest of the Polyglot Bibles, that issued by Brian Walton and his fellow editors in 1657, and in its counterpart the *Critici Sacri*, edited by John Pearson and others in 1660, which reproduced a great number of those commentaries which had established effectively the literal and grammatical sense of the Scriptures.

Some words from Walton's defence of his *Biblia Polyglotta* in 1659 may formally conclude this account of the movement of biblical renewal which Erasmus and his contemporaries had begun. '...the design of the Edition was not only to exhibit to the reader all the ancient and chief Translations, together with the Originals, but also the chief Copies, MS. or others, of both, that so in this Edition the reader might have all or most other Editions, and the best MSS. which he might consult at pleasure....Now care is taken that every private man may have them, and use them as his own.'[1]

[1] Brian Walton, *The Considerator Considered* (1659), reprinted in vol. II, pp. 155–6 of *Memoirs of the Life and Writings of Walton*, ed. H. J. Todd (1821).

CHAPTER III

CONTINENTAL VERSIONS TO c. 1600

1. GERMAN VERSIONS

LUTHER

A German Bible printed by Sylvan Otmar at Augsburg did indeed appear during the year 1518—only a few months after Luther had published his theses. But it belonged to the series of editions of the German translation made in about 1350 and first printed in 1466 by Johann Mentelin at Strassburg. In the next fifty years or so there were thirteen further editions. This translation was not made from the original languages but only from the Vulgate, and was moreover—despite several revisions, especially in 1475 and 1483—clumsy in its linguistic form, and partly incomprehensible. Hence it answered neither of Luther's two requirements for such a translation, that it should be based on the original texts and should use a German comprehensible to all; and it is not surprising that this medieval version did not have Luther's approval. He had already used the Greek original in his lectures on Romans in 1515–16, and the Hebrew in his commentary on Hebrews in 1517–18. And since it was one of his cardinal principles that the Scriptures were the only true key to the faith, it is not surprising either that he decided to translate the Bible into German himself. It seems as if the idea of such a translation was already current in Wittenberg in 1520. Andreas Carlstadt's treatise on the canon (*Welche bucher Biblisch seint*), which was published at Wittenberg in November, said 'Shortly, as I hear, new German Bibles are to be printed'. But it was a whole year before the plan was put into effect.

On his short visit to Wittenberg in December 1521 Luther was encouraged by his friend Philipp Melanchthon, professor of Greek at the university, to translate the New Testament, which was linguistically the less arduous task. He began it as soon as he went back to the

Wartburg. When he returned to Wittenberg, on 6 March 1522, Luther brought with him the first draft, which he had completed in two and a half months; and with Melanchthon, the eminent Greek scholar, he submitted it to a thorough revision. Early in May the printing had already begun, and in great secrecy and with the aid of three presses it was finished shortly before 21 September—hence the name 'September Testament'. This, Luther's first biblical edition, appeared under the title *Das Neue Testament Deutzsch* in an edition of 3000 copies, without the name of the translator, the printer (Melchior II Lotther), or the publishers (the elder Lukas Cranach and the Wittenberg goldsmith Christian Döring). It was a folio, and had twenty-one full-page woodcuts in Revelation from Cranach's workshop, and many woodcut initials; and it cost half a gulden, or 10½ groschen, the weekly wage of a journeyman carpenter.

While the printing of the New Testament was still going on, Luther began work on the translation of the Old Testament. Because of its length, and because otherwise the price would be too high, it appeared in parts. The Pentateuch, again published by Cranach and Döring and printed by the younger Melchior Lotther, appeared in the summer of 1523 at 14 groschen. The second and third parts, the historical and poetical books, from Joshua to the Song of Solomon, and the first separate issue of the Psalter, were printed and published by Cranach and Döring in 1524. Luther's original plan was to include the Prophets in the third part, and the table of contents lists them accordingly, but the difficulty of the translation had already caused such delays to the volume that the plan was abandoned. The conflict with the *Schwärmer* (Anabaptists and others), the Peasants' War, and the resumption of the university lectures which he had suspended on 29 March 1521, kept Luther from the continuous prosecution of his translation. But he used his lectures on the Minor Prophets from spring 1524 to summer 1526 as a preparatory study, and in March 1526 was able to publish the translation of Jonah, in June of the same year Habakkuk, and late in 1527 Zechariah, with a commentary on each. The printer was Michael Lotther.

The translation of Isaiah was begun in 1527 when he was lecturing on this book, but was not published until autumn 1528, partly because of the temporary removal of the university to Jena, so that Luther was deprived of the expert linguistic advice of Melanchthon and the

Hebrew scholar Matthäus Aurogallus. This part, like all subsequent first editions of his Bible, was printed at Wittenberg by Hans Lufft. The continuation of the translation was now held up by Luther's activity as Visitor of the Church, by his acting for the absent Johann Bugenhagen as minister to the town, and by other literary works—for instance the two catechisms and the revision of the New Testament—as well as by sickness. But during his illness Luther translated the comparatively easy Greek text of the Wisdom of Solomon, which was published in June 1529 after revision with the help of Melanchthon. The grave Turkish menace then moved him to deal first with the prophet Daniel, whose vision is taken to represent the Turks—an interpretation of Melanchthon's. This edition appeared in the early summer of 1530, with a dedication to Johann Friedrich, son of the Saxon Elector Johann, and a preface containing an extensive commentary. Luther's translation of the 38th and 39th chapters of Ezekiel 'On Gog' was also applied to the Turks. Luther completed the translation of the remaining Major and Minor Prophets during his stay in Coburg at the time of the Diet of Augsburg (24 April–4 October 1530), but the revision and publication were then delayed by other literary work, the revision of the Psalter early in 1531, another spell of acting for Bugenhagen, and several illnesses. *Die Propheten alle Deudsch* finally appeared in March 1532, published by Christian Döring alone, printed by Hans Lufft and costing 8 groschen. Only the Apocrypha now remained, but though Ecclesiasticus was completed and published by the end of 1532, Luther's illness again caused delay. Publication of the first complete Bible now depended only on finishing the Apocrypha, and to hasten its appearance learned friends at Wittenberg now came openly to Luther's aid. They translated the remaining apocryphal books partly from the Septuagint and partly from the Vulgate, while the reformer contributed only the prefaces. I Maccabees appeared as a separate issue in 1533; and in the second edition was supplemented by the apocryphal additions to Daniel: Susannah, and Bel and the Dragon. The remaining Apocrypha—Judith, Tobit, Baruch, II Maccabees, portions of Esther, the prayer of Azariah and the Song of the Three Children, and the Prayer of Manasses—were translated into Low German by an unknown hand from the High German translators' manuscript and first published on 1 April 1534 in the first complete Low German Lutheran Bible, printed in Lübeck by Ludwig Dietz at

Bugenhagen's instigation. In the autumn of 1534 they appeared for the first time in the complete High German Lutheran Bible, at Wittenberg. The Prayer of Manasses, little regarded in the Middle Ages, but always much prized by Luther, held a special place among the apocryphal books. It was first translated in 1519 by Luther's friend Georg Spalatin, from the Vulgate text—the only one then available—and then by another hand (perhaps Luther's) in 1525 and in 1534 for the complete Bible. During the reformer's lifetime it was reprinted with his own writings dozens of times both in High and Low German, and so gained very wide currency.

Luther's autograph manuscripts give the philologist and the linguistic historian important insights into his creative activity. Fairly complete manuscripts survive—though part now only in transcript[1]—of the second and third parts of the Old Testament; of larger portions of the Prophets (part in fair copy) and fragments of the Apocrypha; but nothing of the Pentateuch and the New Testament. At least in the second and third parts of the Old Testament he used a dark-coloured ink for his first draft, but red ink for the revision which he always carried out with the aid of Melanchthon and Aurogallus. So in these parts Luther's original and the revision carried out with others' assistance are clearly distinguishable.

He was never satisfied, however, with the text as it appeared in the first edition, but always made emendations in the new impressions, which often followed in swift succession. In the New Testament, for instance, compared with the first edition which had appeared only three months before, the December Testament of 1522 has hundreds of corrections. Other editions particularly important for their corrections are those of 1526, 1527 and 1530 (the last was revised with Melanchthon in 1529). For the Psalter, which Luther had revised in 1525 and 1528 by himself or possibly with Melanchthon, he set up in the beginning of 1531 a committee of revision composed of Wittenberg scholars (Melanchthon, Aurogallus, Caspar Cruciger, Justus Jonas) which gave the book its present final form. A similar committee helped in 1534 with the preparation of the complete Bible, with the first to the third parts of the

[1] Luther's holograph manuscript of the translation of the third part of the Old Testament (Job to Song of Solomon) which was once in the Prussian State Library in Berlin, and that of fragments of the Minor Prophets which once belonged to the Gymnasium in Zerbst were destroyed in the last war. The printer's copy of part of Jesus Sirach and part of Hosea are now in the University Library at Breslau.

Old Testament, minus the Psalter, the prophet Isaiah and the Wisdom of Solomon under its special care. It functioned again from 1539 to 1541 in the revision of the whole Bible (except the Apocrypha) and this time Bugenhagen was a member. It also helped with the revision of the New Testament which was started in autumn 1544 but broken off when only Romans, I Corinthians and II Corinthians i–iii had been treated. The 'Bible-corrector' Georg Rörer's statements to this committee (except that of 1534) and the copies of the Bible corrected in his own hand which Luther used for the revision—the Old Testament of 1538/9 and the New Testament of 1540—still exist in the University Library at Jena.

The first complete Bible, a folio, appeared in six parts corresponding to the process of translation, in the autumn of 1534. It was published by the Wittenberg booksellers Moritz Goltze, Bartholomäus Vogel and Christoph Schramm, and printed by Hans Lufft. It had 117 woodcuts signed with the monogram MS, had a Saxon privilege of unlimited duration dated 6 August 1534, and cost 2 gulden 8 groschen—about the price of five calves. It contains the Psalter in the text of 1531 and the Prophets, except Isaiah, substantially in that of 1532; the New Testament, which had been radically revised in 1529, shows, like Ecclesiasticus and I Maccabees, comparatively few corrections. In the four subsequent impressions of the Bible—of 1535 (carelessly printed), of 1536, 1538/9 and 1540—there are comparatively few textual alterations by Luther. The large-scale revision of 1539–41, which affected the whole Bible except the Apocrypha, is only partially reflected in the folio Bible of 1540/1 ('newly revised') and had its first full effect in the splendid Bible of autumn 1541, in a 'median' size of type, and embellished with a new title-page. The edition was of 1500 copies, and the price 3 gulden, and this was the first edition to abandon the earlier division into parts and to publish the whole biblical text in two volumes.

Further improvements, especially in the Pentateuch, are to be found in the single-column Bible of spring 1543, and a small number also in the two-column edition of autumn 1543. On the other hand the revision of autumn 1544, which affected only the early part of the Epistles (up to II Corinthians iii), did not come into effect until the Bible of 1546. The printing was begun during Luther's lifetime but completed after his death, and so the Bible was for centuries erroneously thought to have been corrupted by the intervention of others. For those parts of the

New Testament this Bible is unquestionably to be taken as Luther's final version; but for the remaining portions the 'median' Bible of spring 1545, which Luther did not himself see through the press, and this folio Bible of summer 1546, whose authenticity has again been wrongly questioned in recent times, are of equal authority. In the printing of his Bibles he was much assisted from 1538 onwards by 'the Bible-corrector' Georg Rörer, who supplied the Bibles after 1541 with appendixes from his own hand, which give important information about their printing history, with parallel passages in the margins and for a time with an arrangement of capitals in *Fraktur* or roman as a means of indicating the nature of the contents. He was joined by Christoph Walther as 'under-corrector'.

Apart from these eleven folio Bibles from 1534 to 1546, portions of the Bible were published in quarto or octavo. At Wittenberg in Luther's lifetime there were numerous editions in these formats of the New Testament only or the Psalter, which were almost all printed by Lufft. The publishers also commissioned from various other printers separate editions of Ecclesiasticus and the Sapiential books—Proverbs, Ecclesiastes, the Song of Solomon—which were then held in special affection.

Luther's translation differs basically from the medieval German version in its recourse to the original sources. For the New Testament Luther used Erasmus's Greek text, with his associated Latin translation, in the second edition of 1519. For the canonical books of the Old Testament he used the Soncino edition which had appeared in 1494 in Brescia (Luther's own copy is in the West German Library at Marburg), and also very probably another edition which has not yet been found. His translation of the Psalter is based on the Hebrew edition printed by Froben in 1516; until the early nineteenth century Luther's copy was at Danzig. For the Apocrypha he relied partly on the Vulgate and partly on the Septuagint either in Aldus's Venetian edition of 1518 or in Wolfgang Koepfel's Strassburg reprint of 1526. Apart from dictionaries and grammars, such as Johann Reuchlin's *Rudimenta Linguae Hebraicae* (1506), or independent translations like the Latin version of the Psalter made by Felix Pratensis in 1515, and the German version of the Prophets which appeared at Worms in 1527 (see below p. 105), the Septuagint and the Vulgate were substantial aids. Luther himself said 'If we did not have the Greek and Latin

Bibles, we should not be able to make out a word of the Hebrew today'.[1] For the New Testament he drew upon Erasmus's Latin version and his *Annotationes*. While it is probably true that he did not make substantial use of the medieval German version as revised for Zainer's Bible of about 1475 or in later editions—and the point has been much debated—it seems probable that he was influenced by an oral tradition of German translation which is hard to identify.

As for the sequence of the biblical books, Luther followed Erasmus and not the Vulgate or the old German version in the New Testament in that Acts follows the Gospels, not Hebrews, and the apocryphal Epistle to the Laodiceans is left out. But he placed Hebrews and the Epistle of James, together with Jude and Revelation, at the end of the New Testament instead of before I Peter, and as non-apostolic writings did not give them numbers in the table of contents; appealing in this to the decision of the early Church, as against Erasmus's view. In the Old Testament, on the other hand, Luther's table of contents of 1523 to the historical, poetical and prophetic books followed the order of the Vulgate, not the Hebrew, in that he excluded only those books or passages not found in the Hebrew and in 1534 put these apocryphal books at the end of the Old Testament in the order set by the Vulgate (except that he transposed Tobit and the Wisdom of Solomon and placed the Prayer of Manasses at the very end). This was his first use of the term 'Apocrypha', which he glossed as 'books not to be esteemed as part of the Holy Scriptures, but nonetheless profitable and good to read'. He divided them into two groups: complete books, and isolated passages not contained in the Hebrew text of Esther and Daniel. But in 1534, abandoning his scheme of 1523, he omitted altogether III Esdras and IV Esdras (which is not found in the Septuagint). These two books first appeared in a Lutheran Bible in an octavo edition of 1569 at Frankfurt, translated by the Schwenkfeldian Johan Heyden; later translators were David Wolder, Johann Assenburg, Johann Piscator and Daniel Cramer. Luther also omitted III and IV Maccabees, which are not found in the Vulgate.

Wittenberg Bibles were printed in single columns, or sometimes—as in the medieval versions—in double-column. The text was divided into paragraphs, but without verse-numbering, which was not introduced into Wittenberg Bibles until 1586 (the first German Bible with

[1] Weimar Ausgabe, *Tischreden*, vol. v, no. 5327.

numbered verses appeared in Heidelberg in 1568–9). Luther had already introduced his own prefaces to the individual books in 1522; following in this the example of Jerome. Only the Gospels, the Pentateuch, the historical books of the Old Testament and the Prayer of Manasses lack prefaces. Several were later replaced by new ones: the Psalter in 1528, Revelation in 1530, the Sapiential books in 1534; the preface to Acts first appeared in 1533; the original preface to Ezechiel was supplemented by a further one in 1541; and the preface to Daniel of 1530 was enlarged in 1541 to include an extended commentary on the chapter on Antichrist (chapter xii). To guard against the corruption of his translation he addressed exhortations to the printers in his New Testament of 1530 and the complete Bible of 1541. The first editions already contained in the margins the reformer's short glosses explaining words or defining terms or giving exegetical help; in 1534 and 1541 these were much revised and extended; among other changes, the allegorical interpretations in the Pentateuch were in 1534 mostly omitted. More references to parallel passages were set out in the inner margin in 1539 and 1541. From the beginning Luther concerned himself with the selection of subjects for illustration.

From the outset Luther's translation of the Bible had a striking success, and it is natural that it soon swamped the fragmentary translations from other hands (see below, pp. 104–5). Luther's version owed its wide circulation largely to reprints, especially the editions of parts or single books, which by 1546 outnumbered the Wittenberg editions threefold. These were mostly printed in Erfurt in central Germany and Augsburg, Strassburg, and Nürnberg in the south, and, until the conflict over the communion service in 1527, Basle as well. The language of the version was basically 'middle' German with an infusion of Low German; it was made comprehensible to readers in the Oberland by glossaries which appeared in many south German reprints until the late 1530's (though almost exclusively in the New Testament). There followed occasional modifications of vocabulary in the text itself.

At first so-called 'combined' Bibles had appeared in west Germany and the Oberland from 1529 onwards, supplying the portions not yet available in Luther's translation, the Prophets and Apocrypha, from other versions—Hätzer and Denck's or the Zurich ministers' for the Prophets, Leo Juda's for the Apocrypha (see below, pp. 105–6). But from 1534 Wittenberg became undisputedly the principal source of complete Bibles.

Because of the importance which Low German still had as a literary language, all portions of Luther's version were translated by unknown writers into Low German, usually as soon as they appeared. This happened three times in all to the New Testament. These versions were printed most often at Wittenberg and at Magdeburg, the citadel of Low German printing in the sixteenth century. In spring 1534 the portions were united under Bugenhagen's directions, the Apocrypha still missing being supplied from the High German manuscript translation mentioned above (p. 96), and this first complete Low German Bible was printed by Ludwig Dietz at Lübeck. Further editions, partly revised to comply with Luther's own revisions made in the interim, appeared at Magdeburg in 1536, Wittenberg in 1541 (printed by Lufft), and Magdeburg in 1545. The later editions also were predominantly printed at Wittenberg (ten from 1558 to 1607) and Magdeburg. The last Low German Bible appeared in 1621 in Goslar-Lüneburg.

After Luther's death Wittenberg remained the centre of German Bible-printing. Its massive production—over sixty High and Low German editions of an average of at least 2000 copies each between 1546 and 1600—supplied the German territories far beyond the boundaries of Saxony, and even to the southernmost parts, such as Styria. Its position was safeguarded by a succession of 'privileges' granted by the Electors, and not even the competition offered from 1560 onwards by Frankfurt am Main could shake it. Initially the folio format established in 1534 was used exclusively; but a quarto was produced at Wittenberg in 1575, and the first octavo (which was also the first Wittenberg Bible with numbered verses) appeared in 1586. From 1572 occasional editions used the 'summaries' of Luther's pupil Veit Dietrich: epitomes of the contents, chapter by chapter. Rörer remained responsible for the accuracy of the text until he went to Denmark in 1551; his place as 'Bible-corrector' was then taken until 1574 by Christoph Walther, who was an untiring defender of the integrity of the text. Lufft remained until 1572 the sole printer of High German Bibles—a contemporary estimated his production at 'almost 100,000 copies'. His printing-house was also responsible for the High German editions of the New Testament and the Psalter, while the printing of the octavo issues of the Sapiential books and Ecclesiasticus always remained the perquisite of other Wittenberg printers. Between 1569 and 1579 Lufft also printed three Low German Bibles at

Wittenberg. From 1572 other Wittenberg printers were commissioned to print Bibles. The original composition of the publishing consortium of Goltze, Vogel and Schramm was gradually changed in course of time by death or the sale of partnerships. By far the most important and able of the partners was Samuel Selfisch, who entered the association in 1564 and until his death in 1615 became increasingly influential in its direction.

After the reformer's death various alterations crept into the text and the marginal glosses; and there were considerable variations in wording between the Bibles of 1545 and 1546. The historical reasons for these had been quite forgotten, and so the posthumous Bible of 1546 was regarded as virtually corrupt. All this caused the Saxon Elector August I to order the examination of the authenticity of the text by learned theologians. This investigation led to the erroneous conclusion that the only true and uncorrupted text of Luther's version was to be found in the Bible of 1545, which was therefore taken as the basis of the Wittenberg edition of 1581 which was authorized by the Elector. Thus the Bible of 1545 was given a quite unjustified canonical status, which has had its effects to the present day.

As for the significance of Luther's version, it is far more than a mere translation, for it does not adhere slavishly to the style and syntactical structure of the originals, but is both wholly rendered into German, and at the same time linguistically exact in detail. Luther's principles are set out in his preface to the Old Testament of 1523, in his 'Letter on Translation', and his 'Summaries on the Psalms and on the grounds of the translation'.[1] Luther's Bible was a literary event of the first magnitude, for it is the first work of art in German prose. Luther showed himself to be a poet of genius, and with a true feeling for the properties of other languages—even though he was less of a scholar than his learned collaborators Melanchthon and Aurogallus. The Bible first became a real part of the literary heritage of the German people with Luther. He believed—contrary to the teaching of the Catholic Church—that the Holy Scriptures were the one true key to faith and doctrine, and so his translation was also the sure foundation of the Reformation. In the history of the language his version is also a factor whose significance cannot be overestimated in the development of the vocabulary of modern literary German.

[1] Weimar Ausgabe: German Bible, VIII, 30–2; Works, 30, part II, 632–43; 38, 9–17.

PROTESTANT VERSIONS BEFORE AND CONTEMPORARY WITH LUTHER

Even before the appearance of his own translation, the influence of Luther's reforming ideas aroused a keen desire for a German Bible among the laity who were not skilled in other languages. Luther had for instance expressed the wish in the summer of 1520 that 'every town should have a girls' school, in which the girls should daily hear the Gospel read for an hour, whether in German or Latin'.[1] There had appeared yet another reprint in 1518 of the pre-Lutheran translation, printed at the imperial city of Augsburg, which had been since 1475 the principal source of this version; though from the autumn of 1522 it became the leading source of reprints of the part-issues of Luther's Bible. Not surprisingly, for the old version was found 'un-German', 'dark' and 'difficult', as Luther's disciple Johann Mathesius called it. The Catholic scholar Johann Eck also criticized the translator of the pre-Lutheran Bible in these terms: 'he tried too hard to translate word for word into German, so that he often became impossible to understand, and the simple reader can make no sense of it'. Plainly this version did not meet the contemporary demand. In these circumstances various scholars in central Germany and the Oberland resolved to attempt new versions quite independent of the old one. But each of them confined himself, because of the great linguistic difficulty, to the reproduction of single scriptural books.

For the New Testament Luther's fellow-Augustinian Johann Lang of Erfurt was the first; in the summer of 1521 he produced a translation of Matthew from the Greek (he too had been a critic of the earlier version). In the following year Nikolaus Krumpach, vicar of Querfurt, translated I and II Peter, I and II Timothy, Titus and the fourth Gospel, from the Vulgate. In the same year there appeared both at Leipzig and at Augsburg an anonymous translation of Mark and Luke, after Erasmus's Latin text, together with a reprint of Lang's and Krumpach's translations of the other Gospels. Finally, still in 1522, Galatians was anonymously translated from the Vulgate. There were a few attempts at translation from the Old Testament—mostly incompetent linguistically. The Hebraist Johann Böschenstein who lived in the Oberland produced a few versions from the original: the seven Penitential Psalms

[1] Weimar Ausgabe, 6, 461.

(1520), Solomon's prayer (1523), the Lamentations of Jeremiah and Daniel's prayer (Daniel ix. 3–19) (1529). After the appearance of Luther's translation, Böschenstein translated only one book—Ruth—in 1525. The Augustinian provincial Caspar Ammann of Lauingen on the Danube, and the Augsburg preacher Otmar Nachtgall produced versions of the Psalter in 1523 and 1524 from the Hebrew and Greek respectively. All these translations from either Testament could in no way compare with Luther's, and disappeared from the market as soon as the corresponding part of his version appeared. This process is seen most clearly in the case of Nachtgall's German Psalter; the only edition was printed at Augsburg in August 1524 by Simprecht Ruff and published by Sigmund Grimm. Luther's Psalter appeared in October 1524, and was reprinted by Ruff in the same year.

Nearly all these cases were of books of the Bible which had also appeared in swift succession between 1522 and 1524 in the first parts of Luther's translation (the New Testament and the second and third parts of the Old Testament). But the translation of the Prophets by two Anabaptists, Ludwig Hätzer and Hans Denck, prepared from the original Hebrew and linguistically a considerable success, had a much longer lease of life. It was printed by Peter Schöffer at Worms in April 1527, while Luther's translation was completed a good five years later, in spring 1532. Hätzer's and Denck's translation was the first one based on the original, and, with its preface by Hätzer, was not only reprinted twelve times in all between April 1527 and November 1531 in the west and south German regions, but was also used on several occasions from 1529 onwards, in combination with those parts of the Lutheran translation which had already appeared, to make up complete Bibles—the 'combined' Bible. Luther was critical of this work of the 'mob spirits' (*Rottengeister*) because of their theological principles; nonetheless it is demonstrable that he frequently drew on the 'Prophets of Worms' as an auxiliary, mostly in very difficult passages, and usually for particular words and phrases, though never for long sequences. There is for instance a marginal note in the manuscript of Luther's translation at Hos. x. 14: 'Vide Hetzer.'

The starting-point of the 'Zurich Bible' was the reprinting of the four hitherto separate parts of Luther's version (Parts 1–3 of the Old Testament and the New Testament) by Zwingli's printer at Zurich, Christoph Froschauer. These reprints appeared in folio in the

Swyzerdeutsch dialect in 1524–5, and in 16mo and in octavo, both in Oberdeutsch, in 1527 and 1527/8, but all editions were similar in appearance. They were supplemented in spring 1529 by the two parts still lacking in Luther's translation—the Prophets and the Apocrypha. These were translated in Zurich and printed by Froschauer in separate editions, in folio in Swyzerdeutsch, and in 16mo and octavo in Oberdeutsch. The prophetic books were translated out of the Hebrew by the Zurich ministers, and although they attacked Hätzer and Denck as 'heretics', because of their baptist inclinations, they still made use of the translation itself. Leo Juda translated the Apocrypha by himself, from the Septuagint and the Vulgate. Luther's Apocrypha, which was not complete until 1534, differs from Juda's. Juda included the third and the fourth books of Esdras (the latter being omitted in the Septuagint) as well as III Maccabees (which occurs in the Septuagint only) and omitted three shorter pieces, which did not appear in the Zurich Bible until 1589: the Prayer of Azariah, the Song of the Three Children, and the Prayer of Manasses. He also omitted the apocryphal additions to the book of Esther, which were included from the Bible of 1531 onwards.

Once all six separate parts of the Bible had appeared, Froschauer published the first Swiss Bible in 1530; an octavo meant 'as a handbook for daily use'. This edition differed from Luther in that the Prophets and Apocrypha were an independent translation, and it omitted his prefaces, which had not been used since the 16mo edition of 1527. The poetical books (Job to Song of Solomon) were translated entirely afresh for the great folio edition of 1531, which was to be thenceforward the standard text. The remaining portions adhered basically to Luther, though numerous emendations were made—either linguistic ('to accord with our Swiss German tongue') or textual.[1] After Juda, in collaboration with the converted Jew Michael Adam, had revised the Old Testament thoroughly in 1539–40 for the folio Bible of 1540 and the octavo of 1542, the Swiss Bible remained largely unaltered in its text in succeeding years (except for a revision, of the New Testament only, in 1547). The quarto Bible of 1548 was for decades used as copy text for later editions, and no notice was taken of the numerous improvements which Luther later made to his version. In Zurich Christoph Froschauer, and after his death in 1564 his nephew of the

[1] In 1530 the Apocrypha were placed after the New Testament; in 1531 after Esther.

same name, played the same dominating part as Bible-printers as Lufft did in Wittenberg. When Christoph II died in 1585 the brothers Escher took over the printing-house, and in 1590 it passed into the possession of Johann Wolf. During the sixteenth century Zurich, like Wittenberg, also produced separate issues of the New Testament (thirty altogether), as well as its thirty-two German and ten Latin Bibles. The more convenient small formats were specially popular here from the very beginning. Verse-numbering was introduced in Zurich Bibles in 1589, three years later than in Wittenberg.

CATHOLIC VERSIONS

Luther's Reformation was not only the spur to a larger number of Protestant Bible-translations; it also provoked his Catholic opponents to attempt at three different times to lessen Luther's own overwhelming success in this field by producing their own German versions.

On 7 November 1522 Duke Georg of Saxony, a strict Catholic, issued a special edict against Luther's September Testament. But this had almost no practical effect; nor did the critique drawn up in 1523 at the duke's request by his secretary Hieronymus Emser; it was based on the Vulgate text and directed at Luther's translation of the New Testament—which was based on the Greek original. The critique was in effect a list of some hundreds of alleged 'heretical errors and lies'. The duke was forced to the conclusion that the only effective antidote was a Catholic vernacular translation. Emser was given the task, and though he tried at first to produce an independent version, he soon found that he could not emulate Luther's mastery of language; so he took the text of the September Testament, which he had so violently attacked, as a basis, and corrected it more or less thoroughly to accord with the 'proven old text' of the Vulgate. Hence for a large part Emser's product agrees word for word with Luther's text. The duke provided a foreword dated 1 August 1527, and in the autumn of that year the Dresden printer Wolfgang Stöckel produced an edition in folio of this New Testament. It had illustrations by Georg Lemberger; it also had, in Revelation, nineteen of Cranach's twenty-one extremely anti-Catholic woodcuts which Emser had bought from Cranach for 40 talers. So Emser's edition strongly resembled Luther's of 1522 in its outward appearance as well.

Emser died soon after, in November 1527, but within the next two years six further editions appeared: in the duchy of Saxony at Leipzig, and in west Germany at Cologne and Freiburg im Breisgau. These were Catholic territories where Luther had no influence. In the 1530's there were four further editions at Freiburg, and there was one in 1532 at Tübingen, which was still Catholic at that time. But when the Michaelisbrüder were about to bring out in 1530 an edition in Low German at Rostock in Mecklenburg, Luther, who had several times bitterly castigated the dubious methods of the 'Dresden botcher' Emser, put a stop to the project, with the help of the Duke of Mecklenburg, Heinrich V. Thanks to Luther's part in it, Emser's version had a vigorous life, and was frequently reprinted until well into the eighteenth century.

Johann Dietenberger, at that time Dominican prior of Koblenz, took Emser's Freiburg edition of 1529 (reprinted in 1532 in Tübingen) and added to it the Old Testament 'pericopae', the scriptural lessons read during the Mass. These he took almost verbatim from those parts of Luther's Old Testament which had already appeared, from Hätzer's and Denck's translation of the Prophets, and from the medieval version of the Apocrypha. It was his aim that 'no one should need to buy a whole Bible', but he soon saw that this was no way to undercut the sale of the Lutheran Bible. He was made professor of theology at the University of Mainz meanwhile; and five years after his first venture he decided to make a complete German version 'after the old translation received in Christian churches' (the Vulgate), and he dedicated it to Archbishop Albrecht of Mainz. For the New Testament he simply took over Emser's modification of Luther's September Testament. As Emser had done with the New Testament, Dietenberger at first attempted an independent version of the Old Testament. But the resulting difficulties soon made him desist from this attempt, and for the first three parts of the Old Testament he simply used Luther's version as the underlying text, and corrected it to accord with the Vulgate, occasionally using the medieval German version as an aid. For the Prophets his principal source was the work of Hätzer and Denck, but he also used, spasmodically, Luther's version, which had appeared in 1532, occasionally the Zurich version of 1529, and also the medieval German version, which he used for the Apocrypha as well. In the Apocrypha he reproduced Juda's version of 1529 for the most part; but for Ecclesiasticus he also used Luther's version which had appeared early in 1533. Dietenberger's Bible was printed by Peter Jordan at Mainz in 1534, appearing a few months before the first complete Wittenberg Bible. At first it could hardly hold its own against the genuine Lutheran version, and new editions of it were rare (1540 and 1550 only). But in the period of the Counter-Reformation, when the purchase and possession of Lutheran Bibles were heavily punished, it served as a kind of substitute for the real thing—doubtless because of its close adherence to the text and style of the linguistically successful Lutheran version. In consequence it found a considerable market, then and in the seventeenth and eighteenth centuries. In the second half of the sixteenth century alone it was reprinted at Cologne no less than seventeen times.

Like Emser's work, the translation, ten years later, of Eck, Luther's old opponent, was undertaken not on his own initiative but at the command of his prince. The two dukes of Bavaria, Wilhelm V and Ludwig, rejected Dietenberger's translation because it 'borrowed so much from Luther'; at their command Eck took up the 'heavy work' which he 'would have been glad to have done with'. Like Dietenberger, he took over Emser's New Testament, and confined himself, apart from certain corrections derived from the Vulgate, to converting Emser's linguistic usage into the Swabian dialect 'in words and syllables'—though not particularly consistently. For the Old Testament, however, he made his own independent translation, again into the Swabian dialect, from the Vulgate. The Bible was published by Georg Krapf in Ingolstadt and printed by Alexander Weissenhorn at Augsburg in June 1537. It had little success and during the sixteenth century was only reprinted in 1550 and 1558; this was partly due to the use of the Swabian dialect, which hindered its use outside that province, and partly to Eck's style, which was far too close to the original Latin and made it hard to understand. It is precisely in the comparison with this most unsuccessful version by one of the foremost Catholic scholars of his day that one perceives the true nature of Luther's supreme and unique achievement as a translator.

2. ITALIAN VERSIONS

In the preface to his commentary on the Canticle, published at Venice in 1504, Isaia da Este, a canon of Padua, justified his writing in the vernacular by the consideration that printing had now brought 'tutta la sacratissima Bibbia' to the knowledge of ordinary unlearned people including women. This statement, allowing for exaggeration, is one of several indications that in Italy as elsewhere at this time Bible study was in the air and that there was a public disposed to welcome such fresh translations of the Scriptures as might be offered. And the advance of learning made it likely that these, when they came, would represent an effort to return behind the Vulgate (from which the medieval versions had been made) to the original tongues. But the first important new Italian version did not see the light until 1530.

This was the work of a Florentine layman, Antonio Brucioli (*c.* 1495–1566). Banished from his native city and already suspected of heresy, this remarkable man brought out at Venice in 1530 a New Testament 'di greco novamente tradotto in lingua toscana'; in 1531 a version of the Psalms 'da la hebraica verità'; and finally in 1532 a complete Bible in Italian, done from the original tongues. This work enjoyed a considerable success throughout the sixteenth century, especially with Italian Protestants, though its style is rough and obscure and although Brucioli's scholarship was hardly equal to his pretensions. Indeed, though he knew Greek fairly well he probably had little Hebrew. For the Old Testament he seems to have drawn heavily—without acknowledgment—on Santi Pagnini's interlinear Latin version, printed at Lyons in 1528.[1] Nevertheless, this part of his work, revised by F. Rustici, was incorporated into the first complete Protestant Bible in Italian, issued at Geneva in 1562; for which edition the New Testament was supplied by a revision of the version, made from the Greek, of Massimo Teofilo (see below). By this time Brucioli's New Testament had been reprinted six or seven times—once at Antwerp and twice at Lyons—and there had been several editions of separate parts of his Old Testament. In 1540 Brucioli added three volumes of commentary (later increased to seven) to his Bible, in which his Protestant leanings became evident, though indeed they are already apparent in his preface to the Venice edition of 1532, and in an accompanying

[1] On Pagnini see *Archivium Fratrum Praedicatorum*, XV (1945), 5–51.

dedicatory letter addressed to King Francis I of France. These last are interesting documents, if somewhat naïve and pretentious. Brucioli is contemptuous of all previous versions of the Scriptures 'ne la italica lingua'; and this is understandable, given his date; but his aversion to the traditional rational theology—about which he evidently knew little and cared less—led him on to perilous generalizations on the history of the Church. Christianity had flourished so long as the Scriptures had been taken as the one all-sufficient rule of faith and guide to life; the decline and corruption of 'la christiana republica' began when the door was opened to 'human sciences'—identified with St Paul's *prudentia carnis*. In view of such sentiments as these it is not surprising that Brucioli's Bible was placed on the Roman Index in 1559. Yet he himself never formally broke with the Roman Church.

Soon after Brucioli two friars of the Dominican community of San Marco in Florence came into the field; in 1536, a Fra Zaccaria brought out at Venice a New Testament done from the Greek; and then, two years later, the same printer issued a complete Italian Bible, the work of a man with a reputation for learning in a wide variety of subjects, Santi Marmochini. [1] Marmochini too claimed to have rendered the Old Testament 'dalla hebraica verità', but it is agreed that he probably worked from an already existing version—either from Brucioli or from the Latin version of that other Dominican and greater scholar, Pagnini. In any case Marmochini seems to have been concerned to harmonize his material with the Vulgate. For the New Testament he probably utilized Zaccaria's version. His efforts did not meet with much success, his Bible being only once reprinted, at Venice in 1546, with Job and the Psalter translated afresh anonymously. Meanwhile at Lyons in 1551 a more original work had appeared, a rendering of the Greek New Testament by another Florentine, Massimo Teofilo. Teofilo was a Benedictine, but at some date he seems to have turned Protestant. He was a good Greek scholar and his work was several times reprinted, sometimes along with Erasmus's Latin text; and, as we have noted, it was incorporated into the first complete Protestant Bible in Italian, the Geneva edition of 1562. During the second half of the century a good many other versions of parts of the Bible appeared, some printed outside Italy. None of these had much importance except so far as they represented an effort to keep Protestantism alive in the country; such,

[1] See Quetif-Echard, *Scriptores Ord. Fr. Praedicatorum*, II, 124–5.

for example, was G. L. Pascale's version of the New Testament, printed at Geneva in 1555. The only new Jewish version actually published seems to have been that of Ecclesiastes by David de Pomis (Venice, 1571). Of merely literary interest are Pietro Aretino's version of Genesis and paraphrase of the Penitential Psalms. The fact is that Paul IV's prohibition (promulgated in the Index of 1559 and repeated by Pius IV in 1564) of all printing and reading of vernacular versions of the Scriptures without the express permission of the Holy Office effectively put an end to serious Bible translation by Catholics in Italy for the next two hundred years. It was left to the Protestant Diodati to produce, early in the seventeenth century, the Italian version that was to hold the field unchallenged until the last decades of the eighteenth century.

Giovanni Diodati was born at Geneva in 1576, the son of a Protestant *émigré* from Lucca. A precocious Hebrew scholar, he taught this language at Geneva from the age of twenty-one, and in 1609 succeeded Beza as professor of theology at Geneva, retaining this post until his death in 1649. The first edition of his Bible, *La Bibbia, cioè i Libri del v. e del n. Testamenti...traslati in lingua italiana*, was published at Geneva in 1607. A second edition, revised, with enlarged notes and introductions to the several books, came out in 1641, also at Geneva. In both editions the apocryphal books of the Old Testament are printed after the rest, with a separate introduction (much enlarged in the second edition) but without notes. At the end of the 1641 volume is added a translation in verse of the whole Psalter.

The general accuracy and the remarkable clarity of Diodati's Bible have won it a high place among vernacular versions of the Scriptures. Diodati was an expert Hebraist and a good Greek scholar; moreover, his Italian is lucid and vigorous. His Old Testament is regarded as better than his New Testament, where a Protestant bias is occasionally discernible. His version of the Hebrew Old Testament—the Psalter excepted—only slightly differs here and there from the sense of the Vulgate; in the New Testament divergences are more noticeable, but less than might have been expected. A Protestant touch may be felt, for example, in the rendering of Luke i. 28, 'Bene stii, o favorita; il Signore sia teco' (1641 edition); again in the rendering 'in *cospetto* di Cristo' for ἐν προσώπῳ Χριστοῦ (II Cor. ii. 10); in *insegnamento* for παράδοσις; in *anziano* for πρεσβύτερος. For the rest, Diodati tends to paraphrase rather excessively. With regard to his notes and introductions three points may be noted here. First, the ample introductions, especially those to the books of the Old Testament, are interesting as pieces of Calvinist theology. The human race is seen as divided from the beginning between the elect and the reprobate, and the head of the elect, already in the Old Testament, is Christ the Son of God; it was he who spoke to Moses from the bush, led the Israelites through the desert, gave them the 'paschal sacrament' and the law. There is much stress on the continuity of Old Testament and New Testament. Secondly, with regard to the apocryphal books of the Old Testament, it is maintained that their style alone shows them to be not inspired; and their introduction into the canon is blamed on the Latin and African churches. Thirdly, in Diodati's comments on those texts of the New Testament which might be expected to have offered him occasions for anti-Catholic polemic, he displays in fact a sobriety, a mildness and absence of heat, which is remarkable in view of the time in which he was writing.

Diodati's Bible has been many times reprinted and remained, until the present century, the version commonly used by Italian Protestants.

In conclusion may be mentioned a version of Proverbs by the Jew Ezekiah Rieti (Venice, 1617).

3. FRENCH VERSIONS

In the history of the French Bible there is no Authorized Version, no Luther, no translation which has achieved anything like the universal authority of the standard versions in England and Germany. Both the causes and the consequences of this state of affairs are of some importance. The critical period, that covered by this chapter, coincides with violent theological controversy and religious war, so that neither a Roman Catholic nor a Protestant version could hope to command general acceptance. Moreover, vernacular translation itself became associated in the eyes of the stronger party with schism and heresy. Hence, for example, the Edict of Châteaubriant of June 1551, which forbade, *inter alia*, translation of any part of the Bible and the printing or selling of translations, commentaries, scholia, annotations, tables, indices or epitomes concerning Holy Scripture written during the preceding forty years in any language.[1] Such prohibitions were not effective, but before 1600 only the Louvain Bible received a sort of tacit approval. In the seventeenth century Sacy's translation, which has been in some ways the nearest French equivalent of the Authorized Version, was suspect for its Jansenist origin and never had official sanction (it is noteworthy that, like the Antwerp, Geneva and Louvain Bibles, it was first printed outside France). No Catholic translation since has acquired a dominant status.

Linguistic, as well as political and ecclesiastical, causes played their part. The sixteenth century saw an unparalleled transformation of the French language ('Il escoule tous les jours de nos mains et depuis que je vis s'est alteré de moitié', says Montaigne).[2] In these circumstances any translation soon became archaic, if not unintelligible, and the frequent revisions of both Catholic and Protestant Bibles may be largely ascribed to linguistic reasons. Even so the revisions themselves were never sufficient, and no translation made before the middle of the seventeenth century could satisfy a modern linguistic consciousness. After Sacy Catholics possessed a version which, whatever its other weaknesses, was written in standard academic French, but the Protestants clung to their old Geneva Bible (the 1588 revision with the modifications introduced in 1693, and in the eighteenth century by Martin and Ostervald). The language they learned from it was scornfully described, in Protestant as well as Catholic circles, as *le patois de Chanaan* (Jurieu, preaching at Sedan in 1675, is said to have been incomprehensible because of the archaisms of the Geneva translation).[3] All this is far removed from the continuing and invigorating influence of the Bible on the English language.

With these considerations we are already engaged in consequences, and one result of the absence of a standard version has been that biblical ways of expression have penetrated much less deeply into French than English. Quotation comes less easily when the form of the text is not fixed. For most educated Frenchmen, it is true, the authoritative text is the Vulgate, and readers of Pascal, or for that matter of Gide, will know how often the Latin quotation is preferred to the French.

However, the principal consequence has been the large number of

[1] D. T. Pottinger, *The French Book Trade in the Ancien Régime* (Harvard, 1958), pp. 57–8.

[2] *Essais*, III, ix.

[3] Lortsch, *Histoire de la Bible en France*, p. 129.

attempts to fill the gap. Lortsch counts twenty-four new or original translations of the whole Bible between 1530 and 1900, and still more numerous original translations of Old Testament, or New Testament separately, or of individual books (a total of 206).[1] Such figures can only be approximate, since originality in this matter is almost impossible to define, but it may well be that the number of translations in French exceeds that in any other modern language, and the problem of description becomes correspondingly more complex.

Within this wide range a great division is formed between Roman Catholic and Protestant versions. As we shall see, they are by no means entirely independent, but since Olivetan nearly every translation has been inspired by one or the other communion. Characteristic differences of terminology can be detected: Protestant Bibles usually translate Yahveh as *l'Éternel* (first found in Olivetan, 1535), where the Catholics have *le Seigneur* (Authorized Version, 'the LORD'); they use *tu* for the Catholic *vous* and, in the accounts of the Last Supper, *la coupe* for *le calice*. Sometimes these differences touch on crucial doctrinal points and it is interesting to compare the treatment of such passages as Acts xiii. 2 or I Cor. iii. 15.

Yet another consequence of the multiplicity of versions is the changing response of succeeding generations to the new demands of their time: demands of theological and ecclesiastical movements, of developments in biblical scholarship, of linguistic evolution and literary taste. So in the sixteenth century we find the representatives of evangelical humanism (Lefèvre), Reformation (Olivetan and the Geneva pastors) and Counter-Reformation (Louvain); in the seventeenth the quest for a classical translation, culminating in Sacy, and early applications of modern critical principles (Simon); in the nineteenth the influence of Romanticism (Genoude), the missionary activities of the Protestant Bible Societies, and the growth of impartial scholarship (Renan and Reuss), continued in the twentieth by the Jerusalem Bible and the new Pléiade translation. In this way the many French versions reflect a wide area of spiritual and intellectual history.

So far we have emphasized the multiplicity of versions and the differences between them. However, these differences must not be exaggerated. A complete and independent translation of the Bible is a

[1] *Ibid.* pp. 230–2.

formidable undertaking: human weakness and conscientious scruple alike lead a translator to consult and follow his predecessors. Moreover, this tendency is strengthened by an understandable reverence: changes in the sacred text can only be introduced with reluctance, even if the accepted version is unsatisfactory. The history of the French Bible bears this out in a remarkable way. It has indeed been argued that there is only one main version, beginning with the twelfth-century Psalter and transmitted with modifications from one translator to the next until the end of the nineteenth century.[1] This continuous evolution was observed by Richard Simon as early as 1690: 'il n'y a veritablement qu'une seule Traduction Françoise, qui a ensuite esté retouchée par differentes personnes en differens lieux...'.[2] Subsequent researches have tended to confirm his view, and we shall see how far it can be accepted for the modern period. It may well be that among the earlier versions only Castellio's of 1555 has strong claims to originality.

The modern history of our subject begins in 1523 with the appearance from the press of the great printer Simon de Colines of an anonymous translation of the New Testament, which can be ascribed with a high degree of probability, if not absolute certainty, to Jacques Lefèvre d'Étaples (Faber Stapulensis). The Old Testament was printed at Antwerp in 1528, both together (the Antwerp Bible) in 1530.[3] There were new editions, with considerable corrections, in 1534 and 1541 (the whole work thus coincides almost exactly with the publication of Luther's Bible). It soon caused alarm and was placed on the Index in 1546. Lefèvre is typical of the first generation of French Reformers: a humanist and a good Catholic, protected by the bishop of Meaux, Briçonnet, who shared his ideas, as well as by the queen of Navarre, he sought an internal reformation of the Church.

This somewhat hesitant position is mirrored in his Bible. The whole tone of the Epistle which precedes the 1523 New Testament is Protestant, with its insistence on faith, on the Scriptures and Gospels as the sole repository of truth and on the importance of making them accessible to the common people. A similar note reappears in the 1530 Prologue: 'Paul vasseau d'election...loue magnifiquement les

[1] S. Berger, *La Bible française au moyen âge* (Paris, 1884), pp. vi, 320.

[2] *Histoire critique du texte du Nouveau Testament* (Rotterdam, 1689–90), II, 329.

[3] Plate 18.

escriptures diuines: de ce qu'elles ont pour leur autheur Dieu, qui est toute puissance, toute sapience et toute bonté.' On the other hand, Lefèvre follows the Vulgate (his title runs 'translatee selon la pure et entiere traduction de sainct Hierome'), though he makes some corrections in the New Testament from the Greek, especially in the 1534 edition, where he also adopts some new readings in the Old Testament, based on Robert Estienne's Latin Bible of 1532. The Apocrypha are printed in the traditional order as part of the Old Testament, though here again the 1534 edition goes further, with a note describing them as non-canonical, to be read only for 'la bonne doctrine et prophetie' (approaching the Anglican position, as well as that of St Jerome). Moreover, this is not a wholly independent translation even from the Vulgate: it relies heavily on Jean de Rely's *Bible historiee*, printed in the late fifteenth century.[1] Lefèvre thus forms the vital link between medieval and modern translations.

Though the basis of most of the versions that followed, he cannot be said to possess great literary merit: he is too much inclined merely to transpose Latin words into French. What he has done is to begin the task of comparison with the originals and to present, as he claims, a purer text, stripped of the glosses (or *Hystoires*) which in the earlier versions are inextricably confused with it. One example will suffice (Gen. i. 1 in the 1545 edition of the *Bible historiee*):[2] '...ilz ont trois cieulx de diuerses couleurs: Dont le premier est de couleur de cristal. Le second de blanche couleur ainsi comme neige. Et le tiers ciel de rouge couleur...est le ciel imperial qui est le plus hault.' All this medieval astronomy, which continues at great length, is suppressed by Lefèvre. In the text itself he prunes and clarifies.

Meanwhile in Switzerland reform was proceeding more boldly. On 12 September 1532 the Waldenses held a synod at Chanforans in the Val d'Angrognes (now in Piedmont), to which they had invited the reformers Farel and Saunier. Calvin's cousin, Pierre Robert Olivetan, like Lefèvre a native of Picardy, was probably also present. It was agreed that a new translation of the Bible should be published and that the Waldenses should contribute to the cost. From this decision emerged the Neuchâtel Bible (sometimes called the Bible de Serrières), printed by Pierre de Wingle in June 1535.[3] There can be no doubt that Olivetan was the translator.

[1] See p. 425 below. [2] Paris, G. le Bret. [3] Plate 19.

He begins the first true Protestant version in French with a dedication, in which he declares his intention of presenting it, rather than to a great lord as the custom was, to the Church, 'o paoure Eglise a qui rien on ne presente'. The dedication is dated 'Des Alpes, ce xij[e] de Feburier 1535' and followed by a touching footnote: 'Je te eusse escrit plus amplement: mais tu voys icy le destroict ou ie suis, et de papier et dautres choses.' Then comes an 'Apologie du Translateur' addressed to Farel, Viret and Saunier, disguised in Hebrew or Greek as Cusemeth, Chlorotes and Almeutes. Olivetan's insistence on the barbarism of French compared with 'leloquence Ebraicque et Grecque' illustrates his affinities with contemporary French humanists. But the apology is mostly devoted to a discussion of points of Hebrew grammar, which reveals some knowledge of Hebrew, as well as of German. There is also a Latin preface by Calvin and a table of proper names partly by Bonaventure Des Periers, whose subsequent writings illustrate the strangely mixed origins of the French Reformation.

The question of Olivetan's originality is complicated. In the Apocrypha, now printed separately, he follows Lefèvre with only superficial corrections. In the New Testament he does much the same, with more fundamental corrections, mostly based on the Latin of Erasmus. However, in the Old Testament he has clearly produced a new work, aided by Pagnini, whose Latin version from the Hebrew had appeared in 1528, but often going direct to the Hebrew himself, as his notes testify. He retains Hebraic forms in proper names, including the titles of Old Testament books (for example, Moseh, Jehosua, Jehezekiel, Jehudith) and in the 1538 New Testament he adopts a Hebrew pseudonym, Belisem de Belimakom (no name of no place).

On the whole Olivetan's language is simpler and more French than Lefèvre's. Thus in I Cor. xiii. 2, 6 he has *secretz* and *iniustice* for Lefèvre's *misteres* and *iniquité*. In Matt. xxvi and Mark xiv *calice* is replaced by *hanap* (goblet), changed by the Geneva revisers to *coupe*. Bishops, priests and apostles are called *surveillans*, *ministres* and *ambassadeurs*. The doctrinal significance of these changes is clear.

One innovation is of interest to all readers of the Bible. Olivetan distinguishes by the use of a smaller fount words which are not in the original and have been added by the translator (cf. the use of italics in the Authorized Version).

One of the two Bodleian copies of the Neuchâtel Bible belonged to an official family of Antwerp, Panhuys, presumably Catholic; Calvin's name has been cut out from the preface. This suggests that its diffusion was not limited to Protestant areas.

Throughout the sixteenth century Olivetan's translation was subjected to continuous revision by the pastors of Geneva, and Calvin himself played the leading part in the earlier years. The Bible de l'Épée (Geneva, 1540),[1] so called from the sword on the title-page, is noteworthy for a preface which unites the humanistic and the reforming outlook and is almost in the spirit of Rabelais:[2] it is wrong to withhold the Bible from the masses, since this age has seen the arts flourish as never before, especially printing and machinery, which have put books within the reach of everyone. The Geneva quarto of 1551 has a preface by Calvin, which begins with a panegyric of the Scriptures and a denunciation of the diabolical presumption of those who would keep them from the common people (this emphasis is perhaps characteristic of Calvin). There follows praise of Pierre Robert (Olivetan) and a discussion of the weaknesses in his version which have made revision necessary. Calvin remarks that he has been assisted by Louis Budé for the Psalter, Théodore de Bèze (Beza) for the Apocrypha and a third, unnamed, for the Minor Prophets.[3] In 1553 Robert Estienne printed his French Bible, divided into verses, with more corrections; in 1560 appeared a new revision with the New Testament corrected by Calvin and Bèze, and a posthumous publication of Robert Estienne's (with preface by his son Henri), including independent corrections of the Old Testament. Further editions of the official version, mostly with at least some corrections, appeared for example in 1565, 1567, 1568 (the bilingual *Biblia Latinogallica*), 1570 and 1580.

Finally, in 1588 a committee of Geneva pastors, headed by Bèze and the professor of Hebrew, Corneille Bertram, published the revision which henceforward was the Geneva Bible *par excellence*. The introductory epistle, by Bèze, includes a defence against the charge of creating a diversity of Bibles, and gives a history of earlier French translations from the reigns of Charles V and Charles VIII, a time when, he says, 'n'ayant encores le Seigneur comme ramené au Monde la cognoissance des deux langues originelles...ni poli les esprits par

[1] Plate 25. [2] Cf. *Pantagruel*, ch. VIII.

[3] For Calvin's text see *La Bible française de Calvin*, ed. by E. Reuss, 2 vols. (Paris, 1897).

l'estude des bonnes lettres'. The humanist in him was not yet dead. The revision itself is a linguistic improvement, but tends to pick out readings from earlier editions, including the despised Castellio. For more than a hundred years, until 1693, it remained uncorrected except in minor details, and subsequent Protestant versions owe much to it.

Outside Geneva the splendid series of folio Bibles printed at Lyons by Jean de Tournes between 1551 and 1564 is mainly of typographical interest.[1] The external form is Catholic (Apocrypha with Old Testament; prefaces of St Jerome), but the text, close to the Geneva versions, is undoubtedly Protestant. Jean de Tournes was a convert to Calvinism and the ambiguous character of his Bibles reflects the difficulties of the French Huguenots.

In 1555 Sébastien Châteillon (Castellio) published his translation at Basle.[2] It was savagely attacked by his enemies at Geneva, who describe him in the preface dated 10 October 1559, prefixed to the 1560 New Testament and several subsequent editions, as 'homme si bien cogneu en ceste Eglise tant par son ingratitude & impudence... instrument choisi de Satan pour amuser tous esprits volages & indiscrets'. In fact his translation is the most original of the century and one of the best. His dedication to Henry II of France contains a noble plea for tolerance and moderation in religious questions. These views had been the main cause of his breach with Calvin and Bèze, and had at that moment little chance of a hearing.

He addresses himself primarily to the uneducated (*les idiots*) and therefore systematically gallicizes. The use of such words as *arriere-femme* (concubine), *empellé* (uncircumcized) or *brulage* (burnt offering), together with his native dialect of Bresse, exposed him to ridicule. Such features help to explain the success of the English Bible, but the evolution of the French language has left Castellio far behind. At the same time he is capable of rising to the greatness of his task and of attaining true poetic quality, as a short quotation may show (Ps. civ. 3, 4): 'Tu planchoyes tes sales en eau, e te seruant des nuées pour chariot, marches sur les ailes du vent. Tu fais des vens tes messagers, e du feu flamboyant tes valets.'[3]

[1] Plate 27 shows a Latin edition. See A. Cartier, *Bibliographie des éditions des de Tournes*, 2 vols. (Paris, 1938).

[2] Plate 26.

[3] For a full study see F. Buisson, *Sébastien Castellion*, 2 vols. (Paris, 1892), and especially the appendix by O. Douen, 'Fragment d'une étude inédite sur la Bible française de Castalion' (I, 415–36). For Castellio in general see also pp. 8, 14, 71 above.

The verse translation of the Psalms begun by Clément Marot (forty-nine Psalms, published 1533–43) and completed by Bèze (1551–62) is not exactly a version, but it requires mention because these Psalms became the hymnal of the French Protestants, sung at the stake, in the Wars of Religion and the Camisard revolt, and serving as a signal of recognition everywhere. Ps. lxviii (Bèze) in particular was the Huguenot battle-song. A specimen is Marot's translation of Ps. civ. 3, 4 (cf. Castellio):

> Lambrissé d'eaux est ton palais vousté,
> En lieu de char sur la nue es porté,
> Et les fortz ventz qui parmy l'air souspirent
> Ton chariot avec leurs esles tirent.[1]

On the Catholic side activity was understandably less intense, since, as we have seen, translation into the vernacular was regarded as a characteristically Protestant enterprise. As a counterweight the Louvain Faculty of Theology authorized a translation first printed in September 1550 (the Louvain Bible). It was mainly the work of Nicolas de Leuze, assisted by François de Larben, a Frenchman from the Lyonnais. It was conceived in a very different spirit from the Protestant versions, as Nicolas de Leuze's preface shows:

> Car on voit maintenant...que gens mechaniques, comme foullons, tisserans, massons, charpentiers, marchans, & autres qui d'auenture ne sçaiuent lire ne escripre, veullent iuger de la tressaincte & tresparfonde Theologie, & sur icelle donner leur opinion, en peruertissant souuentesfois la vraie intelligence du texte....

The translation is in fact a reproduction of Lefèvre, with linguistic and stylistic corrections and some borrowings from Olivetan. It was reprinted, revised in 1572 and, heavily revised, in 1578. Now the odd thing is that this revision was based on the Geneva versions and in the majority of passages tested, except where doctrinal points are involved, comes closer to them than to the 1550 Louvain edition. The 1578 version was frequently reprinted in its own right and in the ostensibly new translations of Besse (Paris, 1608), Deville (Lyons, 1614) and Frizon (Paris, 1621). They have no claims to originality.

[1] Full account in O. Douen, *Clément Marot et le Psautier huguenot*, 2 vols. (Paris, 1878–9).

Thus at the end of our period there are two authoritative versions, the Louvain Bible of 1578 for Catholics and the Geneva Bible of 1588 for Protestants. They derive from the same source (Lefèvre) and the Louvain revisions bring the two streams closer together. Both are the inspiration of later versions.

4. DUTCH VERSIONS

The translations of the Bible in the Low Countries tend to reflect the various trends of church life in each period. The nature of the translation itself, the name of the printer and the place where it was printed, even the omission of these particulars: all indicate the situation at a given moment.

Before the Reformation the translations were usually incomplete, and followed the contents and order of Peter Comestor's *Historia Scholastica*. The first printed Bible in the Netherlands was also incomplete, and was based on a fourteenth- or fifteenth-century manuscript. This was the folio Bible printed by Jacob Jacobsoen and Maurits Yemantszoen of Middelborch, and published at Delft in 1477. The name of the translator is unknown, and Dutch scholars are still trying to identify him. Only one complete Bible was printed in this period—by P. Quentell in Cologne about 1478. The language of this version was influenced by the dialect spoken in the eastern provinces of the Netherlands. There were also printed in various places small books containing translations of the Psalms, and the liturgical Epistles and Gospels. The translation is derived from that of J. Schutken, a disciple of Gerard Groot.

With the changes caused by the Reformation, and in the climate of increased interest in the Bible, the number of printed editions increased, and new translations also appeared. Erasmus's Latin text of the New Testament[1] was used as the basis of a Dutch translation published in Amsterdam by Doen Pietersz. In 1522 appeared Joh. Pelt's translation of Matthew, followed in 1523 by the complete New Testament and in 1527 by the Old Testament. The translation was later banned, and the printer summoned to appear in court, but influential friends helped him to escape, in 1532. The general political circumstances in Amsterdam meant that for the time being it played no further part in the Reformation.

[1] Another translation of the New Testament based on Erasmus appeared in 1524 at Delft, printed by (?) C. H. Lettersnyder. It was often reprinted.

Luther's translation also was soon being used, among others by Jacob van Liesveldt of Antwerp whose first complete Bible appeared in 1526. (He was anticipated by a printer of Cologne, H. Fuchs, who had printed in 1525 a Dutch translation of Luther's New Testament, with an introduction defending such translations.) An Old Testament partly based on Luther's translation was also printed in 1525, by H. van Ruremunde of Antwerp. Indeed Antwerp and its printers had for some time been influencing the course of the Reformation. Van Liesveldt's typically Protestant marginal notes, which grew with every reprint, gave his Bibles an increasingly reforming tone. In the end they were fatal to him, for he was executed in 1545. But his Bible was often reprinted elsewhere, and the translation was very commonly used by the adherents of the new movement.

The general political and ecclesiastical situation in the Netherlands, the war of independence against Spain and the associated breach with the Roman Church, were immediately reflected in translations and editions of the Bible. Willem Vorsterman for instance, an orthodox Roman Catholic, published an 'expurgated' edition of Liesveldt's version at Antwerp in 1528. It was proscribed, but many clandestine editions continued to appear. The Roman Catholics therefore decided to publish an authorized version of their own. It was prepared by Nicolaas van Winghe from Henten's Louvain Vulgate of 1547, and it was itself published at Louvain in 1548. It was this translation which was used for Plantin's celebrated and beautiful Antwerp edition of 1566. A further edition, corrected according to the Clementine Vulgate, was printed by Plantin's son-in-law Jan Moerentorf (Moretus) in 1599. This revision was in general use among Roman Catholics for several centuries.

Eventually the southern Netherlands, now Belgium, were subdued by the Spanish and remained part of the Spanish Empire, while the northern Low Countries, now Holland, became independent and Protestant. Before then, while the political circumstances remained uncertain and religious persecution was rife, many leading Protestants fled from the Netherlands, particularly to Emden, just across the German border. It was here that the new Dutch Protestant versions were printed.

Meanwhile Protestantism itself had its divisions. The militant majority were the Calvinists, the 'Gereformeerden'; the Mennonites were a minority, but a distinctive one. Lutheranism never took strong root in the Netherlands; this sprang from the acceptance by the German reformers of the formula 'cuius regio eius religio' at the Peace of Augsburg. German Lutheran theologians tended in consequence to advise the Dutch rebels to submit and accept the religion of the legal Spanish government, and the advice was naturally not well received. Each of the Protestant parties had or required its own translation. The Bible of the Mennonites had grown out of a New Testament published by Mattheus Jacobsz of Cologne and the same printer's edition of the Prophets, both of 1554. The eventual complete edition of the Bible was named the Biestkens Bible after its principal publisher. It was first printed in Emden in 1558 by Steven Mierdman and Jan Gheilliaert; Biestkens published it in 1560, and frequently reprinted it with corrections. It remained the standard Mennonite Bible until the eighteenth century. As the translation followed Luther's for the most part, the Lutherans used it until in the seventeenth century they produced a version of their own.

The Calvinists very early felt the need for a good translation of their own, but had to wait for it until 1637.[1] The first Bible specifically intended for them was published by Mierdman and Gheilliaert. The text was in the main Gheilliaert's work. There were also some other editions which had little success, such as J. Utenhoven's translation of the New Testament (Emden, 1556). For the most part Calvinists used the so-called *Deus-aes* Bible of 1561–2. Godfried van Winghen translated the Old Testament, but his translation was derived from the Liesveldt Bible. The New Testament was translated by 'J.D.', who was probably Jan Dyrkinus.

The *Deus-aes* Bible was often reprinted, first at Emden, and later in several other places. It was first printed in the Netherlands at Dordrecht in 1571 by Jan Canin (or Caen), but it cost him his life. It was later printed very often in the Netherlands. The name *Deus-aes* Bible has its origin in a marginal note by Luther on Neh. iii. 56, in 1534. He said, 'Deus-aes has nothing, six-cinque won't give anything, quater-dry helps greatly'. The reference is to a game of dice; Luther meant that deuce-ace (two-one) meant the lower classes, six-cinque (five) meant the nobility, and quater-dry (four-three) the middle classes. The translation kept its name long after the original note had given offence and been omitted.

[1] In 1595 Marnix of St Aldegonde was asked by one of the Reformed synods and the States General to make a new translation of the Bible, but he died in 1598. His translation of the Psalms is well known.

The Calvinists, who were becoming the dominant party and were acutely aware of their task, could no longer be satisfied with hasty and partial translations, and the demand for a good translation from the original sources became increasingly urgent by the end of the sixteenth and the beginning of the seventeenth century.

5. SPANISH VERSIONS

The first printed Index of the Spanish Inquisition (Toledo, 1551) prohibited the 'Bible in Castilian romance or in any other vulgar tongue', the Spanish New Testament of Francisco de Enzinas and those 'Old and New Testaments, Gospels, Epistles and Prophecies and any other books of Holy Scripture in Castilian romance, French or Flemish or any other tongue which have prefaces, notes or glosses that reveal erroneous doctrines repugnant or contrary to our holy Catholic faith or to the sacraments of Holy Mother Church'. The more thoroughgoing Index of 1559 forbade 'The Bible in our vernacular or in any other, wholly or in part, unless it be in Hebrew, Chaldean, Greek or Latin'. And in another place: 'And because there are some pieces of Gospels and Epistles of St Paul and other parts of the New Testament in the Castilian vernacular both printed and in manuscript from which certain objectionable consequences have followed, we order such books and treatises to be shown and handed over to the Holy Office, whether or not they bear their authors' names, until the Council of the Holy General Inquisition shall determine otherwise.' Their list included some twenty particular items that fell under the general ban, which of course included portions of Scripture as well as the whole Bible. And just as this formidable catalogue proscribed devotional works by St Francis Borgia and Luis of Granada which had been printed hitherto with full ecclesiastical approval, so it also contained some scriptural versions whose purposes were entirely orthodox. Master Jarava's versions of the Penitential Psalms, Songs of Ascents and the Lamentations (1543, 1544, 1546 and 1556) appeared alongside others which, disguised by false imprints, came from the printing-house of Jean Crespin of Geneva.[1]

[1] See *Tres índices expurgatorios de la Inquisición española en el siglo XVI*. Salen nuevamente a luz reproducidos en facsímil de la Real Academia Española (Madrid, 1952).

Bonifacio Ferrer's Catalan translation of the Bible was printed in Valencia, 1478; all available copies were destroyed by the Inquisition before 1500, but a single leaf survives in the Hispanic Society of America's library. The Catalan Psalter (Barcelona, 1480) was reprinted from Ferrer's Bible. The Acts and Catholic Epistles appeared in Portuguese in Lisbon, 1505. The liturgical Gospels and Epistles (William of Paris's *Postilla*) were printed at Saragossa in Spanish in 1485 and at Salamanca 1493; in Portuguese *c.* 1510.[1] The Gospel harmony of Ludolf of Saxony came out in Portuguese in Lisbon 1495; Montesino's Spanish version and his liturgical Epistles and Gospels were first printed at Alcalá, 1502/3, and Toledo, 1512, respectively. The latter, especially, must have helped to satisfy the scriptural hunger of the unlearned pious before the accession of Charles V. Some of Montesino's work, revised and corrected, continued to be reprinted into the seventeenth century. The enormous influence of Erasmus in the 1520's must have stimulated the hunger and created a new demand for vernacular versions of at least the Psalms and Pauline Epistles, if not for the whole Bible. A few Spanish Psalters were produced in the peninsula in Lisbon 1529, 1535, Barcelona 1538, and Burgos 1548. But works such as these mostly appeared in the forties and fifties and were by Protestants or near Protestants and printed in Lyons or Geneva.

Particularly interesting here are two works of Juan de Valdés—*alias* Valdesso—who died in Naples in 1541. His religious beliefs have been much disputed, but he may be called a heterodox Roman Catholic who believed in justification by faith.[2] He had included a version of the Sermon on the Mount in an illuminist dialogue of religious doctrine, printed in 1529 and banned by the Index of 1551.[3] His versions, made from the Greek, of Romans and I Corinthians appeared over the imprint of 'Iuan Philadelpho' of 'Venice' in 1556 and 1557; this was the common disguise of Jean Crespin of Geneva. Though Valdés

[1] *Evangelios e epístolas con sus exposiciones en romance según la versión castellana del siglo XV hecha por Gonçalo de Santa María*, ed. I. Collijn and E. Staaff (Uppsala and Leipzig, 1908).

[2] Fr Domingo de Santa Teresa, *Juan de Valdés 1498(?)–1541. Su pensamiento religioso y las corrientes espirituales de su tiempo*, Analecta Gregoriana (Rome, 1957).

[3] *Diálogo de doctrina cristiana*, reproduction en fac-similé...par Marcel Bataillon (Coimbra, 1925), fols. cii–cviii.

cannot correctly be described as a Protestant, the Protestants found his biblical translations and commentaries useful. These two books were included in the Index of 1559. His other biblical translations perished or had to wait until the nineteenth century before they were printed.

Two different Spanish New Testaments had also been printed before the Index of 1559 was issued. Francisco de Enzinas's version (Antwerp, 1543), made from the Greek text of Erasmus, was suppressed because of its unorthodox marginalia and because he printed in capitals the verses of Romans iii which were often appealed to by the champions of justification by faith. Juan Pérez de Pineda, who seems to have been the principal agent in the publication of Valdés's books at Geneva, published there his own translations of the New Testament (1556) and Psalms (1557). His version of the former was also made from the Greek.

By that time a literal Spanish translation of the Old Testament had been printed by a Jewish press at Ferrara in 1553. The bibliographical problems of this handsome volume, its different authors' names, dedications and colophons, its strange variants in Is. vii. 14, and its other variations have been ably studied recently.[1] The translation was made word-for-word from the Hebrew, and its syntax is therefore peculiar. The abundant archaisms and 'intolerable Hebraisms'—the consequence of its compilation, perhaps, from manuscripts used for instructional purposes in medieval Spanish synagogues—add to this bizarre character. Nevertheless, it sometimes has (as the preface states) 'the gravity that antiquity often has'.[2] This frankly Jewish Bible gave immense help to later translators of the Old Testament, Catholic and Protestant alike. For it was used both by Reyna in the sixteenth century and by Father Scío de San Miguel in the eighteenth; traces of it may easily be seen in Quevedo's literal version of Lamentations i and in the poetic paraphrases of Scripture by Bernardino de Rebolledo in the seventeenth century. There are many later editions of the Ferrara Bible, mostly published for the Jews at Amsterdam.

The first complete translation of the Bible (including the Apocrypha) into Spanish appeared at Basle in 1569 (reissued at Frankfurt in 1602 and 1622). It was the work of Cassiodoro de Reyna, like Pérez de

[1] Stanley Rypins, 'The Ferrara Bible at Press', *The Library*, 5th ser. x (1955), 244–69.

[2] 'Y alla tiene su grauedad que la antiguedad suele tener.'

Pineda a refugee monk who escaped from the Convent of San Isidoro of Seville during the fifties. For the Old Testament he leaned heavily on the Ferrara Bible, the syntax and vocabulary of which he normalized and modernized. This book is known as the Bear Bible, because of the title-page device which shows a bear searching for honey in a tree trunk. It is written in good straightforward prose.

Reyna's reviser, Cipriano de Valera, had also been a monk of San Isidoro. His version differs from the earlier one only in details. The New Testament was printed by 'Ricardo del Campo' (i.e. Richard Field of London) in 1596, and the complete Bible (including the Apocrypha) appeared in Amsterdam six years later. Many later Spanish Protestant Bibles derive from this, including some printed by the British and Foreign Bible Society since 1861. Valera's alterations hardly affect the quality of Reyna's competent prose.

The following table shows how certain key words were translated in the Spanish sixteenth-century versions of the New Testament:

	Vulgate	Enzinas	Pérez de Pineda	Reyna and Valera
Matt. iii. 2	poenitentiam agere	hazed penitentia	enmendaos	enmendaos
Luke i. 28	gratia plena	llena de gracia	has hallado gracia delante di Dios	amada
I Pet. ii. 25	episcopum	curador	Obispo	Obispo

Menéndez y Pelayo pointed out that the Index did not mean the end of biblical translation inside the peninsula. Although Fray Luis de León earned himself four years of imprisonment by the Inquisition because he wrote and circulated a manuscript version of the Song of Songs in the vernacular, his poetical paraphrases of the Psalms and prose translations of shorter texts in his *Nombres de Cristo* (1583) were freely sanctioned. Diego de Estella, Malón de Chaide, Luis of Granada (and a host of others) quoted more or less extensively from the Bible after 1559; and Spanish poets of the seventeenth century were as free to versify the Psalms, Job and the Lamentations of Jeremiah as were Donne, Milton and Nahum Tate. Biblical plays were common on the ordinary stage, and Calderón's sacramental allegories were full of biblical quotations, imagery and incident. Spanish Bibles were forbidden, but any ordinary Spaniard who opened a book of devotion had access to passages of holy writ. In special circumstances licences were granted to the learned to consult the heretical translations. The inquisitorial ban was certainly deplorable, but it did less harm to Spanish religion and to Spanish literature than some people have imagined.[1]

6. THE BIBLE IN EAST-CENTRAL EUROPE

From the early sixteenth century until the late eighteenth the easternmost territories of western Christendom were divided between two States—Poland and the Habsburg Empire. This vast area, stretching from the Baltic to the Adriatic, was inhabited by a great variety of peoples, most (but by no means all) of whom spoke Slavonic languages. To all of them the religious reform movements of the fifteenth and sixteenth centuries gave the incentive to translate the Bible into their own vernaculars. By 1700 the Counter-Reformation had re-established the hold of Roman Catholicism in all these territories except eastern Hungary, where Calvinism was never dislodged. Yet the importance of the new Bible translations remained: the literary languages of all the peoples concerned were affected, often decisively, by the Protestant versions of the Scriptures and sometimes also by the Catholic versions which they stimulated.[2]

Among the Czechs manuscript translations of the whole Bible had existed from the fourteenth century. John Hus (*c.* 1369–1415) and the reform movement named after him attached great importance to the reading of the Scriptures in the vernacular: over fifty complete or fragmentary Bible manuscripts in Czech have been preserved from the fifteenth century. In 1475 the first printed Czech New Testament[3] appeared, though it is uncertain whether it was printed in Bohemia. The first complete Bible to be printed in Czech was issued from the

[1] In giving this account of Spanish Bibles I have used extensively both Darlow and Moule's *Historical Catalogue*, vol. III, and the Spanish translation, published in two volumes in Mexico, 1950, of Monsieur Marcel Bataillon's *Érasme et l'Espagne*. The last paragraph comes from Marcelino Menéndez y Pelayo's *Historia de los heterodoxos españoles*, first printed in Madrid, 1880/2.

[2] Valuable information on all the countries dealt with in this section may be found in T. H. Darlow and H. F. Moule, *Historical Catalogue of the Printed Editions of Holy Scripture in the Library of the British and Foreign Bible Society* (London, 1911), vol. II.

[3] For bibliographical descriptions of all the Czech books referred to see Zd. Tobolka, *Knihopis československých tisků od doby nejstarší až do konce XVIII. století*, I (Prague, 1925) and II, ii (Prague, 1941) and J. Merell, *Bible v českých zemích* (Prague, 1956).

press of J. Kamp in Prague in 1488. Its text was essentially based on the (linguistically rather archaic) version which had grown from Hus's own revision of the text and is represented by many of the manuscripts. Though reprinted a year later at Kutná Hora, Kamp's Bible was soon superseded by another version which, though printed outside Bohemia, exercised a considerable influence on later translators. This was the Bible printed at Venice in 1506 by Peter Liechtenstein of Cologne. The editors of this version (or 'correctors' as they are called in the colophon) were Jan Jindřišský of Žatec (Saaz) and Tomáš Molek of Hradec Králové. They had based themselves largely on the traditional text represented by the two earlier printed Czech Bibles; and their arrangement of the books (including IV Esdras[1] and the apocryphal Epistle to the Laodiceans) was followed for three centuries in all Czech Bibles except those of the Bohemian Brethren. The Venetian Bible was financed by certain citizens of Prague and no doubt intended for circulation among the Utraquists, by now the strongest religious denomination among the Czechs.

Several other Czech versions of the whole Bible or of the New Testament appeared during the sixteenth century; with the exception of the translation by Optát Beneš and Petr Gzel (Náměstí, 1533), which was made from Erasmus's Latin version and not, like its predecessors, from the Vulgate, they offer no new features of importance. Of incalculable significance for the Czechs, however, was the translation of the Bible undertaken by the *Unitas Fratrum* (Bohemian or Moravian Brethren). The Brethren, with their emphasis on practical Christianity and their relative lack of interest in doctrinal disputes, had remained separate from both the Catholic and Utraquist parties; and in the person of Jan Blahoslav (1523–71) they produced a scholar of real eminence. Blahoslav's translation of the New Testament from the Greek was printed by the Brethren at Ivančice in Moravia in 1564, and was the prelude to the translation of the whole Bible from the original languages which was carried out by a group of ten scholars, two of whom knew Hebrew.[2] The Brethren's printing-press had been transferred from Ivančice to Kralice, on the estate of the Žerotín family, one of whom (Jan the elder) had been Blahoslav's pupil. This Kralice Bible appeared in six volumes: volumes I (1579), II (1580), III (1582) and IV (1587)

[1] II Esdras in the English Apocrypha.

[2] One of them, Lukáš Helic, was a converted Jew.

contained the Old Testament; volume v (1588) the Apocrypha; and volume vi (1593) the New Testament.[1] The translators took their text from the Antwerp Polyglot Bible of 1569–72 and called in the aid of various Latin commentaries. Yet they were not concerned only with scholarly accuracy: in their preface to the first volume they state as one of their principal aims that the Czech text should be clear, straightforward, simple and dignified. In this they were brilliantly successful. The Kralice Bible is universally recognized as the finest example of the older Czech language.

The six-volume edition of the Kralice Bible was followed, in 1596, by an edition in one volume which was reprinted in 1613. It was not to be printed again in Bohemia until 1863. After the defeat of the Protestant armies at the battle of the White Mountain in 1620 Bohemia and Moravia were engulfed by the Counter-Reformation. All Protestant writings were proscribed and many copies of them were burnt. The Kralice Bible continued to be treasured by Czech Protestants in exile who also introduced copies surreptitiously into Bohemia for circulation among those who in secret retained their loyalty to the old faith. It was several times reprinted abroad during the eighteenth century—at Berlin, in Silesia where the Brethren now had their main centre, and in Hungary, where the force of the Counter-Reformation was less extreme than in the Czech provinces. In the meantime the Catholic authorities in Prague had felt the necessity to provide their own translation of the Scriptures: all versions subsequent to the Venetian Bible of 1506 were considered to be tainted with heresy; and in 1676 the Archbishop of Prague issued a decree authorizing the publication of a new version. This was made by a group of Jesuits who, while basing themselves on the Vulgate, took into account not merely the text of the Venetian Bible but also that of the 'heretical' Kralice Bible. The St Wenceslas Bible, as this version is called, was printed at the *Clementinum*, the Jesuit College of Prague University, and appeared in three volumes in 1715. This long remained the official Czech Catholic version.

Even after the Emperor Joseph II's Patent of Tolerance (1780) Protestantism never again regained an extensive hold in Bohemia and Moravia, so that the Kralice Bible has remained an 'authorized version' for only a minority of Czechs. But the place that it occupies in the

[1] This was a revision of Blahoslav's earlier translation.

national history is strikingly illustrated by the fact that the leaders of the national revival around 1800 made its language the basis of their efforts to revive the neglected Czech vernacular. The position of the Kralice Bible in the history of the Czech language is comparable with the Authorized Version in England or Luther's Bible in Germany.

In Slovakia important Protestant communities continued to exist throughout the seventeenth and eighteenth centuries: among them the Kralice Bible never ceased to be read in church and home.

The influence of Luther's doctrines quickly spread to Hungary, no doubt partly through the large German element in the towns; and a number of partial or complete translations of the Bible into Hungarian appeared in the course of the sixteenth century. The first Hungarian version of the New Testament to be made from the Greek original appeared at Sárvár near Új Sziget in 1541,[1] the year of the capture of Buda by the Turks. The translator was Johannes Sylvester (Erdösi),[2] a Lutheran who had studied at Wittenberg under Melanchthon.

By the middle of the century the greater part of Hungary was under Turkish rule. In the narrow north-western strip that was held by the Habsburgs the Counter-Reformation made itself strongly felt; to the east, however, in the semi-autonomous principality of Transylvania religious tolerance was the rule, and several versions of the Scriptures were printed there. Between 1551 and 1565 several books of the Bible appeared at Kolozsvár (Cluj, Klausenburg) in the translation of the Calvinist Gáspár Heltai;[3] but it was not until 1590 that the whole Bible appeared in Hungarian. The translator was another Calvinist, Gáspár Károlyi (*c.* 1529–92). He too had studied at Wittenberg. His Bible was printed at Vizsoly in eastern Hungary: that the press there was able to survive despite a viceregal order for its closure was due to the protection of Sigismund Rákóczy, prince of Transylvania, who also provided financial assistance for Károlyi's translation. The scholarly character of this version and its attractive, even if archaic, language

[1] For further bibliographical and other information about the Hungarian versions see K. Szabó, *Régi magyar könyvtár, az 1531–1711. megjelent magyar nyomtatványok könyvészeti kézikönyve* (Budapest, 1879), vol. I.

[2] On Sylvester and his work see the detailed study by J. Balázs, *Sylvester János és kora* (Budapest, 1958).

[3] Originally Caspar Helth. Born in Saxony and originally a Lutheran, he was converted to Calvinism and thereafter wrote only in Hungarian, a language which he had not begun to learn till his twentieth year.

ensured its future as the official Hungarian Protestant version. It was reprinted, somewhat revised, in Germany (Hanau, 1608 and Oppenheim, 1612); and during the eighteenth century a new revision appeared at Leyden (1719) and several times thereafter at Utrecht and Basle. A rival, Roman Catholic, version appeared in Vienna in 1626; it was the work of György Káldi and sponsored by the leader of the Hungarian Counter-Reformation, Péter Pázmány.

The only complete Polish translation of the Bible to be made before the Reformation was a slavish imitation of the Czech version;[1] but here too the advent of Protestantism stimulated biblical scholarship. The Gospels appeared at Königsberg in 1551–2[2] under the editorship of the Lutheran preacher Jan Seklucjan; but the first complete Polish Bible was a Catholic version, that of Jan Leopolita Nicz which appeared in Cracow in 1561. The translation (from the Vulgate) may have been the work of the Dominican friar Leonard, the confessor of King Sigismund Augustus to whom it was dedicated. This was soon overshadowed by the scholarly Protestant Bible printed in 1563 at Brest Litovsk in the Grand Duchy of Lithuania. The Grand Hetman of Lithuania, Prince Nicholas Radziwiłł, known as 'the Black', put up the funds for its publication. The translation (from the original languages) was the work of a committee consisting of Calvinists and Socinians.[3] The sumptuous folio is dedicated, like its Catholic predecessor, to King Sigismund Augustus.[4]

In addition to Lutheranism and Calvinism the antitrinitarian or Socinian doctrine had many adherents in late sixteenth-century Poland and two Bible translations were made for them: the more noteworthy is that made by the Hebrew scholar Szymon Budny and printed at Nieśwież in 1570–82.

The Brest (or Radziwiłł) Bible was also criticized for its supposedly

[1] Known as the Bible of Queen Sophia or Sárospatak Bible (1455).

[2] For further information on early Polish Bibles see A. Brückner, *Encyklopedia staropolska* (Cracow, 1939), vol. I, and Z. Gloger, *Encyklopedia staropolska* (Warsaw, 1900–3; reprinted, Warsaw, 1958), *s.v. Biblia.* Bibliographical descriptions may be found in K. Estreicher, *Bibliografia polska* (Cracow, 1894), XIII, 13 ff.

[3] One member of it was Jan Łaski (John a Lasco), known for his activities in the English Reformation: see *Cambridge History of Poland, from the Origins to Sobieski* (Cambridge, 1950), p. 339.

[4] Himself a Catholic, the king was nevertheless tolerant and indeed sympathetic to Protestantism. Prince Radziwiłł 'the Black' and other Protestant nobles were among his close advisers.

'Arian' marginal notes and was therefore revised by the Calvinist Daniel Mikołajewski and Jan Turnowski of the *Unitas Fratrum*: this version appeared at Danzig in 1632 and became accepted as the official Protestant version. It was several times reprinted in Germany, like the Bibles of the Czech and Hungarian Protestants. The Catholic version of Nicz was replaced by the excellent version made from the Vulgate by Jakób Wujek z Wągrowca (New Testament 1593, Old Testament 1599). Revised by the Jesuits, this translation was approved by Pope Clement VIII and accepted as the official Polish Catholic version at the synod of Piotrków in 1607.

The victory of the Counter-Reformation in Poland was ultimately even more complete than in Bohemia; and it seems symbolic that Prince Nicholas Christopher Radziwiłł bought up copies of the Brest Bible, which his father had had published, and caused them to be burnt with other Protestant books in the main square at Wilno.

Much of the strength of Polish Protestantism had been in the Grand Duchy of Lithuania; and it was not until well on in the seventeenth century that it succumbed. While the Brest Bible had satisfied the Polish-speaking nobility and citizenry in Lithuania the need came to be felt for a version in Lithuanian, in order to win the country people also for the new faith. By a strange twist of events the first Bible ever printed in Lithuanian was produced in London, and even this was unfinished. It was the work of a Polish Lithuanian, Samuel Bogusław Chyliński (*c.* 1633–68), who made it in Oxford from 1657 onwards. He succeeded in obtaining influential support in England for his venture but had to discontinue it when his text failed to gain the approval of the Calvinist synod of Wilno. Only three incomplete printed copies of his Old Testament are extant.[1] The first printed New Testament in Lithuanian eventually appeared in 1701 and the first complete Bible in 1735, both at Königsberg.

A short but far-reaching chapter in the history of the Bible in Central Europe is linked with the activity of the Slavonic printing-press set up at Urach in 1560 by the Styrian Protestant Count Hans Ungnad, with the approval of Duke Christopher of Württemberg. The Lutheran

[1] The strange story of Chyliński's Bible translation has recently been told by S. Kot in the introduction to Cz. Kudzinowski and J. Otrębski (eds.), *Biblia litewska Chylińskiego. Nowy Testament—Chyliński's Lithuanian Bible. The New Testament*, vol. II, Text (Poznań and Wrocław, 1958).

Reformation had gained many adherents in the Austrian provinces of Carniola, Carinthia and Styria where large sections of the population spoke Slovene. The Slovene reformer Primož Trubar[1] was driven into exile and went to Germany where he established close contact with leading Lutherans. In 1557 and 1560 he published at Tübingen a Slovene translation of part of the New Testament (Gospels, Acts, Romans). In the latter year, however, Count Ungnad set up a printing-press at his own residence in Urach near Tübingen for the use of Protestants from Slovene and Croatian territories. Here for nearly five years (1560–4) Protestant books were printed in the Glagolitic, Cyrillic and Latin alphabets. They included a further instalment of Trubar's Slovene New Testament (I and II Corinthians and Galatians) (1561) and a Croatian translation of the whole New Testament by Stjepan Konzul (Istranin) and Antun Dalmatin which was issued in both the Glagolitic (1562–3) and Cyrillic (1563) alphabets. The whole venture aimed at spreading Protestantism amongst all the southern Slavs, even those under Turkish rule: hence the use of both the traditional alphabets. After Ungnad's death in 1564 the Urach press ceased to function; but a complete Slovene Bible, translated from the original languages with reference to Luther's German version by Trubar's associate Jurij Dalmatin, appeared at Wittenberg in 1584. Its text had been approved by representatives of the Estates of the three Slovene provinces; but the opposition of the archbishop of Ljubljana prevented its being printed in that city. Protestantism among the Slovenes and Croats was short-lived; but the books of Trubar and Jurij Dalmatin, the first written in the Slovene language, inaugurated a new chapter in the history of their people.

7. SCANDINAVIAN VERSIONS

When the Reformation reached Denmark and Sweden in the 1520's, Danish and Swedish had already begun to develop as separate languages instead of being, as in the earlier part of the Middle Ages, merely two

[1] Trubar's activities and the work of the Slavonic press at Urach have been well summarized by M. Rupel in L. Legiša and A. Gspan (eds.), *Zgodovina slovenskega slovstva* (Ljubljana, 1956), I, 206–33. For Dalmatin see *ibid.* pp. 237–44. Bibliographical information about the Croatian books printed at Urach may be found in F. Bučar and F. Fancev, 'Bibliografija hrvatske protestantske književnosti za reformacije', *Starine*, XXXIX (1938), 49–128.

dialects of the one East Scandinavian language; for in the same decade Sweden threw off the Danish domination. On the other hand, Norway, which had been the area of the West Scandinavian tongue (spoken also by the originally Norwegian population of the Faeroes and Iceland), remained part of the Danish–Norwegian monarchy and used Danish as a religious language, the old Norwegian merely existing as the vernacular and developing as such in Norway, whereas it retained, to a far greater extent, its original structure and vocabulary in the Faroes and Iceland. In consequence, up to the Reformation we have different traditions in (*a*) Norway and Iceland, (*b*) Sweden, and (*c*) Denmark; but after the Reformation the development of the languages and also the Bible versions follow different lines in (*a*) Sweden, (*b*) Denmark and Norway, and (*c*) Iceland.

Several medieval manuscripts containing biblical texts have survived to show that, just as in other parts of Europe, the Bible was known not only as the Vulgate but also in the vernacular. The most famous is the *Stjórn*[1] (that is, 'Steering' or 'Guidance', namely, of God), consisting of an Old Norwegian translation of Genesis–Kings (with lacunae), probably written about 1300. Others are the Swedish versions of the Pentateuch and Acts from the fourteenth century (generally held to be of Brigittine origin), the likewise Swedish translation of Judith, Esther and I and II Maccabees, 1484 (by Jöns Budde of Nådendal in Finland), and one of Joshua–Judges, about 1500 (by Nicholaus Ragnvaldi of Vadstena); the 'Oldest Danish Bible Version', about 1470, comprises Genesis–Kings.[2] None of these early versions is complete and they are all rather free renderings, since they either abridge the text or offer a paraphrase of it, or even notes on it. They were all made on the basis of the Vulgate.

As far as we can judge from the available material, the Bible translators of the age of the Reformation did not make use of the medieval versions. But, at least in Denmark, there is a close link between the times before the Reformation and the versions called forth by the Reformation: one of the first to translate the New Testament into Danish, the canon Christiern Pedersen, had translated, as early as 1514, the Prayers of the Canonical Hours, including fifty Psalms and the

[1] Edited by C. R. Unger (Christiania, 1862).

[2] *Den ældste danske Bibel-Oversættelse*, ed. Christian Molbech (Copenhagen, 1828) (only Genesis–Ruth).

hymns of Luke i–ii; in 1515 followed a Book of Homilies,[1] with the lessons (Gospels and Epistles) in Pedersen's own translation; both of them were printed in Paris. It is noteworthy that Pedersen says in his preface, 1515: 'Nobody ought to think that the Gospels are more sacred in one tongue than in another: they are as good in Danish or in German as they are in Latin, if only they are rightly interpreted.'

Two years later the Reformation started at Wittenberg, and Luther's version of the New Testament appeared in 1522; in 1524 it was already used for parts of the first Danish translation of the New Testament, by Christiern Vinter and Hans Mikkelsen. The work having been done at the request of the exiled king, the translation is known as *Christian II's Nye Testamente*; it was printed in Wittenberg by the younger Melchior Lotther. Only two years after the Danish, the Swedish people got its New Testament, *Jesus. Thet Nyia Testamentit på Swensko* (1526), printed at Stockholm by the royal press. The authorship is ascribed to either Laurentius Andreae or Olaus Petri, both outstanding figures in the history of the Swedish Reformation. This version is also based on Luther's New Testament (whether the 'September Testament' of 1522 or a later edition is hard to tell), but Erasmus's Greek Testament with its Latin translation (probably the third impression 1522 or a reprint) has been consulted and very often has induced the translator to part company with Luther: the influence of the Vulgate is also discernible. It is generally acknowledged to be a fine specimen of the Swedish of the sixteenth century.

Both these New Testaments, the Swedish and the Danish, were called forth by the Reformation in Germany and served to prepare the soil for it in Scandinavia: Bible reading and Bible translation have played an essential part in the history of the Reformation in all countries. But there was still a decade to go before the Reformation was carried through and the national churches of Denmark–Norway and Sweden were established (1536/7), which was the prerequisite for producing complete Bibles in the national languages. Meanwhile, several people worked on translations of different biblical books. In Sweden, versions of Psalms, Proverbs, Wisdom, and Ecclesiasticus appeared in 1536; they have been ascribed to Olaus Petri, with some degree of probability. Frands Vormordsen, a Dutchman who had come to Denmark as a monk, issued a translation of the Psalms, *Dauids psaltere paa danske*

[1] *Jærtegnspostil* ('Book of Portents').

(Rostock, 1528); he had to resort to Danish friends (among them Paulus Eliae) for help in linguistic matters, but succeeded in creating a very good translation; according to his own statement, he made use of five Latin and two German versions (one of the German is Luther's in its Low German edition), but he displays also knowledge of Hebrew and has consulted the Hebrew text of the Psalms. Of even greater importance was the work of the above-mentioned Pedersen. He began it at Lier, where he lived with the exiled king, with the intention of translating the whole Bible into Danish, for the benefit not only of his fellow-countrymen proper but also of the Norwegians and Swedes. The only two parts of the Bible that were ever published, *Det Ny Testamente* (1529), and *Dauidz Psaltere* (1531) (both printed in Antwerp) used the text of the Vulgate, but are also, as might be expected, dependent on Luther (1522–7), and it is obvious that the master has induced Pedersen to aim at a strict, though not literal, translation, in contradistinction to his earlier works. The first edition of the New Testament had to be followed by another only two years later, and the Psalter was reprinted repeatedly in the Hymn Books of the late sixteenth century (1582–6). The most outstanding Danish reformer, Hans Tavsen, was the first translator of the Pentateuch, which was printed in Magdeburg, 1535, bearing the title *Det Gamle Testamente*, that is, 'The Old Testament': apparently, he intended to translate the whole Bible and he is, in fact, known to have advanced much further; but his manuscripts are lost, only his translation of the *Pericopae* (Lessons) is preserved in his Homily Book of 1539. Hans Tavsen uses both the Vulgate and Luther, but very often goes with the Hebrew text against both. His Danish style is excellent, and it is most regrettable that nothing but the Pentateuch was ever published. Peder Tidemand translated Judges (1539), and Ecclesiasticus and Wisdom (1541).

Such were some of the preliminaries for translating the whole Bible; but others had to be added: the completion of Luther's version and the publication of its Low German counterpart (1534) and, last but not least, the final victory of the Reformation in the Scandinavian countries, when the kings of Sweden (Gustaf Vasa) and Denmark and Norway (Christian III) made Lutheranism the established religion of their kingdoms (Sweden 1536, Denmark 1536, Norway 1537, and Iceland, after vigorous struggles, during 1537–52).

Sweden was the first Scandinavian country to get a complete Bible in the national tongue: *Biblia, Thet är, All then Helgha Scrifft, på Swensko* (Uppsala, 1541) (the so-called Gustaf Vasa's Bible). Its sources are the already mentioned parts of the Bible in Swedish, Erasmus, the Vulgate and, above all, the Luther Bible of 1534 or perhaps the 1539 edition.[1] The famous brothers Petri, Olaus and Laurentius, are generally regarded as the chief translators, but at the moment most scholars are inclined to ascribe the authorship to Laurentius Petri. Luther's authority was immense and his influence on the version is very marked; it is not wholly without reason that students of the Swedish Reformation Bible complain that the comparatively independent approach of earlier translators to the Bible was sacrificed to a dependence on Luther. But the style and wording of the previous attempts were none the less improved upon.

This is the first 'Authorized Version' in Sweden, and it remained, in all essentials, the Church Bible during the following centuries. The work of Bible translation went on, it is true, for some decades: Laurentius Petri was the author of versions of various Old Testament books in the 1560's, and in 1600 a committee appointed by Carl IX had stressed the necessity of a thorough revision (in the *Observationes Strengnenses*). But when the next Church Bible ('Gustaf Adolf's Bible') was printed in 1618, it showed a complete neglect of all the work done since 1541; in substance, though not in outward form, it is the same Bible as its predecessor. The 'Carl XII Bible' of 1703 is also a mere revision, with only a few alterations and emendations; in this shape the Reformation Bible survived many generations of Bible Translation Committee members and remained the Bible of the Church of Sweden until 1917.

The Danish Reformation Bible, called the 'Christian III Bible', was printed in Copenhagen by the printer of the Low German Luther Bible, Ludwig Dietz, in 1550. It is still an unsolved problem to whom the chief authorship should be ascribed; Pedersen had finished a translation of the whole Bible in 1543, and it is widely held, though it cannot be proved, that the 1550 Bible is a revision of his work; Hans Tavsen admittedly had no direct influence on the version. The committee consisted of seven members (Bishop Peder Palladius, Professors Niels Hemmingsen and Johannes Machabæus—the latter a Scot and a friend of Melanchthon's—and Povl Tidemand, together with three others),

[1] Professor Lindblom, *Lunds Universitets Årsskrift* (1941).

and it is impossible to prove whether, or how, they divided the work between them and how far they are dependent on Pedersen's lost version of the whole Bible. The king had ordered that the version should be based on Luther's German Bible, but recent investigations[1] have shown that the genesis of the first authorized Danish Bible is much more complicated. The Luther Bible of 1545 was in fact used, but the members of the committee did not confine themselves to it: the Low German version of 1534 was also consulted, which was only a matter of course since Low German was the mother tongue of the king; the previously published Danish translations of the New Testament, Psalms, and other Old Testament books also influenced its language and style.

The Reformation Bible was followed by a revision and reprint, the 'Frederik II Bible', in 1589, and by another reprint, the 'Christian IV Bible' in 1633. By the time the latter appeared, a new translation from the Hebrew and Greek had already been issued (cf. p. 356), which eventually prevailed as the Church Bible, though it was never formally authorized. But the Reformation Bible, in its latest shape and under the name of *Huus- og Reyse-Bibel*, retained its popularity with the people and was still reprinted in the nineteenth century.

In Iceland, Oddur Gottskálksson, a bishop's secretary at Skálholt who had studied in Norway, Denmark, and Germany, translated the New Testament and had it printed at Roskilde (in Denmark) in 1540. At almost the same time, Gissur Einarsson, the first Lutheran bishop, translated Job, Proverbs, and Ecclesiasticus, using the German Bible as a text. The Reformation Bible is the 'Gudbrand Bible' (1584), named after Gudbrandur Thorláksson (bishop of Hólar, 1571–1627), who was himself responsible for the main part of the Old Testament, which he translated from the German and the Vulgate; in general the New Testament was dependent on Oddur Gottskálksson's. It is a marvellous piece of work: book production had been a national craft in Iceland ever since the last Roman Catholic bishop, Jón Arason, had a press established at Hólar, and the Reformation Bible is its most outstanding specimen. The New Testament was printed separately in 1609.

[1] Bertil Molde, *Källorna till Christian III:s Bibel 1550* (Lund and Copenhagen, 1949), and Peter Skautrup, *Bidrag til Den danske Bibels Historie* (Copenhagen, 1950), pp. 42–58.

CHAPTER IV

ENGLISH VERSIONS OF THE BIBLE A.D. 1525–1611

TYNDALE

The survival of some two hundred manuscripts of the Wycliffite versions, most of them written after the synods of Oxford and London, A.D. 1407–9, is sufficient evidence of a demand for the Scriptures in English which legislation could not stifle. With the invention of printing (even if that did not immediately bring cheap and plentiful copies of the Bible) the galling knowledge that vernacular versions were circulating, sometimes with the consent of the Church, in most European countries must have stiffened determination to get an English translation into print. Further stimulus came from the teaching of Colet at home and from the Reformation in Germany and Switzerland. Simultaneously the quickening of scholarship manifest in the Complutensian Polyglot and Erasmus's Greek Testament meant that no mere rendering of the Vulgate would suffice, although one made from the original languages must provoke greater opposition from ecclesiastical authority. England was fortunate to have in William Tyndale the man who could do what was wanted, a man of sufficient scholarship to work from Hebrew and Greek, with genius to fashion a fitting English idiom and faith and courage to persist whatever it cost him.

PUBLICATION

With an Oxford education behind him (B.A. 1512, M.A. 1515), followed by a period of study at Cambridge, Tyndale went as tutor to the family of Sir John Walsh of Little Sodbury, Gloucestershire, where he not only found himself countering the arguments of Walsh's guests (abbots, deans, archdeacons and divers doctors, says Foxe) by open and manifest Scripture, but also translated Erasmus's *Enchiridion Militis Christiani*. That he knew Erasmus's Greek Testament is indicated by his ringing challenge, 'If God spare my life, ere many years I will cause a boy that driveth the plough shall know more scripture than thou dost', words which echo Erasmus's *Exhortation*, in the 1516 Testament, 'I would wish that the husbandman may sing parts of them at his plough'.

But how secure publication with the approval of the Church, even less likely to be given now that the pressure for vernacular Scripture was linked with new methods of interpretation and new conceptions of authority, in short with a reforming movement more menacing than Wycliffe's? There was one man worth approaching, Cuthbert Tunstall, bishop of London, 'whom Erasmus praiseth exceedingly, in his annotations on the New Testament, for his great learning. Then thought I, if I might come to this man's service, I were happy. And so I gat me to London.'[1]

So in summer 1523 Tyndale arrived in London with a translation of Isocrates to demonstrate his proficiency in Greek; he obtained an interview with Tunstall, who gave him neither patronage nor employment, was helped by Humphrey Monmouth, a wealthy cloth-merchant, despaired of achieving his purpose in England, and set off in 1524 for Germany—to Hamburg, Wittenberg, Hamburg again and Cologne, where he first tried to print his English New Testament. The printer, probably Peter Quentell, had scarcely started on St Mark when Dobneck (Cochlaeus) reported the work to the Senate, who forbade it. Tyndale rushed off to Worms with the sheets. Only one fragment of the Cologne printing survives, and if this quarto edition was indeed completed at Worms, all copies have perished. Soon, however, an octavo edition of 6000 copies was printed there by Schoeffer; it was selling in England by April 1526.

This was too much for the ecclesiastical authorities in England who quickly had the Testament burned at Paul's Cross and tried to destroy all copies at home and abroad, particularly at Antwerp. How, somewhat later, Tunstall bought up the remainder through an intermediary from Tyndale himself, thus supplying him with funds for a corrected edition, is a charming story which should not be accepted exactly as it is told in Halle's Chronicle.[2]

There were reprints before Tyndale put his own hand to a new edition, all apparently printed by Christopher Endhoven of Antwerp

[1] Tyndale's preface to the Pentateuch, 1530.

[2] J. F. Mozley, *William Tyndale*, pp. 147–50.

or his widow: one already in 1526, another about 1530, a third early in 1534. These were so incorrectly set up by the 'Dutchmen' that George Joye was persuaded (as he declared) to edit another reprint for Endhoven (August 1534) which might have been regarded as an act of piety towards Tyndale had he not tampered with the text and had he not known that a revision was being prepared by the translator himself. Though this was published by Martin de Keyser of Antwerp in November 1534, Joye continued active, reprinting his own revision with corrections in January and defending his conduct in the *Apology* of February 1535. Tyndale also revised his 1534 Testament; this G.H. edition, published by Godfrid van der Haghen in 1535, and not the one 'diligently corrected...and finished, 1535', is the final and authentic text of Tyndale's version of the New Testament. Meanwhile he had begun upon the Old Testament.

By 1530 he had completed the Pentateuch which was published on 17 January with the imprint of Hans Luft of Malborow, Hesse. Malborow means Marburg, but the real printer was Hoochstraten of Antwerp.[1] Bibliographically it can be treated as five items, for each book has its own title-page and separate signatures, and, while Genesis and Numbers are black-letter, the rest is in roman type. A revised Genesis appeared in 1534. Besides the Pentateuch, Tyndale translated Jonah (1531), the Old Testament lessons used as Epistles at Holy Communion (with the 1534 New Testament), and Joshua–II Chronicles, which he never saw in print.

SCHOLARSHIP

As a scholar long indebted to Erasmus, Tyndale had decided to translate directly from the original Hebrew and Greek. For the New Testament he used Erasmus's Greek text (not a very good one) in one or more of the early editions (1516, 1519, 1522), with the Vulgate, Erasmus's Latin rendering and Luther's German Testament to help him. His independence has been abundantly proved. If there are enough echoes of Purvey to suggest that he had come across that version or knew phrases current from it, it is certain that he started afresh. 'I had no man to counterfeit,' he said, 'neither was helped with English of any that had interpreted the same', and he spoke the truth.

[1] Mozley, *William Tyndale*, pp. 123–5; M. E. Kronenberg, *Nederlandsche Bibliographie*, 2477.

The other aids he used considerably but critically, confident in his knowledge of Greek, though of course he made some mistakes.[1]

If he had not learned Greek at Oxford, it was easy to do so at Cambridge where Croke was lecturing from 1518 onwards. How much Hebrew he knew when he left England is uncertain; perhaps none. He had ample opportunity to learn it in Germany. While no one's knowledge of Hebrew in the sixteenth century was fully adequate to translate the Old Testament accurately, Tyndale grasped the essentials of Hebrew vocabulary and syntax and sufficiently understood the genius and idiom of biblical Hebrew. For the Pentateuch and historical books he had the Hebrew text, the Septuagint, the Vulgate and Luther's German versions. He could also have referred to the Zurich Bible and Pagnini's Latin version, but seems not to have done so. There were grammars (Pellican 1503, Reuchlin 1506, Münster 1525) and dictionaries (for example, Pagninus 1529), while some access to Jewish traditional scholarship was possible in the rabbinic Bibles of 1516/17 and 1524/5. Although fuller investigation of his use of sources is required, work already done is sufficient to establish his independence of judgment in Hebrew as well as Greek.

ENGLISH

The virtue of Tyndale's English is attested by the survival of so much of it through the intermediate versions into the Authorized Version of 1611. Style and idiom were determined by his object: to make the Scriptures intelligible to the ordinary layman, even to the boy at the plough. He must be modern, clear, homely. To avoid excessive Latinism he must be inventive, yet not consciously literary. Scripture made him happy, and there is something swift and gay in his rhythm which conveys his happiness. In narrative he has had no superior. Coverdale could be more musical, the Authorized Version more majestic, and the Geneva Version could often interpret complicated passages more precisely. Tyndale was sometimes clumsy, using—in contrast with his normal economy—an unnecessary number of words in such phrases as 'Emanuel, which is as much to say by interpreta-

[1] Note Mozley's bold claim, 'By the level of his own day Tyndale was a good Greek scholar, fully as good as Erasmus or Luther', *William Tyndale*, p. 84; for his independence, Westcott, *General View of the History of the English Bible*, 3rd ed., pp. 132ff.

tion as God with us'.[1] He liked variety, with different English words to translate a single Hebrew or Greek word, contrary to the principles to be laid down for the Revised Version, and sometimes overdid it; sometimes, perhaps, he was too colloquial or anachronistic ('babble not much', the 'easter holidays' and 'shire town' are often quoted). Minor blemishes matter little in the light of his positive achievement. He had discovered that 'the Greek tongue agreeth more with the English than with the Latin. And the properties of the Hebrew tongue agreeth a thousand times more with the English than with the Latin. The manner of speaking is both one; so that in a thousand places thou needest not but to translate into the English, word for word: when thou must seek a compass in the Latin.' If this makes too little of that forcing of Hebraisms into English which proved successful only because the Bible became so familiar, it remains true that Tyndale made of the spoken English of his day a fit vehicle for the communication of Holy Scripture and determined the fundamental character of most of the subsequent versions.

OPPOSITION

Why was Tyndale's enterprise so bitterly opposed? To say, because it was unauthorized, merely forces the question back a step. Why did not the English bishops, several friends of Erasmus among them, welcome a translation at once so readable and so scholarly? In general the answer must be that Tyndale's work as a whole, treatises and translations, came before them as part of the Lutheran movement. More particularly, the translations themselves contained, both in their text and in the apparatus of notes and prefaces, matter which was unquestionably intended to promote reform along Lutheran lines. First, the celebrated ecclesiastical words. Tyndale wrote repent, not do penance, congregation, not church, and senior or elder, not priest; and the delicate choice between love and charity for the Christian-Greek *agape* was not for him or his critics a point of rhythm. That Tyndale was largely right does not make their protests unintelligible, and one can feel some sympathy with the fears and perplexities of a conservative bishop. Again, Tyndale printed prefaces which, wherever opportunity

[1] Matt. i. 23 in 1526, changed by Tyndale himself in 1534 into 'Emanuel, which is by interpretation, God with us'.

offered, drove home the basic Lutheran principle of justification by faith (many of the prefaces, notably the important Prologue to Romans, are essentially translations from Luther) and added notes of his own which satirized popes and bishops and pungently attacked many of the distinguishing marks of contemporary catholicism. These have often been quoted; less familiar are the extreme comments on justification, only too liable to misunderstanding in the climate of his day. Moralist bishops of an Erasmian outlook might well see the end of decent Christian conduct in such a note as this on faith, from the table at the end of Genesis: 'Jacob robbed Laban his uncle: Moses robbed the Egyptians: And Abraham is about to slay and burn his own son: And all are holy works, because they were wrought in faith at God's commandment. To steal, rob and murder are no holy works before worldly people: but unto them that have their trust in God: they are holy when God commandeth them.'[1]

But that is only one side of the story. Doctrinal notes were no novelty, rather they had been and still are the normal preference—at times the rule—of the Church of Rome. It was the reformers who were willing to let Scripture speak for itself. Luther's New Testament had few notes, Tyndale's Worms quarto none. The provocative notes of the Pentateuch were themselves provoked by the sharp opposition he had experienced by 1530, and he not only softened them in the 1534 Genesis but also issued his final G.H. Testament without notes. Indeed, in 1531 he had declared that if Henry VIII would 'grant only a bare text of the scriptures to be put forth among his people...be it of the translation of what person soever shall please his majesty' he would 'promise never to write more'.[2] Perhaps the prefaces were more obnoxious than the pin-pricking notes since they offered a Lutheran guide to the understanding of Scripture as a whole. But in England even a bare text was still suspect.

Tyndale's first venture was upset by the magistrates of Cologne. The Worms Testament (6000 copies on sale at about two shillings each) was prohibited by Tunstall in 1526 and by the king in 1530; copies of this and later translations were bought up and destroyed by Archbishop Warham, Tunstall and others, as were the Endhoven reprints. Men who bought or sold them were threatened, sometimes tried for

[1] Cf. pp. 14–16 above.

[2] Pollard, *Records of the English Bible*, XXIII.

heresy, sometimes put to death.[1] Tyndale himself was kept in controversy by Sir Thomas More, Robert Ridley and other scholars and harassed by royal agents. He spent his last year in prison at Vilvorde near Brussels, still bent on translating the Old Testament, and there he died at the stake, leaving the memory of his final prayer, 'Lord, open the King of England's eyes'.[2]

FROM TYNDALE TO THE GREAT BIBLE

Much had happened before Tyndale spoke these words—more versions from Protestants, fresh proposals from conservatives, royal proclamations, the publication of the first complete English Bible.

Two of Tyndale's associates broke with him and undertook independent Bible-translating. In the preface to his *Brief Dialogue* (1527) William Roye says he has translated some of the Old Testament and will complete it; but nothing was published, as Tyndale foresaw. George Joye produced much: the Psalms of 1530 (a translation, probably Joye's, of Bucer's Latin version) and 1534 (certainly Joye's); Isaiah (1531), Jeremiah (1534); Proverbs and Ecclesiastes (both 1535, probably Joye's). So tangled were Joye's relations with Tyndale that one cannot say whether these versions, which do not overlap with what Tyndale left in manuscript, were part of a concerted plan; probably not. Joye was no great scholar and possessed no nicety of taste, but he is an interesting minor figure in the story of the English Bible.[3]

Joye's work was printed abroad.[4] At home the influence of Cranmer and Thomas Cromwell gradually prevailed. In December 1534 the Canterbury Convocation, while anxious that laymen should be kept from public wrangling over the Catholic faith or the meaning of Scripture, actually petitioned the Crown for an English Bible, the translator to be named by the king. So Cranmer divided the New

[1] Pollard, *Records*, XV–XXII. For a good example of the circulation and influence of Tyndale's Worms Testament, see *Plumpton Correspondence*, pp. 231–4, quoted by A. G. Dickens, *Lollards and Protestants in the Diocese of York* (Oxford, 1959), pp. 132–5.

[2] So Foxe. Tyndale's letter to the prison governor, asking for Hebrew Bible, dictionary and grammar, is extant: Mozley, *op. cit.* p. 333.

[3] Samples of Joye's work may be examined conveniently in Mozley, *Coverdale and his Bibles*, pp. 54–9; C. C. Butterworth, *Literary Lineage of the King James Bible*, pp. 75–91, and *idem*, *The English Primers (1529–45)*.

[4] Except Proverbs and Ecclesiastes, London, T. Godfray. Mozley suggests these also were first printed in Antwerp, *c.* 1532 (*Coverdale*, p. 50).

Testament among learned bishops and divines, requiring them to correct *it*, presumably Tyndale. Though most of them produced their stints, the plan failed. Still, the door was ajar for Coverdale.

Miles Coverdale had helped Tyndale with the Pentateuch in 1529 and perhaps followed him from Hamburg to Antwerp, where he may have worked as a proof-reader for Keyser. His first translation was *A Paraphrase upon all the Psalms of David* from the Latin of Johannes Campensis, published anonymously in 1534 and attributable on strong internal and some external evidence to Coverdale. A reprint of 1535 adds Ecclesiastes, again attributable to him on grounds of style. A small start, yet on 4 October 1535 his complete English Bible was published. Remarks in the 1550 edition show that he began it only in 1534 under pressure from Jacob van Meteren, an Antwerp merchant. This 1535 folio, long believed to have come from the press of Froschauer of Zurich, was probably printed by Soter and Cervicorn of Cologne.[1] It exists in two forms, the earlier with preliminaries printed in the text-types, the later with preliminaries in an English black-letter, the form in which it was sold in England by James Nicolson of Southwark who bought the sheets from Meteren. The first edition made no claim to have been authorized by the king.[2]

Coverdale did not translate directly from Hebrew and Greek. His modest preface speaks of lowly and faithfully following his interpreters, five in number according to the *Dedication to the King*. They were the Vulgate, Pagnini's Latin version of 1528 (very literal in rendering the Old Testament), Luther's German, the Zurich Bible in the 1531 and 1534 editions, and Tyndale, or, if Tyndale was not counted, Erasmus's Latin version; he did not use Tyndale's Joshua–II Chronicles. Coverdale's scholarship was not sufficient for an independent choice between authorities on philological grounds. For the Pentateuch, Jonah and the New Testament Tyndale is basic, though much revised; for Joshua–Esther (where Luther and Zurich largely agree) he relies on the German versions, with some preference for Zurich; for Job–Maccabees he trusts to the scholarship of Zurich, here independent of Luther, though

[1] L. A. Sheppard in *The Library*, 4th ser. XVI (1935). But he thinks they printed it in Marburg.

[2] Nicolson's letter to Cromwell, first printed by Mozley, *Coverdale*, p. 111, asks that it may go forth under the king's privilege; Mozley argues, not quite convincingly, that Henry submitted it to the bishops and approved its circulation, without granting a formal licence.

the Vulgate is used considerably for the Apocrypha. His English style is commonly judged by his Psalms, where it is at its best: abounding in music, beautifully phrased. Elsewhere he is generally smoother and more melodious than Tyndale, less given to variation, missing something of his swiftness and native force, but often finding a better phrase. His style tends to adapt itself to the 'interpreter' most in use; hence his coining of Germanic compounds—deadburier, handreaching, righteousnessmaking and the like.[1] It is still a Protestant version, with congregation for church, elder for priest, love for charity. There is some concession to conservatism, however, in the occasional use of penance, and there are no such controversial prologues and notes as in Tyndale. According to Archbishop Parker, Anne Boleyn persuaded Henry to have the English Bible placed in every church, an intention of which there is evidence in the injunctions prepared by Cromwell in 1536 but not issued. Coverdale's Bible was reprinted by Nicolson, with some revision, in 1537 (folio and quarto), by Froschauer for Hester in 1550 and by Richard Jugge in 1553; and there was a separate edition of the Books of Solomon (Nicolson, 1537). But its true continuation was in the Great Bible of 1539.

The intricate story of the English Bible from 1535 is but one aspect of the story of the English Reformation. Apart from repudiating the papacy, Henry did not wish to move far doctrinally, but he approved some practical reforms and wanted to check superstition. He would consider restatement of doctrine in terms conducive to unity and was ready enough to exploit the religious convictions of others for his own political ends, for example by intermittent negotiation with German Protestants. Anne's fall, therefore, while it marked (rather than caused) the end of the first round of negotiations with Germany and was soon followed by the mainly conservative *Ten Articles* (July 1536), did not provoke a sharp reaction. Indeed, the injunctions which accompanied the articles gave some encouragement to the reformers. Jane Seymour was a Protestant, and Cromwell still more powerful. In the episcopal debate preceding the *Bishop's Book* of 1537, Edward Foxe, a mediating theologian, could say: 'The lay people do now know the holy scripture better than many of us; and the Germans have made the text of the Bible so plain and easy by the Hebrew and Greek tongue that now many things may be better understood without any glosses at all than by all

[1] The above conclusions are largely those of Mozley, *Coverdale*, pp. 78–109.

the commentaries of the doctors.' Henry himself had instructed Convocation to determine all things by Scripture and not by custom and unwritten verities, a phrase which may suggest the influence of Cranmer.[1] About a vernacular Bible he was cautious, but open to persuasion. In August 1537 Cromwell could tell Cranmer that the king would authorize an English version which the archbishop had just submitted for licence 'until such time that we the bishops shall set forth a better translation which I think will not be till a day after domesday'.

This 'new translation and of a new print, dedicated unto the king's majesty', a folio printed in Antwerp and published in England by Grafton and Whitchurch, purported to be the work of Thomas Matthew. Internal and external evidence combine to prove it a composite version edited by Tyndale's friend, John Rogers.[2] The Pentateuch is Tyndale's (1530, not 1534) with little change; so is Joshua–II Chronicles, now first printed; Ezra–Malachi and the Apocrypha are Coverdale's, with some revision to the middle of Job and only the slightest thereafter; the New Testament is Tyndale's in the G.H. edition of 1535. Rogers translated only the Prayer of Manasses, closely following Olivetan's French version. More interesting than the text, except Joshua–Chronicles, are the accessories, which drew upon Lefèvre and Olivetan. There are some 2000 notes, a few of them Rogers's own, some Coverdale's, many Tyndale's, some Luther's, many from other continental scholars: Erasmus, Lefèvre, Pellican, Oecolampadius, Olivetan, Bucer. Less sharp than Tyndale's, these are still sufficiently controversial to make us wonder why Henry did not insist on a bare text.

What the king permitted, many bishops were ready to enforce. Some required every parish church to procure an English Bible, others ordered their clergy to read a chapter daily in English and Latin, for which a Latin–English New Testament of 1538 was useful. As printed by Regnault in Paris it was Coverdale's work, the English of 1535 brought nearer to the Vulgate text. Two careless, half-pirated, editions of it, got out by Nicolson before Regnault's, caused Coverdale much pain. Then came the royal injunctions of 5 September 1538 which

[1] The debate is reported in John Foxe, *Acts and Monuments*, Book VIII.

[2] W. T. Whitley, *The English Bible under the Tudor Sovereigns* (1937), attributed it to a real Thomas Matthew of Colchester, but his argument has generally been rejected, for example by Mozley and Butterworth.

commanded the clergy to set up in every parish church (parishioners paying half the cost) 'one book of the whole Bible of the largest volume in English'.

There were now two complete Bibles in circulation, Coverdale's (1535 and 1537—the quarto claiming to have the king's licence) and 'Matthew' (1537, 1500 copies printed). The former could not satisfy the scholars, not being made from the originals; the latter would offend the conservatives by its notes and its origin, for Tyndale's share must soon be detected.[1] Besides, insufficient copies were available. Better to meet both objections by revision than to provoke dissatisfaction by reprinting. It is generally agreed that the Bible of the largest volume prescribed by the injunctions was the Great Bible which, after unexpected delays, became available in quantity late in 1539. This official Bible was planned by Cromwell, with Cranmer's approval. Coverdale was the editor, Grafton and Whitchurch the publishers. It was to have been printed, for purely technical reasons, in Paris, and was begun by Regnault under the direct supervision of Coverdale and Grafton. Sheets were sent to Cromwell in June, August and December 1538. Then the Inquisitor-General of France intervened so that, in Grafton's words, 'not only the same bibles being xxv c. in number were seized and made confiscate, but also both the printer, merchants and correctors with great jeopardy of their lives escaped'. Pressed by the English ambassador, Francis I compromised. Manuscripts, paper, type and printers, but not the confiscated sheets, might go to London. The Apocrypha, but not much else, remained to be done in England. Perhaps the Bible was not generally on sale until November, when it was priced 10*s*. unbound, Whitchurch having secured a privilege which compensated for the rather low price.

The widespread desire for a version made from the original tongues determined Coverdale (on Cromwell's instruction?) to revise 'Matthew', not his own Bible of 1535. A conciliatory intention was shown by dropping some of its more provocative elements: the Protestant table of principal matters (Olivetan's), the Luther–Tyndale prologue to Romans and other prologues, and the marginal notes. Words or sentences from the Vulgate not justified by the original were

[1] Royal Injunctions of November 1538 forbade the printing or importation of English Bibles with notes or prologues unless authorized by the king (Pollard, *Records*, XXXVII).

added in small type 'to content those that herebeforetime hath missed such' in English Bibles, but Tyndale's Protestant renderings of the ecclesiastical words were retained. The title-page shows Henry enthroned, handing the Word of God to Cranmer and Cromwell for distribution to clergy and laity amid cries of 'God save the King'. Coverdale was in a hurry. He could not revise every part of the composite 'Matthew' in the light of every work of contemporary scholarship. In general he used Münster's annotated Hebrew–Latin Bible of 1535 to correct the Old Testament and Erasmus for the New, leaving his own Apocrypha almost as in 'Matthew'. More thorough revision of Job–Malachi—his own work of 1535 and much in need of it—had to wait for the second edition. Münster and Erasmus brought greater precision into Tyndale's share of 'Matthew' and greatly improved Coverdale's earlier translation. Linguistically they drew him away from many of the German idioms which he had adapted from Luther and Zurich and were responsible for an increased use of Latinisms, a step towards the Authorized Version. If some of Tyndale's vitality disappears, especially by reduction of his variations, there is compensation in the frequent minor improvements.

Supported by royal and episcopal injunctions the new Bible was in great demand. For the second edition (April 1540), which became the standard text, Cranmer wrote an impressive preface (hence 'Cranmer's Bible'). Five more editions were published by Grafton and Whitchurch in 1540 and 1541.

Not that opposition ceased. Enthusiasm was matched by indifference or could itself make trouble by flouting the injunction to 'avoid all contention and altercation therein, but to use an honest sobriety in the inquisition of the true sense of the same, and to refer the explication of obscure places to men of higher judgment in Scripture'. Few bishops were Protestants, and royal policy changed with the Catholic Six Articles of 1539 and the fall of Cromwell in 1540. It is perhaps some measure of Cranmer's influence that the Great Bible was not withdrawn and that a new order to put it in all churches was made in 1541. Episcopal dissatisfaction came to a head in 1542 when Convocation determined upon another revision, the existing version to be corrected by the Vulgate. Gardiner proposed much Latinizing terminology (cf. p. 205) and perhaps, by going too far, gave Cranmer his chance, for Henry decided to refer the revision to the universities—and nothing was done. On the other hand, no more Great Bibles were printed in Henry's reign, and an Act of 1543 prohibited the use of Tyndale or any other annotated Bible in English and forbade unlicensed persons to read or expound the Bible to others in any church or open assembly.[1] Henry was not against English in church, as the English Litany of 1544 and the King's Primer of 1545 show. He was working for a uniformity in worship and doctrine which would presumably have included a new standard English Bible had he lived longer. While 'one uniform manner of praying' was envisaged in the preface to the English–Latin edition of the Primer (*S.T.C.* 16040), the *Necessary Doctrine* or *King's Book* of 1543 set a standard of doctrine. But when he died in 1547 more Protestant influences quickly prevailed. At once Edward VI renewed the injunction to place the Bible in every parish church; there were many new editions of the Great Bible and the earlier versions, and worship was governed by the Book of Common Prayer in English (1549, 1552). Under Mary, despite Standish's plea to parliament, 'Thousands have been brought from the true meaning of God's word through the English Bible: therefore away with it', there was no formal prohibition, though much destruction, of vernacular Scriptures.[2]

CAXTON, THE PRIMERS, MORE, TAVERNER, CHEKE

Some brief notice must be taken of versions outside the main stream. While English Bibles were still prohibited, Caxton included much biblical history in his *Golden Legend*, first published in 1483. The translations were his own, from the Vulgate, but, although many passages were quite close to the text, it was impossible for the reader to know, without checking, what was biblical and what was not.

More important was the series of English Primers which, from about 1529, contained many Psalms together with substantial prayers taken out of the Bible and passages from the Gospels, for example, the

[1] Yet in 1543 Convocation ordered that the Bible should be read through in English, chapter by chapter, every Sunday and Holy Day after *Te Deum* and *Magnificat*.

[2] Standish's *Discourse* (1554) is quoted by Mozley, *Coverdale*, p. 293. Further details of the fortunes of the English Bible, 1539–58, will be found there (pp. 261–305) and in Pollard, *Records*, XL–XLV.

Passion story. Some of them contained also the Epistles and Gospels which, in 1538, Shaxton had ordered to be read in English at High Mass in his diocese. And there were several separate editions of the Psalter.[1]

In 1539 a revision of 'Matthew' was published. It was made at the request of the printers by Richard Taverner, a scholarly lawyer and a supporter of Thomas Cromwell. His version of the Old Testament is insignificant, for he knew no Hebrew and what corrections he made were introduced mainly from the Vulgate. But his Greek was good. His style is terse and vigorous, more Anglo-Saxon even than Tyndale's; but excessive literalness sometimes results in obscurity. Though he coined some phrases which survive in the Authorized Version, his influence upon the later versions was quite small.[2]

In principle Sir Thomas More favoured the translation of Scripture. 'Nor I never yet heard any reason laid why it were not convenient to have the Bible translated into the English tongue.' But there should be provisions against abuse, and he suggests that the bishop should control its distribution, allowing one man to read Matthew, Mark and Luke, but not John, another to read Ephesians, but not Romans; he might 'to some man well and with reason restrain the reading of some part and from some busybody the meddling with any part at all'. So in the *Dialogue* of 1528 (printed 1529). Five years later, in the *Apology*, he is 'of the same opinion still...if the men were amended and the time meet therefore', a significant qualification. He is now more inclined to insist that a vernacular Bible is not necessary to salvation. He believed he had seen pre-Wycliffite versions in use by ecclesiastical permission, but, when challenged by Barnes, failed to substantiate his claim. Short of an authorized translation, he preferred the unlearned layman to be content with devotional books like 'Bonaventure', that is, Nicholas Love's *Mirrour of the Blessed Lyf of Iesu Crist*, first printed by Caxton (1486), and Walter Hylton's *Scale of Perfection*, Wynkyn de Worde (1494). Tyndale's version he attacked in his *Dialogue* (1528), which was followed by Tyndale's *Answer* (1530), and More's *Confutation of Tyndale's Answer* (1532–3), and *Apology* (1533).

[1] The Primers and similar books are examined with particular reference to their biblical texts in C. C. Butterworth, *The English Primers (1529–45)*. See also C. Hopf, *Martin Bucer and the English Reformation*, ch. VI.

[2] Despite the arguments of H. H. Hutson and H. R. Willoughby in the *Crozier Quarterly* (1939).

More himself experimented with Bible-translation, and the occasional renderings in his *Four Last Things* (1522) are interesting in that they precede Tyndale's, which they resemble. More and longer passages occur in the devotional treatises which he wrote in the Tower. Here he translates from the Vulgate and is influenced by its vocabulary and word-order, but in the main his English is homely and racy like that of Tyndale, with whose version More was by this time well acquainted. And, having no doctrinal controversy in mind, he does not even keep consistently to the Latinized technical terms. He uses chalice and cup, messenger and apostle. R. W. Chambers, who compares the versions of John xiii. 2–17 in More's *Treatise on the Passion* (1534), and Tyndale's 1534 New Testament, concludes that 'they both write the same English'.[1]

Sir John Cheke, professor of Greek at Cambridge and tutor to Edward VI, went far beyond Taverner in his determination to put the Greek Testament into non-learned, non-Latin English. Apostle becomes frosent, proselyte freshman, crucified crossed. He also advocated a reformed spelling: taak mi iook on iou. His translation of Matthew and Mark i, made about 1550, remained in manuscript at St John's College, Cambridge, until it was published in 1843.

THE GENEVA BIBLE

That persecution stiffens faith is among the commonest lessons of history. But these lessons are rarely learned, and Mary can hardly be expected to have foreseen the brevity of her reign and the utter collapse of her religious policy. At Geneva some zealously Protestant exiles, led by John Knox, were making provision for their own religious needs and, maybe, for their missionary return to England. In 1557 they produced English versions of the New Testament and the Psalms, in 1559 a revised Psalter, in 1560 a complete English Bible. While these were understandably marked by a Calvinism distasteful to ecclesiastical authority even in Elizabeth's reign, the Authorized Version was to benefit greatly from their erudition. For Geneva was humming with

[1] F. E. Hutchison, 'Sir Thomas More as a Translator of the Bible', *Review of English Studies*, XVII (1941), 1–10, on which the above is partly based; R. W. Chambers, *On the Continuity of English Prose*, E.E.T.S. no. 186 (1932); A. I. Taft's edition of the *Apology*, with introduction and notes, E.E.T.S. no. 180 (1930); Mozley, *William Tyndale*, pp. 77–80, 89–98, 212–38; W. E. Campbell, *Erasmus, Tyndale and More* (1949).

biblical scholarship: 'the store of heavenly learning and judgment' Whittingham called it, 'the place where God hath appointed us to dwell'. Calvin was writing commentaries there and Beza studying the Greek text. French and Italian versions were being prepared simultaneously with the English, to their mutual advantage.[1]

The New Testament of 1557 was the work principally of William Whittingham, later Dean of Durham, who took as his basic text not the Great Bible but Tyndale, perhaps in Jugge's edition of 1552, and revised it 'by the most approved Greek examples and conference of translations in other tongues'. Superseded in 1560, it exercised no direct influence upon the Authorized Version. The 1557 Psalms was also superseded by the 1559 revision which was incorporated into the 1560 Bible.[2]

This Bible, printed at Geneva by Roland Hall, was a most remarkable book. Its evangelical intention and scholarly methods are indicated in a lengthy preface. It is a new version because 'considering the infancy of those times and imperfect knowledge of the tongues, in respect of this ripe age and clear light which God hath now revealed, the translations required greatly to be perused and reformed'. It endeavours 'to set forth the purity of the word and right sense of the Holy Ghost for the edifying of the brethren in faith and charity'. Reverently keeping the propriety of the words it follows the Apostles in constraining Gentile readers to the lively phrase of the Hebrew and often 'reserved the Hebrew phrases notwithstanding that they may seem somewhat hard in their ears that are not well practised and also delight in the sweet sounding phrases of the holy Scriptures'. The simple reader is encouraged by variant translations in the margin 'which may also seem agreeable to the mind of the Holy Ghost and proper for our language'. Additional words required by English idiom are printed in italics, the 1557 Testament having introduced this distinction into the English Bible. Chapters are divided into verses so that concordances may be profitably used; principal matters are distinguished by ¶; there are arguments to each book and chapter, headnotes to each page, and brief annotations upon hard places gathered 'both by diligent reading of the best commentaries and also by conference with the godly

[1] See pp. 110, 119 above, 441–5 below.

[2] Butterworth detected the similarity to Jugge (1552), *Literary Lineage*, pp. 159–61. It must be left to Dr J. D. Alexander of San Francisco to give the details of his discovery of the 1557 Psalms.

and learned brethren'. There are text-figures and maps, a table for the interpretation of Hebrew names and one of principal matters, so that 'nothing (as we trust) that any could justly desire is omitted'—a touch of complacency perhaps, but essentially a statement of fact with pardonable pride. Unlike most of its predecessors it was a quarto, handier and cheaper than the folios, and for the first time the English Bible was printed in roman type.[1]

The translators, Whittingham, Gilby, Sampson,[2] had much new work to help them. The foundation of their Old Testament was the Great Bible (1550 edition), which they revised in the light of the Hebrew–Latin Bibles of Pagninus (1528, and in Stephanus's Latin Bible, Geneva, 1557) and Münster (1534/5) together with the more recent Latin versions of Leo Juda (1544) and Castellio (1551) and Olivetan's French Bible, then under revision at Geneva. They were sufficiently good Hebraists to form their own judgment and were perhaps the earliest English translators to make first-hand use of Rabbi David Kimḥi's commentary, though they may have known him only through Pagninus. The 1557 New Testament was further revised, with much more attention to Beza's Latin version of 1556, already used by Whittingham. Their Greek text was that of Stephanus as in the *editio regia* with its collection of variants (Paris, 1550) or in that of Geneva, 1551, the first to have verse-numbers.

The whole Bible was substantially revised, but the Pentateuch and historical books (largely Tyndale's work) needed less drastic handling than the remainder. For the Apocrypha they were helped by the French version made by Beza for the 1551 revision of Olivetan and by Baduel's Latin translation printed in Stephanus, 1556–7. Devotion to *Hebraica veritas* produced a few pedantries like the proper names: Izhák, Iaakób and the momentarily puzzling Ahashverosh (Ahasuerus), and some hard expressions, as they admitted. But, besides their greater accuracy, they discovered many good phrases which were to stay. Of accuracy Job xix. 25 is a good example, with 'he [my redeemer] shall stand on the earth' for 'I shall rise out of the earth' (Great Bible). Among

[1] See pp. 436, 444 below.

[2] Evidence as to the translators is early, but imprecise. Whittingham was probably their leader and the 'I' of the 1557 preface. Anthony Gilby was celebrated *ex trium principalium linguarum notitia* and wrote commentaries on Micah and Malachi. Sampson was a good scholar, later Dean of Christ Church. Coverdale may have helped for a short time.

phrases coined are: 'smote them hip and thigh', 'he swalloweth the ground', 'a little leaven leaveneth the whole lump', 'the proportion of faith', 'cloud of witnesses'. To the Authorized Version of I Corinthians xiii it contributes 'for we know in part and we prophesy in part', 'childish things', 'in a glass darkly' and other minutiae.

The prefatory material and the notes—which were in large part derived from the French Bible, itself revised by Calvin and published at Geneva in 1558—are sometimes distinctively Calvinist, a trend which is marked where it might be expected, as in the interpretation of Romans ix–xi, but crops up elsewhere also. Thus the margin reads at Romans ix. 15, 'As the only will and purpose of God is the chief cause of election and reprobation: so his free mercy in Christ is an inferior cause of salvation and the hardening of the heart an inferior cause of damnation'; but Psalm cxlvii. 20 also has the comment, God's 'just judgment...appointed the reprobate to eternal damnation'. Even so, a false impression of this tendency is established when modern scholars put the most controversial notes together to make the point. With their continual emphasis upon justification by faith alone and their frequent jibes at Rome, the notes of the original 1560 Geneva Bible are as a whole generally Protestant in intention rather than specifically Calvinist. They do not, for example, stress presbyterian polity. In 1576, however, Laurence Tomson revised the New Testament, introducing still more of Beza's readings and interpretations from his critical (but sometimes rashly conjectural) Greek text with Latin version and commentary, published in 1565. The notes which he added, largely taken from Beza, do indeed strengthen the Calvinist flavour, and not only in the matter of predestination. Polity becomes prominent. On Ephesians iv. 11, where the 1560 notes are brief and untendentious, he has, 'He reckoneth up the ecclesiastical functions, which are partly extraordinary and for a season, as Apostles, Prophets, Evangelists, and partly ordinary and perpetual, as Pastors and Doctors', and 'Pastors are they which govern the Church, and Teachers are they which govern the schools'. On I Tim. v. 17, 'There were two kinds of Elders, the one attended upon the government only and looked to the manners of the Congregation, the other did beside that attend upon preaching and prayers, to and for the Congregation'. Another major change was the addition in 1595 (and substitution from 1599) of Junius's full and violently anti-papal comments on Revelation.

In one form or another, the Geneva Bible was to have a long history, running to at least 140 editions—Bible or Testament—until the last of 1644. Its handy comprehensiveness made it the family Bible of the English people and it was the first Bible printed in Scotland (Edinburgh, Bassandyne, 1579); in both countries the majority welcomed its strong Protestantism, even its Calvinism. It not only superseded the Great Bible but also retained its popularity against the Bishops' Bible and, for a generation, against the Authorized Version.

Elizabeth's injunctions of 1559 had again required the provision of the whole Bible of the largest volume in English for every parish. No one must be discouraged from reading any part of the Bible (a rejection of the restrictions once proposed by More) but rather should be exhorted to read it, though 'no man to reason or contend, but quietly to hear the reader'. This was still the Great Bible; reprints of 1562 and 1566 met increased demand. At first Archbishop Parker and his colleagues did not object to the Geneva Bible, particularly for reading at home, and the queen granted John Bodley an exclusive patent to print it for seven years. Perhaps Parker had other plans from the beginning, for the patent enjoined that the Bible 'be so ordered in the edition thereof as may seem expedient' to the bishops of Canterbury and London, and in 1561/2 Cox of Lincoln was pressing for a new episcopal revision. Although Parker and Grindal recommended a renewal of Bodley's licence in 1565/6, no Geneva Bible was printed in England until 1576. The return of Marian exiles eager for a more thorough reformation of the Church of England on a Calvinist pattern made its popularity a matter of concern to moderate men like Parker, and it is a reasonable conjecture that, besides planning a new translation, he meant Bodley's reprints—to Parker a stopgap—to appear without the 'bitter notes' and other of the accessories.[1]

THE BISHOPS' BIBLE

Parker's own project came alive in 1566, just after Bodley's application. Clear instructions were given to the contributors, who were mostly bishops: they were 'to follow the common English translation used in the churches and not to recede from it but where it varieth manifestly from the Hebrew or Greek original', to follow Pagninus and

[1] For Bodley's privilege and for Cox see Pollard, *Records*, XLVIII–L.

Münster 'for the verity of the Hebrew' and 'to make no bitter notes upon any text or yet to set down any determination in places of controversy'. Unedifying passages should be marked 'that the reader may eschew them in his public reading', and offensive words should be altered. The work was quickly done, with varying degrees of thoroughness or freedom in different books, and the Bishops' Bible was handsomely printed by Richard Jugge in 1568. The New Testament was on thicker paper, to stand wear; the illustrations included portraits of Elizabeth, Leicester and Burghley! Parker, who took for himself the preliminaries, Genesis, Exodus, Matthew, Mark and II Corinthians–Hebrews, thought that contributors would be more diligent, as answerable for their doings, if their initials were printed after their books; but this was not done consistently.

The translation was a compromise—a dignified and 'safe' version for public reading, a sign that the bishops were not unmindful of their responsibilities, in scholarship an improvement upon the Great Bible, less radical than Geneva but willing to learn from it. A single verse, Isa. liii. 11, illustrates its relation to its English sources and successor; Isaiah, with Jeremiah, was translated by Robert Horne, bishop of Winchester:

Great: With travail and labour of his soul shall he obtain fruit, and he shall be satisfied;
Geneva: He shall see of the travail of his soul, and shall be satisfied;
Bishops': Of the travail and labour of his soul shall he see the fruit, and be satisfied.
A.V.: He shall see of the travail of his soul, and shall be satisfied;

Great: by the knowledge of him which is my righteous servant he shall justify the multitude,
Geneva: by his knowledge shall my righteous servant justify many,
Bishops': My righteous servant shall with his knowledge justify the multitude,
A.V.: by his knowledge shall my righteous servant justify many,

Great: for he shall bear away their sins.
Geneva: for he shall bear their iniquities.
Bishops': for he shall bear their sins.
A.V.: for he shall bear their iniquities.

Horne's words are all in either the Great or Geneva Bible; for the sense he is guided by Geneva, but keeps words from the Great. The Authorized Version almost equals Geneva; the Revised Version almost equals the Authorized Version. All these English versions keep close to the Hebrew text, against the Septuagint.

This version is no violent reaction from the Calvinism of Geneva. Its doctrinal notes, though fewer, are strongly Protestant (for example, on Heb. xiii. 14, retained from Geneva, 'our altar, which is thanksgiving and liberality, which two sacrifices or offerings are now only left to the Christians'); the ecclesiastical words remain (elders, not priests, repentance, not penance, congregation in Matt. xvi. 18 for church, though not always, Geneva itself having frequently used church); and the interpolations from the Vulgate introduced into the Great Bible are mostly eliminated. But 'bitter' attacks on the Catholic hierarchy are dropped. Parker asked Elizabeth to authorize this Bible alone for reading in church, since 'in certain places be publicly used some translations which have not been laboured in your Realm, having inspersed divers prejudicial notes'. He wanted 'to draw to one uniformity'. The text was considerably revised in 1572, a special feature being the printing of the Psalter from the Great Bible parallel with the Bishops'. Then, as now, the Prayer-Book Psalter, Coverdale's version, was too deeply loved to be abandoned, and in subsequent editions (except 1585) this alone was printed. The revision of 1572 chiefly concerned the New Testament, in deference to the scholarly criticism of Giles Lawrence, professor of Greek at Oxford. Though not in itself a work of high merit, the Bishops' Bible is important as the official basis of the revision of 1611.[1]

THE RHEMES-DOUAY BIBLE

Meanwhile English Roman Catholics were working upon a vernacular Bible at their College at Reims. Allen, its first president, gave biblical studies a large place in the curriculum. To meet the Protestant challenge, priests must be ready to quote Scripture in the vulgar tongue since their adversaries have every favourable passage at their fingers' ends; they must know the passages 'correctly used by Catholics in support of our faith, or impiously misused by heretics in opposition to the Church's faith'. Moreover, there was danger that Catholics would read heretical translations for want of better. Accordingly, in 1578 Gregory Martin began his Catholic version, translating two chapters

[1] The Bishops' Bible has been less thoroughly studied than the other major versions. For the documents see Pollard, *Records*, L–LII and for scholarly comment, Westcott, *History*, pp. 230–44.

daily which were reviewed by Allen and Bristow. The New Testament was published in 1582, quarto, Rhemes, John Fogny.[1]

Its principles are explained in a preface. The appearance of an English Bible, required by circumstances, does not imply that Scripture must be available in the mother-tongue. It is translated from the Vulgate which possesses ecclesiastical authority and is the least partial text, 'truer than the vulgar Greek itself'. The translators follow it precisely, risking unfamiliar Latinisms and not presuming to mollify hard places 'for fear of missing or restraining the sense of the Holy Ghost to our phantasy', whereas Protestants use 'presumptuous boldness and liberty in translating'.

Though Martin started from Latin, he watched the Greek, occasionally putting it in the margin. He also made extensive use of the English versions which he condemned. In some points of scholarship—faithfulness to the Greek article, conjunctions and tenses—he introduced improvements which were accepted into the Authorized Version. But his literalness sometimes produced sheer unintelligibility, while many words and phrases can have been meaningful only to those who already understood the Latin. True, numerous ecclesiastical words were familiar enough in their Latin dress—penance, chalice, altar, host—and Martin could not foretell which of his novelties would justify themselves in use. Many of his Latinisms (perhaps not of his novelties) contributed to the majesty of the Authorized Version. Still, a version which renders Philippians ii. 10 'every knee shall bow of celestials, terrestrials and infernals' was not likely to satisfy the plain man. Nor did it.

If ever a vernacular Bible was combative and tendentious, this was—in its Vulgate basis, the version itself, the marginal notes, the lengthy annotations. 'Very plain and outspoken language', says Father Pope, 'necessarily highly controversial'. Every opportunity was taken to press the distinctive teachings of Rome against 'the intolerable ignorance and importunity of the heretics of this time...the false and vain glosses of Calvin and his followers'. Wherever possible the authority of St Augustine, so dear to the reformers, is adduced to support Catholic teaching. As was natural in the circumstances there are straightforward notes on the sacrifice of the Mass, priesthood, the

[1] See especially J. G. Carleton, *The Part of Rheims in the Making of the English Bible* (Oxford, 1902); Hugh Pope (ed. Bullough), *English Versions of the Bible* (St Louis, 1952), and Pollard, *Records*, LIII–LIV; and cf. pp. 211–13 below.

primacy of Peter, penance, counsels and precepts, etc.; others are tart or playful as when the Corinthian speakers of tongues are 'much like to some fond Linguists of our time, who think themselves better than a Doctor of Divinity that is not a Linguist' (that is, doctrine should govern translation).

The Old Testament was not published until 1609/10 (two volumes, Doway, Laurence Kellam); the preface explains that it has been 'lying by us for lack of good means to publish the whole'. Begun by Martin (†1584) it was completed by Allen and Bristow (probably, for there is little exact evidence); Worthington contributed the notes, few but sometimes long, and not usually controversial. The version had been based on the unofficial Louvain Vulgate (1547, ed. Henten), but was 'conformed to the most perfect Latin edition', the Sixtine–Clementine of 1592. It is scholarly (within its limits), but often excessively literal, at its worst in the Psalms. It came too late to influence the Authorized Version.

The New Testament was reprinted in 1600, 1621 and 1633, the whole Bible in 1635, and not again before Challoner's revision of 1750. There need be no fear that the few available copies would be found in the hand of every husbandman.

In 1582 Martin also published *A Discovery of the manifold Corruptions of the Holy Scriptures by the Heretics of our days, specially the English Sectaries*, which was quickly answered by William Fulke's *Defence of the sincere and true Translations of the holy Scriptures into the English Tongue*. In 1589 Fulke published a volume in which the Rhemes and Bishops' versions were printed side by side, with his replies to the doctrinal notes of the former. Contributions to the debate, which ranged over canon, text, renderings, ecclesiastical words and doctrinal interpretation, were made by William Whitaker, *Disputatio de Sacra Scriptura* (Cambridge, 1588), George Wither, *View of the marginal notes of the popish Testament* (1588), and Thomas Cartwright, whose *Confutation of the Rhemists translation, glosses and annotations* was published posthumously in 1618. Fulke's second work was probably in the hands of many of the makers of the Authorized Version.

THE AUTHORIZED VERSION (KING JAMES BIBLE)

The continuing popularity of the Geneva Bible and the comparative failure of the Bishops', together perhaps with Broughton's criticism of the latter, set a problem to Whitgift and his colleagues; and there is extant a draft Act of Parliament, composed during his primacy, for 'one setled vulgar translated from the originall' which foreshadows some of the methods eventually adopted.[1]

But it was the Puritans who provided the immediate occasion of the Authorized Version. In January 1604, at the Hampton Court Conference, John Reynolds 'moved his Majestie, that there might bee a newe translation of the Bible, because those which were allowed in the raignes of Henrie the eight, and Edward the sixt, were corrupt and not aunswerable to the truth of the Originall', the reason for specifying these older versions being their use in the Book of Common Prayer. Accepting Bancroft's qualification that no marginal notes be added (James himself had been annoyed by what he considered seditious comments in the Geneva Bible), the king approved Reynolds's proposal and constituted himself its patron. It is quite likely that Reynolds was only making a move in opposition to the Prayer Book itself and would have been content if—*per impossibile*—the Geneva Bible had been authorized. If this is the case, James was more than a patron; he was the motive force behind the new translation, the more so as the bishops were not immediately favourable to the project. 'If every man's humour should be followed', said Bancroft, 'there would be no end of translating.' But, as the preface to the Authorized Version tells us, 'his Royall heart was not daunted or discouraged for this or that colour, but stood resolute'. On 22 July he told Bancroft that he had 'appointed certain learned men, to the number of four and fifty,[2] for the translating of the Bible'. How they were selected is not known. Perhaps the

[1] Pollard, *Records*, LIX. Hugh Broughton, an eminent but eccentric Hebraist, translated Daniel (1596), Ecclesiastes (1605), Lamentations (1606), Job (1610), and published *An epistle to the learned nobilitie of England touching translating the bible* (1597) and many works on points of detail. He was not chosen among the Revisers. See Brit. Mus. *Guide* to Bible Exhibition (1911), nos. 105–6, for his proposals to Cecil.

[2] In fact, forty-seven names are known. For details see Westcott, *History*, pp. 112–14, 343–50, and Daiches, *King James Version*, pp. 139–66, and for the Hampton Court Conference, William Barlow, *The summe and substance of the conference* (1604).

universities made proposals. They had been chosen by 30 June and probably through Bancroft, as the Authorized Version preface suggests. The king now requested Bancroft to help make provision for their expenses and to instruct other scholars to send in their observations.[1]

The translators were formed into six companies meeting at Westminster, Cambridge and Oxford, with the work distributed among them as follows: (1) Westminster, Genesis–II Kings; (2) Cambridge, I Chronicles–Ecclesiastes; (3) Oxford, Isaiah–Malachi; (4) Cambridge, Apocrypha; (5) Oxford, Gospels, Acts, Apocalypse; (6) Westminster, Romans–Jude. Scholarship, especially Hebrew scholarship, had much improved in England since the mid-sixteenth century. The excellent continental scholars Fagius, Tremellius and Chevalier had been brought over to teach Hebrew at Cambridge, the early dictionaries and grammars upon which Tyndale and his successors depended had been revised or superseded, and there was more knowledge of the cognate languages, Aramaic and Syriac. Increasing familiarity with Jewish commentaries on the Old Testament was an important factor in Bible study and translation. Kimḥi, whose Hebrew is straightforward, was widely and directly known, the more difficult Rashi and Ibn Ezra at least at second hand through the commentaries of Mercier. Among the revisers Edward Lively was a good Hebraist (but he died in 1605), Lancelot Andrewes was regarded as a brilliant linguist, Bedwell was perhaps the most distinguished Orientalist of his day. Other good Semitists were Miles Smith, John Reynolds and Thomas Harrison. Chaderton and Kilby knew the rabbis. Sir Henry Savile, editor of the Eton Chrysostom, was eminent among Greek scholars, Saravia's knowledge of modern languages was a considerable asset. Despite the omission of two of the best contemporary Hebraists, Andrew Willett and the cantankerous Broughton, they were unquestionably a strong team.

Rules drawn up for the companies prescribed that the Bishops' Bible should be followed 'as little altered as the truth of the original will permit', that the translations of Tyndale, Matthew, Coverdale, Whitchurch (that is, the Great Bible) and Geneva be used 'when they agree better with the text than the Bishops' Bible', 'the old ecclesiastical words to be kept, viz. the word Church not to be translated Congregation', and 'no marginal notes at all to be affixed, but only for the explanation of the Hebrew or Greek words which cannot, without

[1] Pollard, *Records*, LX.

some circumlocution, so briefly and fitly be expressed in the text'. According to the procedure proposed in these rules, 'every particular man of each company' was to translate the same chapters, upon which the whole company would meet and agree what should stand; each company would send every book on completion to the other companies; and any differences arising would be compounded by a general meeting of the chief persons of each company. From the Authorized Version's preface and from what the English delegates told the Synod of Dort (1618) it is plain that a somewhat different method was adopted. When each group had finished its portion, twelve men (two from each company) reviewed the whole, and Thomas Bilson and Miles Smith put the finishing touches to the version. Preliminary work took about three years, the meetings roughly another three, so that the translation was able to appear from the press of Robert Barker, the King's Printer, in 1611.[1]

The first edition, a folio in black-letter, is often dubbed the 'He-Bible' from the reading 'he went' in Ruth iii. 15, afterwards corrected to 'she'. Properly it should have the handsome engraved title-page signed by Cornelis Boel, though Barker issued many copies—perhaps not of the first edition—with a woodcut title-border which he had used for the Bishops' Bible (1602) and which introduces the New Testament in the first Authorized Version. After the title comes a fulsome dedication to James, a superb preface, defending the principle of vernacular Bibles and explaining the methods now used, various tables, the (bibliographically distinct) genealogy and map of Canaan, and the table of contents. The Apocrypha are included. There are chapter summaries, headline summaries, numbered verses, paragraph signs, marginal notes (philological only) and cross-references.

Although the Bishops' version was to stand where possible, the truth of the original had to be discovered through the best contemporary scholarship. 'Neither did we think much to consult the Translators or Commentators, Chaldee, Hebrew, Syrian, Greek or Latin, no more the Spanish, French, Italian or Dutch'. The then recent foreign versions are described elsewhere in this volume.[2] For the ancient

[1] Pollard, *Records*, LXII–LXIII and pp. 37–64. For Barker and the Bible patent, see P. M. Handover, *Printing in London* (1960), ch. III.

[2] Note especially the Geneva French Bible, 1587/8 (p. 119), the Spanish of de Reynas, 1569, and de Valera, 1602 (pp. 127–8), Diodati's Italian, 1607 (p. 112).

languages they had, in addition to the books available to their predecessors, two valuable new aids, the Antwerp Polyglot of 1572, with a fresh Latin version of the Hebrew by Arias Montanus, and Tremellius's Bible (1579). The latter, to which they probably resorted more than to any other single book, contained (in the later editions which they used) Tremellius's Latin version of the Hebrew Old Testament with a commentary, Junius's Latin of the Apocrypha, Tremellius's Latin of the Syriac New Testament and Beza's Latin of the Greek New Testament. For their Greek text the translators worked from Stephanus and Beza, without any sure principles of textual criticism to guide them.

If, with the Bishops' Bible as their English starting-point, they rarely went back to the pre-Elizabethan translations, they did make extensive use of Geneva and Rhemes. Geneva contributed clarity and precision, Rhemes (besides its share of improvements in scholarship) affected their vocabulary, which is more Latin than that of their other predecessors. For 1611 their diction was already a little archaistic, though not so as to hinder understanding; it preserved the note of the numinous in the public reading of the Word of God. The beauties of the Authorized Version, notably its increased majesty and the music of its rhythm, have been so often analysed and appraised by students of literature that—as C. S. Lewis well reminds us—it is sometimes forgotten that the effect of the translation depends ultimately on the qualities of the original, and that the majority of its variants result not from literary taste but from the advance of scholarship.[1] For it was of accuracy and intelligibility that the revisers were thinking when they endeavoured to make a good translation better, 'or out of many good ones, one principal good one, not justly to be excepted against'.

Of course their scholarship was not impeccable: their text was still poor, the New Testament not yet based on the chief uncials;[2] their knowledge of Hebrew, for example of tenses and many idioms, was still defective and they had no papyri to help them with the Greek *Koine*; they incurred Broughton's wrath for timidly relegating numerous correct renderings to the margin.[3] But chapter after chapter,

[1] *English Literature in the Sixteenth Century* (Oxford, 1954), pp. 213–15. It has not been found possible to allow space for lengthy illustration of the Authorized Version's language or to compare it in detail with earlier versions. Such comparisons have often been made and may be conveniently sampled in Westcott and Butterworth.

[2] See above pp. 63–4.

[3] *A censure of the late translation, c. 1612* (*S.T.C.* 3847).

particularly in the more difficult books, reveals how well the commissions did their work 'through the good hand of the Lord upon us'.

Strictly speaking, the Authorized Version was never authorized, nor were parish churches ordered to procure it. It replaced the Bishops' Bible in public use because after 1611 no other folio Bible was printed. But from Broughton onwards it met with plenty of criticism. In ordinary private use the comprehensive Geneva Bible long competed with it, while scholars and preachers went on using what they would. So strong a Protestant as Becon had continued to quote the Vulgate in Latin or translate directly from it, while at times he took up Tyndale or the Great Bible apparently as it came to hand. Later, so prominent a reviser as Lancelot Andrewes commonly used the Geneva Bible for his sermons, as did other bishops.[1] Eventually, however, its victory was so complete that its text acquired a sanctity properly ascribable only to the unmediated voice of God; to multitudes of English-speaking Christians it has seemed little less than blasphemy to tamper with the words of the King James Version.

APPENDIX I

THE APOCRYPHA IN THE ENGLISH VERSIONS

The apocryphal books are those which were not included in the Hebrew canon of Scripture but were accepted by Hellenistic Jews and taken over by the early Church as part of the Septuagint; to which must be added II (IV) Esdras, extant only in Latin and Oriental versions.[2] In the Greek and Latin Bibles they were mostly interspersed among the canonical books. Protestant practice, when it does not omit them altogether, has been to put them as a separate block between the Old and New Testaments (so Luther and Zurich, cf. pp. 96, 106).

The preface to the Wycliffite Bible repeats Jerome's statement that

[1] Including Laud! See R. T. Davidson in *Macmillan's Magazine* (1881), quoted in part by Westcott, *History*, p. 107 n. and Pollard, *Records*, LXVI.

[2] Chaps. i, ii, xv and xvi exist in Greek, but are (second-century?) Christian additions. The Authorized Version rejected seventy verses then known only in Oriental versions, but following the discovery of the Latin text they were admitted into the Revised Version as vii. 36–105. They had previously been printed, from Arabic, in Haag's Berleburg Bible (1726–42) and from it in Sauer's Germantown Bible of 1743, the first English Bible printed in America.

the Hebrew canon alone is of divine authority, but in fact includes the whole Apocrypha. Tyndale only translated the passages used as liturgical Epistles. Coverdale has the Apocrypha *en bloc* between the Testaments, except Baruch which he places after Jeremiah. To him these books are not of like authority and reputation with Scripture proper since many places in them 'seem repugnant unto the open and manifest truth in the other books of the Bible', yet they should not be despised, though they need careful interpretation. Matthew reprinted Coverdale's Apocrypha, adding the Prayer of Manasses (popular with reformers, cf. pp. 9, 97) and a preface explaining their inferiority. Prayer and preface were translated from Olivetan's French Bible. Subsequent English Bibles, including the Authorized Version, all had the Apocrypha, usually with Baruch transferred to them; the Douay Bible follows the Vulgate positioning of the books. III Maccabees was added in the 1549 edition of Taverner's Apocrypha, but soon dropped.

Article VI of the Church of England (1562) authorizes the reading of these books (I (III) Esdras–II Maccabees) for example of life and instruction of manners, but not to establish any doctrine. However, much Protestant (especially Calvinist) opinion disapproved of the Apocrypha, which are frequently absent from extant copies of Geneva Bibles, particularly those printed in Holland. In 1615 Archbishop Abbott forbade the issue of Bibles without the Apocrypha, but copies of the Authorized Version surviving from editions of the 1630's often lack them, and were perhaps so purchasable. The first edition of an English Bible deliberately issued without them was probably the Geneva Bible of A. Hart, Edinburgh, 1640, which retains the Prayer of Manasses only and gives reasons for omitting the rest. The Westminster Confession of 1648 pronounced these books 'of no authority in the Church of God, nor to be otherwise approved, or made use of, than other human writings'. In modern times the English Bible has more often been issued without than with the Apocrypha, and this is the rule of the British and Foreign Bible Society (cf. p. 391).

It is not surprising that translation of the Apocrypha was commonly less careful than of the canonical books. Luther had been very free in rendering it. Coverdale allowed many of the Vulgate interpolations, and his Apocrypha were little revised in the Great Bible. Geneva, more scholarly, made much use of Beza's translation in Olivetan's French

Bible (Geneva, 1551). The apocryphal books are the weakest part of the Authorized Version: Scrivener, for example, criticizes them sharply in his *Authorized Edition of the English Bible* (pp. 46–55, 72–4, 140–1).

APPENDIX II

THE BIBLE IN WELSH, ERSE, GAELIC AND MANX

WELSH

Portions of the Bible had been translated from Latin into Welsh during the Middle Ages. The so-called 'Bible in Welsh', an abridgment of the historical books, contained the beginning of Genesis, the story of the Crucifixion and Resurrection (from St Matthew) and the opening of St John's Gospel, with other short passages. But, while the considerable bulk of religious literature in Welsh (including some popular apocryphal narratives of 'biblical' events) may have contributed to a style and vocabulary for any future version of Scripture, the complete Welsh Bible was a product of the Reformation.

There is a story that Richard Davies remembered seeing a Welsh Pentateuch in his boyhood, and another that Tyndale's New Testament was translated into Welsh; if they ever existed they were not printed. Important steps forward were taken by William Salesbury, who published the first Welsh–English dictionary in 1547 (*S.T.C.* 21616), urged his countrymen to petition Henry VIII for a Welsh Bible, and published the liturgical Epistles and Gospels 'put into Welsh by W.S.' in 1551 (*S.T.C.* 21617 = 2983). In the diocese of St Asaph it was ordered, in 1561, that the Epistles and Gospels should be read in Welsh as well as English at the Holy Communion. Next, in 1563, Elizabeth instructed the Welsh bishops to have Bible and Book of Common Prayer printed in Welsh by 1 March 1566 and placed in all parish churches. Salesbury and the printer Waley were given a sole privilege to print the Welsh Bible, Prayer Book and Homilies for seven years. The work was supervised by Richard Davies, bishop of St David's, who had been a Marian exile, was a friend of Cecil and Parker, and was to take a part in the English Bishops' Bible. He had the help of Salesbury and of Thomas Huet, precentor of St David's. Together they translated the New Testament which was printed by

Denham for Toy (not Waley) in 1567 (*S.T.C.* 2960), as also was the Book of Common Prayer, containing the first Welsh version of the complete Psalter (*S.T.C.* 16435). Davies did I Timothy, Hebrews, I and II Peter, James, Huet did Revelation, Salesbury the rest. The version was made from the original Greek, apparently from the texts of Stephanus and Beza, with reference to the Vulgate and the Latin versions of Erasmus and Beza. The Testament contained an English dedication to Elizabeth and an exhortation to the Welsh people by Davies. 'Arguments' to the books were taken from the Geneva Bible and some references and marginal notes were given. According to Thomas Parry, it was fine work in style, idiom and dignity of language, though Salesbury had awkward views on orthography which cut across traditional practice and might confuse readers.

The whole Bible appeared in Welsh for the first time in 1588, a folio published by the deputies of C. Barker (*S.T.C.* 2347). It was the work of William Morgan, later bishop of Llandaff and St Asaph, with a number of helpers, notably Edmund Prys who also made the long popular Welsh metrical version of the Psalter. Davies (d. 1581) and Salesbury had quarrelled, so Whitgift asked Morgan, who had already undertaken the Pentateuch, to be responsible for the whole. The translation, an excellent one which anticipated many of the changes introduced into the Revised Version, was made from the Hebrew and Greek with use also of the Vulgate, Pagninus and the English Geneva Bible. It included the Apocrypha. Linguistically it adopted the manner of the strict poets, not the colloquial use nor the flexible tongue of free poetry; it is dignified, 'a worthy medium for all the variety of literature and history and thought' in the Bible (Parry, pp. 193ff.).

A revised edition of Morgan's Bible came out in 1620 under the name of Richard Parry, bishop of St Asaph, though it was largely the work of Dr John Davies, the learned author of the Welsh grammar (1621) and dictionary (1632). The text was conformed to that of the Authorized Version. With a few modifications, particularly in orthography, this remained the standard Welsh Bible. In Parry's judgment the language is even finer than in 1567 or 1588, though rather mechanical in its correctness. He suggests that it might not have been entirely disadvantageous if the flexible speech of free poetry had been employed (that is, from 1567 onwards) since there would then have been less gap between the literary and spoken tongues of today. On the other hand he recognizes that the Bible came just in time to preserve the pure Welsh, gave the nation a standard tongue superior to any dialect, and has served as an abiding standard of good style.

Significant later Bibles must be reviewed briefly. In 1621 the first edition of Prys's metrical Psalter was appended to the Welsh Book of Common Prayer of 1621, which itself has the 1620 Bible version of the Psalms; in 1630 came the first cheap Welsh Bible ('the Little Bible') made possible by rich Welshmen in London; in 1674 the foundation of the Welsh Trust which established schools, published religious books and brought out in 1677/8 a new edition of the 1620 Bible, edited by Charles Edwards (8000 copies at 4*s*., of which 1000 were given free to the poor); in 1718 the S.P.C.K. Welsh Bible, 10,000 copies, also in connection with the Society's educational work (Griffith Jones was promoting schools to teach the Welsh to read the Bible and the Book of Common Prayer in Welsh); in 1770 at Carmarthen the first Bible printed in Wales, with a commentary by the Calvinistic Methodist, Peter Williams, still popular as a Bible for the home; in 1806/7 the first British and Foreign Bible Society New Testament and Bible in Welsh; in 1842 a Baptist version of the New Testament by John Williams; in 1908 a British and Foreign Bible Society edition with the previous text, but with variants from the Revised Version as notes. Before 1800 the Bible had been printed, in whole or part, thirty-one times in Welsh; from 1800 to 1900 there were some 370 editions, including the American ones. A Welsh Bible revised according to the new orthography was published in 1955.[1]

IRISH

The New Testament was first printed in Irish Gaelic (Erse) in 1602 (*S.T.C.* 2958, fo., Dublin, Seón Francke). A translation had been undertaken in 1573 by Nicholas Walsh, chancellor of St Patrick's, John O'Kearney, treasurer of St Patrick's, and Nehemiah Donnellan. It was completed by William Daniel (O'Donnell), later archbishop of Tuam, who saw it through the press. Five hundred copies were printed from a fount of Irish type (strictly a hybrid type with some sorts for Irish characters) given by Queen Elizabeth to O'Kearney. It had been

[1] Darlow–Moule, *Historical Catalogue of the Printed Editions of Holy Scripture in the Library of the British and Foreign Bible Society*, vol. IV; J. Ballinger, *The Bible in Wales* (London, 1906); Thomas Parry, *A History of Welsh Literature*, transl. from Welsh by H. Idris Bell (Oxford, 1955).

printed, but not folded for binding, when she died, so that it was issued with a dedication to James I. There was then a long gap, though the Book of Common Prayer was printed in Irish, 1608–9, and William Bedel, bishop of Kilmore 1629–42, began work on the Old Testament. In 1681 a fresh translation of the New Testament by Reilly appeared (London, R. Everingham, 500 copies) and in 1685 Bedel's version of the Old Testament was published to accompany it. Both books were printed in a new Irish type cut by Moxon at the cost of Robert Boyle. The Apocrypha were translated but not printed, Boyle objecting. Copies of both Testaments were sent to the Scottish highlands. But since the Irish character was unfamiliar, the whole Bible was printed in Roman type (3000 copies) in 1690, under the direction of Robert Kirke, a Scottish minister.

In 1810 the first British and Foreign Bible Society Irish New Testament was published, in 1817 the whole Bible, a revision of 1690 edited by James McQuige. No complete Irish Bible for Roman Catholic use has been published, though in 1830 the British and Foreign Bible Society version was edited by Edward O'Reilly, a Roman Catholic, for the (Protestant) Hibernian Bible Society. A *Harmony of the Four Gospels* in the Munster vernacular, with the Douay version opposite, was published in 1835, and in 1859 the first part of an Irish version from the Vulgate by John McHale, archbishop of Tuam; by 1861 the Pentateuch was complete, but no more appeared. The Gospels and Acts in Irish translated by Canon O'Leary from the Vulgate came out in 1915, and other unofficial versions of portions of the New Testament have since appeared.[1]

SCOTTISH GAELIC

Apart from some of the Psalms (1659), the publication of the Bible in Gaelic is a comparatively modern development. Copies of the Irish Bible, 1681–90, were distributed in the Highlands. A fresh version of the New Testament into Gaelic was made, from the Greek, by James Stuart, minister of Killin, and published in 1767 by the Scottish Society for Promoting Christian Knowledge (Tiomnadh Huadh, 12°, S.S.P.C.K., Edinburgh, 1767, 10,000 copies). At first regarded as free from Irish idiom, later scholars have found it more Irish than Gaelic in savour. The Old Testament was translated from Hebrew by John Stuart and John

[1] Darlow–Moule, *Catalogue*, III, 790–9; E. R. M. Dix, *The Earliest Dublin Printing* (Dublin, 1901); Shán O'Cúiv, *Irish Ecclesiastical Record*, LXXVI (1951), 284–92.

Smith, and was published by 1801 (4 vols., 1783, 1786, 1787, 1801, S.S.P.C.K.); this was revised in 1807 by Alexander Stewart, since Smith had been too free in translating the Prophets. A further slight revision was authorized by the General Assembly in 1826 (the 'Public Bible', S.S.P.C.K.), and this was considerably revised by a committee in 1902 (S.S.P.C.K.). A version of the New Testament from the Vulgate for the use of Roman Catholics was published at Aberdeen in 1875.[1]

MANX

No trace has been found of a version said to have been made by John Phillips, bishop of Sodor and Man, who translated the Book of Common Prayer in 1610. W. Walker's translation of St Matthew was published in 1748 at the expense of Bishop Wilson, whose catechism was the first book printed in Manx. The Gospels and Acts appeared in 1763 in a version begun by Wilson and revised under Bishop Hildesley. The Epistles and Revelation followed in 1767, the Old Testament in 1773. This was translated by a company of twenty-four scholars, and included Wisdom and Ecclesiasticus. The New Testament was published in 1775, the whole Bible in a tiny edition of forty copies in the same year (S.P.C.K.). The British and Foreign Bible Society published its first Manx New Testament in 1810 and the whole Bible (but dropping Wisdom and Ecclesiasticus) in 1819, 5000 copies.[2]

[1] Darlow–Moule, *Catalogue*, II, 461–7.
[2] *Ibid.* III, 1067–71.

CHAPTER V

THE RELIGION OF PROTESTANTS

THE AUTHORITY OF THE BIBLE

As I walked through the wilderness of this world, I lighted on a certain place, where was a den, and laid me down in that place to sleep; and, as I slept, I dreamed a dream, and behold, I saw a man clothed with rags standing in a certain place, with his face from his own house, a book in his hand, and a great burden upon his back. I looked, and saw him open the book, and read therein.

The well-known introductory paragraph to John Bunyan's *The Pilgrim's Progress* is itself an epitome of the place enjoyed by the vernacular Bible in the religious life of the seventeenth century. J. R. Green's statement that the English people became the people of a book, and that book the Bible, is justified by the evidence. But the vogue of the Bible was no peculiarly insular phenomenon, nor was its use confined to devotional reading. It became the source of doctrine and of worship, no less than of piety and hymnody, the object of close and continuous study on the part of scholars as well as the vade-mecum of ordinary Christian laymen. Nor was its influence restricted to religious issues. It became a proof-text for systems of government and 'an outline of knowledge for boys and girls and their parents' (to adopt a modern phrase) in various fields of human interest, historical, geographical and cosmographical.

At the outset stood its position as the supreme and sovereign standard of doctrine and belief in all churches which had thrown off the Roman obedience. The famous phrase of William Chillingworth, 'THE BIBLE, I say, the BIBLE only, is the religion of Protestants',[1] epitomized the refusal of non-Roman Christians to accept the equation of Scripture and oral tradition required by the Council of Trent. At an early stage in his controversy with Eck, Luther had taken up the position that the Bible alone was authoritative, so that *sola scriptura*

[1] William Chillingworth, *The Religion of Protestants: a Safe Way to Salvation* (Oxford, 1638).

took its place side by side with *sola fide*. Calvin was even more emphatic in his iterated assertion of the same principle. 'Let this then be a sure axiom—that nothing ought to be admitted in the Church as the Word of God, save that which is contained, first in the Law and the Prophets, and secondly in the writings of the Apostles; and that there is no other method of teaching in the Church than according to the prescription and rule of his Word.' But Calvin carried the principle of the sole authority of Scripture further than Luther, by requiring that all ecclesiastical regulations and ordinances must have a positive basis and precept in the Bible. 'I approve of those human institutions only which are founded upon the authority of God and derived from Scripture, and therefore are certainly divine.' In the Thirty-nine Articles of Religion of the Church of England, Article VI declared that 'Holy Scripture containeth all things necessary for salvation, so that whatsoever is not read therein, nor may be proved thereby, is not to be required of any man, that it should be believed as an article of the Faith or be thought requisite or necessary to salvation'. In accordance with this principle, Article XX stated that 'the Church hath power to decree Rites or Ceremonies, and authority in Controversies of Faith; and yet it is not lawful for the Church to ordain anything that is contrary to God's Word written.... Wherefore, although the Church be a witness and keeper of holy Writ, yet, as it ought not to decree anything against the same, so besides the same ought it not to enforce anything to be believed for necessity of Salvation.' During the seventeenth century, divines were much occupied in working out this axiom in great detail and in relation to all parts of systematic theology. For the Reformation and post-Reformation epochs inherited from the Middle Ages the conviction that theology was an exact and autonomous science, together with a passion for the elaboration of doctrine to cover the farthest minutiae of the proportion of the faith. Accordingly, the movement which in the sixteenth century had produced the principal Lutheran, Reformed and Anglican Confessions of Faith was continued in its successor, and characterized by the attempt to leave no point of doctrine unexplained.

Perhaps the best illustration of this process may be seen in the Irish Articles of 1615, largely the work of Archbishop James Ussher. The Thirty-nine Articles of the Church of England were expanded to one hundred and four, and instead of the reticences and general formulae of the former, they proceeded to define exactly the doctrine of the Church of Ireland in respect, for example, of such controverted questions as double-predestination (that is, to reprobation as well as to election). It was not surprising therefore that the Westminster Assembly of divines, summoned by the Long Parliament to meet in 1643, adopted Ussher's Articles as the basis of their work, and adhered with close fidelity to their general sequence, doctrine and language. The Westminster Confession represented, and still remains, one of the most constructive results of the zeal for confessional standards founded upon the Bible. On the other hand, the decrees of the Synod of Dort were evidence of a more unfortunate aspect of doctrinal over-definition. Arising from the conflict of theological opinion between the Arminians or Remonstrants (followers of Jakob Hermandszoon—Latinized as Jacobus Arminius) and the Calvinists or Counter-Remonstrants, which convulsed the political no less than the ecclesiastical life of the United Provinces, the assembly as a national synod convoked to define and defend orthodoxy against heterodoxy, proceeded to accept the straitest Calvinist doctrines concerning double-predestination, the effects of the death of Christ in relation to the redemption of mankind, the fall of Man and the problem of human free-will, and the perseverance of the elect. The result brought not peace but a sword to the Reformed Church, since both schism, exile and persecution ensued, and the acute division of opinion was reflected not only in other Reformed churches in France and Scotland, but also in Lutheran and Anglican circles. Not less unfortunate was the effect upon the fortunes of such famous individuals as Episcopius and Grotius; while among the Huguenots of France, Tilenus, Curcellaeus and Amyraldus were also involved in the conflict. In Lutheran churches the passion for systematization and for the construction of dogmatic outworks as a defence against the Counter-Reformation went far towards the substitution of confessional orthodoxy for vivifying faith, in which *sola scriptura* almost superseded *sola fide*. With some divines the authority of Scripture was extended to embrace its form no less than its contents, as when Calovius called the authors of the several books of the Old and New Testaments *Dei amanuenses*, *Christi manus et Spiritus Sancti tabelliones et notarii*.[1] Furthermore, much time was spent and much heat engendered in the definition of points dividing Lutherans from Reformed, particularly those of predestination and

[1] Cf. p. 12 above.

free-will. The seventeenth century indeed was fecund in works of Protestant systematic theology, of which the *Loci Communes Theologici* in nine volumes of Johann Gerhard of Jena, published between 1610 and 1622, and the twelve volumes of *Systema Locorum Theologicorum* of Abraham Calovius of Wittenberg, published between 1655 and 1672, were illustrative. From such works it was a relief to turn to those of Georg Calixtus of Helmstedt, whose life and writings were dedicated to the ideal of discovering common ground not only between Lutheran and Calvinist but also between both and the Roman Church. From Calixtus and also from Grotius there stemmed the eirenic temper which sought to distinguish fundamentals from non-essentials in the *credenda* of the several churches, and by agreement on the former and the toleration of differences of belief in respect of the latter to prepare the way for the healing of the schisms of Christendom.

But *sola scriptura* was meantime proving itself to be the harbinger not of peace but of a sword; and a sword of such sharpness as to pierce to the dividing asunder of the joints and marrow of Protestantism. Welcomed at first as a principle of defence against the Church of Rome and the decrees of the Council of Trent and expanded to cover a series of outworks in support of the Protestant cause, it was now suffering assault from the rear at the hands of Socinus and his followers. The publication in 1605 of the Racovian Catechism in the Polish tongue, followed during the century by eight Latin translations, three Dutch and two each in German and English, revealed the nature and extent of the threat to orthodoxy. James I of England (who had intervened on behalf of the Counter-Remonstrants in the controversies relating to the Synod of Dort) caused the first Latin version, dedicated to himself without his permission, to be burned in 1614 by order of Parliament. Other methods of refutation, however, were necessary; and for a century and a half a succession of Lutheran and Reformed theologians attacked the catechism. Socinus and his adherents denied the orthodox doctrine of the Trinity and the co-equal Deity of Christ and the Father, together with a number of generally accepted beliefs, such as those in original sin, predestination, vicarious atonement and justification by faith. Notwithstanding the many refutations from orthodox Protestant writers, Socinian views and tendencies spread widely, and offered an obvious and tempting target for Roman Catholic polemic against Protestantism in general.

For did not Arius first, Socinus now
The Son's eternal Godhead disavow?
And did not these by Gospel texts alone
Condemn our doctrine and maintain their own?
Have not all heretics the same pretence,
To plead the Scriptures in their own defence?

The thrust of the Hind at the Panther in Dryden's satire[1] went home, and it became evident that 'The Bible only' was an insecure basis even for so fundamental a tenet of orthodoxy as the doctrine of the Trinity.

If, however, other secondary and subsidiary authorities were to be sought to supplement the witness of the Scriptures, did not this appeal open the door to a wide variety of dangerous opinions? Bossuet's taunt against Protestantism in the *Histoire des Variations des Églises Protestantes* had too obvious an element of fact and truth to be lightly brushed aside as a mere controversial *ruse de guerre*. Calvin indeed had allowed 'that Scripture is self-authenticated, carrying its own evidence along with it, and ought not to submit to proofs and arguments, but obtains the conviction which it merits with us by the testimony of the Spirit'. Did the *testimonium sancti Spiritus* therefore as a matter of fact and experience make men to be of one mind in the understanding of the Bible? During the seventeenth century the appeal to the Spirit was widespread and vigorous. It seemed almost as if Joachim of Flora's prophecy of the age of the *Spiritualis Intellectus* and the resultant emergence of the *Ecclesia Spiritualis* was about to be fulfilled. The *dernier cri* was that the Word must be tried by the Spirit and not the Spirit by the Word, notwithstanding the dangerous possibilities (for example) of George Fox's doctrine of the Inner Light, as 'a light which would, if followed honestly and steadily, infallibly lead to God: and that without the aid of either the Bible or any ordinances'. Under the influence of the Spirit, various Puritan sects shed many of the usages of historic Christianity, by jettisoning the two sacraments of the Gospel, allowing women preachers, and, in the case of the Quakers, abandoning altogether a professional ministry. 'There is a great difference between us and our adversaries', observed the moderate Puritan Richard Sibbes: 'They say we must believe...because of the Church. I say,

[1] *The Hind and the Panther*, II, 150–5, published in 1687 when Dryden was a Roman Catholic.

No. The Church, we believe, hath a kind of working here, but that is in the last place. For God himself in his Word, he is the chief. The inward arguments from the Word itself and from the Spirit, they are the next. The Church is the remotest witness, the remotest help of all.' In vain did Oliver Cromwell urge that God 'speaks without a written word sometimes, yet according to it', and Baxter argues that

> we must prefer the Spirit's inspiring the apostles to indite the Scriptures, before the Spirit's illuminating of us to understand them, or before any present inspirations, the former being the more perfect; because Christ gave the apostles the Spirit to deliver to us infallibly his own commands and to indite a rule for following ages; but he giveth us the Spirit but to understand and use that rule aright. This trying the Spirit by the Scriptures is not a setting of the Scriptures above the Spirit itself; but is only a trying of the Spirit by the Spirit; that is, the Spirit's operations in ourselves and his revelations to any pretenders now, by the Spirit's operations in the apostles, and by their revelations recorded for our use. For they and not we, are called foundations of the Church.

The very popularity of the Bible, thanks to the several vernacular versions, served but to increase the confusion; for, where everyman had a prophecy and an interpretation of hard and difficult passages of Scripture, believed to be a private revelation, the authority of the Spirit was claimed for the most diverse and contradictory theses. Allowing for the degree of exaggeration natural to satire, there might seem sufficient justification for the ironical conclusion of Dryden:

> The Book thus put in every vulgar hand,
> Which each presumed he best could understand,
> The common rule was made the common prey
> And at the mercy of the rabble lay.
> The tender page with horny fists was galled,
> And he was gifted most that loudest bawled.
> The spirit gave the doctoral degree,
> And every member of a Company
> Was of his trade and of the Bible free.
> Plain truths enough for needful use they found,
> But men would still be itching to expound;
> Each was ambitious of the obscurest place,
> No measure ta'en from knowledge, all from grace.

Study and pains were now no more their care,
Texts we explained by fasting and by prayer.
This was the fruit the private spirit brought,
Occasioned by great zeal and little thought.[1]

Nor was the phenomenon confined to Protestants. There was an element of spiritual illumination in Jansenism; and more than a double portion of the Spirit in Quietism and Molinism and amongst the Camisards; and the age which immediately followed the Counter-Reformation has been described as an age of introverts.

In the field of public worship also the Bible became the standard of rites and ceremonies. *Lex orandi, lex credendi* was as important and influential in non-Roman churches as in the post-Tridentine Church of Rome. Luther would admit into his worship any liturgical elements not inconsistent with the precepts of Scripture, whereas Calvin would accept only what the Bible specifically warranted. Even outside the formal liturgical services, whilst Lutheran practice approved the singing of hymns and spiritual songs not contained in Scripture ('merely human compositions' as their opponents stigmatized them), Calvinist praises must be entirely biblical, as represented by the *psaumes français* of the famous metrical Psalter. Indeed, Isaac Watts later was to inaugurate a revolution in respect of psalmody when he contended that 'if we would prepare David's Psalms to be sung by Christian lips, we should observe these two plain rules: first, they ought to be translated in such a manner as we have reason to believe David would have composed them if he had lived in our own day; and therefore his poems are given us as a pattern to be imitated in our composures, rather than as the precise and invariable matter of our psalmody'. Nor was his second principle less revolutionary, namely, the 'grand design' of his endeavour 'to make my author to speak like a Christian'. Another aspect of the conflict of Word with Spirit was reflected in the division of opinion concerning the relative merits of set forms of public prayer and extemporaneous utterances. Controversy broke out whether the Lord's Prayer should be repeated verbatim in public worship, or whether such a use savoured of vain repetitions and the Prayer itself had been intended only as a pattern, 'after this manner pray ye'. On the Continent the differences found expression in the respective litur-

[1] *Religio Laici*, 400–16, written in 1682 when Dryden was a member of the Church of England.

gical rites of the Lutheran and Calvinist churches; and in England the Directory of Public Worship on the one hand, compiled by the Westminster Assembly, represented a compromise settlement between the champions of a fixed liturgy and of free prayers and was rather a Manual than a Liturgy, whilst on the other hand Baxter's Savoy Liturgy was a Presbyterian composition impregnated with biblical phraseology but including also, for example, an *epiklesis* in the Prayer of Consecration in the Order for Communion. The popularity of the Bible ensured that even extemporaneous devotions would be couched in scriptural language and phraseology, mingled with the common speech of the region, so that the influence of the Scriptures penetrated into all branches of public worship.

Amidst the strife of theologians and prophets the still, small voice of the school of Cambridge Platonists made little apparent impression by its advocacy of the Gospel as a way of life rather than a corpus of dogmas, by its emphasis on Reason as a wiser interpreter of the Bible than the Spirit, and by its eirenic plea for agreement on fundamentals and agreement to differ on non-essentials. Not only did the Cambridge churchmen hold that 'reason is the divine governor of man's life' and 'the very voice of God', but they refused also to allow any divorce between the rational and the spiritual, affirming with Whichcote that 'spiritual is most rational'. Similarly they believed reason to be the judge of the authenticity of revelation, holding, again with Whichcote, that 'the written word of God is not the first or only discovery of the duty of man. It doth gather and repeat and reinforce and charge upon us the scattered and neglected principles of God's creation, that has suffered prejudice and damnation by the defect and apostacy of man.' But their position did not rest upon a narrow rationalism. Rather they emphasized with equal force the moral consciousness of man as a sure guide to salvation. 'The moral part of religion never alters', Whichcote further wrote: 'Moral laws are of themselves, without sanction by will, and the necessity of them arises from the things themselves. All *other* things in religion are *in order to* these. The moral part of religion does sanctify the soul, and is final both to what is instrumental and instituted.' Thus the Bible was valuable less as a deposit of doctrine than as a pattern of conduct, interpreted and explained by reason and conscience.

PURITAN PREACHING AND THE POPULARITY OF THE BIBLE

The chief pastoral use of the Bible, naturally, was as the source and basis of preaching, and under its influence the sermon not only became the principal element of Protestant public worship but also changed its form and content. During the seventeenth century the full effect of the widespread circulation of the vernacular Bible was realized, and nowhere more emphatically than in the pulpit. Queen Elizabeth I had cherished a deep-rooted mistrust of preaching and had tried therefore to suppress 'prophesyings'; but even her determination could not succeed, and preaching became a popular fashion during the reign of her successor.

What distinguished the Puritan preachers even more than their doctrinal position was the manner and purpose of their preaching. Discountenanced by those in authority but bent upon saving the world through the foolishness of preaching, directed to provoke a religious revival and ultimate ecclesiastical reform, they were compelled to seek support wherever it might be found among the people. They asserted, as did others, that man could be saved by faith alone. They endeavoured to do this, however, in terms that common men might understand, in expressive images that would move men to repent, believe and begin the new life at once under the leadership of the preacher. Preaching of this type soon came to be called 'spiritual' in contradiction to the 'witty' preaching of the more conservative churchmen.[1]

Typical of this new interest was the foundation at Cambridge towards the end of the sixteenth century of two colleges, Emmanuel and Sidney Sussex, for the express purpose of training preachers of the Puritan tradition. The influence of these foundations became evident in the following century, when lectureships became a popular means of endowing preachers who sat somewhat loosely to the services of the Book of Common Prayer, but whose *forte* was the evangelical sermon. The attempt of Laud to control and silence these lecturers was itself testimony to the extent of their spread and popularity, in London particularly and also in various provincial towns. But amongst Anglican preachers also, the Bible was the foundation of their sermons, though expounded in very different style. Lancelot Andrewes and John Donne were typical, if outstanding, representatives of the Anglican

[1] W. Haller, *The Rise of Puritanism*, pp. 19–20.

tradition of literary preaching, reflecting contemporary fondness for conceit and word-play, buttressing Scripture with patristic citations and even with classical allusions, and embracing contemporary humanism as well as metaphysical argument. Judged however by the comparative popularity of their published sermons, they had to yield the palm to their Puritan counterparts. Moreover, the difference between the two styles of preaching, between 'the Wisdom of Words' and 'the Word of Wisdom', was emphasized by the Puritan aversion to the quotation of human authors in favour of exclusive dependence upon Holy Scripture.

So large was the volume of Puritan sermons committed to the press that Baxter compiled a list of authors which should be found in 'the poorest or smallest library that is tolerable', amounting to fifty-eight in all, and headed of course by the Bible, with an appropriate concordance and commentary. Many of these works had already been despatched across the Atlantic to form part of Elder William Brewster's library, and of the collection of books bequeathed by John Harvard, of Emmanuel College, Cambridge, to the foundation bearing his name in the Cambridge of New England. At the beginning of the seventeenth century there was published Richard Rogers's *Seven Treatises, Containing Such Direction as is gathered out of the Holie Scriptures, leading and guiding to true happiness, both in this life and the life to come; and may be called the practise of Christianitie*, which went into seven editions between 1603 and 1630, and became the classic exposition of the Puritan system of moral and spiritual life. Nor was a succession of preachers lacking to his contemporary John Rogers, of Dedham, who was remembered as 'taking hold with his hands at one time of the canopy over the pulpit and roaring hideously to represent the torments of the damned'. Moreover, the diary of Richard Rogers revealed the applications to his own personal problems of the principles which inspired his sermons; and to his contemporaries, 'the diary, like the autobiography of which it was the forerunner, was the Puritan's confessional'. Through it the preacher schooled himself and prepared his flock to put on the whole armour of God wherewith to withstand all the fiery darts of the Devil. Among famous biblical preachers were Laurence Chaderton, first Master of Emmanuel College and one of the translators of the Authorized Version of 1611, Arthur Hildersham, and John Dod; of the last of whom Fuller wrote that he was 'humble, meek, patient, hospitable, charitable as in his censures of, so in his alms to, others; Would I could truly say but half so much of the next generation'. Before leaving England for the new world across the Atlantic, John Cotton and Thomas Hooker took counsel with Dod whether their duty lay in remaining at home to suffer persecution or in planting the seeds of Puritanism in North America; and Cotton remembered how the advice he received was that 'whilst Peter was young he might gird himself and go whither he would, but when he was old and unfit for travel, then indeed God called him rather to suffer himself to be girt of others and led along to prison and death'. Cotton himself had been converted by Richard Sibbes, another Cambridge Puritan, and only after a ministry of twenty years at Boston in Lincolnshire sailed for America.

The chief pattern of Puritan preaching was 'an admirable plainness and an admirable powerfulness', expressive not only of the themes but also of the style of the Bible. This did not mean that learning was scorned; but that it must be hidden, not paraded, and that its fruits must be presented in a language understanded of the people, which was in fact that of the Authorized Version. Samuel Clarke, the comprehensive biographer of eminent Puritan divines, observed of Samuel Crook, fellow of Emmanuel College and rector of Wrington, Somerset, that he knew 'very well how to set forth καινὰ, κοινῶς, abstruse points plainly, and how to manage κοινὰ, καινῶς, plain truths elegantly'. The structure of the Puritan sermon comprised 'the analysis of the text, the proofs of Scripture for the doctrines, and the reasons and uses'; that is, the preacher first expounded his text in its context, then exemplified the doctrines which it contained by reference to other parts of Scripture, and finally applied them 'to the life and manners of men in a simple and plain speech'. The two most familiar similes of the Puritan preacher were those comparing the spiritual life of Man to a pilgrimage and combat, to wayfaring and warfaring.[1] These formed the theme of countless sermons, in which 'the preachers did indeed endeavour to serve as a kind of general staff to the hosts of the spirit in a campaign against the evil one'. Thus the corporate drama of the human race, which fell before the wiles of Satan in the person of the First Adam and vanquished the Tempter in the person of the Second Adam, was set forth with imagery, similitude and illustration as the individual

[1] Haller, *op. cit.* pp. 142–60.

biography of every human being. This kind of preaching assumed and depended upon a detailed knowledge of the Bible thanks to its circulation in the vernacular. Not the least of the points of vantage from which Puritan doctrine was set forth were the pulpits of Gray's Inn, where Sibbes preached, and of Lincoln's Inn under John Preston, whose eighteen sermons published in 1629 under the title of *The New Covenant* averaged a new edition each year for the next decade.

Naturally, these Puritan preachers and principles proliferated even more in North America. John Cotton has been aptly described as 'something like the primate of the pulpit brotherhood and keeper of the conscience of the civil magistrate', but there the pastors were no longer in a minority as they had been in England and opposed by and to the government. Instead they were in a position of influence and authority, and so were led to translate their religious maxims into terms of politics and society. There also the innate dissidence of Puritanism led to division and schism as the Spirit deviated some preachers from the accepted orthodoxy, thereby becoming the indirect agent of the spreading of the Gospel to newer territories. Roger Williams was moved to seek agreements with the Indians, deducing from the biblical precept that 'God had made of one blood all mankind' the conclusion that there is 'no difference between Europeans and Americans in blood, birth, bodies, etc.', and hoping to convert them from children of wrath to children of grace. Similarly he became the champion of the right of every Christian to interpret the Scriptures in accordance with his own understanding and therewith of the principle of complete religious toleration. 'In vaine', he argued, 'have English Parliaments permitted English Bibles in the poorest English houses, and the simplest man and woman to search the Scriptures, if yet against their souls' persuasion from the Scripture, they should be forced (as if they lived in Spain or Rome itself without the sight of a Bible) to believe as the Church believes.' Both in the old and the new worlds, the Puritan standards were the parent in ecclesiastical matters not of unity but of diversity. In England not only were all the Smectymnuans preachers of Puritan persuasion, but Baxter found in the New Model Army enthusiastic if unlettered preachers of an unrestrained private judgment and individualism, based on the Bible. The prospect of all the Lord's people, that is the saints and the elect, becoming prophets alarmed him: 'Some think the truth will not thrive among us, till every man have leave to speak both in press and pulpit that please; God forbid that we should ever see that day. If ten men's voices be louder than one, then would the noise of error drown the voice of truth.... For the godly, compared with the ungodly, are not near so few as the man of clear understanding in comparison of the ignorant; and they are most forward to speak that know least.' One of the army preachers indeed, Hugh Peters, suffered death at the Restoration for his part in dividing the Word of God in its political relevance. After the Restoration the Anglican tradition of preaching returned in the sermons of Robert South, until a generation later Tillotson introduced a revolution in the pulpit oratory of the established church. Burnet held that Tillotson 'was not only the best preacher of the age, but seemed to have brought preaching to perfection; his sermons were so well heard and liked and so much read, that all the nation proposed him as a pattern and studied to copy after him'. Nor was his reputation confined to England, since his sermons were translated into French and High and Low Dutch. He had devoted four years to 'an exact study of the Scriptures' as the foundation of homiletics and deliberately abandoned contemporary Anglican patterns in favour of his own style.

From another angle the Bible furnished Anglican, Presbyterian and Independent alike with defences of their various forms of church order. Bishop Carleton, a representative of the Church of England at Dort, published in 1624 his *Thankful Remembrance of God's Mercy in an Historical Collection of the great and merciful Deliverances of the Church and State in England, since the Gospel began here to flourish from the beginning of Queen Elizabeth*, in which he found many parallels between the divine protection of Israel and the providential deliverances of England. 'We see God hath made our enemies, his enemies: they cannot fight against us, but they must fight against God; how much then are we bound to honour and serve this great God of heaven and earth that hath shewed such favour to his Church in England.' On the other hand, the Presbyterian found in the Bible that form of church polity which distinguished 'the best reformed churches' and for which therefore the claim of divine right was set forth; whilst in the Covenant relationship between God and the Jews in the Old Testament, the Separatists discovered the pattern of their Gathered Church, bound each to other in a solemn Covenant, 'by a free mutual consent of Believers, joining and covenanting to live as members of a holy Society together in all religious and virtuous duties as Christ and his Apostles did institute and practise in the Gospel'. Perhaps the best example of the pastoral application of Puritan preaching may be seen in the ministry of Baxter at Kidderminster. In addition to his Sunday sermons and his weekly Thursday sermon, he entertained each Thursday evening at his house such members as desired to come; 'and there one of them repeated the Sermon and afterwards they proposed what doubts any of them had about the sermon, or any other case of conscience', whilst 'every Saturday night they met at some of their houses to repeat the sermon of the last Lord's Day and to pray and prepare themselves for the following day'. Further, two days of each week he spent in private catechizing of families; every first Wednesday of the month he held a meeting for parish discipline; and every first Thursday he conducted a meeting of neighbouring ministers 'for discipline and disputation', at which he himself usually produced 'a written determination', after which some of the company adjourned to his house 'with whom I spent the truest recreation till my neighbours came to meet for their exercise of repetition and prayer'. Such was the influence of the Bible on Puritan life and observance in seventeenth-century England.

The popularity of the Bible was further evidenced by the number of versions published after the Authorized Version of 1611.[1] The way had been opened by the Geneva Bible, the size and format of which made it suitable for private devotional reading at home, and in particular the New Testament of 1557 became the first pocket New Testament in English to attain a wide circulation. Not even the Authorized Version challenged the popularity of the Geneva Bible. Moreover, other English translations continued to make their appearance. From Amsterdam in 1616–27 there came the version of Henry Ainsworth, a Brownist, followed by the fully cross-referenced Bible of John Canne in 1647. The popular demand for expositions led to the vogue of paraphrases, of which Henry Hammond's *New Testament Paraphrase* led the van in 1653, whilst in 1675 there appeared a composite work by several Oxford dons in the form of a *Paraphrase of the Epistles*, and in 1702 Daniel Whitby's *Paraphrase and Commentary on the New Testament* enjoyed a circulation of four editions. So great was this fashion that the Arianizers in their turn took up the task, and Dr Samuel Clarke and Thomas Pyle joined in making a paraphrase of the entire New Testament in 1701–2

[1] See also pp. 363–8 below.

and 1725–35. Shortly afterwards, as an orthodox counterblast, the Independent John Guyse issued his paraphrase between 1739 and 1752. In 1685 Richard Baxter had published his translation of the New Testament and Philip Doddridge, the most influential Nonconformist divine of the next generation, issued his *Family Expositor, or a Paraphrase and Version of the New Testament* in 1739. Amongst the Presbyterians William Mace translated the New Testament in 1729 in colloquial style, whilst the Society of Friends produced in 1764 Anthony Purver's *Quakers' Bible*. Amongst Roman Catholics, the Rhemes New Testament of 1582 and the Douay Old Testament of 1609–10 held their place for more than a century, until the appearance of Dr Nary's translation of the New Testament in 1718 (with a preface setting forth his principles of translation), followed by Dr Robert Witham's revision of the Rhemes New Testament in 1730, and by the comprehensive revision at the hand of Bishop Dr Richard Challenor of both the Rhemes and Douay versions in 1749–50. Both the number and variety of these biblical translations testified to the demand for, and interest in, popular versions of the Scriptures.

In other fields than those properly associated with doctrine, worship and ecclesiastical discipline the vernacular Bible occupied the centre of the stage. Side by side with the biblical prose of Bunyan stands the epic poetry of Milton, who chose biblical themes for three of his principal works, *Paradise Lost*, *Paradise Regained* and *Samson Agonistes*. To George Herbert's *Countrey Parson* 'the chief and top of his knowledge consists in the book of books, the storehouse and magazine of life and comfort, the Holy Scriptures. There he sucks and lives. In the Scriptures he finds four things: precept for life, doctrines for knowledge, examples for illustration and promises for comfort.' To this end he employs 'a diligent collation of Scripture with Scripture. For all truth being consonant to itself, and all being penned by one and the self-same Spirit, it cannot be but that an industrious and judicious comparing of place with place must be a singular help for the right understanding of the Scriptures.' Similarly he studies 'commentators and fathers who have handled the places controverted', and thereby 'ploughing with this and his own meditations he enters into the secrets of God treasured in the Holy Scripture'. In private devotion heads of households, whose duty in earlier centuries had been interpreted as the teaching of their families the Apostles' Creed, the *Pater Noster* and the

Ave Maria, now profited by the vernacular Bible to read passages from it, with expositions drawn from favourite commentators or with readings from *The Whole Duty of Man.* Furthermore, biblical phraseology and diction moulded parliamentary oratory, and the speeches of Oliver Cromwell read to modern eyes much more like sermons than political addresses. Indeed both constitutional and social issues were generally veiled and expressed in language and concepts drawn from the Scriptures. Not only the social revolutionaries of the Commonwealth period, but traditionalist writers on political theory, such as Sir Robert Filmer in his *Patriarcha or the Natural Power of Kings Asserted* appealed to the Bible as the foundation and support of their contentions. Even Hobbes found it necessary to cloak the theories of *Leviathan* by a fiction of scriptural argument, whilst Anglican pulpits rang with declarations of the Divine Right of Kings, and of passive obedience as the doctrine of the Cross. Not until the 'Glorious Revolution' of 1688, by its undeniable breach of hereditary succession and the inauguration of an elective, parliamentary monarchy, had driven out of court the traditional theories, did the tone of Locke's writings coincide with the new temper of political affairs, which was to become increasingly secular.

PIETISM

In reaction against biblical dogmatism the Pietist movement in Germany sought to restore the conception of Christianity as a way of life and to provide an escape from the multiplication of theological definitions. In its early phase during the lifetime of Philip Jacob Spener it encountered opposition and even persecution. Among Spener's predecessors may be reckoned John Arndt, minister of St Martin's Church, Brunswick, from 1599 to 1621 and author of *Four Books on True Christianity*, a manual of personal devotion and mysticism, and Valentine Andrea, dean of Calw, who throughout the miseries of the Thirty Years War gave himself to the encouragement of practical piety. But Spener's was the *nomen praeclarum* of Pietism, initially during his long ministry at Frankfurt am Main from 1666 to 1686, where he held *mutua colloquia* or *collegia pietatis* for the exposition of Scripture and mutual spiritual edification, which resulted in a notable religious revival of personal piety. In 1675 he published *Pia Desideria* and in 1677 *Spiritual Priesthood*; and in 1686 was called to Dresden as principal court-chaplain. Here the harvest of his sowing was garnered, and in addition to his pastoral work in Dresden he became spiritual director of a series of pious sodalities founded in various cities for the promotion of religious life. In academic circles his work provoked opposition from Darmstadt, Erfurt, Gotha, Jena, Wolfenbüttel, Hanover, Hamburg and Halberstadt, the traditional guardians of theological orthodoxy. But in the same year as his removal to Dresden, there was formed at Leipzig by August Hermann Francke and Paul Anton a *collegium philobiblicum* for the study of biblical exegesis, which became a school of personal piety and spiritual zeal, somewhat to the detriment of the academic studies of its members, so that the university faculty dissolved the collegium and forbade Francke to deliver theological lectures. There resulted a *diaspora* of the leaders, principally to the electorate of Brandenburg, the hospitable asylum of religious refugees, where in 1691 Spener became provost of the Nicolai-kirche in Berlin and in 1694 the University of Halle was founded, with Francke and Anton amongst its professoriate. The new foundation flourished and expanded rapidly, and became the headquarters of Pietism, basking in the sunshine of civil countenance and theological respectability, and being joined by Christian Thomasius who left Leipzig for Berlin in 1690 and shortly became professor at Halle. From this movement there resulted Francke's orphanage, his Bible society and various missionary enterprises, and the consequent recognition of Halle as the *fons et origo* of Pietism.[1] But, although a great door and effectual had been opened for this variety of Christian good works, there were also many adversaries, ecclesiastical as well as academic. Spener bore the brunt of defence until his death in 1705, after which Francke became the second-founder of the movement. His efforts were unwearying in preaching, conducting meetings of spiritual edification and writing; and his professional lectures were concentrated on biblical themes and on their pastoral application. Pietism was characterized by its emphasis on the need for a theology based on living faith and practical works of piety; and at Halle this emphasis was expressed in the place enjoyed by Scripture as the core of theological teaching and directed towards spiritual edification. Hence the movement became the parent of much controversy within Lutheranism, in which the systematic theologians were ranged against the schools of the prophets and defenders of the traditional position of the

[1] See further pp. 340–1, 461 below.

Word and Sacraments against the champions of spiritual gifts. Pietism indeed was not consciously unorthodox in any point of belief, but its iterated insistence on the primary importance of spiritual gifts and insight, as contrasted with formal theology and academic learning, provoked misunderstanding and opposition. Some Pietists, including Spener himself, were millenarians; and in general Pietism favoured an individualistic expression of religion, an ascetic attitude towards the world and a puritan outlook in matters of conduct. Notwithstanding, its devotion to the exposition and preaching of the Bible presented a valuable and necessary counterpart to the rigidities of many theologians, and undoubtedly kindled a flame of personal and religious life amongst its adherents. Perhaps also it was of equal importance in two of its offshoots, namely in the work of Johann Albert Bengel and of Count Zinzendorf.

Bengel indeed was a theologian of the first rank in Lutheranism, a man also of intense and virile personal piety, whose visit to Halle in 1713 inspired him henceforth with zeal for practical religion. His union of individual piety with sound theological learning enabled him to correct some of the dangerous tendencies of the school at Halle, but his own theological teaching was less a systematic exposition of dogma than a continuous exegesis of Scripture. Moreover, he was significant also in another respect, as a pioneer in textual criticism of the New Testament and as an exponent of the Old Testament as a historical record of God's dealing with men, to be studied historically and with due regard to the circumstances of the times in which it was compiled. Bengel and his followers not only bridged the gulf between theology and piety, but also foreshadowed the later development of literary and historical criticism of the Bible. Count Zinzendorf's contribution was of a different nature and order. He strove to develop the individual religion of Pietism along communal channels, and thanks to his great gifts of organization, he brought together the older Moravian tradition and the more recent Lutheran. Having Spener as a godfather and having been educated in Francke's school at Halle, he was early imbued with the principles and practice of Pietism, and afterwards was transferred to the Lutheran traditions of Wittenberg, where he became a student of law. His capacities as an organizer, together with the prestige and authority resulting from his education, made him in some ways a comparable figure with John Wesley, and also a pioneer in the campaign for Christian unity. Having encouraged the settlement of two families of the Moravian Brethren on his estate at Berthelsdorf, he watched over the growth of the community during the next seven years to the number of three hundred, and established a new settlement at Herrnhut, which became an asylum for persecuted Protestants from all parts of Germany. Here Zinzendorf developed a new interpretation of the principle *cujus regio, ejus religio*, by undertaking the religious oversight of the immigrants and refusing to allow diversity of custom and use to occasion any breach of spiritual unity. Both the religious and constitutional experiments at Herrnhut were of considerable interest and importance and, by his fusion of Moravians and Lutherans, Zinzendorf made a distinctive contribution to the development of Pietism. Pietism was indeed a 'vast and comprehensive' movement, to which a number of individuals brought each his own treasure.

In Spener it combines a certain legal strictness, a scrupulous interest in personal sanctification, with the demand for a more spiritual church system. It meets the ancient vein of mysticism in the Lutheran church,...which to a large extent steps into the inheritance of the medieval mystics. In Francke the legal pietism changes into the Hallensic type, characterized by the insistence on individual, sudden conversion and great practical effects of Christian charity....In Württemberg the deep, meditative spirit of Bengel puts its stamp on a line of development distinguished by its insistence on the study of the Bible, its fruitful work for edification in the scriptural sense. Finally there is the exuberant evangelicalism of Zinzendorf, revelling in the joyful contemplation of the wounds of the Saviour. Moravianism represents the opposite pole to the early school, the pietism of the law.[1]

CRITICISM: RICHARD SIMON AND JOHN LOCKE

Side by side however with emphasis upon and devotion to the Bible, appeal was made during the seventeenth century by both Roman Catholic and Protestant divines to the testimony of the early Church and of the Fathers, in order to establish the orthodox faith against heterodoxy. The terms of the decree of the Council of Trent concerning the equal adhesion of faith and reverence to be accorded to Scripture and unwritten Tradition encouraged this process, for these traditions were defined as those 'which were received by the apostles from the

[1] Y. Brilioth, *Evangelicalism and the Oxford Movement* (Oxford, 1934), p. 10.

lips of Christ himself, or by the same apostles at the dictation of the Holy Spirit and were handed down and have come down to us', and, further, 'as well those pertaining to faith as those pertaining to morals, ...and preserved by unbroken succession in the Church'. The definition led to a search, both extensive and intensive, into ecclesiastical traditions in all matters concerning doctrine, liturgy and ceremonies, in order to ascertain which were apostolic and handed down in unbroken succession in the Church. Naturally, the results were in many respects surprising and disconcerting; and especially in regard to ante-Nicene patristic opinions on the Trinity. Equally naturally, the criticism directed to the Fathers was turned next upon the Scriptures; and before the end of the seventeenth century the first beginnings of a rationalistic approach to the Bible were discerned. The Socinians had already directed attention to the doubtful authenticity of I John v. 7–8;[1] and shortly the entire front of assault was to be widened by works proceeding from a presumably orthodox source. In France the brilliant Oratorian Richard Simon published the results of his biblical studies, which were to earn for him the just designation of 'the father of biblical criticism'. In 1678 there appeared his *Histoire critique du Vieux Testament*, translated into English in 1682, which using the most accurate available texts and the methods of philology reached the conclusion that Moses was not the author of the Pentateuch, but only of the Mosaic law, that the chronology of various parts of the Old Testament was confused, and that within the framework of some of its books, the order of their contents had been transposed. On the other hand, he insisted that, without the aid of tradition, the Bible could be neither interpreted nor understood correctly; and thus becamed involved in controversy with Protestants, particularly Isaac Voss, canon of Windsor, and Jacques Basnage, pastor at Rouen and afterwards at Rotterdam. At the same time he was particularly antipathetic to all Socinians. Notwithstanding, he was dismissed from the Oratory, his book was confiscated by an order of the King's Council and in 1683 was placed on the Index. Nothing daunted, he published in 1689 his *Histoire critique du texte du Nouveau Testament*, in the following year his *Histoire critique des versions du Nouveau Testament*, and in 1693 his *Histoire critique des principaux commentateurs du Nouveau Testament*. Finally in 1702 there appeared *Le Nouveau Testament de Notre-*

[1] The *comma Joanneum*, cf. pp. 11, 59 above, 203, 233 below.

Seigneur Jésus Christ, traduit sur l'ancienne édition latine avec des remarques.[1]

It was hardly surprising that Simon should draw upon his head the indignant protests of both Roman Catholics and Protestants in respect of his cavalier handling of the Old and New Testaments. Despite his appeals to tradition, neither it nor the authority of the Fathers availed anything against the evidences of grammar and philology. Nor would he allow allegorical and mystical interpretations of Scripture to prevail over the literal sense; nor anything whatsoever resembling 'je ne sais quel jargon, auquel on donne le nom de spiritualité'. From the Protestant camp some forty refutations of his works appeared; and from the Roman Catholic side Dryden expressed the general and widespread sense of disquiet:

> For some, who have his secret meaning guessed,
> Have found our author not too much a priest:
> For fashion-sake he seems to have recourse
> To Pope and Councils and Tradition's force:
> But he that old traditions could subdue
> Could not but find the weakness of the new:
> If Scripture, though derived from heavenly birth,
> Has been but carelessly preserved on earth;
> If God's own people, who of God before
> Knew what we know, and had been promised more
> In fuller terms of Heaven's assisting care,
> And who did neither time nor study spare
> To keep this Book untainted, unperplext,
> Let in gross errors to corrupt the text,
> Omitted paragraphs, embroiled the sense,
> With vain traditions stopped the gaping fence,
> Which every common hand pulled up with ease,
> What safety from such brushwood-helps as these?[2]

Moreover, Simon's critical approach to the study of the Bible was soon to be followed by the amorphous yet influential movement of Deism in all its various facets. Locke's *The Reasonableness of Christianity* popularized a new version of Christianity by reducing its doctrine to the lowest common denominator of belief in Jesus as the Messiah, whose advent had been foretold in the prophecies of the Old

[1] Cf. pp. 218–21 below. [2] *Religio Laici*, 252–69.

Testament and whose mission had been authenticated by the miracles of the New Testament. Even this reduced creed was to be measured against the background of Natural Religion and of the religion of Natural Science, so that Revelation in addition to being required to justify itself by Locke's standard, had to present itself as a republication of Natural Religion. For a time indeed the Word of God assumed a secondary position to his works as set forth in the created universe. For whereas the testimony of the latter was universal and ubiquitous, the evidences of Revelation were confined to sacred books written in dead languages, whose interpretation was not agreed even amongst professed Christians, and which related moreover to distant events which had occurred in remote times and in places far removed from the centres of learning and civilization. Under such handicaps the Bible became a ground of controversy rather than a sure foundation of belief. In particular Locke's summary of Christian doctrine led to a hostile inquiry into the authenticity of Old Testament predictive prophecy and of the miracles of the New Testament. Anthony Collins's *Discourse of the Grounds and Reasons of the Christian Religion* argued that a literal interpretation of Old Testament prophecy was untenable, and therefore a purely allegorical interpretation must be accepted. Similarly, Thomas Woolston's *Six Discourses on the Miracles of our Saviour* contended for a mystical and allegorical explanation of the miracles instead of a factual and historical.[1] Orthodox champions enjoyed a fair measure of success in defending their position against such adversaries; and in the person of Thomas Sherlock approached a more modern exposition of Old Testament prophecy. But the assault on the Bible extended to all its parts and books; and during the protracted controversy a surprising number of guesses were put forward which subsequently found favour with biblical scholars of the nineteenth century, working with a better critical equipment; such as the denial of the Mosaic authorship of the Pentateuch, the composite authorship of the prophecy of Isaiah and the observation of the similarities as well as the differences between the Synoptic Gospels. Dr F. R. Tennant was justified in describing this rationalistic approach to the Bible as 'the beginning of modernity in English theology'. But, although the opponents of Deism lacked the magic theory of evolution in religious thought and of progressive revelation, which in the nine-

[1] On this controversy see chapter VII below.

teenth century was the key to open so many doors, they constructed learned and solid defences of the Bible, in accordance with the temper of their times. Unfortunately, their complete disregard of tradition led to a widespread vogue of Arianism, since the doctrine of the Trinity embodied in the *Quicunque Vult* could not be supported by scriptural evidence and phraseology alone, as Dr Samuel Clarke's *Scripture Doctrine of the Trinity* sufficiently established. While therefore the testimony of prophecy was generally accepted and the evidence of miracles firmly maintained, on points of doctrine much uncertainty and heterodoxy prevailed, and tradition was rejected as an ancillary support.

> Must all tradition then be set aside?
> This to affirm were ignorance or pride.
> Are there not many points, some needful sure
> To saving faith, that Scripture leaves obscure,
> Which every sect will wrest a several way?
> For what one sect interprets, all sects may.
> We hold, and say we prove from Scripture plain,
> That Christ is God; the bold Socinian
> From the same Scripture urges he's but MAN.
> Now what appeal can end the important suit?
> Both parts talk loudly, but the rule is mute.[1]

In view of the confusion alike of opinions and of tongues on various doctrinal issues, apologists tended to fall back on the position that Scripture contained all things necessary for salvation, and that such things were comparatively few in number; in fact

> ... that the Scriptures, though not everywhere
> Free from corruption, or entire, or clear,
> Are uncorrupt, sufficient, clear, entire,
> In all things which our needful faith require.[2]

It must be admitted, however, that much of this controversy became arid no less than dull, unprofitable as well as tedious. Accordingly, just as Pietism arose in protest against the theological hair-splitting and passion for over-definition in Lutheranism, so Methodism swept away the rationalistic disputes which had overcome English theological discussion. Indeed the Evangelical revival, in both its Arminian and Calvinistic forms, alike within and without the Church of England,

[1] *Religio Laici*, 305–15. [2] *Ibid.* 297–300.

changed the character of religious life and thought. By its insistence on the fallen state of mankind and the consequent need of redemption, it taught the necessity of a Redeemer whose nature was fully divine, and thereby thrust into the limbo of outmoded controversies all speculations concerning the relationship of the Three Persons of the Trinity. Indeed this revival by its emphasis on soteriology played the same part in current controversies as did Athanasius's standpoint in relation to the theories of Arius. The Bible accordingly was restored to its position of authority and popularity as the foundation of doctrine and the inspiration and source of piety, until the nineteenth century witnessed a further assault upon its authenticity at the hands of the new movement of literary and historical criticism. Meantime, however, it resumed its traditional prestige as the fount of study on the part of learned divines and as the vade-mecum of Christian in his pilgrimage from the City of Destruction to the City of God. Both the humble pilgrim of Bunyan's allegory and the theologian of the schools lived by its teaching and died by its consolation. During the troubled epoch of controversy and unsettlement which followed the Reformation, the Bible was indeed the book of books.

> If on the Book itself we cast our view,
> Concurrent heathens prove the story true,
> The doctrine, miracles; which must convince
> For Heaven in them appeals to human sense....
> Then for the style, majestic and divine,
> It speaks no less than God in every line....
> To what can Reason such effects assign,
> Transcending Nature, but to laws divine?
> Which in that sacred volume are contained,
> Sufficient, clear and for that use ordained....
> The unlettered Christian, who believes in gross,
> Plods on to heaven, and ne'er is at a loss....
> The few by Nature formed, with learning fraught,
> Born to instruct, as others to be taught,
> Must study well the sacred page, and see
> Which doctrine, this or that, does best agree
> With the whole tenour of the work divine,
> And plainliest points to Heaven's revealed design.[1]

[1] *Religio Laici*, 146–67, 322–31.

CHAPTER VI

THE BIBLE IN THE ROMAN CATHOLIC CHURCH FROM TRENT TO THE PRESENT DAY

THE COUNCIL OF TRENT

The first task of the Council of Trent was to delimit the spheres of Scripture and Tradition in the transmission of Catholic doctrine. For centuries the Church had been content with a rough-and-ready arrangement whereby Tradition (in the shape of the baptismal catechesis) introduced a believer to the doctrines of the faith, while Scripture was used at a later stage to test, to amplify and to collate those doctrines. Thus it was that St Thomas had said, in a much-abused phrase, *sola canonica scriptura est regula fidei*: only canonical Scripture—as distinct from apocryphal writings—is the (or a) rule of faith (*lectio* VI in John xxi).[1] But doctrines which were accepted alone or mainly on the authority of Tradition were not unfamiliar. It was these doctrines which were the main objects of reforming attacks: purgatory, the invocation of saints, the conversion of the bread into the Body of Christ, infant baptism and the sacramental character of marriage. Hence the Council had to start by making its position clear on the value of Tradition as contrasted with Scripture.

After sharp discussion the Council came to the decision that it received and held in honour *pari pietatis affectu ac reverentia*, with equal devotion and veneration, the books of Scripture and the divine and apostolic traditions (that is, those coming from Christ or the apostles) which concerned faith or morals. It did not mean that each book of Scripture was inspired in exactly the same way, as some modern theologians have claimed, for the Council was not comparing book with

[1] For St Thomas's attitude to Tradition, see G. Geenen in *Dict. théol. cath.* XV, 738–60, where, in spite of Aquinas's well-known dependence upon Scripture, it is claimed that his Christology is principally Greek and his sacramental theology a theoretical justification of the practices of the Latin West.

book but the body of Scripture with the body of apostolic tradition. In the debate some of the bishops wanted the word *simili* to be used in place of *pari*, but their emendation was not accepted, and the decree was finally carried by 32 against 20. Of the opposition, eleven wanted the word *simili*, four had other emendations, three were uncertain and only two were quite opposed. At the formal session (8 April 1546), one of these, Nacchianti, bishop of Chioggia, was not prepared to say *Non placet*, but contented himself with the word *Obediam*. It is true, as some modern theologians have pointed out, that in drafting the decree the Council rejected a form of words that would have canonized the view that the doctrine of the Church was transmitted *partly* in Scripture and *partly* in Tradition. It refrained for the moment from deciding the question whether there were doctrines that had come down through Tradition only, or through Scripture only, but this suspension of judgment did not prevent the Council at later sessions (for example, the 24th, when dealing with the sacramental character of marriage (Denzinger, 970)) from basing its teaching in practice on Tradition alone. It should indeed be clear that, if the Church holds to a certain doctrine by Tradition, it is often possible to discover this doctrine adumbrated in the spiritual sense of some passage of Scripture, but the knowledge that such is truly the spiritual sense of that passage will usually come from Tradition, for the very notion of a spiritual sense requires that it belong to the words of Scripture, not literally, but because God put it there without the knowledge of the human author and made its presence known by a distinct revelation. Thus the Council appealed to Mark vi. 13, not as proving but as adumbrating the institution of the sacrament of Last Anointing, holding that it was established in Tradition that these anointings done by the apostles in the public life of Christ were not themselves sacraments but pointed forward to the sacrament that he instituted later on. A relationship of type and fulfilment exists between many Old Testament and New Testament passages, and in the opinion of many theologians there can be in the New Testament types of the present age. The literal meaning of the passage in Mark does not say that this is true of it, and if Christ meant the episode to carry that message, he must have made the thing plain by some teaching not recorded in Scripture.

One doctrine which manifestly came from Tradition alone was the teaching that so many books and no more made up the canon of the

Scriptures. By attaching an anathema to the decree which laid down the canon, the Council made it clear that this list of books was to be accepted as part of the teaching of the Church and not merely as the result of a historical inquiry. The Church, of course, has always presented the Gospels to an inquirer as historical evidence for the existence and activities of Christ, and at this stage they are treated as historical works and no more; but when the act of faith has once been made, then it is proper to accept from the Church an authoritative teaching on the question how far God's written word extends. In this way the word of God in the Bible, though higher in dignity than any Tradition by the fact that it has come from God by direct inspiration (whereas apostolic traditions have come down through the general assistance given by the Spirit to the Church), may be seen to depend on Tradition, not in itself but in so far as our knowledge of it is concerned. Hence the Council could fairly claim that Bible and Tradition were to be received *pari affectu*, with an equal reverence from believers. The canon was not discussed at length in the Council, though there was some debate about certain fragments—the ending of Mark, the passage in John vii. 53–viii. 11 and others—and the archbishop of Armagh (Robert Wauchop) urged that a separate decree be issued with a list of such of these as were held to be canonical, but this was not agreed to.

The question of the biblical canon was for the Council primarily a juridical one. The Council of Florence had already approved the full canon of books (that is, the Septuagint canon for the Old Testament and the complete list of epistles in the New Testament), and it was merely a question of reaffirming what Florence had said. But at this point some of the bishops claimed that the decree of Florence was not a true conciliar decree, being issued after the Greeks had left and lacking the words *Sacro approbante concilio*. The legates sent to Rome to have the original of this bull for the Union of the Jacobites at Florence sent to them, and they were able to show that it had been drawn in proper form and did not lack conciliar status, but after thus serving the Council's turn the document was unfortunately lost. The further question, whether in the decree of Trent anything should be said about the status of books within the canon (that is, of the deuterocanonical books), was left to one side. Writing on 16 February 1546, the day after the debate, the legates report to Rome that there was general agreement not to enter into that question (*Acta*, x, 382) and the notice in the official account of proceedings (*Acta*, v, 10), recording that there was a majority in favour of putting the books all on an equal footing but that nothing was put into the decree about it, seems to agree with this. The fact that the words *pari pietatis affectu recipit* do not appear in the decree, but in another place, where they establish an equality between Scripture as a whole and Tradition, has led some theologians into a short-sighted attempt to twist the story of the Council. The legates cannot have been mistaken when they wrote that there was agreement not to enter into that difficult matter (*concordandosi quasi tutti a non entrare in quelle difficoltà*).

When the Council began to debate the problem of vernacular translations of the Bible, it was faced with a situation that differed widely from country to country. In Italy there had been as many as ten different versions made, between Malermi's of 1471 and the end of the century, and the making of a new Latin version by Santi Pagnini in 1528 led to a new crop of Italian versions made from it. In Germany Luther, who died just as Trent was debating the problem of the Scriptures (February 1546), had utilized a fashion of the times; when everyone was making versions of the Scripture, he would use the opportunity to set out his own doctrines more fully. The same was done in Italy by the new version of Brucioli (Venice, 1532), which was at once denounced by Catharinus as being under the influence of Bucer. In England there had been the strictest prohibition against unauthorized versions ever since the Council of Oxford (in 1408) had condemned the version associated with Wycliffe. France had more recently imposed such a prohibition, at the Synod of Sens in 1528. Cardinal Pacheco and his theologian, Alfonso de Castro, put the Spanish point of view at Trent, calling vernacular Bibles 'mothers of heresy'. When an attempt was made to reason with him by pointing out that a complete prohibition of them would not be acceptable to the Catholics of Italy, Poland and Germany, while to permit them would alienate the Spanish and French, and therefore the subject should not be legislated upon, he was not prepared to go further than to suggest that, where the habit had already taken root of having vernacular Bibles, only portions of the Bible should be allowed, such as the Psalms and the Acts, while on no account should the Epistles or Apocalypse be put in the hands of all and sundry. This opposition caused the Council to turn to an obvious way out, that of prescribing that all versions should carry annotations and of arranging for the setting up of lectureships in Scripture. Pole, who was one of the legates at Trent, had long set an example in expounding the Scriptures, being accustomed to comment on the Pastoral Epistles and other Pauline writings to his numerous household of ecclesiastics daily after the evening meal. The drafting of the decree on Scripture-lectureships owed much to Pole and Cervini. It was debated during May 1546, and the Christian humanists at the Council saw to it that the arguments put up by conservative interests (such as the claim that monks were contemplatives and that therefore lectures on Scripture were not needed in monasteries) were swept aside. Much care was taken to see that the lectureships were endowed and would therefore be taken up. In its long existence, the Council came to supersede some of its own legislation, for the decree concerning seminaries (1563) went much further than the order to found lectureships in each diocese; but here again the initiative had been taken by Pole, who in his Synod of London (1556) had legislated for such establishments in England.

The problem of the Vulgate could be said to have arisen out of that of the versions, since some at least of the contenders did not look beyond the Latin to the Greek and Hebrew originals, and for these it was largely a question of deciding whether the Vulgate was a sound basis for a translation into the vernacular. The debate had begun even before the Council, for Martin Dorpius had challenged the appeal made to the Greek by his fellow-Dutchman, Erasmus. Dorpius had countered the advice, cited from Augustine, to go to the Greek for guidance to the sense of Scripture, by the answer that in Augustine's day the Greek was not so corrupt as it now proved to be, nor was the Vulgate entrenched by so long a period of prescription. Erasmus waved all this aside with the remark that he could scarcely believe that Dorpius was sincere in what he said about the Greek codices; but it cannot now be denied that Erasmus was working with very imperfect Greek manuscripts. He was told by a friend in 1521 of an ancient Vatican codex (the now famous B) from which the *comma Joanneum* was missing (*Letters*, IV, 530), and again in 1533 Sepulveda told him roundly that the Greek manuscripts he had followed in the New Testament were thoroughly corrupt; a list of some 365 places was sent to him where B was in agreement with the Vulgate against the Greek manuscripts he had himself followed (*Letters*, X, 307). To this Erasmus replied that one of the conditions of the union of Greek and Roman churches at Florence had been that the Greeks should conform their readings to those of the Latin Vulgate. This extraordinary tale he professed to draw from the *Bulla aurea* of the union, where, needless to say, it is not to be found (*Letters*, x, 355). Sepulveda was at the time working with Cardinal Cajetan on a revised text of the Greek New Testament and it seems quite certain that his sharp reaction against Erasmus would have been known to those who took part in the deliberations of Trent. Even today it sometimes happens that the papyri give readings that are in agreement with the Old Latin and the Vulgate though opposed to all pre-existing Greek manuscripts. An example of this can be found in 𝔓 65 and its reading at I Thess. ii. 10. It is not surprising, then, that Trent was not anxious to abandon the traditional Vulgate; the very fact that Erasmus and Sepulveda were at odds about the Greek text would make that text seem very difficult of attainment in an authentic form.

But what exactly did the Council mean by declaring the Vulgate authentic? It should first be noted what the decree omitted to say. It did not say that the Vulgate was by Jerome nor distinguish it from the Old Latin; it did not call for its revision; it did not say what its relation was to the original Greek and Hebrew texts. The sense of the declaration was to make the Vulgate a reliable source of dogmatic arguments for theological teaching and debate. The ground of this reliability was not its relation to the originals, close or otherwise, but the fact that it had been for so many centuries in constant use for this purpose by the Church, which could not have used it for so long without engaging thereby its supreme teaching authority. Richard Simon cites Bellarmine on this decree: 'He very judiciously answers Calvin . . . that that Council meddled not with the originals, which are still of the same authority they were before, but that the Church . . . had only ordered that the ancient Latin translation should be preferred before the modern ones.' Calvin, in his *Antidote to the Council* (1547) made merry over the Vulgate Psalms; he claimed, too, that Trent had decreed that the Fathers were not to be listened to when they gave a version of Scripture that differed from the Vulgate, but this was to ignore the second part of the Tridentine decree, where it was laid down that the interpretation of Scripture (and every version is an interpretation) was to follow the unanimous teaching of the Fathers. Calvin said this took away all liberty from the Church, but he cannot have realized how few passages of Scripture found the Fathers really unanimous.

It cannot be denied that the extremist views of some theologians in later times pressed the use of the word *authenticum* as applied to the Vulgate, as if it made all other texts and versions superfluous. One can find in Bañez (*Commentarius in 2–2ae*: 11: 2) the view that it would be theologically temerarious to attempt to correct the Vulgate by the Greek or the Hebrew originals. Ignorance of the proceedings at Trent, after the death of the last participants in the Council, led to these misunderstandings. Actually the Council had decided to throw upon the pope the burden of revising the Latin, Greek and Hebrew texts (*Acta*, x, 468 and 471; also v, 128). The Vulgate, as the legates said, was a generic term and they had simply decided that 'the old was better' for dogmatic purposes, since it had never been found heretical, as some of the new versions had already been found to be. At Rome the Council's decree was not well received, for it did nothing to indicate that the Vulgate was in need of revision, nor did it make any attempt to distinguish between the clearing away of defects in the text due to its transmission and to the carelessness of scribes and the much greater task of remedying its defects as a version, by collating it afresh with Greek and Hebrew. It was realized that in this second work there would be need not to overestimate the Greek and Hebrew texts then available, as Erasmus had done.

Stephen Gardiner was not far from the point of view of Trent when he wrote (in June 1547): 'Religion hath continued in them [Latin and Greek] 1500 years. But as for the English tongue, itself hath not continued in one form of understanding 200 years; and without God's work and special miracle it shall hardly contain religion long, when it cannot last itself' (*Letters*, 121). His list of words that should be left in their Latin form, or put into English speech in the most exact manner possible, bears some resemblance to the list which the Rhemes translators put at the end of their work, of 'words which might not conveniently be uttered otherwise'. Gardiner read out his list during the debates of 1542 about the misleading nature of some parts of the English Bible, and it may well be that a memory of this event came down to Gregory Martin, working at Reims in 1580. There were humanists on either side in the Reformation struggles, and, just as Cranmer borrowed some of the ideas of Erasmus, it is not surprising to find Henrician bishops such as Gardiner and Tunstall contributing ideas to the Catholic side.

A PIONEER SCRIPTURE ENCYCLOPAEDIST

Sixtus of Siena (1520–69), a convert Jew who after some time as a Franciscan relapsed into heresy and was saved from the stake by the future Pope Pius V and then joined the Dominicans, produced in 1566 a great tome which he called *Bibliotheca Sancta* and which was a complete guide to the Bible. He said that he was impelled to write it by the confusion that was being spread—not so much by the malice of heretics as by the greed of publishers—through the appearance of so many spurious works of the Fathers and commentators; some of his examples are striking enough, including as they do Justin, *Quaestiones ad gentes*, Origen, *Paraphrasis in Iob*, and Ambrose, *Explanationes in Apocalypsim*. The first two books of this work give an account of the canonical writings in the Bible and of those works which have sometimes passed for Scripture. Here he uses for the first time the term 'deuterocanonical' for the books of the Old Testament which are outside the Hebrew canon and for some portions of the New Testament; but he is rather confused in his description of what the term meant. He says indeed that it covers writings which were some time in doubt since they had not been brought to the knowledge of the whole Church in apostolic times, but this will certainly not apply to books like Judith and Ecclesiasticus. On Tobias he notes that he had himself seen a Hebrew version, a manuscript brought from Constantinople, which agreed largely with the Greek but in which the whole narrative was in the first person. On the apocryphal writings he rejects such obvious frauds as the Gospel of Nicodemus, but accepts the letters of Paul and Seneca. He gives a list of the books of the Talmud and of its charges against the Christian doctrine. Sixtus was a pupil of Ambrosius Catharinus, a Dominican of independent views who spent much of his time attacking the opinions of his dead confrère Cajetan. Sixtus did not follow his master blindly, calling his writings against Cajetan *valde acres*, but he was swayed by him to refuse to accept Cajetan's exposure of the pseudo-Dionysius.

Sixtus's third book deals with the senses of Scripture and the methods of interpretation. He accepts a twofold literal sense, either proper or metaphorical, and a mystic or spiritual sense which can be divided into many varieties. He considers translation under the heading of methods of interpretation, and after a long list of methods he comes in the twenty-third place to the Scholastic method of the Middle Ages which he defines as 'the exposition of the sacred books in the manner of the Jurisconsults'. First, concordances of words are to be built up, then distinctions introduced of shades of meaning, next a continuous narrative is to be constructed with the help, if needed, of profane historians, and in the fourth place postillas, that is, the rendering of the literal and spiritual sense, while in the fifth place disputations are to be started upon points that arise out of a text and carried through in the manner of the *Summa*. It is significant of the new, humanist attitude that this method is put in so lowly a place by Sixtus. His fourth book is a short dictionary of writers on Scripture, where the notices of Augustine, of his own master, Catharinus, and of Thomas Aquinas are of interest. Thomas he commends as the next-best to Augustine: *Augustini animum migrasse in Thomam...communi adagio iactatum* (*est*). Books five and six give a detailed commentary on select passages from Old Testament and New Testament which are more open to misunderstanding, and the last two books then deal with heresies that have arisen through the repudiation of single books of New Testament or Old Testament or in connection with the Scriptures generally. He follows Catharinus in regarding as Pelagian the commentaries on the Pauline Epistles ascribed to Jerome; he is vehement against the new Latin versions of Münster and Castellio, the one so rough in its rendering of Hebrew names that a Latin cannot get his tongue round them, the other so effeminate in turning the language of the Canticle into that of Catullus that the divine love of Christ for the Church is not allowed to appear, while the Father is described as Jove, *Gradivus* or *Caelicola*. The work of Sixtus was in its third edition by 1586 and it had an immense influence on the theological revival of the Counter-Reformation. Though he did not consider the problem of inspiration *ex professo*, a chance remark of his about II Maccabees (*libri fides non ab auctore sed ab ecclesiae catholicae auctoritate pendet*) led to a new theory of inspiration being advanced by Lessius.

SIXTUS V AND THE BIBLE

The edition of the Septuagint produced in Rome in 1587 under the orders of Pope Sixtus V was a by-product of the Council of Trent. At the Council Pole had urged, thinking more imperially than most of the bishops, that authentic texts should be prepared in Greek and Hebrew as well as in the Latin Vulgate (*Acta*, v, 65). His proposal attracted some support, and was passed on to the pope, along with the recommendation that a definitive text of the Vulgate should be prepared in Rome. It was the Greek that was the first to appear. The story of its making is of interest as it was in some ways a rehearsal of the episode of the Vulgate of Sixtus V, an episode that has been so much misunderstood. When still a cardinal, Sixtus had in 1578 approached his predecessor Gregory XIII with the proposal that a standard text of the Septuagint be issued. A commission was therefore appointed, under the presidency of Carafa and including such scholars as Sirleto, and set to work on the *Codex Vaticanus*, which was collated with various Roman and Medicean manuscripts; the work was finished in the second year of the pontificate of Sixtus, and it must have been with great pride that he launched the published work in 1587. His decree expressed the hope that the work would help to the understanding of the Vulgate and of the Fathers, and a *ne varietur* clause was added to it. The work had a great fortune and remained the standard edition for about three centuries, being reprinted many times (in England by Daniel in 1653, in Walton's Polyglot in 1657, again in 1665 and often later). Even the discovery of Alexandrinus did not shake the foundation on which it was based, and subsequent editors (except Grabe in 1707) took the same way as it had followed, adopting the *Vaticanus* as the basic text.

The success of the Septuagint may have led Sixtus to think that the Vulgate could be dealt with as easily. There had been work going on since 1561, under Sirleto's direction, which was a remote preparation for a new edition. Various scholars had been copying into the margins of a chosen printed Vulgate (that of Henten of Louvain) the variants they noted in ancient codices which they inspected. In 1586, as work on the Septuagint was coming to a close, Sixtus named Carafa the head of a Vulgate commission, and it was possible in two years to put together an edition that drew upon all these collations. The work was presented to Sixtus late in 1588 or early in 1589, but he showed much displeasure at it and decided to see the matter through himself. As he said in the Constitution *Aeternus ille* prefixed to his edition, he felt it was the work of others to advise, but his to choose from among the alternatives submitted that which was best. Some changes were for the good; works not in the canon of Trent were omitted (such as III and IV Esdras and III Maccabees), and the New Testament was remarkably free from misprints, but the Old Testament left more to be desired. Num. xxx. 11–13 was entirely omitted, perhaps by mistake, but as the passage was used by moral theologians to argue that husbands could annul the vows of chastity which their wives might make without their consent, and as in this disputed question St Bonaventure and St Thomas were on opposite sides, it does not seem entirely impossible that some interested party was responsible for making so clean a cut of three verses, especially as there is no warrant for the omission in any manuscript. One of the great faults of the new version was that it changed the system of reference, having indeed a division into verses as well as chapters, but not following the same system as had been made popular by the edition of Stephanus. This cause alone might have moved the Cardinals to attempt to have the work withdrawn. Nestle's suggestion (in 1892) that this opposition was due to some *odium theologicum* between Bellarmine and the pope reads like an aftermath of the *Kulturkampf*.

Sixtus was impatient for the release of the printed work and the accompanying Constitution was dated for 1 March 1590, although the printing of the Bible did not finish until 10 April of that year. The first few copies were sent off to Catholic princes on 31 May. Before the time of grace allowed (four months in Italy and eight months outside) had elapsed and before the Constitution could come into force, Sixtus was dead (27 August 1590), and on 5 September the cardinals forbade the sale of the new Bible. Thus it was never the case that Sixtus's desire for the imposition of a uniform edition reached fulfilment, and his legislation that henceforth this book must be regarded as *the* Vulgate—a question which Trent had left open when it made its *generic* decree about the authenticity of the Vulgate—was never in fact operative. An over-zealous Inquisitor at Venice had already gone to work to have the Latin Bibles in bookshops there withdrawn from sale in favour of the new work, but the pope had (7 July 1590) assured the Venetian government that this act was premature.

On 7 February 1591 the new pope, Gregory XIV, set up a new commission of cardinals and theologians (including William Allen and Bellarmine) to revise the Bible of Sixtus and to advise him on what could be done to restore the situation, which Sixtus had left in confusion. Even after the publication of his Vulgate Sixtus was sending out tiny correction slips which were to be pasted over the misprints (Plate 35). Sometimes he sent a special messenger to see to the job being done. He also thought, according to Bellarmine, of more extensive revision of his work, to which he had devoted himself, body and soul, for many months before his death. The new commission returned (as they had been told) to the work of Carafa's men and made their revised text depend more on the ancient manuscripts where Sixtus had rather followed the printed editions of Henten and Stephanus. No doubt some of the trouble was due to a natural conservatism, Sixtus not wanting to disturb a reading which was familiar to Catholics from long use, even though it might have little support in the manuscripts. In modern times, the controversies over the new Latin Psalter introduced by Pius XII in 1944 might show the same forces at work. Thus, at Wisdom viii. 17 the Carafa commission had decided on *immortalitas est in cognitione sapientiae*; Sixtus went back to the earlier printed text, giving *immortalis est in cogitatione sapientiae*, but then he wavered and accepted the word *immortalitas* as a correction. Hesitation of this kind was, in spite of his vehemence of character, not uncommon in Sixtus, and it may be true that, as Angelo Rocca, one of his counsellors in this business, asserted, at the very end he wished to make his first edition serve as an experimental text on which comments might be made by Catholic scholars everywhere, so that a more definitive edition could then be made. Pastor (*History of the Popes*, XXI, 215–18) inclines to accept this, and also gives a full account of the uncertainties about the bull. One indication of the incomplete state of the text can be seen at John i. 3–4, where the words *quod factum est* are left 'in the air', having a comma before and after them, so that the reader can take them with what precedes or with what follows as he may please. Toletus, whose commentary on John appeared in 1588, and who was advising Sixtus in his work, says that he cannot make up his mind which reading is correct here, and it would seem that Sixtus could not do so either.

The Clementine Bible represented an attempt to incorporate the work of the Carafa commission into the received text of the earlier printed editions. It departed from the text that Sixtus had printed in a great many places, but it bore the marks of haste in the number of misprints it included, having been rushed through to take the place of the edition of Sixtus which had been called in. It received the name of Clement VIII, who had succeeded to the short-lived Gregory XIV, and who issued on 9 November 1592 the bull which introduced the new work. Unlike Sixtus, he did not insist that all preceding editions be now discarded, and he gave the privilege of printing the new work to the Vatican press for no more than ten years, thus showing some deference to the Spanish king's desire to protect the printers of Flanders. When all minutiae are taken into account, it has been estimated that there are 4900 variations between the Vulgate of Sixtus and that of Clement. Bellarmine, who had a large part in the making of the Clementine Vulgate, began in 1615–17 to make collations for a new edition of the Greek New Testament, but the work was never carried to completion. There was also an abortive attempt to edit the Hebrew Old Testament about this time. The place of England in all this affair of the Sixtine Vulgate was probably quite considerable. Olivares, the Spanish ambassador in Rome, wrote to his king (7 May 1590) that he had heard from Toletus that Sixtus had made changes in his new Bible, in one place omitting five whole lines (this must have been Num. xxx. 11–13, the only large omission), which he thought would comfort the heretics and warrant the calling of a general council. On the other hand, he wrote (28 April 1591) that Cardinal Allen had been put on the commission for revising the work of Sixtus and that he was one who had a better understanding of those things and would resist change. So it is clear that the English exiles were exerting themselves to guard against danger to Catholicism in Britain. The Rhemes version of the Vulgate had been made from the pre-Sixtine text in 1578–82 and immediately thereafter its translator, Gregory Martin, had been involved in polemics about the corruption of the text of Scripture. His version will be discussed below, but it is necessary here to notice the stir it caused. In 1582 he produced *A Discovery of the manifold corruptions of the Holy Scriptures*. In this he attacked Beza for changing the text:

Another way is to alter the very original text of the Holy Scripture by adding, taking away, or changing it here and there for their purpose; so did the Arians in sundry places and the Nestorians in the first Epistle of John, and especially Marcion, who was therefore called the mouse of Pontus, because he had gnawen as it were certain places with his corruptions, whereof some are said to remain in the Greek text until this day....Thus you see how the mouse of Geneva knibbleth and gnaweth about it, though he cannot bite it off altogether.

In 1583 Fulke replied to Martin. Cartwright also was at work on the same task (though his book did not appear till much later), and in 1588 G. Wither attacked the annotations of the Rhemes version. Fulke followed this up in 1589 with 'a confutation of all such arguments, glosses and annotations', while in 1588 E. Bulkeley had produced *An answer to the frivolous and foolish reasons set down by the Rhemish Jesuits*. With all this before him, Cardinal Allen may well have been alarmed when he learned that Sixtus was making changes in the text of the Vulgate. With Fulke already proclaiming that 'the swinish Jesuits trample the good pearls of the Greek copies under their filthy feet', it is easy to imagine what could be expected if Sixtus's work went through. No wonder that Allen turned to the Spanish ambassador for help in this emergency; he must have felt extreme embarrassment.

The Rhemes version has much greater merit than is now generally allowed. It has been compared with the Authorized Version in a very careful study by James Carleton (1902, *The Part of Rheims in the Making of the English Bible*). Martin did not neglect the Greek text, but in his work began a marked improvement on the previous English versions in the notice taken of the presence or absence in the Greek of the definite article and of the particle δέ, an improvement that the translators of King James were happy to accept. The Latinisms which are so often brought up against Rhemes are sometimes failures, but it is largely owing to the Rhemes version that one can now speak in English of 'apprehending a malefactor and treating him contumeliously', and many other such words have become naturalized in English through this version. The preface claims that the editors

> have used...no more licence than is sufferable in translating of holy Scriptures, continually keeping ourselves as near as possible to our text, and to the very words and phrases which by long use are made venerable, though to some profane or delicate ears they may seem more hard or barbarous...acknowledging with St Jerome that in other writings it is enough to give in translation sense for sense, but that in Scriptures, lest we miss the sense, we must keep the very words....Moreover we presume not in hard places to mollify the speech or phrases, but religiously keep them word for word and point for point, for fear of missing, or restraining, the sense of the Holy Ghost to our phantasy.

In spite of this it must be admitted that in such lofty passages as the description of the fall of Babylon (Apoc. xviii. 4–24) Gregory Martin showed that he could write with power. All the rhythms of his speech in this passage and elsewhere have been destroyed by the revising hand of Bishop Challenor in the eighteenth century, and the Douay version as it is now known has lost much of what Martin gave it. The Old Testament was begun as soon as the New Testament was finished (in 1582) and Martin seems to have worked on it, doing a stint of two chapters a day, until his death in 1584, but it was not published until 1609–10, when the college had moved from Reims to Douai, whence the whole version later took its name. The annotations of the New Testament were compiled by Richard Bristow and those of the Old Testament, along with the parts of the version which Martin had left unfinished, were made by Thomas Worthington. Martin is ultimately responsible for such familiar English phrases as 'striveth for the mastery', 'evil communications', 'to publish and blaze abroad', 'the one shall be taken and the other shall be left', 'compassed about with an army', 'to set at nought', 'the fatted calf', etc.[1]

THE GREAT COMMENTATORS

The Golden Century of Spain was marked by a great florescence of Scripture studies in that land, the Spanish exegetes of the period from 1560 to 1630 surpassing those of other lands. Alfonso Salmeron, S.J. (1515–85) was one of the original companions of St Ignatius; he had been present at all the debates of Trent and his *Commentaries on the New Testament* (in sixteen volumes) were published (Madrid, 1597) after his death, representing the fruit of some forty years of pulpit-commentary on the Scripture. Salmeron began this form of expounding the Scriptures at Verona in 1548, taking one book at a time and working through it for a general audience, and the practice became very common among the early Jesuits. Among his pupils at Naples he had the Cardinal Carafa who was afterwards to take charge of the revision of Septuagint and Vulgate. Juan Maldonado (1534–83) taught theology and philosophy for a long time at Paris, but when the Jesuits were driven out of the university there, he retired to Bourges and began to compile his *Commentary on the Gospels* (published 1597), which was finished after his death by Fronton du Duc. His advice to theological students was exacting. After their morning devotions they

[1] On the Rhemes–Douay Bible, see pp. 161–3 above.

should spend the first hour of the morning in reading the New Testament in Greek and the first hour of the evening in reading the Old Testament in Hebrew, if they could. He was strongly patristic in his exegesis, but never refused to accept and use an explanation of a passage that commended itself to him when it happened to come from a heretic author. Francis Toletus (1532–96) did manage to have his great *Commentary on John* published in his lifetime (1588), though his unfinished work on Luke did not appear until 1600. In all these cases the authors were themselves too much taken up with the work of expounding and consulting to put the notes they used into readiness for publication, and the issuing of these great works was really due to the insistence of Claudius Aquaviva, the General of the Jesuits. Toletus was a pioneer in having his commentary printed separately from the notes on the text of John, in a fashion that is now common. On the Old Testament the great Spanish authority was Francis Ribera, S.J. (1537–91), the confessor of St Teresa, who wrote the life of the saint, after having taught her the Scriptures. His main work was on the Minor Prophets (1587) and was the fruit of sixteen years of teaching at Salamanca. His later work, on the Apocalypse, on Hebrews and John, appeared after his death. Benedict Pereyra, S.J. (1535–1610), another of the same group, wrote on Daniel, Genesis and Exodus, and then, yielding somewhat to the controversial exigencies of the time, produced *Selecta in Paulum* and *Selecta in Apocalypsim*, in this last work going out of his way to show that Mahomet was not to be regarded as Antichrist. Behind all these Spanish Jesuits stood Benito Arias (1527–98), called, from his native Sierras, by the name Montanus, who carried through in five years (1568–72) Philip II's plan of a new Polyglot, printed by Plantin of Antwerp. The merit of this work was that it brought within reach of all European scholars the Syriac New Testament, printing it with a literal Latin version alongside and with a version in Hebrew at the foot of the page. Walton was content to borrow largely from Arias in the making of his Polyglot, and although Richard Simon says of Arias that in his revision of Pagnini's Latin version of the Hebrew Old Testament: *quot correctiones, tot corruptiones*, the work is on the whole done with care and skill.[1]

The publication of commentaries on the grand scale could not have proceeded so far in the latter part of the sixteenth century if there had

[1] See further pp. 54–5 above.

been no market for them. This was largely created by the teaching of Scripture in the new universities of the Counter-Reformation. In the *Constitutions* of the Society of Jesus (Part IV, ch. 14), it was laid down by St Ignatius that in Jesuit universities there should be lectures on Old Testament and New Testament and on the scholastic theology of St Thomas. There were to be professors of Greek and Hebrew (*ibid.* ch. 12), and if Jesuit students began to learn these languages, one of the motives for their study was to be to be able to defend the Vulgate as the approved version of the Church. Ignatius indeed would have set down this as the only motive, but he was over-persuaded by Salmeron and Lainez. The result of these prescriptions can be seen in the programme of studies in many of these new establishments, where, as at Cologne in 1570, one lecturer would go through the Gospels and Acts lecturing for two hours twice a week, while another would begin with Romans and go through the Epistles and Apocalypse on three other days of the week. Here the Old Testament was not considered, save for a series of lectures on the Psalms, but at Ingolstadt in 1575 the programme gives it equal space with the New Testament, a four-year plan being arranged thus: 1575, Psalms; 1576, Hebrews and James; 1577, Isaiah; 1578, Luke and I John. The next four years were to cover Genesis, I Corinthians and II Thessalonians, Job and John.

The French biblical epics of the seventeenth century owe much, as has been claimed by Mr Sayce (*The French Biblical Epic*, Oxford, 1955), to the four versions of Josephus which appeared in France between 1558 and 1598, but on the Catholic side it might be said that they owed still more to the new generation of commentaries that appeared at the same time; and the long Baroque poems of Saint Peres on Tobias and Joseph (1648), of Coras on Jonah, Joshua, Samson and David (1660–5) and of Saint Amant on Moses and Joseph (1653–8), would not have been quite the same had it not been for that most Baroque of commentators, Cornelius a Lapide. In Germany this Baroque popularizing of the Scriptures went down to a lower level of education than in France. Village Passion-plays had been customary in some parts of Germany since the days of Magdalena Beutler (1407–58), a mystic of Freiburg, and the Jesuit drama had something to build upon there, in the expectation of the populace, that did not exist to such an extent in France. The efforts also of the Capuchin Martin von Cochem (1634–1712) at popularizing the stories of the Bible left their mark on the devotional literature of the next two centuries. Another work of immense influence in popularizing the Gospels was the *Adnotationes et Meditationes* of Jerome Nadal, one of the early Jesuits (1507–80). The work contained reflections on all the Gospel-texts that are read in the Roman missal throughout the year. It also contained 153 large engravings of the events commented upon, and these, made by Flemish artists and craftsmen, not only set a standard for works of devotion but also exerted great influence on the later Baroque artists. Concentration on the momentary reaction of the characters in a scene (for example, there are five pictures for the story of the Prodigal), on what it felt like to be there, shutting out all illustration of the theme by appeal to typology (no use of parallel episodes from the Old Testament being possible here as it had been, for example, in the windows of King's College chapel at Cambridge), all these are signs of what the Baroque would later become. The book was brought out in 1593; it had several reprints, Italian and French versions were made, and the book was used in China and the Middle East.

Cornelius a Lapide (or van den Steyn, 1567–1637) was the universal commentator of the Baroque age, and himself in his profusion partook of its spirit. It is true that the commentary of Estius (or van Esten, 1542–1613) on the Epistles would have been found in most Catholic libraries of the age, but the Baianist tendency of this Douai professor led to his being relegated into a lower place. A Lapide was a man of wide learning and calm disposition, and although his works now seem marred by his credulity in accepting many a legend from apocryphal sources in his anxiety not to throw away anything that might serve to interpret the sacred text, one can still find much valuable insight in the 'canons of interpretation' which he lays down before starting to comment on any particular author. Thus, for St Paul, he will assert that negative general propositions in his Epistles may be understood absolutely, but that positive generalizations are often to be taken with a condition that is not expressed. So too, in St Paul the adverbs and conjunctions that would indicate causal connection or comparison between two clauses in a sentence are often omitted in Hebrew fashion and have to be supplied by the reader. Following Jerome he sees at times the presence in Paul (as at Col. ii. 18) of a Cilician Greek usage. Underlying the contrasted words about the Cross (I Cor. i. 23) as stumbling-block, or folly or wisdom, he will see an elaborate Hebrew pun on the words used. But above all he is copious, giving as many interpretations as he thinks can reasonably be defended and catering for all types of readers, much as the Baroque church was calculated to appeal to every type of worshipper. His commentary covered all the books of the Bible save for Job and the Psalms, where he does not seem to have wished to challenge the popular works of Pineda (1597) and Bellarmine (1611) respectively. The Latin commentary has been reprinted at least twenty times and various versions have been made of parts of it, there being an English version of the Gospel-commentary and of that on I and II Corinthians, Galatians and the Epistles of John, made by T. W. Mossman in 1876.

THEORIES OF INSPIRATION

During the sixteenth and seventeenth centuries there was a steady movement among Catholic theologians away from the theory of the verbal inspiration of the Scriptures. Leonard Lessius, picking up a hint from Sixtus of Siena, went so far as to defend (at Louvain in 1585) the view that 'a book such as II Maccabees, written by human industry without the aid of the Holy Spirit, may afterwards, if the Holy Spirit give testimony that it contains nothing false, be ranked as Holy Scripture'. As Lessius had taken part in controversies about Baius and had made enemies among his disciples, it was not to be wondered at that he was now pilloried by these enemies for his temerity. Bellarmine did not quite like the view of Lessius but thought it could be defended, and Lessius later revised it, withdrawing the reference to Maccabees and saying that the theory represented a hypothesis about what God might do, not a claim to describe what he had in fact done. Soon, however, Jacques Bonfrère (1573–1642), who was for some time rector of the Scots College at Douai, returned to the original view of Lessius, claiming that some of the lost books of Scripture had originated from unaided human efforts and after having enjoyed official approbation for a time had been allowed to perish. He argued from the way in which citations (such as that from Aratus in Acts xvii. 28) are taken up into a book of Scripture that a whole book could in similar fashion be given a subsequent approbation by the Church, under the guidance of the Spirit, and thus become part of canonical Scripture. The chief gap in his argument is the omission of the difference between the inspired writer (who is inspired to choose this or that citation) and the church council or other authority which might deliberate upon accepting a whole book as inspired. The council could not in Catholic doctrine claim to have such close assistance from the Spirit as an inspired author, for its decrees would not themselves be part of Scripture, even though they might be regarded as irreformable. Bonfrère, in spite of this error (which was condemned much later on at the Vatican Council), was something of a pioneer in developing, as a by-product of the Molinist theory of divine assistance to the human soul *a simultaneo*, a theory of concomitant inspiration, according to which the Holy Spirit did not impose his words on the human writer but, while leaving him inwardly free, managed to secure by use of the divine foreknowledge that he did not in fact write anything which the Spirit did not want him to write. If the human writer thus had liberty not only in deciding to write or not to write (*libertas exercitii*) but also liberty to choose his words (*libertas specificationis*), it is easy to see that a theologian could now look for signs of the human author in Scripture which a strict theory of verbal inspiration would deny to him. It is fair to add that Bonfrère did not claim that a human author would produce the whole of his inspired book in this freer way; there might be passages where the Spirit fell back on dictation of the words for some particular reason. But the link that was now (1625) set up between the problem of inspiration of the Scriptures and the controversy about divine grace was to be the source of many later theological debates. In the meantime the new views on the liberty of the inspired writer were much used in controversy with Protestant champions of dictation-theories.

Richard Simon (1638–1712) was one of the most original minds of his century.[1] He was a Molinist in his view of inspiration and had a great admiration for the Jesuit scholars Maldonado and Mariana. He became a member of the French Oratory in 1662, but left that body in 1678, just after the publication of his first great work, the *Critical History of the Old Testament*. He was an erudite orientalist and a logical thinker, but, as he himself said: 'Infelix eruditio est scire quod multi nesciunt: multo etiam infelicior scire quod omnes ignorant.'[2] He was a long way ahead of his time and the condemnation of his works as

[1] See also pp. 193–5 above.

[2] 'It is the misfortune of the learned to know what many do not know; it is their calamity to know what no one knows.'

soon as they appeared meant that the chance of using them to defend orthodoxy against the new rationalism of Spinoza—which is what he intended—was lost. The fact of their condemnation led to their being quickly translated into English, but they found as many contradictors among Anglicans as he had had among the Catholics of France. It was Vossius from Windsor who persistently attacked him in a series of pamphlets. His method is summed up in the verse which his English translator put at the head of the work:

> To vindicate the Sacred Books a new
> But onely certain method you pursue
> And showing th' are corrupted, prove 'em true.

His defence of textual criticism (in a time when the Swiss *formula consensus* of 1675 had declared that all vowel-points and accents were from the Holy Spirit as much as the words of the text of Scripture) was thus worded by his unknown English translator: 'The Catholics, who are persuaded their Religion depends not onely on the text of Scripture but likewise on the Tradition of the Church, are not at all scandalized to see that the misfortune of Time and the negligence of Transcribers have wrought changes in the Holy Scriptures.' He rejected the *Letter of Aristeas* and its fable about the origin of the LXX, and in general was not a great admirer of that version, though of Aquila he says that his work is rather a dictionary of the Greek equivalents of Hebrew words than a translation. Morin, who was his senior and mentor among the Oratorians, had a strong bias in favour of the LXX, but Simon argued that Jerome's version, which so often went according to the Hebrew, could never have found such approval in the Church if the LXX had been held to be of so absolute an authority. He found fault with Augustine for preferring the science of numbers and of music to profane history as aids to the understanding of the Bible, and with an eye on Origen he remarked: 'Many have been out who have modelled their notions according to the Platonist books.'

His greatest innovation was the theory of the existence of public scribes among the Jews from early times. He can cite Theodoret (on Joshua x. 14 and in his preface to Kings; *P.G.* LXXX, 473 and 529) for the view that both works were written in later times, being compiled from contemporary annals which the public scribes had written down. Simon regarded both scribes and later authors as inspired and conceived of their relationship very much as that which could have existed between St Paul and his secretaries. He found a predecessor in Andrew Maes (Masius), whose *Commentary* on Joshua (1574) had put forward the outline of this theory, and had applied it to the Pentateuch. Pereyra and a Lapide had given a nodding assent to some of the ideas of Maes, while the *Systema theologicum* of La Peyrère (1655) had described Numbers as a *farrago apographorum congesta*. This latter died at the Paris Oratory just one year before Simon published his book, and was not alive to protect his disciple from the storm that arose when a more sweeping use of such ideas was made. Simon appealed to Exod. xviii. 14 and Deut. xxxi. 19 for evidence that Moses had kept some kind of annals which a later author could have worked up into the present text. What is perhaps of more importance for the history of criticism is that Jean d'Astruc, the doctor of Montpellier who in 1753 hit upon the clue of J and E for the study of Pentateuch sources, was an amateur disciple of Simon.

Simon had his shortcomings. He can say roundly that there are no manuscripts surviving of the Old Latin version of the Old Testament, a claim that the patient work of the Benedictine P. Sabatier (1743–9) was to disprove. He had a sharp wit which made him enemies, especially among the gentlemen of Port Royal, whom he accused of using tendentious words to translate certain key-phrases of St Paul. Citing Eusebius (*H.E.* IV, 29) on Tatian he can say: 'This custom of making the Apostles speak better Greek than they did in their writings is very ancient', while of Nicholas of Lyra and Thomas Anglicus he says wistfully: 'These great men had the misfortune to be born in a time when learning was at an ebb.' Ten of Simon's works were put on the Index, largely through the influence of Bossuet and the Oratory, and he retired to pastoral work and finally to his home at Dieppe. Though at some points he presents a parallel to the Abbé Loisy two centuries later, their two lives do not match as do those of Plutarch's parallel heroes. Simon never wavered in his allegiance to the Church and was aiming all the time at constructive criticism. The reputation of Simon has grown among his countrymen, as may be seen by comparing the notice of him given in the *Dictionnaire de la Bible* of 1912 with the study of him published in 1951 by the Sulpician, R. Deville. The burden of the former notice is that Simon was a compound of lies and vanity and that Bossuet was right to have him condemned, while the latter bears witness to a great 'revirement d'opinion' in his favour among Catholics in France. Ironically enough the writer in the *Dictionnaire de la Bible* ascribed to Simon a view of inspiration which really belonged to Henry Holden and which Simon did his best to combat. Henry Holden, an English priest and doctor of the Sorbonne, put forward in his *Analysis of Divine Faith* (1658) the following view of inspiration:

It is to be noted that the special and divine assistance which is given to the author of every such book as the Church receives for the Word of God doth only extend itself to those things which are doctrinal, or at least have some near or necessary relation to them. But in those things which are written by the bye, or have reference to something else not concerning religion, I conceive the author had only such a divine assistance as other holy and saintly authors have (p. 61).

This was undoubtedly the original of what later became Newman's system of *obiter dicta* which were by him excluded from the scope of biblical inspiration. Simon, who does not name Holden but refers guardedly to 'a theologian of Paris' (where the book was published in Latin as well as in English), says roundly that this view is opposed to the New Testament view of inspiration and is fraught with dangerous consequences. For himself, he would extend inspiration to the whole content of the Bible, including the changes which it may have undergone (in certain books) at the hands of such editors as Ezra, but not to those changes which are due to the negligence of copyists and the erosions which the passage of time brings to any written work. Holden took his theory of *obiter dicta* from the notorious *episcopus vagans* Marcantonio de Dominis (who exchanged his bishopric of Spalato for a canonry of Windsor and afterwards returned to Rome, where he died). De Dominis had devised an exceedingly subtle theory of the relation between Bible and Church, and this was part of it. It is an article of faith, he said, that all parts of Scripture which contain revealed truths are of divine authorship, but that this or that book is part of Scripture is a matter of human testimony. Concerning the parts of the Bible which do not contain revealed truths but simply narrate facts of history (such as the fact that Christ claimed to be Son of God) de Dominis says that these too depend on human tradition, but that it is a certain tradition. He does not say how he can be sure of this, and while making much play with the notion of an *authentic* narrative, he fails to distinguish between authentic in the sense of belonging to the man whose name it bears and authentic in the wider sense of being an accurate account of what took place. Holden, who had his own reasons for putting forward what he thought might be acceptable to Protestant opinion in England (where the formation of an Anglo-Catholic church on Gallican lines was being canvassed during the Commonwealth), took up the ideas of de Dominis but did not manage to remove their inconsistency. 'Scripture as such is not the word of God, but contains and proposes to us the word of God', was the ultimate conclusion of de Dominis; Holden accepted this but without being able to say what criterion enabled him to distinguish where revelation ended in the text and the non-inspired matter began. The attempt to find the distinction between divine and human in Scripture on a physical basis by measuring off passages clearly led to a dead end. It would hardly have been undertaken had not de Dominis been anxious to find some way of outflanking the Catholic position on the necessity of divine tradition.

JANSENISM AND THE BIBLE

The principal event of the eighteenth century in which the Catholic Church had to develop her teaching on the Bible was the long struggle with the Jansenists over the bull *Unigenitus*, which (issued in 1713) was contested step by step by those it condemned until 1756. Later still, Pius VI had to condemn the same errors when they had been revived by the Italian Jansenists at the pseudo-synod of Pistoia (1794). Quesnel and the other Jansenists, quite apart from their heretical views on grace, had built up a whole system of theology and this was condemned piecemeal by the bull, though the individual propositions listed were not given each its individual note of condemnation. Instead, the list concluded with the sentence which declared that the propositions listed were variously heretical, near to heresy, scandalous, offensive and so on. Thus the condemned propositions about Scripture cannot be said to state what all Catholics must regard as heresy; they are most probably among the less important errors in the list, being perhaps due more to the Jansenist desire for a rapprochement with the Protestants than to their logical coherence with the Jansenist system. Seven propositions (Denzinger, 1429–35) deal with the reading of the Scriptures. The Jansenists held that Scripture-reading was for everyone, that the obscurity of the Word of God was no excuse for any layman neglecting this duty, that it should be practised on Sundays, and that the denial of the Scriptures to any of the faithful was a kind of excommunication. The Church at that period, while anxious for the spread of education, was aware that education was far from being universal, and, in view of the obscurity of Scripture 'which the unlearned wrest to their own destruction', she held that it was safer to have less Scripture-reading than more heresy. There was no desire to hold back the spread of education. One might instance the founding of schools by the English Jesuits at Bury St Edmunds, Lincoln, London (one at the Savoy and one in Fenchurch Street), Newcastle, Welshpool and Edinburgh during the brief reign of James II as evidence to the contrary. During the same reign it seems that copies of the Rhemes–Douay Bible, with the royal arms on the binding, were placed in such chapels as the English Catholics ventured to open, in such places as Preston or Holywell. It was only the plain text that was thought harmful; versions that carried annotations or extracts from patristic interpretation were always allowed. In missionary work it was generally desired to make the newly converted acquainted with some of the simpler books of the Bible and to keep them from the Apocalypse and similar books until they were mature. Jewish practice, which reserved the Canticle for those over the age of thirty, was not very far removed from this, even without the theological reasons of Catholicism.

The synod of Pistoia went further than Quesnel and held (Denzinger, 1567) that only incapability excused a man from sin if he neglected to read the Scriptures. In condemning the synod, Pius VI attached a qualifying clause to each proposition condemned, and this one was labelled false, rash and provocative, but *not* heretical. It was clearly seen to be much more a matter of opinion than of doctrine, and in matters of opinion like this the Church was habitually conservative. As the synod went on (in the next sentence) to urge parish priests to read the *Commentaries* of Quesnel to their parishioners, it can be seen that the Jansenists were now not so much enamoured of the plain text as before.

CATHOLICS AND THE BIBLE SOCIETIES

During the wars that followed the French Revolution the Church was very much on the defensive, and the founding at this very time (1804) of the British and Foreign Bible Society seemed to aggravate a situation in which the Church was already imperilled.[1] The activities of Paterson and Pinkerton, agents of the Society, in northern Europe, and especially in Russia (1812–15), caused Pius VII to send a letter of warning to the archbishop of Mogilev in 1816, saying that the multiplicity of vernacular versions, made without regard to the Catholic rules of interpretation and at times corrupted in a heretical sense, did more harm than good (Denzinger, 1602–6). At the same time the editions of the Greek New Testament by the Catholics Gratz and Scholz in Germany (1821 and 1830) showed that there was no attempt made to check well-intentioned study of the Bible. The dispute over the printing of the deuterocanonical books in the Bibles of the British and Foreign Bible Society (1824–6) led Leo XII to repeat the warnings of his predecessor (Denzinger, 1607–8), while Pius IX in 1844 (Denzinger, 1630–3) had to deal with the Bible-smuggling activities of the Scottish settlers at Leghorn, who under the Free Church minister Robert Stewart and others carried on a considerable business of clandestine distribution with the aid of Italians belonging to the Waldensians.

Pius IX found fault with the Bible Societies for their attitude of indifference to the fate of the books they distributed; they did not care what the purchaser made of the text that was thus set before him. The answer to this was obviously to form study-groups to consider the meaning of the sacred text, and then the nucleus of a new church was at once created. The rise of such bodies as the Jehovah's Witnesses (which grew out of just such study-groups) is an indication that random distribution of the Bible does have some of the consequences which the popes foresaw. The great growth of missionary activity in the nineteenth century made these problems of Bible distribution very much more acute, and the vast number of Christian sects indigenous to Africa is primarily due to such premature circulation of an uninterpreted Bible. The Orthodox Church in Greece reacted in an exactly similar way, declaring the LXX the sole permitted version of the Old

[1] Cf. ch. XI below.

Testament that could be used by its members and even succeeding in having a clause inserted in the Greek Constitution of 1911 that forbade the use of Scriptures in modern Greek. Much of the trouble could have been avoided if more neutral versions had been adopted at the outset by the Bible Societies. Thus the choice was unfortunate of the Italian version made by the Calvinist Diodati in 1607, of which Richard Simon said that it was more like a paraphrase than a version and that Diodati's notes were those of a theologian and not those of a critic.[1] In the Levant it has been found possible for the Society to distribute an Arabic version of the Scriptures that was prepared by the Jesuits of Beirut, thus saving much waste of effort.

SCIENCE AND THE BIBLE

The conflict between Catholic teaching about the Bible and scientific thought began with the Galileo affair (1616–33) but did not become at all serious until the nineteenth century. The whole story of Galileo cannot be examined here, but it may be said that *doctrinally* the Church did not take up in that affair any position which science showed later to be wrong. A personal precept was put upon Galileo not to teach certain opinions, but Bellarmine, the cardinal who in a private interview communicated the precept to Galileo, himself declared in a letter to the Carmelite Foscarini in 1615: 'If there was a real demonstration that the sun is in the centre and that the earth goes round it, then one would have to proceed with much care in expounding the places of Scripture which seem to be contrary to that, and it would be better to say that we do not understand them than to declare that false which has been demonstrated.' The lesser theologians whose opinions weighed with the Roman tribunal in 1616 were not so careful, and the theological climate of the times, when any suggestion of a blemish in the Scriptures was likely to upset the faith of the uneducated, did not admit of much latitude of opinion. In China, whither the missionaries had brought the theories of Galileo, no such restraint was imposed, and the missionaries joyfully reported that with the hypothesis of Galileo they had made correct calculations for an eclipse, while the system of Tycho Brahe had not proved so accurate, and the Ptolemaic quite erroneous. Another new factor in the Galileo story which was brought to light by

[1] Cf. pp. 112–13 above.

an Italian canonist on the occasion of the tercentenary of his death (1942) was that he was finally proceeded against in 1633 on the score not of heresy but of *heretica pravitas*, a wider offence, which differed from heresy much as loitering with intent might be said to differ from a felony; the concept was used in those troubled times but passed out of judicial practice in the more settled times which followed. All these new factors make it quite impossible to accept the old estimates of the Galileo affair, and it has always to be remembered that it was never made a precedent for dogmatic pronouncements in the sequel.

The codification of much scriptural knowledge in the biblical encyclopaedias which appeared in the eighteenth century (that of R. Simon in 1712 and that of Dom A. Calmet in 1734) meant that much was passed on which might otherwise have perished in the French Revolution, but it also meant that somewhat narrow views, produced by the condensation of the encyclopaedia articles, were passed into circulation, and it was these narrow views which were so often the settled convictions of those who had in the nineteenth century to meet the new scientific theories face to face. The first reaction was to produce what is now known as Concordism, an attempt to save the appearances of Scripture by a most liberal dosing of the evidence with hypotheses for which there was and could be no support. Thus the six days of creation were thought of as real days but with such intervals of time between them as would admit of the gradual process of the production of life in the way the geologists described it. Similarly, a pre-Adamite race was postulated, which could be used to account for the early skeletons found and then conveniently die off before the arrival of Adam on the scene. The biblical account of the appearance of tillage and the working of metals among men was carefully synchronized with what the archaeologists reported. Not all Catholics were carried away by Concordism, even in the height of the Colenso dispute, and Newman in particular was unimpressed by it. In 1861 he wrote in the draft of a work he was preparing on inspiration:

I am not proposing to comment on Scripture, nor am I proposing to reconcile Scripture with the conclusions of human sciences; so far from it that I would rather contend that there is little to reconcile, because there is as little as possible common between them. I am to adjust rather than to reconcile; that is, I aim at showing how theology sits easy (if I may use such an expression) in its own domain, without any fear, as time goes on, of any collision between itself and secular knowledge, as regards the statements of the Written Word, provided each party will but consent to remain within its own boundaries.... Nothing that human science or inquiry can discover is able to reach, for confirmation or for damage, those sacred truths and facts which the voice of the Church, or of her Doctors and schoolmen, or of her Bishops and people *in orbe terrarum*, has recognized and declared to be dogma in the Written Word (Seynaeve, p. 70*).

NEWMAN AND INSPIRATION

Newman was working with an idea of inspiration which owed a good deal to Holden, whom he had studied. Part of his confidence in the complete non-interference of science and Scripture was due to Holden's theory that inspiration simply meant a guidance that kept the writer sound in faith and morals and left him to do his best with the history and science of his times. The whole trend of Catholic theological opinion, at least since Augustine, had been to allow that in matters of physical science the inspired writers spoke as men of their own time with the circumscribed ideas of their contemporaries, but the question of historical writing was differently regarded. Out of this obscurity in Newman's work was to come the misunderstanding that contributed in some measure to the Modernist crisis, when at the end of the century that movement had arisen from other causes.

Manning, no less than Newman, was ready to defend Holden in his mistaken view of inspiration. There is a passage in chapter III of Manning's *Temporal Mission of the Holy Ghost* (1865), where the relation of the Holy Spirit to the written Word of God is being considered, in which he says that Holden's orthodoxy can be defended though at the expense of his consistency. In fact, the opposite appears to be the case. Holden was consistent but unorthodox. Manning recognized that some French theologians of his own day followed Holden in thinking that inspiration secured the freedom from error of the inspired writers only when they dealt with matters of faith and morals, but he held that this was not a true conclusion from what Holden said. There can be little doubt that in this point Newman was right and Manning wrong in the way each tried to understand Holden. It was part of the difficulty of the times that neither of them was able to rise above an 'atomic' view of Scripture, which treated it as so many isolated bits of statement put together by the inspired writers; the subject of the literary genus of the various books of the Bible never fell under consideration. Had Newman theorized about these literary genera in the manner of a modern theologian, he would never have gone in for Holden's *obiter dicta*.

The mature expression of Newman's view on inspiration came in 1884 in an article contributed to the *Nineteenth Century* for February of that year. This set out, with considerable elaboration, what was in essence the Holden theory. It was immediately subjected to serious theological criticism by Dr Healy of Maynooth in the March issue of the *Irish Ecclesiastical Record*. In May there appeared a tract by Newman entitled *What is of obligation for a Catholic to believe concerning the inspiration of the canonical Scriptures*. Dr Healy prepared a reply, which was, however, not published at the time, only seeing the light in his *Papers and Addresses* (1909) long after Newman's death. In place of his own rejoinder Healy was persuaded by friends to content himself with the printing in the *Irish Ecclesiastical Record* of an English version of a chapter from the work of Cardinal Franzelin on inspiration. To have done more would have been invidious, as he had himself been made a bishop in the course of the controversy. Newman had moved forward somewhat since his draft scheme of 1861. He now took within the ambit of inerrancy those historical statements of inspired writers which were in some way linked with dogmatic teaching. It is indeed clear that the Gospel recording of the fact that Christ suffered under Pontius Pilate could hardly be left outside, and there are many other historical statements that fall within the same class. But Newman still classed such statements as the dictum of St Paul that he had left his cloak at Troas with Carpus among the *obiter dicta* which might be false with no detriment to the inspiration of the work. Defining an *obiter dictum* as 'a phrase or sentence which, whether a statement of literal fact or not, is not from the circumstances binding upon our faith', Newman did not make it easy to recognize when an *obiter dictum* had been met with. If there was profane evidence of an error in the statement, then it would no doubt be open to the user of his theory to say that here was an *obiter dictum*, but such use would be simply to treat the theory as a convenient escape-clause in the whole teaching about inspiration. Had Newman said that there were certain literary forms, such as historical fiction or the Jewish haggadic midrash, in which the writer did not bind himself always to write what was true, he would have given a positive test for setting up a limit to inerrancy, but at that time no thought was given to literary genera.

Newman was also in error in saying that two councils (Trent and the Vatican) had taught 'that the divine inspiration of Scripture is to be assigned especially to matters of faith and morals'. Trent had taught that the Vulgate version might be used with safety in these matters of faith and morals, but the very word *inspiration* is not mentioned in the decree of Trent (Denzinger, 783–6). In the Vatican council the Tridentine decree had been reiterated, and an additional pronouncement had been made to the effect that the books of Scripture were not accepted as canonical by the Church because they had been produced by the unaided wit of man and then crowned or canonized by the authority of the Church but because under the inspiration of the Holy Spirit they had God for their author and as such had been committed to the Church. This addition was made at the Vatican council in order to exclude as heretical the theory of 'subsequent inspiration' as it had been taught by Bonfrère and had been revived by J. Jahn of Vienna and by Abbot Haneberg of Munich in 1860. There is nothing in the Vatican decree which justifies Newman's claim, and one can only suppose that in his old age (he was then 84) he had misread Trent and had taken it for granted that the Vatican had reiterated the decree of Trent. Confusion about the true purport of the Tridentine decree on the Vulgate persisted until 1943. Lessius, the originator of the 'subsequent inspiration' theory in its simpler form, was declared by the proposer of the decree to be outside its scope (Mansi, *Acta Conciliorum*, LI, 47 and 283), but soon afterwards Leo XIII carried things to a logical conclusion and decided in his encyclical on Scripture (Denzinger, 1952) that it would be meaningless to call God the author of Scripture unless it was admitted that he had given the human writer antecedent motion to write and a concomitant help in the carrying out of his task.

Leo XIII published his encyclical in 1893, and although he said plainly that it was wrong to limit inspiration to matters of faith and morals, or to allow that the inspired author was guilty of any error, he did not use the term *obiter dictum*, and various attempts were made to argue that the theory of Holden and Newman had not been condemned. It was possible to find an occasion for the encyclical in an article of a French theologian, Mgr D'Hulst, who had frankly abandoned the complete inerrancy of the Bible, but the death of Newman on 11 August 1890 was at least the removal of an obstacle to the pronouncement, for Rome would hardly have condemned his view in his lifetime as cardinal. These speculations were brought to an end only in 1943 when the encyclical *Divino afflante* of Pope Pius XII made clear beyond any doubt that *obiter dicta* as a theory had been set aside:

Certain Catholic writers...dared to restrict the truth of sacred Scripture to matters of faith and morals alone, and to consider the remainder, touching matters of the physical or historical order, as *obiter dicta*, and as having no connection whatever with faith. These errors found their merited condemnation in the encyclical *Providentissimus*... (*Acta apostolicae Sedis*, 1943, 298).

One of Newman's ideas about Scripture was taken up by Leo XIII, for it is recounted in Ward's *Life of Cardinal Newman* (II, 477) that he was once asked what he would do if he became pope and he replied with some gravity that he would set up commissions for biblical matters and for the early history of the Church. One cannot be sure that Newman advised Leo in this sense, but it seems likely, though neither of them could have then (in 1880) foreseen what the Modernist crisis would bring.

THE MODERNIST CRISIS

The Modernist movement was an amalgam of disparate and sometimes conflicting interests, and the principal English Modernist, George Tyrrell, was not really interested in biblical questions. Baron von Hügel, who had sought Newman's advice over difficulties of Scripture in 1884, was much more concerned to circulate the ideas of the Abbé Loisy in England and Italy; in fact he acted as a general post-office for the movement. One of the causes of confusion at the time was that in the encyclical *Providentissimus* Leo XIII had outlined what was to be the correct attitude for a Catholic exegete towards the conclusions of the physical scientist, and had then added: 'It will be advantageous to apply these ideas to cognate disciplines, especially to history.' No indication was given of the closeness or otherwise of the analogy, and it was possible for exegetes in all good faith to suppose that they had been given the signal to begin a process of scaling down the historical value of the Old Testament. Thus, apart from the Modernists, who had for the moment panicked under the stress of the new archaeological and textual discoveries that began about 1890, there was a group of moderate men in the Church who proceeded to abandon some of the positions that were still jealously guarded by conservative exegetes. The school of S. Étienne at Jerusalem had been founded by Père Lagrange in 1890 and in 1892 the *Revue biblique* began to issue from it; ten years later, at Toulouse in 1902, Lagrange gave his famous course on 'Historical method in the Old Testament' which presented a detailed working out of the analogy between the statements in the Old Testament about physical science and those which purported to be historical. Here the consideration of the literary genera was for the first time suggested, though not as the main principle for overcoming discrepancies between the Bible and the findings of historians. In the same year appeared Lagrange's *Livre des Juges*, which was the first volume in a series of commentaries designed to cover all the books of the Bible (the *Études bibliques*), a series that is not yet complete. From 1891 there had been appearing also the parts of the *Dictionnaire de la Bible*, the editor of which, the Abbé Vigouroux, was the chief representative of the conservative school of exegesis.

On 30 October 1902 Leo XIII set up the Biblical Commission, with an Anglo-Irish Franciscan, Fr David Fleming, as its secretary. Its purpose was, as Newman had already suggested, to encourage Catholic scholars in their study of the Bible, to act as a clearing-house for ideas and opinions, to use all the new helps to exegesis that were now becoming available, while at the same time guarding against anything which would appear to go against the true sense of Scripture, where that was established by the unanimous teaching of the Fathers and doctors of the Church. The Apostolic Letter *Vigilantiae*, which set up the Commission, was one of the latest acts of Leo XIII, who died on 20 July 1903. The first decisions of the Commission (Denzinger, 1979–80) were both concerned with general questions touching the historical character of the Bible. To the questions whether it was lawful to appeal to tacit or implicit citation of sources to excuse the inspired writer from having fallen into historical error, and whether it could be allowed that certain books which appeared to be historical were so only in appearance, negative answers were given, though in each case an escape-clause was added. One might say that there was a citation if there was evidence that the writer was quoting and if he showed that he did not adopt the citation as his own declaration. One might also allow (subject to the judgment of the Church) that in certain cases parable, allegory or some other non-historical form of writing was being used, if the evidence really pointed to that. These answers were given in 1905, and towards the close of that year Fr David Fleming was replaced as secretary by the Abbé Vigouroux and by Abbot Janssens, O.S.B., who jointly edited the deliberations of the commission until 1914. During this time a number of decisions on the character of individual books of the Bible came forth, which were due to the widespread publicity which the Modernists attracted to themselves, but which the present secretary of the Commission (Athanasius Miller, O.S.B.) has characterized in the following terms: 'In so far as there are proposed in the decrees of the Commission opinions which are not directly or indirectly linked with the truths of faith or morals, the exegete obviously has full liberty to prosecute his researches and to evaluate his findings, though always with due regard to the teaching authority of the Church.'[1] One might compare the difference between the Commission's attitude of 1907 and 1955 with that between the treatment of Galileo in Rome and in China; where the climate of opinion was charged with peril, there had to be restraint, but where no such tension existed, there could be liberty.

Pope Pius X soon turned the Biblical Commission into an examining body, empowering it on 23 February 1904 to confer by examination the degrees of Licentiate and Doctor in Scripture. It was soon found necessary to supply students with the means to prepare for such degrees, and on 7 May 1909 the Biblical Institute was founded in Rome and entrusted by the pope to the Jesuits. At first it prepared its students for the examinations of the Commission, but after a time it was given the right to confer its own degrees, and thus two parallel examining bodies now exist, with slightly differing characteristics and with all the advantages that come from two different centres of initiative existing in the same place. Pius XI, on 27 April 1924, ruled that those who teach Scripture in seminaries must have at least a Licentiate in Scripture from one or other of these bodies, and thus the ideas of Trent on the equipping of Scripture lecturers at last came to full fruition.

[1] *Benediktinische Monatschrift* (1955, p. 49). His assistant, A. Kleinhans, O.F.M., included the same statement in an article he wrote in *Antonianum* (1955, p. 64) on the same subject.

When errors concerning Scripture drew on to threaten the doctrines of the Church, the Holy Office became the proper organization to deal with the matter, since the Biblical Commission was after all meant rather for the proper forwarding of biblical studies than for the control of heresy. Thus the Holy Office had in 1897 (13 January) issued a decree denying that it was safe to call in question the authenticity of the *comma Joanneum*. The decree was published in *The Tablet* (8 May 1897) and was accompanied by the comment that Rome had now spoken and that the question was settled. On 5 June von Hügel wrote to the editor to protest that he had just returned from Rome where he had spoken about the decree to 'twenty or more Catholic specialists', who all took the decree to be an *ad interim* pronouncement and in no way final. *The Tablet* replied with a leading article on 12 June, saying that the decree was a disciplinary decision, about the safety of teaching a particular view, and was in no way irreformable, and, most surprising of all, that it was dealing with the text of the Vulgate, not with that of the original Greek. There is some reason for thinking that Cardinal Vaughan (who then controlled *The Tablet*) had higher authority for publishing this article. At all events, no hindrance was put by Rome to the later appearance of various learned articles by A. Bludau or of a monograph in 1905 by G. Künstle, both of which ascribed the origin of the words to the fourth century. Then in 1927 (Denzinger, 2198) the Holy Office issued a gloss on its former decree to say that it was simply meant as a brake on rash speculation (*ut coerceretur audacia privatorum doctorum*) and not as a final decision. Nonetheless, it has often figured in the armoury of the controversialist as one of the ultimate missiles. The Holy Office on 3 July 1907 also issued (Denzinger, 2001–24) in the decree *Lamentabili* a catalogue of theological errors concerning exegesis to be found in the works of Loisy, and this decree was afterwards confirmed by the special authority of the pope, but in the encyclical which he issued (*Pascendi*, on 8 September 1907) the exegetical errors of the Modernists are less noticed, the main charge being against their idea of the Church and of the nature of dogma.

RECENT DEVELOPMENTS AND DISCUSSIONS

Modernism vanished in the smoke of war that drifted over Europe in 1914, but it left the Church with some way yet to go in finding a *principle* of solution for the problem of the divine and human elements in Scripture. The Modernists had made the Scriptures all too human, denying like some latter-day Nestorians that the Written Word was united or associated in a substantial way with the nature and activity of God, while some of the conservative exegetes had been going to the opposite extreme and asserting that all in the Scriptures was entirely divine, down to the choice of metaphors and of grammar. Eventually a middle way was proposed in the encyclical *Divino afflante* of 30 September 1943. Here the comparison of the Incarnate Word and the Written Word was brought in, almost by chance, at the end of a long passage about the literal sense (*Acta apostolicae Sedis*, 1943, p. 316), but it has been taken up, first in the *Catholic Commentary on Holy Scripture* (36*j*), and by many others since, notably in a book (1958) by J. Levie, S.J., of Louvain, *La Bible, parole humaine et message de Dieu*, whose title embodies the principle itself. The principle can be found clearly in tradition, but it had been lost sight of in the days of Modernism, or rather had been rejected by Cardinal Billot and upheld only in the *De Scriptura sacra* (1910) of J. Bainvel, S.J. It provides a means of grouping together the various 'exemptions' which are allowed to the inspired author, mistakes in grammar, use of inaccurate citations, choice of strange metaphors (as in Ecclus. xx. 4 and xxx. 20), use of literary genera which depart from strict history, stylized grouping of facts in historical narrative, and so on. All these are so many signs of the humanity of the writer, which has to be perceived even though God is guiding him, for otherwise the books would all be alike and one would have to say that their style was always the best possible. Reference to the Incarnation provides also a means of saying where this condescension must stop. As in Christ there was humanity without sin, so in the Scriptures there is to be found the humanity of the writers without formal error; that is, they do not put forward as their own assertion that which is false. This principle would exclude the presence in Scripture of aetiological writing such as Ovid indulged in with his *Fasti*, but not of a primitive type of history (in the first eleven chapters of Genesis), of which one cannot either affirm or deny the historical character without applying to them the norms of a literary genus which does not fit them.... To say *a priori* that they are not historical in the modern sense would imply that they are not historical at all, whereas they tell in language that is simple, full of imagery and adapted to the understanding of a less-developed human race the fundamental truths that are at the base of the work of salvation.

In these terms the secretary of the Biblical Commission (J. Vosté, O.P.) wrote in 1948 in a public letter to Cardinal Suhard, thus making an application of the principles included in the encyclical of 1943.

The occasion of the writing of that encyclical (*Divino afflante*) was a curious manœuvre by an ultra-conservative ecclesiastic in Italy, who after having had his commentaries (thirteen volumes, covering Genesis to Ecclesiasticus) put on the Index, wrote under a pseudonym a tract in which he argued that the Church should not bother about anything but the Vulgate, that textual criticism was a massacring of the Bible, that study of Hebrew and Syriac was only an occasion of pride, and that exegesis should consist in the meditative elaboration of allegories out of the Latin text. This he circulated to the pope and all the cardinals, early in 1941, and the reaction it provoked must have surprised him. What had happened in the interval since the Modernist crisis was that so much evidence of the early literature of the Near East had come to light that it was now possible to study their literary genera in a way that had been impossible before, and the task that had been glimpsed by Lagrange in 1902 and by von Hummelauer in 1904 could now be undertaken with some hope of progress. But how slow some theologians were to admit the incarnational principle in exegesis may be seen from the fact that one of the chief Roman theologians was in 1936 ready to allow that while the study of literary genera was a help to exegesis, they should not be appealed to as a defence of the inerrancy of the Scriptures. The encyclical *Divino afflante* said the opposite.

The work of distributing copies of the Scriptures had been fostered by Pius X in Italy, through the Society of St Jerome, while in England the Catholic Truth Society produced its 'halfpenny gospels' in the nineties. In 1897 Catholic candidates were allowed by the Oxford Local Examination Board to take papers in their own version of the New Testament and manuals for their use were forthcoming. In England, France and Germany much care has been given to the making of new and better versions in the recent past, while Spain has since the end of the civil war done much to promote widespread study of the Scriptures, besides producing the Greek and Latin New Testament of J. Bover, S.J., which with those of Merk and Vogels reaches a high standard of competence. Biblical associations have sprung up, an American one being founded in 1937, which sees to the publication of a *Catholic Biblical Quarterly*, just as the Spanish society does the *Estudios bíblicos*, while the bibliographical service rendered by the periodical of the Biblical Institute (*Biblica*, founded 1920) is valued by all scholars. A revision of the *Dictionnaire de la Bible* (which has covered the letters A–P) while not dealing with many minor topics treats the major questions in a manner quite different from that of Vigouroux and the older editors. In English-speaking countries the appearance in 1953 of the *Catholic Commentary on Holy Scripture* after ten years of patient collaboration marked the end of an epoch, during which Catholics slowly emerging from their catacombs had to struggle to gain knowledge of the Scriptures, and the beginning of a new period, wherein they can hear the Word with joy and study daily to see if these things be so.

The most recent debate among Catholics seeks to clarify the relation of Scripture to Tradition, especially by examining the way in which the decree of Trent on this subject was made (see the first section of this chapter). Professor Geiselmann[1] of Tübingen has drawn attention to the change made in the draft decree, where the words declaring that the truth of Christ's good news was contained *partly* in the Scripture and *partly* in Tradition were changed into a more neutral statement, that it was to be found in the one *and* in the other. He argues from this that the Council rejected, or at least refused to accept, a view of Scripture and Tradition as two separate entities, leaving room for the view (which he has revived from J. E. Kuhn, a disciple of Möhler) that the *whole* of revelation is in the Scripture and the whole equally in Tradition. It is impossible now to show from the *Acta* of Trent why the wording was changed. It was criticized by Bonucci, the Servite General, in the debate of 23 March 1546, but, when a list of doubtful points in the draft was drawn up on 29 March, to be voted on one by one, this was not among them; and yet in the final version of the decree the

[1] H. Bacht, J. R. Geiselmann, H. Fries, *Die mündliche Überlieferung* (Munich, 1957); J. R. Geiselmann, *Die Tradition in der neueren Theologie*, III (Freiburg, 1959); P. Lengsfeld, *Überlieferung, Tradition und Schrift in der evangelischen und katholischen Theologie der Gegenwart* (Paderborn, 1960) (with full bibliography).

change is made. The other phrase in the decree which sums up the relation of Scripture and Tradition is the very core of the decree, where it is said that the Council *receives* (in the legal sense) Scripture and Tradition with equal reverence. This phrase was called impious by Nacchianti, bishop of Chioggia (see above, p. 200), in the final debate of 5 April. In reply, Cardinal de Monte said that he would call in the theologians and, if they supported Nacchianti, the decree would be changed, but, if not, he must apologize to the Council for his words. Pole commented drily that he had prefaced them with *videtur* and so might be excused (*Acta*, I, 45 and V, 72). That night the secretary was busy with the legates until 7 p.m. (*Acta*, I, 533); Ambrose Catharinus was in consultation with them, and the decree was changed.[1] But this phrase that had been called in question by Nacchianti was not changed, and it is hard to see what else *was* changed, save for the *partim*... *partim* phrase. Was this a mere drafting concession, which might seem to satisfy the opposition while leaving intact the substance of the decree? Or was it a change of substance? If the latter, one would expect the other phrase (about receiving both) to be altered too, as it was this phrase that was immediately under fire. As it was left standing in the decree, it must be said that the historical probabilities are against Geiselmann. To receive Scripture and Tradition with equal reverence implies that they are two distinct entities; if they were identical in content, one would expect them to be received with the same reverence (*eadem*, and not *pari*).

On the wider question of how far it can be said that the whole of revelation is in Scripture, Geiselmann does not really advance beyond the position of Bellarmine, for both would admit that every doctrine can be found in Scripture in some generic way at least, Bellarmine saying (*Controversiae*, I, iv, 10) that, as Scripture teaches us to consult the Church in what may be doubtful, it can be said somehow to contain all needful doctrine, and Geiselmann saying that Scripture is *relatively* sufficient, having at least the premisses and connecting links (*Anknüpfungspunkte*) of all dogmas, which are then made explicit by Tradition. The growth in clarity about the spiritual sense of Scripture, which is one of the marks of the present age, may in the future close the gap that still exists between the disputants; it all depends on what one means by *being in* Scripture.

[1] His published works make it clear that Catharinus was opposed to the view that the whole of revealed truth can be found in the Scriptures.

CHAPTER VII

THE CRITICISM AND THEOLOGICAL USE OF THE BIBLE 1700–1950

CRITICISM OF THE TRADITIONAL USE BY RATIONALISTS

It is not unjust to trace the origins of biblical criticism in the modern sense back to the Renaissance. The liberation of men's minds from the dead weight of authority and tradition made it inevitable that, sooner or later, the Bible would cease to be treated, as it had been throughout the Middle Ages, as a supernaturally guaranteed revelation beyond the scope of rational inquiry. The Reformation, in the sense that it was a by-product of the Renaissance, assisted rather than hindered the process, for in their critical approach to the Bible, as in other matters, Luther and Calvin ranged themselves on the side of those who upheld the right of private judgment against an externally imposed authority. 'The Protestant writers against Rome were forging the weapons which were soon to be used against themselves.'[1]

The attempt of their successors to invest the Bible with the authority that the Church had lost was therefore bound to be little more than an ineffective effort to turn back the clock. A new spirit had come into western life and thought which was prepared to challenge every assumption and question every assertion. Men were no longer prepared to limit their inquiries to the narrow confines prescribed by traditional orthodoxy and ecclesiastical protocol. Whether they accepted Reason or the Spirit as their guide they acknowledged as their ultimate criterion nothing but the establishment of the truth.

In 1700 science as we know it today was still in its infancy, but the scientific spirit was already at work. Enough had been established to make it plain that the earth, to say nothing of the universe, was a much

[1] L. Stephen, *English Thought in the Eighteenth Century*, I, 79.

larger place than medieval Europe had imagined. Columbus and Vasco da Gama had brought new territories within men's ken which raised questions both as to the concept of Christendom and the geography of Genesis. Copernicus and Galileo had not only sown seeds of doubt as to the cosmogony of the Pentateuch, but their treatment by the ecclesiastics had reflected on the intellectual integrity of the Church.

Yet it was not until the nineteenth century that science came to play a major role in biblical studies, both as an avowed opponent and as a useful servant. In the eighteenth century too little was known with certainty about the natural world, and too little of what was known appeared to impinge directly upon biblical narratives, to make a frontal attack on the Scriptures primarily scientific in character. Such criticism as the eighteenth century produced arose more from the free play of reason upon the sacred texts in the liberal atmosphere of post-Renaissance Europe. It was the exercise of common sense in an age which prided itself on its enlightenment and which queried the apparent inconsistencies and contradictions, the intellectual absurdities and moral ambiguities of Scripture.

Already in the seventeenth century Bacon and Descartes, while both professing orthodoxy, had raised doubts as to the authority of the Bible, in so far as they insisted on the supremacy of reason as the ultimate criterion. Among the philosophers, Hobbes in his *Leviathan* had disputed the Mosaic authorship of the Pentateuch, and Spinoza had maintained that the Bible must be treated like any other book. Within the Church itself, Peyrère and Richard Simon in France had come to the same conclusion as Hobbes.

But it was above all the work of Pierre Bayle (1647–1707), driven from his native France to Holland, where he spent most of his life, and of John Locke in England (1632–1704), which laid the foundations of eighteenth-century rationalist criticism of the Scriptures. Mark Pattison rightly points out in his essay on 'Tendencies of Religious Thought in England, 1688–1750' that in eighteenth-century English theology 'rationalism' had a vastly different connotation from its later nineteenth-century use which largely obtains up to the present day.

Then it was not a system of beliefs antagonistic to Christianity, but an attitude of mind which assumed that in all matters of religion reason is supreme. 'Rationalism was not an anti-Christian sect outside the Church making war against religion. It was a habit of thought ruling all minds, under the conditions of which all alike tried to make good the peculiar opinions they might happen to cherish. The Churchman differed from the Socinian, and the Socinian from the Deist, as to the number of articles in his creed: but all alike consented to test their belief by the rational evidence for it.'[1]

Bayle, under the subtle guise of defending orthodoxy, made revelation appear so unreasonable that the Deists of the first half of the eighteenth century had more than enough ammunition with which to attack the traditional approach. His *Dictionnaire historique et critique* published in 1697, as well as his lesser works, sought to remove religious beliefs both credal and biblical from the sphere of rational understanding, and, on the pretext of thereby exalting the value of unquestioning faith, made it difficult for people living in an age where reason was prized as the supreme value not to ask whether in fact revealed religion was not unacceptable to civilized man. His method, writes Bréhier, 'consiste à priver de tout point d'appui dans la nature et dans la raison humaines les thèses métaphysiques et religieuses, si bien que, avec une continuelle affectation d'orthodoxie, Bayle les renvoie à la seule autorité divine dont elles se réclament'.[2]

Among these 'thèses religieuses' was the authority of Scripture. 'On emploie l'Ecriture à soutenir le pour et le contre', said Bayle, and took great pains to point out the different interpretation given by Catholics and Protestants to the allegedly authoritative text. With obvious relish he contrasted the moral standards of David, the apple of the Lord's eye, with the behaviour of a virtuous atheist. His pretext of defending the faith deceived few, and his vast scholarship with its sceptical implications made a deep impression not only in Holland but in France and England.

His contemporary, John Locke, was equally influential. His fundamental position is expressed in the well-known quotation from his *Essay on the Human Understanding* (1690).[3]

> Reason is natural revelation, whereby the eternal Father of light and fountain of all knowledge, communicates to mankind that portion of truth which he has laid within the reach of their natural faculties; revelation is natural reason enlarged by a new set of discoveries communicated by God immediately; which reason vouches the truth of, by the testimony and proofs it gives that

[1] *Essays and Reviews* (1860), p. 257.

[2] *Histoire de la Philosophie*, vol. II, part I, p. 300.

[3] IV, 19, para. 4.

they come from God. So that he that takes away reason to make way for revelation, puts out the light of both, and does much what the same as if he would persuade a man to put out his eyes, the better to receive the remote light of an invisible star by a telescope.

As a professedly orthodox Anglican, it was of course part of Locke's business to show that reason and revelation were not opposed. The title of his book on *The Reasonableness of Christianity* might have been adopted as the slogan for the controversy which raged in England for the next half century. Both Deists and churchmen were agreed that reason was the basic criterion. What was disputed was whether, in addition to the natural religion which was common property, there was also a supernatural communication of revealed truth, and if so what were its limits. Within this framework the contest ranged from Hume's rejection of any supernatural element whatever to the orthodox 'hewing and chiselling Christianity into an intelligible human system which they then represented, as thus mutilated, as affording a remarkable evidence of the truth of the Bible'.[1]

Christianity had to be 'proved' to be 'true', and the aspect of the Bible that was of most concern was its credibility. It is significant that the first blast of the trumpet in the Deist camp was sounded by the appearance of a book called *Christianity not Mysterious* in 1696. Its author, John Toland, an Irishman, took the view that there could not possibly be anything mysterious in Christianity since mystery was contrary to reason. Absurdities in the biblical records must therefore be eliminated, and Toland proceeded in his next work to excise those parts of the New Testament which appeared to him to be incomprehensible. For this he came under heavy fire from the orthodox champions of the faith. In his view, however, it was a 'blamable credulity and a temerarious opinion' to believe 'the divinity of the Scripture or the sense of any passage thereof without rational proofs and an evident consistency'.[2]

It was no doubt in an attempt to prevent the rot from spreading that a new statute was enacted in 1698 which directed among other provisos that anyone who 'shall deny the Holy Scriptures of the Old and New

[1] *Tracts for the Times*, vol. II, no. 73. Quoted by Pattison, 'Tendencies of Religious Thought in England, 1688–1750', in *Essays and Reviews* (1860), p. 258.

[2] *Christianity not Mysterious*, p. 37. Quoted by Stephen, *English Thought in the Eighteenth Century*, p. 107.

Testament to be of divine authority' should be debarred from holding public office for the first offence and on the second offence should be sentenced to three years' imprisonment. In Scotland, in the previous year, an able student, Thomas Aikenhead, had been hanged in Edinburgh at the age of eighteen for uttering wild statements such as that Ezra was the author of the Pentateuch, that Moses had learned magic in Egypt and that the Apocalypse was an allegorical book about the philosophers' stone.

Repressive measures of this kind had some effect. Criticism was discouraged for a time although some writers adopted the subterfuge of insisting that since literal interpretation of the Scriptures led to patent absurdities, the Bible must obviously have been meant to be interpreted allegorically. The net result of this was, of course, to draw more attention than ever to the irrational elements in the Old and New Testaments. How could the essentially time-conditioned figure of Jehovah, as presented in the Bible, at worst a Jewish tribal deity, at best the creator and ruler of a midget globe, be reconciled with the God of the philosophers? Addison might be content to see the hand of the 'great Original' in the wonder of the starry heavens and to write:

> What though in solemn silence all
> Move round the dark terrestrial ball?
> What though no real voice nor sound
> Amidst their radiant orbs be found?
> In reason's ear they all rejoice
> And utter forth a glorious voice,
> For ever singing as they shine
> 'The hand that made us is divine'.

But did the same divine hand make clothes for Adam and Eve in the Garden of Eden, muzzle the lions in the den for Daniel's protection, and send the bears which gobbled up children for making fun of Elisha? If this was revealed truth was there any option for thinking men but to reject it?

This was the nub of the Deist controversy as it affected biblical studies. Traditional harmonists like Whiston were prepared to say that 'the creation of the world in six days, the universal deluge and the general conflagration as laid down in the Holy Scriptures' were 'perfectly agreeable to religion and philosophy'. But Whiston was perhaps the last wholehearted supporter of the Chillingworth thesis in his day. Most of the orthodox opponents of Deism not only shared its presuppositions but accompanied its exponents much of the way.

It was an ill-matched contest. On the side of orthodoxy were ranged, after Locke, men of the intellectual calibre of Berkeley and Butler, supported powerfully by Addison, Pope and Swift. Even the lesser lights, Bentley, Clarke, Leland, Law, and the rest, were more than equal to all that the Deists could produce in the way of champions, except Shaftesbury and Bolingbroke. Stephen claims that on the side of Christianity there 'appeared all that was intellectually venerable in England' and dismisses the Deists as 'a ragged regiment, whose whole ammunition of learning was a trifle when compared with the abundant stores of a single light of orthodoxy'.[1]

Nevertheless, it was the contribution of less notable members of the 'ragged regiment' like Collins, Woolston, Tindal, Dodwell and Middleton, rather than the more powerful names of Shaftesbury, who did not concern himself much with biblical questions, and Bolingbroke, whose contribution was made when the battle was nearly over, which put orthodoxy on its mettle and rightly brought to the light of day and into the fierce heat of controversy many critical questions regarding the Scriptures which had hitherto been avoided.

The net result of the Deist controversy, as it affected Holy Scripture, was to leave the traditional view of the authority of the Bible in a much weakened position. It is of little moment that on paper the victory went to orthodoxy. Its champions were abler and it was supported by the powerful assistance of law, tradition and convention. But to bandy about the sacred texts in public dispute, and to make the Scriptures the small change of pamphleteers, was at once to unseat the Bible from the pedestal on which it had been placed in the seventeenth century. The awe and reverence with which its exaltation into the seat of infallible authority had surrounded it were soon tarnished in the rough and tumble of debate.

Even if every argument of the Deists had been routed, whether by taking refuge in allegorism or by refuting it with superior dialectic, the damage had been done. Something that had been largely sacrosanct had been discussed, attacked and defended as if it were some common man-made philosophy. Orthodoxy, at the end of the battle, stood firmly entrenched behind its battlements, but the breaches in the walls had

[1] *English Thought in the Eighteenth Century*, p. 87.

been repaired with such makeshift materials that a few well-placed shots in the next engagement would lay its defences wide open. New and more deadly enemies in the shape of science and higher criticism were already on the march. But first the details of the preliminary skirmish with the Deists must be recorded.

Anthony Collins, a country gentleman of mild temper with some pretensions to scholarship, and who was much influenced by Locke and Bayle, was already known as a controversial writer when he drew upon his head a storm of abuse from Bentley and Swift by his *Discourse of Freethinking* published in 1713. Collins, as a good Deist, advocated freedom of inquiry and religious tolerance, at the same time deploring superstition, with which, at least by implication, he coupled supernaturalism of any kind. One of the pillars of his argument for liberty of opinion was the vast variety of possible interpretations of Scripture, and, although his orthodox opponents denied his conclusions and dubbed him an atheist, they had to concede that the older Protestant view of verbal inspiration was no longer tenable. Collins retreated to Holland to avoid the Olympian thunder of his formidable opponents, but returned to the fray ten years later with a much more damaging attack on the traditionalists. This was his *Discourse of the Grounds and Reasons of the Christian Religion* published in 1724.

It was a reply to an extraordinary effusion from the pen of William Whiston, whose undoubted eminence as a professor of mathematics was not matched by his dabblings in the field of theology. He had written an *Essay towards restoring the true Text of the Old Testament and for vindicating the Citations made thence in the New Testament* (1722), in which he had attempted to account for the fact that many of the Old Testament prophecies quoted in the New Testament had apparently had a meaning imposed on them which they did not originally have.

This, according to Whiston, indicated that the text of the Old Testament had at some point after the apostolic age been tampered with by Jewish enemies of Christ, who had altered the prophecies in such a way that they should not seem to imply what the New Testament writers claimed that they did imply.[1] By adducing evidence from various sources, but largely by his own conjectures, Whiston attempted to 'restore' the Old Testament texts to their original form, thereby

[1] Cf. above p. 10.

ensuring that the prophecies quoted in the Gospels and Epistles harmonized completely with the Messianic interpretation given to them.

Collins had no difficulty in exposing the absurdity of Whiston's methods, but his main purpose was more radical. He insisted that the truth of Christianity must stand or fall by its fulfilment of prophecy. If the events recorded in the Gospels were not in fact accurately foretold in the inspired words of the prophets then Christianity had no validity. But then Collins went on to point out, so far in agreement with Whiston, that the prophecies quoted in the New Testament did not bear the sense which Christianity had imposed on them. We must conclude, therefore, and here he parted company with Whiston, that they were never intended to be taken literally but allegorically. But having made this apparently innocuous claim, Collins went on so successfully to expose the extravagances of allegorism and, with his tongue in his cheek, to show how easily the most unlikely Old Testament prophecies could be twisted into clear prognostications of New Testament events, that it was quite obvious that his real intention was not to confirm the authority of Scripture but to shake it.

His *Discourse* provoked no fewer than thirty-five treatises in reply, mostly from stout defenders of the literalist standpoint. The debate raged fast and furious. Collins struck back with his *Literal Scheme of Prophecy considered* and obviously derived great enjoyment from the controversy he had started. Perhaps his most significant contribution, from the angle of biblical criticism, was his recognition that the book of Daniel is not a forecast of post-exilic history but a contemporary document written during the reign of Antiochus Epiphanes.

The traditional view of the Bible was attacked from a different quarter by Thomas Woolston, a fellow of Sidney Sussex College, Cambridge. There is some evidence that he was mentally unbalanced, but his six *Discourses on the Miracles of our Saviour*, published between 1727 and 1729, sold 30,000 copies and evoked sixty pamphlets in reply. It is difficult to know what to make of these *Discourses*. They do not read like the arguments of a sane man, but they were so judged by the churchmen who attempted to refute them, and by the court which fined Woolston £100 and sentenced him to a year's imprisonment.

Like Collins, Woolston advocated the allegorical interpretation of Scripture but for different reasons. He maintained bluntly that, regarded as historical events, the miracles of the New Testament were so fantastic that no reasonable person could believe them possible. The only truth in the miracle stories was spiritual truth. Having therefore made the claim that he is a true believer, with Origen and Augustine as his mentors, and that he is an enemy only of those who would interpret the Bible literally, he can proceed to make the most outrageous assertions about the Gospel narratives.

He comments on the healing of the Gadarene Demoniac: If Jesus had been accused of bewitching a flock of sheep as he did the swine, 'our laws, and judges, too, of the last age would have made him to swing for it'.[1] The Cursing of the Fig Tree makes him ask: 'What if a yeoman of Kent should go to look for pippins in his orchard at Easter and because of a disappointment cut down his trees? What then would his neighbours make of him? Nothing less than a laughing stock; and if the story got into our Publick News, he would be the jest and ridicule of mankind.'[2]

The reference to the angel in the story of the miracle at the Pool of Bethesda moves him to remark: 'An odd and a merry way of conferring a Divine mercy. And one would think that the angels of God did this for their own diversion more than to do good to mankind. Just as some throw a bone among a kennel of hounds for the pleasure of seeing them quarrel for it, or as others cast a piece of money among a company of boys for the sport of seeing them scramble for it, so was the pastime of the angels here.'[3] Jesus behaves like a 'strolling fortune-teller', and some might even conclude that he and his mother were probably drunk at the Wedding Feast in Cana, and that the Resurrection was a cleverly managed fraud on the part of the disciples.

As opposed to these grotesque conclusions, which he alleged to be inevitable if we treat these stories as in any sense historical, Woolston argued that the only possible approach to the miracles was to treat them as allegories of the mystical union between Christ and the believer. Whether he really did so regard them, or whether he was a complete sceptic, it is hard to say. What is quite certain is that many to whom it had never occurred to doubt the divine character of the works of Jesus, and the inspired record of them in Holy Scripture, were shaken in their belief, and found themselves asking questions which orthodoxy had difficulty in answering.

[1] *Disc.* I, 34. Quoted by Stephen, *English Thought in the Eighteenth Century*, p. 232.
[2] *Disc.* III, 7.
[3] *Disc.* III, 43.

Bishop Smalbroke, for example, can scarcely be said to have offered an adequate solution to the problem of the miracle of the Gadarene Demoniac by saying that the purpose of the transference of the demons from the madman to the swine was to terrify the local inhabitants for their lack of faith 'so that even this permission of Jesus to the evil spirits was amply compensated by casting a whole legion of devils out of one person—that is, by suffering about three of them to enter into each hog, instead of about six thousand of them keeping possession of one man'.[1] The same bishop, in answering Woolston's disbelief in the power of faith to remove mountains, quotes a series of examples from the Fathers of mountains having been removed, concluding with testimony from Marco Polo that a Christian in Persia removed a mountain at 'a very critical juncture'.

Another typical contribution from the side of Deism came from Matthew Tindal, a fellow of All Souls, Oxford, who published in 1730 the first volume of a work called *Christianity as Old as the Creation*. The manuscript of the second volume which would have appeared posthumously was suppressed by a wary bishop,[2] who doubtless thought that enough damage had been done already. Tindal expressed at length the basic difficulty of eighteenth-century rationalism, that of reconciling any form of historical religion with the austere and impersonal concept of an Almighty Creator, Ruler and Lawgiver. How can this Supreme Being be accommodated with one who according to the current Christian doctrine chose to reveal his nature and purpose in an obscure corner of the earth to a barbaric tribe, and in a series of trivial and sometimes outrageous laws and anecdotes?

True Christianity, said Tindal, is surely essentially reasonable. It consists of the simple truths that are common to all religions. The Gospel and the natural law are one and the same, and any suggestion of a special revelation through the Bible is superfluous. Since true religion means 'doing good' we may well find better guidance in Confucius than in the Sermon on the Mount.

If revealed religion satisfies reason it may be accepted, and in so far as it conforms to this standard Christianity is 'as Old as the Creation'. But in so far as the Old Testament advocates such 'unreasonable' practices as circumcision and animal sacrifice, records such 'unreason-

[1] *Vindication of Miracles*, p. 203. Quoted by Stephen, *English Thought in the Eighteenth Century*, p. 235.

[2] Gibson of London.

able' stories as that of Balaam's talking ass, or Elijah preventing rain, or holds up for our approval massacres of Israel's enemies, it may safely be discarded as superstition and priestcraft. In a more guarded way Tindal disposes of those doctrines of the Church which were based on 'unreasonable' New Testament evidence. 'It's an odd jumble', he says, 'to prove the truth of a book by the truth of the doctrine it contains, and at the same time to conclude those doctrines to be true because contained in that book.'[1] Tindal's thesis elicited no fewer than one hundred and fifty replies, many of them content to point out the more obvious flaws in his argument while accepting most of his premises, which was a fair indication of how far orthodoxy was prepared to travel along the same road as the Deists.

After the Tindal controversy, the excitement caused by the attack of the Deists on the authority and infallibility of the Bible tended to die down. Deism itself fell into disrepute, perhaps not so much because its advocates had been routed by abler disputants on the side of orthodoxy, but because it was a barren and colourless creed which took insufficient account of the facts of history and experience. In the field of biblical criticism, however, it had raised doubts and started inquiries which were not so easily answered, and which were continued under other than Deist auspices as the eighteenth century advanced.

Little new was added by Thomas Chubb, a decent tallow-chandler from Salisbury, who surprised everyone by writing a large number of Deistic tracts of quite considerable merit. He had much to say by way of criticism of the narratives of both Old and New Testaments, and denied the literal inspiration of the Scriptures. But as he boasted that he knew neither Latin nor Greek, to say nothing of Hebrew, his critical apparatus was obviously not of the highest order. Thomas Morgan, a physician who was writing about the year 1740, has some harsh things to say about that 'most grossly ignorant, and most stupid people' Israel, a priest-ridden, superstitious race. These same Jews corrupted the Gospel of Christ, which was the 'pure religion of nature', despite all the efforts of Paul, whom Morgan describes as 'the great free thinker of that age, and the bold and brave defender of reason against authority'. We are perhaps not surprised to learn after these remarks that 'true Christianity' was carried on by the Gnostics!

[1] *Christianity as Old as the Creation*, p. 164. Quoted by Bury, *History of Freedom of Thought*, p. 144.

Henry Dodwell, in his *Christianity not founded on Argument* (1741), attacked the presupposition of many churchmen that all that was wrong with Deism was that it went too far. Dodwell claimed that reason had very little to do with Christianity. The latter had to be accepted as a matter of faith. Christ and the apostles did not argue the early Christians into the Faith, they bade them accept it. Reason and authority of this kind are incompatible. It is therefore absurd for Christian divines to claim that if reason is allowed free rein men will generally accept the biblical revelation and the dogmas dependent on it.

Certainly Peter Annet would have claimed that reason and faith were like oil and water. In a pamphlet published in 1744 called *The Resurrection of Jesus examined by a Moral Philosopher*, he has no doubt as a dispassionate inquirer that the Gospel narratives are hopelessly contradictory, the apostles completely unreliable, and the event wholly incredible. Conyers Middleton, a parson with strong leanings towards Deism, may be said to have closed this stage of the controversy between biblical orthodoxy and rationalism. In 1748 he published his *Free Inquiry into the Miraculous Powers which are supposed to have existed in the Christian Church through several successive Ages*. His avowed aim was to query the existence of miracles in general in the history of the Church but, by asking the pertinent question as to when the Church ceased to have the power to work miracles, he encouraged more radical minds to question the validity of biblical miracle stories as well.

The Deist controversy had undoubtedly shaken the traditional view of the authority of Scripture. Few were prepared to go all the way with violent critics like Woolston and Annet, but few on the other hand were still prepared to claim that every word of the Bible must be accepted literally. Allegorism provided a convenient loophole. Churchmen and Deists would differ as to the extent to which the records exhibited flaws and inconsistencies but few on either side would have denied the validity of the concept of revelation or the right of reason to examine it. Natural and revealed religion continued to exist in uneasy association. It was left to the second half of the century to produce more far-reaching attacks and a more radical scepticism than anything the Deists had ventured.

Joseph Butler (1692–1752), the Church's ablest apologist against Deism, seems himself to have contributed unwittingly to the rise of this deeper scepticism. He attempted to defend the validity of revealed truth by drawing attention to the unsatisfactory aspects of natural religion. There are doubtless problems for the rational man within the field of the biblical revelation, he argued, but there are no fewer problems when we examine the natural order. Butler's own deduction from this was that we must be content to confess our ignorance of the ways of God in both cases and acknowledge that we are in the presence of mystery beyond our understanding. It was, however, equally possible to draw another conclusion, namely, that if neither revelation nor reason could indicate a completely just and beneficent providential order, one might ask, Was there any good and all-wise Providence at all?

David Hume (1711–76), for example, could see nothing beyond a 'blind nature, impregnated by a great vivifying principle, and pouring forth from her lap, without discernment or parental care, her maimed and abortive children'.[1] The God of the Old Testament is merely the product of anthropomorphism and superstition, and the biblical miracles, like all others, to demonstrating the impossibility of which Hume devoted an essay, are simply based on mistaken evidence.

The brilliant irony of Edward Gibbon (1737–94) did not fail to accomplish what he obviously intended, namely, to discount the supernatural character of Christian origins. In particular, the miraculous elements in the Gospel narrative came in for his sardonic comment. Orthodoxy, however, was persuaded with Paley (1743–1805) that a Divine Watchmaker was capable of inserting a screwdriver from time to time to speed up or slow down the mechanism which he had started.

Eighteenth-century rationalism in England ended with a large volley from the blunderbuss of Tom Paine whose *Age of Reason* began to appear in 1793. His chief significance is not that he added anything new to the arguments of his predecessors, but that he said it in a way that the ordinary man could understand. He made no pretensions to scholarship, indeed he confessed that when he wrote the first part of his book he did not even possess a Bible. When he did eventually procure a copy he found it 'much worse than he had conceived'.

He railed in crude terms against the equally crude presentation of the Bible with which he was familiar. 'Whence could arise the solitary and strange conceit that the Almighty, who had millions of worlds equally

[1] *Dialogues concerning Natural Religion*, II, 446. Quoted by Stephen, *English Thought in the Eighteenth Century*, p. 328.

dependent on his perfections, should quit the universe and come to die in our world because they say one man and one woman had eaten an apple?'[1] Of the Old Testament he writes: 'When we read the obscure stories, the cruel and barbarous executions, the unrelenting vindictiveness with which more than half the Bible is filled, it would be more consistent that we called it the work of a demon than the word of God. It is a history of wickedness that has served to corrupt and brutalise mankind: and for my own part I sincerely detest it, as I detest everything that is cruel.'[2] The New Testament is similarly dismissed. He confesses that he has never found anywhere 'so many and such glaring absurdities, contradictions and falsehoods as are in these books'.[3]

The *Age of Reason* was a much headier mixture and, in the eyes of orthodoxy, a more dangerous portent than the contemporary biblical criticism of Unitarians like Priestley (1733–1804), who put the New Testament writers on a level with Thucydides and Tacitus, or Evanson (1731–1805), who dismissed most of the New Testament itself as either unintelligible or immoral. It is perhaps not surprising that Bishop Watson entitled his reply to Paine *An Apology for the Bible* (1796), and although George III is said to have commented that he 'was not aware that any apology was needed for that book',[4] the State was so alarmed at the effect which Paine's book was having on the masses that his publishers were heavily fined and sent to prison.

While the biblical experts of the period contented themselves with an examination of the 'Evidences' in an attempt to prove the integrity and authenticity of the records, and while, as Johnson put it, that type of Old Bailey theology flourished in which the apostles were being tried once a week for the capital crime of forgery,[5] the second half of the eighteenth century had brought to light a sharper and more uncompromising opposition to orthodoxy than anything the Deists had offered. Unlike the earlier decades of the century, however, the heavy artillery was this time not on the side of the angels. Hume, Gibbon and, in his own turbulent way, Paine, were more than a match for churchmen who either felt themselves obliged to defend a thesis in which they did not wholeheartedly believe, or who were bigoted enough to refuse

1 *Age of Reason*, I, 44. 2 *Ibid.* p. 13.

3 *Ibid.* II, 74. Quoted by Stephen, *English Thought in the Eighteenth Century*, pp. 460–2.

4 Bury, *History of Freedom of Thought*, p. 171.

5 Pattison, 'Tendencies of Religious Thought in England, 1688–1750', in *Essays and Reviews* (1860), p. 260.

to recognize that there was any case to answer. Most of them well deserved Gibbon's verdict on them, as opponents 'victory over whom was a sufficient humiliation'.

It was in this second half of the eighteenth century that across the Channel the most devastating campaign of all was waged by the redoubtable Voltaire. It is said of him that at the age of three his godfather, an abbé, taught him a poem in which Moses in particular and religious revelations in general were derided as fraudulent.[1] The lesson was taught to an apt pupil. Voltaire absorbed not only all that Bayle could teach him, but was also profoundly influenced by Locke and the English Deists. His battle against intolerance and superstition was waged in the more repressive atmosphere of Catholic France and he brought all the power of his satirical pen to bear upon the 'infamy' which Christianity, as he knew it, was perpetrating on men's minds. Voltaire was a Deist, but there was no room in his Deism for any compromise with the Christian revelation, which he described as an 'absurd and sanguinary creed, supported by executions and surrounded by fiery faggots'.

The Bible did not escape his shafts. He notes geographical contradictions in the Old Testament and remarks: 'God was evidently not strong in geography.' In the drama of *Saul* (1763) he pours scorn on David and Samuel, the men of God, contrasting them unfavourably with Saul and Agag. When Samuel accuses Saul of failing to exterminate the Amalekites, Agag asks him: 'Your god commanded you? You are mistaken. You mean your devil.'

Anti-Christian Deism of this kind expounded by such a brilliant advocate, or even its milder form as professed by Rousseau, led inevitably to the atheism of Holbach, Diderot and the Encyclopaedists, but the Revolution soon faced France with more existential issues than biblical criticism. In Germany, on the other hand, it was the Aufklärung, under the influence of English Deism, and stimulated by the patronage of Frederick the Great, who surrounded himself with French rationalists, among them pre-eminently Voltaire, which directly fathered the rise of that radical type of 'higher' biblical criticism of which Strauss and Baur became the prime exponents. Edelmann, who attacked the concept of inspiration, and Bahrdt whose *Letters on the Bible* followed the normal rationalist pattern, ought to be mentioned

[1] J. M. Robertson, *Short History of Freethought*, p. 337.

in this connection, together with Herder, Reimarus and Lessing, who were pioneers of the later and more scientific critical approach.

Despite the fact that at the height of the Deist controversy the two opposing factions had bombarded each other with gusto, the conflict between rationalism and orthodoxy in the eighteenth century had been on the whole an unimpassioned intellectual battle of wits. In an age that was marked by an absence of enthusiasm, and by a common acceptance of the paramount authority of reason, the two sides had too much in common to make either feel that the issues were matters of life and death. True, there was legislative restraint on the more outrageous utterances of the Deists. Fines and imprisonment were not unknown. But on the whole the controversy leaves us with the impression of having witnessed a polite disputation between educated and comfortable contestants, most of whom were prepared to admit that much could be said on both sides.

The Deists after all believed in a God who was not much more abstract than the kind of God who was proclaimed from many pulpits. Churchmen, too, shared the slightly superior attitude of all polished and civilized Europeans towards the crude ongoings of Levantine nomads. Nor were they any happier about the moral ambiguity of many of the acts of the patriarchs, kings and prophets of Jehovah's people.

They fought for the view of the Scriptures which they had inherited as men defending a cause for which they must apologize, waging war with their heads but not with their hearts. Of course they maintained the supreme authority of the Bible, its inspiration and infallibility, and the primacy of revealed religion. But they had modified these claims with so many reservations and qualifications, that by the end of the controversy the words no longer meant what Chillingworth and his generation had understood by them. The religion of Protestants was no longer simply the Bible, but the Bible as understood by moderate and cultivated men, who were prepared to find ways and means of smoothing the rough edges of this slightly embarrassing bedfellow. As Gibbon said of their attitude to the articles of faith, they 'subscribed with a sigh or a smile'.

By the beginning of the nineteenth century, however, a reaction had set in in England. Orthodoxy had seen the red light. In the latter decades of the century, the opposition had ceased to skirmish on the flanks and had struck at the centre of the line. Hume and Gibbon, especially the latter, had done grave damage to the prestige of the Christian faith. Across the Channel, the violence of the French Revolution, with its anticlericalism and political radicalism, was an alarming portent of the times. It was one thing for a reasonable English churchman to denounce the errors of popery; it was quite another thing to see blatant secularism enthroned in place of a Christian monarchy.

It was this basic fear of the overthrow of the established order in Church and State which accounted for the fury of the opposition to Paine's *Age of Reason*. The Revolution had come to England! Atheism was being fed to the masses! Bishop Watson and his moderate friends might be content to answer this challenge with an *Apology*, but most churchmen felt that a more proper reply was to repair as quickly as possible the damaged fabric of Creed and Bible by a reassertion of the principle of authority, which in the case of the Bible meant a more intransigent conception of its divine inspiration. When the very basis of Christian civilization was being threatened abroad, and similar tendencies had begun to manifest themselves at home, it was high time to have done with apologetic and, with the help of the State, to ensure that Church and Bible recovered their old place as the pillars of English society.

These prudential considerations would, however, have made little headway had they not been supported by the genuine religious dynamic of the Evangelical Revival. It would be safe to say that Wesley, Whitefield and their disciples were as little influenced by a concern for the maintenance of the established social structure as they were moved to provide an antidote to Hume and Gibbon. They were bent on revitalizing the dry bones of the Church by the power of the Spirit, bringing men face to face with Christ, and reforming the godless ways of contemporary society. Their preaching of a full-blooded salvation, with heaven and hell, grace and damnation, went hand in hand with a literal acceptance of the Scriptures as the very Word of God. They had neither time nor place for those dilettante questions which interested the Deists and their orthodox opponents. Here was the Gospel, kindling men's hearts, changing their lives, winning their souls. Who cared, amid these mighty evidences of God's presence, in this day of Pentecostal miracle, to linger over academic wrangles about the Bible that could not save a single soul from sin?

So the religious life of England was carried into the nineteenth century on a new note of enthusiasm, and with a personal living faith that for the most part ignored the questions that Deism had properly asked about the historical basis of that faith, and that were to be raised again from a new angle by the more powerful and persistent voices that were already audible in the field of natural science.

CRITICISM OF THE TRADITIONAL USE BY SCIENTISTS

The nineteenth century cannot lay claim to be called the beginning of the scientific age on the ground that it was only then that men began to study Nature and to discover its secrets. Men had been doing that from the beginning of history, and the myths of ancient peoples were often concerned with this very problem of accounting for the mysteries that surrounded them. But it was only in the nineteenth century that it came to be recognized that man cannot be treated as a separate entity from the world in which he lives, that he is subject to the same physical laws and processes as govern the universe, and that 'scientific methods of observation, induction, deduction and experiment are applicable, not only to the original subject matter of pure science, but to nearly all the many and varied fields of human thought and activity'.[1]

This recognition proved to be a two-edged sword as far as biblical studies were concerned. For while it led on the one hand to the wholly desirable application of scientific method to the study of the sacred texts, and the fruitful results of textual and literary criticism, it also produced a head-on clash between 'Science' and 'Religion' which generated more heat than light, and did much to stultify the beneficial effect which scientific biblical scholarship ought to have had. Although this controversy is now almost a century old, and the issue with which it was mainly concerned was already settled in favour of science before the battle started, its echoes have lamentably persisted to the present day and religion has suffered incalculable harm from the myopic attempts of some of its more obscurantist devotees to regard the battle as still in progress and science as an enemy which must still be resisted.

The scientific insights and discoveries of Copernicus, Galileo and Kepler had been accommodated to Scripture by a process of reinterpretation. Seventeenth-century men of science, and most contemporary

[1] Dampier-Whetham, *History of Science*, p. 217.

philosophers, saw no conflict between scientific thought and religious belief. Descartes, when accused of having devised so perfect a theory of cosmic mechanism that Providence was no longer necessary, claimed that the mathematical laws of nature had been laid down by God. Even Hobbes, who dismissed religious beliefs as superstition, and based his philosophy only on what natural science had established, still wanted to retain the Bible as the foundation of a religion which should be enforced by the State. 'The fundamental theistic assumption was made by all enquirers not for the purposes of apologetic, but because it was regarded as one of the universally accepted data with which any theory of the cosmos to be true must necessarily conform.'[1]

In the following century, which may well be called the age of Newton (1642–1727), it was not the master or his disciples who were responsible for converting his scientific conclusions into a basis for a mechanical philosophy. Many of the French Encyclopaedists chose to interpret Newton in this way, and we may recall Laplace's reply to Napoleon, who commented that in his *Mécanique Céleste*, based on Newton's *Principia*, he had not even mentioned the Creator: 'Je n'avais pas besoin de cette hypothèse-là.' Newton himself, however, held that all his research served only to enhance the wonder of the universe and the wisdom of its Creator, and in England, after his day, both churchmen and Deists subscribed to this verdict.

Thus scientific thought and revealed religion, liberally interpreted, were able to exist side by side. It was perhaps the English genius for compromise which made this possible in a way which the more logical minds of the French could not fathom. Even with the swing back to biblical orthodoxy which took place in the first half of the nineteenth century, it does not appear that churchmen regarded the revolution in scientific thought which was taking place in the fields of mathematics, physics and chemistry as in any way incompatible with a firm adherence to the doctrine of the verbal inspiration of Holy Scripture. There was admittedly an alarming growth of materialism, which was felt to be traceable partly to the practical science which had brought about the industrial revolution, and partly to continental influence, which in its turn was the fruit of the impact of scientific thought upon philosophy, but on the whole science and religion continued in uneasy association for several decades.

[1] Dampier-Whetham, *History of Science*, p. 162.

There were, however, more formidable opponents than mathematicians and physicists still to be encountered. It might be possible to maintain that the biblical view of God and man had been unaffected by Copernicus's dethronement of the earth from its pre-eminence in the universe, or by Newton's recognition that the heavens were subject to the same mechanical laws as could be observed in everyday experience, but a like ambivalence was excluded in the fields of geology and biology, where new knowledge came into such obvious conflict with the text of Holy Scripture that a clash could not be avoided. Indeed it is probably true to say that for the ordinary man, then as now, what the astronomers, physicists and mathematicians had to say about the nature of the universe was so abstruse that it made little difference to his traditional ways of thought. He still regarded mankind as the sole purpose of creation and this planet as the centre of the universe, as the plain words of the Bible had taught him.

But when geologists began to make assertions about the age of the rocks which were clearly incompatible with the chronology of Genesis, or when biologists claimed that man was the end product of a vast evolutionary process, involving the whole animal kingdom, and not the result of a unique creative act of God, this was no longer a matter for academic discussion but a frontal attack on revealed truth, in which every ordinary Christian believer felt himself to be involved.

Whatever reservations may have existed in the minds of the learned, the simple church member had no doubt that the universe and its inhabitants had been created in six days as described at the beginning of Genesis, and to be more precise, as John Lightfoot of Cambridge had calculated from the biblical data in 1642, that the creation of man had taken place at 9 a.m. on 23 October in the year 4004 B.C. The poet Cowper expressed the resentment of the ordinary churchman against the claims of the geologists when he wrote:

> Some drill and bore
> The solid earth, and from the strata there
> Extract a register, by which we learn,
> That he who made it, and revealed its date
> To Moses, was mistaken in its age.

If therefore geologists discovered fossils which pointed to a vastly different conclusion about the age of the earth it must be that God or perhaps the Devil had hidden them there to test men's faith. Geology, however, like Laplace, had no need of that hypothesis. Already before the end of the seventeenth century John Ray had maintained that fossils were not *lusus naturae* but remains of living organisms, that their presence indicated that the earth's surface had undergone prodigious changes, and had suggested that it would be difficult to reconcile these facts with the Genesis version of Creation.

This particular argument does not appear to have featured in the biblical controversies of the eighteenth century, however, and it was not until the cumulative evidence produced by Hutton, Cuvier, Lamarck and, above all, Lyell showed beyond all possible doubt that the antiquity of the earth was a scientific fact and that life had existed upon it for countless ages, that it became obvious that the biblical account of Creation was unhistorical.

Sir Charles Lyell in his *Principles of Geology*, first published in 1830–3, tried hard to accommodate his geological findings to the Genesis stories by postulating a succession of creative acts. Cuvier had up to a point succeeded in allaying the fears of the faithful by his theory that the earth had suffered a series of violent cataclysms which had altered its surface and destroyed its inhabitants. This appeared to make it possible to accept the Genesis story of the Flood, although it was not easy to reconcile it with a six-day Creation. In 1863, however, Lyell published his *Evidence of the Antiquity of Man*, in which he presented decisive proof of the existence of the human race on this planet long before the biblical chronology allowed. Again it was possible to adjust the interpretation of Genesis in the case of the earth itself and other forms of life by expanding the six 'days' into six 'ages', but in the case of man the statutory date had been fixed at 4004 B.C.

The net result of geological evidence was undoubtedly to shake the current acceptance of the infallibility of Scripture, but it did not finally dispose of the possibility that, at some remote point in pre-history, Adam and Eve had been specifically created, as the Bible recorded, to inaugurate the human race. It was left to the biologists, and above all to Charles Darwin, to remove that last prop from the tottering structure of scriptural orthodoxy.

Meanwhile it is an indication of the growing alarm among Christian people over the upsetting of traditional views by developments in the field of science, that the Earl of Bridgewater in 1839 bequeathed a large sum of money to the President of the Royal Society, to provide for a series of treatises to be written by experts in theology and science, demonstrating that the Christian revelation and the new knowledge were not incompatible.

It was unfortunate for the purpose of the bequest that the contribution of one of the scholars, William Buckland, the geologist, raised more controversy than it allayed by throwing overboard the traditional cosmogony and dating of the Creation, declaring that the Bible did not contain 'historical information respecting all the operations of the Creator', and insisting that in view of the clearly established age of the earth and the obvious development that had taken place upon it, the Genesis narrative could not be precisely reconciled with the findings of science. But even without Buckland's contribution, there was so much diversity of opinion among the authors of the treatises that they tended only to increase the general bewilderment.[1] The years 1859 and 1871 are of peculiar significance in the Science-*versus*-Religion controversy regarding the historicity of the early chapters of Genesis. In 1859 appeared Darwin's *Origin of Species* and in 1871 his *Descent of Man*. It may serve to explain something of the violent reaction which they produced, the passion with which churchmen sought to rebut their arguments, and the general consternation they caused to simple people, if we notice the views of two responsible, and presumably representative, ecclesiastics in these very years.

In 1859 the subject of the Bampton Lectures was 'The Historical Evidences of the Truth of the Scripture Records'. Their author, Canon George Rawlinson, spoke of the revolution that had taken place in 'the whole world of profane history' due to the science of historical criticism. Scholars in that field had made it plain that it was no longer possible to treat 'the campaigns of Caesar and the doings of Romulus, the account of Alexander's marches and the conquests of Semiramis' as being on the same level of historical value. 'The views of the ancient world formerly entertained have been in ten thousand points either modified or reversed.'

But did this revolution of thought apply to that part of ancient history which recorded the story of Israel's beginnings? Most certainly not. It was quite clear from the chronology of Genesis that there were only five steps between Adam and Moses. A nation could quite easily

[1] C. E. Raven, *Natural Religion and Christian Theology*, I, 173–4.

retain its traditions for five generations. Thus 'Moses might, by mere oral tradition, have obtained the history of Abraham and even of the Deluge at third hand; and that of the Temptation and the Fall at fifth hand.' We may conclude, therefore, that 'we possess in the Pentateuch not only the most authentic account of ancient times that has come down to us, but a history absolutely and in every respect true'.

In 1871 the bishop of Ely, writing in the *Speaker's Commentary* on the book of Genesis, gave it as his considered view that 'the history of Creation in Gen. i–ii. 3 was very probably the ancient primeval record of the formation of the world' which 'may even have been communicated to the first man in his innocence'.[1]

It is not to be wondered at, therefore, that the combined effect of Darwin's two volumes, as significant a landmark in the history of scientific thought as Newton's *Principia*, and coming as they did as the climax of what ultra-conservative religious opinion could only regard as a series of diabolical attempts on the part of the scientists to discredit the Bible, the Church and God, was to rally to the side of the traditional view of Genesis not only those who were afraid to face new and disturbing ideas, but honest believers, clerical and lay, who felt that if Darwin were proved right and Genesis were proved wrong, then the majesty of God and the dignity of man had gone for ever, and the whole Christian scheme of salvation would collapse like a house of cards.

Thus Bishop Wilberforce roundly declared that the 'principle of natural selection is incompatible with the Word of God'. Mr Gladstone thundered: 'Upon the grounds of what is called evolution God is relieved of the labour of creation, and in the name of unchangeable laws is discharged from governing the world.' Less exalted but equally outraged believers echoed the impassioned *cri du cœur* of one of their spokesmen: 'Leave me my ancestors in Paradise and I will allow you yours in the Zoological Gardens.'

Yet much of what Darwin said was not new, and none of it was intended as an attack on the Christian religion. It would seem as if the explosion was caused by a growing tendency to arrogance on the part of some scientists, and an increasing sense on the part of churchmen that they were fighting a losing battle against science.

Buffon, in France, had ventured the opinion a century before that

[1] J. Estlin Carpenter, *The Bible in the Nineteenth Century*, pp. 455–7.

'had it not been for the express statements of the Bible, one might be tempted to seek a common origin for the horse and the ass, the man and the monkey'.[1] Indeed the idea of some kind of evolutionary process in nature was as old as the Greek philosophers. Revived at the Renaissance, it had been ventilated by philosophers from Bacon to Herbert Spencer, and by naturalists before Darwin from Buffon to Chambers, including Darwin's own grandfather, Erasmus Darwin.

But it was the genius of Charles Darwin himself which found in Malthus's *Essay on Population* the clue which led him to combine the principle of evolution with the theory of natural selection. Here then seemed to be the answer to the mystery of origins which had for so long baffled both science and philosophy. Here, it was felt, was an explanation which was at once rational and scientific, which tallied with the findings of the geologists, and which in the eyes of all who were not blinded by dogmatic assumptions disposed once and for all of such unsatisfactory premises as a six-day creation in 4004 B.C., a universal Deluge, a literal Adam and Eve, and as a corollary, the historical character of the early chapters of Genesis.

No one was more surprised than Darwin himself at the acclaim with which his *Origin of Species* was received. He had modestly anticipated a sale of 1250 copies. These were in fact sold out on the day of publication. The appearance of the *Origin of Species* has been variously described as a flash of lightning or a bolt from the blue. The preface to the German translation asked the almost apocalyptic question: 'How will it be with you, dear reader, after you have read this book?' It was as if the keystone had at last been placed on the edifice that science had been so patiently building, or as if the last piece of the jig-saw puzzle had now been supplied.

Many hailed the book because it expressed clearly and systematically ideas that had long been taking shape in their minds. T. H. Huxley was not speaking for himself alone when he said: 'The *Origin*...did the immense service of freeing us forever from the dilemma—Refuse to accept the Creation hypothesis, and what have you to propose that can be accepted by any cautious reasoner? In 1857 I had no answer ready, and I do not think that anyone else had. A year later we reproached ourselves with dullness for being perplexed with such an enquiry. My reflection when I first made myself master of the central idea of the

[1] Dampier-Whetham, *History of Science*, p. 201.

Origin, was, "How extremely stupid not to have thought of that!"'[1] Not only Huxley but 'the world was weary of unquestioning faith in Genesis, and was hungry for explanations'.[2]

Many, in the tradition of Hume and Paine, welcomed Darwinism because it appeared to drive another nail into the coffin of the Christian religion. In Germany, characteristically enough, *Darwinismus* became more Darwinian than Darwin, and Haeckel used it as the pillar of his monistic philosophy. Others, for less commendable reasons, found support in the idea of the 'survival of the fittest' for the *laissez faire* policies of Victorian industrialism and imperial development, and greeted with enthusiasm a doctrine which appeared to them to justify the principle of every man for himself. Not a few theologians saw in Darwin's conclusions evidence which harmonized with the scientific criticism of the Pentateuchal sources which was already in progress.

But if support for Darwin was strong, and in the long run decisive, opposition was equally immediate and much more vocal. It is doubtful if the furore would have been half so violent if Darwin, who was no controversialist, had not found a champion in T. H. Huxley. This doughty exponent of evolution, natural selection, and the cause of science in general, had that kind of journalistic flair in writing and popular appeal in debate which magnified the whole issue into one of Science *versus* Religion, Evolution *versus* Moses, New Knowledge *versus* Biblical Obscurantism. He aptly called himself 'Darwin's bulldog', and certainly he had all the courage and tenacity of the breed. He revelled in dialectic, adducing with obvious relish evidence from science and the Bible alike, to confound the churchmen who denounced Darwin and all his works with a vehemence which could hardly have been greater had he been Antichrist himself.

The shocked incredulity of the devout is well reflected in the comment of a country clergyman, whose son presented him with a copy of the *Origin of Species* as a Christmas gift just after its publication. 'I cannot conceive', said the old parson, 'how a book can be written on the subject. We know all there is to be known about it. God created plants and animals and man out of the ground.'[3]

[1] Dampier-Whetham, *History of Science*, p. 299.

[2] G. P. Wells, in *Great Victorians*, p. 159.

[3] Quoted by J. Y. Simpson, *Landmarks in the Struggle between Science and Religion*, p. 177.

It has been noted by most historians of the period that it was not so much a controversy between Darwinism and the Book of Genesis as between Darwinism and Milton's interpretation of Genesis. Men of simple faith tended to think of Creation not in terms of the serenely majestic fiat of Genesis i: 'And God said, let there be...' but rather in the vivid imagery of the seventh book of *Paradise Lost*:

> The earth obeyed, and straight
> Op'ning her fertile womb, teem'd at a birth
> Innumerous living creatures, perfect forms,
> Limb'd and full-grown: out of the ground up rose,
> As from his lair, the wild beast, where he wons
> In forest wild, in thicket, brake, or den;
> Among the trees in pairs they rose, they walk'd;
> The cattle in the fields and meadows green;
> Those rare and solitary, these in flocks
> Pasturing at once, and in broad herds upsprung,
> The grassy clods now calved; now half appear'd
> The tawny lion, pawing to get free
> His hinder parts, then springs, as broke from bonds
> And rampant shakes his brinded mane; the ounce,
> The libbard, and the tiger, as the mole
> Rising, the crumbled earth above them threw
> In hillocks: the swift stag from under ground
> Bore up his branching head....

This partly explains why in 1864 the Oxford Declaration, denouncing all who denied that the whole Bible was the word of God, and that the wicked would be punished everlastingly, was signed by no fewer than eleven thousand clergy. Conversely, the Declaration makes sense of Huxley's half-serious, half-comic reply to Lord Ernle, who commented on the amount of 'vinegar and mustard' which he contrived to introduce into his disputations with orthodoxy: 'My dear young man, you are not old enough to remember when men like Lyell and Murchison were not considered fit to lick the dust off the boots of a curate. I should like to get my heel into their mouths and scr-r-unch it round.'[1]

The famous meeting of the British Association in 1860 where Huxley gleefully made havoc of poor Bishop Wilberforce's arguments for a literal acceptance of the Genesis narratives was perhaps his

1 'Victorian Memoirs and Memories', *Quarterly Review* (April, 1923).

greatest triumph. The temper of the debate may be judged from the fact that when, at one point in his address, Wilberforce wanted to know whether Mr Huxley was related to an ape on his grandfather's or on his grandmother's side, Huxley slapped his thigh and murmured to his neighbour: 'The Lord hath delivered him into my hand.'[1]

Mr Gladstone, who rashly ventured into the fray, was equally ill equipped to face this sparkling opponent. Disraeli with more wisdom contented himself with the observation that if he had to choose between the Book of Genesis and the *Origin of Species* and to say whether man was an angel or an ape, he, Disraeli, was 'on the side of the angels'. The fact that the two foremost politicians of the Victorian era felt obliged to take part in the discussion at all is a measure of the nation-wide interest in the issues at stake.

The Church as a whole showed up badly. Its spokesmen defended propositions which they ought to have known to be untenable. But given as a basic thesis that Holy Scripture was verbally inspired and literally infallible, plus the fact that at first blush Darwinism seemed to eliminate God entirely from the created world, and to rob man of everything except a common ancestry with a monkey, perhaps the religious reaction was not surprising. As Dean Church said at the time, when people are in a panic they tend to behave 'more like old ladies than philosophers'.[2]

By the end of the nineteenth century the fury of the battle over Genesis had largely subsided, although the private war between Gladstone and Huxley had latterly been transferred to the territory of the Gadarene Swine. The idea of an evolutionary process in the natural world had, with modifications, become an accepted canon, although the weaknesses in the hypothesis of natural selection were already apparent. The attitude of the Church to Darwinism had on the whole reached the third stage of Whewell's dictum that 'every great scientific discovery went through three stages. First, people said, "It is absurd", then they said, "It is contrary to the Bible". And finally they said, "We always knew it was so".'[3]

There was a growing recognition that Science and Religion were not mutually destructive but were two different approaches to ultimate

[1] Raven, *Science, Religion and the Future*, p. 43.
[2] M. C. Church, *Life and Letters of Dean Church*, p. 154.
[3] A. L. Moore, *Science and the Faith*, p. 83.

truth, and that many scientists were men of deep religious convictions and not blasphemous iconoclasts. The Church admitted that by and large in the Genesis controversy science had been right and orthodoxy had been misguided. Darwinism, robbed of the crudities of some of its presentation, was seen to enhance the wonder of the created world and the providential order of its Creator. The Christian scheme of salvation had not suffered from science establishing man's kinship with the animal kingdom. More particularly the narratives of Genesis, since they could no longer be regarded as a scientific account of world origins, were equally no longer a millstone round the necks of scholars who were free to inquire into their real significance.

But obviously Darwinism of itself would not have brought about this changed attitude on the part of the Church. Scientists were not yet exhibiting that humility in face of the increasing mystery of this unpredictable universe which in the twentieth century has made the relationship between science and religion so much more fruitful and healthy. At the end of the nineteenth century science was still too self-assured and self-sufficient. Had there been no other factors at work churchmen would inevitably have been driven more and more to defend the doctrine of the infallibility of Scripture, as the only bastion against what seemed to be an increasing tendency towards a mechanical and materialistic interpretation of the universe which left no room for revealed religion.

CRITICISM OF THE TRADITIONAL USE BY THEOLOGIANS

Happily, however, science had been proving itself to be the handmaiden of biblical studies in a more effective if less spectacular way. Throughout the century, there had been developing a new approach to the Bible, based on scientific methods of historical and literary criticism, which in contrast to the strident clamour and often trivial superficiality of the Genesis controversy, was able in the end to present the Church with a rational and intelligent alternative to a dog-in-the-manger adherence to the doctrine of the verbal infallibility of Scripture. In this the principle of evolution found its proper place. It is no more than the truth to say that it was the patient labours of the 'Higher Critics', despite their occasional excesses of enthusiasm, which not only made possible an eventual rapprochement between scientists and churchmen, but rehabilitated the study of the Bible in the eyes of men of intelligence everywhere, who had felt that the Church's insistence on a literal acceptance of the Scriptures made any kind of reasonable faith impossible.

In an essay called *The Lights of the Church and the Light of Science*, published in 1890,[1] T. H. Huxley made one of his typically uncompromising attacks on 'the historical trustworthiness of the Jewish Scriptures', arguing that if it is conceded that the Old Testament is not a factual record in all its details, then the whole structure of Christian dogma inevitably collapses since its foundations rest upon 'legendary quicksands'. Unfortunately he was able to quote, with much approval, part of a sermon by H. P. Liddon delivered in St Paul's Cathedral in the previous year which is based upon the same premise. In his sermon, the Chancellor of the Cathedral had confronted with the authority of Christ's own words those who sought to take account of recent scientific insights by affirming that the truth of the Old Testament did not lie in the scientific or historical accuracy of its narratives.

> For Christians [said Liddon] it will be enough to know that our Lord Jesus Christ set the seal of His infallible sanction on the whole of the Old Testament. He found the Hebrew Canon as we have it in our hands today, and He treated it as an authority which was above discussion. Nay more: He went out of His way—if we may reverently speak thus—to sanction not a few portions of it which modern scepticism rejects. When He would warn His hearers against the dangers of spiritual relapse, He bids them remember 'Lot's wife'. When He would point out how worldly engagements may blind the soul to a coming judgment, He reminds them how men ate, and drank, and married, and were given in marriage, until the day that Noah entered into the ark, and the Flood came and destroyed them all. If He would put His finger on a fact in past Jewish history which, by its admitted reality, would warrant belief in His own coming Resurrection, He points to Jonah's being three days and three nights in the whale's belly.

The preacher dismisses the possibility that Jesus may have been arguing *ad hominem*, and goes on to say that those who would suggest that Jesus himself spoke from limited knowledge

> will find it difficult to persuade mankind that, if He could be mistaken on a matter of such strictly religious importance as the value of the sacred litera-

[1] In *Science and Hebrew Tradition*, pp. 200–38.

ture of His countrymen, He can be safely trusted about anything else. The trustworthiness of the Old Testament is, in fact, inseparable from the trustworthiness of our Lord Jesus Christ; and if we believe that He is the true Light of the world, we shall close our ears against suggestions impairing the credit of those Jewish Scriptures which have received the stamp of His Divine authority.

Well might Huxley link this pronouncement with that of Rawlinson in his Bampton lecture of 1859, quoted above (p. 259), pointing out that in these thirty-one years not only the new insights of natural science but also the application of the scientific method to historical criticism, the discoveries of archaeologists, and the work of textual scholars, which ought to have revolutionized the traditional approach to the inerrancy of Scripture, might as well never have happened for all the attention that was paid to them by orthodoxy.

Characteristically he comments on the utterances of Liddon and Rawlinson,

If the 'trustworthiness of our Lord Jesus Christ' is to stand or fall with the belief in the sudden transmutation of the chemical components of a woman's body into sodium chloride, or on the 'admitted reality' of Jonah's ejection, safe and sound, on the shores of the Levant, after three days' sea-journey in the stomach of a gigantic marine animal, what possible pretext can there be for even hinting a doubt as to the precise truth of the longevity attributed to the Patriarchs? Who that has swallowed the camel of Jonah's journey will be guilty of the affectation of straining at such a historical gnat—nay, midge—as the supposition that the mother of Moses was told the story of the Flood by Jacob; who had it straight from Shem; who was on friendly terms with Methuselah; who knew Adam quite well?

Huxley is well aware that Liddon's sermon was not only a protest against the scepticism of scientists but against the growing volume of critical opinion among English theologians themselves, who were finding the infallibility of Scripture an impossible concept. He recognized only too well the desperate last-ditch character of Liddon's position, and that biblical scholarship within the Church had little sympathy with it. It suits his argument, however, as well as his pugnacious temper, to brush aside as equivocations the views of such theologians as the authors of *Lux Mundi*, which had just appeared. He assumes the pose of the blunt and simple scientist, who calls a spade a spade, and asks whether the biblical narratives are historical or unhistorical, true or false. There is no middle way, no loop-hole of parable, type or allegory. 'The books of ecclesiastical authority declare that certain events happened in a certain fashion: the books of scientific authority say they did not.'

Mercifully by 1890, however, Liddon's trumpet gave but an uncertain sound. There were other voices within the Church, proclaiming in ever-growing volume that Liddon's position was as untenable as Huxley's, and that the Church must in penitence for its past obscurantism recognize that the Spirit was leading it, through the new knowledge that science had made available, into a deeper understanding than either of these two protagonists had begun to realize of what was meant by the truth of the Bible.

Thus in his Bampton lectures in 1885 F. W. Farrar had said:[1] 'No conception more subversive of Scriptural authority has ever been devised than the assertion, that in the Bible we must accept everything or nothing.' Having paid a handsome tribute to Darwin he went on: 'The students of science have exercised a mighty influence over theology, were it only that by their linear progress and magnificent achievements they have stimulated that spirit of inquiry which for many centuries had only gyrated within limits prescribed too often by the ignorance of priests.' Admitting that the characteristic attitude of religion towards new insights of science had been one 'first of fierce persecution, then of timid compromise, lastly, of thankless and inevitable acceptance', he affirmed his belief that 'true science and true religion are twin sisters, each studying her own sacred book of God, and nothing but disaster has arisen from the petulant scorn of the one and the false fear and cruel tyrannies of the other'.

In the light of this great outburst of new knowledge, said Farrar, it was 'imperative that new principles of inquiry and modern methods of criticism should be extended to those records of revelation in which it was certain that nothing could suffer which was intrinsically truthful or divine'. He acknowledged the great debt which English scholarship owed to the critical work which had been done by continental, and, in particular, by German theologians. He confesses that the conservatism with which their views had been received in England had been so cautious that it had 'not seldom proved itself to be retrogressive'.

'Fifty years ago', he says, 'the Shibboleth of popular orthodoxy was

[1] *History of Interpretation*, pp. 421 ff.

the indiscriminate anathema of "German theology".' But there had been at least some English scholars who had been sufficiently perceptive to see that it was possible 'to love the Bible as a book which contains the word of God, and yet to read it...as a book...written by human hands'....'These men during all their days had the honour to endure the beatitude of malediction. They were pursued by the attacks of no small portion of the clergy, and of those who called themselves the religious world.' But 'so far from being disturbed or shaken by their free, glad and earnest investigations, it is by means of these very investigations that the Bible has triumphed over keen ridicule, over charges of fiction, over naturalist explanations, over mythical theories, over destructive criticism'.

Ever since Astruc in 1753 discovered the double strand of Priestly and Jahwist tradition in the book of Genesis,

> criticism, both historic and philological, has been applied to every narrative and every section of Scripture. Many of its results have taken their place among valued truths; many of its assertions have been triumphantly refuted. It has overthrown false human theories, it has not shaken so much as the fringe of a single truth. But the notion of verbal infallibility could not possibly survive the birth of historic inquiry, which showed in Scripture as elsewhere an organic growth, and therefore a necessary period of immature development.

Then, having listed some of the generally accepted critical conclusions about the biblical documents, Farrar ends with what might well be called the confession of faith of higher criticism: 'Where the Spirit of God is there is liberty. All these questions have been under discussion for many years; yet to multitudes of those who on these questions have come to decisions which are in opposition to the current opinions, the Bible is still the divinest of all books and the Lord Jesus Christ is still the Son of God, the Saviour of the World.'

When Farrar delivered his Bampton Lectures in 1885 he could speak with the confidence of one who knew that the battle of higher criticism was as good as won. The vast body of English laity and many of the clergy may still have been untouched by the change that was to come over biblical studies in the last two decades of the nineteenth century. In 1880 Alfred Cave could still speak of 99 per cent of the biblical scholars in England, Scotland and America as supporting the

Mosaic authorship of the Pentateuch. 'In 1880 it was still possible for orthodox Bible scholars in England to consider higher criticism as the temporary form taken by infidelity in Germany and confidently to predict the scholarly victory of tradition.'[1]

But ten years later Cave's percentage would have had to be radically altered. What the combined effort of Deism, Rationalism and Evolution had failed to achieve had been accomplished by the patient labours of the theologians themselves. Undoubtedly the end result had been influenced, as indeed were the biblical critics, by the ideas propounded by the advocates of these three concepts, but of themselves, as has been seen, the supporters of these views had tended rather to consolidate orthodoxy in defence of the verbal inspiration of the Scriptures.

Quite otherwise, however, was the effect when Christian scholars of obvious piety and sound learning set themselves to the task of examining the biblical records with the avowed intention not of destroying but of strengthening their authority to the greater glory of God. But it took the best part of a century and a half for their work to command general recognition. England, for reasons which can readily be understood, lagged behind the Continent in its acceptance of a critical approach to the Bible, and orthodoxy there and in Scotland sowed dragons' teeth in a series of heresy hunts during the nineteenth century. But the future lay clearly with those who saw that only by patient and painstaking subjection of the biblical records to scientific study could they retain any authority in a scientific age, which would no longer be satisfied with the evasions and subterfuges to which orthodoxy had to resort in order to defend a thesis that was patently untenable.

In the modern world, literary criticism of the Bible, that is, the examination of its contents with a view to determining the date, authorship, integrity and character of the various documents, which, since J. G. Eichhorn first used the term at the end of the eighteenth century, has been generally called the 'higher', as distinct from the 'lower', or textual criticism, is normally reckoned to have begun with Jean Astruc. It was this physician to Louis XV, whose *Conjectures sur les mémoires originaux dont il paroit que Moyse s'est servi pour composer le livre de la Genèse* was published anonymously in Brussels in 1753, who by distinguishing the use of Yahweh and Elohim in Genesis, and explaining

[1] W. B. Glover, *Evangelical Nonconformists and Higher Criticism in the Nineteenth Century*, p. 36.

the fact by suggesting that two original documents had subsequently been combined, laid the foundation for all subsequent Pentateuchal criticism and inaugurated the scientific method of studying the Scriptures in general.

The impetus to this kind of approach had come from the rationalistic tendencies of eighteenth-century thought, and ultimately, of course, from the revolt against authority which characterized the Renaissance. But that during the century and a half following Astruc the movement gained momentum until the position was reached which Farrar outlines in his Bampton lectures, was due to the fact that in the early nineteenth century there was the added emphasis on historical criticism and the inductive methods of natural science. Not only was the Bible studied as a collection of literary documents which presented the same problems as other ancient writings, but also the record of Israel's history was removed from its splendid isolation and considered against the background of the rapidly growing knowledge of its contemporary setting. Moreover, under the influence of the evolutionary principle, the religion of the Bible came to be seen as part of the sweep of history, and the concept of progressive revelation became a yardstick for evaluating its claims.

In his review of nineteenth-century criticism, Farrar observes that 'the English Church, since the days of Bede and Alcuin, has rarely, perhaps never, been in the forefront of Scriptural studies' and goes on to ask whether there had been 'a single English commentary before the last generation, except the *Isaiah* of Bishop Lowth, of which one could say without extravagance that it struck out a new line or marked a new epoch'. T. K. Cheyne in his *Founders of Old Testament Criticism* does not concede even as much. Pointing out the singular fact that the Deist controversy, which aroused so much commotion on biblical matters in England, failed to produce any significant critical movement there, although its influence on the development of German critical studies was considerable, Cheyne mentions as the only three English scholars who showed any talent for Old Testament criticism before the beginning of the nineteenth century Warburton, Lowth and Geddes.

The first two he dismisses briefly and allows Geddes alone the honourable title of one of the founders of biblical criticism. He does, however, admit that Lowth's *Isaiah*, published in 1778, in which he worked on the then novel assumption that Isaiah and the rest of the prophets spoke primarily to the people of their own time, had a marked effect on German criticism although in England Lowth remained a *vox clamantis in deserto*.[1]

Alexander Geddes, a Roman Catholic priest from Aberdeenshire, found the north of Scotland an unpropitious climate for his liberal opinions. He settled in London, found a sympathetic patron, and became quite a figure in society. His life work, however, was the preparation of a new translation of the Bible, to which he intended to attach critical and explanatory notes. The first volume appeared in 1792, but its radical views on the origin of the Pentateuch aroused equal opposition from Roman Catholic and Protestant orthodoxy. Further volumes intensified the clamour, and Geddes was suspended from his ecclesiastical office. He died in 1802 with his work unfinished. Many of his critical views have long since been superseded but his basic position and his grasp of critical methods entitle him to be regarded as one of the most notable of the eighteenth-century *avant-garde* of higher critics.

Apparently almost alone in England at that time, Geddes was in close touch with German scholarship, and it is to Germany that we must turn to find the real pioneers of higher criticism both in the Old and in the New Testament. Herder, 'more poet than theologian, and for that reason all the more lovely', as Reuss said of him, had combined in his *Letters on the Study of Theology* (1780) a sympathetic approach to the human element in the biblical revelation with a clear recognition of the problem of harmonizing the Gospels. He asserted the priority of Mark and the interpretative character of the Fourth Gospel.

Herder's contemporary, Lessing, had considerable influence on subsequent scholarship, not least by his strong advocacy of the right to criticize the biblical documents, emphasizing that the faith of the Church depended on its Founder and not upon the record of his activity. His play *Nathan der Weise* was a dramatic presentation of his plea for liberty of opinion in all matters of theology. Both of these contributions had found their origin in the outcry which was raised by his publication in 1774–8 of the *Wolfenbütteler Fragmente*. These consisted of extracts from a manuscript which had been entrusted to Lessing, at that time librarian at Wolfenbüttel, by the daughter of H. S. Reimarus,

[1] *Founders of Old Testament Criticism*, pp. 2ff.

lately professor at Hamburg, after her father's death, and Lessing had published them without indicating either the identity of the author or how far he was in agreement with his opinions.

Reimarus stood in the direct rationalist tradition in his sceptical attitude to the miraculous elements in the Gospels, and it was his suggestion that the disciples stole the body of Jesus, to bolster up their fraudulent story of his Resurrection, that brought down most thunder on Lessing's head. But Reimarus broke new ground, as Schweitzer rightly reminded German liberalism in 1906,[1] by insisting on the eschatological features in the Gospels and the Jewish character of the setting. That he concluded from the evidence that Jesus was a deluded visionary, whose Messianic venture ended in disaster, does not detract from his importance for subsequent Gospel criticism. Another late eighteenth-century pioneer of criticism was Semler, whose great merit is not so much that he produced one hundred and twenty-one volumes in his lifetime but that he gave the impetus to the historical approach to biblical criticism, and, by drawing attention to the antagonism between the Jewish and Gentile factions in the early Church, provided the Tübingen School with their favourite yardstick.

Before turning to the nineteenth century, however, when higher criticism reached its full flood, with the Tübingen School riding on the crest of the first great wave, mention should be made of J. G. Eichhorn, grammar school headmaster at the age of twenty-two, professor of oriental languages at Jena a year later, friend of Herder and Goethe, and versatile *littérateur*, who made the whole Bible his province. It is fitting that this influential scholar, who gave higher criticism its name, should have distinguished himself by publishing critical introductions to both Old and New Testaments. The former, which in its day was as epoch-making as Wellhausen's *Prolegomena*, earned him the right to be called the father of modern Old Testament criticism. He reached independently the same conclusion as Astruc about the interwoven narratives in Genesis, but his criteria were more extensive and his examination was more methodical. It was by following his clues that Pentateuchal criticism in the following century reached its classical formulation.

The first half of the nineteenth century was characterized by the emergence of an extremely radical approach to the New Testament on the part of German scholarship. This had its origin in the University

[1] *Von Reimarus zu Wrede*: English trans. *The Quest of the Historical Jesus* (1910).

of Tübingen and its chief exponents were D. F. Strauss and F. C. Baur. It was in the wholly secular atmosphere of the German universities, unhampered by the ecclesiastical restraints of their English counterparts, that the requisite degree of intellectual freedom could be obtained for the expression of critical views which, to most supporters of the traditional view of the Bible, seemed little short of atheistic.

Yet the Tübingen School, as it came to be known, was as much the child of Christian pietism as of secular rationalism. The latter element was undoubtedly present, and the legacy of the Aufklärung is an important explanatory factor. But at the same time, this critical movement, which so outraged conventional orthodoxy, was for the most part the work of men whose aim was to understand the Bible and not to destroy it, to enhance its value and not to undermine its authority.

The traditionally looser relationship between Church and State in Germany, as compared with England, led to the possibility of greater freedom of belief existing side by side with genuine private piety. Dogmatic theology and institutional religion alike tended to be subordinated to pietistic individualism. Yet even this more propitious climate for biblical criticism was not enough to save D. F. Strauss from sharing the fate of other prophets and pioneers of new and unwelcome ideas.

Schweitzer says of him that to understand him one must love him. 'He was not the greatest, and not the deepest of theologians, but he was the most absolutely sincere.'[1] It is characteristic of Strauss that he went straight to the heart of the question as to the possibility and propriety of criticizing the Bible by singling out the Gospels for his attention. For him this was the crucial issue, and it is for his work on the life of Jesus that he is best remembered.

Schleiermacher had set the tone for this blend of rationalism and pietism in approaching the Gospels with his dictum in *Über die Religion* (1799): 'The holy books have become the Bible in virtue of their own power, but they do not forbid any other book from being or becoming a Bible in its turn.' In place of the absolute authority of Scripture he asserted the absolute authority of Christ: 'The person of Jesus Christ, with all that flows immediately from it, is alone absolutely normative.'[2]

Schleiermacher's own *Leben Jesu*, compiled from his lecture notes

[1] *The Quest of the Historical Jesus*, p. 68.

[2] F. Lichtenberger, *History of German Theology in the Nineteenth Century*, pp. 86, 137.

and published in 1864, thirty years after his death, approached the miraculous element in the Gospels from the old rationalist standpoint. A more uncompromising exponent of last-ditch rationalism was the Heidelberg theologian Paulus, whose *Life of Jesus*, published in 1828, was based on the assumption that 'the truly miraculous thing about Jesus is himself, the purity and serene holiness of his character'. The so-called Gospel 'miracles' are simply dismissed as the product of credulity, illusion or misunderstanding.

It was the great merit of Strauss, and a measure of his importance for biblical criticism, that he would have none of this rationalism masquerading as theology, as a means of coming to terms with the problems presented by the Gospels. It was largely through his attack upon them that the *Lives* of Schleiermacher and Paulus were soon forgotten. With his own *Leben Jesu*, published in 1835, it was a different story. For with this book he at the same time made himself famous, ruined his career, and started a movement which was to change the entire direction of New Testament study for the rest of the century.

The novelty of Strauss's approach to the Gospels is that he cuts the Gordian knot which had baffled both rationalism and orthodoxy. So long as both sides assumed that biblical narratives must be accepted as factual records, there could be no hope of agreement, or of an end to constant battles. Rationalism, whether anti-clerical or in theological guise, would continue to insist that biblical history must be subjected to the same tests as secular literature, and that incidents which were patently improbable, or which were contrary to nineteenth-century man's understanding of the laws of nature, must have some natural explanation. On the other side, biblical orthodoxy would continue to insist that since these facts were to be found within the sacred Scriptures, ordinary criteria could not be applied. Strauss in the preface to his *Leben Jesu* offered another solution.

Orthodox and rationalists alike [he said] proceed from the false assumption that we have always in the gospels testimony, sometimes even that of eye-witnesses, to fact. They are, therefore, reduced to asking themselves what can have been the real and natural fact which is here witnessed to in such extraordinary ways. We have to realize that the narrators testify sometimes, not to outward facts, but to ideas, often most practical and beautiful ideas, constructions which even eye-witnesses had unconsciously put upon facts, imagination concerning them, reflections upon them, reflections such as were natural to the time and at the author's level of culture. What we have here is not falsehood, but misrepresentation of the truth. It is a plastic, naive, and, at the same time, often most profound apprehension of truth, within the area of religious feeling and poetic insight. It results in narrative, legendary, mythical in nature, illustrative often of spiritual truth in a manner more perfect than any hard, prosaic statement could achieve.

On the basis of this principle, Strauss applied himself to the task of examining the Gospel narratives with German thoroughness in a vast work of over fourteen hundred pages. Each incident and every possible interpretation of it, whether rationalist or orthodox, was meticulously considered. But for want of proper criteria, depending on a careful analysis of the sources and on sound standards of historical criticism, it was inevitable that subjectivism should become the yardstick. Strauss taught his successors to recognize the influence of the Messianic theology of the early Church in forming tradition, and showed clearly that account must be taken of legendary elements and pious accretions, not only in the Old Testament, which had already been admitted, but in the New Testament as well.

Where he erred, however, was in failing to show any good reason, apart from personal predilection, for deciding what was probably fact and what was probably fiction. The historical Jesus tended to disappear completely, and in the hands of Strauss's disciples was replaced by the Christ-myth. For himself, Strauss was content to rest his Christian faith on the idea of God-manhood, which through the imposition of myth and legend upon the essentially unknowable Jesus, had entered into man's consciousness as the ultimate goal of humanity.

This Hegelian attitude towards the Founder of the Church did not satisfy either the theologians or the simple believers. It did not even satisfy Strauss himself, and after some attempts at modifying his views he gave up his Christian faith altogether. He had been removed from his teaching post at Tübingen as a result of the fierce criticism which his *Leben Jesu* had aroused, and his subsequent chequered career and final break with Christianity confirmed his opponents in their hostility towards his views. The total of 40,000 signatures which were attached to a petition to the Swiss government not to appoint Strauss to the vacant chair of dogmatics at Zurich in 1839, suggest considerably more than theological disapproval and something more akin to the anti-Darwinian panic of twenty years later.

It was left to Baur, who had in fact been his teacher at Tübingen, to see that the real weakness in his brilliant pupil had been that his intuitions had not been matched with adequate critical tools. Baur made it his business to provide them. He maintained that the question as to the authenticity of a narrative cannot be answered until a prior question has been asked, namely, what is the point of view of the writer? In most cases it is impossible to say whether this or that event recorded in the Gospels happened precisely as it is recorded. What we can do, however, is to try to discover the author's bias. If we can ascertain what sort of a man he was, what his purpose was in writing, what were the great issues in which he was involved, we are then in a better position to eliminate the personal equation and to arrive at a closer approximation to the objective reality which lies behind the record.

Baur applied this *Tendenz-kritik* to the whole of the New Testament. It provided him with a criterion which relegated the Fourth Gospel, as a product of Christian gnosticism, thinly disguised as a life of Jesus, to the end of the second century. Above all it supplied him with an apparently infallible standard by which the Pauline epistles might be judged. He rightly saw that the great issue in the early Church was between the narrower Jewish-Christian party and the universalist missionary zeal of St Paul. Equally correctly he saw evidence of this struggle throughout the New Testament, and recognized that the freeing of Christianity from the fetters of Judaism was largely the work of Paul. His thesis led him astray, however, when it made him assign most of the New Testament to the second century, when the cause which Paul espoused had triumphed, and to date nothing earlier than A.D. 70 which did not bear evidence of being written with an anti-Judaizing bias.

The Tübingen School, of which Baur was the founder, rallied many disciples and likewise stirred up many opponents. The dependence of the critical methods of Baur, as of Strauss, upon Hegelian dialectic was a basic weakness, and the movement as a whole has not unfairly been described as 'a false start, led by philosophy instead of science'.[1] Yet it performed a necessary task. However wrong were its conclusions, the Tübingen School laid the foundations of a critical method for dealing with the New Testament, which could be developed and improved, as indeed it was continuously in Germany throughout the century, despite

[1] C. C. McCown, *The Search for the Real Jesus*, p. 53.

some opposition in the universities and grave misgivings on the part of the Church at large. But largely by virtue of its initiative, literary and historical criticism of the New Testament had come to stay. The radical temper of Tübingen had a considerable effect in Holland where the Christ-myth was later to flourish, and it would doubtless have made a greater impact in France had not Renan's *Vie de Jésus* (1863) provided a local storm-centre.

In England, on the other hand, the new German critical movement had a cool reception. F. C. Conybeare, writing in 1910,[1] was satisfied that he could explain why.

> The Germans, and in a measure the French, have for the last hundred years been making serious efforts to ascertain the truth about Christian origins. Our own divines, amid the contentment and leisure of rich livings and deaneries, and with the libraries and endowments of Oxford and Cambridge at their disposal, have done nothing except produce a handful of apologetic, insincere and worthless volumes. The only books which in England have advanced knowledge have been translations of German or French authors, and not long since our well-endowed professors and doctors of divinity greeted every fresh accession to Christian learning—when they could not ignore it and maintain a conspiracy of silence—with dismal howls of execration and torrents of abuse.

Allowing for the somewhat unsympathetic attitude to the Establishment of a work published under the auspices of the Rationalist Press Association, Conybeare's verdict is not far removed from that of F. W. Farrar. George Eliot, who translated Strauss's *Life of Jesus* into English in 1846, complained that no 'respectable' English publisher would contemplate its publication 'from a fear of persecution'. But even she found much of it 'repulsive', especially his 'dissecting the beautiful story of the crucifixion'.[2]

There were, however, more reasons than clerical and academic complacency or even obscurantism behind English indifference to the German critical movement. Admittedly, insular prejudice played some part at a time when almost anything from Germany was treated with suspicion. But more important was the fact that the first impact of higher criticism upon the general public in England was through the translation of Strauss's *Life of Jesus*. It was difficult for the ordinary

[1] *History of New Testament Criticism*, p. 97.

[2] J. W. Cross, *George Eliot's Life*, ch. 2.

churchman to see that there was any difference between the rationalism of Strauss and the rationalism which had been so recently and triumphantly routed in the Deistic controversies of the preceding century. This was simply the old mixture in a new bottle, worse still, a bottle with a foreign label. It could thus be safely disregarded.

A movement that began by laying irreverent hands upon the most sacred part of the Bible, that subjected the life of our Lord to analysis and dissection, that brushed aside the miraculous elements in his birth, his ministry, and his Resurrection, could be nothing but a deliberate attempt to discredit the Christian faith and degrade the person of its Founder. At best this new higher criticism from the Continent could be dismissed as the 'attenuated intellectuality of Germany which soars away through thin air', at worst, denounced as 'German rationalism', or, as Spurgeon preferred to call it, 'the German poison'.

Popular orthodoxy felt that it had much more need to rally to the defence of the faith against the attacks of geology and biology upon the Book of Genesis, than to concern itself with these unknown pedants who cut up the Bible with 'German scissors'.[1] England had to wait until her more discerning scholars in church and university had sifted the probable from the improbable, and, having taken the measure of German thought, converted its heady effervescence into the more sober nourishment of English ale.

Among those scholars who were in touch with German criticism in the first half of the century, and who introduced something of its spirit and methods into England, were Connop Thirlwall, later bishop of St David's, who translated Schleiermacher's *Essay on the Gospel of St Luke*, and Edward Pusey, who was said to be one of the only two people who could read German in Oxford in his day.

Thirlwall, in introducing his translation, not only dismissed the theory of verbal inspiration as untenable, and urged the necessity of allowing for the element of poetry and parable in the Gospel narratives, but, more important, applied the historical method to their evaluation. Pusey, who had studied in Germany under Eichhorn and Schleiermacher, and mildly commended a modification of the traditional view of the plenary inspiration of Scripture in matters of detail where no doctrinal issues were involved, found himself charged with a radicalism

[1] Glover, *Evangelical Nonconformists and Higher Criticism in the Nineteenth Century*, pp. 37ff.

which he hotly repudiated. Milman's *History of the Jews* (1829), which dared to treat Old Testament characters as human beings in their historical setting, was greeted with anger and alarm, but was not without positive effect.

More than to any of these, however, it was left to Coleridge to make England aware of the current trends of the German critical movement. Both in his *Table Talk* and in the posthumous *Confessions of an Inquiring Spirit*, biblical questions are dealt with on the basis of cautious acceptance of its assumptions. Coleridge maintains that the traditional theories of inspiration are meaningless: that the faith of a Christian does not depend on the authenticity of this or that part of the Bible: that miracle-stories must be judged on their merits.

The authority of Scripture, said Coleridge, is in its truthfulness, its answer to the highest aspirations of the human reason and the most urgent necessities of the moral life....Its literature must be read as literature, its history as history. For the answer in our hearts to the spirit in the Book, Coleridge used the phrase: 'It finds me.' 'In the Bible there is more that finds me than I have experienced in all other books put together. Whatever finds me brings with it an irresistible evidence of its having proceeded from the Holy Spirit.'[1]

Thomas Arnold applied the lessons he had learned, both from Coleridge and also directly from German scholars, to a historical evaluation of the biblical evidence in his *Essay on the right Interpretation and Understanding of the Scriptures* (1831). He insisted that Christian faith, 'which is the guide and comfort of our lives', must not be confounded with 'all questions of science, of history and of criticism', and that it is impossible to understand the Bible if it is regarded as in 'all its parts of equal authority...and like the Koran, all composed at one time, and addressed to persons similarly situated'.[2]

Thus, although in a strict sense higher criticism did not become a live issue in England until the second half of the nineteenth century, the way was being prepared by scholars and men of letters, who, though not prepared to pursue every will-o'-the-wisp that drifted from across the Channel, were nevertheless willing to sit at the feet of the continental theologians, and to mediate their insights with characteristic Anglo-Saxon conservatism, in the belief that this new light

[1] *Confessions of an Inquiring Spirit*, Letter 2.

[2] Arnold's *Sermons*, II, 429, 481.

could in the long run lead only to a deeper appreciation of the divine revelation in Holy Scripture.

The few years around 1860 were indeed momentous for England in the field of biblical studies and more than ordinarily disquieting for orthodox opinion. In 1859 Darwin's *Origin of Species* had appeared, to be followed a year later by the calamitous Huxley–Wilberforce debate at Oxford. In the same year the publication of *Essays and Reviews*, a collection of papers by seven churchmen, six of them ordained, under the leadership of Benjamin Jowett, afterwards Master of Balliol, revealed the fact that dangerously advanced critical opinions in biblical matters were not confined to the wicked scientists and agnostics. Two years later, in 1862, came the first part of a treatise on the Pentateuch by the learned and godly bishop of Natal, John William Colenso, from which it appeared that the rot of radical criticism had reached even the episcopal bench. The crowning horror came in 1863 with the English translation of Ernest Renan's *Vie de Jésus*, hot on the heels of its hostile reception in France on the part of churchmen of all persuasions.

Renan's *Life of Jesus* made a much greater impact on the general public than that of Strauss. It was short, popular and sentimental. Schweitzer has indicated its two major weaknesses. 'It is Christian art in the worst sense of the term—the art of the wax image. The gentle Jesus, the beautiful Mary, the fair Galileans who formed the retinue of the "amiable carpenter", might have been taken over in a body from the shop-window of an ecclesiastical art emporium in the Place St Sulpice.'[1] More important, perhaps, is the objection that Renan was basically a sceptic, who built up a 'Jesus of history' largely on the material contained in the Fourth Gospel, in the authenticity of which he did not himself believe.

In the eyes of English orthodoxy, however, neither of these factors was as important as the fact that here was a distillation of all the heresies of which the German higher critics had been guilty. Renan had mastered their method, assumed their conclusions, and had now clearly demonstrated, by his blasphemous treatment of the Person of Christ, the inevitable end of laying impious hands upon the sacred texts. The Church had a duty to its people to protect them in their ignorance from this insidious undermining of their faith by criticism.

[1] *The Quest of the Historical Jesus*, p. 182.

It did not help to commend the authors of *Essays and Reviews*, or Bishop Colenso, to the defenders of the verbal inerrancy of the Bible, that the translator of Renan's *Life of Jesus* bracketed their names with Renan and F. W. Newman, the Unitarian, describing Renan's opponents in France as obscurantists, or that he claimed that 'the great problem of the present age is to preserve the religious spirit, whilst getting rid of the superstitions and absurdities that deform it, and which are alike opposed to science and common sense'.[1] What were these 'superstitions and absurdities'? Was it merely that the historicity of Jonah or Noah's Ark was at stake? Were not ultimately also the Virgin Birth, the Resurrection, and the Divinity of our Lord?

The Frenchman might be dismissed by orthodoxy as a renegade Roman Catholic, as readily as the Tübingen School had been written off as rationalistic infidels, but Jowett with his associates and Colenso were a different proposition. Here was the viper striking at the bosom which had nurtured it. Browning vividly sketched the danger to the Faith:

> The candid incline to surmise of late
> That the Christian faith may be false, I find;
> For our Essays-and-Reviews debate
> Begins to tell on the public mind,
> And Colenso's words have weight.[2]

So while simple believers trembled for the ark of God, the clergy, led by the bishops, sounded their trumpets and dashed to its rescue.

The seven 'Essayists' were denounced as the *Septem contra Christum* and two of them were sentenced to be suspended for a year by the Court of Arches, a decision which was later reversed by the Privy Council. Colenso, who was known as the 'wicked bishop', and was charitably described by an episcopal brother as 'doing the Devil's work', was deposed from his diocese. This sentence, too, however, was annulled on appeal to the Privy Council.

It is an indication of the irrational panic that swept over orthodoxy at this time that the views put forward by the Essayists were an extremely mild version of the higher criticism which was flourishing in Germany. The Essayists merely contended that the Bible should be examined like any other book; that Hebrew prophecy is not predictive; that parable, poetry and legend are permissible ways of conveying

[1] Translator's preface. [2] From *Gold Hair*.

biblical truth, and that many of the apparently historical narratives of the Bible should be so regarded. All that Colenso had done was to examine the structure of the Hexateuch in the light of the patent absurdities and discrepancies which, when its narratives were treated as sober history, were obvious even to the untutored Zulu who started the bishop off on his researches, and made him turn his attention to the work of Old Testament scholars in Germany.

Yet the 'terror and wrath'[1] which were aroused by such critical treatment of the Scriptures become more explicable when it is remembered that Dr Burgon, the future Dean of Chichester, was expressing the normally held view when he delivered the classic formulation of the doctrine of the infallibility of the Bible from the pulpit of the university church at Oxford, during the controversy which followed the appearance of *Essays and Reviews*. 'The Bible is none other than the voice of Him that sitteth upon the throne. Every book of it, every chapter of it, every verse of it, every word of it, every syllable of it, (where are we to stop?) every letter of it, is the direct utterance of the Most High. The Bible is none other than the Word of God, not some part of it more, some part of it less, but all alike the utterance of Him who sitteth upon the throne, faultless, unerring, supreme.'[2] Burgon, as was said at the time, had smitten the Philistines 'with the jawbone of an ass'. It is doubtful whether such an uncompromising return to Chillingworth's position was ever again made by a responsible churchman.

On the Continent, New Testament scholarship, stimulated by the radical conclusions of Strauss and Baur, proceeded for the rest of the century to digest, acclaim, oppose or improve on them. Gospel criticism produced a plethora of *Lives of Jesus* and the question of the dating, authenticity and integrity of the other New Testament writings was hotly debated in an admirable atmosphere of intellectual freedom. If the *Lives of Jesus* succumbed to the prevalent fashion of *Liberalismus*, and tended to under-emphasize the particularism and supernaturalism of the Gospels, the criticism of the rest of the New Testament tended towards a more conservative evaluation of the documents than had been advocated by the Tübingen School.

In the field of Old Testament studies, Eichhorn's successors, Ewald,

[1] Estlin Carpenter, *The Bible in the Ninteteenth Century*, p. 34.

[2] Burgon, *Inspiration and Interpretation*, p. 89.

Vatke, de Wette, Hupfeld, Graf, and many more in Germany, with Reuss in France and Kuenen in Holland, developed and extended the field of criticism, and from the raw material of their conjectures, false and true alike, a relatively unified body of conclusions gradually emerged.

By the end of the century, biblical criticism on the Continent had achieved a considerable measure of stability. Much of this was due to the two great German scholars who, more than any others, consolidated the critical insights of their predecessors and incorporated them in their works. Julius Wellhausen, in his *Prolegomena zur Geschichte Israels* (1878), did not indeed write the last chapter in the long story of Old Testament criticism, and many of his conclusions have had to be modified in the light of later research, but his fundamental critical position has not been departed from and the Graf–Wellhausen analysis of the Old Testament has been broadly accepted as the basis for all subsequent study. In New Testament criticism, Adolf Harnack performed a similar service in a series of monumental works which range over the whole of early Christian literature.

Both these men, brilliant, creative, and prolific, commended themselves to their times not least by presenting their conclusions in the contemporary idiom. Wellhausen did not stop at literary and historical criticism of the Old Testament, but proceeded to interpret the history of Israel and its literary deposit in terms of current evolutionary theory, while Harnack's theological liberalism undoubtedly over-simplified his conception of the Person and Work of Christ and gave rise to his humanist conception of the Kingdom of God as well as his optimistic forecast of an imminently Christian world.

But if twentieth-century biblical criticism takes issue with Wellhausen and Harnack, it is on the grounds of their subjective interpretation of the results of their scientific study of the biblical texts, and not because of their basic methods of literary and historical analysis of the documents. Wellhausen finally established the composite nature of most of the books of the Old Testament; disposed of the Mosaic authorship of the Pentateuch and identified its four major strands of tradition; defined the three great consecutive stages of Israel's history and demonstrated the formative power of the prophets in its religion and its literature. Similarly, Harnack's nineteenth-century interpretation of the message of the New Testament had as its foundation critical insights which have not since been seriously challenged: the priority of Mark; the two-source hypothesis as the solution of the synoptic problem; the distinctive character of the Fourth Gospel; the gradual growth of the canon and the progressive Hellenization of the Palestinian Gospel.

In England, too, by the end of the century, the 'assured results of criticism' began to be spoken of. The process had been assisted by the appearance of the Revised Version. It was difficult to maintain the Burgon position when it was clearly demonstrated that the biblical manuscripts revealed a vast variety of textual variations, and that in many important passages the evidence was inconclusive. A further important contributing factor was the work of the Cambridge Triumvirate, Lightfoot, Westcott and Hort, with the later addition of William Sanday of Oxford, in the field of New Testament criticism. From the middle of the century onwards this remarkable combined force of textual and literary scholars had been assimilating the results of German biblical studies and propagating them with typically English moderation.

They accepted the principles of higher criticism, and employed them in their work, but tempered their conclusions with a conservatism which did much to allay the fears of the faithful and paved the way for a more widespread recognition of the necessity for scientific study of the Scriptures. Similarly, from 1880 onwards it was undoubtedly because there were men of the mental and spiritual calibre of S. R. Driver and George Adam Smith to mediate the results of German Old Testament criticism that the fruits of these labours gradually won general acceptance.

It is true that English biblical scholarship throughout the whole history of the progress of higher criticism during the nineteenth century was, compared with continental scholarship, unadventurous and unoriginal. But there were undoubted advantages in the fact that the scholar at his desk in England had to be more mindful of the worshipper in the pew than was the case in Germany. The incidence of genuine distress among simple believers in England must have been considerably lower, even if the ecclesiastical dignitaries appear to have had more than their share of apoplectic seizures. It was a further gain that the path of higher criticism in England was not littered with the debris of untenable hypotheses and erratic conjectures, as it was in Germany.

More important, perhaps, in view of the considerable strength of nonconformity in England, is the gratifying fact that the battle for higher criticism was won without a schism on this issue within any of the denominations. This last gain was undoubtedly due not only to the conservative character of English criticism and the obvious sincerity of its exponents, but also to the fact that no fundamental theological doctrines were involved. Solid opposition from the evangelicals did not therefore materialize. Similarly, the Anglo-Catholic party, the other quarter from which a hostile reception might have been expected, was reconciled to the new approach by the wise and enlightened leadership of Bishop Charles Gore and the other contributors to *Lux Mundi* (1889), the high church counterpart of *Essays and Reviews*.[1]

The last few decades of the century were, however, not without the excitement of controversy, and there were some doughty last-ditch defenders of traditional scriptural orthodoxy. The three greatest preachers of the period were all antagonistic to the new approach. Canon Liddon has already been noticed. Charles Haddon Spurgeon was more sure of the truth of the Bible than of the truth of contemporary science. If geology conflicted with Genesis, then so much the worse for geology.[2] Spurgeon was genuinely concerned about what he felt was a decline in evangelical conviction and doctrinal soundness among his nonconformist brethren. This, he argued, was partly due to 'modern thought', and in the 'Down Grade' controversy, which he initiated, and which ended in his secession from the Baptist Union, he constantly reiterated his belief that the verbal inspiration and inerrancy of Scripture was an essential bulwark against the inroads of secularism and 'the inventions of men', including 'the supposed discoveries of the so-called higher criticism'.

It was from similar practical motives that the spread of higher criticism in England was resisted by Joseph Parker of the City Temple.

I am jealous lest the Bible should in any sense be made a priest's book. Even Baur or Colenso may, contrary to his own wishes, be almost unconsciously elevated into a literary deity under whose approving nod alone we can read the Bible with any edification. It is no secret that when Baur rejected the Epistle to the Philippians as un-Pauline, Christian Europe became partially paralysed, and that when Hilgenfeld pronounced it Pauline Christian Europe resumed its prayers. Have we to await a communication from Tübingen, or a telegram from Oxford, before we can read the Bible?[3]

[1] See above, pp. 281–3.

[2] Glover, *Evangelical Nonconformists and Higher Criticism in the Nineteenth Century*, p. 163.

[3] J. Parker, *None Like It*, pp. 72–3.

Parker had already been involved in one of the two other controversial issues between the time of the Colenso case and the end of the century. In 1865 Sir J. R. Seeley had published anonymously a life of Jesus, to which he gave the title *Ecce Homo*, and which was at once furiously attacked as a danger to the Faith. Although sufficiently orthodox to satisfy so exacting a critic as Mr Gladstone, the book smacked too much of Renan in its emphasis on the humanity of Jesus and in its stress on his teaching, at the expense of his work for man's salvation, to please most of the conservative evangelicals. Lord Shaftesbury denounced it as 'the most pestilential volume ever vomited forth from the jaws of Hell' and Parker published a counterblast entitled *Ecce Deus*, in which he presented the aspect of Christ which in his view Seeley had overlooked, basing his conclusions on the inerrancy of the Gospel records.

The last great issue of the century, which was at the same time mercifully the last of the heresy hunts, ended in the shameful deposition in 1881 of William Robertson Smith from the chair of Old Testament studies in the Free Church of Scotland college at Aberdeen. Robertson Smith ranks with the greatest Old Testament scholars of the century. Not the least of his achievements was that he was largely responsible for introducing the substance of German Old Testament criticism to this country in the form of popular lectures and books. It was, however, his contributions to the ninth edition of the *Encyclopædia Britannica* which led to his trial by libel before the Free Church Presbytery of Aberdeen, on the grounds that his article on the Bible, which in fact expounded the views which Wellhausen was shortly to express in classical form in his *Prolegomena*, denied 'the immediate inspiration, infallible truth, and divine authority of the Holy Scriptures'.

Smith's defence was that none of these qualities of Scripture, which he affirmed, was inconsistent with higher criticism. He appealed to the reformers against the travesty of their doctrine of Scripture which verbal infallibility constituted. The Bible, he maintained, was the Word of God only in the sense that it *contained* the Word of God. Through faith it revealed God himself and not merely truths about him. Infallibility and authority belonged primarily to the Word of God and only secondarily to the human record which enshrined it. Since revelation is historical and cumulative, all parts of Scripture, even the most unlikely, belonged to the substance of the Word of God. In such a record of God's revelation of himself in history human error and imperfection were inevitable.[1]

Smith cleared himself of the formal charges of heresy, and thus demonstrated finally that theological orthodoxy was compatible with higher criticism. But his evangelical soundness did nothing to allay the fears of his opponents, who regarded his continuing adherence to radically critical views as a danger to the Church at large and in particular to the young men whom Smith had to instruct. He was therefore removed from his chair on a vote of no confidence by the Free Church General Assembly. The trial and subsequent controversy, which lasted from 1876 to 1881, had aroused wide interest far beyond Scotland. It did much to make higher criticism better known to the general public, and the 'German poison' was robbed of much of its terror when it was seen to be dispensed by a scholar of such unexceptionable theological correctness. It is significant that when a similar attempt was made twenty years later, in the same Free Church of Scotland Assembly, to discredit another distinguished Old Testament scholar, George Adam Smith, clerical timidity and obscurantism were soundly defeated.

It had become clear by the beginning of the twentieth century that there could be no return to a view of Scripture which rationalists, scientists and theologians themselves had shown to be impossible. It had further become plain that nothing had been lost in the process except inadequate and unsound theories of the nature of biblical revelation, authority and inspiration. Many of the conclusions of the nineteenth-century critics have since been discarded, but the solid gain to scholarship has been enormous.

Mention has already been made of the distinctive contribution of Wellhausen and Harnack towards a truer assessment of the structure of the Old and New Testaments and of the judicious appraisal of the conclusions of continental historical and literary criticism by British commentators of the stature of S. R. Driver and George Adam Smith in the Old Testament and of J. B. Lightfoot and B. F. Westcott in the New Testament. By their pastoral concern and personal piety combined with their scholarship they illuminated the sacred texts for the ordinary reader of the Bible and persuaded him that the new knowledge

[1] Glover, *Evangelical Nonconformists and Higher Criticism in the Nineteenth Century*, pp. 117ff.

led to an enhancement of the revelation contained in holy Scripture and not to its disappearance. No modern commentator can begin his work without first mastering the insights of these giants.

Similarly in the field of textual criticism the twentieth century stands in debt to scholars of the calibre of Tischendorf in Germany who produced no fewer than eight editions of the Greek New Testament and Westcott and Hort in England whose definitive edition of the New Testament in 1881 marked the end of twenty-eight years' labours. Scholarship of this quality, as of Kittel in the Old Testament, whose *Biblia Hebraica* appeared just after the turn of the century, gives the measure of the lasting achievements of what to so many seemed to be a period of disintegration and destruction. It is not too much to say that the nineteenth-century critics, both 'higher' and 'lower', have provided us with the indispensable foundation for any proper appreciation of the Bible and with the tools with which modern scholarship must work as it seeks by fresh insights to discover new facets of the truth enshrined within the sacred canon.

To describe the twentieth century as the post-critical era is permissible only if it implies that the solid achievements of the nineteenth-century liberal scholars are accepted as the basis for further study. It cannot be regarded as a legitimate description if it implies that criticism has ceased or ought to cease. Brunner's words in this connection are worth recording: 'It is in keeping with God's choice of a small insignificant and uncouth people, and with his revelation of his profoundest mystery on the Cross at Golgotha, that he gave us his word in a literary document which will give the critics, in the legitimate exercise of their task, enough to do for generations to come.'[1] Critical study of the Bible must of necessity continue so long as men seek to bring new knowledge and fresh insights to bear upon the sacred texts.

In the last fifty years or so scholars have continued to develop the positive findings of nineteenth-century criticism in a variety of ways. The Graf–Wellhausen hypothesis of four major sources in the Pentateuch has been carried further in a fissiparous direction by Eissfeldt, Morgenstern and Pfeiffer, and the same methods of literary dissection have been applied to other books of the Old Testament. In reaction against what was apparently an endless and sterile process of fragmentation Gunkel forsook this analytical method and maintained that rather

[1] *Philosophy of Religion*, p. 156.

than examine the 'documents' and their original components, scholarship must betake itself to a study of the *Sitz im Leben* from which the documents sprang.

In the case of the Old Testament the basic material for study was, he maintained, the tradition of song and story, of myth and legend, which existed in oral form long before written sources of any kind appeared. This concentration on oral tradition, the value of which had first been seen by Alexander Geddes but which had been lost sight of in favour of study of the written sources since Astruc, led Gunkel and later Gressmann further into an identification of literary 'forms' or types in the Old Testament narratives, which again went back to the eighteenth century for its origin, since Herder had first suggested that the poetic spirit expresses itself in certain distinctive forms which later become standardized at the written stage.

The contemporary Scandinavian school of research into the 'history of tradition' in the Old Testament springs from Gunkel's insights. Wellhausen's four documents—J, E, D, and P—cease to be regarded as clearly definable units which can be dated and assigned to individual authors or editors and become blocks of oral tradition crystallized into literary form over a long and indefinite period of time. In association with this view the Uppsala School, notably Engnell and Haldar, have developed their distinctive theory of the importance of the cult-prophets as the moulders of Old Testament literature. This reinstatement of the formative significance of priest and liturgy in the construction of the Old Testament has been a necessary corrective to the nineteenth-century concentration on the paramount role of the prophet.

Less promising would appear to be the emphasis of the 'myth and ritual' school, led by the Norwegian scholar Mowinckel, on the Babylonian New Year Festival as the clue to the understanding of many features in the Hebrew psalms, although his contention that a parallel 'enthronement' of Yahweh took place annually at a Jewish New Year ceremony has led to much fruitful study of the significance of kingship in Israel. It is not without interest that the work of S. H. Hooke and A. R. Johnson in this connection goes back through Johannes Pedersen to the instigator of the anthropological approach to the Old Testament, the nineteenth-century victim of biblical obscurantism, William Robertson Smith.

Within the range of the New Testament, criticism has likewise continued profitably in the last half century. In the succession of Harnack, B. H. Streeter pursued the investigation of the structure of the Gospels with striking results. His advocacy of Proto-Luke, as a first draft of Luke's Gospel, has met with less acceptance than his enlargement of the nineteenth-century two-source hypothesis as a solution of the synoptic problem. Streeter's view that four 'documents' lie behind the existing synoptic Gospels—two documents containing the material peculiar to Matthew and Luke as well as the recognized basic documents of Mark and Q—has not been universally subscribed to, but that four distinct sources must be recognized whether oral or written is still a basic presupposition of Gospel study. Bussmann's subsequent identification of eight sources appeared to be leading New Testament criticism along the same barren track as had stretched before Pentateuchal criticism prior to Gunkel.

Accordingly, it is not surprising that Gunkel's approach to the Old Testament was followed and improved on by a group of German New Testament scholars just after World War I. K. L. Schmidt, Martin Dibelius, and Rudolf Bultmann, working independently, initiated, as the exponents of Form-criticism, one of the most significant developments in New Testament study since the beginning of this century. Schmidt contented himself with dissolving Mark into a collection of isolated *pericopae*, strung together like pearls on a string in no recognizable chronological order, while Bultmann and Dibelius proceeded to classify the Gospel material into categories of varying reliability based on the form of each isolated incident. This was in effect based on an acceptance of Gunkel's principle of the *Sitz im Leben* as being the criterion for judging the provenance and original form of any Gospel narrative.

Most scholars would accept the basic contention of the *Formgeschichtler* that the Christian community has coloured the transmission of Gospel tradition to some extent, and that missionary enterprise rather than biographical interest governed the assembling of the stories and sayings in the Gospels. More hesitation would be felt about subscribing to the Form-critics' claim to be able to judge the historical reliability of a particular incident on the basis of its classification into one or other of the categories which Form-criticism claimed to be able to distinguish. Fewer still—at least among Anglo-Saxon scholars—

would follow Bultmann in his further attempt to 'demythologize' the Gospels, where his historical scepticism leads him to divest the record of the life and ministry of Jesus of almost everything except the most banal and pedestrian occurrences of birth and death. C. H. Dodd, T. W. Manson and Vincent Taylor, in contending for the substantial historical reliability of the Gospels on critical grounds, reflect the inability of the ordinary Englishman to follow the Teutonic mind along a line which seems to be able to combine historical scepticism about the life of Jesus with a devout faith in the person of Christ. Strong support for a more conservative approach has more recently come from Riesenfeld, who concludes that the sayings of Jesus as presented in the Gospels bear clear evidence of a single creative mind, rather than of a theology-making community.

The flood of nineteenth-century lives of Jesus continued into this century, but without doubt Albert Schweitzer's survey of past attempts in this direction and his original demand for a recognition of the eschatological element in the Gospels, which the liberal picture of the 'Jesus of history' had tended to disregard, restored the correct balance, even if it overstated the case, in much the same way as Barth's *Römerbrief* paved the way for a truer assessment of the mind and significance of St Paul.

As a background to this bare outline of the main trends of biblical criticism within the last few decades notice must be taken of the prodigious results in the field of biblical archaeology. In this scholars of Europe and America have amassed evidence of the utmost value for a better understanding of the milieu in which old Israel fulfilled its destiny and the new Israel was brought to birth. In Egypt, Mesopotamia and Palestine itself monuments, inscriptions, tablets, pottery and artefacts discovered above and below ground have shed unexpected and welcome light on most aspects of biblical history and literature. Once again the twentieth century has entered into the legacy of nineteenth-century scholarship. Grotefend's successful deciphering of Babylonian cuneiform, like Champollion's identification of Egyptian hieroglyphics, opened the door to a vast area of new knowledge illuminating the biblical story. The Tell el Amarna tablets and the Elephantiné papyri, both discovered before the turn of the century and having direct bearing on Egypt's relations with Asia at periods when the biblical evidence is none too clear, are matched by the fascinating discovery a mere thirty years ago of the Ras Shamra tablets which revolutionized the conception of Canaanite religion as a primitive form of nature worship and revealed it as the mortal danger to Yahwism which the prophets battled with for centuries. Excavations at Nineveh and Babylon, Mari and Ur, Hazor and Jericho, Megiddo and Lachish have all contributed by the skilful interpretation of the evidence which these sites have revealed to widen and deepen our knowledge of the biblical period, and in a variety of ways to confirm the general picture which the Bible presents.

Nor has this patient service of scholarship been confined to critical examination of the solid evidence of brick and stone. The sands of Egypt at Oxyrhynchus and elsewhere have disgorged masses of biblical and non-biblical papyri, and the Chester Beatty collection and the Rylands fragment of St John's Gospel represent only the most sensational discoveries in a vast new field of investigation. The finding of the Dead Sea Scroll of Isaiah and the skill with which the contents of the jars at Qumran have been examined may be regarded as proof that Tischendorf's great discovery of the *Codex Sinaiticus* and its subsequent study set the pattern for a new chapter in biblical scholarship which links the present day through the great nineteenth-century textual and critical scholars with the eighteenth-century pioneers.

Alongside this varied range of Old and New Testament studies, among which a developing interest in rabbinical literature and the Aramaic origins of the Gospels must also be mentioned, twentieth-century scholarship has recently turned its attention more and more to questions of biblical theology. The controversies of the past two centuries have borne fruit and the conclusions that have emerged from them are being used as a base from which to advance to more positive results. The 'assured results of criticism' have indeed disposed of a wrong approach to the Bible. The task of biblical scholarship in this century is to recover the right approach, in the light of the mass of new knowledge, to such problems as the nature of biblical authority and revelation, the unity of the Bible and the function of the Bible in the Church. The basis of such study may be expressed in some words of P. T. Forsyth, which crystallize the transition from Chillingworth's position to that of twentieth-century biblical scholarship: 'The Gospel, and the Gospel alone, is the religion of Protestants.'

CHAPTER VIII

THE RISE OF MODERN BIBLICAL SCHOLARSHIP AND RECENT DISCUSSION OF THE AUTHORITY OF THE BIBLE

THE RISE OF MODERN BIBLICAL SCHOLARSHIP

During the century and a half in which modern methods of study have been applied to the task of biblical research the achievement of scholarship has been positive and immense. Inscriptions and documents contemporaneous with the biblical writings have been discovered; ancient languages can now be read whose existence was unknown or barely suspected by scholars a hundred years ago. It is today possible to compare biblical religious and social ideas and practices with those of other ancient peoples who lived alongside Israel and who influenced and were influenced by the development of Jewish and Christian thought and worship. Modern archaeological, philological and 'history-of-religion' methods have resulted in the accumulation of a mass of knowledge which illuminates every page of the Bible, while at the same time the development of the critical, literary and historical study of the biblical books themselves has brought about a complete revision of traditional notions about their relation to one another. It is impossible here to catalogue the results of these researches, but it is necessary to say something about their rise in the nineteenth century and their consequences both for biblical interpretation and for Christian theology in general in the twentieth. One thing has happened as a result of the rise of modern biblical research in the nineteenth century, and it affects every school of biblical interpretation in the western world today: it is no longer possible to ignore the discoveries of the scientific investigators, the archaeologists, philologists and workers in the sphere of the history of religion (loosely called 'comparative religion'). This in itself implies a change of attitude towards the Bible which is of the greatest theological significance. All confessional or other types and schools of biblical interpretation take seriously such matters as, for example, the discoveries at Qumran, and they await eagerly or anxiously the publication of such new source materials as the Gnostic texts discovered in Upper Egypt in 1946, now in the Coptic museum at Cairo. That the theologians of every developed school of thought throughout western Christendom are aware of the importance of such things is evidence that the Bible is no longer held to be a sacred revelation having nothing in common with the religious literature of non-Christian peoples; it possesses no sacrosanct immunity from the investigations of historical science. This changed attitude towards the Bible is itself a testimony to the achievement of scholarship in the biblical field. How has this change come about and what are its implications for theology?

The thought of our own times has been shaped by the two great intellectual revolutions of the modern period—the scientific revolution of the sixteenth and seventeenth centuries, and the revolution in historical method which was the great achievement of the nineteenth century. The two revolutions are not indeed separate and distinct things; perhaps we should think rather of one great reorientation of the human mind, which began with the Renaissance and is still continuing. It began with the rise of what we today call the natural sciences; and by the nineteenth century it had embraced the sphere of history and what are now called the human sciences. However we account for it, the emergence of the modern scientific study of history in the nineteenth century was a distinctively new development, to which there was no real parallel in earlier centuries. There had indeed been a long line of literary and philosophical historians in previous centuries, but from Herodotus to Gibbon there is little sign of an awareness of historical *method* in the modern sense. There had been a considerable accumulation of historical facts, as every reader of Gibbon is aware; but the distinctive contribution of the nineteenth century was lacking: there was no sense of a real development in historical process. Between the time of Gibbon and that of Macaulay a revolution in historical understanding had occurred. For Gibbon there was no essential difference between the age of the Antonines and that of the English Georges; there was no development, only decline. For Macaulay, on the other hand, history was no longer 'static' but moving; there was an awareness of the emergently new. With the perhaps unavoidable exaggerations of the new historical outlook, as expressed, for instance, in the later nineteenth-century doctrines of progress and the perfectibility of mankind, we need not concern ourselves. It is necessary for our purpose only that we should note the revolution which had taken place in men's view of history, without which historical method in the modern sense could not have been developed.

It was inevitable that the new sense of historical development and the consequent new methods of historical study should have been applied to the study of the Bible and of Christian origins generally. Indeed, it may fairly be claimed that theologians and biblical scholars were as much responsible for the development of the modern study of history as were scholars in any other field. Before the middle of the nineteenth century the new historical approach to the Bible and to Christian doctrine was already presenting sensitive minds with an agonizing challenge to re-think all their theological presuppositions. We need look only at two of the greatest—perhaps the two greatest—prophetic Christian thinkers of the age, Newman and Kierkegaard. Newman was aware of a problem of development in doctrine which could not have been suspected by the theologians of previous centuries. How could the faith once delivered to the saints be said to have developed in the way in which historical inquiry indicated that it had developed, without becoming in the process a different faith? Kierkegaard, most clearly perhaps in the *Unscientific Postcript*, reveals a deep scepticism concerning the possibility of genuine historical knowledge; he is driven to formulate his doctrine of the contemporaneity of the Christ-event because he cannot find a firm historical foundation for faith. A problem of history had now arisen, a problem of which previous generations of theologians had been unaware. It is the question which, above all others, modern theology since the days of Newman and Kierkegarad has been compelled to face. What becomes of the certainty of the revelation if its foundation is only the shifting sands of the relativities of history? To put the question in another way, if the Bible is merely the written deposit of only one line of religious development which took place in the Fertile Crescent in ancient times, what grounds are there for attributing to it an authority which other religious movements do not possess? What becomes of the claim that the Bible is the sole authoritative revelation of the divine nature and purpose for the world?

One important consequence of the nineteenth-century revolution in historical understanding was the rise of 'historical' theology and its separation from 'systematic' theology. Unlike the latter, historical theology did not concern itself with ultimate questions or 'live' convictions. Its outlook was strictly scientific, and science does not deal with ultimate or existential questions and convictions. The scientist, *qua* scientist, is fully occupied with the detailed investigation of his strictly limited field of study; and the intensive concentration upon it of all his energies leaves him with little time for meta-scientific questions. Hume and Kant might debate the question whether or how scientific knowledge is possible; but the physicists and chemists and biologists, absorbed in the extension of knowledge within their own chosen field, listen with scarcely half an ear to what the philosophers are saying. They know that scientific knowledge is possible; they are amassing it daily, and the remarkable achievements of technology and medicine are sufficient pragmatic justification of their belief in the possibility of scientific knowledge. Similarly, the students in the new disciplines of historical theology may find their attention absorbed in their detailed investigations: they are establishing the true text of a biblical writing, or laying bare the influences of Babylonian cosmology upon Hebrew religious ideas, or tracing the development of patristic Logos-theology, or performing a thousand similar research projects; and they often have little time to consider the further questions of systematic or philosophical theology. Even dogmatics can be handled as a discipline of historical theology; it becomes the 'scientific' investigation of the process of the formulation of Christian dogmas. In all such study the research worker himself may remain uncommitted; like all scientific workers he must have an open mind and speak as he finds. There thus emerged a characteristic figure of the late nineteenth- and early twentieth-century theological faculty, more common perhaps in England than in Scotland or America, and commonest of all in pre-Nazi Germany: the academic theologian who was not interested in theology—if by theology is meant a living system of committed faith, articulated by the operation of the believing mind as it thinks theologically. Historical theology played a very important role in the age of bitter denominational controversy at the end of the nineteenth and the beginning of the twentieth centuries, since it was only upon this basis that scholars of different confessional allegiances could collaborate in research and teaching as members of the same university faculty; the 'ecumenical' approach had not then arisen. It is not surprising that the age of denominational quarrelling should have been followed by the age of historical theology, which, though it is no longer the dominant point of view, has left its legacy behind it—a legacy which includes at least one insight of permanent and unchallenged value: that every question of historical development must be investigated with as truly impartial or scientific a detachment as human investigators can bring to bear upon it. Today it would be generally agreed that historical theology is an important part of theological inquiry, but it is not the whole of it: the Bible is not only a field for the ingenious exercise of modern historical methods; it must be studied also by means of other, less detached, theological disciplines.

The late Professor H. R. Mackintosh described the nineteenth century as more important for Christian theology than any century since the fourth. It witnessed the development of a new situation which required the fashioning of an entirely new theological method. At the end of the eighteenth century, as throughout it, the traditional conception of divine revelation was still everywhere accepted in western Christendom: Catholics and Protestants alike conceived of revelation as contained in inerrant propositions written down in the Bible by authors who were directly inspired by the Spirit of God. By the end of the nineteenth century this traditional view was no longer possible for those who had accepted the implications of what we have called the revolution in historical method. A new schism had arisen in Christendom, and it cut right across the old lines of division between the several historic confessions or denominations. Some of the conflicts that arose within the different churches have been described in the last chapter; here we are concerned with the theological issues that were at stake rather than with the details of the controversies that took place.

The main issue was whether the new historical approach to the understanding of the Bible should be accepted or rejected. There were, of course, conservatives and modernists in all the confessions; but of the historic denominations into which western Christendom had been divided since the Reformation it was only the Roman Catholic Church in which, after the suppression of the modernist movement associated with the names of the Abbé Loisy and Father George Tyrrell in the early years of the present century, the new approach was formally and officially rejected. The position of the Roman Catholic Church has been described in chapter VI of this volume, and it is therefore unnecessary to discuss it here. Within the major non-Roman churches there remained a minority of those who rejected the new approach, although by the turn of the century the effective leadership in these churches had decided in its favour. A few of the smaller Protestant sects remain today almost wholly conservative in this regard. With the many and various near-Christian apocalyptic sects, whose position rests upon non-biblical additions rather than upon a scholarly exegesis of the Christian Scriptures, we shall not concern ourselves at all.

THE NEW PRINCIPLE OF EXEGESIS

The rise of modern biblical scholarship presented the Church with a new principle and method of biblical exegesis, such as was not and could not have been in use before the nineteenth-century revolution in historical method. The main difference between the exegetical situation up to the end of the eighteenth century and that which has existed since the latter half of the nineteenth century can be stated quite simply. First, before the nineteenth century it was almost universally assumed that the whole Bible was equally true, since the Holy Spirit of God was the real author of the Scriptures in every part; whereas from the nineteenth century onwards it was possible, indeed necessary, to admit that the Bible was not everywhere equally true, but that there were different and indeed contradictory conceptions of God's nature and of human responsibilities in its different parts. Secondly, before the nineteenth century it had been widely assumed that the Bible contained the written revelation of God to the world, and that in fact God's revelation of himself was something which he had communicated to mankind in the form of propositions written in a book; whereas after the nineteenth century it has become increasingly difficult to believe that revelation is primarily a matter of propositions *about* God at all. Of course, before the nineteenth century there had been doctors of the Church who knew very well that the real content of the divine revelation was God himself, not propositions about him; but during the eighteenth century the insights of a Luther or a Pascal had been buried under the weight of Protestant or post-Tridentine scholasticism, and revelation had come to be generally identified with revealed propositions about God. The nineteenth-century revolution in historical method made necessary the formulation of a fresh view of what revelation consists in. If revelation is not to be identified with propositions written down in a book, what then is the content of it? Some would consider that the answering of this question is the primary task of theologians in the twentieth century.

It is not difficult to see that the rise of modern biblical scholarship must also have necessitated the abandonment of traditional methods of scriptural exegesis and the development of new ones. The assumption that the Holy Spirit was the real author of the whole Bible made it unnecessary for earlier commentators to pay close attention to the style, historical setting, or even the original intention of the human author; the Hebrew prophets were, of course, speaking to a particular historical situation in their nation's life, but that was of no great interest to any save scholars; the only important matter was that their words were the speech of God addressed to all human beings in all ages and in all places. In the eighteenth century there had not as yet emerged the awareness that the actual meaning of the words of the Bible was so intimately bound up with the historical situation in which they were written that their true import could not be understood apart from a sound appreciation of their original intention at a particular time and place. In other words, the significance of the fact that the Christian revelation was a *historical* revelation was not yet properly understood. If the biblical revelation be historical, as the nineteenth century came to understand history, then a new type of exegesis will be required to elucidate the Scriptures, namely one which is based upon sound historical scholarship. It will no longer be possible to treat the words of the Bible as timeless truths addressed to the world at large (except, of course, when a general ethical rule, or something of the kind, is being deliberately asserted), since their real meaning cannot be understood apart from their historical context. It is no longer admissible to quote a proof-text from any part of Scripture as if it were a word of God directed towards the subject of a current discussion. Nor can it be permissible to place passages from different parts of Scripture side by side, in order to establish a meaning, without asking whether in fact the same meaning was intended by the different authors in their different historical contexts. In fact, a new and strict control of exegesis was involved in the acceptance of the historical method: no longer, for instance, could one find a scriptural basis for the doctrine of the Trinity in Isaiah's 'Holy, holy, holy', or (to take a more up-to-date illustration) justify racial discrimination on the basis of the early chapters of Genesis.

There were losses as well as gains amongst the consequences of what we may call the new historical control of biblical exegesis. Amongst the losses must be reckoned the gradual decay of the ordinary Christian's sense that he can read the Bible for himself without an interpreter and discover its unambiguous meaning. One factor at least in the decline of Bible reading on the part of individual Christians must surely be that the Bible came to be regarded as a book for experts, requiring an elaborate training in linguistic and historical disciplines before it could be properly understood; if it needed expert knowledge before it could be read, it was best to leave the Bible to the experts, like so many other things in a world of specialization. The layman would be satisfied if, every now and then, some expert would bring him up to date in the conclusions which the research workers had reached; he could thus be spared the trouble of reading the Bible for himself, since he would be unlikely to profit by his own inexpert flounderings. The Bible all at once became a difficult book, a specialist's book, not a book for working men and women; the new principles of exegesis were not easy to practise. And indeed it must be admitted that during the last century the Bible has become a difficult book in this sense: a hundred years ago the simple Christian found many obscurities in the prophets or St Paul, but he believed that what was lacking to him was spiritual understanding, since the divine word must have a patent and illuminating meaning to those whose eyes were open to the light; today the modern reader knows that he cannot understand what Jeremiah or St Paul is talking about because he does not know enough about the historical background: he tends often to be hardly aware of a need for spiritual understanding. The task of reconciling the old truth with the new one is not easy, yet it is becoming more generally acknowledged that both spiritual insight and historical understanding are necessary for the accomplishment of sound biblical exegesis.

The historical control of biblical exegesis, however, brings with it certain definite gains. Chief among these is perhaps the reduction of the subjective element in biblical interpretation, or at least the possibility of such a reduction. The original meaning of many scriptural passages in the light of our modern understanding of their historical context is now no longer in dispute, whereas until after the end of the eighteenth century many passages could not be understood in this way at all. For instance, Isaiah xl–lv and the Book of Daniel can now be understood more intelligently because of what modern scholarship has shown us of the circumstances in which they were written and the intention of their authors in writing them. Historical information is the best antidote to the uncontrolled subjectivism which formerly interpreted such prophecies as if they were cryptic divine revelations of the future course and predestined end of world history. Again, genuine historical understanding removes the very serious difficulties created by the traditional view, which held that all parts of Scripture were equally true because they were all equally the direct utterance of God himself. Once the nineteenth century had given birth to the conception of history as developing, not static, it was no longer necessary to believe that the divine command to Saul to slaughter the women and children of the Amalekites was as adequately revelatory of the character and purpose of God as the love-commandment of the Sermon on the Mount. It became possible, indeed necessary, to discriminate between two such apparently equal and binding commands of the Law as (say) Exod. xx. 15 ('Thou shalt not steal') and Exod. xxii. 18 ('Thou shalt not suffer a witch to live'). The lack of a soundly historical principle of interpretation in the seventeenth century resulted in witch-burnings that might serve to remind us of the very great practical importance of sound principles of scriptural interpretation in a community which takes the Bible seriously as the revelation of the will of God. The new type of historical exegesis brought relief of mind and conscience to many Christians in the nineteenth century and afterwards, a relief which the older methods of alleviating the apparent asperities of the Word of God had never convincingly provided.

Amongst the methods which earlier centuries had found most useful in the treatment of such passages of Scripture as might offend the sensitive conscience or the enlightened understanding of Christian people the allegorical method of biblical exegesis was pre-eminent. The allegorical interpretation had done for the cultured and philosophically minded Fathers of the ancient Church what the historical method was to do for the Victorians and their successors: both methods helped to reconcile the scriptural teaching with changed views of the universe, whether Ptolemaic or Copernican, whether Stoic or Darwinian, and they made it possible to explain away ethical injunctions and practices which no longer commended themselves to the enlightened conscience. But the allegorical method had never really proved satisfactory to the mind of the Church at large, because it accomplished too much. It was subjective; there was no adequate criterion for its control, so that Aquinas and most of the ancient and medieval doctors of the Church had to insist that the literal meaning of the text was always to be regarded as primary and must never be displaced by the allegorical. This insistence, of course, robbed the allegorical method of exegesis of one of its chief attractions; but it continued to be used throughout the Middle Ages to provide scriptural support for doctrines and practices for which direct literal sanction could not be found. For this reason Luther condemned the allegorical method as a 'beautiful harlot' which seduced men into supporting 'popish' errors that were entirely contrary both to the letter and the spirit of the Bible.[1] In Protestantism generally the allegorical method was renounced and in the seventeenth and eighteenth centuries there prevailed everywhere a literalist biblicism which often prevented the true meaning of Scripture from being perceived. The only question to be discussed was not whether the whole Bible was to be literally received but how fanatically literalist one had to be in all matters of doctrine, ethics, congregational worship and church government. Whether the Church should be governed by bishops or presbyters or whether Christian folk might play tip-cat on Sunday were matters of salvation or damnation, and such issues were to be settled solely by the exegesis of scriptural texts. With what grateful relief would the High Anglicans of the seventeenth century have welcomed the liberation from the dead letter of the scriptural text, if only they could have glimpsed the light that was to be brought by the rise of the historical method in the nineteenth century! But the dawn was not yet, and a century of Protestant scholasticism was to supervene before the contributors to *Lux Mundi* and their successors could develop by means of the new historical method of exegesis the freedom from a dead literalism for which the Caroline divines had contended.

How then, shall we describe the new exegetical method which arose in the nineteenth century? In a word the new hermeneutical principle

[1] See further pp. 24–6, 79 above.

was this. Before we can determine the meaning of any given passage of Scripture we must first ascertain with the aid of every scientific skill at our disposal what its original meaning was for those who first formulated it and first received it. Then we must understand its significance in relation to its place in the development of the biblical revelation as a whole. Only then shall we be in a position to comprehend its meaning for us in the changed situation of today; this latter task will require deep, even prophetic, spiritual insight, which does not come simply by the acquiring of scholarly techniques. Only when we have thus understood the meaning of the scriptural text for ourselves can it be said to be revelation for us; only then can we preach it, live by it, and test it in our lives. Something of this kind is implicit in the use by Christians of the methods of historical exegesis, although the matter might be expressed in several different ways. At once we shall recognize that certain great problems are raised by the new method. These will become more apparent and more urgent as we follow the course of the development of theology in the twentieth century in its particular relation to the question of the authority of Scripture and of the right method of establishing scriptural truth; to trace this development will be the chief aim of the following sections of this chapter. Here we may isolate one aspect of the problem raised by the new historical method of exegesis: how can a revelation which is thus immersed in the relativities of history be said to be a finally authoritative revelation? How, if we begin from the scientific investigation of historical events and utterances, are we to reach the absolute truth of God? Or in its simplest form the question becomes, 'How can the authority of the Bible be maintained in the light of our modern knowledge of its actual origin and history?' In what way can it be said to possess an authority above that of other religious compositions? We shall consider the various answers which have been given to this question in the course of the century or so of theological development which has followed the rise of modern scientific biblical research.

There is, however, one general consideration which ought to be noted before we proceed to this investigation, if only to explain why our subsequent remarks must range over a wider field than that of biblical hermeneutics in the narrow sense. The rise of the modern historical method in the nineteenth century has brought about a revolution in the whole field of theological thinking, not merely a change in the methods of biblical exegesis. The nineteenth century initiated not only a historical revolution but also a revolution in theological method, as we have already suggested. No theological discipline remains in character and method what it had been up to the end of the eighteenth century. This truth may be especially illustrated from the study of dogmatic or systematic theology itself, which is the climax of all the theological disciplines. Until the end of the eighteenth century the task of systematic theology had been conceived of, as the title itself implies, as the systematization of all the variously expressed truths that were to be found in the Scriptures. Since the Bible was thought of as a collection of revealed truths, the very oracles of God himself, the task of the systematic theologian was to arrange these truths into a coherent order. It was clearly necessary to sort out all the various propositional truths contained in the Scriptures, to show that any apparent discrepancies were not real contradictions but only different aspects of a larger truth, and then to arrange them logically according to the fundamental principles of interpretation which underlay the various biblical books and which bound them into a Book, 'the Word of God written'. Aquinas and Calvin would not have disagreed in thus regarding the proper task of the theologian. But, since the nineteenth century, such a conception of the nature and task of systematic theology has no longer been possible for those who have accepted the revolution in theological method occasioned by the rise of modern historical and critical biblical scholarship. No one theological method has been adopted and followed by the various types of theology from Schleiermacher at the beginning of the revolution, to, say, Barth or Bultmann in our own times; indeed wide differences are discernible in their approach to the theology of revelation. The cruciality of the question about theological method has not always been perceived in recent years, but today there is a growing recognition of the need for a critical discussion of methodology before the task of systematic construction can be profitably attempted. The various methods implicit in the main types of modern theology will, it is hoped, become apparent as our investigation continues. A comparative critique of various recent or contemporary theological methods will be attempted, even if in the nature of the case it cannot be conclusively accomplished.

THE CONSERVATIVE REACTION

As has already been pointed out, in Protestant theology a substantial opposition to the new exegetical and theological methods has developed. Not only have certain sects remained strongly conservative, but within the major non-Roman churches considerable elements have rejected the new historical approach. We may for convenience' sake refer to these elements under the general title of 'conservative evangelicalism'. We are concerned only with the conscious, articulate theology which is aware of the issues involved, and not with the many forms of theologically illiterate evangelicalism which proliferate throughout western Christendom. The doctrine of Holy Scripture upheld in articulate conservative evangelicalism is often referred to as that of 'verbal inspiration' or 'plenary inspiration'. It is also often called 'fundamentalism', especially by its detractors. This latter term, however, is not entirely satisfactory, since the word historically denotes much more than a particular theory of scriptural inspiration and authority. The word 'fundamentalism' owes its origin to a series of tracts entitled *The Fundamentals*, written by eminent evangelical leaders (including James Orr, B. B. Warfield, H. C. G. Moule and G. Campbell Morgan) and widely distributed in the English-speaking world with the aid of American money. The first appeared in 1909. The series ranged over many doctrines besides that of the inspiration and authority of the Scriptures, and thus 'fundamentalism', though the word is now often taken to denote a particular view of scriptural inspiration, originally signified the whole system of conservative evangelical doctrines and polemics.

It is important to notice that the conservative evangelical doctrine of the plenary inspiration and verbal inerrancy of the Scriptures is only one strand of a closely twisted rope of distinctively evangelical doctrines, which are all bound up with one another and cannot adequately be considered apart. These doctrines include the penal or substitutionary theory of the Atonement, the necessity of personal experience of salvation and of conversion, the imminence of the literal return of Christ in judgment, and, of course, the verbal inspiration of the Bible. Little stress is laid upon certain other scriptural doctrines, such as the necessity of the sacraments of baptism and the eucharist, the visible unity of the Church as the Body of Christ, corporate salvation in the Church, the priestly character of the Church and its ministry, the oblations of the Christian royal priesthood, and so on. The sectarian character of thorough-going conservative evangelicalism is seen especially in its insistence upon purity of doctrine as a condition of fellowship; many conservative evangelicals will not engage in joint enterprises of evangelism with Christians who do not subscribe to their doctrines and virtually cut themselves off from fellowship with their own church while cultivating an intense religious association with like-minded members of other denominations. The ecumenical temper and the ecumenical movement are not naturally congenial to them.

While in no way denying the positive aspect of the conservative evangelical devotion to the person of Christ as Lord and Saviour, it is probably nevertheless right to think of this kind of conservative evangelicalism as essentially a reaction. In saying this it is not implied that the outlook is reactionary in a pejorative sense, though its opponents have made free use of such words as 'obscurantist' in connection with it. In the first place it represents strongly the Protestant reaction against those elements of medieval Catholicism which the Reformers rejected in the sixteenth century. But historically evangelicalism is also a reaction against Protestant scholasticism, which was dominant in the eighteenth century, towards a warm and personal experience of salvation. Beyond this it is also a reaction against the new historical criticism, especially in its excesses. In each of these reactions its positive affirmations were both necessary and salutary; it witnessed to essential insights into biblical truth which had been in danger of being lost altogether. But like every reaction it carried over into its own system certain of the more questionable aspects of the attitudes from which it resiled. It retained much of the individualism of the late medieval period; it retains that intellectualist notion of revelation as consisting in revealed truths which characterized Protestant (as well as Catholic) scholasticism; and it takes over from nineteenth- and twentieth-century ideology the notion that there can be only one kind of truth, namely, 'scientific' or literal truth. It is with this third aspect of its character of reaction that we are here primarily concerned, and we must take careful note of the significance of the phenomenon of literalism in a scientific age.

The immense prestige of science and its spectacular achievements in the spheres of technology and medicine have accustomed twentieth-century men and women to think of scientific knowledge (of the type of the natural sciences) as the only kind of genuine knowledge, or at least as the ideal of all knowledge. It has become part of the ideological air which they breathe to assume that scientific truth is the only kind of truth and that the only means of ascertaining truth, even the truth of religion, is by means of the scientific method. If scientific method has not as yet been able to verify religious statements, then religion must be held to be a matter of opinion, and everyone must be allowed the indulgence of his own private views. There is no authority in religion, because as yet there is no scientific means of verifying the truth of its claims. In such an atmosphere as this it becomes difficult to understand that religious truth is not primarily a matter of verifiable propositions about God and human destiny, but is rather an existential awareness of man's situation as over against God and the world, which can be expressed and communicated only under the forms of imagination and symbol. The conservative evangelical reflects the spirit of the age in agreeing that there is only one kind of truth, namely the literal or scientific; if the Bible is true, it must be literally true, since there is no other kind of truth than the literal. Hence he feels that to admit that (say) the stories of Gen. i–xi are not literally true means that they are in fact false and that the Bible is therefore fallible and its claim to impart saving truth inadmissible. Therefore he must defend the literal truth of the Scriptures. If the latter were abandoned, we would be back once more in the morass of allegorism and subjectivism. Once we understand the dominance in our society of the central dogma of scientific-humanist ideology, that scientific truth is the only kind of truth, we shall realize that it is not, after all, a strange paradox, but is in fact a natural concurrence, that logical positivism, the literalist interpretation of Scripture, and Bultmann's efforts to demythologize the Gospels should all have appeared as characteristic ways of coming to terms with that dogma in the mid-twentieth century.

Nevertheless, there is on the part of many conservative evangelicals today a willingness to enter into discussion with theologians who do not subscribe to their system of doctrine; and even if the discussion tends to be polemical rather than ecumenical in tone, it indicates a readiness to listen as well as to assert. Then, too, there is an apparent willingness among conservatives to admit the necessity of lower criticism, or the attempt to establish the original text of the biblical documents by means of scholarly research. The Scriptures, it is admitted, possess inerrancy only 'as originally given', and thus it is not necessary to claim that any particular text known to us is endowed with plenary inspiration. Though it is not usual to agree that the accommodation of the Spirit's communication to the personal characteristics of the individual scriptural writer is such as to admit of any danger of misunderstanding or error in the writing, there is often a clearer recognition of the human individuality of the inspired authors as manifested in the varieties of style and presentation in the biblical literature. There is even a tendency in certain quarters to refuse to be pinned down to a literalistic type of exegesis; factual truths may be represented in a symbolic manner. Thus, it is argued, biblical references to the earth as standing on pillars above 'the pit' to which the dead go down, or standing beneath the ceiling of heaven above which God and his angels dwell, need not be taken literally; these are only forms of speech, like our everyday references to the sun's 'rising' and 'setting', and are not to be taken as implying that the Bible upholds a cosmology that is at variance with modern science. Of course, if this reasoning were extended and developed, there would be little to distinguish the conservative evangelical view of Scripture, not indeed from the extremer liberal views, but from the view held by many theologians who do not accept the doctrine of the verbal inspiration and inerrancy of the Scriptures. It would seem that many conservatives today are no longer severely literalist in the interpretation of cosmological texts in the Bible, and for that reason they resent the application of the word 'literalist' to their type of exegesis; yet it would also seem that as far as historical texts are concerned their interpretation remains undeviatingly literalist. Nevertheless, it is an advance to admit that it is not what the Scripture actually says that is inerrant and infallible, but what God intends the Scripture to say to us. The intention of Scripture, it is sometimes admitted, can be discovered only by honest and painstaking exegesis; the meaning which God, as the true author of the Scriptures, intends to convey to us is apprehended only when through the illumination of the Holy Spirit we discern the deep symbolic truth beneath the literal sense of the words. With such a view theologians of other schools would not quarrel, though they might plead for a clearer and franker articulation of it.

The powerful attraction of the doctrine of the plenary inspiration of

Scripture in our scientific age is itself testimony to the devastating effect upon the traditional concept of revelation which the nineteenth-century revolution in theological method has had. In a time of great confusion and uncertainty in religious thinking it is natural that many should seek to find assurance in a retreat to the older or pre-revolutionary position. But this, of course, is just what cannot now be done. The contemporary doctrine of plenary inspiration is not really the same view as that which prevailed up to the end of the eighteenth century. Until then there was no serious alternative, short of complete scepticism, to the traditional view of revelation, just as before Copernicus it was not a rational possibility for men to adopt any alternative cosmology to the Ptolemaic. But the position of a man who insists after the Copernican revolution that the sun goes round the earth is not really the same position as that of the pre-Copernican astronomers. He has in fact taken up an attitude to evidence which the pre-Copernicans had not been able to consider, and which would in all reasonable probability have caused them to modify their Ptolemaic views, if they had had access to it. His attitude to the authority of Ptolemy is quite different from theirs; for them Ptolemy was the only known standard of truth, and accepting Ptolemy did not involve rejecting Copernicus. In the same way the claim, so frequently made, that the conservative evangelicals are maintaining the historic or traditional position is only formally true; the traditional position did not in fact reject evidence which in the nature of the case its pre-nineteenth-century adherents could not have considered. When a far-reaching revolution occurs, no man can be the same after it, however conservative he may strive to be, as those who lived before it; his mind and total outlook have been conditioned in a new way by the necessity of having had to take up an attitude towards the new and revolutionary element that has now appeared. There is an important sense in which the doctrine of the plenary inspiration of the Scriptures in the twentieth century is a new doctrine; nor should it be forgotten that it today carries a passionate emotional and polemical overtone which was not and could not have been associated with pre-nineteenth-century belief in the sufficiency and divine authority of the scriptural revelation. Thus, to take an illustration, in Bishop Butler's *Analogy of Religion* (1736) it is everywhere assumed that the Bible is throughout divinely and infallibly inspired, even when Butler is appealing to reason to support his argument and is refraining from citing revealed truth; but it is hardly open to doubt that, had Butler lived in the nineteenth instead of the eighteenth century, he would have accepted the new theological method, as did his great successor in the see of Durham, J. B. Lightfoot. It is strictly inadmissible to claim (as is sometimes done) the authority of those theologians who lived before the nineteenth century in support of the theory of the plenary inspiration of Scripture as it is put forward in its twentieth-century form.

THE LIBERAL ATTITUDE

By 'liberal' in this connection must be understood the attitude of those who accepted the new principles of historical criticism and exegesis and welcomed them as affording relief from the moral and intellectual difficulties of biblical literalism. Their relief is comparable to that which St Augustine acknowledged himself to have felt when he first encountered the allegorical method as employed by St Ambrose in the exposition of the Old Testament. In their case, as in his, a new type of exegesis removed the obstacles which were met with in the literal interpretation of the Scriptures; but it had the great advantage over the allegorical method of freedom from subjectivism, since it was controlled by seemingly objective or scientific historical standards. The use of the word 'liberal' in this connection must not be taken as referring only to those types of theology known in their continental setting as 'liberal Protestant' and in England as 'modernist'; for in England and elsewhere many theologians of the Catholic outlook (or Anglo-Catholics) and many Liberal Evangelicals could truly be described as 'liberal' in the sense that they accepted the new historical-critical exegesis and yet they found that it yielded a firm biblical basis for an unreduced faith. On the continent of Europe the new historical criticism had been developed and virtually monopolized by theologians of the liberal Protestant school (of whom Sabatier and Harnack were the types), so that 'liberal' and 'liberal Protestant' were more or less synonymous terms. In the extremer liberal Protestant view Jesus was a simple Jewish ethical teacher whose uncomplicated faith in the Fatherhood of God and the Brotherhood of Man was subsequently overlaid by Hellenistic accretions and was thus transmogrified into Catholicism, the 'religion about Jesus'—a mystery-religion with the dying-and-rising

Galilean carpenter as its cult-hero. Loisy had used the same critical principles as those by which Harnack had sought to establish his view of the 'essence of Christianity' and had brilliantly shown that those principles did not support the liberal Protestant theory. But the liberal movement in Roman Catholic theology, which was led by Loisy, was condemned by the papal encyclical *Pascendi Gregis* in 1907, and it was left to Anglican theologians to show that the new criticism was not incompatible with the historic faith of the Church. A notable contribution to this end is to be found in *Essays Catholic and Critical*, a volume of fifteen essays published in 1926 under the editorship of E. G. Selwyn, subsequently dean of Winchester. The essayists, who at the time would have been broadly styled Anglo-Catholic, maintained that the terms 'catholic' and 'critical' were not mutually incompatible but were complementary and that the use of modern critical methods established the truth of the traditional catholic doctrines of the Person of Christ and of the necessity of the Church. They thus took up a position over against that of the Churchmen's Union (or Modern Churchmen's Union as it was called after 1928), which on the whole represented within Anglicanism the liberal Protestant position and which described its standpoint as 'modernist'. The use of the word 'modernist' in this connection, though intelligible enough, is nevertheless historically paradoxical, since it was first used at the beginning of the century in a pejorative sense to describe the position of Loisy and his associates; and this position, as we have indicated, was developed in opposition to the standpoint of Harnack. Nevertheless, the word 'modernism' in England has generally come to be equated with liberal Protestantism of the Harnack type. The important point to notice here, however, is that in England and in the Anglican communion at large the word 'liberal' did not necessarily mean 'liberal Protestant' in the continental sense; and this was largely due to the Anglo-Catholic theologians who continued the line of development suggested by the *Lux Mundi* essayists and also to the Liberal Evangelicals of the school led by V. F. Storr (d. 1940), which published a less influential volume of essays entitled *Liberal Evangelicalism* (ed. by T. G. Rogers, 1923).

The discussion of the new conception of scriptural revelation, necessitated by the development of the critical method, turned largely upon the use of the word 'inspiration'. Like so many other words which have figured prominently in theological controversy, the word 'inspiration' is hardly a biblical word at all. It occurs in the Authorized Version of the New Testament only at II Tim. iii. 16, and in the Revised Version not even there. The conception of 'inspiration' entered Christian thought in post-biblical times from Greek sources; it originally belonged to pagan ways of conceiving of the divine *afflatus* which took possession of a prophet or sibyl, who then uttered the communication of the god in a prophetic frenzy. Such a notion was, of course, far from the mind of the author of II Tim. iii. 16 ('every scripture inspired of God', R.V.), who was thinking rather along Hebraic lines with Gen. ii. 7 in mind: God breathes life into the dead letter of Scripture. However, the conception of the Scriptures as inspired by the Spirit of God passed into traditional Christian thought and terminology, and it was natural that the question raised by the new critical approach should be discussed in terms of the character of scriptural 'inspiration'. Great interest had been focused upon the question by Gore's essay in *Lux Mundi*, which was entitled 'The Holy Spirit and Inspiration'; and it was this essay which especially emphasized the break with the conservative views of Pusey and the Tractarians. The conservatives were gravely perturbed by Gore's acceptance of the new critical approach to the Old Testament. But the tide could not be turned and the new position was formulated in W. Sanday's Bampton lectures (1893) under the title *Inspiration*. Sanday (1843–1920), who was successively Principal of Hatfield Hall, Durham, and Dean Ireland's Professor of Exegesis and Lady Margaret Professor of Divinity at Oxford, had cautiously and painfully worked out his own position in regard to the critical approach to the New Testament, and his influence upon Anglican thought was considerable. For the conservatives the words of Scripture were inspired; and the Bible, thus verbally inspired, was inerrant. With patient exposition enriched by his immense scholarship Sanday showed why such a view was impossible in the light of modern knowledge.

If, then, the Bible is not 'verbally inspired', or if it is not the *words* of Scripture that are inspired, in what sense may Christians speak of the inspiration of Holy Scripture and therefore of its authority? Sanday's answer is that it is the *writers* of the scriptural books who are inspired, not the words which they wrote. The words of Scripture can be said to be inspired only in a secondary or derivative sense, since God's action is personal, not mechanical; it is action upon the minds and hearts of the men to whom he communicates his truth. That truth they must express under the forms of understanding and under the literary conventions which are available to them in their day. The experience of divine inspiration which they have enjoyed is the *revelatum*, the objective gift which they have received; the words in which they seek to communicate their experience are their own. Thus, while they could not have found the words which they wrote in Scripture had not God given them a religious experience of surpassing power, we need not attribute to the Holy Spirit of God any errors or infelicities of expression which may appear in their writings. Nor need we be surprised if we find that there is a gradual evolution of religious ideas, so that the earlier is far transcended in religious truth and value by the later. Thus we may speak of 'degrees of inspiration' and of 'progressive revelation'.

The new view of inspiration, thus developed with much learning and deep sincerity by Sanday, and embraced by increasing numbers of influential leaders and teachers in the English churches, expressed the spirit of the nineteenth-century revolution in historical method in two principal ways. First, it allowed for a *real* development in historical revelation: God revealed his truth as men were able to understand it, and there is *real* progress in religious apprehension between, say, the age of the Judges and that of the great 'writing' prophets. The conception of 'progressive revelation' enabled the enlightened and sensitive modern conscience to understand why it was necessary that the Bible should record the partial gropings and even the positive misconceptions of earlier ages; the Bible is the record of the religious education of the human race, as God guided men's progress from primitive animism or warlike nationalism to prophetic monotheism and universalism. Every partial insight of Israel's long religious development was gathered, when at last men were prepared and able to receive it, into the final revelation of his truth which God gave to the world in Jesus Christ. And secondly, Sanday regarded his new theological method as *inductive*, and therefore as being in harmony with the scientific temper and method of the age. Theology was no longer a deductive science, logically inferring its truths from a series of inerrant propositions within the Bible; it was an inductive science, reaching its conclusions as the result of a wide and scientific induction from the available evidence. It starts from the consciousness of the scriptural writers and analyses the evidence which they themselves present to us concerning the nature and content of their religious experience. It infers that the individual writers are in fact directed by a larger Mind, a central Intelligence, which gives unity and purpose to the biblical writings as a whole. Only thus can we account for the remarkable unity of the many and various books of the Bible written, as they were now known to have been, over such a vast span of time and in such widely different circumstances. The fact of divine revelation through a series of inspired writers is thus not a matter of unsupported speculation or of dogmatic assertion but is one of empirical inquiry and verification. Modern historical method can show that in the biblical history there appears a unique succession of religious geniuses, who were the bearers of an experience so intense that they possessed the power to communicate it and the truths which they inferred from it to all subsequent generations. The truths which are recorded in the Bible are the legacy to us of inspired men, whom God himself had chosen to be the instruments of his revelation. That is why the Bible is authoritative for us. Behind it lies the authority of religious genius, the authority of teachers who had a genius for the knowledge of God, and whose writing therefore possesses an objectivity of reference which, if it cannot be demonstrated, can at least be tested by historical critical research and by the psychological examination of the consciousness of the men whose insights and experience are communicated through the words of the Bible.

The strength of the appeal of such a view as this, as it had been developed by the turn of the century, is obvious. It enabled men to believe in the reality of the divine revelation in the Bible in an age in which the new knowledge had shown the traditional view of scriptural revelation to be untenable. It allowed for the full exercise of the critical faculties of scholars and their freedom of research. It was in entire harmony with the *Zeitgeist*, the spirit of the age, which was one of optimism and of strong belief in the power of man—with or without divine aid—to realize all the splendid potentialities of his nature in the coming years; 'progressive revelation' was the key to the understanding of the Bible, just as belief in progress was the key to the understanding of history or of society. And, though there were those who sought to utilize the new conceptions of 'degrees of inspiration' and 'progressive revelation' in the service of an advanced liberal Protestant position, it could be, and indeed was, accepted *ex animo* by those who, like Sanday himself, believed firmly in the catholic doctrines of the Creed. Thus, though the twentieth century, as it advanced, uncovered difficulties which made it impossible to regard the liberal theory of inspiration as a final and satisfying account of the matter, the theory proved to be most serviceable as a 'caretaker' or interim view in the period between the breakdown of the older literalist theory and the rethinking of the theology of revelation in the twentieth century. It saved many from losing faith in the biblical revelation altogether, and it was advocated with a warmth and enthusiasm by its supporters which brought a new conviction concerning the truth of the Gospel to many who had come to think that the Christian belief in revelation had been discredited. It had rendered one great service: the new theological movements of the twentieth century accepted unquestioningly the principle of the scientific criticism of the Bible. The liberals had shown that the new historical method was not destructive of sincere Christian faith, even though they failed themselves to construct a durable and satisfactory theology of revelation.

With the development of religious thought in the twentieth century the defects of the liberal view of biblical authority have become obvious enough. Most theologians today seem to agree that the non-biblical category of 'inspiration' is not adequate to the elucidation of the doctrine of biblical revelation. Whether in its conservative form of 'inspired words' or in its liberal form of 'inspired men', it cannot adequately express the full biblical truth of God's self-communication to mankind. Until it is carefully examined, it looks as though it will describe to us the mode of God's self-communication to his chosen prophets; but upon examination it is found that it does not do so. The conservatives nowadays usually deny that divine *dictation* was the mode of communication, though they insist that the result of the communication was to produce an inerrant record of God's words, *as if* they had been dictated; but they offer no alternative theory of the mode of the divine communication, and they do not tell us what form 'inspiration' takes. Similarly, the liberals promised an analysis of the inspired religious consciousness of the men of genius through whom the revelation came; but it is hardly an exaggeration to say that the psychology of religion has thrown no light on the mysterious processes by which the revelation of God is communicated to his prophets or by which the knowledge of God is born in the heart of the simple believer. Perhaps it would be sounder to try to say what is meant by biblical revelation or by the authority of the Bible without the aid of a category of interpretation which strictly belongs to a non-biblical religious system and which inevitably therefore could not elucidate the distinctively biblical understanding of revelation by the Word of God.

The category of 'religious experience' has also been severely criticized by theologians in the twentieth century. Sanday himself met the objection that he was founding the authority of Scripture upon the religious experience of men who had been dead for a long time by reasonably pointing out that the new approach had made the men of the Bible live again, as real persons in real history, confronted by the same problems and moved by the same passions as we ourselves, and capable (as may be empirically verified) of communicating their experience and understanding of God to men in every age. But it is nevertheless not apparent that the authority *of the Bible* can be established in this way; what is established is the authority of a religious experience, and this is not what the Bible itself is concerned with. If the Bible is authoritative because it is inspiring, why should not other inspiring literature be read in our churches along with the Bible—a suggestion which has in fact often been made by liberal Christians? Should those passages in the Bible which are not particularly inspiring be excised, and should we not use a biblical anthology?

Again, the notion of 'progressive revelation' has been widely recognized to stand in need of modification. No one today would wish to deny that there are different levels of insight in the various strata of the Bible; there is such a thing as the historical development of theology in the Bible. But the category of progress, or the nineteenth-century conception of universal evolution, does not seem strictly to apply in the sphere of religious truth. Recent biblical research would lead us to hesitate before we speak of the insights even of the great prophets as being 'higher' than those of the J writer (or 'tradition') in Genesis; did not J present in his own 'primitive' way an insight as profound, as ultimate, as anything which we find in the Deutero-Isaiah, even though he clothed it in childlike, pictorial language? The truth would seem to be rather that insights into God's character and into man's relationship with God are independent of relative priority or lateness in an evolutionary series. Shakespeare is not more profound than Aeschylus or Luther than Jeremiah. There is something artificial about the conception of progress in awareness of existential truth. The apprehension of this kind of truth is today widely recognized to be independent of whether a man's cosmology is primitive or scientific, Ptolemaic or Copernican. There is a sense in which, though there is progress in scientific knowledge, there is not necessarily an equivalent progress in men's existential awareness of their personal being as standing over against, yet in the presence of, their Creator, who commands their obedience. It is through reflection upon such considerations as these that many theologians have concluded that 'progressive revelation' does not give us an adequate account of the knowledge of God as it is encountered in the scriptural writings. There is the further difficulty also that the conception of progressive revelation does not account for the finality of the biblical disclosure of divine truth. What answer can be given to the question why the revelation of God finished about the end of the first century A.D., when the last book of the New Testament was written? Many of the more extreme liberal theologians, indeed, would have denied that the biblical revelation was final in this sense. They would have said that God has revealed himself in post-biblical times in many new ways—through science and philosophy, art and literature, and so on; but in so doing they would have abandoned the claim that the Bible is unique, and would have made it merely an instance, though perhaps a very important instance, of God's general revelation of himself to the world.

It is such considerations as these that have led, rightly or wrongly, to general dissatisfaction in the mid-twentieth century with the liberal view of the authority of Scripture. That view, it is widely held, does not adequately account for the historic Christian conviction that the Bible is the unique and final communication of God's truth to mankind, despite the intentions of those who, like Sanday, first developed it. The defect of the liberal view in the eyes of its more vehement critics in recent years is that it makes man the judge of revelation; man becomes the lord of the Scriptures, since they are inspired and authoritative only if he judges them out of his own experience so to be. In this way the objective character of biblical authority, which is the very matter to be elucidated, is in fact rendered problematical.

THE DIALECTICAL THEOLOGY

Dissatisfaction with the prevailing theology of religious experience was widely felt by the time that the First World War had ended. In England the Congregationalist divine P. T. Forsyth (1848–1921) had powerfully criticized the presuppositions of theological liberalism, but it was not until some years after his death that his writings received the recognition that they deserved. The event which really 'rang the bell'—to use his own widely quoted metaphor—was the publication of Karl Barth's *Römerbrief* in 1919. Barth (b. 1886) was then a Swiss country pastor, and it should not be forgotten that it was from a pastoral standpoint that he was driven to criticize the prevailing liberal attitude and to reassert the emphases of the Reformation which liberal theology had obscured. He found himself in sympathy with earlier thinkers who had rebelled against the prevailing humanism of the nineteenth century, especially Kierkegaard and Dostoievsky, and he became the leading figure in the school of 'dialectical theology' which developed in the second quarter of the twentieth century. Other members of the school included Emil Brunner (b. 1889), F. Gogarten (b. 1887) and E. Thurneysen (b. 1888), though not all the members of the school would have regarded themselves as Barth's disciples. The term 'dialectical' in this connection arises from the theological method which the members of the school had in common: they criticized the scholastic (whether Protestant or Catholic) method which makes God an object of man's theological apprehension and reasoning, and they criticized also the negative method of mysticism, which declares that only what God is *not* can be stated. The *via positiva* and the *via negativa* must be transcended by a third method, the *via dialectica*, which asserts 'yes' and 'no' at the same time. God is not to be known as an object, like other objects which we can know and reason about; yet there is a knowledge of him which is more than an assertion of negatives: God is known as Subject, as Thou, if he mysteriously and miraculously reveals himself to men in his own unconditioned freedom. Thus, the knowledge of God cannot be written down in propositional form, whether unsystematically as in the words of the Bible, or systematically as in credal formulations or dogmatic systems. God is known as the 'Thou' who addresses us in personal encounter. Such knowledge of God cannot be analysed by psychological techniques and classified as 'religious experience' or anything of the kind; it is uniquely personal and cannot be scrutinized by the 'objective' methods of science. The influence of Kierkegaard's existentialism is apparent in the theologians of the 'dialectical' school. Within the school, however, there are differences of emphasis, and if we here deal with Barth as its most widely influential member, we must not forget that on certain important matters other members of the school would disagree with him. Thus Brunner disagrees with Barth's view that, apart from Christ, man is totally ignorant of God and is not responsible to him, and that the divine image in man is totally obliterated. Against this Brunner would hold that the *form* of the image remains, though the matter is entirely lost; that is to say, man remains formally a creature responsible to God, but materially he is incapable of making a right response at all. From an Anglo-Saxon point of view Brunner's modification of the Barthian extremism seems only a timid compromise, and perhaps for this reason Brunner's influence has been slighter than Barth's in the English-speaking world, although his standpoint may be said to be one degree nearer to it. Barth's influence in the English-speaking world was greatest in the 1930's. Today he has few wholehearted disciples; nevertheless his impact has been incalculable in changing the direction of theological development in Britain and America. It may well be as a prophet, who himself forthtold the Word of God in the troublous days of the Barmen Declaration (1934), that Barth will be chiefly remembered, rather than as the author of the elaborate theory of revelation contained in the massive volumes of *Die Kirchliche Dogmatik*.

Barth starts from the assumption that man, since the Fall, is totally ignorant of God, that all his natural faculties are perverted, including his reason and conscience, and that he therefore has no 'point of connection' with God at all. Many biblical scholars doubt whether this position is scriptural, since it denies the general biblical view that, though man is in rebellion against God, he is nevertheless responsible to God, being aware, however dimly, of the demand which God's law makes upon him even while he is disobeying it. But from this anthropology Barth's theory of revelation follows remorselessly and consistently. There is no such thing as 'general revelation' or 'natural knowledge of God'. It has been pointed out that Barth's 'man' is not 'biblical man' but is the modern atheistic man, the man who mistakenly thinks of himself as ignorant of God, not responsible to God, self-reliant and autonomous. Since there is thus an absolute gulf between man and God, only God can make a bridge or connection. That he does so is sheer grace, mystery and miracle. Revelation creates in man the capacity for the reception of itself—creates it *ex nihilo*, since man had lost all capacity for the knowledge of God through his sin. The means of this miracle of revelation is the Word of God, a subject on which Barth has written at great length, especially in the second half-volume of his *Dogmatik* (English translation, *Church Dogmatics*, II, 2, Edinburgh, 1956, 'The Doctrine of the Word of God'). It is difficult to epitomize the contents of the 884 pages of this 'half-volume', to say nothing of the many other places in which Barth has dealt with the theme. Our particular interest is the question of the relation of the Word of God to Holy Scripture.

Barth speaks of the Word of God as being in three forms. It is revealed in Christ, proclaimed in the act of preaching and written down in the Bible. It is the first of these forms which is primary and unequivocal. The revelation of God is supremely the incarnation of God in Jesus Christ. 'God's revelation takes place in the fact that God's Word became a man and that this man has become God's Word.' The incarnation of the eternal Word, Jesus Christ, is God's revelation. Revelation is 'a miracle that has happened'; it is 'the miracle of Christmas'. In Jesus Christ God comes forth out of his profound hiddenness, comes down and conceals himself in our humanity, and finally unveils himself at Easter in the miracle of the Resurrection. The Virgin Birth indicates and the Empty Tomb verifies that God has spoken to us men; revelation is the disclosure of the hidden God in his Word, Jesus Christ. Revelation thus means that we know something which we could not otherwise have known; and this emphasis seems to impart an intellectualist appearance to Barth's conception of revelation. Revelation is knowledge, saving knowledge, even though it is not knowledge in propositional form; it is knowledge miraculously imparted, rather than (as many would think) knowledge which comes from man's obedience to God's command.

What, then, is the relation of revelation, or of the Word of God in this primary sense, to the preached Word or the Word in the Scriptures? In its primary sense revelation is prior to preaching and Scripture. The preached Word and the written Word are 'signs' which point us back to 'the miracle of Christmas', to the incarnation of the

Word in Jesus Christ. Signs are pointers which do not contain the thing to which they point, and God's Word cannot be contained in human words, whether spoken or written, since God utterly transcends all human activity, and is always 'over against' human works. God does not work through men, whether in culture, science, politics or revelation. The 'signs', the human words, written or spoken, point back to God's revelation in the incarnate Jesus Christ, and that revelation is unconditionally independent of all human action, co-operation or comprehension. Thus, the words of the Bible are not to be identified with the Word of God; they are human words, not words which God has spoken or is speaking to us, since God does not work through or by means of human agents. Whether in fact this is what the Bible itself teaches is questionable; but, granted Barth's 'atheistic' anthropology, it is an integral part of his theology of revelation. As human words the words of the Bible are, like those of any historical documents, open to investigation by the techniques of modern historical and critical science. Such science can serve a useful purpose in investigating the historical Christ of the New Testament, provided that it is clearly recognized that the 'real historical Christ is none other than the biblical Christ attested by the New Testament, that is, the incarnate Word, the risen and exalted one, God manifested in his redeeming action as the object of his disciples' faith'.

In this conception of the proper function of the historico-critical method we may discern a shrewd and penetrating insight, and one which constitutes perhaps the most valuable contribution which Barth has made to the development of modern theology. It is Barth's demonstration of the fact that the historico-critical method is not necessarily bound up with the presuppositions of liberal theology which may well turn out to have been his most significant theological discovery, though, of course, others such as P. T. Forsyth had made the discovery before 1919. It is especially at this point that Barth's influence has been widely and weightily felt, and it is doubtless this aspect of Barth's teaching which Anglican (or Anglo-Catholic) theologians like Sir Edwyn Hoskyns found so stimulating in the articulation of their own views. Barth reinforced from an unexpected quarter the conviction of many High Anglican theologians, to which we have already alluded, that the historical Christian faith was in no way threatened but rather established by the frankest and fullest employment of the critical method.

Barth himself may have thought that he was reasserting the basic principles of Reformation theology; whether he was in fact so doing may be left to the judgment of Luther- and Calvin-scholars to decide; what concerns us here is the importance of Barth's achievement in dissociating the critical method from the liberal presuppositions of those who had first used and developed it. Besides this achievement it is relatively unimportant that other distinctive and extreme elements in Barth's teaching have been widely criticized in Scandinavia, in the English-speaking world and elsewhere—his 'atheistic' view of man, his rejection of general revelation, his intellectualist theory of revelation by the Word of God, his conception of the relation of law and Gospel and his consequent 'Christological' view of political and sociological duties. Barth has helped to show us that critical methods are themselves a matter of indifference, as far as faith and unbelief are concerned; God's saving grace and the miracle of revelation are not susceptible of investigation by human scientific techniques. The presuppositions which the investigator brings to his 'scientific' study of the Bible or of the Gospels will determine what he finds there. These presuppositions or principles of interpretation are not contained in or given by the use of the historico-critical method itself. If we are looking for a 'Jesus of history', a simple Jewish ethical teacher or religious genius, we shall doubtless find one, but he will be the creature of our imagination, since we possess no sources for a life of Jesus out of which a 'neutral' historian could construct an objective biography: 'the Gospels are testimonies not sources'. But criticism is not *per se* committed to 'chasing the ghost of an historical Jesus in the vacuum behind the New Testament'; it may equally well assist us in the task of reaching an exact and discriminating understanding of the apostolic testimony of the New Testament, which is the affirmation of that marvellous light into which God has called us out of darkness.

EXISTENTIALIST THEOLOGY

The shadow of Kierkegaard falls not immediately behind him in his own century but strangely and hauntingly across the twentieth century. Not only is the dialectical theology strongly influenced by Kierkegaard's treatment of the problem of the relation of history and revelation, but even more explicitly 'existentialist' interpretations of the

New Testament have made their appearance in recent years. The most influential of these is that of the great German New Testament scholar, Rudolf Bultmann, who was a professor at Marburg from 1921 to 1951. In his *Die Geschichte der synoptischen Tradition* (1921 and 1931) he developed and employed the method known as the Form-criticism of the Gospels in such a manner as to lead to an extreme scepticism concerning the possibility of our knowledge of the words and deeds of the historical Jesus. In his *Jesus* (1926) he already displayed his existentialist leanings by making the call to 'decision' almost the only significant feature of the Person and work of Christ. In his *Theologie des Neuen Testaments* (1948–53), the work of his mature years, he traced the evolution of Christian theology from its obscure beginnings in the simple call to decision of a Jewish carpenter-rabbi, through its transformation by contact with Jewish apocalyptic fanaticism and Hellenistic speculation, to its fully developed outcome in the Gnostic Catholicism of the second century A.D. The original call to an existential decision had somehow been metamorphosed into a Hellenistic-Gnostic mythology about a Man from Heaven who had descended to earth to rescue fallen humanity by imparting saving *gnosis* and defeating the evil Powers who rule the world, and who had finally ascended again to heaven when his mission was accomplished. Clearly, if one holds such a conception of the theology of the New Testament as this, the only thing to do is to 'demythologize' it with a view to recovering the original message of Jesus, liberating it from all the mythical accretions which it had attracted. This is precisely what Bultmann proposed to do in a lecture first published in 1941, *Offenbarung und Heilsgeschehen* (subsequently also known under the title *Neues Testament und Mythologie*). Rarely has so short a work produced such a volume of controversy and discussion.[1]

A very definite view of the authority of the Scriptures is implied in existentialist theology. But before we turn directly to this theme, it may be useful to make two clarifications. First, Bultmann has accepted Heidegger's existentialist analysis of the human situation: man's condition is that of 'fallenness', until he takes the existential decision by which he discovers, or rather creates, his proper freedom, worth and

[1] English readers will find the original paper of Bultmann together with some of the criticisms which it provoked in the work edited by H. W. Bartsch and translated by R. H. Fuller under the title *Kerygma and Myth* (London, 1953).

self-hood. In his 'natural' or 'fallen' state the individual, cast into a world of fortuitous and meaningless circumstances, is the pawn of impersonal forces which rule his life and to which he submits in subservient and uncomprehending anxiety. Bultmann, however, parts company with Heidegger in thinking that it is not by their own existential decision that individual men find their salvation in an otherwise meaningless universe, but that this salvation is found by them only in their encounter with Jesus, God's Word in history, the 'Christ-event'. The one incontestable historical truth about Christ in history is that, ever since the days of the first apostles, men have found in their existential encounter with him freedom to be themselves and release from subservience to hostile, impersonal forces and from the fear of suffering and death. The second important consideration that we should notice follows from this. Bultmann is at heart an evangelical preacher. His aim is to confront twentieth-century people with the saving fact of the death of Christ. He is poles apart from those modernists who said that it is only Christ's teaching about the Fatherhood of God and the Brotherhood of Man that matters, and that it is of little importance whether or not Christ ever lived, since the truth associated with his name is contained in these two doctrines, however they first came to be formulated. It is, for Bultmann, man's encounter with God in the death of Christ which is the saving fact, and thus salvation depends upon a present relation with a historical reality, the Christ-event. In the interest of this evangelical truth Bultmann will demythologize the Gospel. The Cross of Christ is in every age a scandal, because it means pouring contempt on every human pride in man's ability to save himself. Christianity must always contain a scandal, and the theologian's task is to see that the scandal of Christianity is the right scandal, not a series of adventitious scandals which inevitably deter the modern man from believing. Those who have been brought up with the modern scientific world view must not and need not be scandalized by being asked to believe in miracles, in the Virgin Birth or the Empty Tomb, in the mythology of a God-man who descended from heaven, imparted saving *gnosis*, rose from the dead and ascended again into heaven. The whole first-century mythology is today a false scandal, and it is no part of the Gospel of salvation. The preacher today must confront his contemporaries with the scandal of the Cross and no other.

Clearly this view involves a quite different attitude to the Bible from any of those which we have considered above. It is indeed through the Bible that we encounter the saving Christ-event, and therefore the Bible is for existentialist theology in some sense the Word of God to man. It is through this book and no other that man in fact comes to the saving, existential decision: so much is a matter of historical determination and verification. The Bible is human testimony to the divine action in history for our benefit. But this testimony becomes true for us only if we perceive our need of this benefit, as something which we cannot accomplish for ourselves. Apart from an original awareness in man of his own predicament, a recognition of his 'fallenness', the divine message of the Bible will pass him by. Bultmann thus disagrees with Barth's view that man is so utterly fallen that he has not only no point of connection with God, no faculty for apprehending God's revelation, but also indeed no knowledge of his own fallenness or need of salvation. On the contrary Bultmann would say that man's existential *Angst*, his quest for significance, security, status—even though he seeks these things in monstrous and idolatrous gods or demons of his own devising—is nevertheless evidence that his being is turned towards the God he cannot name. The disturbing awareness of a Thou who confronts us as both demand and promise is the precondition of our understanding of the Bible. The Bible articulates this awareness for us; it expresses our own self-knowledge better than we could express it for ourselves. When we read the Bible, we recognize that it is explaining to us our own existential predicament. Man's basic question about his own existence—not the abstract questions of the philosophers about human nature in general but the anxious, shuddering question of the individual who stands before the abyss of nothingness—is answered by the Bible, not in general philosophical terms but as the answer of a Thou to a thou. Thus, it is only the man who, as he approaches the Bible, is anxiously aware of himself as a problem (and there is no human being who is untroubled by this question of his existence), who will find the word which the Bible contains for him: the word of condemnation and forgiveness. The Bible does not speak to us objectively, that is, in general terms which philosophers can understand; it speaks to us in all the passionate subjectivity of our loneliness as we face the problem of our existence.

Thus, what we find in the Bible is not a revelation of theological truths, nor infallible sentences from which doctrines may be systematized, nor yet an objective history of events which happened a long time ago. Nor is the Bible a collection of the inspired writings of religious geniuses, capable of imparting something of their remarkable religious experience to us. If it is the objectification of anything, it is the objectification of the encounter of the individual soul with the disturbing Presence in whom at last salvation is found: the Bible is the drama of man's existential encounter with God, mythologically presented under the forms of Hebrew or Hellenistic cosmology and mythology. God reveals himself in the Bible, not to the scientific intellect, but through a man's subjective awareness of what is happening to himself in his encounter with the Thou who summons him to existential decision. God does not communicate knowledge about himself to reason in general, but he reveals himself in faith to the man who freely decides to obey his summons. God does not make incursions of a supernatural kind into the natural order so as to convince by miracles the doubting intellect of those who refuse the existential decision; God's power and divinity are known only by those who trust and obey. God can be known only in subjectivity, that is, not as he is in himself or as he is related to nature, but only in relation to us in our human predicament.

Certain definite hermeneutical principles follow from Bultmann's conception of God's revelation of himself through the Scriptures. First, we are not to look for truth about science, cosmology, history or philosophy in the pages of the Bible, since the Bible does not speak to us about impersonal, objective truths. We may distil a good deal of information from the Bible about the history and ideas of the Hebrews or of the early Christians; but this information is only of academic interest unless it becomes a means by which the real or subjective message of the Bible is brought home to us. In Bultmann's view, needless to say, the scholarly study of the Bible is of great value in helping us to perceive the deep existential issues which confronted the men of the Bible in their day, and so in helping us to perceive these issues in relation to our own personal existence. Secondly, since God reveals himself only in our awareness of our existential predicament, the Bible becomes divine revelation for us only in those places in which our reading or hearing of it makes our predicament clear to us; what does not challenge us to personal decision in face of the divine summons is not strictly 'Bible'. As Luther considered only that to be truly

'Bible' which speaks to us of Christ ('was treibt Christum'), so Bultmann might say that only that is 'Bible' which speaks to us of our human predicament and its resolution; the Bible is Holy Scripture for me where it shows me God's answer to my need. Thirdly, it will be a hermeneutic principle that awareness of one's existential predicament is a prerequisite of the understanding of the Bible, and that the Bible itself creates such an explicit awareness. But the Bible could not create such awareness if men were not already implicitly or subconsciously aware, even in their unauthentic existence, of the possibilities of a better understanding of their true existence. Fourthly, all that does not 'speak to our condition' in this sense must be frankly labelled 'primitive cosmology', 'mythology', 'Gnostic speculation' or 'pre-scientific guess-work', as the case may be. Adventitious scandals must not be allowed to prevent modern man's coming to true self-understanding through the reading of the Bible. It is the task of scientific biblical scholarship to remove these adventitious scandals by showing how the real message of the Bible came to be wrapped up in its pre-scientific envelope and by demythologizing it.

In this view of biblical revelation Bultmann certainly emphasizes much that contemporary theologians seem generally inclined to agree needs emphasizing. In calling attention to the *existential* character of biblical truth, he is reasserting what the Bible itself asserts and what has needed to be rediscovered in many periods of Christian history: 'the God of the Bible is not the God of the philosophers and scientists', in Pascal's words, 'but the God of Abraham, the God of Isaac and the God of Jacob, my God and thy God'. Bultmann restates this timeless insight with uncompromising vigour. But theologians, including New Testament scholars, do not for the most part find it necessary to be so sceptical about history that what has been dissolved as historical truth (the miraculous works and historical resurrection of the Jesus of history) must be brought back again as existentialist philosophy. Bultmann, the evangelical preacher, has been so constrained by Bultmann the liberal Protestant biblical critic, that he has been driven to seek in existentialist analysis the truth of the Gospel which originally concerned God's action in history by the resurrection of Jesus from the dead. Bultmann was never able to discard those dogmas of liberal Protestant ideology (such as that miracles cannot happen because of some so-called 'scientific' laws) which drove him into a denial of the apostolic testimony concerning history; his version of New Testament theology does not commend itself as satisfactory to many younger theologians who have never been dominated by scientific-humanist ideology, and who believe (as Bultmann cannot) that God has in fact acted by making 'an incursion into our world'.

CONTEMPORARY TRENDS

In this section we can do no more than call attention to certain tendencies which have developed during the last two or three decades and which are relevant to the task of reformulating the conception of biblical authority. One might speak of them collectively under the heading of 'biblical theology', a phrase which is sometimes used to denote the general standpoint of which these trends are in some sense the expression. But it would be misleading to suggest that there exists a definite school of 'biblical theologians'; it would be impossible to name the 'founder' or recognized leader of any such school. We are concerned rather with certain tendencies or attitudes which are, as it were, 'in the air' in the mid-twentieth century and which express themselves in many different forms.

First, there is abroad a marked determination to take seriously the attitude of the Bible towards itself. That is to say, there is today a widespread awareness of the danger of interpreting the Bible by means of categories and presuppositions which are drawn from some ideology or dogmatic system which has not itself been submitted to a rigorous biblical critique—such as, for instance, the nineteenth-century notion of 'progress', or the modern ideological atheistic conception of human nature, or existentialist philosophy, or a preconceived dogmatic system. The last-mentioned item raises a question which constitutes a disputed issue in contemporary theological discussion: the relation of dogmatics to scriptural exegesis. The discussion is much more vigorous on the Continent of Europe (and perhaps in Scotland) than it is in England, where the traditional preoccupation of theologians with 'historical theology' has led to a relative neglect of the study of dogmatic theology. Of course, all theologians would claim that they take seriously the attitude of the Bible towards itself; but the claim must be critically examined. The scholastic dogmatic systems of 'fundamentalism' (in the sense of a close-knit pattern of doctrines, as described above) or Barth's *Dogmatik*—or any dogmatic system whatever—all claim to derive their principles of interpretation and hence their dogmas from the Bible alone; but it is clear that they cannot all be doing so without remainder. At one extreme there are those who would reject dogmatics altogether and substitute for it scriptural exegesis; at the other there are those who believe in a dogmatic system based upon the divinely guaranteed tradition of the Church which alone is able to interpret Scripture aright and indeed to supplement it. But in the middle are those who strongly reaffirm Luther's principle: *scriptura interpres scripturae.* They know that it is impossible to approach the Bible in an absolutely presuppositionless frame of mind; everyone is moulded by some tradition and is infected by some current ideology; yet in their view it is the theologian's duty to be as free from non-biblical presuppositions as he can and to criticize his own assumptions as rigorously and honestly as possible. In this way critical scholarship and biblical exegesis will no longer be at variance with dogmatics, for 'biblical theology' will have passed over into dogmatics. No longer will it be necessary to say with W. Janasch that 'dogmatic theologians and New Testament critics have two quite different New Testaments before them'.[1] Dogmatics will have been restored to its traditional and proper place at the summit of the hierarchy of all theological studies. This, at least, is the ideal, even though its realization may not yet be in sight. There would today be wide agreement with the view that dogmatics must concern itself with the critique of theological method itself; it must ask whether the method of any particular theologian or school is capable of doing justice to the biblical revelation or only to some explicit or concealed non-biblical philosophy or ideology. Thus, H. Diem in his *Dogmatics*[2] seeks to demonstrate how dogma can serve exegesis as the starting-point for the examination of the biblical text and provide evidence for its exegetical verification. Dogmatic

[1] Quoted from E. Käsemann, 'Probleme der Neutestamentlichen Arbeit in Deutschland', in *Die Freiheit des Evangeliums und die Ordnung der Gesellschaft*, Beiträge zur Evangelischen Theologie, Bd. xv (1952), p. 138, in H. Diem, *Dogmatics* (Edinburgh, 1959), p. 39 (English trans. of *Dogmatik: Ihr Weg zwischen Historismus und Existentialismus* (Munich, 1955), as Bd. II of *Theologie als kirchliche Wissenschaft: Handreichung zur Einübung ihrer Probleme*, by Hermann Diem). W. Janasch is quoted from *Theologische Literaturzeitung* (1951), p. 5. Käsemann's article, and its discussion by Diem, are of great interest in this connection.

[2] See previous footnote.

theologians are becoming more aware of the danger of ignoring the problematic character of their basic assumptions and are engaging in a discussion of comparative theological methodology. A notable contribution to this discussion is made by G. Wingren of Lund in his work translated into English under the title *Theology in Conflict* (Edinburgh, 1958).

A second characteristic of recent thinking about biblical authority has been the interest in the question of the relation between historical event and divine revelation. The late R. H. Lightfoot in his Bampton lectures for 1934 (published in the following year under the title *History and Interpretation in the Gospels*) underlined the question which had already become acute on the Continent with the development of the method of investigation known as Form-criticism; how could the truth of our eternal salvation be derived from the shadowy lineaments of a Jesus of history who was but dimly discernible behind the mists of community tradition and theological interpretation which veiled him from our view? Bultmann himself, one of the leading form-critics, had, as we have seen, taken refuge from the negative implications of his own method and presuppositions in locating the salvation-message of the Gospels in the challenge to individual existential decision. More recent scholarship has found it possible to discover a very much greater measure of historical reliability in the tradition of the apostolic Church as it is recorded in the New Testament.[1] But, even so, because Christianity is a historical religion and offers historical events as the ground of its beliefs, the question of the relationship between history and faith will remain an issue of vital importance. For that reason, it is argued, Christian theology necessarily involves a doctrine of history, just as it involves a doctrine of man or a doctrine of revelation.[2] The most rigorously scientific historical methods must continually be applied in the investigation of Christian origins. But history, it is now well understood, is always a matter of selection and interpretation; and 'bare facts', even if they could be arrived at without *some* principle of interpretation, are not in themselves salvific. If historians demonstrated that a man rose from the dead in the days of Pontius Pilate, what would this strange fact have to do with us? The world is full of inexplicable

[1] See, for example, H. Riesenfeld, *The Gospel Tradition and its Beginnings* (London, 1957).

[2] See John McIntyre, *The Christian Doctrine of History* (Edinburgh, 1957).

things, but they are question-marks, not solutions. It is the interpretation of the fact which makes it significant. It is the apostolic witness to the facts which reveals their importance for us, and witness in the biblical sense always includes meaning.

We are thus led into a third area of discussion in current thinking about the biblical revelation, the question of the relation of history and witness. The biblical history is not simply bare facts but involves the interpretation of facts. It asserts not merely that Israel came out of Egypt or that Jesus rose from the dead, but that God brought Israel out of Egypt and raised Jesus from the dead. When this is said, we have passed from history to *Heilsgeschichte*, from the record of events which secular historical method can investigate to an interpretation of events which requires elucidation by theological method. Events as such are not salvific and history is not theology, even though there is the closest possible relation between event and salvation, between history and theology. This relation is of very great importance and the discussion of it constitutes one of the leading theological issues today. Behind the theological issue there stands the fact which calls not only theology into being but the Christian community itself, its life and worship, its preaching and ministering, as well as its thinking. This fact is that the biblical history itself is kerygmatic, is proclamation; history is the bearer of the Gospel of salvation. To recall the biblical history is to remember the mighty acts of God for man's salvation. To accept the biblical history is to accept the witness of the prophets and apostles by which it has come down to us; it is to understand not merely that certain things happened but that these things happened for our salvation. In the Bible itself history, as is increasingly stressed today, partakes of the character of recital: 'A Syrian ready to perish was my father, and he went down into Egypt...and Yahweh saw our affliction...and Yahweh brought us forth out of Egypt...and brought us into this place, a land flowing with milk and honey' (Deut. xxvi. 5–9). God had established a testimony in Israel, which was to be told to the generations to come, proclaiming the wondrous works which he had done (Psalm lxxviii. 3–7). As in the Old Testament, so also is it in the New; history is important as the bearer of *kerygma*, the proclamation of the mighty acts of God for the salvation of his people. 'The God of our fathers raised up Jesus, whom ye slew, hanging him upon a tree. Him did God exalt with his right hand to be a Prince and a Saviour...

and we are witnesses of these things' (Acts v. 30–2). The Bible in both Testaments is the witness of those who 'saw and believed' the things which God did in their day (cf. I John i. 1–3); and this is why the Bible is different from all other books, even from the great Christian classics. It is eyewitness testimony to God's saving action in history; and therefore inevitably the canon of the Bible is closed when the sum total of the witness of the community which had known the apostles at first hand has been collected together. Anthologies of Christian religious experience would not be 'Bible' in this sense of being the bearer of kerygmatic history. For those who regard the authority of the Bible as residing in the authority of the historical *kerygma* which it contains it is clear that it is unnecessary to appeal to its qualities as a work of religious geniuses, capable of evoking religious experience in us. It is equally clear that its authority does not lie in its power to challenge men to existential decision, even though it may be true that this is what it does. The Bible is not primarily concerned with the experiences and decisions of the individual. In the biblical view the individual is significant only as a member of the people of God. The individual acquires status, dignity and worth in view of his membership of the people who can declare that God brought *us* up out of the land of Egypt or that *our* eyes saw and *our* hands handled the word of life. It is our membership of the people of God which makes the biblical history significant for us, because it is *our* history that we are reciting, not the history of people long dead or of a foreign nation. The Bible is the Church's book, and apart from the Church's faith and worship its meaning cannot be understood from the inside, or as it is in its essential character.

A fourth area of current discussion is that which is connoted by the word 'inspiration'. While it is no longer generally supposed that the investigation of the religious consciousness is likely to lead to a satisfactory psychological explanation of inspiration, it is of course agreed that the prophetic and apostolic understanding of the meaning of the events of the biblical history is entirely due to the revealing action of God. Revelation is a mystery, like all the miraculous works of God. It is God alone who can open the eyes of faith, whether of the prophets and apostles of old or of those who read or hear the biblical message in subsequent generations. As Calvin so clearly stated the matter, 'the same Spirit who spoke by the mouth of the prophets must penetrate our hearts in order to convince us that they faithfully delivered the message with which they were divinely entrusted'.[1] If 'inspiration' means the mystery of the *testimonium Spiritus Sancti internum*, rather than a theory of how revelation comes to us, there is no objection to the use of the word. In his Bampton lectures for 1948 Dr Austin Farrer has proposed a suggestive reinterpretation of the traditional conception of inspiration.[2] The propositions written down in the Scriptures express the response of human witnesses to divine events, not a miraculous divine dictation. But these events are not in themselves revelations, but require interpretation. This is given in the form of images—the great dominating biblical images, fulfilling the basic or archetypal image-structure of the human mind as such, like those of the King, Kingdom of God, Son of Man, Covenant, Sacrifice, and so on. Dr Farrer holds that 'divine truth is supernaturally communicated to men in an act of inspired thinking which falls into the shape of certain images'. Without the great interpretative images there could be no supernatural revelation. 'The great images interpreted the events of Christ's ministry, death and resurrection, and the events interpreted the images; the interplay of the two is revelation. Certainly the events without the images would be no revelation at all, and the images without the events would remain shadows on the clouds.' There has been considerable discussion in recent times about the function of the imagination in the receiving, articulation and communication of religious or ultimate truth, and probably many today would acknowledge the importance of image-thinking in religious apprehension. They might further agree that the inspiration of the prophet in this sense is formally analogous to the inspiration of the poet or artist. Religious truth can be expressed more adequately under the forms of imagination—symbol, image, myth, drama, parable, liturgical rite and sacramental action—than in the propositional sentences of the intellect. But probably many would draw back from Dr Farrer's apparent acknowledgment of the 'plenary inspiration' of images. It may be true that 'the stuff of inspiration is living images', but it need not therefore be denied that, as the intellect is liable to err when it seeks to express the meaning of 'divine events' in propositional form, the imagination also is capable of error, when it strives to express truth in the form of images. There seems no stronger reason to believe that the Spirit implants 'infallible' images in the minds

[1] *Institutes of the Christian Religion*, Bk. I, ch. VII, par. 4.

[2] *The Glass of Vision* (London, 1948), especially lecture III.

of the prophets than that he implants infallible sentences. Indeed, progress in religion (if we may be allowed the expression) may in fact be largely concerned with the purification of images and symbols, a constant demythologizing of misleading and inadequate myths, and a putting in their place not indeed of propositional statements but of more adequate images and myths.

Consideration of the biblical imagery leads us into a fifth area of recent discussion, namely, the question of typology. This may be briefly defined as the doctrine that the coming of Jesus Christ and his Church were foreshadowed in the persons and events of the Old Testament. Before the rise of critical scholarship in the nineteenth century the richly typological interpretation of the ancient Fathers had been somewhat neglected in favour of a mechanistic conception of the predictive element in the Old Testament, which goes hand in hand with the notion that revelation is written down in the propositional statements of Scripture. The traditional argument from prophecy was based upon the mechanistic notion of prediction: if Isaiah of Jerusalem had predicted the release of Jewish captives from Babylon by Cyrus the Persian, or if Daniel at the time of the Exile had correctly predicted the rise of the Seleucid potentates, then the Scriptures must be infallibly inspired by supernatural means. The rise of modern historical method destroyed the argument from prophecy in its traditional form. During the twentieth century, however, it has been increasingly realized that a powerful apologetic may nevertheless be based upon the fulfilment of the Old Testament in the New. This fulfilment is one of types or images rather than a literalistic coming to pass of verbal predictions. The great images of the Old Testament—King, Priest, Prophet, Messiah, Servant, and many more—are 'reborn' in the New. They have been moulded in the crucible of Israel's history, although they include literary and even legendary figures, part history and part imagination: Adam, Abraham, Moses, Joshua, David, Elijah, the Servant of the Lord, the Son of Man. They belong to Israel's history, and to no other nation's, even though they fulfil the universal gropings and the unexpressed desire of all nations. Many of these images, such as those of King or Man-Adam, were ancient even when they were first adopted in the earliest days by prophetic minds in Israel, who demythologized them and pressed them into the service of the knowledge of Yahweh. In addition, however, to these images, which are figures of persons, there are also the great type-situations—the Flood, the Exodus, the Exile, the Return, and so on. These situations gave rise to the great images of salvation, thus moulded in the crucible of Israel's history, which become in the Old Testament vehicles of divine revelation and are found to be a kind of analogical rehearsal of the New Testament drama of incarnation and redemption. Recent study of the New Testament, especially of the Gospels, has shown that those who developed the tradition of the words and life of Jesus, and those who wrote it down in the four Gospels, were all powerfully affected by the Old Testament types and images; and the Gospel tradition took the forms which we know because of the theological-typological interests of the apostolic witnesses and interpreters of the divine saving events. This new study of the Gospels, which has arisen about the middle of our century, is beginning to make the older schools of source-criticism and Form-criticism appear rather old-fashioned. If this new approach to the Gospels is correct, it was the failure to understand St Luke's typological scheme which led the source-critics to postulate the document Q, a hypothesis which would now no longer be required. The importance of theological insight in the work of critical scholarship is once again strikingly illustrated.[1]

Of course, as is to be expected, there are wide differences of view amongst contemporary theologians over the question of how far typological interpretation should be carried. As in the patristic period there is always the danger that typology may degenerate into allegorism and run out into uncontrolled subjectivism. Most Anglo-Saxon scholars would probably hold that this happens in the writings of scholars such as W. Vischer,[2] who discerns in almost every verse of the Old Testament a truth fulfilled in the New, often in a most detailed sense. Such work is full of deep spiritual insight and is of great value for devotional reading and meditation, but it can hardly be taken seriously as biblical interpretation. It is admittedly difficult to decide at which point typology passes over into allegory, and different interpreters do not draw the line at the same point. On the whole there seems to be general agreement that typology differs from allegorical interpretation because, unlike the latter, it points to an objective

[1] See especially *Studies in the Gospels*, ed. by D. E. Nineham (Oxford, 1955).

[2] See his book *The Witness of the Old Testament to Christ* (London, 1949), English trans. of *Das Christuszeugnis des Alten Testaments* (Zurich, Bd. 1, 1934).

historical parallel between the type and its fulfilment.[1] If there is no real historical analogy between the Old Testament event and the New Testament situation which it foreshadows, there is no true typology. In contrast to the Hellenistic or Alexandrian variety of allegorical exegesis, biblical typology seeks to disclose genuinely historical patterns within the scriptural framework; there must be a real and intelligible correspondence between type and antitype. Such patterns, however, are discerned by a kind of poetic insight rather than by the use of any 'objective' scientific criteria; but this does not imply that the patterns or fulfilments are not real enough. It means, however, that the same kind of 'inspired' vision must be present in us if we are to apprehend the genuine analogies which the New Testament writers have perceived between the life and work of Jesus Christ and the quite different yet genuinely analogous pattern of divine action in the history of Israel. It is widely acknowledged that the Gospel-writers enjoyed poetic vision in this sense; and we may, if we wish, call such vision 'inspiration'. It would probably also be widely allowed that the early Christian community as a whole must have possessed a remarkable poetic discernment to enable it to articulate its *kerygma* in the great biblical images as we find them recast in the New Testament and re-enacted in the liturgy of the Church.

A final area of discussion, which should be mentioned, is that of the question of the authority of the Bible in political and social affairs. Every Christian confession, as is well known, interprets the ethical, social and political teaching of the Bible not only according to its own ecclesiastical tradition but also according to the prevailing ideological climate: *cuius regio eius interpretatio*. The poignant reality of this situation is not perceived until Christians meet one another across the confessional frontiers. After the Second World War the necessity of such ecumenical confrontation was obvious, and scholars from different confessions and many lands have come together in a series of ecumenical study conferences under the auspices of the Study Department of the World Council of Churches. A symposium, containing contributions by leading representative theologians from all the main confessions except the Roman, has been published, dealing with 'the biblical authority for the Churches' political and social message

[1] See *Essays in Typology*, by G. W. H. Lampe and K. J. Woollcombe (London, 1957); also *Allegory and Event*, by R. P. C. Hanson (London, 1959).

today'.[1] More recently the discussion of biblical authority in this realm has centred upon the theme of 'the Lordship of Christ over the Church and the World', and groups of biblical scholars and theologians from different confessions and from many parts of the world have been investigating it together. The view is often expressed that this world-wide discussion of biblical authority in relation to the practical tasks and political responsibilities of Christians living in the world is one of the most fruitful enterprises which have been initiated by the World Council of Churches since its inception in 1948. The document entitled 'Guiding Principles for the Interpretation of the Bible', which was drawn up by the Ecumenical Study Conference held at Wadham College, Oxford, in the summer of 1949, has received world-wide study and has already in a sense become a historic document.[2] It is significant because never before had such a deep agreement upon the principles of biblical interpretation been reached and formulated by representative scholars of such widely divergent confessions. This ecumenical inquiry into the *practical* authority of the Bible is a recent development, and it is too early to attempt an assessment of it; but there are grounds for expecting that it will prove an increasingly important method of biblical study in the coming years.

[1] The English edition is *Biblical Authority for Today*, ed. by Alan Richardson and Wolfgang Schweitzer (London, 1951).

[2] It may be found on pp. 240–3 of *Biblical Authority for Today*, mentioned in the preceding footnote.

CHAPTER IX

CONTINENTAL VERSIONS c. 1600 TO THE PRESENT DAY

1. GERMAN VERSIONS

PROTESTANT VERSIONS

It is plain from the history of the Bible that every age has attempted to come to fresh terms with it, to form its own image of it. This is also true of Luther's version of the Bible, which has been the one most commonly printed and by far the most widely accepted in Germany during the period under review.

The linguistic superiority of Luther's Bible had moved Calvinists such as Tossanus and Pareus—especially in the Palatinate and Frankfurt am Main—to print the text and to add, instead of Luther's, prefaces and glosses of their own which had an entirely different spirit. Lutherans protested against this, particularly in Württemberg. But Johannes Piscator went even further, for he also dispensed with Luther's translation, and produced a most uneven one of his own in 1602–3. It was still being printed in Berne in the nineteenth century.

The Thirty Years War both hampered and helped the dissemination of the Bible. The losses were enormous, and the subsequent general poverty made it hard to replace them. The more handy and cheaper formats came into common use as well as the folios. Bible printing ceased entirely in Wittenberg, and the most important printing towns were now Lüneburg, Nürnberg and Frankfurt am Main. In the very middle of the war Sigismund Evenius promoted the production of one of the most important German bibles. The first printing of this 'Weimar Bible', with its many notes, accessories and pictures, was commissioned by Duke Ernst the Pious of Gotha in 1640 at Nürnberg. Though not cheap, it went through more than a dozen editions in 150 years.

After the war the dissemination of the Bible increased. It was not merely a matter of replacing losses; there was a widespread longing for the Bible. In the confusion of war parishes had often remained without a minister to preach to them. The parishioners had had to read and expound the Bible to each other, and thus had come to see it afresh as the Word of God. A new approach to the Bible grew up: no longer as the book of teaching, but as the book of consolation. The things which should have helped towards a clearer understanding—prefaces, notes, glossaries—were now more and more often omitted by the printer; eventually even the pictures were left out. This explanatory matter, partly derived from Luther, had been revised, altered or omitted by the publishers as they saw fit. Now it was left out altogether; and this made it plain that the Bible was now read in a different spirit.

Spener's treatise *Pia desideria* (1675) gave expression and new impetus to this tendency. The spiritual movement of Pietism now began to concern itself in its own way with the Bible.

One hundred and fifty years had passed since Luther's death, during which his translation had been altered in various ways, not all consistent with each other, by the printers. From 1690 Johannes Dieckmann had sought to reconstitute Luther's original text. But a judicious revision in the light of contemporary usage was also necessary. A. H. Francke, founder of the Orphanage at Halle and one of the most influential of the Pietists, made recommendations to this effect in *Observationes biblicae* (1695), but met only opposition, even in his own circle.

The demand for Bibles was great, as the example of Württemberg shows. Bible printing began there only in 1675, but by the end of the eighteenth century some 300,000 Bibles and portions of Bibles had been printed there.

A layman, an official of the State of Brandenburg, Carl Hildebrand, Baron Canstein, came forward in 1710 with his *Ohnmassgeblicher Vorschlag*, a 'private proposal' that the poor should be provided with Bibles at very low prices. There were already societies which issued Bibles cheaply or for nothing. Canstein's aim was to print them cheaply. He set up his *Bibelanstalt*, in association with Francke's Orphanage, with his own money and private contributions. First the New Testament, later the whole Bible, was set up in type and kept standing; the impressions were large, the Prussian postal service gave free carriage. The published price was lower than the cost of production; the *Bibelanstalt* was not a commercial undertaking which must show a profit; charitable contributions had to cover the losses. Some three million Bibles were printed at Halle in the eighteenth century, and another million or so came from other German presses.

These Halle editions provided a bare text with short summaries, and scarcely any prefatory matter; the layout was economical, the paper bad. More expensive editions were also printed, on better paper. Since the total demand could scarcely be met, the operation was not in competition with ordinary printers.

Many publishers adopted the Halle text, which followed Dieckmann's Stade Bible; it became almost the standard text. It was several times carefully revised at Halle in the course of the eighteenth century.

It was the Canstein *Bibelanstalt* which first enabled the Bible to become the book of all evangelical Christians in Germany. To make it cheap, the aids to comprehension which had been provided in the glosses and prefaces of Luther and others were omitted. The Bible was also taken in a sense quite different from Luther's—far less Christocentric.

Men's minds were now more independent, and many began to go their own way even in the understanding of the Bible. The 'mystical and prophetic' Bible edited at Marburg by H. Horche, and the Berleburg Bible in eight volumes edited between 1726 and 1742 by J. H. Haug, were revisions of Luther's text with their own expository matter, pietistic and separatist in intention. Count Zinzendorf, founder and 'bishop' of the *Brüdergemeine* at Herrnhut, himself translated the New Testament freely from the original, giving it a Moravian complexion. J. L. Schmidt's Wertheim Bible had materialist glosses, and was suppressed after the Pentateuch appeared in 1735. C. F. Bahrdt's translation of the New Testament (*Die neuesten Offenbarungen Gottes*, Riga, 1772–5) was often exact, but more often gave a sense derived from his own 'enlightened' views. Fresh study of early manuscripts, which was leading towards a new basic text of the New Testament, influenced new versions such as Heumann's of 1740 and J. D. Michaelis's of 1790 (he had already translated the Old Testament in 1769). J. A. Bengel's posthumous translation of 1753 was intended as a version complementary to Luther's. Pietists of Württemberg prized his New Testament for many years. W. M. L. de Wette provided a scrupulously scholarly translation of the whole Bible in 1809–14; it remained in use longer.

The number of Bibles printed in Germany in the eighteenth century was large, but insufficient. The circulation of the Bible and its study were greatly increased by the founding of the *Deutsche Christentumsgesellschaft* in Basle in 1780. In the stresses of the Napoleonic era the demand for the Bible was quickened. The British and Foreign Bible Society was founded in 1804 in London, the *Privilegierte Württembergische Bibelanstalt* in 1812 in Stuttgart, in 1814 in Berlin and Dresden the Prussian and the Saxon *Hauptbibelgesellschaft*, and then others in rapid succession, each to provide its own territory with Bibles. The new foundations were inspired by London, and heavily subsidized with Bibles and money. In addition to these, Canstein's *Bibelanstalt* was still active. In order to reduce costs, the new societies used both stereotyping and the mechanical printing press invented by König in 1812. They were helped by subscriptions and State support, as well as postal concessions. The prices were low, the impressions large, many Bibles were presented by supporters, and still the German societies were not able to supply Germany's needs. For a long time London had to help out, for even private contributions did not reach the level common in England.[1]

Prices had sunk so low that publishers could not now compete in the trade, and gave up almost entirely. The societies took over the whole production, and the earlier variety now changed, partly because of the inevitable use of stereotyping, into uniformity. The more expensive editions were distinguished by their better quality, and no longer offered aids to comprehension.

Co-operation with London was destroyed by the battle over the Apocrypha between 1824 and 1826. Until well into the eighteenth century many Lutheran Bibles had still contained the books III and IV Esdras and III Maccabees as a supplement to the Apocrypha, though they had neither been translated nor admitted by Luther, but had slipped into Lutheran Bibles in the last third of the sixteenth century. Now the dispute was about all the apocryphal books, which were rejected by many. Societies which printed Bibles including the Apocrypha could not be supported. The German societies took an independent stand, remaining nonetheless in friendly relations with London. The larger part of the Lutheran Bibles circulated in Germany

[1] Cf. below, ch. XI for the Bible societies in general and also for the difficulties over the Apocrypha.

was still printed abroad until the end of the century. Catholic versions were also printed, but only for a few years; co-operative work across confessional frontiers could not be sustained longer than that. In Berne Piscator's translation, mentioned above, was printed; in Zurich the often revised text of the Zurich Bible.

The Bibles were sold through the parishes and by representatives of the societies; only later were they sold through trading channels. They had no explanatory matter; aids to comprehension had to be sought elsewhere—in church services, and in Bible-reading fellowships. For a long time the evangelical Christian remained defenceless against the attacks of science, the belief in progress, and atheism. The ruling doctrine of verbal inspiration brought him into opposition with the findings of natural science, producing chronic uncertainty, rigid conservatism, or the abdication of all attempts to understand and apathy.

The revision of Luther's text urged long before by Francke was attempted. Preparatory studies had appeared since about 1800; many suggestions had been made for its improvement. By 1850 Luther's text was being circulated in some ten different forms; revision and the establishment of a standard text were essential. The task was commissioned in the first place by the Church Conference at Eisenach in 1861; the actual work of revision was completed in 1883, and the final form was approved in 1890. Public interest was very keen and the revisers had to meet many objections; yet afterwards they were thought to have been too cautious. The critical reception of the revision showed something of the estimation in which Luther's Bible still stands in Germany. It has great majesty of style and it is intimately connected with the history of Luther's Church; it is feared that much of the evangelical spirit will be lost if Luther's Bible is no longer the standard translation of the Evangelical Church.

It was otherwise in German-speaking Switzerland, and many who were not content with the revised Lutheran Bible looked towards Zurich, where there was no such sense of obligation towards a translation made once and for all. In Zurich the Bible had been constantly revised to bring it into line with current scholarship, for instance in 1660–7, and most radically in 1772 when rationalist editorial matter had been added; in this form the Bible had been first printed by the Bible Society in 1817. It was revised once more in 1860–8 and 1882, and newly translated from the original texts between 1907 and 1931.

There were still further translations, especially of the New Testament, of which a few may be mentioned here. In the tradition of de Wette, Emil Kautzsch, the Old Testament scholar, and his colleagues produced in 1894 an Old Testament which turned the results of criticism to account.

In 1875 appeared Carl von Weizsäcker's translation of the New Testament, intended as an aid for scholars and often reprinted since. Heinrich Wiese attached an *apparatus criticus* with variant readings to his New Testament (1905, with subsequent editions) and so did Ludwig Albrecht in 1920. Carl Stage's translation of 1896 was more free, often startlingly so. F. E. Schlachter's Miniature Bible, translated in 1905, went to great lengths to give an accurate rendering, like the Darbyite Bible of Elberfeld in 1855.[1] Hermann Menge translated the whole Bible with philological exactitude and into good German from 1923 onwards, and this version like Luther's was reproduced in Braille. Adolf Schlatter's translation of 1931 was the rich harvest of a lifetime of exegesis.

The number of copies of the Lutheran Bible printed in the nineteenth century rose sharply to thirty million copies. By 1900 only the Bible societies remained in the field, and they sought in every way to give the Bible the widest possible currency, for example by producing illustrated Bibles—especially the illustrations of Julius Schnorr von Carolsfeld, Wilhelm Steinhausen, and Rudolph Schäfer.

In 1912 the Stuttgart Bible Society celebrated its centenary by publishing its 'Jubilee Bible', which gives Luther's text with notes by South German ministers. It was a bold step in a new direction, but unfortunately there has as yet been no remodelling of these notes to take account of modern views. In 1935 was published the 'Children's and Family Bible'; an abridged text with notes.

Though no one regarded the notes as binding, there was a demand for such assistance, which is otherwise to be found only in new versions, extensive works of biblical reference, and commentaries. With the printing of these Bibles the Bible societies took up the task which had fallen to them with the cessation of printing by commercial firms.

[1] J. N. Darby, founder of the strict 'Darbyite' sect of the Plymouth Brethren, translated the New Testament into German 'aus dem Urtext' (1855) and the whole Bible, without Apocrypha, by 1871. He also made French versions, New Testament 1859, Old Testament 1885.

The Revision of the Lutheran Bible of 1892 had not given complete satisfaction. Criticism was especially directed at the too conservative treatment of linguistic usage. A new commission was set up only twenty years later, and quietly completed its task. This revision was finished in 1912, and since then the title-page has read 'newly revised'.

In the 1920's preparatory work began for a new revision on the same principles as the first. These terms of reference permitted a good deal of scope in their interpretation, so that yet another revision may very well be necessary before long. The disturbance of the life of the Church by the National Socialists also hindered this work, so that it was only completed for the New Testament in 1938. It was received with interest, and above all it provoked Kurt Ihlenfeld's collective work *The Book of Christianity*. The war prevented the prosecution of the work, and especially its printing. Bible societies were destroyed by bombing, and printing was almost totally crippled by controls and lack of paper.

After the war, the demand was greater than ever, and was at first met with the co-operation of Christians in other countries. For a long time they contributed supplies of Bibles and raw material. Conditions are by now almost entirely back to normal. Today the Bible Society of Altenburg prints in the German Democratic Republic, the *Hauptbibelgesellschaft* in Berlin, the *Privilegierte Württembergische Bibelanstalt* in Stuttgart, the *Cansteinsche Anstalt* at Witten an der Ruhr. Among other translations the very modern translation of Friedrich Pfäfflin, first published in 1939, and the Zurich Bible are most popular. The New Testament in Luther's and other translations is also issued in the form of illustrated newspapers.

The work of revising the Bible was taken up again after the war. The German text in the stage it had reached in 1938 and the Greek text edited by Nestle were taken as the basis of a new revision, which was adopted for the New Testament in 1956 and since then has been published. The Old Testament is to follow in a few years.

Luther's Bible, now more than four hundred years old, and little altered in its language, is still the bond which unites German Evangelical Christians. Other translations have appeared, but have soon become obsolete while Luther's text has remained in use, and will long remain deeply influential.

ROMAN CATHOLIC VERSIONS

Challenged by the Protestant attitude to Scripture and the abundant dissemination of vernacular Bibles, the Church of Rome began to produce its own translations more freely. In 1630 Caspar Ulenberg revised Dietenberger's version, and this, after further revision by Catholic scholars at Mainz in 1662, became the standard Bible for German Catholics, going through some fifty editions. (An unusual production was the *Biblia Pentapla* of 1710, which printed five translations of the Old Testament in parallel columns: Ulenberg, Luther, the Reformed version of Piscator, the version of John Athias, a Jew, and the Dutch States-General Bible. The Old Testament included the Apocrypha and the New Testament had its own Apocrypha.)

More central to the life of the Church was the pertinacious attempt of the brothers Karl and Leander van Ess to promote Bible study. Their version of the New Testament, made from the Greek and published in 1807, was welcomed by the laity but met with clerical opposition and was placed on the Index, partly because it had no notes. In later editions, which were numerous, the text was revised to fit the Vulgate, with alternative renderings from the Greek put at the foot of the page. The Old Testament, from the Hebrew, was published in two parts. In the first, Genesis–Esther (1822), the variant readings of the Vulgate were given in German at the foot of the page; in the second, Job–II Maccabees, 1836, a complete German version of the Vulgate was given below the translation from Hebrew. The whole Bible appeared in 1840 in two forms, one with the Old Testament translated from Hebrew without notes, the other with a version of the Vulgate Old Testament below the version from Hebrew; in both the New Testament was a translation from the Vulgate with variants from the Greek put below. Leander van Ess criticized the Tridentine decree concerning the Vulgate, edited the Vulgate (1822–4), the Septuagint (1824) and Greek New Testament (1827), and called upon the clergy to familiarize their people with the Bible.[1]

A very popular version, based on one begun by H. Braun in 1786, was that of J. F. Allioli, first published in six parts, 1830–7, and frequently reprinted; it was made from the Vulgate, but footnotes drew attention to variants in the original tongues. Besides frequently

[1] In his *Ihr Priester, gebet und erkläret dem Volke die Bibel* (1825).

reprinting Luther's Bible, the British and Foreign Bible Society assisted the circulation of Van Ess's and Allioli's New Testaments, together with other Roman Catholic versions—J. Gossner's (from 1815) and J. H. Kistemaker's (1825; B.F.B.S. from 2nd ed. 1834)—and, from 1855, circulated Van Ess's Bible, without the Apocrypha. The Regensburg Roman Catholic Bible Society, founded in 1805, was suppressed in 1817 just after Pius VII had forbidden Catholics to use Bibles published by the Protestant societies; but by then it had put into circulation half a million copies of the Regensburg New Testament (1808), a version made by M. Wittmann of that city. Throughout the nineteenth century numerous translations were published with the approval of the bishops, most of them made from the Vulgate. The liturgical movement of the twentieth century has endeavoured to stimulate Bible reading by the Catholic laity; and the periodical *Bibel und Liturgie* was founded in 1926 to bring worship and Bible study together. Noteworthy among modern translations are the Grünewald Bible (1924–6; 7th ed., 1956) of P. Riessler (Old Testament) and R. Storr (New Testament), the Herder Bible (1935 onwards, a set of commentaries on the German text), and, among versions of the New Testament, those by Keppler (1915), Rösch (1921), Tillmann (1925–7), Karrer (1950) and Sigge (1957).

2. FRENCH VERSIONS

In the seventeenth century there were few attempts to produce new Protestant translations in French. Only two deserve brief mention, those of Jean Diodati (Geneva, 1644) and Samuel des Marets (Amsterdam, 1669). Diodati follows the earlier Geneva version, bringing the language up to date and endowing it with greater clarity. He is not afraid of trying out new renderings, based on his own earlier Italian translation. Des Marets's claims are slighter: he reproduces the 1652 edition of the Geneva version with some corrections, and his Bible is distinguished mainly by the extensive notes and the typography of the Elzeviers. The Academician Valentin Conrart revised the Marot and Bèze translation of the Psalms in order to make it more acceptable to contemporary taste. His revision, published in 1677–9, was censured by the Synod of Charenton and failed to displace the now traditional stanzas.

On the other hand Catholics grew much more active under the combined influence of the great Catholic revival of the first half of the century; of linguistic development and codification, which made the sixteenth-century versions barely readable; and of literary classicism, which had a similar effect. Attempts to produce a version in harmony with the new spirit were numerous, though few got further than the New Testament or individual books. In 1643 Jacques Corbin published a complete translation from the Vulgate, described by the theologians of Poitiers as very elegant and very literal and by Richard Simon as 'rude et barbare dans les expressions'.[1] In 1647 appeared François Véron's translation of the New Testament. The Abbé de Marolles, an indefatigable translator, published the Psalms and Canticles in 1644 and a New Testament based on Erasmus in 1649; by 1671 he had finished the Old Testament up to Leviticus xxiii, when the enterprise was abruptly stopped by order of the Chancellor Séguier—official suspicions had not disappeared. The Song of Songs and some of the Prophets (Lamentations, Daniel, Jonah, Nahum) appeared later (1677–8). In 1655 the General Assembly of the Clergy planned a new translation, which might have become a French Authorized Version. It was entrusted to Père Amelote, but only the New Testament appeared (Paris, 1666–70). Other partial translators of eminence were Godeau, bishop of Vence (New Testament, Paris, 1668); Bossuet (Revelation, 1689; Song of Songs, 1695); and the Jesuit Père Bouhours (New Testament, Paris, 1697–1704). The eccentric Bordeaux New Testament of 1686 is remarkable for the openings it afforded to Protestant controversialists (for example, *messe*, Acts xiii. 2; *Purgatoire*, I Cor. iii. 15).

But all these seem failures when compared with the outstanding translation of the period, the Bible which came from the Jansenist circle of Port-Royal and is chiefly associated with Isaac Le Maistre de Sacy. Serious work on it began in 1656–7 at the conferences of Vaumurier between Sacy, his brother Antoine, Arnauld, Nicole and the Duc de Luynes. Racine describes the division of labour.[2] The New Testament was completed between 1657 and Sacy's arrest (13 May 1666) and he began the Old Testament in the Bastille (1666–8).[3] Séguier refused to grant a privilege for the New Testament; it was

[1] *Histoire critique du texte du Nouveau Testament* (Rotterdam, 1689–90), II, 353.

[2] M. de Sacy faisoit le canevas...M. Arnauld étoit celui qui déterminoit presque toujours le sens. M. Nicole avoit devant lui saint Chrysostome et Bèze, ce dernier afin de l'éviter (*Œuvres*, Grands Écrivains de la France, vol. IV, 1886, p. 624).

[3] Sainte-Beuve, *Port-Royal*, 6th ed., II, 348 ff.; G. Delassault, *Le Maistre de Sacy et son temps* (Paris, 1957), pp. 151 ff.

probably printed by Daniel Elsevier at Amsterdam and bore the imprint of Gaspard Migeot at Mons (the Mons Testament, 1667).[1] The Old Testament appeared at intervals between 1672 and 1696 (Paris).

The Mons Testament begins with a long preface by Sacy, in which he praises the Louvain version, against the errors of the Calvinists, but observes that revision is necessary on linguistic grounds. He goes on to state clearly the dilemma of every translator of the Bible: either to follow the sense and neglect the letter, or to follow the letter and neglect the sense. The solution is to be both free and literal, and he gives rules for this difficult undertaking. The whole preface is full of the spirit of humility and scrupulousness, but also of excessive self-examination and self-justification, which characterizes Port-Royal. Sacy was a typical and saintly figure, well qualified for his task: '[Jansénius] répétoit souvent qu'il iroit jusqu'au bout du monde avec saint Augustin; et moi, disoit M. de Saci, j'irois avec ma Bible.'[2] The translation itself is marked by correctness, elegance, a preference for abstract words and a tendency to dilute and paraphrase, to smooth out the ruggedness of biblical language. All this is an expression of French literary classicism and may be paralleled in the biblical plays of Racine.

Sacy was sharply criticized by contemporaries. The Jansenist Barcos reproached him for removing the obscurity which the Holy Spirit had deliberately put into the Scriptures.[3] This was in accordance with the Jansenist conception of a hidden God, and Sacy himself shortly before his death expressed similar doubts.[4] The textual critic Richard Simon attacked the absence of consistent principle: the translation was made from the Vulgate, but corrections from the Greek were introduced unsystematically.[5] Bossuet disliked the 'politeness' which was foreign to the original.[6] In spite of such strictures, Sacy's Bible enjoyed great success. Pascal quotes it in the *Pensées*, having seen parts of it before his death in 1662.[7] It has remained one of the most popular French translations and has even been used and circulated by Protestants.

[1] Plate 41.
[2] Fontaine, *Mémoires*, quoted by Sainte-Beuve, *Port-Royal*, II, 332.
[3] Delassault, *Le Maistre de Sacy*, p. 163.
[4] Sainte-Beuve, *Port-Royal*, II, 365.
[5] *Histoire critique du texte du Nouveau Testament*, II, 414ff.
[6] Delassault, *Le Maistre de Sacy*, p. 157.
[7] J. Lhermet, *Pascal et la Bible* (Paris, 1931), pp. 246ff.

Richard Simon's New Testament (Trévoux, 1702) is perhaps the first example of a scholarly and non-sectarian translation. Simon was an Oratorian and translates the Clementine Vulgate, but he was in friendly relations with Protestant leaders and adopts many Protestant readings (for example, *coupe* for *calice*). The translation was accused by Bossuet of Socinianism,[1] and here as in his other works Simon may be regarded as a precursor of eighteenth-century Deism.

The eighteenth century, though productive of much biblical scholarship (for example, Calmet, Le Long), was not a favourable time for translation, especially on the Catholic side. This was a period of stagnation in the French Church, and the intellectually dominant *philosophes* were unsympathetic. At no other time perhaps has the Bible been condemned on grounds of literary taste (Voltaire). Two translations of the New Testament from the Vulgate stand out among several attempts, those of Barneville (1719) and Mésenguy (1729).

Among Protestants there was more activity, though it was confined to refugees or Swiss (*le style réfugié*, like *le patois de Chanaan*, was much criticized). Beausobre and Lenfant produced an accurate translation of the New Testament from the Greek (Amsterdam, 1718) and Le Cène a complete Bible, marked by the Socinian and Pelagian tendencies of the time (Rotterdam, 1696–Amsterdam, 1741). Two translations have achieved a wider fame and are indeed the most familiar of all, especially perhaps to English readers, because of their adoption as the standard texts of the Bible societies. They are those of David Martin (Amsterdam, 1696–1707) and J.-F. Ostervald (Neuchâtel, 1744; the 1724 Amsterdam edition did not claim to be a new translation). Both simply revise and modernize the accepted Geneva versions of 1588 and 1693. They are dull to read, having lost the vigour of the sixteenth-century versions without acquiring the classical form of Sacy. Ostervald is rather more independent and more modern, but he is guilty of toning down and bowdlerization.

The nineteenth century opened with Chateaubriand's *Génie du Christianisme* and a new revival of Christian sentiment. The Bible which responded to the needs of the Romantic generation was that of the Abbé de Genoude (1815–24). Genoude knew Hugo and was a close

[1] Mangenot in Vigouroux, *Dictionnaire de la Bible*, II, 2369. On Simon see also pp. 193–5, 218–20 above.

friend of Lamartine, who in the dedication of *La Poésie sacrée*[1] describes him as 'le premier qui ait fait passer dans la langue française la sublime poésie des Hébreux'. After such praise the translation itself is rather disappointing, being mainly an adaptation of Sacy, but with greater conciseness and simplicity.

About the same time the British and Foreign Bible Society began its work in France (Paris agency, 1820) and with the French and Swiss societies formed on its model inspired some translations and a wider interest in the Bible. Henceforward new or partly new versions are very numerous. Of the nineteenth-century Protestant translations the most popular has been that of Louis Segond (Old Testament, 1874, completed 1880). It is largely a revision of Martin and Ostervald, thus illustrating the tenacity of the Geneva tradition which began with Olivetan in 1535. From 1874 to 1881 Édouard Reuss, professor of theology at Strassburg, published his translation, which stands high for its erudition, but in the mingling of text and commentary almost returns to the medieval pattern. It is not for the general reader. On the Catholic side the Abbé Crampon (Tournai, 1894–1904) has occupied a position similar to Segond's. More gifted translators than these have attempted parts of the Bible: Lamennais (Gospels, 1846); Renan (Job, 1859; Song of Songs, 1860; Ecclesiastes, 1882); Loisy (Job, 1892; New Testament, 1922). Renan confined himself to the books with which he was most in sympathy; his translations of these are original and remarkable.

Of more recent translations, that published in the Bibliothèque de la Pléiade and edited by Édouard Dhorme is likely to be of interest as following in the line of Simon and Reuss. So far only two volumes have appeared (1956–9). But the most notable of contemporary translations, and possibly the best of all French translations, is the Jerusalem Bible (1948–54), made by the Dominican École Biblique de Jérusalem. It is, like the Authorized Version, the work of a team, and it may be that this is the most satisfactory solution. It is distinguished by historical accuracy, a resolute attempt to translate into modern, even colloquial, French without reference to earlier translators, and an honesty which prefers to omit rather than reconstruct corrupt passages (for example, Exod. ii. 25). The Psalms, translated by the poet Raymond Schwab, are particularly good, and all metrical passages, not only the Psalms, are

[1] *Méditations poétiques*, XXX.

rendered in metrical form. A specimen is the passage already quoted from other translations (Ps. civ. 3, 4):

> tu bâtis sur les eaux tes chambres hautes;
> faisant des nuées ton char,
> tu t'avances sur les ailes du vent;
> tu prends les vents pour messagers,
> pour serviteurs un feu de flamme.

It seems that in the Jerusalem Bible the problem of producing a translation at once accurate, readable and modern has found a solution.

3. DUTCH VERSIONS

The great event in the history of the Dutch Bible was the completion of the States-General Bible (*Statenvertaling*). With Calvinism now altogether dominant, the Dutch Reformed Church at the Synod of Dordrecht (Dort, 1618–19) decided to have a new translation made from the original text. The principal translators were, for the Old Testament Joh. Bogerman and William Baudartius, for the New Festus Hommius and Antonius Walaeus. This monumental work, published in 1637 at the expense of the Government, the States-General, remained of value to Dutch Protestantism for centuries, though in the course of years improvements were made. In the eighteenth century it was adopted by the Mennonites in place of the Biestkens Bible.

The Lutherans, however, came forward in 1648 with a version of their own, basically Luther's German Bible translated into Dutch by Adolf Visscher. This was revised in 1823 by Alberti and Klap, and Lutherans continued to use it, revised from time to time, until 1951. In 1696 the Old Catholics received for the first time their own translation of the New Testament, prepared by E. de Witte. A complete Bible was published in Utrecht in 1717. This was replaced in 1732 by a version with annotations based on the work of A. van der Schuur, amplified by H. van Rhijn.

During the nineteenth century the Reformed Church tried repeatedly to introduce a revised translation, since the language of the *Statenvertaling* was becoming more and more obsolete, and progress in knowledge of the biblical languages, as well as the development of biblical criticism, increased the demand for a new version. Some recognition was earned by the translation of Professor J. H. van der Palm (1818–30) and by a translation of the New Testament, the preparation of which was promoted by the Dutch Reformed Church in 1868. But they never became popular. For many people the rather antiquated diction of the *Statenvertaling* had acquired something of the character of a holy language. A somewhat better reception was given to the Leyden translation made by professors of the theological faculty (among them Kuenen, Oort and Hooykaas) who belonged to the liberal wing of Protestantism; the Old Testament appeared in 1899–1901, the New in 1912. It was a good professional translation in modern language, but never came into general use, though it played an important part in liberal circles.

The Roman Catholics also set to work on a better translation. Moerentorf's was out of date. Among the new translations published that of the New Testament by J. Th. Beelen, 1859–66, must be mentioned. Its language resembles that spoken in Flanders, which is also true of the version of the Old Testament in which several translators collaborated. This edition was used mainly in Belgium. The Roman Catholics of the Netherlands brought out their own translation, the so-called Professors' Bible (1894–1910), published in 'sHertogenbosch. A new version which aroused great interest and which is now in general use among Roman Catholics was published by the Peter Canisius Association (New Testament 1929, Old Testament 1936–9) and has been reprinted several times.

A well-known Protestant translation of the present century is that of Obbink and Brouwer, an abbreviated edition of the Old Testament by H. Th. Obbink (1924) and a New Testament by A. M. Brouwer (1921–7). But the great renewal came with the translation made at the instigation of the Dutch Bible Society. The New Testament appeared in 1939, the complete Bible in 1951; it has already been reprinted again and again. This is now the modern translation generally recognized by all Dutch Protestants, so that it has a more or less ecumenical character.[1] In connection with the Dutch language there should be mentioned a Frisian version by Dr G. A. Wumkes (1933) and a translation into South African Dutch (Afrikaans) of the same year.

1 The Old Catholics now use a Bible with their own translation of the New Testament, but with the Old Testament taken from the new Protestant version.

4. SPANISH VERSIONS

The inquisitorial ban on vernacular prose translations of the Scriptures continued during the seventeenth and part of the eighteenth centuries. Verse translations of portions of them continued to appear in Spain during this period. Valera's Bible was reprinted in Amsterdam in 1625 and his New Testament in 1708; the Ferrara Bible was reprinted wholly or in part at least ten times before 1762. Occasional Spanish versions of the Old Testament or parts of it for the benefit of the Sephardim in the Near East were printed in Hebrew characters in Constantinople.

In 1778 Pius VI authorized A. Martini's Italian translation. Anselmo Petite's Spanish New Testament appeared in Valladolid, 1785, and the Inquisition's Index of 1790 duly permitted similar translations. The whole Bible, including the Apocrypha, was translated by Father Felipe Scío de San Miguel in ten volumes, Valencia, 1790–3. Another Roman Catholic translation by Father Félix de Torres Amat, bishop of Astorga, appeared a few years later (eight volumes, Madrid, 1823–5). The latter possibly consisted of a revision of an unpublished manuscript of a Jesuit named J. M. Petisco who died in 1800. Both these Bibles were often reprinted. A Mexican version of the Bible of Vence came out in 1833. Since the Spanish Civil War, Bibles by Nácar-Colunga and Bover-Cantera have been published in Madrid.

Valera's New Testament was reprinted four times in England between 1806 and 1817. The early Protestant versions printed for circulation in Spain and Latin America consisted of the Scío text without its notes. Blanco White revised this version in 1820, and George Borrow printed a Madrid edition of it in 1837. Later Protestant Bibles in Spanish have usually consisted of revised versions of Valera's text, printed in London, New York, Paris, and—occasionally—Madrid. There were, however, others: H. W. Rule, a Methodist, translated and printed the Gospels (Gibraltar, 1841), and other parts of his New Testament were printed later in London; the Spanish Quaker Usoz translated Isaiah in 1863; Baptist versions of the New Testament were printed at Edinburgh between 1855 and 1860. The revised Valera was the Bible most frequently found in Spain before 1936.[1] The circulation of Protestant versions in Spain always depended on the whim of the authorities and only prospered when the government was anti-clerical.

[1] A fresh revision was published by the British and American Bible Societies in 1960.

The Portuguese *princeps* of the New Testament (by João Ferreira d'Almeida) was printed at Amsterdam in 1681, reprinted Batavia 1693 and Amsterdam 1712. The Old Testament appeared in instalments printed by the Danish Mission at Tranquebar between 1719 and 1753. A Roman Catholic Portuguese New Testament by Father Antonio Pereira de Figueiredo was printed in 1781 and the Old followed in 1790. Both these versions were revised and reprinted during the nineteenth century. In Madrid, 1838, Borrow edited Oteiza's version of St Luke's Gospel in Guipuzcoan Basque; his gipsy version of the same Gospel (1837) remains a linguistic curiosity. The Penitential Psalms in Catalan appeared in Perpignan in 1802. The Catalan Protestant New Testament of J. M. Prat was printed in London 1832 and was later reprinted in Barcelona and Madrid. During this century there has been a considerable growth of Catalan versions, thanks largely to two Roman Catholic Bible societies and to the Montserrat Benedictines. Two complete translations have been issued by the societies, and the very scholarly Benedictine version with commentary, begun in 1926, had reached twenty-one volumes in 1961, in spite of the fact that publication was interrupted between 1936 and 1950.[1]

5. SCANDINAVIAN VERSIONS

The Bible versions of the sixteenth century had aimed at giving the Holy Scriptures to the common people in their native languages. The concern of the seventeenth century—not inappropriately called 'the Learned Century'—was different: the Reformation Bibles were criticized for being inaccurate in their rendering of the original texts, and in most countries attempts were made at procuring more scholarly versions. The following centuries were therefore left with the task of trying to combine the advantages of both traditions of translation.

In Sweden, the committee of 1600 had had no influence on the editions of 1618 and 1703. The demand for a revised version became loud about 1750, but it was not until 1773 that Gustaf III appointed a new committee of twenty-one members (Carl Linnaeus was one of

[1] See Darlow and Moule, *op. cit.*; Menéndez y Pelayo, *op. cit.*; W. Canton, *A History of the British and Foreign Bible Society*; and the *Spanish Encyclopaedia*'s articles on Petisco, Scío and Torres Amat. I have not been able to see March, *¿La Biblia de Torres Amat es del P. Petisco?*

them); this committee became a permanent institution, its most important achievement being the '1883 års normalupplaga' of the New Testament (printed in 1884), based on the *textus receptus* and very faithful to the Greek, but at the expense of Swedish idiom. It was never authorized for liturgical use, but only recommended for schools and Bible classes; the Old Testament appeared in a similar edition in 1904. The nineteenth century also saw some private translations. Finally, in 1917, an entirely new version, based on the modern critical editions of the Hebrew and Greek texts, was authorized by King Gustaf V as the Swedish Church Bible.

In Denmark the work took a somewhat different course. In 1605–7 a wholly new translation, based on a solid knowledge of Hebrew and Greek, was made by Professor (later also Bishop) Hans Poulsen Resen. It is a very accurate rendering, but lacks the impetus and appeal of the Reformation Bible and was not unjustly felt to be too difficult. Resen's contemporaries would not recommend it for authorization as a Church Bible, though it was regarded as an excellent instrument for students. The same is true of the revised edition of the Resen Bible, by Hans Svane, later archbishop, the Svaning Bible of 1647. During the next 150 years there was continuous competition between the popular Reformation Bible and the 'learned' Bible of Resen–Svane. Efforts were made to replace both of them by a fresh translation, and a committee published the results of their efforts in 1742–52, but without getting them authorized; several attempts were also made by private persons, the best known being the New Testament translations by Bastholm, 1780, and O. H. Guldberg, 1794.

The year 1814 inaugurates a new epoch: Norway was severed from Denmark and entered into a personal union with Sweden which was to last till 1905. In 1814 also, the Danish Bible Society was founded, and with it came a strong desire for a modern version. The result was a revision, 1819, of the New Testament of Resen–Svane, which was printed together with the Svaning Old Testament of 1647 until 1871, when a revised version of the Old Testament was authorized. Thus the 'learned' Bible had eventually won the day. But it could not be expected to meet the needs of the religious revival of the nineteenth century, and it is no mere coincidence that precisely that century saw an astonishing series of private translations by churchmen, scholars, and men of letters. The most conspicuous are those by J. C. Lindberg (the complete Bible), 1837–56, and Bishop Skat Rørdam (an annotated New Testament), 1886. The authorized New Testament of 1819 was revised anew in 1907.

Our century has seen the publication of an entirely new Bible. Professor Buhl's critical version of the Old Testament, 1910, gave rise to a committee which translated the Old Testament afresh from the Hebrew text (authorized in 1931); a corresponding version of the New Testament was authorized in 1948, and one of the Apocrypha in 1951. The Danish Bible Society has also provided a Faeroe Bible (the Gospel of St Matthew 1823, the New Testament 1931, the complete Bible 1948) and a Bible for Greenland.

Norway started on a revision of the Church Bible in the same year as Denmark, 1819, but managed to revise not only the New Testament but the whole Bible. The nineteenth century is, however, characterized by the revival of the native language for literary purposes; the 'Danish–Norwegian' language was in use all through the century, though it developed along lines of its own, and the translation produced at the request of the Norwegian Bible Society (the Old Testament 1842–87; revised edition 1891; the New Testament 1870–1904), was not so different from the Danish Bible as not to be understood by Danes, and the New Testament in particular was, to some extent, used in Denmark as well. But the outstanding feature of Bible translation in Norway is the revival of the vernacular as a biblical and liturgical language ('nynorsk', 'landsmål'). Professor E. Blix translated the New Testament into New Norwegian in 1889 (with the aid of Ivar Aasen), in 1921 the whole Bible was available, and in 1938 it took its final shape in the genuine Norwegian language. For students' use, Professor Mowinckel has translated and annotated, in co-operation with other scholars, the Old Testament (Genesis–Proverbs, 1929–55) and in 1945 Professor Lyder Brun issued a version of the New Testament; both are in modern Norwegian, but not in 'landsmål'.

The Reformation Bible of Iceland was superseded by a revision made by Bishop Thorlákur Skúlason (1627–55); he based his revision on Resen's Danish translation,[1] not to the profit of the Icelandic, which was lamentably marred by Danisms. A translation of the New Testa-

[1] According to Bishop Helgason, *Islands Kirke fra Reformationen til vore Dage* (Copenhagen, 1922), p. 76; his opinion is disputed by Haraldur Níelsson, *Studier tilegnede Frants Buhl* (Copenhagen, 1925), p. 188.

ment by Jón Vídalín (bishop, 1698–1720) was never printed. Steinn Jónsson translated the Danish Bible into Icelandic in 1728, but it was generally regarded as a linguistic and typographical monstrosity and could not compete with the 'Thorlák Bible', which was still reprinted. The complete Bible was printed again by the British and Foreign Bible Society in 1813, but a few years later the Icelandic Bible Society was founded, and a new translation of the New Testament appeared in 1827, printed in Videyjar Klaustur near Reykjavík; the complete Bible was issued in 1841 (Videyjar), and again in 1859 (Reykjavík). This was very soon revised, and an improved edition was printed in Oxford (New Testament and Psalms 1863, the whole Bible 1866) at the expense of the British and Foreign Bible Society. An entirely new edition, Reykjavík, 1912, is the present Church Bible of Iceland. A new translation is in progress.

6. ITALIAN VERSIONS

When Benedict XIV, by a decree of 13 June 1757, permitted the reading and printing of vernacular versions of the Bible—if approved by the Holy See or published, with orthodox notes, under the supervision of a bishop—the way was reopened to Italian Catholics to recover some of the ground lost during their prolonged inactivity in this matter. By far the most important result of the new liberty was the version of Antonio Martini (1720–1809), but two other contemporary translations are worth noting for their historical interest: a drastic revision of Malermi's Bible by A. Guerra, a professor of theology at Padua (Venice, 1773), and an Italian version of the Port-Royal Bible, with notes by Le Maistre de Sacy (Venice, 1775–85). Both of these versions were Jansenistic in tendency. They were eclipsed by the great work—as it deserves to be called, despite its obvious limitations—of Martini. This gifted but unassuming Tuscan priest was moved to undertake his version chiefly by a pastoral concern: his aim was to provide an accurate yet popular version of the Vulgate, with notes adapted to the religious needs of ordinary educated Catholics. And this modest intention he certainly carried out. His version of the New Testament was published at Turin, in six volumes, 1769–71, with a dedication to Charles Emmanuel III of Savoy; the Old Testament followed, in sixteen volumes, between 1776 and 1781. In 1778 Pius VI, after some hesitation,[1] gave the work his official approval in a letter which Martini printed in volume nine. In 1781 Martini was made archbishop of Florence; and a final revised edition of his Bible was published in that city between 1782 and 1792. It has been often reprinted, wholly or in part, and in 1885 it was given the status of an Italian classic, a 'testo di lingua' by the Accademia della Crusca. Shorn of its notes, it has been used by the British and Foreign Bible Society.

Martini's version was made from the Vulgate, but, in the case of the New Testament, with careful reference to the Greek text and with tables of variant readings. He knew little Hebrew. His notes show him well read in the Fathers; but in general his aim was doctrinal and moral instruction rather than thorough exegesis. His style lacks force, but is polished and clear. The great merit of Martini's version is that it supplied the Church in Italy with a decent literal rendering of the Vulgate which has remained in use down to our own day.

Of nineteenth-century Catholic translators the following may be mentioned: G. B. de Rossi (1742–1831) and G. Ugdulena (1815–72) for their merit as scholars, C. M. Curci (1809–91) for the popularity of his versions. De Rossi, the celebrated hebraist, translated the Psalms, Ecclesiastes, Job, Lamentations and Proverbs (all published at Parma, 1808–15). The learned Ugdulena, a Sicilian priest and a gifted scholar, allowed himself to be too distracted by politics (he was a fervent Garibaldian) to take his version of the Old Testament further than II Kings. C. M. Curci's fame in other spheres attracted a wide public to his renderings of the Gospels from the Greek (Naples, 1879) and of the Psalter from the Hebrew (Naples, 1883); but neither version is important.

In S. D. Luzzatto (1800–65) Italian Jewry produced a great hebraist. Professor of Hebrew at the Rabbinic college of Padua from 1829, Luzzatto was working at a version of the Old Testament when he died. He had completed an Isaiah (Padua, 1855 and 1867), a Job and a Pentateuch (Trieste, 1853 and 1859–60 respectively; the Pentateuch was reprinted with a critical introduction and Hebrew commentary, Padua, 1871). His work was finished by a number of rabbis and published as *La Sacra Bibbia volgarizzata da S. D. Luzzatto e continuatori* (4 vols., Rovigo, 1868–75); a severely literal version, it has remained almost unknown to non-Jewish Italians. More esteemed as

[1] For the circumstances, see Cesare Guasti, *Opere* (Prato, 1899), v, 734–8.

literature are the versions of another Jewish scholar, D. Castelli (1836–1901): Ecclesiastes (Pisa, 1866), the Canticle and Job (Florence, 1892 and 1897).

Of more recent translators of the Bible from the original tongues the following should be noted. S. Minocchi (Catholic inclined to Modernism): the Psalms (Rome, 1905); Gospels (Florence, 1900); Isaiah (Bologna, 1907). G. Ricciotti (Catholic): Jeremiah, Job, the Canticle (Turin, 1923, 1924 and 1928); St Paul's Epistles (Rome, 1949). G. Luzzi (Protestant): the whole Bible (12 vols., Florence, 1921–30). A complete version from the Hebrew and Greek is being edited by the Pontifical Biblical Institute; so far published are the Pentateuch (Florence, 1943–8), and *I libri poetici* (the work of A. Vaccari, Rome, 1925).

CHAPTER X

ENGLISH VERSIONS SINCE 1611

ACCEPTANCE OF THE KING JAMES VERSION

The King James version of the Bible was a revision of prior English translations. In their preface, the scholars who were charged to make this revision show that they were fully aware that their work would encounter strong opposition:

Zeale to promote the common good...findeth but cold intertainment in the world....Many mens mouths have bene open a good while (and yet are not stopped) with speeches about the Translation so long in hand, or rather perusals of Translations made before: and aske what may be the reason, what the necessitie of the employment: Hath the Church bene deceived, say they, all this while?...Was their Translation good before? Why doe they now mend it? Was it not good? Why then was it obtruded to the people?

For eighty years after its publication in 1611, the King James version endured bitter attacks. It was denounced as theologically unsound and ecclesiastically biased, as truckling to the king and unduly deferring to his belief in witchcraft, as untrue to the Hebrew text and relying too much on the Septuagint. The personal integrity of the translators was impugned. Among other things, they were accused of 'blasphemy', 'most damnable corruptions', 'intolerable deceit', and 'vile imposture', the critic who used these epithets being careful to say that they were not 'the dictates of passion, but the just resentment of a zealous mind'.

But the attacks were negligible. The King James version quickly displaced the Bishops' Bible as the version read in the churches. The Geneva Bible continued to be printed until 1644, and only gradually fell into disuse. English Bibles which contained the King James text and the Geneva notes were published in Holland in 1642, and in England in 1649, 1679, 1708, and 1715.

No evidence has been found that the King James version received final authorization by Convocation or by Parliament or by the King in Council. But it did not need that. Bishop Westcott, writing in 1868, said:

From the middle of the seventeenth century, the King's Bible has been the acknowledged Bible of the English-speaking nations throughout the world simply because it is the best. A revision which embodied the ripe fruits of nearly a century of labour, and appealed to the religious instinct of a great Christian people, gained by its own internal character a vital authority which could never have been secured by any edict of sovereign rulers.[1]

MAINTENANCE OF THE TEXT OF THE KING JAMES VERSION

The first issue of the King James version contained some typographic errors, such as 'hoopes' for 'hookes' (Exod. xxxviii. 11). In Exod. xiv. 10 three whole lines were repeated: 'the children of Israel lift up their eyes, and beholde, the Egyptians marched after them, and they were sore afraid'. 'Strain at a gnat' (Matt. xxiii. 24) is a mistranslation which was almost certainly a printer's error.

From time to time minor amendments were made in the text. As early as 1616, 'approved to death' (I Cor. iv. 9) was changed to 'appointed to death', which had been used by Tyndale, Coverdale, the Great Bible, and the Bishops' Bible. Among changes made in 1629 were 'Jew' to 'Jewess' (Acts xxiv. 24), 'helps in governments' to 'helps, governments' (I Cor. xii. 28), 'runne with patience unto the race' to 'run with patience the race' (Heb. xii. 1). In 1638 'There is no man good, but one, *that is* God' was changed to '*there is* none good but one, *that is*, God' (Mark x. 18).

Not all changes were as careful as these; the majority were simply the errors of careless printers. A 1631 edition omitted 'not' in Exod. xx. 14, which then read 'Thou shalt commit adultery'. A duodecimo edition with the imprint of Robert Barker, 1638, had many errors, such as 'Belial' for 'Bilhah' (Gen. xxxvii. 2), 'wives' for 'wiles' (Num. xxv. 18), 'slew two lions like men' for 'slew two lion-like men' (II Sam. xxiii. 20), 'purifying sores' for 'putrefying sores' (Isa. i. 6), 'shamefulness' for 'shamefastness' (I Tim. ii. 9). The imprint of this edition was false, said William Kilburne in his essay, *Dangerous Errors in several late Printed Bibles to the great scandal and corruption of sound and true religion* (1659). It had been printed in Holland, and was typical

[1] B. F. Westcott, *A General View of the History of the English Bible* (3rd ed. 1911), p. 121.

of the editions imported from that country. But in six editions printed in England by Hills and Field in the 1650's, Kilburne claims to have discovered some twenty thousand errors.

Notable for careful editorial work in the interest of securing an 'authentique corrected Bible' were the Cambridge editions of 1629 and 1638. More comprehensive corrections and amendments were made by Dr Thomas Paris, Cambridge, 1762, and by Dr Benjamin Blayney, Oxford, 1769. 'These two editors', Scrivener wryly observed, 'are the great modernizers of the diction of the version, from what it was left in the seventeenth century.'[1]

SEVENTEENTH-CENTURY PRIVATE VERSIONS

Henry Ainsworth, minister of the separatist English congregation at Amsterdam, 1593–1622, was a Hebrew scholar in his own right, who translated the Five Books of Moses, the Psalms, and the Canticles. His renderings were often too literal to be good English, but his version of the Psalms came with the Plymouth Pilgrims to America.

In 1645 Dr John Lightfoot, preaching before the House of Commons, urged it 'to think of a review and survey of the translation of the Bible', that 'the three nations might come to understand the proper and genuine study of the Scriptures, by an exact, vigorous, and lively translation'. In 1653 a bill was enacted by Parliament expressing the fear that revisions and new translations might be made and published by individuals, 'which if it should be done on their own heads, without due care for the supervising thereof by learned persons sound in the fundamentals of the Christian religion, might be a precedent of dangerous consequence, emboldening other to do the like'. A committee of scholars was appointed to examine any proposed revision, without whose authority it could not appear. The committee was instructed to 'seriously consider the translation of Mr H. Ainsworth' and 'any other translations, annotations, or observations', and to 'consider of the marginal readings in Bibles, whether any of them should rather be in the line'. The project was revived in 1657, and assigned to the care of Bulstrode Whitelocke, Commissioner of the

[1] This statement is from the informing and exhaustive introduction to Scrivener's critical edition of the Authorized English Version, entitled *The Cambridge Paragraph Bible* (1873).

Great Seal, at whose home the committee often met. 'Excellent and learned observations' were made on some mistakes in the King James Bible, 'which yet was agreed to be the best of any translation in the world'. The dissolution of Parliament and the restoration of the Stuart dynasty put an end to the proposal.

In the meantime the era of 'paraphrases' had begun. Dr Henry Hammond, Oxford scholar, friend and chaplain to King Charles I, prepared a *Paraphrase and Annotations on the New Testament* which was published in 1653 and often reprinted, the last edition being in four volumes, 1845. Three Oxford dons, Abraham Woodhead, Richard Allestry, and Obadiah Walker, wrote a *Paraphrase on the Epistles of St Paul*, issued anonymously in 1675, and in a 'third edition' in 1708, bearing the authors' names and edited by Dr John Fell, bishop of Oxford. Richard Baxter also published a *New Testament with a paraphrase and notes*, in 1685.

The vogue of 'paraphrases' inserting bracketed explanatory material into the text of the King James version continued in the eighteenth century, with publications by Dr Daniel Whitby (1703); Samuel Clarke (1701) and Thomas Pyle (1717–35); and John Guyse (1739–52). Guyse opposed the Arianism of Clarke and Pyle; his three-volume *Exposition of the New Testament in the form of a Paraphrase* was published in a sixth edition in 1818.

FREE RENDERINGS IN CONTEMPORARY STYLE

In 1729 Daniel Mace, a Presbyterian minister, published *The New Testament in Greek and English...corrected from the Authority of the most Authentic Manuscripts.* His corrections of the Greek text were in the direction of sound scholarship; but his English version was too obvious an attempt to copy 'the humour of the age'—the pert, colloquial style which was then fashionable. Examples are: 'When ye fast, don't put on a dismal air as the Hypocrites do' (Matt. vi. 16). 'If any man thinks it would be a reflexion upon his manhood to be a stale batchelor' (I Cor. vii. 36).

In 1768 Dr Edward Harwood published *A Liberal Translation of the New Testament; Being an Attempt to translate the Sacred Writings with the same Freedom, Spirit, and Elegance, with which other English*

Translations from the Greek Classics have lately been executed. He stated that his aim was 'to clothe the ideas of the Apostles with propriety and perspicuity', and replace the 'bald and barbarous language of the old vulgar version with the elegance of modern English'.

Harwood's version of the *Magnificat* is: 'My soul with reverence adores my Creator, and all my faculties with transport join in celebrating the goodness of God my Saviour, who hath in so signal a manner condescended to regard my poor and humble station. Transcendent goodness! Every future age will now conjoin in celebrating my happiness!'

And the *Nunc dimittis*: 'O God, thy promise to me is amply fulfilled. I now quit the post of human life with satisfaction and joy, since thou hast indulged mine eyes with so divine a spectacle as the great Messiah.'

At the Transfiguration, Peter remarks: 'Oh, Sir! what a delectable residence we might establish here!'

Less expansive but quite as pretentious was *A New and Corrected Version of the New Testament*, by Rodolphus Dickinson, published at Boston, Mass., in 1833. The author condemns the 'quaint monotony and affected solemnity' of the King James version, with its 'frequently rude and occasionally barbarous attire'; and he declares his purpose to adorn the Scriptures with 'a splendid and sweetly flowing diction' suited to the use of 'accomplished and refined persons'. Examples are: 'When Elizabeth heard the salutation of Mary, the embryo was joyfully agitated' (Luke i. 41). 'Festus declared with a loud voice, Paul, you are insane! Multiplied research drives you to distraction' (Acts xxvi. 24).

SECTARIAN TRANSLATIONS

Gilbert Wakefield, a dissenter both in theology and in politics, dissented also from Dr Harwood's 'diffusive' style. His *Translation of the New Testament* (1791) stayed close to the King James version, making changes only when 'some low, obsolete or obscure word... some coarse or uncouth phrase...demanded an alteration'. Other editions appeared in 1795 and 1820.

Archbishop William Newcome, in *An Historical View of the English Biblical Translations* (1792), urged that revision of the King James version be authorized. He published a harmony of the Gospels in Greek (1776), and in English (1800); a revision of the Minor Prophets

(1785) and of Ezekiel (1788). His New Testament was printed in 1796 and published in 1800, with the title *An Attempt towards revising our English Translation of the Greek Scriptures, or the New Covenant of Jesus Christ: and towards illustrating the sense by philological and explanatory notes.* It was based upon Griesbach's critical edition of the Greek text; and the English text was set in paragraphs, with the verse numbers on the margin. Quotation marks were used for direct quotations.

The translations by Wakefield and Newcome were in no sense sectarian. Yet both are sometimes listed as Unitarian. The facts are that the Unitarian Society for Promoting Christian Knowledge sought to produce a version of the New Testament 'divesting the sacred volume of the technical phrases of a systematic theology which has no foundation in the Scriptures themselves'. Wakefield was approached, but his death in 1801 caused the Society to look elsewhere. It was decided to adopt Newcome's text as the basis for the Unitarian version, to be edited and adapted by Dr Thomas Belsham. This was published in 1808 as *The New Testament in an Improved Version, upon the basis of Archbishop Newcome's New Translation; with a corrected text.* Newcome had died in 1800, and could not object; Bishop Stock, who was a relative of Newcome, protested, but to no effect. The fifth edition, 1819, bears the title *Unitarian Version* on the back.

A Translation of the New Testament from the Original Greek Humbly attempted by Nathaniel Scarlett, Assisted By Men of Piety and Literature: with Notes (1798) divides the text into sections, each with a section title. It also 'personifies' the text, putting the names of the speakers as in the text of a play, and assigning the narrative portions to 'Historian'. And it uses 'immerse' instead of 'baptize' wherever the word occurs.

The most determined effort to secure an 'immersion' version of the Scriptures was that of the American Bible Union, organized in 1850. Its revision of the New Testament was published in 1864, a second revision in 1865, and a third in 1891. Revisions of various Old Testament books were published at intervals from 1856 to 1879. In 1883 the Union was merged with the American Baptist Publication Society, under whose auspices the work was completed, newly revised, and a translation of the Bible published with the subtitle *An Improved Edition (Based in part on the Bible Union Version)* (1913). Though it is an excellent translation, it met with a small sale. Its device of using 'baptize (immerse)', with the thought that the reader might take his choice, did not prove to be popular.

CATHOLIC TRANSLATIONS

The Rhemes New Testament, 1582, was published in a 'Fourth Edition' in 1633. A second edition of the Douay Old Testament, 1609–10, appeared in 1635. Both were published by John Cousturier at Rouen in France. There were no further editions until the eighteenth century.

At Dublin, in 1718, appeared a translation of the New Testament from the Latin Vulgate, 'with the Original Greek and divers translations in Vulgar Languages diligently compared and revised', by Dr Cornelius Nary. In 1730 Dr Robert Witham, president of the college at Douai, published a revision of the Rhemes New Testament. Each of these volumes has an extended preface, explaining the principles of biblical translation which have been followed. Witham did not hesitate to criticize Nary as well as Rhemes. For example, in I Thess. iv. 6 he rejects 'in business' or 'in any matter' in favour of 'in the matter'. Here he clearly relies upon the Greek text; and he anticipates the revised versions of the present time.

A folio 'Fifth Edition' of the Rhemes New Testament appeared in 1738, with some revisions for which Dr Richard Challoner, who had been associated with Witham at Douai, was probably responsible. Consecrated as bishop in 1741, he was appointed vicar-apostolic of the London District in 1758, serving until his death in 1781. He revised the Douay Old Testament twice (published 1750 and 1763); and the Rhemes New Testament five times (published 1749, 1750, 1752, 1763, and 1772). Father Hugh Pope, in his *English Versions of the Bible* (1952), says: 'English-speaking Catholics the world over owe Dr Challoner an immense debt of gratitude, for he provided them for the first time with a portable, cheap, and readable version which in spite of a few inevitable defects has stood the test of two hundred years of use.'

Dr John Lingard, English historian, made a translation of the Gospels from the Greek, published as 'by a Catholic' in 1836. In America, Archbishop Kenrick made a new revision of the Rhemes–Douay Bible, published in six volumes, 1849–60.

Twentieth-century Catholic versions include a translation of the

New Testament from the Greek, by Father Francis A. Spencer, 1937; the Westminster version, translated from the original tongues, of which the New Testament was completed 1913–36, while the Old Testament, beginning with the publication of Malachy in 1934, is still in process; the revision of the Challoner–Rhemes version of the New Testament, under the auspices of the Confraternity of Christian Doctrine, 1941; a new translation of the Old Testament into modern English, from the original Hebrew, also sponsored by the Confraternity, beginning with the publication of Genesis in 1948 and now approaching completion; and a new translation of the Bible from the Latin Vulgate, in a style quite his own, by Monsignor Ronald Knox, 1944–54.

THE MOVEMENT TOWARD REVISION

In 1753 Robert Lowth published in Latin his Oxford lectures on *The Sacred Poetry of the Hebrews*, under which title they appeared in English in 1787. In 1778, now bishop of London, Lowth published *Isaiah: a new Translation, with a preliminary Dissertation, and Notes.* His work opened a new vista for the interpretation and translation of the Old Testament.

John Wesley's translation of the New Testament (1755) was based upon a fresh and independent study of the Greek text. An 'Anniversary Edition' published in 1953 compares it with the Authorized Version, showing that he made twelve thousand changes, and stating that three-quarters of these were accepted by the revisers in the 1870's. His judgment with respect to the Greek text was usually sound; for example, he omitted 'through his blood' in Col. i. 14 but retained it in Eph. i. 7.

Three popular eighteenth-century translations were: of the New Testament, by Philip Doddridge (1739–56); of the Gospels, by George Campbell (1789); of the Epistles, by James MacKnight (1795). In 1818 a New Testament was published in London which combined the text of Campbell and of MacKnight with Doddridge's version of the Acts and Revelation.

A copy of this London publication fell into the hands of Alexander Campbell in Bethany, Virginia, who took it as a basis for the translation of the New Testament which he published in 1826, the other major basis being the critical Greek text of Griesbach. He continued to revise this translation up to six editions, and it has been often reprinted. Its most obvious defect was its English diction. Campbell tended to substitute ornate words of Latin derivation for the ordinary words of common use. 'A city situate on a mountain must be conspicuous' is a needless elaboration of 'A city set on a hill cannot be hid'. 'Whosoever commits murder shall be obnoxious to the judges' is a correct statement in archaic legal language, but is almost sure to be misunderstood by the reader.

Noah Webster, the American lexicographer, had high regard for the King James Bible. Its language, he said, 'is in general correct and perspicuous; the genuine popular English of Saxon origin; peculiarly adapted to the subjects, and in many passages, uniting sublimity with beautiful simplicity'. But he called attention to the fact that it contains many words which have changed in meaning. 'A version of the scriptures for popular use should consist of words expressing the sense which is most common in popular usage, so that the first ideas suggested to the reader should be the true meaning of such words according to the original languages. That many words in the present version fail to do this, is certain.'

Webster's revised version, entitled *The Holy Bible, containing the Old and New Testaments, in the Common Version, with Amendments of the Language* was published in 1833. There were some one hundred and fifty words and phrases which he found to be erroneous or misleading, and which he corrected in the various passages where they appeared. Practically all of these have been changed by later revisers also, who found his judgment sound as to the need of change, and in most cases accepted the corrections he proposed. He substituted 'who' for 'which', when it refers to persons; and 'its' for 'his', when it refers to things. He used 'Be not anxious' for 'Take no thought'; 'food' for 'meat'; 'ask' for 'demand'; 'hinder' for the obsolete sense of 'let'; and various words appropriate to the context for 'prevent' in its obsolete sense of 'go before'. He used the term 'Holy Spirit' instead of 'Holy Ghost'.

As far as it went, Noah Webster's revision of the English Bible was sound. It pointed the way that revision should take in matters of English usage. For a time it was used in many Congregational churches; a second edition was published in 1841, and three editions of his revision of the New Testament were printed in 1839, 1840, and 1841.

But then it faded from public view, and now it is almost forgotten. It made too few amendments to challenge attention; it was not adopted for general use in the public worship of the churches; and it did not go far enough, in that it was based almost wholly upon English usage, and did not push behind this to the problems with respect to the Greek text of the New Testament that were emerging in the 1830's and 1840's.

The movement towards revision gathered strength from 1830 on, with the new light upon the Greek text afforded by the work of Lachmann and Tischendorf. James Scholefield, regius professor of Greek at Cambridge, published *Hints for an Improved Translation of the New Testament* (1832, re-edited in 1836 and in 1849). Canon William Selwyn, in Convocation, and Mr James Heywood, in the House of Commons, 1856, proposed an address to the Crown, praying for a royal commission; but 'neither the clerical nor the lay mind was prepared for such a leap in the dark'. Selwyn presented his case to the public in his *Notes on the proposed Amendment of the Authorized Version* (1856, re-edited 1857).

Ernest Hawkins, secretary of the Society for the Propagation of the Gospel, convinced that an actual example was needed, drew together, in the summer of 1856, five scholars who agreed to undertake the revision of the Authorized Version of St John's Gospel. They were: Henry Alford, later dean of Canterbury; John Barrow, principal of St Edmund Hall; C. J. Ellicott, later bishop of Gloucester and Bristol; W. H. G. Humphrey, vicar of St Martin-in-the-Fields; and George Moberly, later bishop of Salisbury. They met regularly at St Martin's vicarage, and the result of their co-operation was published in 1857 as *The Authorized Version of St John's Gospel, revised by Five Clergymen.* This was followed by the Epistle to the Romans, the Epistles to the Corinthians, and subsequently the Epistles to the Galatians, Ephesians, and Philippians.

Among other publications contributing to the movement toward revision were Conybeare and Howson's *Life and Epistles of St Paul* (1852); Dean R. C. Trench's admirable work *On the Authorized Version of the New Testament, in connexion with some recent Proposals for its Revision* (1858); E. H. Plumptre's article on 'Version, Authorised' in Smith's *Dictionary of the Bible* (1863); an article by Dean Alford in the *Contemporary Review* for July, 1868, and his own revision, *The New*

Testament, newly compared with the original Greek, and revised (1869). With these should be associated two books published by members of the Revision Committee as its work was getting under way: C. J. Ellicott, *Considerations on the Revision of the English Version of the New Testament* (1870); and J. B. Lightfoot, *On a Fresh Revision of the English New Testament* (1871).

THE REVISED VERSION

In May 1870 the Convocation of the Province of Canterbury decided to undertake 'a revision of the Authorized Version of the Holy Scriptures', and appointed a committee, divided into two companies, to do the work. The Convocation of the Province of York had declined to participate. The New Testament company began work on 22 June, and the Old Testament company on 30 June. The New Testament company began with twenty-four members, added four, and lost four by death or resignation; its chairman was C. J. Ellicott, bishop of Gloucester and Bristol. The Old Testament company began with twenty-four members, added thirteen, and lost ten; its chairman from 1871 on was E. H. Browne, bishop of Ely. Forty-eight of the sixty-five members of the committee were Anglicans; seventeen were of other communions. The Revised Version of the New Testament was published on 17 May 1881; that of the Old and New Testaments together on 19 May 1885.

Naturally, the work of the New Testament company bore the full brunt of criticism. This centred, not so much upon their decisions concerning the Greek text, where they had the expert help of Westcott and Hort, as upon their English. The revisers' ideal of 'faithfulness' in translation was a meticulous word-for-word reproduction of the Greek text in English words, using the same English word for a given Greek word whenever possible, leaving no Greek word without translation into a corresponding English word, following the order of the Greek words rather than the order natural to English, and attempting to translate the articles and the tenses with a precision alien to English idiom. The result is that the Revised Version is distinctly 'translation English'. It was unnecessary, for example, to change the third petition of the Lord's Prayer to read, 'Thy will be done, as in heaven, so on earth'. Or to change the statement concerning Jesus in Mark i. 28, 'And immediately his fame spread abroad throughout all the region round about Galilee', to read, 'And the report of him went out straightway everywhere into all the region of Galilee round about'.

The work of the Old Testament company was more calmly received, in part because they dealt more cautiously with the English of the King James version and did little to amend errors in the Massoretic Hebrew text. For example, the content of Saul's prayer to the LORD in I Sam. xiv. 41, omitted by homoioteleuton from the Hebrew, but preserved in the Septuagint and Vulgate, is completely ignored.

Both companies were somewhat hampered by their instruction that the alterations to be introduced should be expressed, as far as possible, in the language of the Authorized or earlier English versions. The attempt on the part of nineteenth-century scholars to rewrite a classic of sixteenth-century English in such a way that its misleading archaisms would be removed but not missed, because they would find other sixteenth-century terms to put in their places, could hardly result in an unlaboured and natural translation.

At some points the revisers unnecessarily introduced archaisms that are not present in the Authorized Version. They increased the use of such words as 'howbeit', 'peradventure', 'holden', 'aforetime', 'sojourn', 'must needs', 'would fain', and 'behooved'. They joined the word 'haply' to the word 'lest' in seventeen cases where the Authorized Version did not have it. The Authorized Version uses the preposition 'toward' 320 times, but has 'to God-ward', 'to us-ward', and 'to you-ward' three times each, 'to thee-ward' once, and 'to the mercy seatward' once. The revisers of 1881 inserted the archaic '-ward' in four additional passages: 'to us-ward', Rom. viii. 18; and 'to you-ward', Gal. v. 10, Col. i. 25, I Thess. v. 18.

In spite of all criticism, however, the Revised Version is a milestone in the history of the English Bible. It was the response of sound scholars to the more accurate knowledge of the ancient text and its meaning which was becoming available in the nineteenth century. As such, it was of great significance. In general aim and method, the Revised Version pointed the way for future translators. It established the principle that Hebrew poetry is to be translated as poetry, in characteristic parallelism; and in the New Testament it broke the hold of the Greek *textus receptus*.[1] It still meets the need of those who desire

[1] The revisers did not adopt any existing Greek text. Their readings were published in the Oxford *Greek Testament* of 1881.

a meticulously exact, literal, word-for-word translation of the Hebrew and Greek—provided they remember that the revisers of the 1870's lacked the resources afforded by the discoveries of the past eighty years.

THE AMERICAN STANDARD VERSION

On 7 July 1870 the two Houses of Convocation voted 'to invite the co-operation of some American divines' in the work of revision. In response to this invitation, an American Revision Committee was organized on 7 December 1871 and began work on 4 October 1872, after the first draft of the revision of the Synoptic Gospels had been received from England. Dr Philip Schaff, Union Theological Seminary, was president of this Committee; Dr William Green, Princeton Theological Seminary, chairman of the Old Testament company; and Dr Theodore Woolsey, Yale University, chairman of the New Testament company. The committee had thirty-two members, of whom it lost seven by death or resignation; and it represented nine communions—Protestant Episcopal, Presbyterian, Congregational, Baptist, Methodist, Reformed, Lutheran, Unitarian, Friends.

The American committee had opportunity to review and comment upon both the first and second drafts of the revision, and many of its suggestions were adopted. It was agreed that 'if any differences still remain, the American Committee will yield its preferences for the sake of harmony; provided that such differences of reading and rendering as the American Committee may represent to the English Companies to be of special importance, be distinctly stated either in the Preface to the Revised Version, or in an Appendix to the volume, during a term of fourteen years from the date of publication'. It was further agreed that for this term of fourteen years the American committee would recognize as authorized only those editions of the Revised Version published or approved by the University Presses of England. It was understood that the American committee 'assume no responsibility in regard to the action of the American Churches, or in regard to any term beyond the period of fourteen years'.

In accordance with this agreement the American committee prepared an appendix containing by no means a complete list of their recommendations which had been rejected, but a minimum list of those which they deemed to be of sufficient importance to record, in the hope that they might ultimately be incorporated in the text. After the publication of the Revised Version of the Old Testament in 1885 the American committee continued its organization, to take such action as should be called for at the expiration of the fourteen-year period.

In 1881 and 1882 unauthorized editions of the Revised Version of the New Testament were published in New York and Philadelphia, which incorporated those of the readings preferred by the American committee which had been recorded in the appendix. In 1898 the Oxford and Cambridge University Presses published a similar edition of the Revised Version of the Bible for the American market, with a preface referring to it as the American Revised Bible. These editions were unacceptable to the American committee, since they contained only the preferences included in the appendix, which had purposely been reduced in number.

The committee had continued its work somewhat desultorily in the closing years of the 1880's, but resumed full activity in April 1897. Nine of the members of the committee survived, and these prepared, from the records of the committee, the revision which it had proposed. In 1901 this was published as *The Holy Bible containing the Old and New Testaments translated out of the original tongues, being the version set forth A.D. 1611 compared with the most ancient authorities and revised A.D. 1881–1885. Newly Edited by the American Revision Committee A.D. 1901.* It was copyrighted to protect the text from unauthorized changes. This edition contained the full body of the American committee's preferences, and published in an appendix the readings which they displaced.

The nine members of the American committee who rendered this service were Professor William H. Green, of Princeton, chairman, and Professor George E. Day, of Yale, secretary, of the Old Testament company; President Timothy Dwight, of Yale, chairman, and Professor J. H. Thayer, of Harvard, secretary, of the New Testament company; and five biblical scholars from the faculties of other theological seminaries—John DeWitt, New Brunswick; Charles M. Mead, Andover; Howard Osgood, Rochester; Joseph Packard, Alexandria; Matthew B. Riddle, Hartford.

TRANSLATIONS IN MODERN SPEECH

Andrews Norton, conservative Unitarian and professor at Harvard, was one of the outstanding biblical scholars of America in the first half of the nineteenth century. His *Translation of the Gospels, with Notes* was published in two volumes, 1855, two years after his death. It is in straightforward contemporary language, including the use of 'you' instead of 'thou', with the other changes which this entails. Leicester A. Sawyer published a translation of the New Testament in 1858, in which he adopted contemporary usage except in the language of prayer, where he retained 'thou' and its concomitant archaisms.[1]

Ferrar Fenton, a London business man, made the translation of the Bible into modern English a lifetime avocation. His translation of Paul's epistles was published in 1883, and other portions from time to time thereafter, leading to *The Bible in Modern English* (1903). The value of his work lies not so much in his particular renderings, which are sometimes erroneous or amateurish, as in its keeping alive and furthering the general idea.[2]

Popular translations of the New Testament into modern English have been *The Twentieth Century New Testament*, by an anonymous group of scholars (1898–1901, revised 1904); *The New Testament in Modern Speech*, by R. F. Weymouth (1903); *The New Testament: a New Translation*, by James Moffatt (1913); *The New Testament: an American Translation*, by Edgar J. Goodspeed (1923). Weymouth's translation has been twice revised by other scholars, and remains the most conservative of the group. The translations by Moffatt and Goodspeed are more colloquial, the first with a British tang and the second in American everyday language.

Moffatt put forth a translation of the Old Testament in 1924, and a final revision of his translation of the Bible in 1935. In 1927 an American translation of the Old Testament appeared, by J. M. Powis Smith and three other scholars; and in 1931 this and the Goodspeed New Testament were published together as *The Bible: An American Translation.*

[1] See the biographical sketches of Norton and Sawyer in *Dictionary of American Biography*.

[2] For further details on Fenton's translation, and on other modern versions which must here be treated summarily, see E. H. Robertson, *The New Translations of the Bible* (London, S.C.M. Press, 1959).

The Riverside New Testament, by William G. Ballantine (1923, revised 1934), stands next to Weymouth as thoroughly modern yet conservative in literary quality. *The Four Gospels, a New Translation*, by Charles C. Torrey (1933, revised 1947), reflects his view that an Aramaic original underlay the Greek text, and contains a compact essay on 'The Origin of the Gospels'.

The New Testament: A Translation in the Language of the People, by Charles B. Williams (copyrighted in 1937), was acquired and published by the Moody Bible Institute, Chicago, in 1949. It is a modern translation by a competent scholar, which happily is trusted by folk of conservative theological views. The New Testament 'in plain English', using a small and simple vocabulary, by C. Kingsley Williams, appeared in 1952.

The New Testament in Basic English (1941), and *The Basic Bible* (1949), prepared under the direction of Professor S. H. Hooke, are cramped by the narrow limits of the word list, but most readers will agree with the prefatory note that the translation is straightforward and simple. And underlying it is sound biblical scholarship.

The New Testament Letters, prefaced and paraphrased, by Bishop J. W. C. Wand, was published in Australia in 1943 and in London in 1946. The introduction says that the work 'may be called either a free translation or a close paraphrase'. In any case, it has no extravagances of paraphrase, and has many qualities of sound free translation.

A new translation from the Greek of *The Four Gospels*, by E. V. Rieu, was published in 1952 as one of the Penguin Classics. It is accurate and readable, and its introduction is an informative essay upon the problems of the translator.

At present, the most popular of the translations into modern speech is *The New Testament in Modern English*, translated by J. B. Phillips (1958). It brings together into one volume his four previous translations, which began with the publication of *Letters to Young Churches* (1947). Phillips is the most free among the modern translators who refrain from wordy paraphrase. An example to which he refers in the foreword is Rom. xvi. 16, where the Authorized Version has 'Salute one another with a holy kiss'. This is retained by the Revised Version, Weymouth, and Moffatt. Others change 'Salute' to 'Greet', but keep kiss'. Phillips has 'Give one another a hearty handshake all round for my sake'.

THE REVISED STANDARD VERSION

In 1928 the copyright of the American Standard Version was acquired by the International Council of Religious Education, and thus passed into the ownership of the churches of the United States and Canada which were associated in this council through their boards of education and publication. The council included forty major denominations.

The council appointed a committee of fifteen scholars to have charge of the text and to undertake inquiry as to whether further revision was necessary. After two years of investigation and experiment, this committee recommended that there be a thorough revision of the version of 1901, which would stay as close to the Tyndale–King James tradition as it could in the light of our present knowledge of the Hebrew and Greek text and its meaning on the one hand, and our present understanding of English on the other.

In 1937 the revision was authorized by vote of the council, which directed that the resulting version should 'embody the best results of modern scholarship as to the meaning of the Scriptures, and express this meaning in English diction which is designed for use in public and private worship and preserves those qualities which have given to the King James version a supreme place in English literature'.

Thirty-two scholars served as members of the committee charged with making the revision, and they secured the review and counsel of an advisory board of fifty representatives of the co-operating denominations. Dean Luther A. Weigle, Yale University, was chairman of the committee and of each of the two sections. James Moffatt, Union Theological Seminary, as executive secretary, also served as a member of both sections. Dean Willard L. Sperry, Harvard University, was vice-chairman, and was succeeded in that post by Millar Burrows, Yale University, who served with both sections. The thirty-two scholars came from the faculties of twenty universities and theological seminaries. Except for one Jewish scholar, all were active members of evangelical communions: Baptist, Congregational, Disciples, Friends, Lutheran, Methodist, Presbyterian, Protestant Episcopal, and the United Church of Canada.

The Revised Standard Version of the New Testament was published in 1946. The Revised Standard Version of the Bible, containing the Old and New Testaments, was published on 30 September 1952.

Its publication had been authorized by the National Council of Churches, through vote of its General Board.[1]

The principles underlying this revision are stated briefly in the preface to the Revised Standard Version, and are set forth in more detail in two pamphlets: *An Introduction to the Revised Standard Version of the New Testament* (1946), and *An Introduction to the Revised Standard Version of the Old Testament* (1952).

The revision of the translation of the Old Testament is based upon the consonantal Hebrew and Aramaic text as preserved by the Massoretes. This is corrected, when necessary, in the light of the ancient versions; and, in cases where it is evident that the Hebrew text has suffered in transmission and none of the versions provides a satisfactory restoration, by cautious emendation. No single printed edition of the Greek text was followed for the New Testament, though the readings adopted are as a rule to be found in Westcott–Hort or in the text or margin of the seventeenth edition of Nestle's *Novum Testamentum Graece* (1941). In both Testaments use was made of the latest discoveries, both as to the text and as to the vocabulary, grammar, and idioms of the biblical and related languages. In Isaiah, for example, the Revised Standard Version has thirteen readings drawn from the complete manuscript of Isaiah which is the best preserved of the Dead Sea Scrolls discovered in 1947. In Rom. viii. 28, the decisive evidence for the Revised Standard Version rendering was afforded by the Chester Beatty Papyri discovered in 1931: 'We know that in everything God works for good with those who love him.'

Like the King James Version, the Revised Standard Version has endured some misrepresentations and attacks. But these have withered under honest scrutiny. They are answered in *An Open Letter concerning the Revised Standard Version*, published by the National Council of Churches. Over twelve million copies of the Revised Standard Version were sold within ten years. Most of the denominations in the NCCCUSA, and many not in its membership, use the Revised Standard Version in their work of Christian education, and it is widely used by the churches in public worship.

[1] In 1950 the International Council of Religious Education merged with other bodies to become the Division of Christian Education of the National Council of the Churches of Christ in the U.S.A.

THE APOCRYPHA

The Apocrypha were included in the King James Version, 1611. Special committees were appointed in 1879–84 to revise the translation of these books, and the Revised Version of the Apocrypha was completed and published in 1894.

In 1913 a group of scholars, under the leadership of R. H. Charles, published two massive volumes of *The Apocrypha and Pseudepigrapha of the Old Testament* in English. Most of the books appear in a fresh rendering, but for some the Revised Version was adopted. In 1938 Edgar J. Goodspeed published *The Apocrypha: An American Translation*, in modern English.

In response to the request of the General Convention of the Protestant Episcopal Church, October 1952, the National Council of the Churches of Christ in the U.S.A. authorized revision of the English translation of the Apocrypha. Ten scholars accepted this assignment, in accordance with principles and procedures similar to those followed for the Revised Standard Version Old and New Testaments. Dean Weigle was chairman, and Bruce M. Metzger, Princeton Theological Seminary, secretary, of the Apocrypha Section. The Revised Standard Version of the Apocrypha was published on 30 September 1957.

THE NEW ENGLISH BIBLE

The initial facts are summarized as follows in the bishop of Winchester's preface to the New Testament in this version (Library edition, 1961, p. v):

In May 1946 the General Assembly of the Church of Scotland received an overture from the Presbytery of Stirling and Dunblane recommending that a translation of the Bible be made in the language of the present day. As a result of this, delegates of the Church of England, the Church of Scotland, and the Methodist, Baptist, and Congregationalist Churches met in conference in October. They recommended that the work should be undertaken, and that a completely new translation should be made, rather than a revision, once previously contemplated, of any earlier version. In January 1947 a second conference, held like the first in the Central Hall, Westminster, included representatives of the University Presses of Oxford and Cambridge. At the request of this conference, the Churches named above appointed representatives to form the Joint Committee on the New Translation of the Bible. This Committee met for the first time in July of the same year. By January 1948, when its third meeting was held, invitations to be represented had been sent to the Presbyterian Church of England, the Society of Friends, the Churches in Wales, the Churches in Ireland, the British and Foreign Bible Society, and the National Bible Society of Scotland: these invitations were accepted.

The Bishop of Truro (Dr J. W. Hunkin) acted as Chairman from the beginning. He gave most valuable service until his death in 1950, when the Bishop of Durham (Dr A. T. P. Williams, later Bishop of Winchester) was elected to succeed him....

The actual work of translation was entrusted by the Committee to four panels dealing respectively with the Old Testament, the Apocrypha, the New Testament, and the literary revision of the whole. Denominational considerations played no part in the appointment to membership of these panels.

The director of the whole undertaking was Dr C. H. Dodd, formerly Norris-Hulse Professor of Divinity in the University of Cambridge, who was also chairman of the New Testament panel.

The resulting version of the New Testament was published on 14 March 1961, in the year of the 350th anniversary of the publication of the Authorized Version in 1611. At the time of writing, work on the Old Testament and Apocrypha is still going forward.

The distinctive character of this translation is due above all to the fact that it was at once a translation made straight from the original Greek, and also carried the collective authority of all the participant Churches and scholars. By contrast, most, if not all, of the previous English translations direct from the original were by individuals or, at most, a free-lance body; while the Authorized and Revised versions, though carrying collective authority, and, of course, using the originals, nevertheless leaned heavily on already existing English versions.

The intentions of the New English Bible are defined in some detail in the introduction by C. H. Dodd (Library edition, 1961, pp. vii ff.). Here it need only be said that it aimed at rendering the original so far as possible into idiomatic English, free alike from archaisms and from transient modernisms. This raised a host of difficulties. Despite the great advances in the understanding of New Testament Greek since the earlier English versions were made, much uncertainty remains. In literal and unidiomatic translation it is possible to avoid decisions over obscure passages. But idiomatic translation necessitates decision. Consequently, the line between translation and paraphrase sometimes waxes faint. For instance, Col. iii. 9f., quite literally, runs: 'do not lie to one another, having stripped off the old man with his deeds, and having put on the new which is being renovated into knowledge according to the likeness of the one who created him'. What is intended by 'into knowledge'? The New English Bible makes a clear decision, with the slightly paraphrastic: '...the new nature, which is being constantly renewed in the image of its Creator *and brought to know God*'. When the translators' panel was divided in opinion, a minority (even of one) could always claim a marginal alternative: Col. ii. 15 offers an exceptionally varied margin, reflecting the ambiguity of the Greek. Occasionally, the Greek seems to be deliberately ambiguous, with the intention of conveying a multiple meaning—a familiar feature of Johannine style. Here the translator may be hard put to it to be ambiguous enough. In John iii. 8 the translators were compelled, like their predecessors, to use both 'wind' and 'spirit' to represent *pneuma* (with the footnote *a single Greek word with both meanings*).

One area where idiomatic translation brought considerable change was that of 'Semiticisms'. Semitic idioms in both Testaments have become naturalized in English, but usually as more or less conscious 'biblicisms', such as 'children of light', 'sons of wrath', and numerous other phrases with loosely attached, adjectival genitives ('the hope of your calling', etc.). These were replaced, where possible, by idiomatic English equivalents.

To have tried to construct a complete Greek text before starting would have delayed the work indefinitely. Instead, the translator who prepared the initial draft of any passage did his best to mark and discuss the major textual *cruces* in it; and when the whole panel met to revise the draft, these *cruces*, together with any others then brought up, were debated, and decisions were reached. The translators were conscious of the fluid state of textual criticism, and of the impropriety of assuming any one codex, however ancient, to be necessarily the best in a given passage. They were enjoined by their commission not to resort to conjectural emendation unless it were impossible to make sense otherwise; and in fact it was never used, although some members were strongly tempted more than once. The margin was kept as clear as possible of minor variants not substantially affecting the sense.

The translators' panel sent each completed draft to the literary panel, who returned it with suggested stylistic improvements, and, when agreement was reached, the resultant draft went forward to the joint committee of the Churches for approval. At no point was the independence of the translators' convictions ever restricted by the representatives of the Churches. The measure of understanding and co-operation ultimately reached between the translators' panel and the literary panel yielded a version which is on the whole clear and readable. No doubt it lacks the individuality of a rendering by a single lively mind, but it carries a certain compensating weight, both of combined scholarship and of joint authorization.

CHAPTER XI

THE BIBLE AND THE MISSIONARY

For nearly two thousand years the missionary work of the Church has been essentially Bible-centred, and that in three senses: the Bible has been the source of inspiration and of spiritual nourishment for the missionary himself; it has also been the basis of the worship of the Church into which he sought to bring pagan or non-Christian tribes or individuals; and (to a larger extent than is commonly recognized) it has been a means of evangelism in itself.

From the end of the period of oral transmission the Church was dependent for authentic knowledge of Christ on the apostolic witness enshrined in the Epistles and Gospels. The final definition of the canon, followed by the provision of an authoritative version of the Latin Scriptures by St Jerome, was, therefore, an important step both for the inner life of the Christian community and for its expansion into the pagan world. The facts to which successive generations of Christian missionaries have borne witness are not merely matters of subjective experience: they are rooted in history, and in a history which is recorded uniquely in the documents which comprise the New Testament, read in the context of the Old Testament. Moreover, it has been the consistent witness of the Church in every age that these records contain not only an account of the coming of Jesus Christ and of his work for man's salvation, but also an authentic Word of God to the human soul. The missionary, therefore, has been bound to the Bible by a threefold cord: his own spiritual life and his authority as a messenger of the Gospel depended on his own knowledge of the Scriptures; the message he sought to proclaim and the Church into which he brought his converts was centred on the Bible; and the written Scriptures were a means by which the Gospel could lay hold of the minds and hearts of men and women, sometimes more effectively than by any word of his own. The first of these strands binding the missionary to the Bible has been common to all Christian witness: the emphasis laid on each of the other two strands has varied. Broadly, in Catholicism the emphasis has been laid on the Church and on the Bible as understood within the

Church, while in Protestantism the stress has fallen on the Bible and on the Church as created and recreated by the Word of God enshrined in Scripture.

The Reformation, in its religious aspect, brought the Bible into the centre of faith and of controversy in a quite new way. The reformers appealed to Scripture as warrant for their criticism of current faith and practice and as the all-sufficient ground for the reforms which they began by advocating and ended by instituting, even at the cost of schism. The consequent religious strife absorbed an immense amount of energy both within the Catholic Church and outside it; but, whereas the Protestant sects were too fully occupied in the struggle for survival to have much thought for the evangelization of the non-Christian world, one important element in the Counter-Reformation was a new outburst of missionary zeal. One expression of this was the formation in 1540 of the Society of Jesus, a religious order pledged not only to the normal threefold rule of monastic life but also to strenuous spiritual discipline and absolute obedience to the pope in all things. The Jesuits went wherever they were told to go, and by the time St Ignatius died in 1556 they had their outposts in America, Africa and Asia as well as in most parts of Europe. The shock of the Reformation thus greatly stimulated Catholic missionary activity, and the results were given permanent form when, in 1662, the Sacred Congregation of Propaganda was formed in Rome, followed in 1627 by the setting up of a training centre for Catholic missionaries by Pope Urban VIII. This may be taken as the beginning of the modern Catholic missionary enterprise and its relation to the Bible shows a predominant emphasis on two of the strands which connect the missionary with the Scriptures: the Bible remained the basis of the missionary's personal devotion and the chief objective was to get people into the Church (or back into the Church if they had fallen victim to heresy) so that they might be exposed through the worship and discipline of the Church to the saving facts of the Gospel as enshrined in Holy Scripture.

The missionary activity of the Protestant Churches emerged much more slowly. That is not to be wondered at, for the battle for religious freedom fell more heavily on them than on the ancient Church and the wars of religion were matters of life and death. Moreover, the Protestant churches were seldom in direct contact with non-Christian cultures, apart from Judaism and European Islam, whereas Catholic missions were closely allied to the imperial expansion of Spain, Portugal and France, as these powers pushed out into the New World which the Age of Discovery was beginning to reveal. Further, the harsh lines of Lutheran and Calvinistic doctrine needed to be softened and modified by Pietism and Puritanism, and the whole movement energized by the Evangelical Revival, before the full missionary power of Protestantism could be released.

Nonetheless, as soon as the Protestant nations began to develop as maritime powers they showed concern for the conversion of the natives of the countries visited by their ships in their search for trade. It is to the Netherlands that the honour belongs of making the first translation of any part of the Bible into a non-European language, and it is significant that the man who achieved this was neither priest nor minister but trader. In 1629 Albert Cornelius Ruyl, an agent of the Dutch East India Company, translated the Gospel of St Matthew into Malay and later added St Mark. Seventeen years later, in 1646, another merchant, Jan van Hasel, put the other two Gospels into this language and, in 1652, the Psalms and Acts were added. Finally, Melchior Leydekker, a Reformed pastor, and his colleague, P. van der Vorm, completed the translation of the Old and New Testaments in 1735. This translation remained the master version in Malay for many years and was produced both in roman and in arabic script. The motive behind this effort was the desire to make available to the inhabitants of the Malay peninsula the Book in which they could discover the truth of the Gospel. It shows an important difference of emphasis: whereas the Catholic missionary sought to bring people into the Church so that there they might learn the Gospel, the Protestant missionary (whether layman or minister) sought to give people the Bible in the language they could read so that they might discover for themselves the truth of the Gospel and the Church might be born among them by the impact of the Word of God.

Netherlands traders were also responsible for the beginning of translation into Formosan Chinese (1661) and into Sinhalese (1739). In the New World, John Eliot, working among the Mohican Indians, prepared the first version in any North American Indian tongue (1663) and Danish missionaries translated the New Testament into Eskimo (Greenland) in 1766. A beginning was also made on the languages of India by another Danish missionary, Ziegenbalg, who completed the New Testament in Tamil in 1715.

About the beginning of the eighteenth century, two events may be recorded as prophetic of that immense missionary expansion which was to mark the Protestant world in the next century; one was the formation of the Moravian Brotherhood under Count von Zinzendorf at Herrnhut in 1722, the other was the foundation in England of two closely related societies—the Society for Promoting Christian Knowledge (1698) and the Society for the Propagation of the Gospel in Foreign Parts (1701). The Moravian Brotherhood was heir and successor to the Bohemian Brethren who had suffered persecution or lived under precarious toleration since the middle of the fifteenth century. Herrnhut was a focal point in the Pietist Movement which began, in the later part of the seventeenth century, to make headway against the formalism into which Protestantism had fallen in the course of its struggle for survival. The Moravians were a close-knit missionary brotherhood, destined to have a decisive influence on John Wesley and thus to affect the Evangelical Revival in England. Under their influence von Canstein founded his Bible Institution in Halle in 1710 and Callenberg set up his *Institutum Judaicum* in the same city in 1728: both were vitally interested in the provision of Christian literature for Jews and Muslims.[1]

The two English societies were closely connected with one another. The S.P.C.K. formulated its aims as 'to promote and encourage the erection of charity schools in all parts of England and Wales; to disperse, both at home and abroad, Bibles and tracts of religion; and in general to advance the honour of God and the good of mankind, by promoting Christian knowledge both at home and in other parts of the world by the best methods that should offer'. The S.P.G. was formed to assist in the missionary work initiated by the S.P.C.K. by providing ministrations for British people overseas and by seeking to evangelize the non-Christian races of the world. Both societies were confined to members of the Church of England, and in their close fellowship we see clearly the pattern of the missionary work of the future: the provision both of Bibles and of missionaries for the enlarging witness of the Church overseas and at home. Yet it was to be another hundred years before the spiritual life of the Churches, whether in Britain or on the continent of Europe, would be strong enough to support a systematic missionary effort which would affect the life of the world.

[1] Cf. above, p. 340.

The decisive element, lacking up till then, was supplied by the Evangelical Revival. This was nothing less than a rediscovery of the sources of spiritual power through a return to biblical faith and piety. Some of the leaders were men such as John Fletcher, Henry Venn, William Romaine and John Newton, who remained within the Church of England in spite of the doubtful hospitality extended to them by their Church. Others, such as the Wesley brothers, were in the end compelled to form their own ecclesiastical organization. All, however, were men whose whole religious life had been transformed by a fresh study of the Bible and who bent their energies to persuading people not only of the truth of the Gospel but of the necessity of nourishing their lives at the sources of the Gospel in Scripture. It was out of this movement, which none could doubt was a movement of the Spirit, that there came that fresh conviction of the universality of the Gospel which was to make the nineteenth century so notable a landmark in the expansion of Christianity. The fact that the new spirituality had been so closely connected with the recovery of biblical truth meant that the Bible moved into the centre of faith and practice again in a way which ensured that it would be at the very heart of the new movement when it came.

The implications of the new evangelical grasp on biblical truth were not, however, generally accepted by the leaders of the various denominations with ease or speed. The inroads of an arid Calvinism had gone too deep. When William Carey made his passionate plea for the formation of the Baptist Missionary Society, he was met at first with the rebuke, 'Sit down, young man; when God wishes to convert the heathen, He will do it without your help!' Nonetheless, the enterprise was launched, and Carey sailed for India in 1793, there to undertake a work which still shocks us into incredulity by its scope and variety, above all in the field of Scripture translation.

At the turn of the century all the major British missionary societies came into existence in rapid succession: the London Missionary Society (the only interdenominational venture of its kind) in 1795, the Church Missionary Society in 1799, the Methodist Missionary Society in 1813 and, as handmaid to them all, the British and Foreign Bible Society in 1804, growing directly out of the Religious Tract Society (1799) and having as its sole aim the production and distribution of the Scriptures in the languages of the world. Thus, in a matter of two decades and while England was in the throes of one of the major crises of her history in the Napoleonic Wars, the pattern of the modern missionary movement was laid down—a group of determined men in charge of missionary recruitment, finance and propaganda, together with equally determined men dedicated to the task of supplying the Church with the basic necessity of its work, the Holy Bible in the vernacular. From then onwards the two enterprises marched together, mutually dependent and drawing strength from the same source.

THE BIBLE SOCIETIES

The foundation of the British and Foreign Bible Society at a meeting in the London Tavern, Bishopsgate, on 7 March 1804, was more than the beginning of a national institution: it was the birth of a world-wide movement of Bible translation, printing and distribution which was destined to draw into its orbit men and women of many different nations and languages and of most, if not all, Christian traditions. The origins of the Society lay, it is true, in a religious revival which had affected Great Britain more directly than other nations and, in particular, in the challenge of a very practical and localized need; yet, in the very act of meeting that need, the founders of the Society had their eyes already on the wider need of the world. Moreover, personal contacts between the leaders of the Evangelical Revival in this country and the leaders of the Pietist movement on the Continent meant that there were potential allies already available as soon as the design of a Bible Society had taken shape. The truth of this situation has always been dramatically symbolized in the story of the first move towards the launching of the Society. The Rev. Thomas Charles was a notable figure in the Evangelical Revival in Wales and one to whom, more perhaps than to any other single person, the rising passion for education in the Principality owed both its stimulus and its satisfaction. When he journeyed to London in the winter of 1802, it was to lay before the committee of the Religious Tract Society the desperate need of Wales for Bibles in the Welsh language—a need which the S.P.C.K. was unable to meet. The demand, as he reported it, was clearly beyond the capacity of the Religious Tract Society also, but in the course of the discussion a question was raised which was to be the charter of the Bible Society movement. For when the Rev. Joseph Hughes suggested that 'a society might be formed for the purpose—and if for Wales, why not for the Kingdom; why not for the whole world?' he provided the spark of imagination needed to set something new in motion. Fifteen months later, with the support of that influential group of wealthy laymen who had already earned the name of 'the Clapham Sect' and which included such men as William Wilberforce, Lord Teignmouth, Charles Grant and Zachary Macaulay, the British and Foreign Bible Society was formed 'for the wider distribution of the Scriptures, without note or comment'. In its title, if not in the modest description of its aims, the new Society declared its concern for the whole world—a concern which found expression a few months later in the publication of the Gospel of St John in the language of the Mohawk Indians. In its constitution—which has remained without substantial change—the Society also gave pledges to the future, for it was thoroughly interdenominational, governed by a committee consisting of fifteen Anglican and fifteen Free Church laymen, together with six representatives of foreign (that is, European) Churches.

It was the emphasis on the central place of the layman in the new project which probably accounted for the phrase attached to the aim of the Society which stipulated that the Bibles must be produced 'without note or comment'. Previous generations had seen enough Bibles, put out both by Roman Catholic and Protestant authorities, with tendentious notes in them, and memories of the theological controversies of the seventeenth century were still green. The new Society did not wish to get involved in such discussions: its sole concern was that men should have access to the sources of Christian faith in the Bible, rather than to any one interpretation of the Gospel itself. Interpretation has always been regarded as the duty of the Churches; the Society is concerned with the provision of Scriptures. Thus, what to us might well seem to be a restrictive clause, shutting out the possibility of helpful notes on the meaning of texts and words, was in origin both a necessary condition of wide, interdenominational co-operation and a charter of freedom from theological controversy.

The success of the movement was immediate and remarkable. In England, Wales, Ireland and Scotland local groups, known as 'Auxiliaries' of the parent Society, grew up, each pledged to do all that it could to distribute the Bible in its locality and to raise funds for the national enterprise. The cause was such that all denominations felt able to support it (although there were those who looked askance at a body which deliberately and tenaciously insisted on the equal part played in its work by the Church of England and the Nonconformist bodies). Representatives of the Society toured Europe—even before the battle of Waterloo brought the war to an end—seeking support wherever they could find it. Thus, as early as May 1804 a German Bible Society was formed in Nürnberg, although it had to move to Basle two years later on the renewal of hostilities between France and the Allies—a move which served to stimulate Bible Society activity in Switzerland. Two Scottish missionaries, Paterson and Henderson, on their way to the Far East, were held up in the Netherlands and Denmark, where they were able to start Bible societies which still flourish. Later, Paterson got through to Russia and, through the good offices of Prince Galitzin, persuaded the Tsar to sanction the formation of the Russian Bible Society in 1812 and to give it his patronage—although this Society was disbanded fourteen years later. In France, after the end of the war, a young Catholic took the initiative in starting Bible distribution, his books being supplied by the London Society; while in Greece the authorities of the Orthodox Church at first welcomed the movement wholeheartedly and gave their full support to representatives of the British Society. In the western hemisphere, Bible societies grew up in Philadelphia, Connecticut, Massachusetts, New Jersey and New York, so that by 1814 there were already sixty-nine such organizations in existence, and in 1816, when the American Bible Society was formed, it had already established bases in more than one hundred cities and states. Thus in ten or twelve years a network of agencies was set up sharing with the parent Society in London both responsibility and enthusiasm for the work.

For the most part these agencies concentrated their efforts on the distribution of the Scriptures in their own countries, where indeed the need was urgent; but the lands which had growing colonial responsibilities were soon involved in a programme of production in foreign languages. This was true of the Netherlands, as might be expected of a maritime nation, and of America: it was above all true of the British and Foreign Bible Society, with its centre in London at the heart of a growing empire.

The hope of avoiding controversy by excluding 'note or comment' from the publications of the Society was justified, but storms gathered round another matter during the 1820's and finally broke in the great 'Apocrypha Controversy' which rocked the organization for five years. Ever since the Reformation the status of the apocryphal books included in the Vulgate (in spite of St Jerome's protests) had been questioned or bitterly contested in Protestantism, and the most determined opponents of any recognition of the Apocrypha as 'Scripture' were the followers of John Calvin. When the Bible Society came into existence it accepted the fact that there was a difference of practice on this matter and continued to include the Apocrypha in its editions for countries where it was the custom of the churches to use these books. Thus, continental editions destined for Lutheran countries, and Greek editions for the Eastern Orthodox lands and copies of the Authorized Version for English use contained the Apocrypha. (Even the famous 'Mary Jones Bible' on view at Bible House in London shows her signature on a free half-page at the end of the Welsh translation of Maccabees!) But the Scottish Auxiliaries took strong exception to this practice: did not the Westminster Confession say in round terms that 'the books commonly called Apocrypha, not being of divine inspiration, are no part of the canon of the Scripture; and therefore are of no authority in the Church of God, nor to be any otherwise approved, or made use of, than other human writings'? So the battle was set and at the end of a long engagement the Society was prohibited from publishing the Apocrypha or aiding any other society in the publication of Bibles containing the offending books (1826). This, however, did not prevent the Scottish Auxiliaries from forming their own National Bible Society of Scotland; a decision which resulted in the cause receiving greater support in Scotland than would have been forthcoming had London remained the exclusive centre of British Bible Society work.

Another argument which ended in secession concerned the application of theological tests to workers in the Bible Society. There were those who held that nobody should be employed on such work except those who could profess Trinitarian belief. The main body of the Society, however, remained of the opinion that anybody who was willing to give honest support to the central aims of the Bible distribution should be used and encouraged. The minority seceded and in 1831 formed the Trinitarian Bible Society.

In spite of these storms of contrary opinion, the work grew steadily throughout the nineteenth century, so that when the Society celebrated its centenary in 1904 it found itself the centre of a vast system of subsidiary organizations spread throughout the British Empire and outside it, either definite auxiliaries of the parent Society or independent national bodies still looking to London for supplies; and in contact with (sometimes in friendly rivalry with) other great 'missionary' Bible societies, such as those centred on New York, Amsterdam or Edinburgh. As the Christian Churches pushed steadily on with the task of evangelization, the burden on the societies grew and the possibilities of conflict over general policy in places where more than one such agency was at work became acute. Thus, in South America both the British and Foreign Bible Society and the American Bible Society had large undertakings in the distribution of Scriptures in Spanish, Portuguese and some of the South American Indian languages; in China, again, both of these Societies and the Scottish Society were at work; in Indonesia, the Netherlands Bible Society, the British and Foreign Bible Society and the National Bible Society of Scotland all had considerable commitments, while a similar situation obtained in the Near East where the principal agencies were those of Britain and America. The independent expansion of societies with identical aims clearly must lead to confusion and wastage, and in the past fifty years two developments in policy have been carried out, each designed to avoid overlapping and to foster common planning. The first was the formation of joint agencies in which two or more Bible societies pooled their resources in the field and took agreed shares in the production programmes involved; and the second was the formation, after the Second World War, of 'The United Bible Societies' as a permanent means of common counsel and planning between the chief executive officers of the Bible societies. The former step has frequently been followed by the development of a 'National Bible Society' (as, for example, in India, Korea, or Brazil), still dependent on the pioneer societies for support but seeking to enlist the co-operation of nationals of the country concerned in meeting their own needs. The second was an important development both within the Bible societies and in relation to world missionary strategy, for it reproduced on a world scale the relationship between churches and Bible societies already proved to be fruitful nationally: alongside the World Council of Churches (now including within its organization the International Missionary Council) there is a world organization of Bible societies, independent in structure but in close co-operation with the official international organ of the churches.

One other development calls for mention: the part played in the total enterprise by the British Dominions has so much increased in the last fifty years that today the contribution both in money, book production and distribution of Scriptures by the Bible Society in Canada, South Africa, Australia and New Zealand is valued at approximately a quarter of the total budget of over a million pounds annually.

THE BIBLE SOCIETIES AND THE MISSIONARY

From the beginning there was the closest possible co-operation between missionaries in the field and the Bible societies. This relationship became the closer as these societies developed the policy of planting agents in Africa or in the Far East so that they might be in continuous and direct touch with the needs of the expanding Church, but it was always a necessary relationship. At the time of the formation of the British and Foreign Bible Society, for instance, William Carey and his companions (chief among whom were Marshman and Ward) were already established in Serampore, though excluded from the rest of India by the opposition of the East India Company. The Bible Society immediately established contact with them and gave assistance in two ways—by contributing generously towards their expenses (to a total of £27,230) and by publishing the results of their labours. That these were extensive is shown by the startling fact that, before Carey's death in 1834, he and his colleagues had translated some part of the Scriptures into no less than thirty-four Asiatic languages. Again, when Robert Morrison went to China in 1807 (as a servant of the East India Company, since China was closed to western missionaries) and began the dangerous and laborious task of putting the Bible into Chinese, he could rely on the sympathy and ready help of the Bible Society, with which he was in constant touch throughout his astonishing enterprise. Meanwhile, Henry Martyn had gone to Calcutta and begun work on what is still the basic text of the New Testament in Persian (completed in 1815) besides doing valuable studies in Hindustani and Arabic. Adoniram Judson added to his efforts as a pioneer missionary in Burma the immense task of translating the Bible into Burmese (1835). John Williams visited the Pacific Islands and put portions of the Scriptures into Raratongan (1828). All the great missionary pioneers were able to rely on the vivid interest and support of the societies of which the British and Foreign Bible Society was the first.

THREE PHASES OF TRANSLATION WORK

Three phases may be distinguished in the story of Bible translation in which the Bible societies have worked closely with missionaries in various fields. The first and most obvious was the putting of the Scriptures into languages which had a written form and in which there was already a considerable literature, such as those of India, China, Burma, Korea and Japan. Each such venture is a story in itself and in most instances the translation preceded the opening of the country to organized missionary work. China remained closed to missionaries until the middle of the nineteenth century, but Robert Morrison's translation of the New Testament was ready by 1814. Japan did not open her doors to the West until 1853, yet pioneer translations into Japanese had been made as early as 1837 (St Francis Xavier is said to have translated selections during his visit to the country, 1549–51, and the Jesuits to have had a complete New Testament before 1613. These Catholic translations perished, however, when missionaries were expelled from Japan in the middle of the seventeenth century). Korea remained sealed off from the West until 1882, but two Gospels were translated into Korean some years before that. Indeed, so important did missionaries deem the impact of the written Word that copies of the Scriptures actually preceded them into forbidden territory. Thus, when at last western missionaries were admitted to Korea they found a considerable number of Christians in Seoul, awaiting baptism, who had been converted by copies of Gospels smuggled in across the Manchurian border. More recently the same method has been adopted in Tibet where the whole of the first edition of a Bible which had taken almost a hundred years to prepare and which was published in 1948 has been distributed, in spite of the fact that missionaries are not allowed into the country; and there is some evidence that copies have found their way into lamaseries and are being studied by the monks.

The second phase of translation work opened with the exploration of the interior of Africa and the beginning of the vast missionary activity which has absorbed thousands of lives in that immense continent. This brought men up against the problem of the unwritten language and the quest for words in which to express the Christian Gospel in tongues which might be very poor in abstract nouns. A man might have to search for years before he found the right term for even the simplest and most fundamental of Christian concepts. The names connected with this daunting enterprise are legion—Livingstone, Stanley, Mackay, Moffat, Steere, Crowther, to name only a few—and the work is still going on. With a sure instinct such men felt that until they had got the Bible into the language of the people among whom they were working, there could be no stability for the Christian Church which they were trying to build, and until their people had a literature they themselves would never truly be a people. So, wherever the Christian Gospel was carried, there men set to work to make the Scriptures available and to teach the people to read. Not for nothing were Mackay's converts in Uganda known as 'Readers'.

The problems involved in this phase of the work were—and still are—most formidable. What, for instance, was to be done about an alphabet where none existed? Some of the early pioneers invented a system of signs for this purpose. James Evans, working among the Cree Indians of North America, made a special syllabary consisting of simple triangles, dots and circles, and did his own printing, with a hand-made press and ink made out of a mixture of whale oil and soot, on paper manufactured from the inside of birch bark. But this invention of special alphabets was soon abandoned in favour of some modification of the roman script, with special signs for the more peculiar sounds.

A more serious difficulty is the discovery of the right terms for basic biblical conceptions. The translator of the Bible into Luba-Katanga (for South-east Congo) had to spend years looking for the right expression for 'Holy Spirit' because, although this language abounded in words for 'spirits', they all had the wrong connotation or the wrong associations. One day he discovered that there was at the court of the local chief an official, known as 'Nsenka', whose function it was to meet those who had business with the chief, find out what they wanted, conduct them into the royal presence and act as their advocate and intercessor. It occurred to him that the functions which the Nsenka fulfilled on a human and tribal plane were exactly those assigned by Christian theology to the Holy Spirit and expressed in the words

'Comforter', 'Advocate' and 'Intercessor'. He therefore adopted the term and turned it to Christian usage in his translation. Moreover, divergence of social habit may make the biblical term mean the precise opposite—as, for instance, in the translation of 'Behold, I stand at the door and knock' for people among whom knocking is either unknown or else a sign of enmity. Or there is the recurrent problem of what to do about such basic symbols as 'sheep' and 'shepherd' for a people who have never seen a sheep and have no shepherds. Yet, in spite of these formidable difficulties the work has gone on from the middle of the nineteenth century to the present day, a matter of endless patience, trial, revision, and tentative use, until some portion of the Bible exists in an intelligible form in over 300 African languages, and in many other tongues which formerly existed exclusively in spoken form. The experience of Africa could be paralleled in South America and the Pacific Islands, where the American Bible Society has played a dominant part.

The third phase in Bible translation has only recently opened. It was only natural that, in the attempt to put the Scriptures into the languages of the people among whom they were working, missionaries should at times have produced what was in fact a dialect translation, without noting its similarity to neighbouring forms of speech. Today there is a search for the common languages underlying different dialects, and a number of 'Union' or 'Standard' versions have been prepared in the hope that one translation may serve a much wider area. Thus, whereas before 1950 there were three different translations of the Bible into Swahili, the great East African language, there is now a Union version so devised as to be understood over the whole of the mainly Swahili-speaking area from the East coast almost to the Great Lakes. Whether this movement will be successful or not it is still too early to say, but it betokens a great new exercise in linguistic study, and it might well have very great cultural consequences.

The Bible societies have differed somewhat in the methods used in this essentially scholarly work. The British and Foreign Bible Society has always regarded the missionary as the chief agent in translation and has from time to time subsidized the work so that the translator might be set free from other responsibilities. The Netherlands Bible Society, on the other hand, has always trained its own translators and sent them out to work alongside the missionary while being responsible for this one linguistic task. Again, all the missionary Bible societies employ a specialist at their headquarters whose task it is to keep in touch with translation work wherever it is being done, to make the experience of one translator available to others and to consult with experts in the particular group of languages concerned (for instance, in London, with the School of African and Oriental Languages in the University of London, and similar bodies). The societies differ also in the way in which this expert on translation works. The American Bible Society acts on the principle that translation can only be done, or even rightly judged, in the field, and therefore sends its Translations Secretary on frequent and prolonged tours; while the British and Foreign Bible Society tends to leave the working out of problems to the people on the spot. One of the advantages following from the formation of the 'United Bible Societies' is precisely that these differences of method can more easily be checked against one another to the benefit of all.

Wherever possible, translators work from the Hebrew and the Greek. Many of those concerned, however, have insufficient knowledge of these languages to translate direct into the new tongue they are working on. They therefore (if they are British, or at least English-speaking) use the Authorized and the Revised Versions, with any or all modern English translations, as a basis, and check their work against any already existing versions in cognate languages. The translator works with a team of native assistants whose job it is to say what a given word or idea conveys to their minds and to scrutinize the translation from the standpoint of a native-born speaker of the language used. Recently a new tool for translators has begun to be fashioned in the form of a Greek–English diglot of the New Testament, containing the Greek on one side of the page and a modern translation close to the original on the other, so that those whose knowledge of Greek is not sufficient for them to work direct from that version may still be able to check their English against the Greek.[1]

The task of translation is initially difficult, and it is never finished. Language is not static and men's knowledge of a foreign tongue is never complete. Even the most established versions reach a point where they are out of line with current speech; and if that is deemed to be true now of the Authorized Version, which was made by Englishmen, much more must it be true of translations not made by nationals

[1] The British and Foreign Bible Society has published in this form Mark (1958), Matthew (1959), John (1960), the General Letters (1961), Luke (1962).

at all. One feature, therefore, of the present work of the Bible societies is the revision of the earlier versions and particularly of those current in Asia, and wherever possible these revisions are being made by native Christian scholars. Thus, a Chinese version is under preparation by a Chinese scholar able to work direct from Hebrew and Greek into his own language, and a new version in Bengali is in the hands of an Indian scholar similarly equipped. Again, after the Second World War, the Japanese Bible Society, supported by the American Bible Society and the British and Foreign Bible Society, took the unprecedented step of discarding a revision in 'classical' Japanese in favour of a new version in 'colloquial' form, in order to bring the Bible closer to the common speech of men—and this, again, was the work of a distinguished group of Japanese Christian scholars.

Bible translation provides a rough gauge of the success of the missionary enterprise in different parts of the world. The generalization needs to be qualified in certain respects—particularly in relation to the Islamic countries, where it scarcely applies at all—but it would seem that the appearance of a Gospel or other single book of the Bible in a 'new' language was an indication that the Church (in one form or another) was at grips with its essential task among those people: the language has been mastered at least to the stage when a first essay may be made in expressing the truth of the Gospel in the mother-tongue of the people. When, after a decade or two, the New Testament is completed, its appearance usually indicates the emergence of a Christian community speaking that particular language: that is, there has been a response to the Gospel and a believing community has come into existence. When, very much later, the complete Bible appears, it betokens a degree of permanence in the Christian community: the Gospel has taken root in the life of the people. Finally, the revision of a Bible comes at the point where the Christian community has attained a measure of maturity and possesses native members capable of critical appraisal of the text in the light of a real understanding of the Gospel.

THE USE OF THE BIBLE IN EVANGELISM

The translation of the Scriptures, fascinating and complicated as it is, represents only a necessary first stage in the work of Bible distribution. The object of the Bible societies is to get the book so translated into the hands of the people who can read it, whether they are Christians or not.

To this end three methods have been used: first, the distribution of Scriptures (particularly Gospels) by missionaries as part of their own evangelistic work; second, the employment by the Bible societies themselves of agents, known as colporteurs, whose task is to take the books to the people; and, third, the encouragement of 'voluntary colportage' on the part of native Christians as one essential aspect of their normal witness to the Faith. In all three the principles on which the Bible societies have operated have been, first, that books should not normally be given away (since people do not value what they get for nothing); but, second, that nobody ought to be debarred from possessing the Scriptures simply by lack of money. In practice this has meant fixing the prices of the books according to what the average person could afford to pay—a difficult estimate, made after such consultation with people on the spot as might be possible—and generous discounts to agents who were prepared to make Scripture distribution a serious part of their work. In addition, *ad hoc* grants of books for free distribution have been frequently made where conditions justified this procedure. This has meant that there has always been a deficit on the enterprise, viewed as a commercial transaction, and this deficit (in the case of the British and Foreign Bible Society) now amounts to over £350,000 a year, which represents the sum which must be raised by voluntary contributions from the Christian public.

The chief instrument of evangelistic distribution has been the single Gospel or other book of the Bible. That is why, in the figures for distribution, the number of so-called 'portions' is so very much greater than the number of New Testaments and Bibles. These latter normally only become relevant and useful at a later stage, when the purchaser has been interested by reading a Gospel. The early missionaries made Scripture distribution an essential part of their work, and it still remains true that those who are engaged in direct evangelism in a pagan or non-Christian environment rely on the Scriptures as a major instrument. Not unnaturally, however, it has been the colporteur who has been the hero of Bible Society literature: he is usually a native of the country, a man of humble origin but of deep personal conviction; he goes out alone, day after day, with his bag of books, often uncertain of his reception, and he has adventures. Broadly speaking, it has been the colporteur who has carried the main burden in Muslim countries and in the Far East, while the missionary has done most of the work in Africa, where colportage is only just beginning. This is not surprising in view of the fact that literacy has had to grow from zero in Africa, whereas there has been a literate class in Asian countries for generations. Again, allowance must be made for the longer history of the Church in India compared with the comparatively recent growth of Christianity in Africa; and, in fact, it is in India that the most determined effort is now being made to lay upon the ordinary member of the Church the obligation to witness to his faith through the distribution of the Scriptures.

By whatever method the Bible societies have operated, the annual circulation reported by all of them together has reached the total of some twenty-five million books. The vast majority of these books are single Gospels or 'portions', but roughly three and a half million are New Testaments and the same number complete Bibles. In any one year this distribution takes place in some 500 languages. This result must, however, be set against the fact that some twenty-five million people learn to read each year, so that the annual distribution is only just keeping pace with the rise in literacy.

The number of languages used by mankind was estimated twenty years ago (by the French Academy of Sciences) at 2796. India alone has over one hundred, Africa at least 400, and there are many still unidentified spoken by small groups of isolated people in places such as New Guinea. All the Bible societies together have so far (1962) produced some part of the Scriptures in 1181 tongues: the whole Bible in 226, the New Testament in 281 and some book or books in another 674. Of these translations one hundred are in languages spoken in India and three hundred in African languages. It is probable that many of the 1600 languages as yet untouched belong to small tribes and groups of people, so that the 1181 translations recorded represent the languages spoken by about four-fifths of the population of the world.

THE IMPACT OF THE BIBLE

It is very difficult to estimate the effect of this steady output of biblical literature which has been going on with increasing volume for more than a hundred and fifty years. That there is great wastage is only to be expected. Not everyone who is persuaded to buy a Gospel or a New Testament reads it, and some put the books to ignoble uses, or simply forget all about them. In attempting some assessment, we shall deal with the impact of the Bible on individuals, on churches and on the non-Christian cultures in which the churches exist.

The impact of the Bible on individuals is of course varied and largely dependent on the cultural background. A Muslim, for instance, approaches the Scriptures usually with a bias in favour of a sacred book, since he is himself a child of the Koran; yet there may be a violent reaction if the first book he encounters is the Gospel according to St Mark, with its uncompromising opening, 'The beginning of the gospel of Jesus Christ, the Son of God', which at once raises the traditional antipathy of the Muslim towards the suggestion that God could ever have a son. There is thus need of some discrimination in the selection of books for distribution among non-Christians. Yet the use of the Scriptures for evangelistic work has been one of the most important factors in Islamic countries and has often been possible when direct preaching was ruled out. Cases of conversion remain rare, but there is evidence, particularly perhaps in Persia, of a considerable body of secret or partial believers, nourished by the reading of the Bible. In contrast, Hinduism is a hospitable religion, able to absorb ideas from other sources without discomfort and without remarkable effect. On the other hand, the tribal life of Africa is so close to the conditions described in the Old Testament that there tends to be a ready acceptance of Old Testament ideas and a rather greater resistance to the New Testament. Yet, when all allowance is made for background and conditioning factors of all kinds, it remains true that there is a steady volume of evidence that the written Word can be of decisive influence in the conversion of men and women. Such converts or inquirers invariably attach themselves to a Christian community, in which they can receive further instruction in the Faith, but their first impulse towards Christianity comes from the records themselves. Moreover, there are instances where a whole Christian community has been created out of paganism or non-Christian religion by the witness of the Scriptures. This is true not only of the church in Korea, to which reference has already been made, and which is still an intensely Bible-centred community: it is also true of the Batak church in Sumatra and of the Protestant churches in South America, most of which owe their existence to the devoted work of pioneer colporteurs carrying the Spanish or Portuguese or Indian versions to remote places.

The impact of the Bible on churches is perhaps a more familiar theme, for the Bible has always held a central place in Christian devotion, and an untried community in an alien environment can hardly be expected to grow in depth and understanding without access to the sources of Christian faith. The vital importance of the Bible in sustaining the faith of the Church always becomes evident in time of persecution. Mackay's 'Readers' in Uganda were able to stand up to fierce persecution and, though many died, the Church survived. In Madagascar, during the persecution which continued for over twenty years (1836–61) Christians not only kept their faith alive by secret Bible reading but showed such vitality that the Church increased tenfold under the experience. More recently, the Formosan hill tribes, almost untouched by Christianity before the Second World War, resisted Japanese pressure and emerged with firmly planted Christian communities, based on nothing but the study of the Japanese version of the Bible, read and pondered in secret but with amazing effect. In Kenya, under the threat of Mau Mau, it was the Christians whose life was most deeply rooted in the Bible who stood firm against all attempts to get them to take the oath. The toughness of the indigenous churches would seem to depend on the degree of devotion to the Bible. The organization of a church, even its ministers and priests, may be destroyed or dispersed without ultimate disaster so long as the Bible is there.

While persecution or acute crisis may thus reveal the closeness of the link between spiritual vitality in the Church and the study of the Bible, in more untroubled times the matter is usually more complicated. The Bible may become a mere part of the public worship of the Church, with little more than a superstitious impact on the hearers. An intense concentration on Bible study, coloured by a particular, narrow interpretation, may increase and intensify sectarianism. On the other hand, it has been the experience of people active in the Ecumenical Movement, when fundamental problems have been discussed by representatives of very different Christian traditions, that the more central the Bible has become in such discussions the more they have become aware of a common heritage. There is thus evidence that the apostolic testimony, as contained in the New Testament, is a potent means by which a divided Church can rediscover its lost unity. This, however, must be set against the fact that the great rift, which runs through all denominations, particularly in the Anglo-Saxon countries, divides people precisely on the question of their understanding of the Bible as the revealed Word of God.

When we come to the impact of the Bible on non-Christian cultures, the data are even more confused and uncertain. On the one hand, the emphasis laid by Protestant missions on the knowledge of the Bible has tended to make the Christian group more highly literate than the rest of the community. The Christian stress on education, expressed in countless schools and colleges which owe their origin to missionary enthusiasm, derives from the conviction that only a literate Christian can fully enter into his faith and that literacy in the community at large is an asset in the propagation of the Gospel. Thus, literacy and the open Bible have gone together. Moreover, the fact that the first literature to appear in many hitherto unwritten languages has been the Bible has meant that the main themes of the biblical message have entered into the general consciousness at least of those who have learnt to read, even though they have not necessarily become Christians. Apart altogether from the religious message of the Scriptures, the contribution of translation into the vernacular to the task of nation-building can hardly be overestimated. Even among those peoples who already possessed a great literature, the wide dispersion of the Christian writings in their languages has had an indefinable effect on the basic ideas and values in their culture. It is, for instance, at least significant of a change in the ideal of the 'good man' that the highest praise given to Mahatma Gandhi, even by Hindu writers, was that he was 'Christ-like'. This, of course, is nothing new: it was the ethical ideal enshrined in the Jewish Scriptures and to some extent embodied in the Jewish community which attracted many to the synagogue in the first century and induced them to become 'god-fearers'.

On the other hand, too much cannot be built on this wide, diffused influence of Christian literature. It may, indeed, militate against the deeper impact of the Bible on the souls of men by making them familiar with the externals of the faith and thus the more reluctant to commit themselves to the more fundamental truth. Out of this situation there may also come a criticism of the Christian Church for being so unlike the ethical ideal discovered in the Gospels that the contradiction robs the Church of authority. This may be salutary for the Church, but it may also indicate a complete unawareness of the depth of the biblical diagnosis of man's malady and a disregard for the biblical teaching about sin.

One notable example of the impact of the Bible on a non-Christian culture is provided by Japan. The Christian community in that country still numbers less than half a million out of a population of over ninety million people. Yet the circulation in Japan, recorded in 1957 (not an unusual year), amounted to more than 78,500 Bibles, 713,000 New Testaments and more than a million Gospels and other single books. Since the publication in 1955 of the Bible in colloquial Japanese, something like half a million copies of the New Testament have been sold each year. Japan is one of the most highly literate countries in the world and there are said to be ten thousand bookshops serving its passion for literature—a passion raised to white heat by the collapse of the cultural and religious life of the people after the defeat of 1945. In the search for a new foundation for their national life, the Japanese people are looking not only to the Christian Scriptures but also to Marxism, and the outcome is not yet foreseeable. The effect, however, of this exposure of thousands of minds to the Christian writings cannot be negligible at a time when the old culture is in almost total flux.

Outside Protestantism there appears to be a revival of interest in the Bible which may well be of the greatest importance, not only for the preservation of what unity is left to European culture but also for the better understanding between churches of different traditions. In Greece movements have been at work in recent years which have encouraged the reading of the Bible among Orthodox Church people, and the American Bible Society has given large gifts of the New Testament in Modern Greek for use in the armed forces and the prisons, as well as in the parishes. A modern translation of the New Testament into Russian has been undertaken by members of the Russian emigration centred on Paris. Meanwhile, in the Roman Catholic Church, new editions of the Bible in French have been issued in France and Belgium, and the late Cardinal Innitzer actively supported a notable Bible study movement in Austria, which was guided by an Augustinian monk, Father Parch. How far such movements will go it is not yet possible to foresee but they may be further evidence of the wide recognition of the fact that the strength of a church, particularly under duress and difficulty, depends on the place it gives in its life to the study of the Bible.

ASSESSMENT

Protestantism has laid great stress in its missionary work on the Bible, both as a source of strength for the Christian and as a means of evangelization: it has acted in the faith that where the Word is proclaimed, whether by preaching or by Scripture distribution, there the Holy Spirit will be at work and the Church will be created. This policy has not lacked critics, particularly among Catholics, for it seems to be a highly dangerous invitation to private opinion and sectarianism. The recent movements in the Roman Catholic Church referred to above do not betoken any departure from this opposition to a policy which makes the Bible available to the generality without the guidance of the Church. The dangers thus indicated are very real, as anybody who is at all aware of the proliferation of sects both in Europe and overseas must admit. It is possible for men to misunderstand the Bible, or to understand only one part of it and to form movements and religious bodies on the basis of that partial understanding, and then to add arrogance to error. This is not just a tragic event of the past which has effect in the present: the fact is that the types of religion which are spreading most rapidly in the modern world are those associated with the more extreme and even bizarre sects, based on a one-sided interpretation of the Scriptures.

The fact that, for good or ill, the Bible has become a public document for practically the whole of mankind is bound to raise large questions concerning the nature of the authority which can rightly interpret Scripture. For masses of people in the western world—and for many in the Christian churches—the Bible is no longer self-explanatory because for them the doctrinal framework within which it was once understood has collapsed and they need guidance in reading it. This will become increasingly true of other parts of the world as western, industrial civilization spreads and 'the acids of modernity' work in men's minds. Thus the necessity for interpretation—and the complexity of the task—is likely to grow more urgent with the years. There is, therefore, no longer any issue between Protestant and Catholic concerning the need for an interpretative authority: the question centres on the nature of the authority to be accepted.

This is an issue which properly lies outside the scope of this chapter, but it is clearly of vital importance for the Christian missionary both in the work of translating the Scriptures (which in itself involves interpretation) and in the task of enabling men and women to understand the Scriptures which are now so widely disseminated among them. All Christian denominations have in fact some ultimate authority in matters of faith and practice, whether this is the Episcopate, the General Assembly, the Synod or the vaguer authority of 'sound scholarship'. One of the central tasks in the reformation of Christendom may well be the development of an organ of interpretation common to all the Churches which will be sufficiently flexible to respond to the deepening insights of biblical scholarship and at the same time strong enough to bring a greater coherence to the varied understandings of the Bible which are current among Christians. In this task the experience of the missionary in his unending effort to bring non-Christians to the sources of Christian faith in Holy Scripture should be taken fully into account; for he is at the growing-point of the Christian Church, where the Gospel makes fresh impact on the life of mankind.

STATISTICAL SUMMARY OF THE WORK OF TWO OF THE LARGER BIBLE SOCIETIES

NOTE: In this summary the second column gives the number of languages in which the Society published some portion of the Bible between the date of its foundation and the date selected for comparison; the third gives the distribution figures for that year and the last the total expenditure involved in the year selected.

THE BRITISH AND FOREIGN BIBLE SOCIETY
(founded 1804)

Date	Languages	Distribution: Bibles	Distribution: New Testaments	Distribution: Portions	Total cost £
1854	152	570,656	744,801	52,071	119,257
1904	378	1,057,154	1,449,808	3,190,399	255,639
1954	825	1,258,385	830,513	4,517,488	1,306,594

THE AMERICAN BIBLE SOCIETY
(founded 1816)

Date	Languages	Bibles	New Testaments	Portions	$
1854	9	256,128	493,307	454	211,248.66
1904	32	290,847	440,209	1,100,040	456,999.69
1954	101	1,005,254	1,639,087	12,643,693	2,701,564.86

TOTAL WORLD CIRCULATION
(carried out by all the Bible agencies, exclusive of commercial houses)

	1957
Bibles	3,599,347
New Testaments	3,240,936
Portions	18,126,593
Total	24,966,876

CHAPTER XII

THE PRINTED BIBLE

The invention of printing was as important for the Bible as it was for all literature; but its significance has often been misinterpreted, largely because modern conceptions and preoccupations have been imported into the context of early printing. The earliest observers went to the heart of the matter, as they saw it. 'He prints as much in a day as was formerly written in a year' said Campano, bishop of Teramo, of the fifteenth-century printer Ulrich Han. Printing was a means of speedy, and soon of cheap production. Speaking of the Bible, a French translator added that there was now no excuse for the literate believer if he was not familiar with the Word of God.

Writers nearer our own time, but before modern bibliographers had made their systematic investigations, found a deeper significance, which is still advanced. The concept of the edition, a scholar's concept which has taken five hundred years to elaborate, is projected backwards into the first years of printing as if it were the perfect outcome of a sudden transformation. Where once the scribe had produced his single copy—perhaps inaccurately transcribed, interpolated or tendentiously altered, and taken from another single copy subject to the same vicissitudes, and so on back through innumerable stages—there was now supposed to be the modern succession of accurately printed editions, each an improvement on the last if not faithful to it. Within each edition all copies were supposed to be identical.

Reflection suggests objections. Both printing and writing are manual operations, and each is as accurate as the operator makes it. There is no reason inherent in the process why writing should provide a less faithful transcript, and Jewish scribes had long evolved an attitude of reverence to the text which elevated copying to a ritual and made inaccuracy a blasphemy. Though it might be argued that the numbers of copies printed at a time made collaboration easier between scholars, since a reference to page and line of a printed book would make discussion quicker, this is only partly true. The medieval scribes had a process of duplication; the transcription of an exemplar was capable of producing copies that tallied line for line; and in any case the Bible had its own system of reference long before printing began and needed this kind of help less than any ordinary book.

So much for principles. When we come to examine actual practice the apparent disparity between the processes is again diminished. By the time printing was invented, manuscript copying had evolved safeguards against its potential deficiencies; for a book lectured on in the schools it was important that copies must tally in essentials, and it was for this reason that the very widely used system of the *pecia* was developed. On the other hand it was some time before the potential scholarly advantages of printing, as distinct from its economic advantages, were understood—and much longer before they were exploited. It is as well to say now that it was not until the eighteenth century or even later that editorial technique and general printing practice had advanced to the point where it was possible—and even then it was not common—to produce an edition in the modern sense: that is, printings where all the copies could be collated and shown to have no variants of any significance. This general statement admits of qualification; some printers have always striven for uniformity and accuracy. But both qualities can be thought of as relative, and it is reasonable to believe that our ideal of the edition, of literal accuracy, the diplomatic transcript or the quasi-facsimile, would have struck the practitioners of an earlier age as unnecessary, pedantic and wasteful. Taken as a whole, the statement can stand until some scholar has collated all the known copies of an early edition and pronounced them identical. This is a vast labour; it has been partially accomplished in some cases, and it would only have been prosecuted because the variants disclosed are so substantial and rewarding. The most notable case, and the most interesting to the reader of English, is the First Folio of Shakespeare's plays. Some eighty copies in the Folger Shakespeare Library of Washington have now been collated. None is identical with all the others; the variants are in many cases substantial; and it seems as if the business of editing Shakespeare's text can only now be begun. Where a variant is apparently insignificant for the text, it may still tell something of the process of printing, and this may permit further deduction about the nature of the underlying text.[1]

[1] The notes of Fredson Bowers's *Textual and Literary Criticism* (Cambridge, 1959) are a convenient source of references to the principal studies, mostly by American

The relevance of this to Bible printing is plain. In any age the Bible text must be accurate; during the Reformation—and after, for that matter—a false text could produce false doctrine, and that might entail damnation. For their contemporaries the texts of Shakespeare or Dekker, providers of mere entertainment and members of a despised profession, might very well be ill-printed and no harm done. But printing practice, like the rain, fell on the just and the unjust alike. Though the modern textual scholar is unlikely to apply his techniques and his collating-machines to a scriptural version no longer current, we can infer the same standards in Bible printing. There is good evidence.

English printing, of course—late, derivative, provincial and sometimes incompetent, carried out by ill-educated artisans in ill-equipped shops—seems almost to have sunk into the decline of the seventeenth century without having gone through the blossoming of the sixteenth. It is not to be directly compared with the best that Italy, France and Switzerland could do. But the difference is of degree, not kind. What we know from the evidence of the texts and from contemporary accounts allows a general picture of early printing practice to be reconstructed. It is destructive of modern preconceptions. In the narrative which follows cases will be illustrated as they arise. It is useful first to give a general account of those features of early printing which make it from one point of view unsatisfactory. It is not a matter of calling the great men of the heroic age of printing to the bar and convicting them of negligence. Many of them did not fall short of the standard they set themselves; rather they fall short of standards evolved since, and by their help. But since authority, accuracy and freedom from piecemeal corruption are the cardinal points in Bible printing, standing even before functional or aesthetic qualities, an account of Bible printing must put them first and dwell on them.

EARLY PRINTING PRACTICE

Printing has these stages: the preparation of copy, composition (the setting-up of type), correction, presswork (printing off), and the dispersal of the type. The book you are now reading, after leaving

scholars and mostly in the journal *Studies in Bibliography*. For Charlton Hinman's work on the First Folio see especially 'Variant Readings in the First Folio of Shakespeare', in *Shakespeare Quarterly* (July 1953).

the editor's hands, underwent further stages of checking by the printer's staff before it was set up; then two successive stages of proof were read, by the editor, by the contributor, and by the printer's readers. At each proof corrections were made. When the entire book had thus been checked several times, the type was all printed off in an uninterrupted succession of units of sixteen pages (octavo sheets). From the point of view of consistency and accuracy, it is important to note that printing was not started until proofing and correction were complete, and that it was not interrupted to make last-minute changes. Errors remaining are due to human frailty, and are to be found in all copies of the edition: they cannot be attributed to the sequence of operations. Barring extreme accidents, the only variants between copies are due to the damage of type in the press; they are unlikely to be significant. Modern Bibles are subjected to an extra proof-reading against a master copy of a standard edition; the type is 'plated' (see below, p. 466) before printing, for extra wear and to safeguard against the displacement of type on the machine or in storage.

This sequence evolved as the result of two processes: the increasing mechanization of printing in the nineteenth century, and the accumulated experience of editors, authors and conscientious printers. The first printers had everything to learn by trial and error, except what manuscript production could suggest to them. It is illogical as well as incorrect to point out that early books were conditioned in many respects by manuscripts and at the same time to suggest that printed books were an immediate advance on manuscripts.

The first Bible was set from a manuscript, and its text could be no better than its exemplar. Like a manuscript, it was produced page by page; the pages being grouped in quires of folded sheets. Different pages were set simultaneously by more than one compositor, as different sheets of a manuscript could be written simultaneously by more than one scribe. Here is one source of inconsistency and occasionally of error: for compositors had their personal styles and conventions in matters of spelling, punctuation and abbreviation. Such inconsistencies were not at that time regularized; and accidentals can sometimes affect the sense.

Early proof-reading has had at least one book devoted to it, but remains in some respects tantalizingly ambiguous. Certain tendencies emerge. The corrector of the press was, at first at least, a learned man, but his principal function was the preparation of copy: he was in fact an editor. There seems to have been a tacit assumption that if this part of his duty was well done, the other part—the correction of proofs—was correspondingly lightened. Nonetheless the copy he provided for the compositors was most often 'corrected' copy: a manuscript or a printed book with corrections, deletions and insertions in his own hand—just the kind of copy which leads to misunderstanding by the compositor (see the case of Benoist, p. 447 below). It is possible that copy was sometimes read aloud to the compositor; it is established that the proofs were often read back to the corrector by reading-boys, while he followed his own copy. The possibilities of error here are enormous: either from homophones, ambiguous pointing, mis-hearing or hasty following. It is probable that the proofs were sometimes read character by character rather than currently; it is plain that this precaution would be abandoned when time was short. Reading-boys are a legacy from the scholarship of the time; they were Erasmus's normal method of collating manuscripts. What is more, reading-boys (or rather girls) are still to be found in some printing-houses, though it should be axiomatic that proper checking can only be done by ocular comparison of copy and proof; and if the reading is at all critical it must allow pauses for thought and for comparison with other parts of the book (which in the early days would either be already printed off or not yet set). It is an often told tale that Plantin's daughter Madeleine, aged thirteen, read proofs of the Royal Polyglot in all the tongues to Montanus. Even if she were a prodigy, the proofs could not have been well read by modern standards, yet Montanus was conscious of exceeding the standards of the time.

These stages, then, allow abundant opportunity for ordinary error or straightforward corruption of the text, and they should be added to the kinds of strictly typographical error to which the compositor is prone—letters inverted, letters taken from the wrong compartment of the 'case', and so on. Of these lapses the most celebrated in English printing history was the omission of the word 'not' in the seventh commandment of the 'Wicked Bible' of 1631, for which Robert Barker and Martin Lucas, the King's Printers, were fined £200 and £100 respectively. It can be argued that errors so obvious are less dangerous than small ones ('we' for 'ye' in Acts vi. 3, in the Cambridge Bible of 1638; repeated in subsequent printings, and wrongly thought to be a deliberate act of anti-clericalism).

Where a printer had a proofing-press—and they are rarely mentioned—or where an editor or corrector was demanding, type could be corrected until it was right, before printing began. But many printers had one or two presses only, and final proofs were pulled on the press which was to be used for the printing, and which could not long be allowed to stand idle. This is so often the case that it is reasonable to think that some of our difficulty today in extracting a precise sense from the evidence about proofing is due to a confusion in the early printers' own minds about the difference between a proof-sheet, which we should segregate or destroy, and the first sheet off the press. There is a strong presumption in many cases, and certainty in others, that while the first sheet was being read for errors, further sheets were being printed. Philip II of Spain, punctiliously interested in the progress of Plantin's Royal Polyglot, subsidized by himself, asked to be sent a 'proof' of each forme. It stands to reason that Plantin would not wait until the sheet had gone from Antwerp to Spain, been read and corrected by the king, and the corrections returned. What Philip got was the first sheet off the press, and he might have got the early pages, but not the late ones, in time for any errors he noticed to be mentioned in the list of errata, which would be printed last of all. Meanwhile Montanus was doing the real proof-reading as well as he and Madeleine knew how.

In most cases proof-reading and presswork went on concurrently. Errors might be noticed, the press would be stopped for correction of the type, and printing would then go on. If the errors were thought to be less than hair-raising, paper was too expensive for the sheets in the uncorrected state to be wasted, and they might be included in the finished book. The first corrected state was not necessarily the last. Nor—to complicate the matter—would the bound copies of the book consist entirely of sheets in one state; the first sheet might be uncorrected; the second in the second state, others in the third, and so on. The possibilities of variation were thus enormous. Many of the variants might be insignificant, but whole lines might be left out, the word 'not' be inserted or deleted, and so on. The net result was that the scholar, who could see obvious errors for himself, could still be deprived of confidence in his text simply because he did not know where it might be defective.

The best hope for the eminent reader was to be presented by the author with a hand-corrected copy. The author's other remedy was to print a list (or in Erasmus's and Bellarmine's cases, a volume) of errata. If he took the whole matter light-heartedly he prefaced the list with a statement like 'The ingenious have not only judgment to discern, but courtesy to pass over small faults. The most remarkable are the following...'. A note of unction was sounded by the printer of a French Bible of 1540: 'Finally, friend and reader,' he says, 'we beg you in your Christian modesty to look well on our labour, which indeed as much through the scantness of time as for several other reasons has been more troubled than we can well say now, and if there be some things not well done according to our art, it will be your duty to suffer the whole with kindly charity.' As for the errata, it was a natural consequence of the process of proofing and correction that some of the errors listed were already corrected in certain copies; that some errors were not noted; and that the list itself contained errors.

The dreadful consequence for Bible printing of the prevalence of press-variants is that reprints which took as exemplar one copy of an earlier edition reproduced only the variants in that copy but not others, as well as producing their own variants. Especially during the seventeenth and eighteenth centuries, when the maintenance of a qualified corrector was a burden which the printer was often eager to dispense with (p. 460), the verifying of reprints was often done by the compositor or by an unqualified person. Indeed the best proof-reader available was the master-printer himself, in many houses; and even if he was competent he was usually harassed by his other duties. (For another cause leading to hasty proof-reading, see p. 447.) The result was a proliferation of errors and variants, from printing to printing, and a steady debasing of the text. This is especially true of the English Authorized Version.

In a gloomy moment Samuel Berger once said of the manuscript Vulgate 'all the changes to Alcuin's text of the Gospels were for the worse....In the hands of the correctors of St Martin of Tours it became the most vulgarized and bastardized text imaginable. I do wrong to speak so: the whole of the Middle Ages was devoted to interpolating it and disfiguring it even more.' The arrival of printing for a long time facilitated and speeded the process of corruption, as well as providing the instrument by which corruption might eventually be stayed.

The Printed Bible

FROM THE BEGINNINGS TO THE REFORMATION

THE VULGATE

It is no longer possible to say that the Latin Bible was the first book ever printed, but it is still reasonable to suppose that Gutenberg's early works were a kind of rehearsal for his masterpiece. Little is known with certainty of the 42-line Bible, or of the 36-line Bible which is assumed to have been printed later. But a fair amount can be inferred. Cutting of the types of the 42-line Bible probably began in 1449 or 1450;[1] setting began in 1452 and the printing may have been finished in 1455. In the later stages of production six compositors were at work simultaneously; four started, beginning at folios 1 and 129 of volume I and folios 1 and 162 of volume II; two were brought in later. The characteristic conventions of each allow his work to be identified. This division of labour indicates accurate 'casting off': that is, the compositor knew in advance the exact number of pages his portion of copy would make; but this particular skill was already known to scribes. At the least, the system required skill in dovetailing together the portions by different hands, unless an unsightly blank were to be left at the bottom of the last column of each man's 'stint'. If the calculation was badly made, the text sometimes suffered. It is also noteworthy that the early sheets of both volumes were set more than once—perhaps three times: which suggests that the size of the edition was increased after the first sheets had been printed off and the type dispersed, so that the extra copies could only be printed from reset type. It is understandable that this kind of operation also produces variants and errors.

Some forty copies of this Bible still exist. Estimates of the total number printed vary from 240 on paper plus 30 on vellum to 54 on paper plus 16 on vellum. Professor Ruppel suggests a total of 185 copies. Certainly the edition must have been small by our standards. The mere demand on the paper and vellum supply of the time must have been unprecedented: the book made 340 folio sheets, and allowing two sheets per hide, each vellum copy must have required the skins of 170 animals. The outlay on this alone must have made serious inroads

[1] Fifteenth- and even sixteenth-century dates should be treated with some reserve. Most of the printing dates in this chapter are derived from Darlow and Moule, *Historical Catalogue*.

on the capital available. The decision at a late stage to print perhaps 30 more copies on paper may have followed anxious figuring, where the increased expense was weighed against the increased revenue. The selling price is not known, but it is a safe assumption that Gutenberg's prices were high. In those days buying a large manuscript Bible on vellum was like buying a house today—as much an investment as a commodity. Whether Gutenberg made a profit on his and his partners' outlay is doubtful; he seems to have died relatively poor.

It is not certain whether he was responsible for the 36-line Bible which may have been printed in Mainz or Bamberg, between 1457 and 1461. The book itself is typographically and economically a regression. The smaller number of lines per page increases the amount of paper or vellum required by 38 per cent; the setting is not as good as that of the 42-line Bible; the type itself is older. Logically one would assume that it preceded the other, but it has been suggested that the 42-line Bible is the copy-text, for the 36-line Bible repeats its errors. Thirteen copies survive, which suggests a smaller edition.

The 42-line Bible has been rightly praised for its distinction of form and the quality of its workmanship. Its beauty lies in its simplicity, and that was due to necessity rather than choice. It is often pointed out that early books were modelled on contemporary western manuscripts. But what else could they have been modelled on? As far as Gutenberg was concerned, that was what books looked like; older manuscripts or those of other traditions were at that time inaccessible to him. Comparison with manuscripts suggests that printers only followed them as far as they were able to. With only one size of type, with the inflexibility caused by the need to contain the type in rigid rectangles, usually unable for economic reasons to print in two colours, without initial letters or titling founts, the printer was forced for at least a generation to make a virtue of the necessity for simplicity. He could print the text in a good letter in good black ink on good white paper, setting the words closely together as the scribes had done, dividing his page with a good space between the two columns, and imposing the page of type in the medieval manner, with a comparatively narrow text-area held well up on the page by a large margin at the foot. But for colour, for the articulation of a long text, for any decoration which broke the rectangle of the text, he had to call in the rubricator. True, early printers did print in two colours at times; but printing in red as well as black doubled the number of impressions. Paradoxically, it was cheaper to call in the hand-worker, whom printing was later to oust. As for the *Glossa ordinaria* (Plate 5), that triumph of the scribe's art, it was not until the 1480's that the printer had either the necessary types or the skill in 'making-up'[1] a complicated page to produce in hard metal the same arrangement.

By the end of the fifteenth century, Bible printing, like printing itself, had spread over the trade-routes from the first centres in Germany. Germany remained important, of course; of the hundred-odd editions of the Vulgate (Hain lists 109, but some others may have been entirely lost) and apart from Mainz itself, fourteen came from Nürnberg, thirteen from Strassburg, seven from Cologne, two from Speyer, one from Ulm. A little further afield, seventeen came from Basle. But Venice produced seventeen, and after the late 1470's Lyons produced nine. Paris produced only one, but became a leading centre in the next century. Inevitably, the printed product shows steady emancipation from early technical restrictions, increasing versatility, increasing economy and fitness for use. By the time of the Reformation the printed Bible had already become an article of ready commerce, available in convenient formats and with a considerable body of aids to study incorporated with the text.

Venetian printers in the 1480's produced Vulgates of remarkable compactness. They were in fact little larger than the celebrated octavo, the first Bible in this format, produced by Froben in 1491. This book has as many lines on the page—fifty-six—as many a folio, and remains very readable; but the achievement had been long prepared and was soon surpassed. Otherwise the book is notable for its failure to economize in the use of rubrication. Other octavos followed at once; the format was obviously convenient. It remained the smallest until the early years of the sixteenth century. Then there was a series of attempts to produce miniature editions. The first, a small octavo printed by Hopyl of Paris in 1510, was appropriately called *Biblia exigue molis ac plures in partes divisibilis* (Plate 8 *a*)—which explains its novelty. Though folio Bibles had often been bound in more than one volume as a convenience for the user, this was the first case in which such a division was

[1] 'Make-up' is the arrangement of constituent parts into a whole page: headline, text, small type, illustrations. At first it meant simply placing two columns of text side by side. The sixteenth-century page became exceedingly elaborate.

the basis of the whole design. The small page only allowed a single column, but blackletter was still used, and typographically the book can be thought of as the traditional medieval page divided into quarters. In 1523 Prevel, also of Paris, produced the New Testament in two even smaller editions, both minute 32mos. Again blackletter was used, and again the design is only apparently novel. Events showed that there was no future in these smaller blackletter books; they were superseded by small books in roman type.

The design of the 'traditional' page was based on the integrity of the column of type, and it could only permit the kind of modification to which Prevel and Hopyl submitted it; which amounted to a simple slicing of the page into four quarters, which then became successive pages. In early Bibles it is rare, almost unheard of, for such spacing as there was to be carried right across both columns, though exigencies of cast-off and make-up do produce an occasional blank space in the column. The articulation of the text entirely depended, until approximately 1515–20, upon the use of large initials for book-openings and smaller initials for chapter-openings. Editorial incipits and explicits were supplied, but they were printed in the same type as the text, and could only be picked out by the prefixed paragraph-mark (¶). At first all these features were supplied by hand, together with page-headings and folio-numbers; they were often written in red, which gave them added prominence. From the typographical and economic point of view, it is interesting to trace the clearly discernible process by which more and more was achieved in type-metal and in a single impression, leaving less and less for the rubricator. Occasionally in the 1460's and 1470's large printed initials are to be found in German-printed Bibles. The compactness of the Venetian editions printed from 1475 onwards was achieved by using markedly smaller sizes of type (it is a common fallacy that it was the pressure of the Reformation which changed Bibles from 'unwieldy folios' to 'handy octavos'). Many printers used the large size originally intended for printing the Canon of the Mass—and hence called 'canon'—for the first lines of books and for the page-heads (single-word book-titles, at first printed on the recto only). The larger size of type, though printed in the same ink, seems to have an added intensity of black; and when printed woodcut initials had become common, in the late 1490's, this colour was thus carried right across the column, making the book-openings particularly easy to find (Plate 7).

The chapters had always been divided in printed Bibles; the division itself, Berger says, dates from the thirteenth century. At first the printer had been content to leave a blank line for a rubricated heading and a large space for the initial. Very soon a simple chapter-number was printed, not usually on a line by itself, but tucked at the end of the last line of the preceding chapter, if it left a little space. The chapter-number was to hold this position tenaciously until well into the sixteenth century. Scribes had of course been free to place the numbers in, and to allow initials to project into, the margin, where they are easily seen. For some time printers were unable for technical reasons to use the margin, and when they learnt the knack no bible-printer ever placed the chapter-number there except once: Froben's heirs' folio of 1530, which is consciously modelled on Greek manuscript practice.

Chapter-summaries were then printed, the first instance probably being Zainer's folio printed at Ulm in 1480. He printed them in the large size of type. Later printers used the normal size of type for summaries, and in the early sixteenth century sometimes used a third, smaller size. A Bible printed by Herbort at Venice in 1484 seems to have introduced into printing the system of dividing chapters into sections by posting the letters A, B, C, D and so on down the margins. Herbort had also printed some marginal references in 1483. It soon became common to print references to parallel passages in the margin. Folio-numbers were printed at least as early as 1478, though they were printed in large roman numerals, and tended to reach unwieldy numbers such as CCCCCLXVIII; it was not until Froben's first edition of Erasmus's New Testament in 1516 that a book of Scripture had each page numbered in arabic figures.

By the end of the fifteenth century it had become easy to refer to a Bible, and the system of reference was 'built in' and not added by the rubricator. The page-headings in a large size of type indicated which book was printed below; a very large woodcut initial and a line of the same large type indicated a new book; the smaller initials indicated chapter-openings. Above these smaller initials were printed the chapter-summaries; above them, usually at the right-hand side of the column, were the chapter-numbers. The A-B-C-D division narrowed the search to about fifteen lines (Plate 7 shows the entire system). Yet all this was managed with great economy of space, for the system depended on variation of 'colour' rather than space. The best Bibles of the time achieve an effect of great solidity: the columns succeed each other, even, full and black from Genesis to Revelation without stopping for breath, so to speak. This is the essence of the medieval book, and it is entirely appropriate to the Bible of the time. Had not Bernard spoken of the *unitas scripturarum*? Here it is made manifest.[1]

When the transition from II Maccabees to Matthew, through Jerome's prologues to the New Testament, had been made without a break or a line of space, and when the New Testament might very well in consequence have begun half-way down the second column of a left-hand page, it comes as a shock to find in a quarto Bible printed by Lucantonio di Giunta of Venice in 1511 the firm announcement

Explicit Secundus liber Machabaeorum
Explicit vetus testamentum
Finis

followed on the next page by a frontispiece to the New Testament—a Nativity—which counterbalances the frontispiece to the Old Testament—the Six Days of Creation, copied from the illustrations to the Malermi Bible (p. 425). But the new Bible has other new features. In particular the canons of Eusebius are also printed between the two Testaments, and are set out in a colonnade printed in red. This, probably the first instance in printing, is a revival of a very old practice indeed; the canons were set out in the same kind of romanesque colonnade in manuscripts of the Carolingian period. Such antique influences were soon to transform the design of books, including—for a time—the Bible.

Long before the Reformation the early printers and editors had begun to add other aids to the reader. It is not fanciful to say that they increased as the printers' ability to deal with them also increased. From very early times—for instance in Sweynheym and Pannartz's folio of 1471—a table of interpretations of proper names was appended. This was a heritage of much earlier scholarship; it was also one of the most persistent of adjuncts to the printed Bible. The same folio also has an editorial preface by J. Andreae, bishop of Aleria, and a Latin translation of the *Letter of Aristeas*. An early (?1473) edition by Richel of

[1] For a fuller treatment of Bible design, see M. H. Black, 'The Evolution of a Book-Form: the Octavo Bible from MS. to the Geneva Version', in *The Library* (March 1961).

Basle gives Menardus's guide to the contents of the Bible, the table of canons, and some marginal references. Herbort's edition of 1484 gives registers before each Gospel, with references to the chapters. A folio of 1486 by Drach of Speyer gives a table at the end of the volume listing the scriptural readings through the liturgical year (this was most common at the time in German vernacular Bibles). In 1487 Kesler of Basle produced a Bible with other editorial matter which was so frequently used later as almost to be standard apparatus: the little treatises *de translationibus* on the history of the text and *de modo intelligendi sacram scripturam* on medieval exegesis. In 1486 Pruss of Strassburg printed the first Bible with a title-page; another edition of 1489 had a title announcing that it had concordances and the interpretation of Hebrew terms. It also had a kind of table of contents at the beginning. Froben's octavo of 1491 advertised itself as *superemendata*; in the preliminary pages were the *ad divinarum litterarum verarumque divitiarum amatores exhortatio*, mnemonic verses on the order of the books, a table of contents, the interpretation of Hebrew names, and the two treatises mentioned above. From 1492 there were added the *Tabula alphabetica* of the minorite Gabriel Bruno: these were metrical lists summarizing the contents of the whole Bible; in 1494 another table by Villadeus was added. During the remaining life of the blackletter Vulgate (until the mid-1540's) some or all of this accumulated *plenus apparatus* was standard equipment.

These were ordinary editions with no particularly scholarly pretensions. From 1472 there was also a succession of editions of the *Glossa ordinaria*. The first ones merely printed the exposition, assuming that the reader had the text open beside it. In 1481 text and gloss were printed together for Jenson at Venice, in four large volumes. In 1483 Renner of Venice produced another edition, which is comparable in arrangement with the manuscript editions: islands of text in a medium size of type, with an interlinear gloss, and all around a sea of commentary in a smaller size. The best and best-known editions were printed for Koberger, and give Lyra's diagrams, which were to have such an influence on later iconography. The succession of editions of the *Glossa* was rapid: perhaps fifteen were printed by the end of the century, and Koberger is said to have printed 1500 at a time, so the sale was brisk. (Sweynheym and Pannartz claimed to have printed 275 copies of all their books; by 1478 Leonard Wild was able to print 930 copies of a

Vulgate.) A Venetian edition of 1495 has a treatise *de libris biblie canonicis et non canonicis*.

The great triumph of pre-Reformation scholarship was of course the Complutensian Polyglot, printed at Alcalá in six volumes between 1514 and 1517, and probably published in 1522 in an edition of 600 copies. It was conceived in 1502, and the New Testament was printed before Erasmus's edition of 1516; it can be seen as the culmination of some fifty years of editing and printing the Bible in more and more scholarly forms. It was also the first complete Testament printed in Greek. (Greek types had been first used in the 1460's, in brief quotation; continuous texts followed in the mid-1470's; the first book entirely in Greek was the *Epitome* of Lascaris, printed in Milan in 1476.) The Complutensian New Testament used a Greek fount of the kind called Jensonian or Graeco-Latin: based on the formal upright hand without the ligatures of western manuscripts. By the time it appeared, the type had already been superseded in public estimation by Aldus's Greek, mentioned below (p. 426). In 1509 Henri Estienne had printed in Paris Lefèvre's *Quincuplex Psalterium*, the first edition of any part of the Scriptures to give the Massoretic verse-division, and using some Hebrew and Greek type. Aldus had planned a triglot Old Testament, and produced a specimen, but got no further. From 1488 editions of the Hebrew Scriptures had appeared, printed by learned Jews. There were four Hebrew Bibles in the fifteenth century.[1] As with Greek, western printers had from fairly early times had a few Hebrew characters for quotations. The first books entirely in Hebrew were, naturally enough, printed by Jews for the use of their own communities—of which the richest were in Italy and Spain. The first dated book entirely in Hebrew was Rashi's Commentary on the Pentateuch, printed in Reggio in 1475. When the Jews were driven from Spain in 1492, and from Portugal in 1498, Italy remained the principal centre, especially Soncino. In Venice, the Christian Bomberg settled in 1517 and produced the first Talmud. A Genoese Polyglot Psalter of 1516 gave Hebrew, Greek, Arabic and Chaldee texts. The Complutensian has been mentioned in chapter II; here it is sufficient to say that it represents the greatest technical achievement, and required the greatest range of typographical equipment and compositorial skill used on any Bible until Plantin's Royal Polyglot of 1569–72.

[1] See above pp. 48–50.

THE VERNACULARS

It is not sufficiently emphasized that the printing of vernacular texts long preceded the Reformation in several countries. In a few it was an isolated occurrence: two Czech Bibles appeared at Prague and Kuttenberg in 1488 and 1489; a Catalan translation was printed at Valencia in 1478, but was proscribed and burnt, and no complete copy survives. Another translation appeared in 1492 in Barcelona. A Dutch 'Bible' which contained only the Old Testament without the Psalter was printed at Delft in 1477. It was followed in 1480 by the Psalms. The 'Bibel int corte', a translation of the French *Bible historiée*, did not follow until 1513; and then it was, like the original, far from a complete text. But the countries with a real tradition of vernacular printing are Germany and Italy, while France produced several editions which claim attention, though the text was still not a full translation.

The oldest tradition is the German. The first edition was printed by Mentelin of Strassburg in 1466; and by 1522 fourteen High German and four Low German editions had appeared. It has been calculated that altogether 8000–10,000 copies were printed: which indicates a considerable market, when it is remembered that early editions probably cost (as Vulgates also must have cost) the equivalent of a town house, or fourteen fattened oxen. From the evidence of bequests, most vernacular Bibles were owned by laymen—which is what one would expect. But it is worth noting that the preface to a French Bible of 1510 says:

> Since idleness is the enemy of the soul it is necessary for all without occupation to read by way of pastime some good tale or other book of sacred learning. You may read this present book, which is the Holy Bible which has been translated from Latin into French adding nothing but the pure truth as it is in the Latin Bible and omitting nothing but such things as ought not to be translated. And the translation has been made not for the clerkly, but for lay folk and simple religious and hermits who are not as well lettered as they ought to be.

Because of this mixed aim, part evangelical, part purveyance of honest pastime, it is the early vernacular Bibles which have illustrations. No Vulgate except the Glossa had illustrations before 1511; the man who can read Latin scorns such aids, though he is willing to use Lyra's diagrams of the Temple, or Ezekiel's vision, and the differing interpretations of these scholarly concerns offered by the Jewish commentators. German Bible illustration began with a stage-army of conventionalized prophets, apostles and evangelists inhabiting woodcut initials. The two great editions now thought to have been printed at Cologne from 1478 by Bartholomäus Unkel for a company consisting of Johan Helman, Arnold Salmonster and possibly Koberger[1] introduced an important tradition. Only the Old Testament was illustrated, and later Bibles copying this superb series tended to establish a canon which overlooked the New Testament.

In all but minor respects the arrangement of the German Bibles was similar to that of the Vulgate. There was a tendency to sell them in parts, especially the Gospels and the Psalter. The Psalms themselves had a peculiarly German arrangement, each Psalm being preceded by a *titulus* and a reference to the opening words of the Latin version; this suggests that devotional reading of the Psalms, linked to the liturgical year, was carried on at home (German- and Dutch-printed Bibles had a special tendency to incorporate lists of the Gospel- and Epistle-readings *per anni circulum*). As with the Vulgate, an attempt was made to reduce the size of the book. Early German Bibles tended to be huge cubes of board and paper, almost impossible to carry and even to use. From 1478 the bulk was greatly reduced in several editions from Augsburg; the last, of 1518, is almost exactly the same size as Luther's first editions, which are commonly supposed to be the first really portable editions.

By Luther's time the German Bible had entirely dispensed with the rubricator. All initials were printed, and they are usually magnificent; William Morris imitated some of them in the nineteenth century. The expense of illustration was to some extent compensated by the complete absence of marginal notes. There seems to have been a marked fall in prices, which is perhaps best expressed by saying that where buying a Bible had once been like buying a house, it was now more like buying a car (in Europe).

German Bibles were printed—as was thought appropriate to the vernacular—in German varieties of blackletter, and they were to remain so. Two early Vulgates were printed in the fifteenth century in the new, or as the innovators would have it, the antique 'roman' letter. But as often happened, a novelty appealing only to the *avant-garde* was

[1] Severin Corsten, 'Die Kölner Bilderbibeln von 1478', in *Gutenberg Jahrbuch* (1957).

at first unacceptable to the majority, and died for lack of support. It is all the more striking that Italian vernacular Bibles were from the start and almost exclusively printed in roman. The first edition of Malermi's translation was printed at Venice in 1471 by Wendelin of Speyer. Perhaps the most important was the edition of 1490, with illustrations. This set was obviously influenced by the Cologne Bible, and in its turn influenced many later series which were printed in Vulgates, especially in Lyons.

Bible printing came to France through Lyons, which was the financial centre of France, and a trading-town so well placed for contact with Italy and Switzerland, and thence with Germany, that it long disputed the supremacy of Paris, and was an established printing-town before Paris, in spite of the early attempt to set up academic printing there. Two small books were printed at Lyons in the early 1470's, giving the New Testament, or such portions of it as the old *Bible historiée* reproduced. They were extremely simple typographically; square books with the text printed in long lines, using only one size of a formal blackletter. There was no editorial matter apart from *incipits* and *explicits*, and the chapters were unnumbered. In 1478 a complete *Bible historiée* was printed at Lyons. This was an advance; the longer text is printed in double column, and there are illustrations copied from the Cologne–Malermi series. But the text was still a mere summary of the Scriptures, with interpolated moralization. It was not until about 1498 that Antoine Vérard began his series of magnificent French Bibles. By now the text was more extensively translated, and the whole book commonly occupied two volumes. These editions were printed in the sloped and angular *lettre bâtarde*; the woodcuts are numerous and the initials often fine. The interpolated glosses are progressively abandoned, but the prefaces become more evangelical, in one case stating explicitly that the only way to eternal glory is by the word of Christ, and that word must be seen, heard, understood, put into effect and treasured in the heart; which is more than can be done by merely listening. To be pondered, it must be accessible and read; and here, the translator adds, it is; 'you cannot therefore be excused for ignorance of our faith'. Plainly the old *Bible historiée* has here undergone an intensification of purpose. It was eventually killed by the newer translations, but it went on being reprinted until at least 1546, surviving like other earlier forms long after it had been potentially replaced by something less spacious and agreeable, but much more narrowly effective.

THE INTRODUCTION OF ROMAN TYPE

In the sixteenth century new translations nearly always mark important typographical as well as scholarly or doctrinal changes. The first edition of Erasmus's diglot *Novum Instrumentum*, printed by Froben of Basle in 1516 (Plate 10), liberates into Bible printing those new aspects of book-production which we call 'Humanist'. We have already noticed early stirrings: Sweynheym and Pannartz's folio of 1471 in roman type and Giunta's Bible of 1511, which could only have been printed by someone who had seen Carolingian Gospel-books and Italian humanist manuscripts. Froben's book introduces the combined influence of Byzantine calligraphy and those antique conventions which had already been revived in the West in Carolingian times: in the Greek type copied from Aldus's, in the decoration, in the general shape and imposition of the type area on the page, and in the system of articulation. These influences were to be seen successively in the Venetian style of printing (mostly secular books), then at Basle, then at Lyons and Paris. They can easily be summarized: each book of the New Testament tends to begin a new page, like chapters in most modern books; the book-titles are set out in inscriptional roman capitals, in lines of decreasing length, the first preceded by an Aldine leaf or other ornament; page-headings are in roman SMALL CAPITALS, well spaced, with the page number at the outer edge in arabic numerals; decorative head-pieces are common above book-headings, and title-pages and the first page of text tend to be surrounded with a renaissance or even a paganistic border, usually in white on black; the lines of text tend to be long and the whole text-area to present a single wide unbroken rectangle. There are even small differences like a tawny shade of red for the decorative rubrication, where the northern style used a true red. Roman or italic type is *de rigueur*. The unmistakable inscriptional capitals of Basle were soon to be copied by every printer with 'modern' pretensions. Aldus's Greek type, which Froben copied, was based on the sloped and informal commercial and correspondence 'hand' of fifteenth-century Byzantine scribes and teachers of Greek. The type so faithfully followed its flourishes, ligatures and contractions that the compositor found himself faced with founts made up of more than 400 characters. This was a formidable obstacle to speed, and could only have been accepted in an age of cheap labour. At least the type, wiry and cursive, went well with Aldus's matching italic, which was for a time the height of fashion. Unfortunately it set a pattern for Greek types for 300 years, until the Cambridge Great Porson Greek of 1826.

The reprints of Erasmus's Latin New Testament which swiftly followed introduced this whole ready-made style, which was profoundly to influence Bible printing for a short time. These octavos were mostly in italic; though at least two printers, Knoblochtzer of Strassburg and Cervicornus of Cologne, produced in 1523 and 1525 typographical 'mules' giving Erasmus's text in blackletter, but with many of the new conventions of humanist articulation. These were sports. The New Testaments in italic were attractive books, and it is important to note that they were in a sense the most 'modern' books of Scripture ever printed; that is, they represent the most extreme departure from the traditional medieval design. Representative are Cratander's New Testament (Basle, 1520), Froben's editions of the early 1520's, and Wolf's complete Bible of 1522 (Plate 13). It will be noticed that the chapter-number at least has remained obstinately traditional.

So many new traditions were started in the 1520's that it is better not to give a confused chronological survey but to isolate the strands. Italic Testaments were first; but this priority and their novelty gave them no advantage. Occasional Bibles and Testaments were printed in italic until the 1550's, but they are of only local interest. The movement, if it can be called that, had a brief flourishing and died very rapidly. This was largely because of the competition from other sources, which came into operation very shortly after. One may also single out certain inherent defects in the books themselves. In the first place Erasmus's text satisfied neither conservatives nor reformers; after the flourishing of the 1520's the editions, mostly from Antwerp, become rare, and stop in the 1550's; superseded itself, it may be that the typographical trappings so obviously associated with it suffered from its eclipse—certainly the printers of new translations and editions made a point of giving each a recognizable typographical identity or affinity. Secondly, the Aldine italic is less economical of space than the old blackletter or the new small roman, and is certainly less easy to read in large amounts (blackletter is in fact very readable when one is used to it). Third, the articulatory system of these books, though engaging and clear, is wasteful of space. Only one Bible, Wolf's, took the Erasmian form, largely of course because Erasmus never produced an Old Testament: which may have been decisive. Had he done so the style would probably have had to be modified anyway, to accommodate it.

So these books died, and their place was taken by a multitude of contenders. The first, to take Latin Bibles first (and they remained until the end of the century the largest single concern of the important printers working for the international market) were the small Bibles produced at Paris in roman type from 1523. These books, like Hopyl's of 1510, faced the problem of reducing the Bible to portable format and solved it by dividing the whole text into as many as seven separate volumes. The format chosen was 16mo; so each little volume was hardly bigger than one of our modern pocket diaries. Three or four would go into a capacious pocket. The first of these editions came from the press of Simon de Colines; but the real credit is probably due to Colines's stepson Robert Estienne, who was foreman at the time. It was the first of Estienne's many editions of the Bible. This format was much used during the century; Estienne himself found that it did not suit his scholarly purposes and used it little, but other French printers produced many more, and the series had its highest achievements in Lyons in the 1550's, especially in the hands of Frellon and Gryphius. It is also the forerunner of the Geneva Testaments in the vernacular (for instance Conrad Badius's first edition in 1557 of the English Genevan New Testament). Illustration and decoration were added, to produce exquisite little books. They were something like the printed books of hours printed at the time at Paris and Lyons: charming accessories of private orthodox devotion.

In 1522, the year before Colines's first 16mo, Luther had published his New Testament: the September Testament being followed by his own December Testament (pp. 95–7; Plate 14), and—with remarkable speed—by reprints in Basle and elsewhere. Van Liesveldt of Antwerp printed a Dutch Gospel-book in octavo in 1522, and in 1523 printed the Epistles, while Van Bergen of the same town produced an octavo New Testament translated from Luther's. Editions in German and Dutch now began to appear at short intervals—though much more rapidly in Germany, of course. Between 1522 and 1524 there were fourteen reprints of Luther's New Testament at Wittenberg, and sixty-six others at other towns. In 1523 there also appeared Lefèvre's French New Testament, printed by Colines, in blackletter, and soon followed by other editions from Antwerp (Plate 18). In 1526 Tyndale's New Testament was printed at Cologne and Worms, and followed by editions from the Low Countries (Plate 15). The general tempo of printing and publication had been immensely stimulated by the outbreak of open conflict.

THE BOOK TRADE IN THE REFORMATION PERIOD

This was only possible because during the previous seventy years the ancient trade of bookselling had been so consolidated and expanded, and the new enterprise of publishing had so developed, that the allied book trades were now ready to cope with the new situation. Printing the Bible had from the beginning required considerable capital; it also demanded an organized market to dispose of the greatly increased numbers of copies. It may be that Gutenberg's obscurity and his putative business failure were due to the obvious lack of confidence of his backers and the comparative infancy—the extreme localization—of the retail trade. But while the *stationarii* had primarily existed in a few centres of organized learning or courtly refinement, to lend a small number of books, partly for private copying by the reader himself, books had now become a trade commodity. Publishers of a sort had existed from the start, since capital was needed: more money was needed then and later to print a big book like the Bible than was needed simply to set up a press. From the 1480's onwards the great businesses like Jenson and Company, Koberger, the Giunta clan, Birkman of Cologne, Luther's publishers Cranach and Döring, Kerver and Petit of Paris, had organized a truly international trade, based on credit-sale and payment by bill of exchange and barter in kind. Koberger in Nürnberg had printers working on commission for him in Basle and Lyons and other towns; he had correspondents, agents and depots in most countries, including England.

There was of course less specialization in the trade than there is now. A poor printer, without working capital, would work for rich publishers, being supplied with paper or type or illustrations and being paid by the printed sheet. But a successful man would be at once printer, publisher, bookseller and even papermaker and binder; he could commission work from other printers; and would exchange part of an edition for works by other publishers, selling the rest in his own shops or at the great fairs, of which the Frankfurt fair was the most important. The centres of distribution were still the main centres of all trade; the widest possible diffusion was accomplished with the help of itinerant vendors or 'mercuries'—who inevitably played an important part when the authorities chose to ban this or that work, and who became so effective that regulation of the book trade was made inevitable. But the mere multiplicity of the authorities—even in countries like France which had achieved a degree of centralized government—meant that a shrewd printer-publisher could use one great man to shield him from the others, for a time at any rate (see below, p. 448).

The authorities for their part had even before the Reformation taken steps to control the production of books, and to prevent the spread of seditious publications. It may have been the Cologne Bible of 1478 that provoked Sixtus IV to send a brief to the University of Cologne praising it for its zeal in suppressing heretical works, and giving it the right to exercise censorship. The brief refers specifically to the 'foolish simplicity of women, who arrogate to themselves the knowledge of Scripture'. Certain townships had already set up censoring bodies to supervise what was printed there before Leo X issued his bull of 15 May 1515 requiring bishops and inquisitors to read books before they were printed in their dioceses. The Reformation inevitably produced evasions of the regulations. In order to make retribution easier, it was in most countries made an offence to produce a book without the name of the author and printer and the place of publication. Edicts to this effect were repeated so often that it is plain that they were disobeyed; and the printer still had an easy way out; he could print a false name and address (though it was not very adroit of Tyndale's printer to adopt the name of Hans Lufft, when it was soon known throughout Europe that Luther's printer was called Lufft).

The first book-burnings of the Reformation took place in 1521. In 1524 the bookseller Herrgott was beheaded in Leipzig; an Anabaptist printer was burnt at Nürnberg in 1527. In 1529 an edict by the Emperor proscribed the works of the chief reformers, and also the New Testaments printed by Van Bergen, Van Ruremonde and Zel. While he was about it he also proscribed all books printed in the last ten years without the authors' or printers' names, and for good measure any book savouring of heresy. The penalty for not surrendering such books could be burning for men, burial alive for women. Moreover it was forbidden to print any part of the Scriptures in the vernacular, or any book on ecclesiastical matters without approval. In 1550 the death penalty was introduced for reprinting the books proscribed in 1529. Both in the Empire and in France (where the printer Dolet was burnt in 1544 with his books) attempts were made to prevent sedition at its source by policing the printing trade itself. Master printers were made responsible for their men, or printing was confined to certain towns. But in an age when a clandestine press could be dismounted and carried about with comparative ease, and where the small printer managed with a minimum of equipment and could supply his own labour, authority could only hope to stop the biggest gaps. It should not be thought that the reformers, where they gained control, were slow to make their own rules: it was the City Council of Geneva that burnt Servetus. But for our immediate purpose there was one important difference: the Zurich regulations of 1524 specifically permit the printing and selling of the Scriptures.

It is important to keep in mind this background of increasing legislation and control over an industry which was naturally constituted of small sources of production with a wide network of distribution, and hence fairly elusive. It was the large and well-equipped shops which were most affected. They were few but well known, and they produced the important work. For printers in the highest class, the choice was between doing inoffensive work, and living in peace, or moving to a reformed town (as Estienne did), or living on a constant tightrope of diplomacy, dissimulation and frank hypocrisy, with periods of convenient absence, like Plantin. The smallest printers could keep moving, but the most that they could contribute that is of interest here was the hasty reprint of another man's New Testament. The conditions of the period are thus basically against the scholarly work that most interests us; it is all the more remarkable that so much was done. For the Reformation brought into play the two strongest motives: idealism and love of gain. As for the latter, there was no doubt where the profit lay. In Leipzig Wolfgang Stockel, who chose, or had, to print Emser's anti-Lutheran New Testament, complained to the City Fathers of the censorship, saying that printers would be ruined if they could not print what they could sell, or had to print what they could not sell.

The impulse to make a quick profit had two important effects. It meant, in an age where there was none but local copyright, very speedy diffusion of a popular work. It also meant hasty work, and inaccurate printing. Luther called printing 'God's highest and extremest act of grace, whereby the business of the Gospel is driven forward; it is the last flame before the extinction of the world'. He thought otherwise when he saw what the printers of hasty reprints had done with his work. The preface to his Bible of 1541 said of them 'For since they look only to their own greed they ask not how truly or falsely they have reprinted it. And I have often found when I have read the reprinted edition that it is so garbled that in many places I have not recognized my own work, and have had to revise it again.' In a splendid Lutheran phrase, he added *Sie machens hin rips raps: es gilt Gelt.*

LUTHER'S BIBLE

Wittenberg had not been a printing town of any importance before 1522; certainly it did not compare with the main centres of Bible production at that time—Paris, Lyons, Basle and Antwerp. Luther's presence made all the difference. The first printer, Rhau-Grünenberg, printed some early works for Luther, but he was slow and inefficient, so Luther persuaded an old acquaintance, Melchior I Lotther of Leipzig, to send his son Melchior II to Wittenberg in December 1519. Lotther printed the September and December Testaments in 1522, and some later editions in High and Low German, being joined by his brother Michael in 1523. Meanwhile other printers had been attracted to the town, and naturally hoped for work by Luther or his colleagues. An enterprise of the size of Luther's translations needed capital; the publishers Cranach and Döring supplied it, having a monopoly of the reformer's first editions for some time. Their appointed printer supplied them; the others had to hope for sub-contracted work or for reprints. The Lotther partnership broke up between 1524 and 1528, and the bulk of Bible printing was transferred to Lufft, who took on the Old Testament text where the Lotthers had left off. Lufft became the supreme printer in Wittenberg until 1572. This was an immense undertaking: between 1534 and 1620 about 100 editions of the Bible came from Wittenberg—a total production of perhaps 200,000 copies (not counting issues of single Testaments and books; if they are included with the product of other towns the number of editions rises to 430). The only printer whose output compared with Lufft's at the time was Christoffel I Froschauer of Zurich, whose firm, carried on by his nephew Christoffel II, was official printer to Zwingli and the town, and between 1530 and 1585 produced ninety-five biblical editions. Froschauer's eminence sprang from the variety of his output: Bibles in Swiss German, German, Latin, English and Italian, in blackletter, roman and italic. Beside him Lufft's production seems more parochial, but Zurich was of course better placed to serve an international market. Lufft's concentration meant that he produced at least 88,000 folio German Bibles alone—forty-four editions each averaging 2000 copies. The September and December Testaments of 1522 were probably printed in editions of 3000 or even 4000 copies each; but after the first rapid sale it was more a matter of supplying a steady market. With the text still being revised no printer would wish to print very large editions and so run the risk of having his stock made worthless by a later revision, which helped to stem corruption of the text, or by cheap reprints from other towns, which swiftly undid the good of each revision. The speed and unreliability of reprinting led Luther to invent a trademark with the warning 'This sign is a guarantee that books bearing it have passed through my hands'.

At one time Luther was hard pressed to keep up with his own printers, who were printing the successive parts of the Old Testament as he did the translation. The first part was published in late August 1523; by 24 October it had been reprinted in Augsburg. There was a recurrent danger that early sheets of unfinished books might be stolen from the warehouse, taken to a town where the publishers' privilege had no validity, and reprinted. This happened with the *Postillae*. Luther was moved eventually to a sardonic preface in 1530: 'I beg all my friends and foes, my masters, printers, and readers, let this New Testament be mine. If you lack one, then make one for yourselves.... But this Testament is Luther's German Testament.'

Just before the publication of the first complete Lutheran Bible in 1534 the office of publisher was transferred to Vogel, Goltze and Schramm, who took over Döring's privilege, valid throughout Saxony. The shares in the partnership were variously bequeathed and transferred until 1626. It was in fact an early privileged Bible-press, somewhat comparable to that in England (see pp. 455–7 below). The obviously profitable monopoly, though it was not exempt from competition from printers in other German territories, was counterbalanced by some care for authoritative printing, and did not lead to inflated prices: the first complete Bible cost 2 gulden 8 groschen; that of 1540 cost 2 gulden 3 groschen. Prices rose later, but this should be ascribed to the general rise in prices in the late sixteenth century. Luther continued to revise the text, but the printers of reprints were none too careful what edition they took as copy-text or what errors or variants they introduced. The text was therefore in great danger of corruption after Luther's death. The edition of 1545 was the last he saw through the press; it was therefore accorded great respect; at least one later edition had '1545' on the title-page for commercial reasons. The whole situation was reviewed in the late 1570's. Until then the greatest defender of the purity of the text was the corrector Christoph Walther, who had succeeded Georg Rörer, called to Denmark in 1551. Walther was an extreme conservative who wished to preserve every minute detail of Luther's text and style. He would not permit the numbering of the verses because Luther had not numbered them, so this innovation was delayed until 1586. He criticized the editions of Frankfurt and Jena for inaccuracy, and their printers retorted in kind. The Duke of Saxony eventually intervened; Luther's manuscript corrections were collated with a printed text of 1560; in 1580 the edition of 1545 was pronounced authoritative. The decision was wrong, for the text of 1546 was better. The whole discussion, as related by Dr Volz, shows that the printing and editorial practice of the time made the stabilization of an authoritative text virtually impossible: indeed the concept was imperfectly understood. But the authorities at least recognized that the problem existed, and this alone set them in advance of their time.

From the typographical point of view Luther's Bible, and more especially the New Testament, was immensely influential. It set one great pattern for reforming Scriptures. The little octavo reprints of the New Testament with their characteristic layout and illustrations were widely copied by their equivalents in other languages. It was tactless of course; an orthodox magistrate, if he had ever seen a copy of Luther's New Testament, would immediately recognize Lefèvre's or Tyndale's or the Dutch vernaculars as based on the same design (Plate 15). They proclaimed their sympathies, and if it helped the sale, it also helped repression. The style owed a great deal to the 'modern' typography which Erasmus had introduced. Luther, Lefèvre and Tyndale all used the long line and the well-differentiated book- and chapter-openings. The use of blackletter much diminishes the effect of modernity for us, but it was still accepted as the normal medium for printing in the vernacular, while roman type was still associated with classical eloquence. Since lines of blackletter capitals are almost indecipherable, headings tended naturally to be set in a larger size of blackletter minuscules. German printers at first set the text in the round Schwabacher and headings in the Fraktur which is still familiar to us; this relationship was eventually reversed.

The similarity between these reforming Gospel-books must be attributed first of all to conscious imitation of the Lutheran model; but it must not be forgotten that it was also due to the simple fact that the same printers very often printed in several languages. Martin De Keyser's name appears as Martin Lempereur in French Testaments, as Martin Emperor in English, as Martin Imperator in Latin; this industrious and bold printer of Antwerp was a natural choice when it came to commissioning the printing abroad of works which were forbidden at home. For Colines soon found it expedient to cease printing Lefèvre's text; it was too dangerous. It was never possible in the 1520's to print an English Gospel in England; and after the early ventures in Cologne and Worms it was natural that Tyndale and his sympathizers in the Low Countries should choose printers on the north-eastern seaboard for the most direct access to England. The notable rise of Antwerp as a printing centre from the 1530's onwards must be ascribed to its general prosperity as the principal trading and financial town of Europe (and printing gravitated naturally to such centres) and to its happy political situation, which was markedly particularist until it was brought to heel by the Spanish in 1576—after which the 'independent' printing centres were Emden, Leyden and Amsterdam. Antwerp's geographical situation was of course ideal for the importation of books into England. They were sent in bales of flat sheets, or rolled up in barrels. The difficulty of identifying a consignment of books in a miscellaneous cargo could only be overcome by diligent search or by information from spies who told the customs authorities what tradesman's mark to look for. In all, Antwerp was the source of the Danish New Testament of Pedersen in 1529, of twelve editions of Lefèvre's

French text, the Spanish New Testament of Enzinas (1543), and a reprint of Brucioli's Italian text, as well as reprints of Tyndale's English text—quite apart from the steady flow of Latin texts.

THE VICTORY OF ROMAN TYPE

The Lutheran format was of course designed for New Testaments; when it came to printing the whole Bible the Wittenberg printers could only use the same design as long as they were issuing the Old Testament and New Testament in several parts. It became extremely uneconomical when the whole Bible was issued in one volume (after 1534 in German, 1535 in English, 1530 in French, 1526 in Dutch). The printers, unable to devise a radically new design, were then forced back into modifications of the traditional blackletter format of the fifteenth century. Indeed the German printers did not acquire the art of the octavo Bible until the seventeenth century; their Lutheran editions were often more cumbersome than those of the fifteenth century. It was in the printing of the Latin Bible, which was in any case carried forward by the finest typographers of the day, that the design of the printed Bible was most advanced. The achievements of these printers were then made available to the vernaculars by the Geneva Bibles. But where, as in Germany and the Scandinavian countries, the abiding influence was the Lutheran Reformation and the Lutheran Bible, printing never underwent the later influence. Thus was established the great division into 'Genevan' and 'Lutheran' which—apart from some individual designs for Roman Catholic versions—governed Bible printing until today. The Lutheran design is illustrated in Plates 14, 15, 21, 34; the Genevan in Plates 32 and 36.

We have seen that Colines had made a start in 1523 with his 16mo in roman. In the late 1520's printers began to produce one-volume Bibles in roman. In 1526 Cratander of Basle printed an edition of the Complutensian Latin translation of the LXX, a quarto, which owes something to the traditions of italic printing and something to the blackletter Vulgate. It is plainly a transitional product; so is Robert Estienne's folio Vulgate of 1528. In the same year appeared Pagnini's important translation, a quarto printed by Du Ry of Lyons. This is the first Bible in which the verses were numbered, though the system was not the one in use today. The printer approached the problem without diffidence, but without imagination, as Plate 17 shows. The text is printed continuously; the verse-numbers are placed in the margin, and the division is indicated in the text by a heavy paragraph-mark. This gives the page an unfortunate plague-stricken appearance; it was not however to be expected that a typographical problem of this sort would immediately be solved in a way both practical and pleasing. In the event this Bible had no immediate successors, though it was influential editorially. No other Bible marked the verses throughout for another thirty years, though the Psalms were occasionally numbered and divided—most successfully by Estienne in 1528. Pagnini also printed the apocryphal books together in a section between the Testaments.

In 1530 Froben's heirs printed a folio in roman which shows an uncompromising adherence to the 'modern' style. It uses single column: more, it uses a very wide solid rectangle of type which occupies with great assurance a formidable text area (it is unfortunately hard to read). The startling innovation is the virtual absence of any break in the text for chapters, and the 'Greek' habit of placing the chapter-numbers and italic summaries in the margin. The Psalms are differently treated, and their articulation may well have influenced Estienne in his next Bible. Robert Estienne's folio of 1532 marks an epoch. It is quite simply the most remarkable and original typographical treatment of the Bible ever printed. It had an immense influence on other printers, who promptly adopted both his text and his design. (We may note here that it was common in the sixteenth century for the opponents of dangerous innovators to counter their editions by producing others which imitated them closely in appearance and even used their text, castigated and with polemical editorial matter. Thus the Louvain Bible in several editions was closely modelled on Estienne's; while Emser's German text aped Luther's in appearance but offered 'the 607 marked places where Luther has violated and distorted the text of the New Testament and where he has wrested it into an unchristian sense by false glosses'. These were unreflecting tactics, for they advertised the texts in question, and made it harder for the simple person to distinguish between the orthodox and the dangerous.)

Estienne's design is reproduced in Plate 23, which is taken from the folio of 1532. That of 1540 incorporates refinements of detail which may have been borrowed from another Froben folio of 1538, which itself obviously copies Estienne. The 1540 folio thus has a claim to be considered the most beautiful Bible ever printed. The most striking thing about the page is obviously the page-head, in gros-canon roman; the characters are by or after Garamond, the prince of letter-cutters. In the early books of the Old Testament the heading includes a 'running-head' alluding to the content of the page below. Estienne invented this feature, as far as Bibles are concerned, and it was imitated by countless printers in many languages. But the setting-out of the text, and the articulation of the books and chapters, are also original—though it should be noted how much the use of a large minuscule for the page-head owes to the blackletter tradition, and that the chapter-heading at the right-hand edge above the initial is also basically traditional. The Psalms were set out *per cola et commata*, and so were certain poetical passages in other books.

Certain standard adjuncts to Estienne's Bibles should also be mentioned. The preliminary pages tend to show two evangelistic features, a little preface *Ad sacrarum literarum studium exhortatio ex sacris literis*, and a short epitome headed *Haec docent sacra bibliorum scripta*, and set out in a most characteristic way. The adoption of these two features by later printers can be taken as an indication of reforming sympathies; and in 1551 the Edict of Châteaubriant expressly forbade the printing or selling of books, commentaries, scholia, annotations, tables, indexes, epitomes or summaries of Holy Scripture and the Christian religion written during the past forty years. At the end of the Bible were two indexes and a revised glossary of Hebrew names and terms, both much copied. With succeeding editions Estienne's apparatus of notes grew, and even in 1532 some of the marginal notes are to be found swelling across the foot of the page—a novelty in those days. In 1540 he introduced his splendid delicate illustrations of the subjects Lyra had first illustrated. These are also to be found in Luther's Old Testament, but it was usually Estienne's set which later printers copied.

Estienne had a four-year privilege, but it was only valid for the French realm. Hence De Keyser was able in 1534 to copy Estienne's design and use his text at Antwerp. Boullé did the same at Lyons in 1537. Froben's heirs' folio of 1538 has been mentioned. In 1541 Colines produced a modification of the design at Paris; in 1543 Froschauer printed the first edition of the Zurich Latin Bible using the same design, and followed it with a reproduction in quarto in 1544. Examples could be multiplied.

All this while the *bien pensants* among the Paris printers, the *libraires jurés* who produced for the Faculty what the Faculty was accustomed to use, had gone on printing small blackletter octavo Vulgates. Of their kind they are extraordinarily good; compact, closely set, well inked and impressed. The most notable printing-house was that of Kerver. The series faltered in the 1530's and probably came to an end in 1543. It is reasonable to suppose that it was Estienne's doing, for in 1534 he had produced an octavo in a minute roman type (Plate 24). It was not the first octavo Bible in roman; Froschauer had produced a German text in 1530, but that was an isolated venture. It was Estienne who really set the fashion.

It must be admitted that functionally his octavo was not an advance. His very small type is more difficult to read (and to print) than the corresponding size of blackletter; for the latter, of its nature, carries more ink and—to lapse into jargon—its shorter ascenders and descenders permitted a greater x-height.[1] Estienne's 'garamond' had ascending and descending strokes of the same proportions as in larger sizes of type, so that the characteristic, or body, parts of the type are extremely small. The type was naturally delicate in design; it could not be heavily inked, or the bowls of the letters would fill with ink; nor could it be heavily impressed, or there was danger of damage to the face. The appearance of the page is thus very grey; it is an 'eye-breaker'. But the book was small and handy; it offered the best text available, and the use of roman was presumably indicative of a modernist attitude. Hence it won, and blackletter was finally ousted in Latin Bible printing. The result was momentous, for it eventually affected the printing of vernacular texts, which came (with the exception of those whose typographical and doctrinal origins were German) to adopt not only roman type but also the design of page which now began to evolve from Estienne's designs of 1532 and 1534.

But this is to anticipate. During the late 1520's and the 1530's blackletter was still used for the vernacular except in Italy. Here Malermi's version was joined by the more radical version of Brucioli, which first appeared as an octavo New Testament at Venice in 1530. There were a few folios of this translation, but it is mainly associated

[1] Literally the height of the minuscule x: the body-part of the letter.

with smaller formats giving the New Testament only—which is characteristic of reforming texts, and had been so since the dualist heresies of the Middle Ages. These books are, by the standards of contemporary French printing, archaic. It is noteworthy that Antwerp printers produced at least one edition of Brucioli's text in their characteristic Lutheran–Erasmian style, and that those have evangelistic prefaces and tables of Gospels and Epistles. After the 1540's Bible printing seems to have been suspended at Venice (there were 800 trials for heresy there between 1547 and 1600) and a new centre, Lyons, takes over. The Lyonnese printers now mainly produced 16mo New Testaments, some in italic, in their charming style. The town was of course as handy for trade with Italy as Antwerp was for England.

Lefèvre's French translation appeared entire in 1530; a large blackletter folio of traditional though elaborate design by De Keyser. A second edition of 1534 borrows Estienne's prefatory matter and running-heads, and his interpretation of Greek and Hebrew names. Folios, octavos and 16mos continued to come from Antwerp for a while, but the printers soon turned to Olivetan's version. This first appeared in 1535 as a large blackletter folio, printed by Pierre de Wingle, who had left Lyons for Neuchâtel for his religion's sake. (Neuchâtel had been reformed by Farel in 1530, and de Wingle had been invited there by the reformer. The town was also associated with the *affaire des placards*, which so incensed François I that he first ordered the total suspension of printing in France and then relented, deciding instead to regulate the trade most strictly.) The cost of printing the Bible was borne by the Vaudois. It is a very big book, suitable only for lectern use. The design is traditional, but uses Estienne's running-heads. The title of the New Testament gives the specifically Protestant, or rather Puritan, form 'The New Testament of our Lord and only Saviour Jesus Christ' which came into use in other languages through the Genevan versions. Basically this first Olivetan Bible is too cumbrous an instrument for any vigorous evangelical movement.

Dutch Bibles form a tradition of their own. The design of the books is naturally linked with German models: the small octavo and 16mo New Testaments resemble the Erasmian model as taken over by Luther; the large folios are very similar to the German ones, but have great elaboration of detail. They were often illustrated, the illustrations being usually after German models. One noteworthy characteristic is the habit of including elaborate calendars in black and red (cf. the English 'Matthew' Bible printed in Antwerp in 1537 by Crom, and even early editions of the Authorized Version printed in England in the next century). Since some of Lefèvre's early editions came from Antwerp, some of the evangelistic preliminaries and accessories derived from the French reforming movement also appear, and were also transmitted into English Bibles through Dutch printing.

The freedom of Dutch printers was not absolute. From time to time the authorities reined in the independent municipalities. A Dutch printer, Van Liesveldt, who produced numerous vernacular Bibles and Testaments, was executed in 1546. Tyndale himself had been burnt in what is now Belgium in 1536. An edict of 1546 prohibited the sale of Bibles printed in Brabant in the previous twenty years, and Dutch-printed Bibles are to be found with false imprints ascribing them to Basle or to Germany. In particularly difficult times the only recourse was to German printers, some at Cologne, but more often at Emden, a centre of extreme heterodoxy. For the historian of printing, following the evolution of the design of the Bible, these northern printing towns are particularly interesting as a kind of focus, where traditional designs are influenced first by the German and then by the newer French models, and these are disseminated into other countries: France and England and even Italy. There resulted a conflict between the Lutheran and the newer models: the one characterized by the use of blackletter, the old vehicle, the other by roman type, which was gradually carried over to the vernaculars. It helped to decide the issue that Antwerp ceased to be the principal centre for international Bible printing, and that its place was taken by Geneva.

THE GENEVA VERSIONS

The great scholar-printers of the early part of the century, above all Estienne, had fairly quickly secured the ascendancy of roman in Latin Bibles. Estienne's octavo of 1534, small and very handy, showed an obvious example to printers who wished to produce pocket editions which would also proclaim a general intention of modernity. In 1536 Jean Girard of Geneva, later to be publisher to Calvin for a while, printed an octavo edition of the New Testament in the Olivetan version in roman. Editions of the Bible soon followed. At first they were indeterminate or transitional in style, but soon one can trace the gradual evolution of a new form—always assisted of course by what was currently being achieved by adaptors of Estienne's design in the parallel development of the Latin Bible. An edition of the French by Girard, a quarto of 1546, uses Garamond's type and Estienne's arrangement of the book-headings. At the end of the volume there is a glossary which the orthodox would feel to be sectarian, though the definitions always base themselves on the original tongues; giving the sense of words like *Église*, *prêtre* and so on. This was the first of an armoury of offensive or defensive weapons to be added to the text. In 1550 Estienne left Paris, driven to leave his home and a place of honour in his trade by the troubles which the Faculties of Louvain and Paris had caused him on account of his editions of the Vulgate. In 1551 he printed a 16mo Greek–Latin New Testament with the verses numbered and divided. In the next year he produced a French–Latin octavo New Testament on the same plan. In 1553 he printed a folio French Bible which is the first Bible to use his verse-division throughout. It is a characteristic book, though unusual for him in setting italic chapter-summaries between the chapter-headings and the text. This device strikes us as specifically modern, but it has reached us because it was adopted as standard treatment by the Genevan versions. It ends with the tendentious glossary. In the next year Crespin printed an octavo French Bible in small roman. The verses were not yet divided, but the italic chapter-summaries were used.

Editions now began to follow each other very fast, and not only in French. In 1555 Estienne had had printed for him the first Latin octavo Bible to incorporate his verse-system. The verses do not begin separate lines, but are divided by a ¶-mark: another reminder that Estienne was a powerful traditionalist as well as an innovator; even his most advanced designs have stronger links with the medieval scribes' conventions than had the products of the humanist printers of Basle. Having introduced verse-division, which does more than any other innovation to disintegrate the old unity and regularity of the column of text by dividing it into irregular units, Estienne attempted at first to keep the column intact by not separating the verses. There is another motive, of course: economy. A verse may end with a half-line of space; throughout the whole Bible this means a considerable increase in the total space occupied, if each verse is to begin a new line.

In the same year a Latin Bible printed by Michael Sylvius for Frellon and Vincent of Lyons separates the verses. The outline of the column was further dissolved by printing the verse-numbers clear of the column to the left, and indenting the first line of each verse (cf. Plate 32). For some time there was uncertainty about the best way of indicating verse-divisions. Plantin, for instance, who began to print Bibles in 1559, soon developed a system which he used consistently: a thin rule was printed between the columns; the verse-numbers for both columns were printed on each side of the rule; in the text the division between the verses was indicated by a small symbol printed as a 'superior', like a modern footnote reference. Plantin went for economy in his small formats, and it is noticeable that he took the fine 'old faces' modelled on Garamond's and recast them on a smaller body with shortened ascenders and descenders. This produces a compact type, and gets more matter on a page; it could even produce—to do him justice—a more readable page, since it allowed, as a corollary, a larger face on the same body as before. But some beauty was lost, and in the cheese-paring seventeenth and eighteenth centuries the mutilation and condensation of types was carried to extremes, and he had shown the way.

The Geneva Bibles opted for the separation of the verses; and very soon a remarkably consistent design emerged, coupled with a formidable set of accessories. In 1556 Barbier of Geneva produced a French octavo Bible which has joined to it at the end two indexes; 'Eighty-nine Psalms of David in French rhymed verse, 49 by Clement Marot and 40 by Théodore de Bèze' with printed musical notation; a form of common prayer covering among other matters the sacraments; and the Geneva catechism. Geneva Bibles had also printed Calvin's preface 'That Christ is the end of the Law' before this date. Another Bible of 1559 by Barbier and Courteau is in effect the first Geneva Bible which embodies the entire standard format and appurtenances, to be repeated in countless editions, Latin, French, Spanish, English and Italian (Plates 32, 36). The title-page points out that it is 'Newly revised, with arguments to every book, new annotations in the margin.... There are also several diagrams and maps.' The printers also print a preface, what we should call a 'blurb' today, in which the usefulness of the new features is urged. (This was common practice at the time; Estienne tended to expand his title-pages into blurbs.) The preliminary pages give Calvin's preface, and Estienne's summary of Christian doctrine, but the arguments to the books, which had in some previous editions been placed all together at the beginning, are now placed before the book concerned, in italic across both columns, below a book-title of characteristic style derived from Estienne. His running-headlines in the early books of the New Testament are still used. The diagrams are in the tradition begun by Lyra and continued by Luther and Estienne; they are supplemented by new folding maps. Maps are not in themselves new: Froschauer had printed excellent ones, and some Dutch editions also used them; but these particular ones are easily the most common and influential. The Bible ended with the index of Hebrew names, and copies can be found with the metrical Psalms and the form of prayers bound in.

Bibles of this sort thus provided the Genevan congregations with a portable and omnicompetent vade-mecum: handy, readable within limits, up-to-date, heavily annotated textually and doctrinally, with visual aids to comprehension, and at the back all that the reader of this persuasion could wish in the way of spiritual solace. It was the ideal Bible for the isolated believer as well as for the congregation. No other edition offered as much, not even the very large scholars' editions, which confined themselves to scholarly matters. The pattern was transferred to the other vernaculars. Conrad Badius (Estienne's brother-in-law) printed the first English Geneva New Testament at Geneva in 1557; it followed the pattern already established for Testaments. Rowland Hall printed the first Bible in 1560; it was a quarto, but in the larger size faithfully reproduced the pattern (Plate 32). It was soon reprinted, and by English and Scottish printers in their own countries; they were careful to reproduce the original typographical style, even when for lack of roman type or in deference to the conservative taste of the insular British they used blackletter.

Meanwhile Italian versions were also being printed at Geneva—since they could not be printed in Italy. A French–Italian diglot New Testament had appeared in 1555, with numbered and divided verses. The device was taken up by the printers of Lyons, who added their own charming decorative elements. A Geneva-printed quarto of 1562 (Brucioli's version) is perhaps the equivalent of Hall's English quarto. When Diodati's version was first printed in 1607 it was inevitable, since he was a second-generation exile whose home was Geneva, that the Genevan style was adopted. A Spanish translation of the New Testament had been printed in 1556.

The Genevan New Testaments were not as entirely successful as the Bibles. They were in single column, and comparatively wasteful of space. They died with the version itself in England, and printers there and elsewhere came to print separate Testaments in the same formats as Bibles (and indeed to make them separable components of Bibles for economy, instead of setting separately). But the Genevan Bible design has lasted to this day. It is the basis of the standard format for cheap Bibles in most countries of the world.

THE TRANSITION TO THE SEVENTEENTH CENTURY

In the history of Bible printing the sixteenth century is by far the most important. The time of the Reformation and Counter-Reformation coincided with the time when the printing industry had become well organized, more prosperous than in the succeeding century, and conducted by the most distinguished men in its history. No later printers can compare with Froben, Estienne, Plantin, Froschauer or their peers. Some of these men were scholars in their own right; many of them were active in affairs of the time; they were peculiarly receptive to artistic and intellectual movements; they had the good fortune to work at just the right moment in the development of the trade.

The century had started with two kinds of trade: the international marketing of Latin Bibles for students and the clergy, and the more local trade in vernacular Bibles. For the first, the sale had been automatically centred in the university and cathedral cities, which were often trading towns as well. For the second, the sale must have been conducted more through the great fairs—which served both scholarly and lay markets. For a time the *stationarii*, who were the traditional sellers of books and were usually licensed university tradesmen, were supplemented by other tradesmen, mercers and grocers. The grocer, as the name implies, bought in gross and sold by retail, and was not necessarily confined to a narrow range of goods; several early English printers and stationers were members of the rich and important Grocers' Company rather than the small and new Stationers' Company; several French booksellers were Mercers. When the official organs of the book trade had to implement their government-bestowed monopoly, they had to abolish these anomalies, which hurt their own trade and made the dissemination of seditious work more hard to control.

As time went by, the network of publisher-booksellers, with their agents and correspondents in other towns, and with their travelling representatives, very adequately served the trade. The greatest of them were to be found in central western Europe, with its well-developed trade-routes, markets, and exchange and credit systems. As we have seen, trade was subject to supervision and restriction before the Reformation. Part of the restriction was self-sought, as the protection of literary property—what we call copyright. A new edition was usually a large, splendid, comparatively careful and therefore costly affair; but other printers eager to reap where they had not sown did not scruple to reprint in a smaller size on cheaper paper and without the expense of qualified press-correctors. A printer therefore sought for a 'privilege'; it was given him by the local authority, and penalized unauthorized reprints in that territory for a stated period of years. But the territorial limitation meant that a foreign printer could buy a copy of the book at a fair such as that at Frankfurt, take it home and reprint it more or less accurately. The records of the time are full of complaints of this and similar practices. Erasmus's printers for instance deplored his habit of giving 'new editions', usually reprints with a few corrections, to other printers before the first edition was exhausted. This added to the natural hazards of the trade, and was another of the factors which limited the size of editions. The printer produced as many copies as he thought he could safely dispose of in a fairly short time; for New Testaments this usually meant an edition of 2000–4000 copies, and of Bibles 1500–3000 copies (late fifteenth-century editions had varied from 900 to 1500 copies). This seems uneconomical to us; it is a cardinal principle of publishing that the capital cost of composition, especially of a Bible, which is several times as big as most ordinary works, should be divided among as many copies as possible; and of a 'steady seller' it is usual to keep composed type 'standing' and to get as many impressions as possible before incurring the cost of setting again. But matters were very different then; for one thing labour was cheap and materials dear. For another, not even those printers who ran their own type-foundries and had very large stocks of type (Plantin, for instance) could afford to lock up capital in standing type. It was needed for the next book. So it was common practice to maintain a steady rhythm of composition, presswork and dispersal of the type. It often happened—indeed it seems to have been the desirable norm—that a forme of four or eight pages was set, corrected and imposed one day, printed the next day, while the next forme was being set, and then dispersed to provide type for the succeeding formes. It seems to have been the pressman's normal stint to produce about 1500 copies in a day; hence 1500 tends to have been the normal edition size. (A late sixteenth-century regulation in England expressly states that not more than 1500 copies were to be printed of most books.) This cycle had its consequences, some of which have been noted. There was steady pressure on the corrector to have the forme ready by the time the pressmen were ready for it. Consequently correction could be over-hasty. There is even evidence, especially in later centuries, that printers deliberately kept their stocks of type from being too big, since the knowledge that there was enough type available to set several more formes encouraged authors or editors to dawdle with their proofs.

Privileges served the dual purpose of giving limited copyright protection and of helping the general movement towards censorship. But jurisdictions overlapped; they might be imperial, royal, parliamentary, municipal or ecclesiastical. It was this conflict which the French king cut through when he took the granting of privileges into his sole hands in 1563, and other powers did the same at about the same time. Hence confusion was somewhat diminished, but there was still scope for manœuvre. The most relevant of these cases, and the most amusing, since it had a happy and not a fiery end, was caused by René Benoist's French Bible. Charles IX of France gave the book a conditional privilege in 1565 for eight years, stipulating that the text should have the approval of the Faculty of Paris. Benoist simply took the Geneva version and emended it in places; the privilege as printed in 1566 omits the clause about the Faculty, but Benoist no doubt felt fairly safe because eighteen doctors of the Sorbonne gave the text their unadvised approval. Benoist's residual uncertainty caused him to print before the text six *advertissements apologétiques*. Unfortunately the printer overlooked some of Benoist's corrections, so the text appeared in the Genevan sense. The Faculty of Paris took notice; the Dean and three members 'sat on' the Bible, meeting forty-five times. Fifteen of the approbatory doctors were heard, and withdrew their approval. In 1567 the Faculty censured thirty propositions, two in the translation and twenty-eight in the notes. The publishers were ordered to withdraw the Bible, but not the New Testament. Meanwhile Plantin had printed a 16mo French New Testament with Benoist's notes, though revised by Henten, the theologian of Louvain, and approved by three doctors; he had a privilege from the Emperor Philip II. Benoist adopted a stiff-necked attitude to the Faculty when he appeared before it, knowing that he had the support of another authority, the archbishop of Paris. Since his privilege was still in effect, he had the Bible reprinted, with the Latin original, and with more *advertissements*; in 1569 he reprinted the New Testament in a French and Latin diglot and in French. The Faculty was furious; and in 1569 seventy-three doctors ratified the earlier condemnation. Benoist signed an act of submission. A higher secular authority was now called in: a decree of the Privy Council suppressed the Bibles. Benoist countered by appealing to the *Parlement*, which agreed that the Faculty should draw up a list of objectionable passages (a standard delaying tactic); the Faculty refused. In 1572 Benoist was expelled from the Faculty. Meanwhile the New Testament was reprinted at Liège, with a privilege from the Prince Archbishop. Plantin reprinted it as well, but without the notes, and mentioning the imprecise approval of 'the theologians of Louvain'; he also printed the French text, without notes, and this time he had the approbation of 'J. Molanus Apostolicus et Regius Librorum Visitator'. Meanwhile Benoist was airing his grievance in a manuscript pamphlet. The Faculty, long past the end of its patience, went to the supreme authority in Rome, and in 1575 Gregory VIII sent a brief ratifying the condemnation; the Faculty had it printed, and sent copies to other faculties, notably Louvain. Since the brief did not mention Bibles based on Benoist's text and printed outside Paris, the astute Plantin reprinted the Bible in 1578. Printers at Lyons and Rouen did the same, several times. By a stroke of political fortune Benoist, much favoured by the new king of France, Henri IV, came back into prominence with the new reign. In fact he became Dean of the Faculty; and like his monarch, who had felt Paris worth a Mass, felt the Decanate was worth another act of submission. He made it in 1598. Meanwhile other printers went on printing his text. The whole story, as Dr De Clercq tells it, is a copybook example of the mechanics and politics of privilege and authorization; we should not forget that some cases ended with exile and death.

No survey of the printing of the period can avoid comment on the quality of the product. This was the heroic age of printing, in spite of the haste and carelessness of the reprints. Few Bibles are worthy to stand on the same shelf as the monuments of the period—Froben's and Estienne's folios, Plantin's great polyglot, De Tournes's folio Vulgate of 1556 (Plate 27), Froschauer's and Oporinus's folios. The dignified simplicity of incunabula was the product of necessity; now elaboration of form was combined with typographical material of equal quality. It strikes the present-day observer as having been done regardless of cost; the truth is that there is no combination like skilled labour—which happened also to be cheap labour—and good material.

This was to change. Venice had already dropped out of Bible printing. After a brief spell as a Calvinist city, Lyons was reoccupied in 1563 and its output dropped to a fraction of its previous capacity. Antwerp was sacked in 1576 and besieged in 1586; its decline favoured the rise of Amsterdam, and particularly the Elseviers, but Bibles were only a part of their output, and their design was no more than neat and decent. Paris had ceased to be a Bible printing centre, largely because Huguenot printers had now left for freer towns; this was particularly unfortunate because it was in Paris alone, though the printers were reduced in number by regulations designed as much to prevent sedition as to safeguard trading interests, that real concern was shown that entrants to the trade should be well educated. Elsewhere there was a very marked decline in qualifications, even though the trade was in most countries subject to statutory organization. It was always the interest of the State to control a potentially dangerous instrument; in England the Stationers' Company, founded in 1557, was granted the monopoly of printing and expected to police itself or to suffer the consequences. The real effect was, as the printers soon pointed out, to accelerate the process whereby power was centred in the hands of the publishers, who commissioned the printing of books, and whose interest it was to keep the printers to small establishments economically dependent on the buyers of their labour and almost pathetically eager for work at cut prices and with low standards. Similar organizations were set up in 1548 in Venice, about 1570 in Paris, and soon in most European states or cities. Germany sank into the bloodshed and poverty of the Thirty Years War; many printers went under, and the total production of books was greatly reduced. All over Europe the average quality of paper declined, and so did the workmanship, except in the few remaining large establishments like the Elseviers or the Imprimerie Royale in Paris. Except in Holland, trade became largely national; England became self-supporting in printing (though not yet in paper-making—a serious weakness in times of war with France or Holland). The total European production of Bibles declined, though that of England went up. It must of course be remembered that very large numbers printed in the sixteenth century would still be in use.

But it must also be remembered that the number of new editions and fairly careful revisions produced in that century had helped to safeguard the texts. No sooner had the cheap reprints corrupted the text than a new edition 'diligently overseen' appeared, and the process had to be started again. In countries which had their 'authorized' version before 1600, it became at least understood that there was a problem. We have seen that efforts were made, with partial success, to stabilize Luther's text. The next step after recension was constant vigilance: the rector and deans of Wittenberg were exhorted in 1614 to keep a closer watch on printing, and especially on proof-correcting, and a fee was prescribed for the correction of Bible proofs, which had to be undertaken by competent theologians. The provision indicates that the printer was no longer trusted to do it himself.

The Sixtine and Clementine editions of the Vulgate caused Protestants much mirth. Whatever the merits of the editors and their work, it must be said that here was another early effort to solve the problems of providing an authoritative text.[1] The prefatory Constitution of the Sixtine declared that this edition only, printed at the Vatican press, was true, legitimate, authentic and unquestionable; after the expiry of the normal time of privilege it only was to be taken as copy-text, and the provincial inquisitors and bishops were to see that it was faithfully followed, and to give their *imprimatur* on that condition only. This was an optimistic provision, for all evidence shows that faithful reprints of the time were only fairly faithful, and there is nothing like a succession of fairly faithful reprints for corrupting a text. But the mere intention is an advance. The book itself, in its surviving copies, shows that extreme care was taken to correct the more significant misprints by

[1] See above pp. 68, 208–11.

hand (Plate 35). Small slips of paper were pasted over errors, with the true version stamped on; there are erasures and pen-corrections as well. Yet one may permit oneself the assumption that only the worst errors were so treated (some twenty). The same laborious process was followed with the Clementine edition; some thirty-seven errors are corrected by printed slips, six by pen. But the most important source of confusion was altogether overlooked; Michael Hetzenauer in producing his critical edition of the Clementine text in 1906 showed in the first place that the third edition was the least correct (as we should expect) and that in the Sixtine Bible of 1590 and all three editions of the Clementine Bible, of 1592, 1593, and 1598, correction took place while the printing progressed, so that copies of the same edition do not agree in all places. When it is remembered that a copy, with certain variants, of one edition is taken as copy-text for another edition, which also has its own variants, and so on, it is only a reader who is unaware of the whole problem who can place any reliance on any part of the text without an elaborate process of collation—which may reveal trivial discrepancies, or significant variation, or nothing at all.

THE SEVENTEENTH CENTURY

Zurich had had its own text since 1529, Germany had had Luther's version since 1534; Geneva had produced its succession of vernaculars in the 1550's and 1560's; Italian Protestants had the Diodati version in 1607; England got its Authorized Version in 1611; Holland had the States General version in 1636. The lines of religious division were firmly drawn; those countries hostile to reform (France, Spain, Italy, Southern Germany and Austria) naturally prevented the printing of reforming Bibles—indeed few Bibles or none at all were printed there. In the countries of the Reformation it was a matter, after the authorized text had appeared, of printing it for home consumption. Bible printing dwindles from an essential part of religious history, and an important part of the history of the great age of printing, into a minor part of the history of publishing.

In Germany the Thirty Years War robbed Wittenberg of its primacy as the Bible printing town. Lüneburg remained important during the whole century, and the Stern family its principal producers: their first Lutheran Bible came out in 1614, published but not printed by them;

they printed Bibles from 1624. Nürnberg, and later Frankfurt, were important Bible-printing towns; Nürnberg's finest production being the *Kurfürstenbibel* (above p. 339). The principal Frankfurt Bible printer was B. C. Wust, a descendant of the privileged printers of Wittenberg, who bought out the other holders of the patent, and so transplanted the Wittenberg tradition and, as it were, the goodwill to Frankfurt. The patent was renewed in his favour by the new Duke of Saxony in 1657, on the express condition that the title-pages of his Bibles should bear the imprint 'Wittenberg'; the text was to be supervised by the theological faculty of Wittenberg. In twelve years Wust claimed to have printed 30,000 Bibles. But his enterprise soon foundered under financial burdens, and his principal rival Zunner died at much the same time, so in the last two decades of the seventeenth century Frankfurt also declined as a Bible-printing town. After seventy years of inactivity an attempt was made to revive the trade at Wittenberg in 1695, but it came to very little. It goes without saying that all these German Bibles were still printed in the German blackletter, which is still in process of being superseded, and bids fair to linger longest in Bibles. Hence they all look curiously old-fashioned to the foreign eye. The folio editions continued to be very cumbrous.

France is, unfortunately, soon dealt with. Printing had been nominally confined to Paris by late sixteenth-century regulations, and the number of printing-houses reduced to a nominal twenty-four (increased to a nominal thirty-six in 1683 and static until 1789).[1] This extreme but theoretical centralization meant that it ought to have been impossible for French printers within the realm to produce anything which authority might frown on; and although there was official religious toleration until 1685, France was effectively a Catholic country. The Vulgate had, one may guess, been over-produced in the sixteenth century, and any surviving demand might be met from the presses of the Propaganda in Rome, founded in 1622 and a source principally of New Testaments. The situation was unfortunate from our point of view, since only the Dutch were at this time as capable as the French; elsewhere standards had declined. There were only two kinds of French activity in Bible printing: splendid but non-commercial

[1] D. Pottinger, in *The French Book Trade in the Ancien Régime* (Cambridge, Mass., 1958), explains the organization of the trade. The 'official' number of printers was of course exceeded, and printing was carried on outside Paris.

editions like the polyglot of du Perron and Le Jay or the Vulgates printed by the Imprimerie Royale, and the editions of Le Maistre de Sacy's new translation, which had in fact to be printed outside the kingdom and ought properly to be considered as Netherlandish.

The Paris Polyglot, in ten volumes of vast size and weight, was printed by Vitré between 1628 and 1645. It cost a fortune, supplied largely by the lawyer Le Jay, who took it up where the Cardinal du Perron left off. Many copies were pulped in the end, as the sale was unsuccessful. It is principally notable for its decorative elements: initials, maps and plates. The Vulgate of 1640 from the Imprimerie Royale is in eight folio volumes, and the whole text is set in a rather ill-fitting and coarsened descendant of Garamond's gros-canon, set in long lines, only twenty-one of them to the page. The type was never meant for setting a text; it was a titling-fount. When one has recovered from the astonishment of seeing it used this way at all, one is bound to feel that the surprise is the principal point. The text is badly set, with more space between the words than between the lines; the chapter-openings are particularly badly managed. The whole venture shows a decline in the printers' sense of fitness for purpose. A later quarto of 1653 from the same press shows greater control of the material; it is almost good enough to have been printed a hundred years earlier. The Imprimerie Royale was in fact a repository of tradition not always well understood, and of craftsmanship not always well employed; its chief talent at this time was in the employment of the specifically seventeenth-century decorative techniques—mostly copper engraving.

The Port-Royal version, begun by the two Le Maistres and revised by Arnauld, Nicole and others, appeared in thirty small octavo volumes between 1672 and 1695. It was printed by the Elseviers and published by Gaspard Migeot of Mons. In accordance with Catholic practice, notes were added, which accounts for the size of the whole. It was successful; some eight or nine editions (probably of the New Testament only) were printed in two years, and 5000 copies were said to have sold in months. It was put on the Index in 1668. The New Testament occupied only two volumes, and appeared in 1667. It is a charming book; certainly the most attractive of the century; indeed the later version by Amelote copies it typographically as well as textually. (In parenthesis, it should be pointed out that Roman Catholic versions, which have always avoided both the Genevan and the Lutheran layout, were frequently of attractive and individual design, from the original Rhemes New Testament of 1582 to the Knox version in the twentieth century.) After the Revocation of the Edict of Nantes in 1685, the French Huguenots who remained in the country became entirely dependent on secret importations. Even a London printer, Evenigham, found it worth his while to print a 12mo New Testament in the Genevan version in 1686. But the greater part of French Bible printing was done in Amsterdam.

Indeed that town became in the seventeenth century what Antwerp had been in the 1520's and 1530's and Geneva in the 1550's and 1560's. Holland was the only country in Europe where the press was free, and this made the fortunes of the Dutch printers, especially the Elseviers. Amsterdam catered for this international trade, while at the same time sharing with Haarlem, Leyden and Dordrecht the supplying of the home market with the new States General Bible. This was first printed by Van Ravenstein or Ravesteyn at Leyden in 1636–7; and the widow and heirs of Van Ravesteyn remained substantial printers of the version. As it first appeared, it was a large folio, with the text printed in blackletter; roman type was used for marginal notes. Some later editions used roman type for page- and chapter-headings, and there were a few editions entirely in roman; but the main stream of Dutch vernacular printing had always been, and remained, in blackletter, in spite of the sophistication and cosmopolitanism of Dutch printing for the outside world. The likely explanation is that the Dutch Bibles, like the German, never underwent the influence of Geneva; and the old idea that vernacular writings must be printed in the medieval vernacular type thus took until the nineteenth—even the twentieth—century to die out.

England had had its Genevan version since 1560; and its great popularity meant that it survived the arrival of the Authorized Version by many years; the last of some 150 editions seems to have been printed in 1644. Laud's objection to its use probably secured its eventual disappearance; later editions had to be printed in Holland. The version met strong official opposition from the start because of its marginal notes and other editorial matter; it is presumably for this reason, and because the authorities up to the time of Archbishop Parker were more willing to provide Bibles for church use than for private reading, that the earlier English versions were printed in large formats and in blackletter. The influence of Estienne is to be seen in the page-headings; otherwise the books are obstinately and deliberately archaic (the printers had the material to print a roman Bible, or even a small Bible, if it had been demanded of them). But the obvious inference was at last drawn; though the Authorized Version in its first editions was a blackletter folio, it must have been seen that if it was to oust its rival one of the necessary moves was to make it available for popular use in the popular style. A quarto edition in roman was printed in 1612–13, and an octavo in 1613. Blackletter editions continued to be printed until the end of the century: the British and Foreign Bible Society Library has an octavo New Testament of 1704 in blackletter, but it is possible that this like other late blackletter Bibles was an illegal import from Holland. The frequency of blackletter English Bibles declines sharply; by the 1620's the number of editions is slightly smaller than in roman; by 1630 blackletter Bibles are rare; by 1640 very occasional indeed. The standard form in which English Bibles were printed in this century and the succeeding centuries, and indeed today, is based on the Genevan model.

The English book trade had become self-policing under the Stationers' Company. Until 1695 printing was forbidden outside London, the two universities and York, and the trade thus centralized was fairly easily supervised by the Company, which was answerable to the State. But Bible printing was subject to special restriction, and here we touch on the whole problem of the Bible patent. It is best to begin with a short retrospect.

Each of the official versions of the English Bible—the 'Matthew', the 'Great', the 'Bishops''—had been sponsored by high authority, and each authority had delegated the printing to a favoured printer. These printers had been given the kind of privilege that any European printer got when he brought out a new version: the sole right to print for a number of years, with the chance of renewal. The quite distinctive growth of trade monopolies granted by sovereigns to a deserving—or more often an accommodating—subject, was during the sixteenth century applied to English printing. Several kinds of books became the monopolies of certain printers, but it was some time before this applied to the Bible. Richard Jugge had a conditional privilege of the Bishops' Bible; and since the Genevan version, the only real competitor, was (according to Pollard) actively discouraged by Archbishop Parker, who shared with Bishop Grindal the duty of licensing the publication of books on theological matters, this meant a *de facto* monopoly of Bible printing in England until 1575, when Parker died. This explains why John Bodley, who had a privilege to print the Geneva Bible, never used it. The other printers then moved forward to share in a lucrative trade. Christopher Barker specialized in the Genevan version; other printers took advantage of the fact that Jugge had the exclusive right to print the Bishops' Bible only in quarto and the New Testament in 16mo, so that other formats were in theory open to free competition by members of the Stationers' Company. Now Jugge happened to be the Queen's Printer, an old-established office which carried with it the right to print certain official publications; but there is no evidence that at this date the Royal Printer's patent gave an *ex officio* monopoly of Bible printing. Jugge merely had a prolonged privilege to print the Bishops' Bible. But when he died in 1577 his patent as Royal Printer was secured by Christopher Barker.

Barker was protected by Walsingham, and through another influential friend, Thomas Wilkes, he secured a further royal patent in 1577 giving him a complete monopoly of printing in England 'all and singular books pamphlets Acts of Parliament injunctions and Bibles and New Testaments in the English tongue of whatever translation with notes or without notes which heretofore or hereafter are printed by our command...'. As is the lawyers' wont, the language is sufficiently opaque to prompt future litigation, without holding out too obvious a chance of success to either side. Barker now began to print 'cum privilegio' on his title-pages. His monopoly seems to have been respected by other printers, except for John Legate, printer to the University of Cambridge, who set a precedent by printing a Bible and a New Testament in 1591. The ground on which Legate based this infringement of the monopoly was a similarly incautious instrument, the royal charter granted to Cambridge in 1534, which gave the University power to print and sell 'all and all manner of books' provided only that they had the approval of the Vice-Chancellor and three doctors. Legate's initiative was an isolated one for some years. The only hope for the London printers was to work under contract for Barker, for the patent could be deputed to assigns, or leased, or even sold. From 1589 some title-pages read 'Imprinted at London by the deputies of Christopher Barker', from which it may be assumed that

Barker was paid for the use of the patent or commissioned the editions himself.

Barker died in 1599; but he had prudently secured in 1589 a fresh patent for the duration of his own life and that of his son Robert. All the appearances suggest that during his lifetime Barker was sluggish to supply the official Bishops' Bible, but zealous in the distribution of the more profitable, because more popular, Genevan version.

Thus the Authorized Version appeared long after an effective monopoly had been established: and a monopoly which associated the office of Royal Printer with the privilege of Bible printing. It is sometimes thought that because James I is associated with the 'Authorized Version' he therefore conferred the monopoly on his printer; but this is evidently not the case. The Authorized Version is today considered to be 'Crown Copyright', but the process by which it became so is obscure. It is indeed the prerogative of the Crown to print certain books of divine service, on the ground that it is the duty of the head of the State—who in England is also the head of the Church—to control the publication of all acts of State on which established doctrine is founded. This certainly applies to the Book of Common Prayer, whose use is mandatory. But the passage of time has obscured the difference in origin between that book and the so-called Authorized Version, which was in fact never authorized at all. As far as documentary grounds are concerned, the monopoly of the Authorized Version seems to be founded only on the patent of 1577, under whose terms the King's Printer had a right which pre-existed the new version (assuming that the words 'which are printed by our command' do not seriously qualify that right: there is no evidence that James, Parliament or Convocation ever expressly commanded the Version either to be printed or to be used). Nor, it should be pointed out, was the patent designed—as it might reasonably have been in a later age—as an attempt to preserve an authoritative text against the corruption incident to careless printing by venal printers; and it was just as well, for it was the official printers who were careless, as we shall see; it was left to the universities—infringers of the monopoly—to make serious attempts at various times to check the process of corruption.

The early editions of the Authorized Version present bibliographical problems which may not yet be entirely solved. Whether two editions were printed simultaneously in 1611 or whether they succeeded each other in the normal way is comparatively unimportant.[1] The point is that the two editions were printed in rapid succession; and since one seems to have taken the other as copy-text in many places, it was presumably printed second; but by a chain of accidents the sheets of the two editions were frequently mixed, so that during the early years of the new version's life no one copy was certain to agree with all others in all places. This was bad enough; it also happened that the translators had serious shortcomings in their editorial method. Scrivener points out that the use of italic, to indicate words not in the original tongues, was erroneous in the extreme; that the marginal references are inaccurate, and vary in their inaccuracy from edition to edition; and that the references to the Psalms in particular are frequently wrong, since they refer to the Vulgate numbering. The printers complicated the matter by importing more or less portentous misprints (for example, 'Judas' for 'Jesus' in one place, and three lines of text repeated in another). The translators did depute some of their number to see the book through the press; and six or twelve of them seem to have stayed at Stationers' Hall at the Company's charge for some nine months; but their supervision was obviously faulty. They do not seem to have left with Barker a 'sealed copy' or a guaranteed authentic manuscript from which, and from which only, future editions were to be set. Although 'the manuscript copy of the Bible' is recorded as having been twice bought, once by Cambridge and once by Hills and Field, there is no evidence that it had this authenticity or was used as anything but a means of procuring copyright. While there is evidence that some revision was attempted in various early London editions, this was fitful and had no cumulative effect. In short, within a very little time the task of maintaining an uncorrupted text had been made quite impossible; Barker's monopoly, while it might have prevented corruption by others, was not seen to have placed him under a corresponding obligation.

It was the Cambridge printers Thomas and John Buck in 1629, and Thomas Buck and Roger Daniel in 1638, who printed folios which showed a consistent attempt at revision; and the records suggest that the revisers included two of the original translators. During the subsequent textual history of the version, the burden of revision was principally borne by the universities, and notably by Dr Paris of

[1] See A. W. Pollard in *Records of the English Bible* (Oxford, 1911), pp. 66ff., where the views of various scholars are considered.

Cambridge in 1762, Dr Blayney of Oxford in 1769, and finally by Dr Scrivener of Cambridge who produced what was essentially the first true critical edition in the Cambridge Paragraph Bible of 1873, which was successful only because the editor took account of the whole history of the text, and all the vicissitudes to which printers had subjected it. His work was the culmination of a movement which began in the 1830's; a 'fundamentalist' objection had been raised to current editions because they departed from the text printed in 1611, and they also disagreed with each other: it was calculated that there were 24,000 variations between the current editions when they were compared with each other and with the original. A literal reprint by the Oxford Press of the edition of 1611 showed how absurd it would be to revert to that text; while Scrivener showed that at that late stage the text must be subjected to careful editing like any other seventeenth-century text.

The remaining history of the seventeenth-century Bible trade in England is entirely concerned with the extremely involved struggles between the monopolists and the 'pirates'. This phrase over-simplifies the matter, for at times there were contending parties for the patent itself: the various heirs, partners and lessees fell out with each other and resorted to intrigue and even violence, as well as litigation. The Stationers' Company was also interested, because it, like the patentees, suffered from the infringement of various monopolies offered by Cambridge and later Oxford. When the Oxford Press was granted its charter in 1636 the Company negotiated on its own behalf and in association with other patentees a covenant of forbearance, by which the University agreed to refrain from printing certain privileged books in return for an annuity of £200. The King's Printers were to contribute to this in respect of the Bible and Book of Common Prayer. The abolition of the Star Chamber, with its control over printing, and the lapse of the previously existing royal patent, gave the Company an opportunity of invading the Bible monopoly after 1641. In 1644 the Company treated with the current operators of the former patent, and bought the presses and equipment of one partner. The Company had long administered 'stocks': ventures in which members held shares in a joint capital which was applied to profitable printing. The principle was applied to Bibles. A 'Bible Stock' was set up in 1646, and lasted until the time of the Commonwealth. The disputes and periodical arrangements with the universities continued until the end of the century. Various forms of agreement were reached from time to time; when their funds were low the universities could forego their rights for an annual payment; when they felt belligerent they went to law; when they felt diplomatic they agreed to limit their activity.

During the Civil War the trade was much disturbed; restrictions lapsed, but so did protection, and the result was chaos. Under the Commonwealth the right to print the Bible was assigned to the partners Hills and Field, by Cromwell's order of 1656; this accounts for the cessation of the Stationers' Company's activity. Both then and later large numbers of English Bibles printed in Holland were imported; Joseph Athias of Amsterdam claimed that in a number of years he printed more than a million English Bibles. Without any ironical intention the States of Holland gave him an exclusive privilege to print English Bibles for fifteen years from 1670. As far as the ordinary English purchaser was concerned, Dutch Bibles were welcome; especially to those who felt that the English privilege was merely a way of laying a 'vast tax' on the English people. If foreign editions were inaccurate, so were the London ones; to this period belongs the anecdote of the bishop who had to preach in St Paul's, went into a bookshop nearby to buy a London-printed Bible, and found that the text he had to preach on was not in it. Several pamphlets of the time give the historian useful details of the prices charged, and complain of inaccuracies: the most notable of these publications is Michael Sparke's, punningly called 'Scintilla; or a light broken into dark warehouses. With observations upon the monopolists of seven several patents and two charters, practised and performed by a mystery of some printers, sleeping stationers, and combining booksellers...' (1641). It provoked retorts, which Sparke was pleased to reply to, and a running battle went on for years. One of the common complaints was that the privileged printers, having paid large sums of money to powerful people to have their privilege continued, looked about for compensating economies, and hit on the device of doing without qualified correctors or not paying them enough. And indeed the four M.A.'s employed by the King's Printers in the 1630's had had to appeal to Archbishop Laud to be continued in office when they were threatened with lower wages and then with dismissal.

The end of the century saw the real rise of the Oxford Press. The agreement with the Stationers lapsed in 1673—at the time when Bishop Fell was about to reinvigorate the Press. Thomas Guy the speculator and philanthropist who had commissioned Dutch-printed Bibles but found his trade was hindered by searches and seizures, turned to Oxford. There the University had entered into fierce competition with the London printers. Guy and Peter Parker were brought into an existing partnership and Guy and Parker became University Printers in 1684. They were said to have made enormous profits, and were removed from office in 1692—as a result of intrigue by the Stationers, whose nominees were then appointed to the office.

THE EIGHTEENTH CENTURY

Without any doubt the most important figure in eighteenth-century Bible printing was Karl Hildebrand Baron von Canstein, who founded the *Cansteinsche Bibelanstalt* at Halle in 1710. He was in fact a one-man Bible Society almost a hundred years before such institutions became common elsewhere. The Institute is still active today. He published his first New Testament in 1712, and a Bible in 1713, and the editions, or more accurately impressions, followed each other rapidly. His Bibles were extremely cheap; the whole secret of his success was that he kept the composed type standing, instead of dispersing it. Thus the cost of composition, normally a heavy charge, was spread over such a large number of copies that it could be left out of account; and as the concern was not meant to make any profit a Bible could be sold for the bare price of ink, paper and presswork, or at a loss. The corollary was that these impressions were also consistent; they were reasonably accurate at first setting-up and later impressions showed textual improvement rather than deterioration, for the publishers specifically asked to be notified of errors, so that they might be corrected in the type before the next impression. By 1741 the 12mo Bible had reached its 67th impression, by 1749 the 92nd, by 1754 the 105th. The preface to the 92nd impression states that it was printed from the fourth edition; in other words each setting provided some thirty impressions before the type became so worn that it had to be melted down and recast and reset. The publishers point out that in spite of the expense of casting and setting new type, the price had not risen. By 1803 the society had circulated 3,000,000 copies of the Scriptures in German and other languages. There were several formats, of which the 12mo was the most popular. They were notably utilitarian and austere in appearance, with an extremely condensed type, and by the early nineteenth century the paper used was appallingly bad; but this was typical of the paper supply in Europe.

The eighteenth century also saw the appearance of America as a Bible-printing country. There had been a Bible printed in an Indian language at Cambridge, Massachusetts, in 1663; the earliest Bible in a European language was a quarto in German printed at Germantown, Pennsylvania, in 1743 by Christoph Saur. The edition was of 1200 copies, and the price was 18*s*. Further editions by Saur's sons appeared in 1763 and 1776. The preface to the first edition says that the printer (who from his introductions was a man of strong evangelical tendencies) was moved to print it because he saw how many poor Germans came to America without a Bible and how many were born and brought up in the new country with no way of getting one from the old; while the rich provided only for their own families. He took the Canstein Bible as his copy-text because it was 'rich in parallels' and was the most accurate available; he had corrected some hundred misprints, which he mentioned not out of pride but in case misprints might be found in his own work; it showed that 'we are all human'. The Fraktur type was supplied free by the Luther foundry at Frankfurt.

There is a story that a small quarto Bible in English was printed in Boston in 1752; but no copy of it is to be found. Admittedly, the story has it that the imprint of the London and Oxford monopolist Baskett was used; even so it should be possible to identify the book if it really existed and any copies remained. In fact the American market was supplied almost entirely from London. The earliest authenticated American-printed New Testament was produced by Aitken of Philadelphia in 1777, and it was followed by a Bible in 1781–2. Aitken certainly believed his was the first American edition. The Rhemes–Douay translation was first printed in America in 1790, at Philadelphia.

This was a slack time in Europe. French Bibles were printed at Hanover, The Hague, Berlin, Hamburg, Leipzig, London and Basle—presumably their importation had become illegal after 1685. Small Vulgates continued to be printed in France, and naturally benefited from French standards and the new French tastes. The *œil poétique*, or narrow-faced letter designed to avoid the turning-over of lines of poetry, was admirably suited to economical Bible printing. A 12mo New Testament printed by Barbou of Paris in 1767 shows the influence of Fournier's decorative inventions as well; it is a charming book. Ibarra of Madrid printed a New Testament in the same year, and a folio Bible in 1778. This was a full-scale exercise in the new art of which Baskerville (see below) was a pioneer, but it was not as impressive as the original.

The English trade in the eighteenth century was still occupied with the privilege question. The greatest monopolist of the century was John Baskett, who in 1709 or 1711 bought a share in the King's Printer's patent, and in 1712 sought a share in the Oxford privilege. Eventually he was simultaneously University Printer and King's Printer, and even sought a share in the King's Scottish Printer's patent. Since Cambridge was not very active at the time, the whole British Bible trade was virtually in Baskett's hands. He produced some splendid Bibles, especially at Oxford, in what might be called the 'Queen Anne' style of printing; he also produced some erroneous editions—notably the 'basket-full of printer's errors'.

It was at this time that enterprising British publishers were bringing out works of instruction in successive parts of 16 or 32 pages at prices like 3*d*. a number, a method which combined serial- and subscription-publishing. The bolder spirits applied it to the Bible, thinking to avoid lawsuits by the privileged printers by disguising the works as 'A Commentary upon all the books of the Old and New Testaments', 'A new complete history of the Holy Bible as contained in the writings of the Old and New Testament', or 'Expository Notes'. It was a mere detail that the actual texts were included entire. These works were partly successful, to judge by the number of them which appeared from 1720 onwards. There was opposition from Baskett; but at least one publisher, W. Rayner, declared in the preface of his offending publication that 'the word of God ought not to be the property of any one person, or set of men', and that 'the interest of Heaven is in no way concerned, whether God's word be printed by J. Baskett, or W. Rayner'. Fine words; but the interest uppermost in the writer's mind was not Heaven's but W. Rayner's.

During this century, in England at any rate, the verifying of reprint copy (that is, the proof-reading of reprints) was commonly carried out by the compositor himself, and since the Bible had been 'reprint copy' since 1638, the text was steadily debased. In the 1760's Paris of Cambridge and Blayney of Oxford attempted a serious and scholarly revision of the text. Paris's edition was soon succeeded by Blayney's and much of it was destroyed by fire, so it had little effect. Blayney's was less discreet, and was indeed erroneous in many places; it also showed another source of error; first set and printed in quarto, the columns of type were 'lengthened out' to make a folio, and in the process the type was much disturbed and had to be recollated. (The practice of 'lengthening out' seems to have started in the late sixteenth century. It was a way of economizing in composition charges, but carried this grave danger with it.)

Aesthetically, the highest point in English Bible printing so far was John Baskerville's folio printed at Cambridge in 1763 (Plate 43). To achieve his ambition to print a folio Bible, Baskerville had to become University Printer, on not very advantageous terms. The Bible uses his types, paper and ink, and shows his characteristic 'machine-made' finish: very smooth and even in colour and impression, with glossy black ink on smooth paper. The design is traditional, but the quality of material and workmanship is so high, and the conventions are so delicately modified and consistently applied that the result is extremely impressive. Unfortunately the edition of 1250 copies hung fire, and was eventually remaindered.

THE NINETEENTH CENTURY

Until the early nineteenth century printing had advanced remarkably little; indeed it could hardly be said to have advanced at all in things like workmanship and material—nor could any eighteenth-century printer be compared with the great printers of the sixteenth century in the size, equipment or productivity of his shop, or inventiveness in design. The old hand-press had been improved in details: it now printed a larger surface at a time, and slightly faster (some 250 impressions per hour). Papermaking had been improved mechanically in the seventeenth century, but chronic shortages of linen rag—the basis of good paper—had drastically reduced the quality: some of the Bibles printed by the King's Scottish Printers in the late eighteenth century were on such coarse grey paper that they were illegible, and caused an outcry. Above all, printers were hampered by the economic conditions of the trade: printing-houses were small, and the amount of capital needed to set up in a small way was still less than that needed to print a large book; but the printers themselves had no source of working capital, while printing and publishing was still too much of a marginal activity, in the days before universal education, to offer much scope to the investing capitalist. The mechanization of the trade which took place in the nineteenth century revolutionized it; and inevitably Bible printing was one of those branches which would of its nature be most advantaged by the process. For the Bible is one of those books where high initial capital costs ought ideally to be set against a very large manufacturing run indeed, producing a big edition at a low unit cost. We have seen that the chronic shortage of type of the hand-printer, and the slowness of the original printing process, meant that the master-printer was almost inevitably forced to print small editions. He worked from hand to mouth, setting up so many sheets, and working each one off in time to make the type available for the next. He could, if he had the money, order extra-large founts of type, but because of the irregular incidence of particular characters in normal printing, he had always to order at least 30 per cent more than he could use at once. When a compositor announced that he was running 'out of sorts', there would still be that total quantity of characters remaining; more of the exhausted letters could be ordered, but the new supply was subject to the same limitations. Type could not therefore be held in the slow-moving press indefinitely; it was needed to allow the work of the office to proceed.

The invention of a printing-machine which would multiply the rate of impression meant first of all that the same amount of type could be used to produce more impressions in the same time. It meant an increased return on the capital invested in type as well as the capital spent on labour. Where 1500–2000 impressions had been made in a day, it became possible to make the same number in an hour. Admittedly, large capital sums were soon needed to buy machinery; but the investment once made, it could be expected to recover its own cost many times in the working life of the machine. Hence the prospects were now interesting enough to attract capital.

The mechanical press was preceded by two other inventions: stereotyping and the papermaking-machine. In England and Germany the chronic shortage of linen rag meant that the cheaper grades of paper, as used in cheap Bibles, were so bad as to cause illegibility. Efforts were made to produce paper of other materials, principally straw, and to make paper by machine. Matthias Koops had British patents of 1800–1 for making paper from straw, hay, thistles, hemp refuse, flax and bark. He set up a large manufactory in London—the largest in Europe—which produced paper on a commercial scale, but went bankrupt in two years. Meanwhile in 1798 Nicholas-Louis Robert, a clerk in the Parisian publishing firm of Didot, secured a patent for a papermaking machine. The engineers and financiers of England took up his invention; Bryan Donkin made for the Fourdrinier brothers the first practical papermaking machine in 1803. By 1812 ten machines had been made in Europe, costing £715–£1040 each. An American machine followed in 1817, which produced paper 30 inches wide at the rate of 60 feet a minute.

The British and Foreign Bible Society was founded in 1804 (above, ch. XI). By an extraordinary coincidence Lord Stanhope had in the same year perfected his stereotyping process. There had been experiments in the eighteenth century, notably by William Ged, a Scottish goldsmith, who had applied the goldsmith's technique of taking plaster casts to the moulding of the complete surface of a page of type. Ged's invention had been adopted by the Cambridge Press, but had come to very little, for a mixture of reasons, technical, personal, and commercial. Now Stanhope improved the process, still using plaster of Paris. He gave the management of the commercial rights to Andrew Wilson of London. Wilson communicated the secret to Cambridge. So when the British and Foreign Bible Society were proposing to buy a large stock of Bibles, it was natural that they should have decided to wait until the process was in operation, for it promised cheapness, accuracy and quick availability. It was in fact a way of getting stock on the Canstein scale, with a stable text, but without locking up capital in standing type: the type once moulded, casts ('plates') could be taken from the moulds, and impressions multiplied without the expense of resetting. As the whole page of type was reproduced as a single surface, there was no danger of single types dropping out during handling, but corrections could be made to the plates if necessary. For the first time in printing history (except for Canstein's non-commercial venture) successive printings could mean an increase in accuracy. Genoux of Lyons is said to have invented in 1829 the mould of papier-mâché, or 'flan' (anglicized as 'flong') which had advantages of cheapness and durability over the fragile plaster mould.

In 1805 the Cambridge Long Primer New Testament appeared, and the British and Foreign Bible Society bought large numbers, by the standards of the times. A Bible followed in 1806 (Plate 44). By 1808 the process was in use at Oxford, and by 1812 by the King's Printers. In 1812 the Philadelphia Bible Society was founded, and is said to have imported stereotype plates from England and printed Bibles from them. In 1816 Tauchnitz started his stereotype foundry in Germany, and was soon stereotyping Bibles. In 1820 a stereotype edition of the Rhemes New Testament was printed in Dublin and distributed to the poor, to schools, and to hospitals. (It was bound in the now familiar black cloth; it was probably the first instance of the practice. At this time English editions were either sold unbound, or in the lower grades of leather, like roan and calf.)

Friedrich König, inventor of the printing-machine, came to London in 1806, and patented a machine in 1810. In 1811 a sheet of the *Annual Register* was printed by machine. In collaboration with his compatriot Bauer, König built a new machine in 1812–13. *The Times* ordered two such machines, and on Tuesday, 29 November 1814, the whole issue of *The Times* was printed by machine at the rate of 1100 sheets an hour. The invention was rapidly developed, both by König and Bauer, who returned to Germany in 1817, and by competitors. It took some time for enough machines to be built to influence the trade generally. König and Bauer supplied French, German, Danish, Dutch and Russian printing-houses between 1822 and 1830; the *Cansteinsche Bibelanstalt* bought a machine in 1830. In England firms like Applegath and Cowper or Napier supplied the large English printers. Probably the first to be mechanized was Clowes, then of London, a very big business which did much foreign Bible printing for the British and Foreign Bible Society, and which seems to have gone over to machine printing in 1824.[1] In 1834 the Oxford Press installed two perfectors (machines which printed both sides of the paper as it passed through the machine). The Press had six machines by 1837. Early machines could be worked by a hand-swung flywheel; but almost at once steam-power was substituted (by 1835 at Oxford). Cambridge was mechanized between 1838 and 1840.

[1] Marjorie Plant, *The English Book-Trade* (London, 1939), p. 278.

Some figures will indicate the quantity of Bibles now being poured out. In the decade 1837–47 English production was:

	Bibles	Testaments
Queen's Printer	2,284,540	1,971,877
Oxford	2,612,750	2,062,250
Cambridge	895,500	1,111,600

Sales to the British and Foreign Bible Society were:

	Bibles	Testaments
Queen's Printer	1,314,031	1,352,604
Oxford	1,167,711	1,373,130
Cambridge	527,846	737,496

The figures for the Queen's Printer include work contracted out to other printers. It will be seen that Oxford alone produced almost half the total. Indeed this press, which had risen from an annual production of 127,000 Bibles, Testaments, psalm-books, prayer-books and service-books in the whole decade 1780–90, rose to an annual production of 1,066,000 by 1860, and was quite certainly the world's largest producer. The effect of early mechanization in England, combined with the extraordinary activity of the British and Foreign Bible Society, meant that England was the primary producer of books of Scripture, supplying a very large part of the needs of the rest of the world, including the continent of Europe; until well on in the century English Bibles had a ready market in the United States of America as well.

It follows that privileged printing in England was very big business; though the sales by the British and Foreign Bible Society at less than commercial prices kept a strong pressure on the privileged printers to produce Bibles economically and so to keep their prices as low as possible, in order to avoid losing more of the market than was inevitable. (In Germany the activities of the Bible societies virtually eliminated commercial competition.) The privileged presses also competed quite genuinely with each other. As in previous centuries, there were infringements of the monopoly, to the point where it ceased in the end to be a monopoly. The firm of Bagster was founded in 1794, and, taking advantage of the fairly well established notion that a reference Bible or polyglot or any text combined with aids and appendages was not strictly an infringement, soon began to publish polyglots and reference works. The polyglots are an interesting application of stereotyping: one edition of 1831 mounted eight sets of stereotype plates, each a double-column octavo page, on the facing pages of a very large format, and printed them all together. The languages were Hebrew, Greek, Latin, English, German, French, Italian and Spanish, with an appendix of Samaritan and Syrian readings of the New Testament.

There appeared from the 1830's several 'Family Bibles' which were also infringements of the monopoly. A Quaker Bible produced at York in 1828 anticipated Bowdler's treatment of Shakespeare. It announced itself as 'principally designed to facilitate the audible or social reading of the Sacred Scriptures', and passages unsuitable for a mixed audience (that is, capable of bringing a blush to the cheek of the young person) were printed at the foot of the page. In 1836 the great popular educator Charles Knight published his 'Pictorial Bible'. It was 'illustrated with many hundred wood-cuts representing the Historical Events, after celebrated pictures, the Landscape scenes, from original drawings or from authentic engravings, and the subjects of Natural History, Costume and antiquities from the best sources, to which are added original notes chiefly explanatory of the Engravings'. The illustrations show some knowledge of the traditions of Bible illustration (bibliography was beginning to be seriously pursued) but are novel in their informativeness. There are engravings of subjects such as *Ficus caricus* or *Olea europaea*; the narrative scenes are after painters like Reubens (*sic*) and Salvator Rosa. The book in its purple leather binding, elaborately gilt, is still a most desirable possession. Much less so is the edition of 1850. In the interval machine-printing had lowered the standards of taste and workmanship, though the book was now no doubt cheaper. The type is debased, the paper cheap, and the binding is of 'leather cloth'. Knight's Bible was, like some of its eighteenth-century predecessors, issued in parts. This was practically the only way in which the poorest readers could hope to afford a 'Family Bible', that mark of respectability. Knight's own venture was probably not financially rewarding; a later publisher for the masses, John Cassell, issued in instalments an *Illustrated Family Bible* which sold 350,000 copies in six years.[1] A specially bound copy was owned by the Queen.

[1] Richard D. Altick, *The English Common Reader* (Chicago, 1957), p. 303. The whole book is valuable as a study of the interaction of education, publishing, the economics of printing, government control, and so on. S. Nowell-Smith, in *The House of Cassell* (London, 1958), p. 57, says that the *Illustrated Family Bible* cost £100,000 to produce, and sold in penny parts at the rate of 300,000 copies a week. These subscription Bibles were reissued in various forms after first publication.

Three of the illustrations—there were over 1000 in all—were by Doré. A few years later Cassell published in England an English version of Doré's illustrated Bible, first published by Mame of Tours between 1865 and 1866. (At that time Mame was even more highly mechanized than Oxford, and its output was immense; but it was devoted mainly to Missals and Breviaries.)

These illustrated family Bibles were an international phenomenon. Baumgartner of Leipzig had produced in 1836 an *Allgemeine Wohlfeile Bilder-Bibel* 'with more than 500 handsome illustrations in the text'. In America Harper's Illuminated Bible of 1846 was the most elaborately illustrated book yet planned in that country,[1] and the engraver, Joseph A. Adams, was an early experimenter in the electrotyping of wood-engravings, producing by galvanic action a metal-faced replica of the surface of the illustration. The process was perfected by Jacobi of St Petersburg, and, used instead of stereotyping, made possible the printing of very large editions with much less wear than with ordinary type-metal. Used for illustrations, it also made possible the purchase by other publishers of cheap electrotype copies of original woodcuts. The trade became international, and was a strong influence on the growth of illustrated journalism. Cassell in particular throve on the use of 'electros', or *clichés*, as the French called them. An earlier Parisian venture of 1834 had combined the principle of serial publication with the new taste for steel-engravings. This Bible, advertised as an '*édition populaire et de luxe*' of 100,000 copies, appeared in paper brochures of 136 pages, at 3 sous the brochure, or 5 sous with an engraving. Curmer of Paris also produced in 1836 a Gospel-book which made use of the processes of chromolithography, copper-engraving, wood-engraving and steel-engraving. It is very much in the manner of medieval books of hours, with the 'gothicism' heightened.

Perhaps it was inevitable that the technical advances of the time should lead to *tours de force* which are little more than that. The perfection of type-cutting earlier in the century had produced type-faces of very small size and great brilliance, hence called 'diamond', 'brilliant' and 'excelsior'. These were sometimes used on very thin paper, as in 1816 by the King's Printer in London, or in 1846 by Briard of Brussels. In 1834 a New Testament was 'printed and enamelled' by

[1] David Bland, *A History of Book-Illustration* (London, 1958), p. 303. See also figure 268. See also T. L. de Vinne, *Plain Printing Types* (New York, 1925), p. 219.

De La Rue, James and Rudd for Adolphus Richter of London. It was printed in gold on a loaded and glazed paper, in an early form of 'Bible' type. It weighs 11 lb. 6 oz. and is an example of the Victorian gift for making the unspeakable out of the unsuitable. In 1877 at the Caxton Festival, which had a special Bible section, Mr Gladstone exhibited to those present an edition of the Bible bound in morocco, of which not a sheet had existed 24 hours before. This was an Oxford product, and so was the 'Golden' Gospel of John printed in 1881 in an edition of three copies in gold sans-serif type on dark green paper (for a lady with failing sight!). In 1896 there was printed at Glasgow on the thinnest India paper ever made a miniature Bible measuring 2 by 1.5 cm. It was held in a case with a magnifying glass incorporated. All this was really mere exuberance; it was more to the point that in 1864 the British and Foreign Bible Society was enabled by machine-production to produce a Bible which sold for *6d.*, and in 1884 a New Testament which sold for a penny. Eight million copies of this New Testament were sold by 1903.

England, and especially Oxford, was now far and away the world's leading Bible printer. Machines developed to the point where sheets holding 128 pages of type produced thousands of copies per day. Paper had become really cheap and plentiful in the 1860's with the introduction of wood-pulp and esparto-grass as its basis. Type-casting machines produced finished type at a great rate; type-setting machines were beginning to be invented, though their general introduction was not accomplished until the early years of this century. All the operations of binding were mechanized by the end of the nineteenth century.

Even by the time the Queen's Printer's patent lapsed in 1859, when there was sufficient public feeling against the continuance of the monopoly to cause the institution of an inquiry by a committee of the House of Commons, the defenders of things as they were had a fairly powerful argument: it was possible to hold up an Oxford Bible, sold to the British and Foreign Bible Society at *4d.* a copy, and ask how in any circumstances of free competition that price could be bettered. The answer, put by the other side, was that that price was not achieved under the conditions of monopoly supposed to be secured by the patent. When the Queen's Scottish Printer's patent had lapsed in 1839, it had not been renewed, but printing of the Bible had been made free, subject to licensing and supervision by a Board, which was supposed to see that the printers chose a satisfactory copy-text and reproduced it accurately. There had long been antagonism between English and Scottish Bible printers, and some litigation, resulting in a truce by which neither side invaded the territories of the other. But in 1858 one of the Scottish printer-publishers, William Collins, in defiance of the privileged presses, had set up an office in London and began to issue his Bibles there. He was not impeded. Collins gave guarded testimony before the committee; it was another witness who pointed out that the result of his incursion had been that a short time afterwards the prices of Bibles in England had dropped by half. Other witnesses testified that neither supervision in Scotland nor privilege in England had in fact secured absolute accuracy; a good deal of capital was made by anti-restrictionists of the discrepancies between the Oxford, Cambridge and London texts, any of which was accepted as authoritative by the Scottish Board. It was also pointed out in the discussion that the terms of the patent gave the Queen's Printers extraordinarily wide powers. It is hard to believe that those who drafted it really meant to give in perpetuity the powers it seemed to convey; strictly interpreted, it gave the Queen's Printers a total monopoly of all Bibles printed in England, in whatever version or whatever language. These powers had never been enforced except to keep the Authorized Version from other English printers, but there was thus good reason not to perpetuate them, at any rate in the previous terms. The committee finally recommended that the patent be not renewed, since it was not in the public interest, but the casting vote of the chairman was needed to reach this decision, and the patent was quietly renewed in 1860. Under the Demise of the Crown Act of 1911 the patent was made valid during the pleasure of the Crown, and was not therefore subject to renewal in each successive reign. The terms of the present patent are no different, but continued to be applied only to the Bible of 1611, until a dispute over the New English Bible arose in 1961.

The main point that emerged from the investigation was that the bold irruption of Collins into the British market had reinforced the activities of the British and Foreign Bible Society in sending English prices down; so that—whatever had happened before—the British public had the economic benefits both of mechanization and quite fierce competition. The palmy days of privileged printing ended in 1858; the inference is that before that date they had been a little too palmy to be entirely satisfactory.

THE TWENTIETH CENTURY

The nineteenth century so concentrated on the increase of production by mechanical means that aesthetic standards went by the board. Printing in the second half of the century so far lost sight of principles of good design that functional qualities also suffered. The bane of Bible printing was the so-called 'Bible' type-faces, where boldness and blackness were mistakenly thought by the buyer to make for legibility. As far as the manufacturer was concerned, these coarse faces stood up well to the repeated impact of dry paper wrapped round the rapidly reciprocating cylinder, whereas the more delicate 'modern' book-faces tended to break at the weakest places—the thin hair-lines and serifs—and were in any case intended to show to best advantage when deeply impressed by a flat surface into the moistened 'antique' paper of the beginning of the century. The more acute designer-printers, like the American De Vinne, reflecting on the problems of machine-printing were led to conclude that the 'old face' types, derived from sixteenth-century originals with their even distribution of weight of line and curve, were technically as well as aesthetically more appropriate to the new circumstances: types designed on the old principles would last better, and were intrinsically more legible; it only required a change of taste to show their beauty. The change of taste was accomplished by William Morris, who also confused the issues. Morris's practice took a revivalist form for reasons we should now call ideological. He hated the machine, because he associated it with the decline of craftsmanship. His partly sentimental attachment to the fifteenth century led him to use a kind of Jensonian roman or transitional blackletter; the designs themselves are bad in so far as they depart from their originals; they fail the elementary test of legibility. But they were associated with superb decoration and the highest standards of setting and presswork, on excellent paper; his books are undeniably beautiful objects, as long as one forgets their possible use. The distinguished but eccentric eclecticism of the movement was applied to Bible printing in the Doves Press Bible of 1903. It uses a fifteenth-century page-design as well as a pseudo-fifteenth-century type; the press even made use of the rubricator (the great calligrapher Edward Johnston wrote initials for the books). Like Morris's work the Doves Bible was hard to read; and it was not, as Morris's was, highly decorative. One comes away from such work thinking that its principal beneficial effect was to show that it was possible to care deeply about quality in printing, and to make immense effort to secure it. That in itself was a great deal.

The gradual introduction of automatic type-setting and type-casting machines in the first quarter of this century carried with it a programme of research into what might be called the experimental psychology of typography, into the history of type-design (partly in search of suitable revivals) and thence into the basic principles of type-design. The leading scholar, designer and propagandist of the movement was Mr Stanley Morison, typographical adviser to the Monotype Corporation (most book and Bible printing in Europe uses the Monotype machine), to *The Times*, and to the Cambridge University Press. The effect of this work can be seen in two kinds of Bible printing: the 'fine' printing of such large works as the lectern Bible produced by the Oxford Press under Bruce Roger's direction in 1935, and in the now numerous commercial editions in smaller formats in nearly all countries where the Bible is printed.

Roger's folio is one of the great Bibles—in spite of a strong element of what could unsympathetically be called pastiche. It uses his Centaur type, based on Jenson's roman; the page-heads and book-titles are borrowed from Estienne, and the paragraph-marks (the least successful feature) from Pagnini. But the scale, the grace, and the quality of workmanship lift it to the highest plane (Plate 48). The large commercial editions in small formats printed since about 1935 by English, American and European printers (including the two principal German firms, the *Cansteinsche Bibelanstalt* and the *Privilegierte Württembergische Bibelanstalt*) almost uniformly use versions of Mr Morison's Times New Roman, which is to this century what Garamond's was to the sixteenth. It was designed to give maximum legibility with economy, and sufficient robustness to stand up to the very large number of impressions now universal in work like Bible printing. It does not have 'beauty' in the mannered or obvious sense; but is so well calculated to fulfil its function, and well-used provides such a satisfying page, that it will be a long time before it is superseded.

This century can be said to have recovered some ground unnecessarily lost in the nineteenth century. Fully mechanized printing has reached the point of maximum economy, especially as it is practised in the United States of America, where the World Publishing Company of Cleveland, Ohio, now the world's largest producer of Bibles, uses the latest and largest machines in continual operation, worked by three daily shifts. The principal economy to be expected in the future is photographic composition, which will after 500 years eliminate the use of metal types. Function has now been so studied that the printing of the text can only be improved in the minutest detail. But in matters of overall design, and especially in the English-speaking countries, the supremacy of the Genevan model, rendered almost obligatory by the equally long-established practice of verse-division, is a severe handicap. The innate conservatism of the Bible trade means that any experiment seems doomed to financial failure. It can only be with the introduction of new versions that this ossification can be abandoned, as it was for instance in the New English Bible New Testament of 1961. The large formats for lectern use offer greater scope; there is still hope that twentieth-century printers can in this category produce something worthy to be placed beside the work of Estienne, De Tournes, Plantin and Baskerville.

CHAPTER XIII

EPILOGUE

THE CIRCULATION OF THE BIBLE

In A.D. 303 the emperor Diocletian decided to attack Christianity. Unwilling at first to have individual Christians put to death simply 'for the name', he devised means of sapping at the foundations of their corporate life in the Church; he forbade them to meet for worship and ordered that all church buildings should be destroyed, all church plate confiscated, and all liturgical books and copies of the Scriptures burned. Though the deacon Hermes of Heraclea might be confident that even if all copies of the Scriptures should disappear, Christians would be able to rewrite them from memory and to compose even more books to the honour of Christ, the more reflective must have been aware that the preservation of the authentic Bible text was necessary to the life and faith of the Church. Bibles were not quite like sacred vessels, which the generosity of the faithful could easily provide when peace came. Hence the moral problem of surrendering them was a difficult one, and in some parts of the Church, notably in Latin Africa, to hand over (*tradere*, betray) the Scriptures was regarded as an offence almost equivalent to the more obvious forms of apostasy. It is from Africa that we have a little—tantalizingly little—evidence about procedure. Magistrates were looking for corporate church property, not for private possessions. At Cirta, for example, when the Curator of the city went to the cathedral church and demanded the books, one very large codex was produced.

'Why have you given us only one codex? Bring out all the writings (scriptures) you have.' 'We have no more. We are subdeacons, the readers have the books.' 'Show us the readers.' 'We don't know where they live.' But someone gave the required information, and the magistrate went round their houses, collecting four books from one, five large and two small from another, two codices and four quires from a third, and so on: thirty-six in all from six readers.

What proportion of the Bibles or parts of Bibles then existing perished at this time we cannot tell. Some magistrates were loath to enforce the persecuting edicts, some church Bibles must have been successfully concealed, some remained safe in private hands. But if the increasing finds of early biblical papyri warn us not to exaggerate the peril of complete loss, it was certainly necessary to multiply fresh copies when peace returned and churches began quickly to grow in number. Among Constantine's benefactions were fifty vellum copies of the Bible, transcribed under the supervision of Eusebius, bishop of Caesarea, more particularly for the benefit of the churches of his new city, Constantinople. It is assumed by writers of the next hundred years that lay people can without difficulty get hold of Bibles for private study, if they will. 'Get books that will be medicines of the soul', Chrysostom told his people. 'At least procure the New Testament, the Acts of the Apostles, the Gospels.' More surprisingly perhaps, in sixth-century Gaul Caesarius of Arles can press his flock to buy the Bible and read it at home in the dark hours of winter. He does not appear to anticipate any lack of copies, or that they will be impossibly expensive for the farmer and tradesman.

No doubt subsequent centuries brought a declining production in the West, outside cathedrals and monasteries, corresponding to the decline in literacy. But the Greek Bible, in whole or part, was continually being copied in the East, and by the thirteenth century Latin Bibles of small format and at not too high a cost were being turned out on almost a factory scale at Paris. While the text of some classical writings and some Christian Fathers rests upon a handful of manuscripts, or even a single one, there are 240 uncial manuscripts of the Greek New Testament, or parts of it, some of them written in the fourth and fifth centuries.

With the invention of printing the number of Bibles in circulation increased rapidly. By A.D. 1500 at least 120 editions of the complete Bible had been published, mostly in Latin, but also in Hebrew, High and Low German, French, Italian, Catalan and Czech. Sweynheym and Pannartz of Rome printed 275 copies of their two-volume Latin Bible (1471), but by the end of the century editions were generally larger, running up to 1000 or 1500. So something like 100,000 copies had been made available in print. Luther's German New Testament appeared in 1522, and by 1533 some eighty-five editions of it had been published. By 1546, 430 whole or partial editions of Luther's version of the Bible had been put into circulation. In the city of Wittenberg sixty or more editions of the German Bible, averaging 2000 copies each, were printed between 1546 and 1600; one printer alone, Hans Lufft, is said to have produced and sold almost 100,000 copies between 1534 and 1574.

Erasmus tells us that 3000 copies of his first two editions (together) of the Greek New Testament were printed, and Tyndale started on 3000 copies of his first English one. Of the great Antwerp Polyglot of 1572 Plantin printed 960 ordinary copies, 200 better ones and fifty-three special. Very striking is the effort of Antoine Vincent, the Lyons bookseller, to provide every French Protestant with the Psalms in his own tongue. He had 27,000 copies printed at Geneva within a few months in 1561–2 and many more thousands in the same short period at Paris, Metz, Poitiers and Saint-Lô. The *Short-Title Catalogue* of English books printed up to 1640 records 284 editions of the whole Bible in English and 135 of the New Testament, besides other parts. Some of these, it is true, are only variants; on the other hand the list is by no means complete. By the seventeenth century, as we can see from Sparke's *Scintilla* (1641), an impression of 3000 was normal.

These figures are still small, compared with what was to happen later. They resemble rather the gradual acceleration of nineteenth-century Bible sales in distant lands: 5000 New Testaments for the Maoris in 1837, with reprints of 20,000 each in 1841, 1842, 1844, and many similar stories that can be elicited from Darlow and Moule's *Historical Catalogue*. Some figures for German Bibles are given in chapter IX: about 300,000 Bibles and parts of Bibles printed in Württemberg between 1675 and 1800, three million at Halle in the eighteenth century and thirty million Lutheran Bibles printed in the nineteenth century. Chapter XII gives more information regarding Bibles in English, and chapter XI regarding the publications of the Bible societies. The total world circulation by these societies of Bibles in whole or part is now about thirty million annually in over eleven hundred languages or dialects. Up to 1961, we are told, over 8,500,000 Bibles in the Revised Standard Version had been put into circulation (it appeared only in 1952) with millions of New Testaments in addition. Of the New English Bible (New Testament 1961), a first edition of a million was printed, and reprinting began at once. Moreover, Bibles have been cheap since early in the eighteenth century, when many English editions were sold at two shillings or three shillings unbound.

No other book has known anything approaching this constant circulation, for it is broadly true to say that until recently it is only Christians who have cared enough about the propagation of their beliefs to circulate books (the Roman emperors indeed circulated propagandist coins) in the way and on the scale that some States are now beginning to employ.

THE USE OF THE BIBLE

These Bibles have been used. Admittedly, very large numbers of them have been neglected or misused—handed out by colporteurs only to be treated as pieces of waste paper, placed beside beds in hotel rooms and never opened (but who knows?), served out to children in schools or prisoners in gaol with little or no effect. And they might be misused in another way, read, misinterpreted and misapplied; but that is another story. It cannot be doubted that enormous numbers of Bibles have been read with intent to profit from their reading.

WORSHIP: THE LESSONS

A primary use of the Bible is its reading in public worship. In the Jewish synagogue the central act of worship was the reading of the Law first in Hebrew and then in the vernacular with an exposition, as when Jesus read and expounded, in the synagogue at Nazareth, a passage from Isaiah: 'The Spirit of the Lord is upon me, Because he hath anointed me to preach the gospel to the poor;... This day is this scripture fulfilled in your ears.' Round this were gathered psalmody and prayer. The Christian Church, naturally influenced by Jewish practice, developed it in two ways: in the liturgy of the Holy Communion and in the daily Offices. From an early date—perhaps long before Justin Martyr first mentions it in the middle of the second century—the Sunday gathering included the reading of 'the memoirs of the apostles and the writings of the prophets as time permits', following upon which the President preached to the people on the truths contained in the lessons. As Tertullian wrote somewhat later, 'We meet together to bring to mind the divine writings, if current events make us derive a warning from them or recognize some fulfilment of them. In any case, we nourish our faith with the holy words, lift up our hope, confirm our confidence, and establish our discipline by impressing the precepts.'

The determination of fixed patterns of lesson-reading in different parts of the Church is too complicated a story to be told here. The synagogue readings had been regulated. In Palestine, at one time, the Pentateuch was read through consecutively in the Sabbath and week-day readings in the course of three years, with specially prescribed readings for the four Sabbaths before Passover and for certain festivals and fast-days. Christian practice was more complicated. Thus in the Clementine Liturgy of the fourth century lections are taken in sequence from (1) the Law, (2) the historical books, (3) the wisdom books, (4) the Prophets, (5) the Acts, (6) the Epistles, (7) the Gospels; they were read in pairs with Psalms sung between each pair. Lessons might be both numerous and long. In a Syriac lectionary of the sixth century analysed by F. C. Burkitt, the Ascension Day services (not all eucharistic) called for sixteen readings, a total of 444 verses, and there were thirteen lessons on a more ordinary occasion, the last Sunday after Pentecost. In the Greek Orthodox Church the lections were eventually reduced to two, normally Epistle and Gospel, with an Old Testament passage, or another from the New, in addition to or in place of the Epistle at certain seasons; though the Coptic rite retained four New Testament lessons, and the Armenian one from the Old Testament as well as Epistle and Gospel. The West clung for a time to the scheme of three lessons, but from the sixth century the Roman and Ambrosian liturgies normally provided only for the Epistle and Gospel; the Gallican rite kept three lessons, and so did the Mozarabic, used in Spain, and Celtic rites. Where the Old Testament lection was lost, the Christian sense of the unity of the Bible was to that extent impaired, but there was some compensation in simplicity and emphasis.

Side by side with the Eucharist went the development of the Divine Office from its roots in Jewish devotion. 'In the evening and at morning, and at noonday will I pray', said the Psalmist (lv. 18), and for many this was basic, while some might aspire to the 'Seven times a day do I praise thee' of another Psalm (cxix. 164). Tertullian and others of his age speak of prayer at the third, sixth and ninth hours which marked the principal divisions of the day, and gradually what had been commended for private prayer came to be organized as daily public worship, a simple form for the laity and secular clergy, something more elaborate for monks. At such services, the details of which do not concern us now, the Psalms were sung and lessons might be read from the Bible. In time, the necessary material was gathered into the Breviary or Book of Hours. Some of the older Breviaries show how at one time the Bible had been read through systematically in the course of the year, with, for example, Genesis begun on Septuagesima Sunday and Jeremiah read during Passiontide; but in the later Middle Ages, with the increase in the number of festivals, the elaboration of services and the general abandonment of the Offices (or at least public attendance at them) to clergy and monks, the tendency was to reduce the quantity of Scripture read to lections of a verse or two, mere reminders of what might be charitably assumed to be familiar to all present. Thus in the Roman Breviary of the fifteenth century the reading of Genesis in Septuagesima week did not even complete chapter two; on the other hand non-biblical lessons, many of them purely legendary, were much in evidence. Even before the Reformation dissatisfaction was widespread. While some deprecated the extent of the unscriptural lessons, others disliked the repetition of a few Psalms at the expense of the remainder. Accordingly, Cardinal Quiñones, commissioned by Pope Clement VII to reform the Breviary, both simplified the Offices and restored a more regular recitation of the Psalter and a more continuous reading of the Bible. So Genesis (to keep the same example) was once more read in full from Septuagesima onwards. When his Breviary first appeared in 1535 it was enthusiastically welcomed in some quarters—witness its six editions—and hotly criticized in others, particularly at the Sorbonne. A revised form, published in 1537, removed some of the opposition and went through several editions; it was welcomed by busy clergy. However, the more revolutionary elements in it smacked too much of the ideas of the reformers, and it was condemned and suppressed by the Council of Trent. It left its mark upon the later Roman Breviary, upon the Book of Common Prayer, and upon the worship of the Reformed churches.

All the churches of the Reformation laid increased emphasis upon the ministry of the Word, and this not only for edification, but also in worship. Here the Word must be free to act sacramentally, bringing the worshipper into the presence of God.

In the proper Lutheran Sunday service, the Mass, the lessons are the Epistle and Gospel, but hymns based closely on Scripture and a sermon expounding the Word are essential parts of the whole act of worship. In Scandinavian churches the sermons are preached from a set series of prescribed texts; such a text may be quite long, almost providing a further lesson. In Germany the use of the old scheme of lessons (the pericopes) became a matter of controversy which has had a long and fluctuating history. Since Calvin opposed the pericope system, it was dropped by the Reformed churches and a variety of uses was adopted. In Zwinglian churches the Epistle and Gospel were always the same: I Cor. xi. 20–9 and John vi. 47–63; in the German Mass at Strassburg about 1525 the Epistle is either Gal. iii. 3–14 or one chosen by the priest, and 'sometimes instead of the Gospel (John vi. 41–58), one of the Gospels may be chosen and each Sunday a part of a chapter expounded' (not 'such a small and imperfect fragment as it has been the custom to have in the popish Church'); Calvin omitted the Epistle as such, and had the Bible read in course on Sundays, a chapter or more at a time, a practice which was adopted, through John Knox, by the Church of Scotland. Other passages of Scripture, such as the Ten Commandments and the Comfortable Words, were introduced into the liturgy of the Holy Communion. Though the Offices, in their old form, were abandoned by Lutheran and Calvinistic churches alike, provision was freely made for weekday meetings in which Scripture-reading bulked large, and there were many informal gatherings to hear the Bible read in the vernacular. The net effect must have been a considerable increase in the people's knowledge of the content of Scripture.

The Book of Common Prayer of the Church of England has retained the Epistle and Gospel of the Holy Communion. From Advent to Trinity they commemorate the life and ministry of Christ on earth, his death, resurrection and ascension, and the sending of the Holy Spirit, culminating in the commemoration of the Trinity. From Trinity to Advent Sunday the Epistles have, on the whole, a moral and practical bearing, and the Gospels have been frequently chosen to go with them. Most of these Epistles and Gospels are the traditional ones, taken largely from the Sarum Missal. The Sarum Epistles and Gospels had already been published in English, and a step towards vernacular services had been taken when, in 1538, certain bishops ordered that they should be read in English at the Mass itself. The Church of England also retained the Divine Office, simplified to daily Mattins and Evensong, and in these the reading of the Scriptures was to have a great part since (we are told) 'the ancient Fathers...so ordered the matter that all the whole

Bible (or the greatest part thereof) should be read over once every year' for the edification of clergy and people alike. But this godly and decent order has been altered, so that 'commonly when any Book of the Bible was begun, after three or four Chapters were read out, all the rest were unread. And in this sort the Book of Isaiah was begun in Advent, and the Book of Genesis in Septuagesima: but they were only begun, and never read through: after like sort were other Books of holy Scripture used'. In the new order, therefore, the Psalms should be read straight through once a month, the Old Testament, omitting a few passages, once a year, the New three times a year, except the Apocalypse, from which only selections were made. Special lessons, interrupting the reading by course, were provided for a few festivals, but not for Sundays. The Prayer Book of 1559 introduced special lessons for Sundays, and there have been several fresh lectionaries since then. If it is mechanically enforced, the principle of continuous reading can produce inopportune results, and, in any case, distinction between a weekday and a Sunday series, with adequate special provision for festivals, is essential. But the alternative, an anthology principle, has its own weaknesses and dangers.

WORSHIP: SERMONS

The Bible is not only *read* in Christian worship; the Word of God is preached, as it has been from the beginning. This needs no explanation. There was the Jewish precedent for expounding and applying the portion of the Scriptures which had been read. In addition, before any Christian books had been written, there was the need to proclaim the new truth in Christ—the *kerygma*, the Gospel. The Old Testament itself, now claimed as a Christian book, had to be interpreted afresh to show how the Gospel and the Messiah had been prepared for and prophesied, and before long the writings of the apostles and their circle required explanation. Sermons, therefore, have always been in principle a part of Christian *worship*, though sometimes neglected, and as a part of worship they are in principle a means of proclaiming, interpreting and bringing home the practical implications of the Word of God, whether or not they take the form of direct expositions of particular passages.

Preaching in the early Church was, in its own way, very biblical: a strange way, sometimes, to modern ears, with the extreme allegorization which admitted so much that was subjective and fanciful, more eisegesis than exegesis. Yet even this element in it sprang from an acknowledged obligation to justify everything that the preacher wanted to say from Scripture or to find a Christian meaning for passages which, taken literally, seemed quite intractable. Sometimes, perhaps usually, preaching kept to the liturgical Gospel of the day for its starting-point; sometimes preachers took whole books and expounded them minutely over a period of time, often on weekdays. Sufficient to mention such outstanding examples as Origen's homilies, much used by later Fathers, St Augustine's 124 *Tractatus in Joannis Evangelium* and *Enarrationes in Psalmos*, and St John Chrysostom's less allegorical expositions of most of the New Testament. Such sermons either presuppose or are intended to communicate (doubtless something of both) a not inconsiderable knowledge of the biblical text on the part of their lay hearers.

That there was a decline from these high standards both in constancy of preaching and in the quality of the sermons cannot be denied. In the Greek Church (or so it is often said) participation in the rich liturgy of the Eucharist overwhelmed the preaching of the Word. In the West the upheavals caused by the barbarian invasions left a mass of people who needed the simplest instruction, and did not always get it. Caesarius of Arles, himself a very practical preacher for the plain man, never ceased to press his suffragan bishops in Gaul to preach more often. If they, or their clergy, could not compose fresh sermons, let them preach the good old ones; and he obligingly compiled collections for them to use. His people, it appears, were eager enough to hear sermons, though they sometimes distressed him by leaving the church immediately afterwards. Gregory the Great too, is fully conscious of the importance of biblical preaching. Homilies of the Fathers were introduced among the lessons of the Offices, and there must always have been much preaching to monks. What the ordinary people received, and how much, is largely unknown to us, though the strenuous efforts of Charlemagne and his episcopal advisers to revive elementary instruction through vernacular sermons suggests that preaching had dropped to a very low level. The Blickling Homilies illustrate post-Carolingian vernacular preaching in England, and allow us a momentary glimpse of the way the Bible was being used. These are nineteen Old English sermons of the tenth century, mostly composed for special days—the Annunciation, Quinquagesima, Palm Sunday, Easter Day, etc. Several of them are very biblical. That for Ascension Day, for instance, contains a detailed exposition of Acts i. 8–11, while others, without being expository, set out central biblical themes or tell a biblical story. Others, however, are completely unbiblical. That for the Assumption tells a story without any indication that it is not taken from the Bible; Pilate's report on the Crucifixion is included in another without warning that it is not scriptural, and the legend of St Andrew is related as if it were on a par with the biblical account of John the Baptist. In this we may see a serious threat to a biblical Christianity, a threat which was intensified in the centuries which followed by the media of Christian art, such as windows and wall-paintings. Most people had no means of knowing what was, and what was not, in the Bible. When preaching was revived by the zeal of the Friars, it still lacked a firm biblical control and, to that extent, it had lost its original purpose, despite the many benefits it could still bestow. Good as it was that, with their colloquial diction, their anecdotes and *exempla*, the Friars should have restored the sermon to general favour, the recall to the Bible sounded by Wycliffe and later by the reformers was altogether necessary if the Christian faith as understood by the people was not to stray further and further from its origin or degenerate into mere moralism.

The principles of the Reformation and the importance attached to the preaching of the Word have been sufficiently described elsewhere in this volume. To Luther (who wrote a good deal!) the Church is not a pen-house, but a mouth-house. The Gospel, proclaimed *viva voce*, has converting-power; preaching is a means of grace; Word and Sacrament must not be sundered. Besides preaching on the Sunday Gospels, many of the reformers preached their way through whole books as Chrysostom had done. At Zurich Zwingli expounded Matthew, Acts, I–II Timothy, Galatians, I Peter, Hebrews, Genesis; and in his first twelve years Bullinger expounded nearly all the books of the Bible. The intention to be faithful to Scripture may be illustrated from William Perkins's *Art of Prophesying*, first published in Latin in 1592 and much used in England for a century. He gives in summary form the order and sum of the sacred and only method of preaching:

(1) To read the text distinctly out of the canonical Scriptures;

(2) To give the sense and understanding of it being read, by the Scripture itself;

(3) To collect a few and profitable points of doctrine out of the natural sense;

(4) To apply (if he have the gift) the doctrines rightly collected to the life and manners of men in a simple and plain speech.

Though the words chosen may have been simple and plain, the reasoning was often very close, with much subdivision and precise distinctions, recalling scholastic methods of disputation. 'The text is first to be accurately divided', said John Dod, a very popular preacher, in his rules for preaching. Whatever may be thought of the method, it is evident that sermons were closely followed by the congregation, and knowledge of Scripture both inculcated and exercised.

Where taste differed, as with the Catholic congregations of France listening to Bossuet or Massillon or with the hearers of South and Tillotson after (as Burnet said) the impertinent way of dividing texts had been laid aside—where, that is, a sermon was more likely to pick on some leading idea and develop it, a less meticulous wrestling with the *ipsissima verba* of Scripture was required, and discussion after service might turn rather on the value of the 'lesson' than the correctness of the exegesis. But it must not be concluded that such sermons, even the moral discourses of the eighteenth century, were unscriptural. If they are sampled in sufficient numbers it will be found that, though a certain proportion of them pay little attention to the Bible once they have got started and though few of them, perhaps, are what Luther understood by preaching the Word, the regular hearer of them was still kept in touch with the narratives and the teachings of Scripture. This is no place for a history of preaching. The immediate point is that, whatever ups and downs there have been in the quality of sermons, whatever fluctuations in the conception of their proper nature and function, the total effect of continuous preaching throughout the centuries in making the Bible known (we are not yet concerned with any other results) has been great beyond calculation.

SCHOOLS

Another major means of promoting the knowledge of the Bible has been the school. One might indeed say, in reverse, that the Bible has promoted the school in the cultural area with which these volumes are concerned. At first is was not so. Though the Jews were compelled by their own exclusiveness, and perhaps also by the fact that their sacred books were not in a common tongue, to keep their special schools in being, Christians used the public schools of the Roman Empire. The faith must be taught in church and in the family, pagan influences must be counteracted at home. But even the rigorist Tertullian conceded that the Christian child must go to the ordinary school for his general education. Even when Christians were in power, they did not establish a new educational system with new methods and new text-books, eliminating the classics. Broadly speaking, though objections are heard, they took the risk. There was more objection to participation in pagan higher education. Monasteries received children to train as monks, and bishops provided for the training of readers who should proceed in course to higher orders. To some extent such vocational schools were opened to other children, but so far as the scanty evidence allows us to judge, this was nothing like a common practice under the Empire. St Basil was willing to have some 'secular' children in his houses, a concession which might have proved important, had not the Council of Chalcedon put a stop to it. Caesarius of Arles would not allow his nuns to receive girls for their education if they intended to return to the world. There was very little wish to promote a liberal education for its own sake. Rather, there was enough fear of pagan philosophy and literature to expose the Church to the charge of obscurantism. Nevertheless, the necessity of an informed clergy who could explain the faith and expound its Scriptures was recognized, and so was the desirability of a people sufficiently literate to read the Bible for themselves. To a certain extent the former depends upon the latter, since all ordinands cannot be pre-selected. What was intended primarily for the training of the clergy broadened out into a system of elementary education when the State could no longer provide it. One landmark is the Council of Vaison, 529, which instructed the parish priests (that is, no longer only the bishops) to take children as *lectores* and educate them. It is unlikely that much notice was taken of this in Merovingian Gaul, but Charlemagne and his bishops made considerable efforts to promote elementary education, and Alfred followed this up in England. Not that literacy was ever common in medieval Europe, and the Church may possibly be blamed for not having done more. What most children learnt, they had got by rote, not by reading; and what most men knew of the Bible came to them *viva voce* or through art. Still, a beginning had been made, and schools of one kind or another gradually became a normal part of living.

Many reasons contributed to the growth of schools from the sixteenth century, and the general history has often been told. It is difficult to discover how much direct study of the Bible went on in the grammar schools, since, though a religious basis for education was usually taken for granted, the original evidence and modern studies of the subject are mainly concerned with the general and secular elements in the curriculum. In England the opportunity to establish widespread elementary education was lost (so at least A. F. Leach has argued) when the revenues of the suppressed chantries were not applied to that end under Edward VI. So knowledge of the text of Scripture had still to be acquired, by most people, through hearing. Now, however, in Protestant countries especially, they could hear it read in the vernacular. In Scotland, although the aspirations of the first reformers could not at once be realized, many ministers conducted schools in their parishes and 'did bring it about in the Lowland counties that many people, who could not write, could at least read, that the Bible, which was the main text-book of the school, became also the main reading at home' (S. Mechie, *The Church and Scottish Social Development*, p. 136). In England and Wales, long before the State provided for education, the Charity schools, from about 1700, and the Sunday schools, from about 1780, and the elementary schools of the National Society (Anglican, from 1811) and the British and Foreign School Society (undenominational, from 1814, following up Lancaster's work) were teaching thousands of children to read, and in particular to read the Bible. As education this was limited; the immediate point is simply that the Bible became familiar through it. Similarly in the mission field there has always been a strong urge both to produce the Bible in the vernacular and to train converts to read it. It is impossible to assess the effects of Scripture lessons in the State schools of modern times: it depends on so many factors, including the general climate of thought. No doubt the 'wastage' is very great. Experience of Certificate and similar examining suggests that in secondary schools, while poor results are common, a great deal of fruitful work is done, and side by side with much apathy, there is evidence of a serious interest among teachers in fresh methods of 'teaching the Bible'.

Epilogue

PRIVATE BIBLE READING

From church and school to the home. 'In the poorest cottage is a book wherein for several thousands of years the spirit of man has found light and nourishment and an interpreting response to whatever is deepest in him.' Carlyle's words can scarcely be taken literally, nor can the extent of their truth be checked. On the other hand, it would be foolish to discount the significance and influence of private Bible reading. In New Testament thought the purpose of God and the Gospel of salvation are indeed mysteries, but a mystery is a secret which has now been, or is being, revealed. The key to the true meaning of the Scriptures of the Old Covenant is given to men in Christ. Just as every Jew was instructed to read those Scriptures for himself, so now must the Christian read the same sacred books in a new light (*the* new Light), together with the new Scriptures of his Church which explain the old, and are also, in a sense, explained by the old. There was a risk in so disseminating the Bible and encouraging the simple layman to read it. Heresies came thick and fast, and commonly tried to substantiate themselves from the authority of the Bible; or sometimes they caused confusion by questioning the status or the text of particular books. Marcion's knife massacred Scripture. There must have been a temptation to lay down as an official ecclesiastical principle that the sacred books were only for the pundits, the clergy, the scholars. Certainly the Church was compelled to establish safeguards for a correct or orthodox interpretation (with all the problems that involves us in) by stressing the apostolic preaching or tradition, by propounding baptismal creeds and rules of faith (*Regula Fidei*, *Regula Veritatis*) which no exegesis of Scripture must contradict, and, later on, by conciliar decrees against heresies; and certainly there was an expectation that the layman would be guided by his bishop (one sees this early and plainly in Ignatius), who was presumed to be a safe guardian of the apostolic faith. But even amidst the confusions of Gnosticism, the drastic step of denying Scripture to the layman was never taken. On the contrary he was for some centuries spurred on to spend a large part of his time in reading it—and not infrequently he thought the demands unreasonable!

Harnack's *Bible-Reading in the Early Church* (Eng. trans. 1912) provides some valuable illustrations. At a very early date we have whole congregations assumed to know, or enjoined to know, the Scriptures. Clement of Rome may, but need not, have the presbyters chiefly in mind when he writes to the church of Corinth about A.D. 95 and says, simply, 'You know the Scriptures'; Polycarp, not much later, writes to the church of Philippi, 'I trust you are well exercised in the Scriptures'; Irenaeus wants every Christian to eat of every scripture of the Lord, which is the right way to understand the words of Genesis, 'Of every tree of this paradise shall ye eat' (pp. 39, 40, 53). Clement of Alexandria speaks of Scripture readings at home before the chief meal of the day, and wants married people to study the Bible together (pp. 55–6), and from the *De Virginitate* falsely ascribed to Clement of Rome (perhaps third-century) we learn of visits to Christian homes to read the Scriptures. They are mentioned also in the third-century *Didascalia*: Meditate on the words of the Lord continually. If you are rich, and do not need to work for your living, do not wander about wasting your time, but zealously visit your Christian brethren, and meditate on the saving words with them, and learn them. Otherwise, stay at home and read right through the Law and the Histories and the Prophets, and the Gospel which fulfils them all. The *Didascalia* continues with exhortation to avoid heathen literature. In the Bible Christians can find all they need, history, philosophy, poetry, law, science (that is, in Genesis, the beginning of the world). Chrysostom also, at a later date, recommends calling one's neighbours together and reading the Bible with them. Children, too, should be introduced to the Scriptures at an early age. They might make biblical names with their letter blocks, Jerome suggests (*Ep.* 107), and should soon learn the Psalms by heart. 'Place every book of Holy Scripture in the hands of children', is an instruction of the fourth-century Apostolic Constitutions (*op. cit.* pp. 59, 126, 123). In one of his letters (32) Paulinus of Nola describes a 'reading-room' annexed to a church: 'Hic poterit residens sacris intendere libris.' Bibles, or portions, appear to have been available at prices not beyond the reach of the ordinary man, if he was prepared to make some sacrifice. They are a Christian's tools, says Chrysostom, and he cannot afford to go without them. Only the utterly destitute can be excused from possessing them, and they must go assiduously to church to hear the Bible read (*Hom. III de Lazaro*). Besides being read in church, the Bible is distributed by sales, says Augustine ('venalis ferri per publicum', *Enarr. in Psalm.* xxxvi, 1:3), and the stichometry of A.D. 359 was 'drawn up by a publisher of Bibles... in order that the purchaser might not be cheated by unprincipled book-sellers' (*op. cit.* pp. 112, 98, 99, 97). It has already been remarked that Caesarius of Arles could still expect his flock to buy Bibles and read them at home.

It is not to be supposed that these exhortations were always heeded. Some of Chrysostom's appeals were elicited precisely by the complaint that the Church's demands were unrealistic and unnecessary. 'I am tied by the law-courts, I have public business to see to, I am a trades-man, I have a wife, children, a household to look after, I am a man of the world, it is not my business to read the Bible; leave that to those who have forsaken the world' (*De Laz.* III). Chrysostom of course replies that the man in the world has even greater need of the guidance of Scripture. The principle is plain: in the formative years of the Christian Church the Bible was available in the vernacular, it was open, the laity, men, women and children, were expected both to hear it read in church and to read it for themselves at home.

The barbarian invasions changed the situation in Europe, catastrophically in some places, gradually in others. The Church had to deal with an illiterate population, many of them pagans or heretics (Arians) or merely nominal Christians. It is understandable, and it may have been inevitable, that it fell back more and more upon the authority of the clergy and upon instruction in simple formulae of belief and practice. The danger was—and many will think it was not escaped—that these methods would be persisted in too long. However that may be, a time came when the demand for vernacular Bibles and freedom for the laity to read them could no longer be resisted. In England many stories are told (no doubt they could be paralleled elsewhere) of people's desire to hear the Bible read in their own tongue or to possess copies of their own, of the gatherings in churches for informal readings which worried the still dubious bishops. Let one tale stand for the rest (Pollard, *Records of the English Bible*, pp. 268–71, from Brit. Mus. Harley MS. 590). William Maldon was about fifteen when Henry VIII ordered that the Bible should be set up in the parish churches (1538). Immediately after, he says, divers poor men in Chelmsford bought the New Testament and on Sundays 'did sit reading in lower end of church, and many would flock about them to hear them reading of that glad and sweet tidings of the Gospel'. William's father objected to his regular attendance at this, so 'then thought I I will learn to read English, and then will I have the New Testament and read thereon myself, and then had I learned an English Primer as far as patris sapientia, and then on Sundays I plied my English Primer. The Maytide following I and my father's prentice, Thomas Jeffray, laid our money together and bought the New Testament in English, and hid it in our bedstraw and so exercised it at convenient times'. As early as 1536 Bishop Foxe could say in Convocation, 'The lay people do know the Holy Scriptures better than many of us'. In 1538 Cranmer's injunctions to the clergy of Hereford Diocese, *sede vacante*, include the requirement that none of you 'shall discourage any layman from the reading of the Bible in Latin or English, but encourage them to it, admonishing them that they so read it for reformation of their own life and knowledge of their duty; and that they be not bold or presumptuous in judging of matters afore they have perfect knowledge'. The risk is acknowledged, but it is taken, and Cranmer's preface to the Great Bible appeals to the ancient Fathers in support of his injunction. Every one, said Bishop Hooper, 'of what degree so ever he be, should cause his family and children to read some part of the Bible for their erudition, to know God'. With increasing literacy and a plentiful supply of Bibles, Genevan or Authorized, the Puritans could demand even more, and did so, with results that must be touched on later. The Puritan sermon was based solely upon the authority of Scripture, the preacher expected his congregation to apply a biblical test to it, and the laity were encouraged to discuss it afterwards, often with copies or notes which they had made during the service. And that it was not only the Puritans who became familiar with the words of Scripture is evident from its use in writings of all kinds as a universe of discourse which readers, or listeners to speeches, were assumed to be able to follow. As Godfrey Davies has written of the early seventeenth century: 'At that time Englishmen studied the Bible with an intensity probably never equalled, and it is hardly possible to read a speech or writing of any length without perceiving its indebtedness to the Authorized Version' (*The Early Stuarts*, 1937, p. 404). Milton follows, and Cromwell and Bunyan, portraying Christian with a Book in his hand, the Methodists, the Evangelicals, and, with Wilkie's painting of *The Cottar's Saturday Night* to remind us of Scotland, back again to Carlyle and the tradition of Victorian Bible reading. Many Bibles were kept only for show

(Chrysostom had already complained of that), and many had dust on them, as Spurgeon lamented; but the quantity of Bible reading, though incapable of measurement, must have been very great.

It was supported by the reading of sermons, books of devotion, and commentaries on the Bible. The *Short Title Catalogue* and its continuation by Wing quickly reveal the immense quantity of sermons that was published, and the frequency with which they ran into a very respectable number of editions. This was by no means limited to the productions of the Puritans, for the plain style advocated by Tillotson created or met a new taste. The first volume of Tillotson's *Sermons* had already gone into eight editions, and the second into five, before Chiswell paid 2500 guineas (a large sum then for any literary work) for the right to bring out his fourteen-volume edition of 1695–1704; his complete works reached a tenth edition in 1735, and several more afterwards, and a selection of *Twenty Discourses* was in its fourth edition in 1779. Robert South's sermons, preached and published in the seventeenth century, were collected in an eleven-volume edition in 1737–44, and there were new editions in 1823, 1843 and 1865. The great preachers of the nineteenth century—Newman, Robertson of Brighton, Liddon, Spurgeon (to mention English ones only)—have been read by far more people than ever heard them speak. Commentaries, one supposes, go more often to the minister's study, but some kinds of commentary or annotated Bible have enjoyed an immense popularity. In 1708 Matthew Henry, a Presbyterian minister at Chester, began the publication of his *Exposition of the Old and New Testaments*, a devotional and practical commentary which found its way into innumerable homes. It has been repeatedly republished (for example, 1844, 1846, 1857, 1867, 1868, 1878); it was published in a five-volume edition in New York, 1896, again in one volume as recently as 1960. A favourite family Bible was that illustrated from the notes of Stackhouse, Henry and others, published in 1806 and then in frequent editions until it became the Royal Family Bible in 1862. Equally popular was the annotated Bible of Thomas Scott, 'the commentator', an Anglican, whose labours and financial worries are described in Sir James Stephens's *Essays in Ecclesiastical Biography*. Beginning in 1788, his notes were published in weekly numbers, totalling 174. It was calculated that £199,900 was 'paid in his lifetime across the counter' for Scott's theological publications—very little of it to Scott himself—

and his Bible, with notes whose special value lay in the minute comparison of each passage with others which might illustrate its meaning, was reprinted every few years for a long time.

There is another side to the story. It would probably be possible to produce a devastating picture of ignorance, especially in great cities since the Industrial Revolution. Sir George Bell writes that when he was a lieutenant in the Peninsular War, 'I never saw a Bible nor do I remember ever seeing anyone read the Bible, although that is *the* book'. Later, as lieutenant-colonel in the West Indies, he started a Bible class for his battalion (*Soldier's Glory*, 1956, pp. 96, 176). Today it is difficult to balance the extraordinary sales of the Bible against the common reports of almost complete ignorance of it, despite universal, compulsory and free education. Basil Willey went so far as to say, in the 1954 Bible Supplement to *The Times*, that since the Bible societies began their work (*post*, not *propter hoc*!) 'the dissemination of Bibles has proceeded in inverse ratio to the amount of Bible reading done at home'. The school now becomes of major importance. Quite apart from the religious issues, it will be an absurd failure in educational perspective if generations grow up in ignorance of one of the foundations of western civilization.

THE INFLUENCE OF THE BIBLE

What, then, has been the effect of all this Bible reading upon the habits and culture of the western world? A question easy to ask, impossible to answer. To begin with, there is not usually the evidence, the direct evidence of the inner mind of writer or artist or statesman or of the ordinary man taking moral decisions in his daily life. We may know in a general way that so-and-so was a Christian, knew his Bible; only rarely, in proportion to the vast sum of human actions, can we say quite definitely that the thing said or written or done was beyond question determined by the Bible. Often we may conclude that it was so, or regard it as highly probable, or guess it, in view of the influences likely to have borne upon particular cases. Here, however, our own approach to such a judgment has its subjective aspect, affected by our own estimate of the power of the Bible. To the Christian it is of faith that all good things come ultimately from God, and he believes the Bible to be God's special instrument for giving those things, for bringing men into a condition capable of receiving and doing good things. He may be puzzled about the theology of natural man, natural virtues, natural sciences; he may highly esteem the achievements of China or India, Greece or Rome. But at least where the Bible has been at work, he can hardly help presupposing that in large measure thought and action which, on the face of it, might have been inspired by the Bible, were in fact so inspired.

There is another difficulty. When there is evidence or high probability that certain thoughts or actions or ways of life were rooted in Christianity, it is still hard to distinguish between the over-all influence of the Church and Christian tradition and the immediate impact of the Bible. And this is not a book about, nor this chapter an essay on, Christianity in general. Beyond that lies the mystery of what might have been—the impossibility of knowing how our civilization would have developed from Graeco-Roman elements only, or from a mixture of these with oriental but non-biblical cultures, or just what contribution would have been made by Teuton or Slav if they had never come into contact with Church and Bible. On such matters it is not supposed that what follows can be objective or omniscient, or even systematic. It can be no more than a few reflections and suggestions within a very limited knowledge and perspective.

LITERATURE

Before literature there must be language, and it is a help if the language has been reduced to writing. Outside the western world, eagerness for a vernacular Bible has frequently been the cause of this reduction. It was so in Armenia and Georgia and Ethiopia, and in the work of Cyril and Methodius for Slavonic. It happens again and again in modern missionary work. In other instances a vernacular Bible has given new life to a language, a new impulse to vernacular literature, as in Egypt and Syria and Mesopotamia, where Coptic and Syriac had ceased to be literary languages since the time of Alexander the Great. In the ancient West, the Germanic languages owed their first alphabet and their first literary monument to the missionary labours of Ulfilas, who began the translation of the Scriptures into Gothic. But Greek and Latin language and literature preceded, if not the Old Testament, at least the dissemination of the Bible by the Christian Church, and in these respects the Church must for a long time be the learner. Yet pupils instruct their teachers. The Bible and the Christian faith brought new words, new images, new ways of thinking, new themes for meditation, new problems to be wrestled with. In his *Confessions* St Augustine added a profound and original masterpiece to Latin letters which could not have been written without the Bible. Observe the biblical perspective of its opening, and the immediate introduction of the biblical paradox of divine prevenience and human aspiration:

Great art Thou, O Lord, and highly to be praised; great is Thy power, and Thy wisdom infinite. And Thee would man praise; man, but a particle of Thy creation, man that bears about him his mortality, the witness of his sin, the witness that Thou resistest the proud; yet would man praise Thee, he but a particle of Thy creation. Thou awakest him to delight in praising Thee, for Thou has made us for Thyself, and our heart is restless until it rests in Thee. Grant me, Lord, to know and understand which is first, to call upon Thee or to praise Thee, to know Thee or to call upon Thee. But who calls upon Thee without knowing Thee? If he did not know Thee, he might be calling upon another than Thee. Or is it rather that Thou art called upon in order that Thou mayest be known? But how shall they call upon Him in whom they have not believed? or how do they believe without a preacher? And they that seek the Lord shall praise Him. For in seeking Him they find Him, and in finding Him they shall praise Him. Let me seek Thee, Lord, in calling upon Thee, and let me call upon Thee believing in Thee. For Thou hast been preached to us. My faith calls upon Thee, Lord, the faith which Thou hast inspired in me through the manhood of Thy Son and the ministry of Thy preacher.[1]

Greatness in art and literature is a thorny problem. It is not determined by the 'subject-matter', yet the theme can enter into it. In letters, as in the graphic arts, the Bible has 'inspired' far more rubbish than greatness—but so has love. One must distinguish between works which are biblical in that they retell Bible stories or depict Bible scenes and those which, without much direct reference to the Bible, could not be what they are without it. Not many—not as many as one might expect—of the greatest achievements of post-classical literature are biblical in the direct sense, among the very greatest perhaps only *Paradise Lost*. Otherwise, in epic, where biblical subjects might have

[1] Pusey's translation, modified. 'Call upon Thee' really means, 'call Thee to me'. The preacher mentioned at the end is St Ambrose.

seemed attractive, the best poets have turned elsewhere, Christian though they may have been, like Camoens, Tasso and Spenser. It is on the lower slopes that the Bible stories are found: Vida's *Christiad*, Du Bartas's *La Semaine* and *Judith*, Sylvester's *Bethulian's Rescue*, the French biblical epics of the seventeenth century, Cowley's *Davideis*, Klopstock's *Messias*. In modern literature only Thomas Mann's handling of the patriarchal narratives stands out.

The developing drama, so much tied to the Bible (or, rather, the subjects suggested by the Bible) in the Middle Ages, came up against a change of taste, to classical themes, and a change in religious feeling. In Paris the mysteries were suppressed in 1548. Biblical dramas were written in great numbers to replace the old forms, particularly among Protestants in France and Germany. For the details one may go to Hardin Craig's *English Religious Drama of the Middle Ages* (Oxford, 1955), where we are told of twenty-five or more plays on Joseph in French, as many in Italian, and others in Spanish, Dutch and German; of the plays on Judith—eight Latin, twenty French, twenty-six Italian, twenty-three German; of plays on Esther in Latin, French, Italian, Spanish, Dutch, German, Greek, Swedish, Polish, Czech, Hebrew, English; of collections of biblical plays in Latin, perhaps for school use, like the *Terentius Christianus* edited by Cornelius Schonaeus of Haarlem. Beza's *Abraham Sacrifiant* (1550) was popular, and was translated into Latin, Italian, German, Spanish and English. But these plays were mainly didactic in intention. They may have contributed something to the developing technique of the drama, but they do not appear to have had much merit in themselves as literature. Dramatists of greater power occasionally took biblical subjects—Jean de la Taille's *Saul* (1572), Garnier's *Les Juives* (1583), regarded as his best play—but the trend was strongly away from them by the end of the century. Among the Latin plays George Buchanan's *Jephthes* and *Baptistes*, both written in the 1540's, were of some importance.

Scotland took action against the biblical drama by an Act of the General Assembly in 1575: 'Forasmuch as it is considered that the playing of clerk-plays, comedies or tragedies, upon the canonical parts of the Scripture induceth and bringeth with it a contempt and profanation of the same, it is thought meet and concluded that no clerk-plays, comedies or tragedies, be made upon canonical Scriptures, other New or Old, in time coming, other upon the Lord's Day or upon a work day.' Nothing so absolute happened in England, where the medieval mysteries and moralities were succeeded by a number of biblical interludes. There were the plays of John Bale, half of them on biblical themes and mostly lost. There were plays, of various kinds, on Jacob and Esau, Godly Queen Hester, King Darius, on Adam and Absalom, on Joseph and Joshua and Judas, on Samson, Susannah and Tobias, on Mary Magdalen and Pontius Pilate, and several on the Prodigal Son. Most of the early biblical plays have not survived. Whatever we may think of the literary value of those which we know—and at least their experiments have a technical importance—the movement which produced them is significant as an attempt to communicate the Bible and, no doubt, to provide in its stories a counterpart and challenge to the pagan themes of the classical revival. In this respect it may have had more immediate success than we can now judge. But such plays were not to become a normal feature of the English stage. One cannot but remark the lack of similar works by the greater dramatists of the Elizabethan and Jacobean age. Arthur Golding translated Beza's *Abraham* (1575, published 1577) and Dekker adapted Buchanan's *Jephthes* (it is not extant). *A Looking Glass for London*, by Greene and Lodge, is a late morality on the Prodigal Son, George Peele wrote his *David and Bethsabe* (published 1599). In quantity, this does not amount to much, even if we add Henry Chettle's *Tobyas* and Samuel Rowley's *Joshua* on the evidence of Henslowe's *Diary*. Nor did the early fashion return. To go back for a moment to France, Corneille took no biblical subjects; Racine's *Esther* and *Athalie* were his last plays, written for a young ladies' school (this is no aspersion on their quality) after he had abandoned the professional stage. It was not substantially different in Germany, where the greatest dramatists have not often worked with biblical subjects.

One or two examples must suffice to illustrate less direct uses of the Bible. The *Divine Comedy* is a Christian poem, and not in the above sense a biblical one. It is built upon and held together by a theological system. But the Bible is everywhere at work, by citation, in image and in persons, and sometimes architectonically, as in *Paradiso* XXIII–XXVI where, following upon the vision of the host of the redeemed, St Peter, St Paul and St John examine Dante concerning Faith, Hope and Love. The Bible is not decoration to the theology of the poem; you cannot abstract from it:

La larga ploia
dello Spirito Santo, ch'è diffusa
in sulle vecchie e in sulle nuove cuoia,

which brings conviction beyond any logical demonstration:

Ed a tal creder non ho io pur prove
fisice e metafisice, ma dalmi
anco la verità che quinci piove
Per Moisè, per profeti, e per salmi,
per l'Evangelio, e per voi che scriveste,
poichè l'ardente Spirto vi fece almi.

Spenser's *Faerie Queene* is a romantic epic, much indebted to Italian poets very different from Dante. But it, too, is a Christian poem, in which the first book is an allegory of the biblical theme of divine grace by which alone humanity is redeemed and brought to heaven. The Red Cross Knight, who is Holiness, will champion Una, Truth, and slay the old Dragon who is ravaging her father's country. He wins some victories, then is caught unarmed by Pride—without, as Spenser explained to Raleigh, 'the armour of a Christian man specified by Saint Paul *v.* Ephes.', and Una must bring divine aid to him in the person of Arthur:

Ay me, how many perils doe enfold
The righteous man, to make him daily fall?
Were not, that heavenly grace doth him uphold,
And stedfast truth acquite him out of all.

Pride thus defeated, the knight must be taken for rest, instruction and repentance to the House of Holiness:

Ne let the man ascribe it to his skill,
That thorough grace hath gained victory.
If any strength we have, it is to ill,
But all the good is Gods, both power and eke will.

There he is taught by Faith, Hope and Charity, first from Faith's book, signed and sealed with blood, hard to understand:

And that her sacred Booke, with bloud ywrit,
That none could read, except she did them teach,
She unto him disclosed every whit,
And heavenly documents thereout did preach,
That weaker wit of man could never reach,

Of God, of grace, of justice, of free will,
That wonder was to heare her goodly speach:
For she was able with her words to kill
And raise againe to life the hart that she did thrill.

So, like Dante, he can approach the highest Mount, and gaze upon

The new Hierusalem, that God has built
For those to dwell in that are chosen his.

An altogether different use of the Bible is the single allusion, enriching, perhaps deepening, a neutral theme. From multitudes, Keats's *Ode to a Nightingale*:

Perhaps the self-same song that found a path
Through the sad heart of Ruth, when, sick for home,
She stood in tears amid the alien corn.

They depend upon familiarity. What if every reference to Eve or Paradise required an explanatory note!

Finally, most important, and most impossible to discuss or illustrate in a few paragraphs, there is the all-embracing fact that since the appearance of the Bible, the full, Christian Bible, western literature has come to birth in and through a mental and spiritual environment different from those of the East or of classical antiquity. Some of the differences must receive attention later on. To be brief, the relation between God and history, between a personal God and the individual man, between body and mind, between man and nature, between man and man, between man and society, between justice and mercy, between constraint and freedom, between time and eternity—on none of these relations does the Christian think exactly as the non-Christian, since to the former everything turns on the Incarnation. Whether Christian beliefs are accepted or rejected, no thinker, no writer, born within western culture can escape them. There are questions to be wrestled with which classical antiquity had not asked, dimensions to be lived in which it had not discovered. There is more hope, but also a keener tragedy; suffering and joy and love have new meanings.

Part of the point is made by Auerbach in his discussion of Elizabethan tragedy:

In Elizabethan tragedy and specifically in Shakespeare the hero's character is depicted in greater and more varied detail than in antique tragedy, and participates more actively in shaping the individual's fate.... Christianity had conceived the problems of humanity (good and evil, guilt and destiny) more excitingly, antithetically, and even paradoxically than had antiquity.... Shakespeare's ethical and intellectual world is much more agitated, multi-layered and, apart from any specific dramatic action, in itself more dramatic than that of antiquity.

In *War and Peace* Tolstoy does not obtrude speculation in such a way as to destroy the narrative power of one of the greatest of novels, but his epilogue shows that all through he has been pondering, in the light of Christian thought, the issue of freedom and necessity in history and 'the immediate participation of the Deity in the affairs of men', the nature of the motive power in or behind history. Or we may think of Goethe assessing, in *Dichtung und Wahrheit*, the preponderant part of the Bible in his early education. 'When my restless imagination... strayed from one field to another...I loved to take refuge in those oriental religions and become absorbed in the first Books of Moses, and there, amid the scattered shepherd tribes, I dwelt in the greatest solitude and yet with my greatest friends.' Again, of the Bible, 'I loved it and valued it; for to it almost alone did I owe my moral education; and the events, the doctrines, the symbols, the similes, had all impressed themselves deeply upon me'. It was through his struggles with the biblical criticism of his day that he learned how to penetrate to the essence of any significant book, into 'the groundwork, the inner meaning, the sense, the tendency'. 'This conviction, born of faith and sight,... underlay the moral as well as the literary structure of my life, and may be regarded as a well-invested and richly productive capital....' It is not his youthful epic on Joseph that matters, but this biblical pervasion of his greatest works, however unorthodox.

> Ich, Ebenbild der Gottheit, das sich schon
> Ganz nah gedünkt dem Spiegel ew'ger Wahrheit,
> Sein selbst genoss in Himmelsglanz und Klarheit,
> Und abgestreift den Erdensohn;
> Ich, mehr als Cherub, dessen freie Kraft
> Schon durch die Adern der Natur zu fliessen
> Und, schaffend, Götterleben zu geniessen
> Sich ahnungsvoll vermass, wie muss ichs büssen!
> Ein Donnerwort hat mich hinweggerafft....
> Zu jenen Sphären wag ich nicht zu streben,
> Woher die holde Nachricht tönt;

Und doch, an diesen Klang von Jugend auf gewöhnt,
Ruft er auch jetzt zurück mich in das Leben....
Aber warum muss der Strom so bald versiegen,
Und wir wieder im Durste liegen?
Davon hab ich so viel Erfahrung.
Doch dieser Mangel lässt sich ersetzen,
Wir lernen das Überirdische schätzen,
Wir sehnen uns nach Offenbarung,
Die nirgends würdger und schöner brennt
Als in dem Neuen Testament.

ART

It is conceivable that the Bible might have had little effect upon the visual arts, for Christianity (like Islam) might have inherited and preserved the anti-representational spirit of Judaism, and the aesthetic impulses of the northern peoples might have been satisfied with a non-representational art which might then have met those religious instincts or cautions which determine the Puritan attitude to religious art; all this despite the fact that the Bible communicates so much of its teaching by means of images.

But that is hypothesis. Whatever might have been, the event was different; and whatever its origin, Greek or otherwise, the gentile Christianity of the Mediterranean world accepted a historical and representational art, using it at first to shape symbols ('catacomb art') but before long to convey information quite directly, as well as to stimulate feeling. Once the decision of principle had been taken and generally accepted (there were controversies, of course, about its application) the Bible inevitably became a source of inspiration to artists, furnishing them with characters and stories, ideas and images, enriching thought and feeling and imagination.

Inspiration is an ambiguous word. That the painting and sculpture of medieval Europe were to so considerable an extent iconographically Christian does not mean that the individual artist or craftsman was always being inspired, in any deeply personal sense, by the Bible, whether directly or through the Church; nor even that he normally chose his own subject and preferred those which were biblical. Most of them were working within a tradition both of technique and of theme, and very frequently—perhaps more often than not—they were fulfilling a commission which imposed the subject, sometimes with detailed precision. They were not necessarily any the worse for that. It is well established that works of the highest order in painting and sculpture and music have at all times originated in such commissions, and that limitation, by theme or material or other contingency, has in countless instances stimulated an artist's invention. Of setting up traditions within which artists may work the Bible and the Church have no monopoly. The Christian tradition was indebted to Greece and Rome, and a liberation from the bondage of ecclesiastical themes was later to bring new life to the arts. But the Renaissance itself illustrates the importance of 'subject-matter' (*inter alia*) as stimulus to new vision, and it will not be denied that the arts in Europe were developed in close connection with the Church and thereby in some considerable dependence upon the literary and visual themes which the Church drew from the Bible, whether the Church as patron was thinking primarily of making a beautiful offering to God or primarily of instructing and edifying the people. Those who had the will and the power to break with tradition could do so, but they owed their nurture to it.

It would need another pen to fathom the mystery of aesthetic inspiration, to trace the interrelation of genius, feeling and technique with each other and with subject-matter. It is a commonplace that the beauty of a work of art does not lie in the beauty of its subject-matter—that is, in the ostensible, representational, subject, the sense in which the term is here used, though it begs many questions. There is great abstract art, there is great art in which, though it is not abstract, the theme seems to matter little, and there is other great art in which the drive has come from the desire to solve a technical problem. But when that has been said, there is still other great art in which the artist is responding to a subject (still in the objective and representational sense) and in which it is the subject which has drawn out his fullest powers through its significance to or impact upon his whole being. Or he may be unable to communicate with others except through a subject which releases in them aesthetic responses which remain dormant without it. And further, while we freely accept as beautiful, perhaps as perfect in their kind, works of art of slight substance or of which the theme (in the representational sense) is trivial, though we might not hesitate to attribute even greatness to them, yet there is a sense, most difficult to seize, in which the theme has to do with greatness, a fact presumably related to the unity and wholeness of human personality. While many works of religious art are aesthetically trivial, the greatness of many great ones cannot be dissociated from their theme. And since it is not Art but particular works of art which we enjoy, it must, at the very least, be allowed that painters (for example) who could produce works of the highest order quite independently of the Bible have in fact produced many of their greatest works under its inspiration. In such cases the biblical contribution may be directly iconographical, or it may be the impulse to give visual expression to thoughts and feelings aroused by the Bible's handling of ultimate mysteries and realities. It is perhaps sufficient to name Rembrandt.

MUSIC

It is much the same with music. Song and dance, the twin sources of its elaborate forms, are universal. They can both be religious; neither need be. Had Europe preserved no contact with Graeco-Roman or Near-Eastern music (the extent of any such continuity is still a puzzle) the natural impulse to sing and dance would have given rise in time to a fresh development of the art. In fact, European music, like painting, sculpture and drama, grew up with the help of the Christian Church, and therefore of the Bible. It would be a simple matter to write out a long list of settings of biblical and liturgical texts: psalms, hymns, anthems, motets, masses, passions, oratorios. The barest hint of a selection shows how noble the list would be, with the masses and motets of Palestrina, Victoria and Byrd, Monteverdi's *Vespers*, the Passion music of Schütz, the cantatas and Passions of Bach and the *B minor Mass*, with Handel's *Messiah* and *Israel in Egypt*, Mozart's *Requiem Mass*, Haydn's *Creation*, the *Missa Solemnis* of Beethoven, the Brahms *Requiem*, Vaughan Williams's *Sancta Civitas*. This is not essentially a question of illustrative or programme music, for the extent of attention to the pictorial possibilities of single words or phrases or incidents can vary considerably (Bach and Handel and Haydn are quite happy doing things of this kind which lesser men have scorned). Non-biblical themes give just as much opportunity for the expression of most human emotions, and music of unsurpassed quality may need no literary or pictorial stimulus, or the slightest. We are once more plunged into the mystery of genius—feeling—inspiration—technique, and are once more driven to say simply that confrontation with the

Bible, or with liturgical texts which convey the same realities and challenges and aspirations, has in fact brought into being particular works acknowledged to be among the greatest. These particular heights would not have been reached without the 'inspiration' of this particular 'subject-matter'.

Further, since so large a part of the best music has no words and paints no picture, it is to be remembered that, whatever might have been, this absolute music also owes much of its development to experience gained in sacred music. One may instance experiments made in the organization of melody within plainchant, going far beyond what is likely in folk-song or even, at the time, in more sophisticated secular song; contrapuntal devices and fugal forms and textures discovered in the vocal music of the Church and made available to the secular composer; the organist's handling of the chorale, leading by variations and other means to larger musical structures. It is not a point to be pressed too far, since the reciprocal influence of secular music upon sacred has also been important. Yet it is remarkable how much of the history, even the technical history, of western music can be traced to the Christian's desire to sing his faith.

CONDUCT

Great or small, the influence of the Bible upon literature and the arts has been incidental to its own purpose. There is little trace of delight in them for their own sake. Individual writers and craftsmen, we may suppose, took pleasure in their activities, and there is a feeling for the beauty of nature. But neither artistic creation nor aesthetic appreciation are recommended as intrinsic parts of the good life. They are instrumental, they are brought into the service of God and the religious community, they are only spoken of as inspired by the Spirit of God when so used. They have the opportunity to develop, but their development is conditioned by the religious outlook. The assistance given to them by the Christian Church has been one side of the story, and in the event the more decisive; the other side has been limitation, suspicion and fear, not only of the place of beauty within worship but even, as a worldly snare, within the Christian life at all.

As to worship, Augustine dwelt upon the dilemma of a Christian who loves music. There were times when he could wish that all the melodies to which the Psalter was sung might be banished from the Church:

Yet when I remember the tears I shed at the songs of the Church in the days when I recovered my faith, and now when I am moved not by the singing, but by the things sung clearly and with fitting modulation, I acknowledge once more how useful this practice is. I fluctuate between the peril of pleasure and the profit I have proved in experience. I am inclined—though this is not an irrevocable opinion—to approve the custom of singing in church so that the weaker mind may rise by the delight of the ear to the feeling of devotion. But whenever I am more moved by the singing than the thing sung, I confess that I have sinned and deserve to be punished (*Confessions*, x, c. 33).

Many Christians have shared Augustine's experience; some have drawn drastic conclusions from it, and have succeeded in imposing them on others.

As to the place of beauty in life, there is more in the context of Augustine's words than a straightforward fear of being distracted from God when one is trying to worship him wholeheartedly. Augustine makes these remarks in the course of a more general discussion of the desires of the body and the delights of the senses, in which sexual experiences, eating and drinking, attractive scents, music and pictures are placed, apparently, on a par. The delight of music is a delight of the *ear*, which may enervate the *mind*. 'The eyes love beautiful and varied forms, bright and pleasing colours; let them not capture my soul.' Here the puritanism (or whatever it should be called) is unhappily based upon a superficial aesthetic, and Augustine himself rises above it. He cannot approve 'art for art's sake' (as sometimes interpreted) any more than he could have approved 'business is business' or any other slogan which claims an ultimate autonomy for any sphere of life. But, though his fear of entanglement in lower things persists, he provides at least the principle by which all beauty can be brought within the sovereignty and bounty of God: 'But I too, my God and my Glory, sing a hymn to Thee and offer my sacrifice of praise to Him who sanctifies me. All the loveliness which goes through men's souls into their skilful hands comes from the Loveliness which is above our souls, for which my soul longs day and night' (*ibid.* c. 34 *fin.*). Others, with more or less explicit theory and more or less severity of discipline, have turned their backs on the arts as temptations of this world; and in so doing they have believed they could find justification in the Bible.

Conduct, however, is a pre-eminent concern of the Bible. Matthew

Arnold wanted to save the Bible from the theology of the bishops of Winchester and Gloucester, and was sure he knew the way. 'Surely, if there be anything with which metaphysics have nothing to do, and where a plain man, without skill to walk in the arduous paths of abstruse reasoning, may yet find himself at home, it is religion. For the object of religion is *conduct*.... And when we are asked further, what is conduct?—let us answer: *Three-fourths of life*' (*Literature and Dogma*, chap. 1). The right way to think of God is as 'the Eternal Power, not ourselves, that makes for righteousness', and the true greatness of the Bible lies in its proclamation of righteousness, for the proper apprehension of which it is indispensable. We may smile at his anxiety to compute the correct proportion between conduct and culture (is culture a quarter or a fifth or a sixth of life?) and we may rage at his disregard of metaphysics and theology. It remains true that the Bible has been for the western world a book of righteousness, and that the plain man has learned from it, infinitely more than from any other source, how he should behave.

Any attempt to measure the moral influence of the Bible would be presumptuous. We must be content to indicate some of the ways in which it has been at work, if possible without injustice to the moral teaching of Greece and Rome and of other civilizations. Some of its simplest lessons have been among the most far-reaching in effect, lessons which could have been learned from elsewhere, but were in fact taught to most western men by the Bible, either directly or indirectly in the simple moral instruction of the Church. Thou shalt do no murder, thou shalt not commit adultery, thou shalt not steal, thou shalt not bear false witness; speak the truth, hold to your word, help other people, look after the poor, the widow and the orphan—the simple elements of personal ethics on which a decent society depends—these are not specifically biblical, but they have been drummed into us through the Bible, and, despite St Paul's excellent psychology in the seventh chapter of Romans ('I had not known coveting, except the law had said, Thou shalt not covet'), there must have been multitudes of beneficial moral decisions taken 'because the Bible tells me to'. That for centuries generation after generation of Europeans and Americans have learned by heart the Commandments and the Beatitudes and the Parable of the Good Samaritan is a major, though incalculable, factor in their history.

Sometimes the Bible has compelled a choice between its ethic and the ethics of other traditions. Consider marriage and divorce. A well-known book, Fritz Schulz's *Classical Roman Law* (Oxford, 1951) writes thus of it: 'The classical law of marriage is an imposing, perhaps the most imposing, achievement of the Roman legal genius. For the first time in the history of civilization there appeared a purely humanistic idea of marriage as being a free and freely dissoluble union of two equal partners for life.' And of divorce, 'In classical law any marriage, without regard to whether the husband has *manus* or not, can be dissolved by agreement of the spouses or by notice given by one of them...this freedom is the inevitable and indispensable keystone of the classical humanistic law of marriage'. Such, then, was the law of the State within which Christians lived. Even the influence of the Church upon Christian emperors could not secure its abrogation, though Constantine modified the law of divorce considerably and Justinian compromised. In Schulz's words, 'even in Justinian's *Corpus Iuris* the principles of the humanistic law of marriage were maintained'. In practice, however, the Church rejected this law as a norm of conduct, and built up its own canon law on the subject. 'In the course of the Middle Ages the Roman law of marriage was almost completely abandoned in western Europe. On the basis of well-known passages of the New Testament the Church developed an anti-humanistic law of divorce.' Schulz regrets this. 'The classical law of marriage bides its time: it is still a living force', and he welcomes a new tendency to humanize the law of marriage which 'has already achieved remarkable results in Scandinavia', though he continues with an acknowledgment that 'the Roman *humanitas* emphasizing the value and dignity of human personality was inevitably individualistic and thus sometimes came into conflict with the interests of the community'. One might question his historical analysis or contest his values, and the Christian teaching on marriage and divorce can be endlessly discussed. The point to be made here is simply that we have in fact been living with and under a law and practice which entailed a break with Rome and which was drawn from the Bible. Christian interpretation of the Bible was not uniform, and so its discipline was not uniform, divorce law in the East differing greatly from that of the West. In both cases, however, it was in principle biblical, based not only upon particular texts but upon a conception of marriage which, for better or worse, contains dimensions unrecognized by Roman law. This is a very plain instance of the influence of the Bible upon the western way of life, up till now, and of the far-reaching questions posed by any rejection of it.

An interesting example is the attitude to work. The Greek attitude has often been described unfairly and the success of Christianity in dignifying labour has been exaggerated. Moderately stated, however, the contrast is real, and very real dignity is given to work by the Bible. The Greek respected agriculture and some of the crafts, besides military service and politics, but he held some crafts (*technai*) to be vulgar (*banausikai*), while work below the craft level was either left undone or done by slaves. In Xenophon's much-quoted *Oeconomicus* Critobulus wants to know about the *technai*, not all of them, but the most beautiful, those which would be fitting (respectable?) for him; and Socrates is represented as dismissing some out of hand—they are banausic. These are the occupations which injure men's bodies by keeping them indoors and sedentary, even by the fire all day. Such bodies become effeminate, and then the mind weakens. Banausic occupations prevent men from giving time to their friends or to politics; those who practice them become useless for war. So some cities do not allow *citizens* to engage in banausic crafts. There was a prejudice also against retail trade—it was necessary, though no one, Plato said, will earn his living this way if he can help it. So back to the land! One recognizes prejudices which persist in western society, even in so Christian a writer as Jane Austen. Whatever may have been true of fifth-century Athens, it can scarcely be doubted that, with the increase of slavery and with *panem et circenses*, the prejudices grew and touched even what we should call 'the professions'.

The early Christians' outlook was different partly because most of them were poor workers; it might be discounted for that reason. Sometimes, too, they were persuaded to accept work as the penalty due to human sin, though this was a misunderstanding of Genesis, which puts the principle of work before the Fall (ii. 5 and 15, a man to till the ground, to dress and keep the garden) and then points out, quite properly, how much toil sin has put into work. But side by side with these, other aspects of biblical teaching were absorbed. Work is a duty to God and to one's neighbour, and this is what gives it dignity. Even the toil of the Fall, though not the true nature of work, is to be made fruitful as discipline. In itself work can be accepted gladly as a divine ordinance. The Son of God worked as a carpenter. 'My Father worketh hitherto, and I work.' The biblical doctrine of work is open to abuse, and has often been gravely perverted in practice. It is, nevertheless, a clear example of an outlook which contrasts sharply with that of the intelligentsia in late Graeco-Roman civilization, and which has been powerfully effective in Christendom.

If man must work, he must also rest. God worked, and rested on the seventh day. Here is an institution which, however it started, has come to us through the Bible and in a biblical form—a regular day, at short intervals, instead of irregular festivals and holidays, a day both for special religious duties and for rest and refreshment. It has taken some strange forms under the influence of biblicism or a too narrow piety, it has sometimes pressed very hard upon children. But even those who jibe at the puritan sabbath or the English Sunday do not propose to work seven days in the week. Compared with the Greek notion of (as we are told) working when you like, the week has introduced order into a more complicated economic life, while Sunday has protected the worker from continuous drudgery.

Examples, despite the advantages of the concrete, must not divert us altogether from principles, nor, despite much continuity, must biblical ethics be treated as a homogeneous unity. To the Christian theologian the Old Testament ethic speaks predominantly of law and righteousness with an accompanying movement of grace, the New Testament of love, grace and freedom with law and righteousness taken up into them. If on the one hand law is allowed to oust grace, or if, on the other hand, love is so sentimentalized or freedom so libertinized as to sap the foundation of righteousness, the ethic to be derived from the culminating biblical revelation in Christ will be perverted. This has happened all too often. Occasionally a misconceived theology of grace has thrown up consciously and deliberately antinomian groups, fortifying their licence with biblical tags—to the pure, all things are pure. More frequently, the concept of forgiveness through the Cross has been debased. Pardon might be bought or granted, ostensibly, without sufficient care for moral earnestness. 'Le bon Dieu pardonnera; c'est son métier.' Then what purports to be grounded in free redemption through the Cross forgets the abiding 'take up your cross'. The opposite danger, in which a legalist spirit is combined with a fundamentalist acceptance of every detail of the Bible as being free from any human relativism, tends to fasten upon the community ideas, customs, institutions, which it should outgrow and from which the central ethic of the New Testament would set it free. Seventeenth-century Puritanism is the most quoted, but not the only example. Its resolve to submit all life, including politics and economics, to the will of God as revealed in Scripture was noble, and a proper distinction between principles and rules, between the right-for-the-time and the permanently valid, was not wanting in theory. In the Epistle prefixed to the *Laws and Liberties of Massachusetts* (1648) it is written, 'So soon as God had set up political government among his people Israel hee gave them a body of lawes for judgement both in civil and criminal causes. These were breif and fundamental principles, yet withall so full and comprehensive as out of them clear deductions were to be drawne to all particular cases in future times.' Such loyalty bore good fruit. Yet it was—and is—easier to bandy isolated texts than to wrestle with the application of principle, and this is a disloyalty to the nature of Scripture which cannot but yield evil fruit. Among the grave results of this kind of biblicism have been disproportionate severity towards sexual offences, the persecution of 'witches' and heretics, the idea of a holy war, the perversion of the biblical concept of a 'chosen people' and of a man (whether ruler or prophet) 'raised up by God'. A very different charge is that the Bible has been used to bolster up privilege and to reconcile the poor and exploited with 'the Will of God' for them by purely spiritual consolations for the moment and promises of bliss hereafter. The charge is not always fairly put, especially when it is forgotten or denied that the spiritual consolations, which include high moral qualities, were real; but it cannot be lightly dismissed. The problem of doing justice at once to the this-worldly and the other-worldly elements in the biblical ethic is more poignantly illustrated in Vautel's *Mon Curé chez les Pauvres* than in many a moral treatise!

When every necessary qualification and admission has been made, it remains surpassingly true that the Bible has been the pre-eminent source of moral reform, individual and social, for the western world. With Moses behind them, the prophets of Israel fought for and obtained the recognition of the righteousness of God. A jealous God indeed, whose people must worship none other god, yet he could not be satisfied nor his favour won by cult alone. He demanded righteousness. 'Take thou away from me the noise of thy songs; for I will not hear the melody of thy viols. But let judgement roll down as waters, and righteousness as a mighty stream' (Amos v. 23–4). 'Will the Lord be pleased with thousands of rams, or with ten thousands of rivers of oil? shall I give my firstborn for my transgression, the fruit of my body for the sin of my soul? He hath shewed thee, O man, what is good: and what doth the Lord require of thee, but to do justly, and to love mercy, and to walk humbly with thy God' (Micah vi. 7–8). By these men the idea of a binding moral law (which is not peculiar to the Bible) was made to glow with a heat generated by its association with a personal, living and active, God whose will for righteousness is both a demand for holiness and a promise to redeem his people from their sins. When the fire is damped down, we get a prudential morality of justification by the works of the law, a besetting temptation to 'natural' moralist man. But the fire has never been quenched; it has warmed the hearts of those whose labour for men has been part of their duty to God and whose confidence has been in the guidance and support of God. Dr George Trevelyan quotes from Miss M. G. Jones's book on the Charity School Movement: 'Conduct, not dogma, stamped the Puritan of the Eighteenth Century.... He was irresistibly drawn towards the service of man, who through misery or ignorance, or debauchery, deprived God of the glory that was His due.' In fact, dogma is here more important than the citer and the author cited perhaps allow, for the conduct described issued from the dogma, that is, the biblical teaching about God. And if we move into the next century, it will be no injustice to the achievements of reforms on Benthamite, utilitarian, principles if we insist that the public opinion which made their operation possible was more biblically motivated through the work of the Methodists and the Evangelical Revival, both very scriptural in outlook.

That 'biblical' reformers have acted from a sense of responsibility to God implies no lack of love for man. The Bible holds love of God and man together: 'Thou shalt love the Lord thy God with all thy heart, and with all thy soul, and with all thy mind. This is the first and great commandment. And the second is like unto it, Thou shalt love thy neighbour as thyself' (Matt. xxii. 37–9); 'He that loveth not his brother whom he hath seen, how can he love God whom he hath not seen? And this commandment have we from him, that he who loveth God love his brother also' (I John iv. 20–1). In the fullness of biblical teaching God is known, through the Cross, as love, law takes its meaning from love, and love is the spring and the goal of conduct. Social reformers have been apt to criticize the Christian Church for being content with the palliatives of charity instead of pressing for radical changes in which love is expressed through justice. This also is a charge which cannot be lightly set aside. All the same, it is by a true instinct that it has clung to the notion of charity. Fundamentally, the charity (*agape*, love) which is characteristic of the Bible is not a matter of palliatives but of persons. For it is not simply that 'the poor you have always with you', but that we have always to do with persons who, in any adequate ethic and in any moral society, must be treated wholly as persons. This is precisely what the complex societies of today, even when set upon social justice, are finding so enormously difficult. Simultaneous care of body, mind and spirit, of the whole person, eludes their grasp—sometimes even their intention. Nothing could be more obvious than that some modern programmes of social reform fail abysmally in this respect at any stage prior to the Utopias to which they aspire. Personality is crushed on the way.

It is at this point that the pressure of biblical ethics is of the utmost value. God loves his children individually and confers inestimable value upon them individually by loving them. He respects their personality, their freedom, at his own cost. His 'laws' are such as to cherish individual selves while at the same time promoting communities, fellowships, within which selves can grow. Regimentation is contrary to the developed biblical ethic, since personal integrity, which includes both freedom and responsibility, must be respected and fostered. Since it is the whole person who is to be respected, the state aimed at cannot be one only of material satisfactions, or even of intellectual or aesthetic ones, or all these together. Whatever place it gives to these (which some may think inadequate) it is evident that the Bible sets moral and religious qualities above them. Its demand is for a holiness which, however differently expressed, is always a form of love; and it is made quite clear that to those who love, the service of others will entail sacrifice and suffering. Sacrifice and suffering are treated in the Bible not as negative or passive experiences, but as positive and fruitful moral actions.

All these concepts—spiritual personality, grace, freedom, sacrifice, suffering, responsibility—are hard ones. Their relation to each other, for example of prevenient grace to moral responsibility, and their requirements in actual living are most puzzling to work out. Yet they have been the inspiration of western civilization, even though no society has come very near to what they offer and require. The temptation to discard them for something more coherent in logic or more tangible in practice is persistent and severe. Plato or Marx beckon, with systems less than the law of love. The Bible offers no proof, but a faith in the ultimate coherence of law and freedom, justice and mercy, within the being of God, in whose will is our peace.

GENERAL CHARACTERISTICS OF BIBLICAL THOUGHT

From the little which has been said about biblical ethics it will already be evident that they are not expounded as a system developed from autonomous ethical principles. Biblical morality is part of biblical religion, and the religion is set in, or itself creates (it would be hard to say which, but probably the latter) a cosmology. For centuries the Bible provided a cosmology for the West, though one which was increasingly modified as Greek thought was recovered or new knowledge acquired. As a frame of reference it was invaluable to art and literature. Science and philosophy were partly hindered and partly assisted by it. Science was hindered by the biblicism which assumed the opening chapters of Genesis to be scientifically correct and also by ecclesiastical authority when—as was bound to happen—theological systems had been interwoven with cosmological notions so derived. At certain times philosophy was presumably hindered by the domination of biblical and theological presuppositions, and ecclesiastical intolerance has often checked freedom of inquiry. But it is not easy to see that philosophical thinking itself has suffered much from the pressure of the Bible. On the other hand, science has been helped by the zeal of many to investigate 'the wonderful works of God' just because they are God's, and, as is now generally understood, by the assumption of law and order in a universe subject to a purposive Creator. In Whitehead's words, 'Faith in the possibility of science, generated antecedently to the development of modern scientific theory, is an unconscious derivative from medieval theology'. Philosophy has been stimulated not only by the general problems of theism but by some particular elements in biblical thought, for example the nature of persons, especially in their relation to, or 'encounter' with, God, or the peculiarly biblical attitude to transcendence and immanence, or the 'scandal of particularity' in law and history.

The Bible itself provides no system, philosophical or scientific. Postponing for the moment its ultimate significance to Christian faith, we may say that it has contributed to western thought not a system, but a number of insights and insistences which frequently differ from those of Greece or the Far East. Hebrew thought is much more consistently religious than Greek, and its religious outlook is in many respects utterly different from that of the Orient. Many pitfalls await attempts to distinguish Hebrew or biblical thought from other types, particularly, as James Barr's *Semantics of Biblical Language* has recently demonstrated, when the distinguishing characteristics are traced back into the very structure of the Hebrew language. But certain characteristics are unmistakable.

To begin with, the Bible so much prefers the concrete to the abstract, the dynamic to the static, one may almost say the material to the (purely) spiritual, the historical to the philosophical, that it persists bravely in an anthropomorphic presentation of God for the sake of the reality which cannot otherwise be communicated. If this is in a sense poetry, it is quite different from the poetical anthropomorphy of the Olympic gods or the symbols of Hinduism. The portrayal of God in the image of man is the counterpart of the fundamental religious assertion that man is made in the image of God and capable of fellowship with him. By its frank anthropomorphism the Bible has enabled multitudes of men and women to believe that God is their Father who knows them and helps them, and to build their lives on this faith. This is a major fact about the history of the western world. Together with it we must put the Bible's way of protecting the idea of God against the dangers of anthropomorphism. It always preserves the distinction between Creator and creation (hence the urgency of the decision, the crisis, about Jesus Christ). God is other than all that is made, even that which is made in his image; he is holy in himself, not by derivation or participation. With all its concreteness and anthropomorphism, the Bible completely maintains the transcendence of God. And this has been another major factor in western history, not only in justifying worship, but also in stimulating action *ad maiorem Dei gloriam.*

There is no theoretical reconciliation of transcendence and immanence; there is a certainty that God who is utterly holy is nevertheless intensely and unceasingly occupied with his creation, with man, matter and history. Matter is accepted as good because it is the good God's creation. In this acceptance lies the recognition as good in principle of the body, the family, the State, of the arts and crafts and sciences. By some of these the Bible itself sets much store, while others, if they are not as highly regarded as among the Greeks, are not ruled out. In its early days the Christian Church fought hard to preserve this attitude to the material order against various non-biblical spiritualisms and dualisms. There is within the Bible itself, and particularly in the New Testament, a very different dualism, a moral dualism of this-worldly and other-worldly outlooks, which raises many questions about the idea of a Christian culture. There is a great difference, however, between attempting to answer these questions in loyalty to the Bible as it is, and prejudging them by a non-biblical—be it oriental or Greek—attitude towards the material. Here the biblical position, maintained by Judaism and by the orthodox Christian victory over Gnosticism, has been decisive up to the present for western thought and practice.

The concept of man is determined throughout the Bible by the conviction that he is the creation of a personal God, is made in God's image, and is by nature and grace capable of fellowship with God, a fellowship which, in the later stages of biblical religion, is held to be potentially eternal. Such people always matter to God. Human personality is not illusory, or something to be escaped from or sloughed off in order that some higher state of being (or of nothingness) may be reached. Man, if he remains alive at all, never ceases to be man, since it is by his coming to the full stature of manhood that his Creator's purpose is achieved. This understanding of man secures the abiding worth of individual selves, in contrast to much oriental thought and also against the modern temptation to belittle man because the physical universe is discovered to be so vast. The worth of man, however, is not assigned by the Bible to himself in his own right, as in much Greek thought. His 'soul' is not *per se* immortal, his reason is not his divinity. He depends always upon God, and his worst folly and sin is to claim independence. There is indeed a parallel here with the Greek notion of Hybris and Nemesis, which has itself been influential in some phases of western culture; but biblical teaching on the Fall of man, and its searching analysis of sin, have been immeasurably more effectual.

Where God is presented as working purposefully in his own creation, history is necessarily taken with the utmost seriousness, and the more so where it is also believed that in so working out his purpose God, as part of it, respects the freedom of those who are responsible to him. It would be foolish to say that the Greeks were not interested in history, and perhaps too simple to contrast their cyclical conception of it with the linear treatment of the Bible. But the sense in which history mattered to the Greeks differed altogether from the sense in which it mattered to the Hebrews. The Bible sees the whole of history as one *historia sacra*, the sphere of divine action, with human action subordinate to it. To establish this it permits anthropomorphisms superficially naive ('God repented him'). It is unscientific in that it commonly disregards secondary causes and goes straight to the divine will as the immediate cause; it is baffling in its fusion of purpose and result; and it never explains, to the satisfaction of the intellect, how divine law is related to the sovereign freedom of God ('miracles'). Its historical information is often slight and is used uncritically. But its general attitude to the nature of history has stamped itself upon western civilization, in which it has never yet been believed, and acted upon, by the majority of men that history is meaningless or that human efforts are mocked at by a capricious deity or blocked by a blind Fate or determined by wholly material forces.

Biblical confidence in the forward movement of history has been abused. It has been perverted into a glib belief in inevitable progress; it lies behind a number of Utopias (sometimes called Jewish Messianism). What the Bible teaches, when it is taken as a whole, is quite different. There is no automatic progress for fallen men, whose hope is only in divine redemption, on God's terms. The climax of history is judgment, the consummation lies beyond. Biblical realism cuts across optimism and pessimism.

Up to this point certain aspects of biblical teaching have been singled out which appear to have influenced western civilization decisively and which could, and presumably would, continue to influence its future even if the Christian faith were to be rejected. The biblical insights, thought-forms, images, emphases, have become part, a large part, of the western mind. But a Christian must say his last words as a Christian. No piecemeal treatment of the Bible can suffice. It must be allowed its unifying principle: Jesus Christ. Its personal and living God is one who reveals himself in action, and the culminating act is his self-giving in Christ. Biblical acceptance of matter, of flesh, is sealed in the Incarnation. The chosen people is narrowed down into the Christ, with an insistence upon the significance of particularity which scandalizes the 'Greek' even more than the Jew. The meaning of linear *historia sacra* is comprehended in Christ—in the preparation for him, in the central events of his birth, death, resurrection and ascension, in the continuing life of his Body, the Church, through his Spirit, drawing the world into itself and giving itself to the world until the end of history and the consummation which can only be hinted at in apocalyptic imagery and awaited in faith and hope. Man, made in God's image but fallen, is restored by communion with the Image, Christ—but only through the suffering which God's holy love demands and accepts in Christ. Holy love, manifest in Christ, becomes the law of human life.

Today all this is exposed to manifold objections. Some are moral. If this be true, why have 'Christian' societies been so evil? The Christian must feel the force of this criticism, but he can fairly point to the Bible's own teaching on the gravity of sin and on God's costly condescension to human freedom; and he may perhaps be allowed to suggest that, since the time-scale of human life has been so enormously extended backwards, we have to reckon with the possibility that, similarly, the Christian society is scarcely beginning to be born. Some objections are intellectual. To the modern mind the Bible cannot be an easy book. The old Christian Fathers used to say that in it all the necessary things are clear, and faith knows in what sense that is true. It is one of the blessings of the Bible that we do not have to be intellectuals to hear what it says to us. Though Coleridge's 'I do not find the Bible, the Bible finds me' is not an adequate theory of biblical inspiration, it is an excellent statement of fact. But if we do not need to be intellectuals to grasp it, will the intellect of the western world, with the growth of historical, psychological, scientific and other knowledge, relegate the Bible to a place among other edifying books which have had their day? If the finding power of the Bible depended upon its clarity in a logical or scientific sense, that might be its fate. But with its own kind of clarity it combines mystery, the holiness of the transcendent God whose ways are not our ways, nor his thoughts our thoughts, but who, being beyond our finding, has revealed himself in the mystery of the Incarnation. It is his self-giving in revelation and redemption which finds us in and through Christ, and shows us, and lays upon us, the way of eternal truth and life. This is the Gospel which the Bible perpetually proclaims. It is to be found nowhere else. We rejoice in all truth, but to Christian faith—and the Christian does not pretend to dispense with faith—the Gospel is the measure of, the key to, all truth. In the coronation of the British Sovereign the Holy Bible is presented with these words: 'this Book, the most valuable thing that this world affords. Here is Wisdom; This is the royal Law; These are the lively Oracles of God.'

APPENDIX I

AIDS TO THE STUDY OF THE BIBLE

GRAMMAR

HEBREW, ARAMAIC AND SYRIAC

Interest in Hebrew grammar was anticipated by the Massoretes, whose unremitting care for the preservation of the Hebrew text and of the most delicate shades of Hebrew pronunciation issued in serious grammatical work among Jewish scholars of the tenth century (mainly concerned with Arabic). The influence of Arabic grammar is to be seen in the work of Ben Asher, the Massorete of Tiberias. His contemporary, the Gaon of Saadia (892–942) may be credited with transforming Hebrew grammar into something like a scientific discipline, and Judah ben David Hayyug, in eleventh-century Spain, put Hebrew grammar on a permanent basis, particularly by the recognition of the tri-literal root. Abraham Ibn Ezra (1092–1167) carried this grammatical knowledge from Spain to other European countries. Joseph Kimḥi's grammar, *Sefer Zikkaron* (*c.* 1150), was the first exposition of Hebrew grammar in Hebrew. His son, David Kimḥi (d. 1235), produced the Hebrew grammar which was to be the main source of the classical Jewish philology of the Middle Ages. Until the sixteenth century, grammatical aids to enable the Christian student to study the Hebrew text of the Old Testament hardly existed.

There is no extant Syriac grammar before the eleventh century, then that of Elias, Bishop of Tirhan (d. 1049), ed. F. W. A. Baethgen (1880), and *The Net of Points* of Joseph bar Malkon, Bishop of Nisibis, and, most important of all, the *K^e^taba Semhe* of Barhebraeus (the Jacobite Syrian bishop Abu-l-Farag, 1226–86).

The first Christian to publish a grammar was Johannes Reuchlin, whose work may be regarded as the main starting-point of Hebrew studies in the Christian world. His *De Rudimentis Linguae Hebraicae una cum Lexico* (1506), ed. Münster (1537), together with the *De modo legendi et intelligendi Hebraea* (1503) of Conrad Pellicanus, was the basis of the work of Wolfgang Fabricius Capito, *Institutiones Hebraicae* (1525) and Sanctes Pagninus, *Institutiones Hebraicae* (1526). The most distinguished Jewish grammarian of this period was Elias Levita (1468–1549): *Sefer ha-Bahur*, *Pirke Elijahu* and a commentary to Kimḥi's grammar. He, more than any other, spread the knowledge of Hebrew among Christians. He taught, among others, Sebastian Münster who wrote *Epitome Grammaticae Hebraicae* (1520) and

Institutiones Grammaticae (1524), together with an Aramaic grammar (1527). The greatest Christian Hebraist in the post-Reformation period was the elder Johannes Buxtorf, whose *Praeceptiones Grammaticae de Lingua Hebraea* (later entitled *Epitome Grammaticae Hebraeae*) went through twenty editions between 1605 and 1716. Syriac grammars were written by Widmanstad, *Syriacae linguae elementa* (1555), and Andreas Masius, *Grammatica linguae Syriacae* (1571).

The first to use Arabic in a scientific way to illustrate Hebrew grammar, and to treat Hebrew as a branch of the family of Semitic dialects, was the Dutch Albert Schultens, *Institutiones ad fundamenta linguae Hebraeae* (1737). This meant a final break with the rabbinic tradition of the incomparable *lingua sacra*.

Supreme among students of Hebrew grammar was Heinrich Friedrich Wilhelm Gesenius, who published the 1st ed. of his *Hebräische Grammatik* in 1813; 14th–18th editions revised by E. Rödiger, 22nd–28th by F. Kautzsch, 29th by G. Bergstrasser; English ed. of Gesenius–Kautzsch by A. E. Cowley (1898), 2nd English ed. (1910) a revision of the 28th German ed. of 1909. H. Bauer and P. Leander, *Historische Grammatik der hebräischen Sprache* (vol. 1, 1918, but unfinished) made use of the comparative researches of Brockelmann (see below).

Widely used teaching instruments have been, in German, the grammars of Ewald, Olshausen, Böttcher, Stade and König; in French, the grammars of Jouon (1947^2) and Mayer Lambert (1946); in English that of A. B. Davidson, *An Introductory Hebrew Grammar* (1874, 1962^{25}), together with his *Hebrew Syntax* (1894, 1901^3). S. R. Driver's *A Treatise on the Use of the Tenses in Hebrew* (1892) stands out as a classic on a subject in which far-reaching advances have been made since his day.

Nineteenth-century discoveries vastly enlarged the field of Aramaic literature, and transformed the study of the language. G. Dalman, *Grammatik des Jüdisch-palästinischen Aramäisch* (1894) was a pioneering work, and a major achievement was the *Grammatik des Biblisch-aramäischen* (1927) by H. Bauer and P. Leander. The most important Syriac grammars were those of Th. Nöldeke, *Kurzgefasste Syrische Grammatik* (1880, 1898^2), English trans. *Compendious Syriac Grammar...from the second and improved German edition* by James A. Crichton (1904), and Carl Brockelmann, *Syrische Grammatik* (1899, 1938^5). Perhaps those of Rubens Duval, *Traité de Grammaire Syriaque* (1881) and A. Ungnad, *Syrische Grammatik* (1913) should not be unrecorded.

At the same time the comparison of the Semitic languages took on a new importance, as represented in the works of W. Wright, *Lectures on the Comparative Grammar of the Semitic Languages* (1890); H. Zimmern,

Vergleichende Grammatik der semitischen Sprachen (1898) and C. Brockelmann, *Grundriss der vergleichenden Grammatik der semitischen Sprachen* (I, 1908; II, 1913).

GREEK

Throughout the Middle Ages, the Latin Vulgate was so exclusively authoritative in the West that knowledge of Greek was almost lost, apart from a small pocket of tradition in South Italy. In the fifteenth century learned Greeks, induced to settle in Italy, taught the men of the Renaissance. At once the Greek Bible was intensively studied. Erasmus, Theodore Beza and Estienne drew attention to the difference between biblical and classical Greek, a primary issue still.

Among those who explained the peculiarities of biblical Greek as hebraisms were John Drusius, *Ad voces ebraicas Novi Testamenti* (1582) and Sal Glass, *Adnotationes in Novum Testamentum* (1612–16), *Philologia Sacra* (1623), Thomas Gataker, John Cocceius and John Vorst; also E. Palairet, *Observationes in Novum Testamentum* (1752). Others believed differences to be due to the special purity of the biblical language under the inspiration of the Holy Spirit: Sebastian Pfochen, *Diatribe de linguae graecae Novi Testamenti puritate* (1629–33), C. S. Georgi, *Dissertationes* (1726), etc., J. C. Schwartz. Mediating positions were taken by J. H. Böcler, *De lingua Novi Testamenti originali* (1642); J. Olearius, *De stylo Novi Testamenti* (1668); John Leusden, and J. H. Michaelis, *Dissertatio de textu Novi Testamenti graeco* (1707).

First independent, systematic study of the grammar of the Greek Bible by Casp. Wyss, *Dialectologia sacra* (1650), Georg Pasor, *Grammatica graeca sacra Novi Testamenti in tres libros distributa* (1655), and Abraham Trommius in his concordance. Until the end of the eighteenth century, compilations called *Observationes*, of grammatical and lexical parallels of New Testament and classical authors, were common: all kinds of extravagances were considered possible.

G. B. Winer, *Grammatik des neutestamentlichen Sprachidioms* (1822), marks the beginning of a more scientific approach; seventh edition by Gottlieb Lünemann (1867) and English trans., first by J. H. Thayer, Winer–Thayer, *A Grammar of the Idiom of the New Testament* (1869), and then by W. F. Moulton, Winer–Moulton, *A Treatise of the Grammar of New Testament Greek* (1882^{3}). Various editions served two generations of English and American scholars. Last important revision was by P. W. Schmiedel, *Winer's Grammatik des neutestamentlichen Sprachidioms* (1894^{8}). On the same level of scientific achievement was Alexander Buttmann's *Grammatik des neutestamentlichen Sprachgebrauchs* (1857–9)—also trans. by Thayer, *A Grammar of the New Testament Greek* (1873).

Classical philologists had by now come to believe that the Greek of the

Bible was a specimen of the *Koine* spoken by Hellenistic Jews, especially in Egypt. Papyri had been discovered in Egypt since the eighteenth century, but the appearance of documents at Arsinoe in the Fayum (1877)—private letters, wills, receipts of Ptolemaic, Roman and Byzantine Egypt—made possible the revolutionary work of A. Deissmann, *Bibelstudien* (1895), and *Neue Bibelstudien* (1897), English trans. *Bible Studies*, by A. Grieve (1909). He concluded, from the strong resemblance which he observed between New Testament Greek and the language of the inscriptions, that there was no special Greek language of the Bible. This thesis was developed by A. Thumb, who, in his *Die griechische Sprache im Zeitalter des Hellenismus* (1901), first set *Koine* Greek in the evolution of the Greek language from classical times to the present.

The implications of this for the LXX were drawn out by R. Meister, *Prolegomena zu einer Grammatik der LXX* (Wiener Studien XXIX, 1907); R. Helbing, *Grammatik der Septuaginta* (1907), and H. St J. Thackeray, *A Grammar of the Old Testament in Greek*, vol. I (1909).

All subsequent New Testament grammars were influenced by the discoveries. So F. Blass, *Grammatik des neutestamentlichen Griechisch* (1896, 1902^2); English trans. of 1st ed. by H. St J. Thackeray (1898), of the 2nd ed. (1905); 4th ed. revised by A. Debrunner (1913). The 9th ed. of Debrunner is the most elaborate of all grammars of New Testament Greek; English trans. of the 9th–10th ed. by R. W. Funk (1961). The classical grammar in English is that of J. H. Moulton, *A Grammar of New Testament Greek*. I, *Prolegomena* (1906); II, ed. by W. F. Howard (1919–29). Moulton followed Deissmann's lead, and few of the semitisms unexplained from the papyri by Moulton have since been explained from that source. Other grammars dependent upon Deissmann are those of A. Bratti (1908–10), L. Radermacher (1911), A. T. Robertson (1914), and F. M. Abel (1927).

Independent of Deissmann are those who have sought an Aramaic original or sources to the Gospels. Pioneer was G. Dalman, *Die Worte Jesu* (1898, English trans. by D. M. Kay, 1902). Today there is general agreement that biblical Greek is the common Hellenistic Greek of the period, modified by Hebrew or Aramaic influence: so C. F. D. Moule, *An Idiom Book of New Testament Greek* (1953).

LEXICONS

HEBREW

The earliest ʿAruk (lexicon) mentioned in Hebrew literature is that of Gaon Zemah b. Paltoi of Pumbedita (ninth century), dealing however with the Talmud. The first known Hebrew lexicon is the ʾAgron (collection of words) of Saadia, Gaon of Sura (A.D. 913). These, together with the work of Judah ibn Koraish of Tahart (N. Africa), and David ben Abraham, the Karaite of the tenth century, provided the background to the *Mahberet* of Menahem ben Saruk, which was the first lexical treatment in the Hebrew language of the words of the Bible, and for long the principal lexical aid to Bible study in non-Arabic-speaking countries. The peak of lexical achievement in the Middle Ages was the *Kitab al-Usul* ('Book of Roots') of Abu al-Walid ibn Janah, who influenced all later Hebrew lexicography.

The 'Aruk of Nathan b. Jehiel of Rome, dealing with the Talmud, Midrash and Targums (*c.* 1100) is still important. David Kimḥi (1160–1235) based his *Sefer ha-Shorashim* ('Book of Roots') on the work of Abu al-Walid. This, the standard lexicon for centuries, was printed in Italy before 1480 (new ed. 1847). The first Hebrew concordance was also a kind of lexicon.

All this is the background to the decisive change of the early sixteenth century. Protestant scholars began to devote themselves to the study of the Hebrew language, even as the Jewish scholars tended to restrict their attention to the Talmud. Between 1500 and 1800 more than seventy lexicons were produced, amongst which, to judge by the number of editions published, the following were the most widely used: Johannes Reuchlin, *Rudimenta Linguae Hebraicae una cum Lexico* (1506); Alfonsus Zamorensis, *Vocabularium Hebr. et Chald. V.T.*; this formed vol. VI of the Complutensian Polyglot (1515); Sebastian Münster, *Dictionarium Hebraicum* (1523); Sanctes Pagninus, *Thesaurus Linguae Sanctae* (1529); Johann Forster, *Dictionarium hebraicum novum* (1557); Johann Buxtorf the Elder, *Lexicon Hebr. Chald.* (1607); Jo. Cocceius, *Lexicon et Commentarius Sermonis Hebr. et Chald. V.T.* (1669); Christ. Remeccius, *Janua Hebr. Linguae V.T.* (2nd ed. with lexicon, 1704); J. Simonis, *Dictionarius V.T. Hebr. et Chald.* (1752), *Lexicon Manuale Hebr. et Chald.* (1756), ed. J. G. Eichhorn (1793), enlarged by F. S. Winer (1828), English trans. (1832).

The seventeenth century was notable for polyglot lexicons. The first was that of Valentine Schindler, *Lexicon Pentaglotton Hebr. Chald. Syr. Talmudici Rabbinicum et Arab.* (1612), followed by the *Etymologicum Orientale seu Lexicon Harmonicum Heptaglotton* of H. Hottinger (1661), and the *Lexikon Heptaglotton* of Edmund Castell (1669). Albert Schultens (1686–1750) placed the comparison of Arabic and Hebrew on a sound basis, and so influenced all future lexical study. J. D. Michaelis, *Supplementa ad lexicon hebraica* (1786) drew out the implications of the work of Schultens for Hebrew philology.

Wilhelm Gesenius is reckoned as 'the father of modern Hebrew lexicography'. He published his *Hebräisch-Deutsche Handwörterbuch über die Schriften des Alten Testaments* in 1810, the basis of his *Thesaurus philologicus criticus Ling. Hebr. et Chald. V.T.* (1829–42) completed by E. Rödiger

(1853–8), and his *Lexicon Manuale Hebraicum et Chaldaicum in V.T. libros* in 1833. The Latin *Manuale* was translated into English by Edward Robinson, and this formed the basis of *A Hebrew and English Lexicon of the Old Testament*, by Francis Brown, S. R. Driver and Charles A. Briggs (1906), with additions and corrections by G. R. Driver (1953). The 17th ed. of the *Handwörterbuch*, ed. by F. Buhl (1915), remains standard.

Other notable lexicons are those of Julius Fürst, *Hebräisches und Chaldäisches Handwörterbuch über das Alte Testament* (1867); and Ludwig Koehler and Walter Baumgartner, *Lexicon in Veteris Testamenti Libros* (1953, Supplement 1958), presenting all meanings in both German and English. The *Theologisches Wörterbuch zum Neuen Testament* contains articles on all the Hebrew words that underlie the Greek of the New Testament.

GREEK

The Complutensian Polyglot (1522) contained not only a Hebrew but also a Greek–Latin glossary of the New Testament, Ecclesiasticus and Wisdom. Though incomplete and inaccurate, this has the merit of being the first attempt. To Georg Pasor, *Lexicon Graeco-Latinum in Novum Testamentum* (1619) belongs the credit of the first thoroughly scholarly production. Notable also were the *Dictionarium Novi Testamenti* of Ludovicus Lucius (1640) and *Prolusiones de Vitiis Lexicorum Novi Testamenti* of Johann Friedrich Fischer (1791), and the Greek–Latin Lexicon of C. A. Wahl (1822), English trans. by the American Edward Robinson (1825).

The best lexicon before the discoveries of papyri was C. W. L. Grimm's revision of C. G. Wilke's Greek–Latin *Clavis Novi Testamenti* (1868). This was further edited and expanded by J. H. Thayer, *Greek–English Lexicon of the New Testament* (1886).

The new discoveries were first exploited to the full by Walter Bauer, whose revision of Edwin Preuschen's Greek–German lexicon of 1910 established him as probably the greatest name in the field of New Testament lexicography. The 4th ed. (1952), *Griechisch-Deutsches Wörterbuch zu den Schriften des Neuen Testaments und der übrigen urchristlichen Literatur*, incorporating the results of an unremitting search for parallels in Greek literature down to Byzantine times, and bearing Bauer's name alone, was translated into English by W. F. Arndt and F. W. Gingrich, *A Greek–English Lexicon of the New Testament and Other Early Christian Literature* (1957). A 5th German ed. was published 1958.

J. H. Moulton and George Milligan, *Vocabulary of the Greek New Testament Illustrated from the Papyri and Other Non-literary Sources* (1914–29) is based on Grimm–Thayer and makes use of the 1st ed. of Preuschen–Bauer.

The aim of Hermann Cremer in his *Biblisch-theologisches Wörterbuch des neutestamentlichen Griechisch* (1883) was to give the conceptual background to every significant New Testament word (11th ed. revised by Julius Kögel, 1923). This aim is being achieved more completely in the *Theologisches Wörterbuch zum Neuen Testament*, started by Gerhard Kittel in 1932, and still appearing under the direction of Gerhard Friedrich. This contains indispensable lexical material on all the important words of the New Testament (even prepositions and numbers).

CONCORDANCES

LATIN

The word 'concordance', as the title of an alphabetical list of all the words in the Bible with references, seems to have been used first by Hugo de Sancto Claro, whose concordance of the Vulgate was produced about A.D. 1244, and printed, with modifications, in 1479. Sebastian Brant, in his *Concordantiae maiores bibliae tam dictionum declinabilium quam indeclinabilium* (1496), added the work of John of Ragusa on the indeclinable words of Scripture to the concordance of Conrad of Halberstadt (1310).

Many concordances have since been based on this. Probably the best is that of F. P. Dutripon, *Vulgatae Editionis Bibliorum sacrorum Concordantiae* (1838). That of V. Cooraert, *Concordantiae Librorum Veteris et Novi Testamenti...juxta Vulgatam Editionem* (1892) was intended for the use of preachers. None of these gives the Hebrew or Greek originals. Peter Mintert's *Lexicon Graeco-Latinum* of the New Testament (1728) serves as a concordance and gives Greek and, where necessary, Hebrew equivalents.

HEBREW

The Hebrew scholar Isaac Nathan b. Kalonymus of Arles used the work of Hugo de Sancto Claro as the foundation of his concordance to the Hebrew Bible (1437–45), first published by Bomberg at Venice (1523), and designed to assist in polemics against Christian scholars. This is the basis of all later Hebrew concordances. It was enlarged by the addition of a concordance to the Aramaic parts of the Bible and lists of proper names and places, by Marius de Calasto, *Concordantiae sacrorum bibliorum* (1621). It was further edited and improved by Johann Buxtorf the Elder of Basle (1632) in a form which was unrivalled for two hundred years. This in turn was the basis of the two most widely used concordances of the present day: (1) Julius Fürst, *Librorum sacrorum Veteris Testamenti concordantiae hebraicae* (1840), so thoroughly extended and revised that he gave it his own name. B. Davidson's *Concordance of the Hebrew and Chaldaic Scriptures* (1876) is an English version of this; (2) Solomon Mandelkern brought out an entirely fresh revision, *Veteris Testamenti Concordantiae Hebraicae atque Chaldaicae* (1896), and this latter, despite some errors, holds the field. The *Konkordanz zum Hebräischen A.T.* by Gerhard Lisowsky, in co-operation with Leonhard Rost (1958), is a photographic reproduction of the compiler's own handwritten, vocalized textual extracts.

GREEK

I. *The Septuagint*

The first, on the whole Bible, may have been made by the Basilian monk Euthalius of Rhodes (1300); in the West by Conrad Kircher, *Concordantiae Veteris Testamenti Graecae Hebraeis vocibus respondentes...* (1607). Thereafter Trommius's *Concordantiae Graecae Versionis...LXX Interpretum*, including reference to the versions of Aquila, Symmachus and Theodotion, remained standard until all previous concordances were superseded by *A Concordance to the Septuagint and the other Greek Versions of the Old Testament (including the Apocryphal books)* by Edwin Hatch and Henry A. Redpath (1892–7).

II. *The Greek New Testament*

The first were those of S. Birken or Betulius, *Novi Testamenti Concordantiae Graecae* (1546), Henry Estienne (1594) and Erasmus Schmidius (1638).

In 1842 C. H. Bruder published his *Concordantiae omnium vocum Novi Testamenti Graeci*, which was based on the *textus receptus*. This was not superseded until Moulton and Geden produced their *Concordance to the Greek Testament, according to the text of Westcott and Hort, Tischendorf and the English Revisers* (1897). R. Morgenthaler's *Statistik des neutestamentlichen Wortschatzes* (1958) is a unique, statistical analysis, with tables and graphs, of the use of words and their associations in the Greek New Testament.

ENGLISH

The first concordance in English was published by Thomas Gybson, *The concordance of the New Testament, most necessary to be had in the handes of all soche as (delight) in the comunicacion of any place contayned in ye new Testament* (1535). The second was that of John Marbecke, *A Concordance, that is to saie, a worke wherein, by the ordre of the letters of the A.B.C., ye may redely finde any worde conteigned in the whole Bible* (1550). That of Robert F. Herry was printed with later editions of the Geneva Bible. In the seventeenth century the outstanding concordance was that of Clement Cotton (1631), revised and extended by Samuel Newman, *A Large and Complete Concordance to the Bible in English according to the Last Translation* (1643). This was the precursor of Alexander Cruden's *Complete Concordance to the Old and New Testaments* (1738) which formed the basis of modern concordances. It had the advantage, absent from the better modern concordances, of including the Apocrypha. The major modern productions are Robert Young's *Analytical Concordance to the Bible* (1879–84), which indicates the Hebrew, Aramaic and Greek originals, and distinguishes the various meanings underlying a word; and James Strong's *The Exhaustive Concordance of the Bible, together with a comparative concordance of the Authorized and Revised Versions* (1894), which refers only to the English text. The use of a modern electronic computer enabled Nelson's to publish their *Complete Concordance of the Revised Standard Version of the Bible* (1957) five years after the completion of the Revised Standard Version itself.

BIBLE DICTIONARIES AND ENCYCLOPAEDIAS

The earliest attempt at a limited Bible dictionary was made by Eusebius of Caesarea (*c.* 260–340), who compiled a list of geographical names (*Onomastica Sacra*). Jerome carried this further in his two works, the *Liber Interpretationis Hebraicorum Nominum*, and the *De Situ et Nominibus Locorum Hebraicorum Liber*. The first attempt to gather together the immense amount of material separately collected by French, Dutch and English orientalists of the period of the Renaissance was made by the Protestant Johann Heinrich Alstedt, *Triumphus Bibliorum Sacrorum seu Encyclopaedia Biblica* (1625). The *Bibliotheca Sacra seu Thesaurus Scripturae Canonicae* of P. Ravenilli (1650) was in the form of a dictionary to the Vulgate.

The epoch-making name before the rise of the critical movement was that of the French Benedictine Augustin Calmet, *Dictionnaire historique, critique, géographique et littéral de la Bible*, 4 vols. (1720–1), English trans. by S. D'Oyly and J. Colson (1732). This was based on the *Dictionarium Biblicum* of M. Simon (1693). Based on Calmet was Daniel Schneider's *Allgemeines Biblisches Lexikon* (3 vols. 1728–31).

Thereafter the chief Bible dictionaries show the all-pervading influence of the critical movement. First was the *Biblische Encyclopädie* (1793–8), never finished, and then superseded by G. B. Winer's *Biblisches Real-Wörterbuch* (2 vols. 1820), which remained standard for years.

It was now accepted that a Bible dictionary was beyond the capacity of any one man, and the age of composite productions began with the *Real-Encyclopädie für Protestantische Theologie und Kirche*, ed. Herzog (1852–62), 2nd ed. by Herzog and Platt (1877–88), 3rd ed. by A. Hauck (24 vols. 1896).

This was followed by Schenkel's *Bibellexikon* (5 vols. 1869–75), and by E. C. A Riehm's *Handwörterbuch des Biblischen Alterthums* (2 vols. 1874), 2nd ed. F. Baethgen (1894).

The first to produce a dictionary in England, independent of the pattern set by Calmet, was John Kitto, *A Cyclopaedia of Biblical Literature* (1843–5). More scholarly was the *Dictionary of the Bible* by W. Smith and W. Aldis Wright (1860). McClintock and Strong's *Cyclopaedia of Biblical, Theological and Ecclesiastical Literature* (12 vols. 1867–87) was popular in the United States of America. W. Robertson Smith planned an Encyclopaedia Biblica, but much of the material he meant to use was incorporated in the *Encyclopaedia Biblia*, ed. by T. K. Cheyne and J. S. Black (4 vols. 1899–1903). This registered a somewhat radical stage in the progress of biblical scholarship. Less radical but still critical were the works ed. by J. Hastings, *Dictionary of the Bible* (5 vols. 1898–1904), a single-vol. *Dictionary of the Bible* (1898), a *Dictionary of Christ and the Gospels* (2 vols. 1906–8), and a *Dictionary of the Apostolic Church* (2 vols. 1915–18).

In France Roman Catholic scholarship produced the *Dictionnaire de la Bible*, ed. by F. Vigouroux (1895–1912), prefaced with an encyclical of Leo XIII; a *Supplément au Dictionnaire* is still being published.

Other recent dictionaries are the *'Ensiklopedya Mikra'ith, Encyclopaedia Biblica, Thesaurus rerum biblicarum alphabetico ordine digestus* (3 vols. out of five, 1950ff.) in modern Hebrew, and mainly, but not exclusively, by Jewish scholars; *Bibel-lexicon*, ed. by H. Haag (with A. van den Born and others, 1951–6) based on a Dutch production of 1941, and *Svenskt Bibliskt Uppslagverk*, ed. by I. Engnell and A. Friedrichsen (1948–52).

Many encyclopaedias, designed to cover a much wider field, contain important contributions on biblical subjects, and, since the seventeenth century, the encyclopaedia has become so assimilated in form to the dictionary, that the distinction between them is often not obvious. In this category are: *Encyclopaedia of Religion and Ethics*, J. Hastings (13 vols. 1908–26, American ed. 1927); *The Jewish Encyclopaedia*, Singer (1901–6); *Real-Encyclopädie für Bibel und Talmud*, Hamburger (1896–7); *Jüdisches Lexikon*, Herlitz and Kirschener (1927–30); *Die Religion in Geschichte und Gegenwart* (1909–13), 2nd ed. (Gunkel and Zscharnack) largely rewritten (1927–31), 3rd ed. K. Galling in progress; *Encyclopaedia Judaica*, Klatzken and Elbogen (1928–32); *Lexikon für Theologie und Kirche*, Buchberger (10 vols. 1930–8, new ed. in progress).

Appendix I

ATLASES

The first maps of the Holy Land were more in the nature of crude, inaccurate diagrams than what is now understood by scientific cartography. Amongst the earliest are those in Herrmann's *Prologus Arminensis in mappam Terrae Sanctae templi domini ac Sancte civitatis Hierusalem* (1476), seven maps of Palestine in Jacobus Ziegler's *Terra Sancta* (1532) and twelve in C. Adrichom's *Theatrum Terrae Sanctae* (1593). It became common to insert 'maps' in the early Bibles. Thus there was a rough 'map' of 'the Land of promys' in Jugge's revision of Tyndale's version of the New Testament (1552), and another illustrating St Paul's journeys 'with the distaunce of the Myles' in the 1553 edition. In the Geneva Bible of 1560 there were five maps, some closely copied in the Bishops' Bible of 1568. Until the eighteenth century students were mainly dependent upon accounts of the Holy Land given by travellers and pilgrims. Samuel Bochart's *Geographia sacra seu Phaleg et Chanaan* (1646) was the major work of the seventeenth century. Adrian Reland, in *Palaestina ex monumentis veteribus illustrata* (2 vols. 1714) for the first time collected and presented critically all relevant information, ancient and modern. This work contained maps and remained standard until the nineteenth century. Universal atlases of the seventeenth and eighteenth centuries, and especially atlases of the ancient world (Jansson, Chiverius, Cellarius, Horn) usually contained one or two maps of the Terra Promissa and of the Mediterranean world: most skilful were those of N. Sanson. In 1838 the foundations of modern topographical knowledge were laid by Edward Robinson and Eli Smith, whose works 'alone surpass the total of all previous contributions to Palestinian geography from the time of Eusebius and Jerome to the early nineteenth century'—especially *Palästina und die südlich abgrenzenden Länder. Tagebuch einer Reise im Jahre 1838 in bezug auf die biblische Geographie* (3 vols. 1841–2). The first scientific cartographic survey (1 in. to a mile) was made by C. R. Conder and his associates (1871–8), under the Palestine Exploration Fund (founded 1865). The major atlases could now be produced: H. Guthe, *Bibelatlas* (1911, 1926^2), G. Adam Smith and J. G. Bartholomew, *Atlas of the Historical Geography of the Holy Land* (1915), G. E. Wright and F. V. Filson, *Westminster Historical Atlas to the Bible* (1945) and L. H. Grollenberg, *Atlas van de Bijbel* (1954) translated into French by R. Beaupère (1955), and translated into English and edited by J. M. H. Reid and H. H. Rowley (1956).

APPENDIX II

AIDS TO THE STUDY OF THE BIBLE

COMMENTARIES

The earliest known commentaries on books of the Old Testament are those found at Qumran; the most complete is on Habakkuk (probably first century B.C.); there are fragments of many others. The rabbis developed an elaborate exegetical and hermeneutical system. The first New Testament commentary may have been that of the Gnostic Basilides on 'the Gospel', followed by that of Heracleon on John (known by forty quotations in Origen). If the work of Papias called *Exposition of the Lord's oracles* (Eus. *H.E.* III, xxxix) is a commentary, it can claim to be the first orthodox commentary. Otherwise certainly Hippolytus of Rome (*c.* 170–*c.* 236), who wrote commentaries on Daniel and Canticles, has that honour. Origen (*c.* 185–*c.* 254) is the first of the Fathers who may be regarded as primarily a biblical exegete (allegorical): he wrote commentaries on most books of the Bible, of which much on Matthew and John survives, with some sections on Canticles and Romans. Thereafter most of the Fathers wrote commentaries, including Eusebius (*c.* 342, on Psalms and Isaiah), Athanasius (Psalms), Basil (Isaiah i–xvi), Gregory of Nazianzus, Cyril of Alexandria (Isaiah, XII Prophets, John), Apollinarius; Diodore of Tarsus (Genesis), Theodore of Mopsuestia (many books, typical of Antiochene exegesis by his literal and historical emphasis, and held in honour by a succession of Nestorian exegetes), John Chrysostom, Polychronius (Job, Ezekiel, Daniel), Theodoret (Canticles, Daniel, XII Prophets, Epistles of St Paul). Hilary of Poitiers (Matthew, Psalms, Job) inaugurated the succession of Latin exegetes, including Ambrose (threefold sense), Jerome (342–420; first and last a biblical scholar and commentator), Tyconius (Revelation), Ambrosiaster, Pelagius (Epistles of St Paul), Augustine, Cassiodorus, Gregory the Great (*c.* 540–604; on Job—threefold sense). Exegesis then lost its force and originality, giving way to the tendency to compile *catenae*. The most famous of the early catenists, who succeeded one another throughout the Middle Ages, was Procopius of Gaza (*c.* 475–538).

A succession of Byzantine exegetes from Olympiodorus and Oecumenius (oldest Greek commentary on Revelation) in the sixth century, to the catenists of the thirteenth to fifteenth centuries, were important as a group, but none individually outstanding. The Jacobite (monophysite) church of Syria also produced commentators, beginning with Philoxenus, bishop of

Mabbug (*c.* 440–523; on the Gospels), and ending with Abu-l-Farag (Barhebraeus, 1226–86), whose *Horreum Mysteriorum* or 'Granary of mysteries', a collection of scholia on the Bible, is a vast repertory of glosses.

Medieval exegesis in the West showed little originality, and depended mainly on the western Fathers, especially Augustine. Bede (*c.* 673–735) was better known in the Middle Ages for his commentaries than for his *Ecclesiastical History*. With Bede the patristic tradition ends. Raban Maur and Alcuin mainly reproduced their sources. The two most original commentators of the ninth century were Paschasius Radbertus (*c.* 785–860; 12 vols. on Matthew), and John the Scot (*c.* 810–77; on John). After Remigius of Auxerre (*c.* 841–908), there was nothing for over a century. Rupert of Deutz (*c.* 1070–1129; especially on XII Prophets) practised allegorical interpretation, but was the first to dissociate the authority of Scripture from that of the Fathers. The great achievement of the eleventh and twelfth centuries was the *Glossa Ordinaria* which, with the *Postillae* of Nicholas of Lyra, and *Additiones* of Paul of Burgos (fifteenth century), was printed many times between the fifteenth and eighteenth centuries in 6 folio volumes. The key figure was Anselm of Laon (d. 1117) who began, but did not complete, a gloss of the whole of Scripture; he was himself responsible for the gloss on the Pauline Epistles, Psalms, and probably also John. The Gloss became standard in western Christendom; the 'set-book' for students was the Bible and the Gloss.

At the same time the form of 'question' and 'discussion' was developed, for example the *Magna Glosatura* of Peter the Lombard (*c.* 1100–60) on the Pauline Epistles and Psalms, and the *Quaestiones et decisiones in Epistolas S. Pauli* of Robert of Melun (d. 1167). The twelfth century is also the century of the Victorines, especially Hugh (*c.* 1096–1141) who practised a literal exegesis, and, anticipating some Reformation emphases, Andrew (d. 1175) who, influenced by Rashi (1040–1105) the Jewish commentator, made a rigorous attempt to interpret the Bible according to its literal sense. The modern division of the text into chapters is sometimes attributed to Stephen Langton (d. 1228), who produced a series of glosses covering the Old and New Testaments. The twelfth century also saw the appearance of the *Distinctio*, a form of biblical glossary or 'spiritual' dictionary.

In the thirteenth century the biblical studies of the Middle Ages reached their climax of achievement in the universities, and especially in Paris, centre of the Dominicans, Hugo of St Cher, Albert the Great (1200–80), whose commentaries are the most representative type of literal exegesis of the thirteenth century, and Bonaventure, and the Franciscan Nicholas of Lyra (1270–1340). Thomas Aquinas, also a Dominican, and influenced by Albert, wrote commentaries on the Gospels (the *Catena Aurea*), the Epistles, Isaiah, Jeremiah, Psalms, and Job.

Appendix II

The effect of the Renaissance was to release a flood of original classical documents for study. This made for a new concentration on the Greek of the New Testament, and the Hebrew of the Old Testament, thus finally relaxing the exclusive hold of the Latin version. Desiderius Erasmus (1466–1536) was the primary figure in restoring the Greek Testament to the Church; he produced the *editio princeps* of the New Testament (1516), together with Paraphrases and Annotations dealing with words and phrases of the New Testament. A similarly independent Catholic humanist who showed a certain sympathy with some aspects of the Reformation was Lefèvre d'Étaples (1455–1536). He wrote a Latin commentary on the Epistles of St Paul and on the Gospels. The effect of the Reformation principle *sola scriptura* was an outpouring of scriptural exegesis, which the invention of printing made widely available. The tendency was to break with the habit of allegorical interpretation and the threefold sense, and to concentrate on the literal and historical meaning. Luther wrote commentaries on Galatians (1519), Romans, Psalms, and Hebrews, but scriptural interpretation runs through all his work. These, with his German translation of the Bible, and the Prefaces, are, in effect, some of the most influential commentaries of the Reformation. Calvin (1509–64) was pre-eminently a biblical commentator, whose commentaries, on almost the whole of the Bible, fill vols. 23–55 of his works in the *Corpus Reformatorum*. They are highly systematic, and in their constant refusal to read into the text, belong to the modern age. Melanchthon, Zwingli, Theodore Beza, Musculus, Pellicanus, Brenz, Bugenhagen, Bullinger, Bucer, Mercerus, and many others rank as exegetes. Calvin owed most to Bucer. Beza was highly regarded in England, and his readings influenced the 1611 translation. Pellicanus and Mercerus may be said to have created a tradition whose highest point was reached in Vitringa. The Geneva Bible of 1560, which for three-quarters of a century became the household Bible of the English-speaking peoples, contained a marginal commentary.

Post-Reformation exegesis showed deterioration. It tended to be confessional, dogmatic and scholastic. Roman Catholic scholars carried on the dogmatic traditions of the Middle Ages. Among the more distinguished were Cardinal Cajetan (1469–1534; on the whole of the New Testament except Revelation), Juan Maldonado on the Prophets and especially on the Gospels (2 vols. 1596–7), Cornelius a Lapide, on all the canonical books except Job and Psalms (1614–45), Jacques Bonfrère, *Pentateuchus Mosis commentario illustratus* (1631) and Antoine Calmet, *Commentaire littéral sur tous les livres de l'ancien et du nouveau Testament* (1707–16). From 1650 to 1880 no commentator of note.

In the Reformation tradition there were commentaries distinguished for erudition and new principles in illustration and research. Such were the

Annotationes in utrumque Testamentum (8 vols. 1873–84) of Lucas Osiander; the works of John Drusius (d. 1616); the *Annotationes in Vetus et Novum Testamentum et libros Apocryphos* (1642) of H. Grotius, who made a new departure by his method of philological criticism; the many commentaries of Johannes Cocceius (1603–69); the *Critica Sacra* (1650) of Ludovicus Cappellus; the *Harmonica Evangelica* and various commentaries of Jean Leclerc (1657–1736); the *Commentarius in librum prophetarum Jesaiae...* (2 vols. 1714, 1720) of Campegius Vitringa; the elaborate commentary on Job (2 vols. 1737), and on Proverbs of Albert Schultens; the *Gnomom Novi Testamenti* (1742) of Albrecht Bengel, critic of the text of the New Testament; the *Libelli ad Crisin atque Interpretationem Novi Testamenti* (a repository of classical and rabbinic illustration) and edition of the New Testament (1751) of J. J. Wettstein; and the *Mosaisches Recht* (6 vols. 1770–5) of J. D. Michaelis (English trans. *Commentaries on the Laws of Moses*, by Alexander Smith, 4 vols. 1814).

Outstanding English commentators were Henry Hammond, *A Paraphrase and Annotations upon all the books of the New Testament* (1653); John Lightfoot, *Horae Hebraicae et Talmudicae* (6 vols. 1658–78); Edward Pococke, on the XII Prophets (1677–91); Simon Patrick on Genesis–Canticles (10 vols. 1695–1710); Daniel Whitby, *A Paraphrase and Commentary on the New Testament* (2 vols. 1703); and Robert Lowth, Isaiah (1778). Influential expositions of a more devotional kind were those of Matthew Henry, *Exposition of the Old and New Testaments* (1708–10), and Thomas Scott, *Commentary on the Bible* (1788–92).

In the nineteenth century, the critical movement inspired a new outpouring of commentaries, beginning with that on Isaiah (1820–1) by H. F. W. Gesenius, and that on the Psalms (1823) by W. M. L. de Wette. A new feature was the production of *series* of commentaries. Among the more important were: *Kritisch-exegetischer Kommentar über das N.T.*, ed. by H. A. W. Meyer (16 vols. 1832–52; English trans. 20 vols. 1873–95); this series, marked by exact scholarship, and among the most comprehensive in any language, was regularly revised and rewritten. *Kurzgefasstes exegetisches Handbuch z. A.T.* (17 vols. from 1838). The plans of Westcott, Lightfoot and Hort in 1860 led to the *Macmillan Commentaries* on books of the New Testament which include some of the best in the English language. *Biblischer Commentar über das A.T.*, by C. F. Keil and Franz Delitzsch (1861–93). *Kurzgefasster Kommentar zu den heiligen Schriften des A. u. N.T.*, ed. by H. L. Strack and O. Zöckler, from 1886. The *International Critical Commentary*, ed. by S. R. Driver, A. Plummer and C. A. Briggs, from 1895, on the Hebrew and Greek text, critical, and comprehensive. *Handkommentar z. A.T.*, ed. by W. Nowack, from 1892. *Kurzer Hand-*

Commentar z. A.T., ed. by K. Marti (1897–1903). *Kommentar z. A.T.*, ed. by E. Sellin from 1913, and *Kommentar z. N.T.*, ed. by Th. Zahn from 1910. The form-critical standpoint is represented in the *Göttingen Bible*, *Die Schriften des A.T.* under the editorship of Gunkel, Gressmann and Hans Schmidt, and *Die Schriften des N.T.* ed. by J. Weiss from 1905. *Handbuch z. A.T.*, ed. by O. Eissfeldt from 1935, and *Handbuch z. N.T.*, ed. by H. Lietzmann from 1906, by G. Bornkamm from 1947. *Text en Uitleg*, ed. by F. M. T. Böhl and Van Veldhuisen, from 1928. All these, together with the slighter *Century Bible* (on the English text), *Expositor's Greek Testament*, *Westminster Commentaries* (on the English text), *Cambridge Bible* and *Cambridge Greek Testament*, and the *Moffatt New Testament Commentaries*, represent the critical movement in its most confident phase. *Das Alte Testament Deutsch* and *Das Neue Testament Deutsch* are an attempt at more theological exposition. The *Soncino Books of the Bible* are by Jewish scholars. Distinguished Roman Catholic scholarship is represented by *Études Bibliques*, from 1903, founded by M.-J. Lagrange, whose own commentaries on the Gospels, Romans and Galatians are notable landmarks in the Roman Catholic assimilation of critical standpoints. *Exegetisches Handbuch z. A.T.*, ed. by J. Nikel and A. Schulz, from 1911. *Die Heilige Schrift des A.T.*, ed. by F. Feldmann and H. Herkenne from 1923. *La Sainte Bible*, ed. L'École Biblique de Jérusalem, from 1948.

Among the more influential one-volume commentaries, each by a variety of authors, are *Commentary on the Bible*, ed. by A. S. Peake (1919), rewritten as *Peake's Commentary on the Bible*, ed. by M. Black and H. H. Rowley (1962); *A New Commentary on Holy Scripture*, ed. by Charles Gore, H. L. Goudge and A. Guillaume (1928); *A Catholic Commentary on Holy Scripture*, ed. by B. Orchard, E. F. Sutcliffe, R. C. Fuller and R. Russell (1953).

Specially influential individual commentaries within the series have been those of Bernhard Duhm on Isaiah (1892) and Jeremiah (1901), and Hermann Gunkel on Genesis (1901) and Psalms (1926). Outside the series: Julius Wellhausen on Mark (1903), Matthew (1904), Luke (1904), John (1908). Karl Barth, *The Epistle to the Romans* (1918), English trans. of the 6th ed. by Edwyn C. Hoskyns (1933); this may be said to have arrested the more radical phase of biblical scholarship, at any rate in so far as it was associated with a 'liberal' theology. *Kommentar z. N.T. aus Talmud und Midrasch*, by H. L. Strack and Paul Billerbeck (1922–8). *The Fourth Gospel*, by Edwyn C. Hoskyns (ed. by F. N. Davey, 2 vols. 1940); and, on almost the whole of the New Testament, the independent work of Adolf Schlatter (1852–1939).

BIBLIOGRAPHY

CHAPTER I

1. *Luther*

Werke (Frankfurt and Erlangen, 1826–57).
Werke, Kritische Gesamtausgabe (Weimar, 1883 ff.).
Werke in Auswahl (Bonn, 1912–33).
On the authority and interpretation of Scripture:
Bizer, E., *Fides ex Auditu* (Neukirchen, 1958).
Bornkamm, H., *Luther und das Alte Testament* (Tübingen, 1948).
Ebeling, G., *Evangelische Evangelienauslegung* (München, 1942).
Ebeling, G., 'Die Anfänge von Luthers Hermeneutik', *Zeitschrift für Theologie und Kirche*, XLVIII (1951), 172–230.
Ebeling, G., 'Luthers Auslegung des 44. (45.) Psalms', *Lutherforschung Heute* (1958).
Fullerton, K., 'Luther's Doctrine and Criticism of Scripture', *Bibliotheca Sacra*, LXIII (1906), 1–34, 284–99.
Holl, Karl, 'Luthers Bedeutung für den Fortschritt der Auslegungskunst', *Gesammelte Aufsätze*, I (Tübingen, 1928), 544–82.
Howorth, H. H., 'The Origin and Authority of the Biblical Canon', *Journal of Theological Studies*, VIII, 321–65; IX, 188–230 (Oxford, 1907–8).
Kolmodin, A., *Skriftens Auktoritet Enligt Luther* (1919).
Loewenich, W. von, 'Luther und das johanneische Christentum', *Forschungen zur Geschichte und Lehre des Protestantismus*, VII, 4 (1935).
Loewenich, W. von, *Luther als Ausleger der Synoptiker* (München, 1954).
Pelikan, J., *Luther the Expositor* (St Louis, 1959).
Preuss, H., *Die Entwicklung des Schriftprinzips bei Luther bis zur Leipziger Disputation* (Leipzig, 1901).
Quanbeck, W. A., 'Luther's Early Exegesis', in *Luther Today* (Decorah, 1957).
Reu, M., *Luther's German Bible* (Columbus, 1934).
Scheel, O., *Luthers Stellung zur Heiligen Schrift* (Tübingen, 1902).
Schempp, P., *Luthers Stellung zur Heiligen Schrift* (München, 1929).
Schwarz, W., *Principles and Problems of Biblical Translation*, ch. VI (Cambridge, 1955).
Schwarz, W., 'Studies in Luther's Attitude towards Humanism', *Journal of Theological Studies*, n.s. VI (Oxford, 1955).
Thimme, K., *Luthers Stellung zur Heiligen Schrift* (Gütersloh, 1903).

2. *Zwingli*

The Latin Works...of Huldreich Zwingli, English trans. ed. S. M. Jackson, 3 vols. (New York, 1912; Philadelphia, 1922, 1929).
Hauptschriften, ed. O. Farner, etc. (Zürich, 1940 ff.).

Sämtliche Werke, I–XI, Corpus Reformatorum, vols. 88–98 (Leipzig, 1905–35).
Selected Works of H. Zwingli, English trans. S. M. Jackson (New York, 1901).
Zwingli and Bullinger, ed. G. W. Bromiley (Library of Christian Classics, XXIV, London, 1953). [A selection in English, including Zwingli's *On the Clarity and Certainty of the Word of God.*]
Nagel, E., *Zwinglis Stellung zur Schrift* (Freiburg, 1896).

3. *Calvin*

Opera quae supersunt omnia, Corpus Reformatorum, vols. 29–87 (Brunswick and Berlin, 1863–1900).
Opera Selecta, ed. P. Barth and G. Niesel, 5 vols. (Munich, 1926–36).
[The Commentaries were published in an English version by the Calvin Translation Society, 45 vols.]
Calvin: Commentaries, ed. J. Haroutunian and L. P. Smith, Library of Christian Classics, XXIII (London, 1958). [A selection in English with a discussion of Calvin's attitude to the Bible.]
Dowey, E. A., *The Knowledge of God in Calvin's Theology* (New York, 1952).
Wallace, R. S., *Calvin's Doctrine of the Word and Sacrament* (Edinburgh, 1954).

4. *The Anabaptists and the left wing of the Reformation*

Bainton, R. H., 'David Joris', *Archiv für Reformationsgeschichte, Ergänzungsband*, VI (1957).
Bainton, R. H., *Castellio concerning Heretics* (New York, 1935).
Bender, H., *Life and Letters of Conrad Grebel* (Goshen, 1950).
Boehmer, H. and Kirn, P., *Thomas Müntzers Briefwechsel* (Leipzig, 1931).
Brandt, O. H., *Thomas Müntzer: Leben und Schriften* (Jena, 1933).
Hegler, A., *Geist und Schrift bei Sebastian Franck* (Freiburg i. Breisgau, 1892).
Littell, F., *The Anabaptist View of the Church* (rev. ed., Chicago, 1958).
Lohmann, A., 'Zur geistigen Entwicklung Thomas Müntzers', *Beiträge zur Kulturgeschichte des Mittelalters und der Renaissance*, XLVII (1931).

5. *The Word and the Spirit*

Burckhardt, A. E., *Das Geistproblem bei Huldrych Zwingli* (Leipzig, 1932).
Gerdes, H., *Luthers Streit mit den Schwärmern um das rechte Verständnis des Gesetzes Mose* (Göttingen, 1955).
Grützmacher, R. H., *Wort und Geist* (Leipzig, 1902).
Krusche, W., *Das Wirken des Heiligen Geistes nach Calvin* (Göttingen, 1957).
Maronier, J. H., *Het Inwendig Woord* (1890).
Prenter, R., *Spiritus Creator* (Copenhagen, 1946). [For Luther.]
Rupp, E. G., 'Word and Spirit in the First Years of the Reformation', *Archiv für Reformationsgeschichte*, XLIX (1959), 13–26.

Bibliography

CHAPTER II

Allen, P. S., 'The Trilingual Colleges of the Early Sixteenth Century', in *Erasmus* (Oxford, 1934).

Armstrong, E., *Robert Estienne* (Cambridge, 1954).

Bachelet, X.-M., *Bellarmin et la Bible Sixto-Clémentine* (Paris, 1911).

Baumgartner, J., *Calvin Hébraïsant et interprète de l'Ancien Testament* (1881).

Diestel, L., *Geschichte des Alten Testaments in der Christlichen Kirche* (Jena, 1869).

Erasmus, D., *Ratio seu methodus compendio perveniendi ad veram theologiam* (Basel, 1522).

Erasmus, D., *Ecclesiastae sive de ratione Concionandi* (Antwerp, 1535).

Erasmus, D., *Opus Epistolarum*, ed. P. S. Allen, 12 vols. (Oxford, 1906–58).

Estienne, Robert, *Les Censures des Théologiens de Paris* (Geneva, 1866). [Facsimile of the edition of 1552.]

Flacius Illyricus, *Clavis Scripturae Sanctae* (Basel, 1567).

Ginsburg, C. D., *Introduction to the Massoretico-Critical Editions of the Hebrew Bible* (London, 1897).

Ginsburg, C. D., *Jacob ben Chajim's Introduction to the Rabbinic Bible* (London, 1865).

Hirschfield, H., *The Literary History of Hebrew Grammarians and Lexicographers* (London, 1926).

The Jewish Encyclopaedia (articles: Bomberg, Elias Levita, Soncino), 12 vols. (New York, 1901–6).

Kraus, Hans-Joachim, *Geschichte des historische-kritischen Erforschung des Alten Testaments von der Reformation bis zur Gegenwart* (Neukirchen, 1956).

Kukenheim, L., *Contributions à l'histoire de la grammaire grecque, latine et hébraïque à l'époque de la Renaissance* (Leiden, 1951).

Lefèvre, J. (Faber Stapulensis), *Commentarii Initiatorii in Quatuor Evangelia*, Preface (Paris, 1522).

Le Long, J., *Bibliotheca sacra seu Syllabus omnium ferme Sacrae Scripturae editionum ac versionum*, 2 vols. (Leipzig, 1709).

Reuss, E., *Geschichte der Heiligen Schriften des Alten Testaments* (Brunswick, 1890).

Reuss, E., *Bibliotheca Novi Testamenti Graeci* (Brunswick, 1872).

Reuss, E., *Geschichte der Heiligen Schriften des Neuen Testaments* (Brunswick, 1887).

Rooses, M., *Correspondance de Christophe Plantin*, 8 vols. (Antwerp, 1883–1918).

Rosenthal, F., 'The Rise of Christian Hebraism in the Sixteenth Century', *Historia Judaica*, vol. VII (New York, 1945).

Simon, R., *Histoire critique du Vieux Testament* (Rotterdam, 1685).

Simon, R., *Histoire critique du texte du Nouveau Testament* (Rotterdam, 1689).

Simon, R., *Histoire critique des versions du Nouveau Testament* (Rotterdam, 1690).

Simon, R., *Histoire critique des principaux commentateurs du Nouveau Testament* (Rotterdam, 1693).

Tregelles, S. P., *An Account of the Printed Text of the Greek New Testament* (London, 1854).

Walton, B., *Biblia Sacra Polyglotta*, Prolegomena (London, 1655–7).
Widmanstadt, J. A. von, *Liber Sacrosancti Evangelii de Jesu Christo Domino et Deo Nostro*, Preface (Vienna, 1555).

CHAPTER III

German versions

Baring, G., 'Die "Wörmser Propheten", eine vorlutherische evangelische Prophetenübersetzung aus dem Jahre 1527', *Archiv für Reformationsgeschichte*, XXXI (1934), 23–41.
Bornkamm, H., 'Luthers Übersetzung des Neuen Testaments', in *Luthers geistige Welt* (3. Aufl., Gütersloh, 1959), pp. 263–71.
Eis, G., *Frühneuhochdeutsche Bibelübersetzungen. Texte von 1400–1600* (Frankfurt a.M., 1949).
Freitag, A., 'Die Zainerbibel als Quelle der Lutherbibel', *Theologische Studien und Kritiken*, C (1927–8), 444–54.
Goeze, J. M., *Versuch einer Historie der gedruckten Niedersächsischen Bibeln vom Jahr 1470 bis 1621* (Halle, 1775).
Grimm, W., 'Zur Charakteristik der Luther'schen Übersetzung des Buches Jesus Sirach', *Zeitschrift für wissenschaftliche Theologie*, XV (1872), 521–38.
Grimm, W., 'Luthers Übersetzung der alttestamentlichen Apokryphen', *Theologische Studien und Kritiken*, LVI (1883), 375–400.
Grimm, W., *Kurzgefasste Geschichte der lutherischen Bibelübersetzung bis zur Gegenwart* (Jena, 1884).
Leeman-van Elck, P., *Der Buchschmuck der Zürcher-Bibeln bis 1800 nebst Bibliographie der in Zürich bis 1800 gedruckten Bibeln, Alten und Neuen Testamente* (Bern, 1938).
Luther's *Werke, Kritische Gesamtausgabe*, Abt. Deutsche Bibel, Bd. II (Weimar, 1909): *Bibliographie der hochdeutsche Bibeldrucke 1522–1546*; Bd. VI (Weimar, 1929)–XII (Weimar, 1961): *Text des Neuen und Alten Testamentes.*
Mezger, J. J., *Geschichte der Deutschen Bibelübersetzungen in der schweizerisch-reformirten Kirche von der Reformation bis zur Gegenwart* (Basel, 1876).
Pahl, T., *Quellenstudien zu Luthers Psalmenübersetzung* (Weimar, 1931).
Panzer, G. W., *Entwurf einer vollständigen Geschichte der deutschen Bibelübersetzung D. Martin Luthers vom Jahr 1517 an, bis 1581* (Nürnberg, 1783) with *Zusätzen* (Nürnberg, 1791).
Panzer, G. W., *Versuch einer kurzen Geschichte der römisch-katholischen deutschen Bibelübersetzung* (Nürnberg, 1781).
Reichert, O., *D. Martin Luthers Deutsche Bibel* (Tübingen, 1910).
Rosenfeld, H. F., 'Luther, Erasmus und wir', *Forschungen und Fortschritte*, XXIX (1955), 313–17.
Schramm, A., *Die Illustration der Lutherbibel* (Leipzig, 1923).
Vogel, P. H., *Europäische Bibeldrucke des 15. und 16. Jahrhunderts in den Volkssprachen* (Baden-Baden, 1962), 23–51.
Volz, H., *Hundert Jahre Wittenberger Bibeldruck, 1522–1626* (Göttingen, 1954).

Volz, H., 'Zur Überlieferung des Gebetes Manasse', *Zeitschrift für Kirchengeschichte*, LXX (1959), 293–307.

Volz, H., 'Melanchthons Anteil an der Lutherbibel', *Archiv für Reformationsgeschichte*, XLV (1954), 196–232.

Volz, H., Einleitungen zu Weimarer Lutherausgabe, Abt. Deutsche Bibel, Bd. VIII (Pentateuch), Bd. IX² (Historische Bücher), Bd. X² (Poetische Bücher), Bd. XI² (Propheten; mit Exkurs: Hat Luther bei seiner Prophetenübersetzung die 'Wormser Propheten' von 1527 benutzt?), Bd. XII (Apokryphen).

Walther, W., *Luthers Deutsche Bibel* (Berlin, 1917).

Walther, W., *Die ersten Konkurrenten des Bibelübersetzers Luther* (Leipzig, 1917).

Zimmermann, H., *Beiträge zur Bibelillustration des 16. Jahrhunderts* (Strassburg, 1924).

French versions

van Eys, W. J., *Bibliographie des Bibles et des Nouveaux Testaments en langue française des XVme et XVIme siècles*, 2 vols. (Geneva, 1900–1). [An indispensable, though incomplete and not always accurate, descriptive bibliography.]

Mangenot, E., 'Françaises (Versions) de la Bible', *Dictionnaire de la Bible*, ed. Vigouroux, II (1895), cols. 2346–73. [A competent survey, including material which was not available to Reuss.]

Lortsch, D., *Histoire de la Bible en France* (Paris, 1910). [A semi-popular work, written by a Protestant; interesting, but not always reliable.]

Pétavel, E., *La Bible en France* (Paris, 1864). [A useful general survey, written from a strongly Protestant viewpoint.]

Reuss, E., 'Romanische Bibelübersetzungen', *Realencyklopädie für protestantische Theologie und Kirche*, XIII (Gotha, 1860), 91–111.

Reuss, E., 'Fragments littéraires et critiques relatifs à l'histoire de la Bible française', *Revue de théologie* (Strasbourg), 3e série, vols. III, IV, V (1865–7). [These articles by one who was himself a distinguished translator remain after a hundred years the most penetrating study of the history of modern French versions.]

Italian versions

Budé, E. de, *The Life of Giovanni Diodati*, transl. (abridged) by M. Betts (London, 1905).

Hauck, A., *Realencyklopädie für protestantische Theologie u. Kirche*, III, 141.

Luzzi, G., *Bilychnis* (April 1916).

Minocchi, S., *Dictionnaire de la Bible* (Vigouroux), III, cols. 1026–31.

Ricciotti, G., *Encicl. Cattolica*, II, cols. 1558–9.

Vaccari, A., 'Bibbie protestanti e Bibbia cattolica', *Civiltà Cattolica*, 74 (1923), 343–51.

Spanish versions

Bataillon, Marcel, *Érasme et l'Espagne* (Paris, 1937); Spanish translation, 2 vols. (Mexico, 1950).

Boehmer, Eduard, *Spanish Reformers*, 3 vols. (Strassburg–London, 1874–1904).

Canton, W., *A History of the British and Foreign Bible Society* (London, 1904–10).
Fr. Domingo de Santa Teresa, *Juan de Valdés*, 1498 (?)–1541. *Su pensamiento religioso y las corrientes espirituales de su tiempo*, Analecta Gregoriana (Rome, 1959).
García de Santa María, Gonçalo, *Evangelios e epistolas con sus exposiciones en romance...*, ed. Isak Collijn and Eric Staaf (Uppsala, 1908).
Haebler, K., *The Valencian Bible of 1478* (New York, 1909).
Menéndez y Pelayo, Marcelino, *Historia de los heterodoxos españoles*, 3 vols. (Madrid, 1880–2). [Reprinted several times.]
Roth, Cecil, 'The Marrano Press at Ferrara', *Modern Language Review*, XXXVIII (1943), 307–17.
Rypins, Stanley, 'The Ferrara Bible at Press', *The Library*, 5th ser. x (1955), 244–69.
Tres índices expurgatorios de la Inquisición española en el siglo XVI... reproducidos en facsímil por acuerdo de la Real Academia Española (Madrid, 1952).
Valdés, Juan de, *Diálogo de doctrina cristiana*, réproduction en facsimilé...par Marcel Bataillon (Coimbra, 1925).

Scandinavian versions

Bentzen, Aage, *Indledning til Det Gamle Testamente* (Copenhagen, 1941), pp. 407–16.
Engelstoft, C. T., 'Om Udgaverne og Udgivningen af den danske Bibeloversaettelse fra Reformationen til vore Tider', *Nyt theologisk Tidsskrift 1856*.
Gyllenberg, R., *Våra fäders bibel* (Stockholm, 1941).
Hauck, A., *Realencyklopädie für protestantische Theologie und Kirche*, 3rd ed., III (Leipzig, 1897), 146–51, *s.v.* 'Skandinavische Bibelübersetzungen'.
Kulturhistorisk Leksikon for Nordisk Middelalder, vol. I (Copenhagen, 1956), cols. 515–20, *s.v.* 'Bibelöversättning'.
Linton, O., 'Medeltida bibeltolkning', *Uppsala Universitets Årsskrift 1941*, 7:6.
Molland, E., *Norske og danske bibeloversettelser brukt i Norge* (Oslo, 1951).
Níelsson, Haraldur, 'De islandske Bibeloversaettelser', *Studier tilegnede Professor Frants Buhl* (Copenhagen, 1925).
Vogel, P. H., 'Dänische und norwegische Bibelübersetzungen seit der Reformation', *Internationale kirchliche Zeitschrift*, 44 (1954).

CHAPTER IV

Bibliographies

Darlow, T. H. and Moule, H. T., *Historical Catalogue of the Printed Editions of Holy Scripture in the Library of the British and Foreign Bible Society*, part I (London, 1903).
Nijhoff, W. and Kronenberg, M. E., *Nederlandsche Bibliographie, 1500–1540* (The Hague, 1923, 1940, 1942).
Pollard, A. W. and Redgrave, G. R., *A Short-Title Catalogue of Books Printed in England, Scotland, and Ireland and of English Books printed abroad, 1475–1640* (London, 1926).

Bibliography

Reprints

Fry, F., *The First New Testament Printed in the English Language* (Bristol, 1862). [Facsimile of the 1526 N.T.]

Miles Coverdale, Biblia 1535 (London, 1838).

Mombert, J. I., *Wm. Tyndale's Pentateuch... 1530* (London, 1884).

Pollard, A. W., *The Holy Bible: an exact reprint of the Authorised Version 1611* (Oxford, 1911).

Pollard, A. W., *The Beginning of the New Testament translated by William Tyndale* (Oxford, 1926). [Facsimile of the 1525 fragment.]

Wallis, N. H., *The New Testament Translated by William Tyndale 1534* (Cambridge, 1938).

The English Hexapla of the New Testament Scriptures (London, 1841). [This contains the versions of Wycliffe–Purvey, Tyndale, 1534, Great Bible, 1539, Geneva N.T. 1557, Rhemes, A.V.]

Weigle, L. (ed.), *The New Testament Octapla* (New York and Edinburgh, 1962). [This contains Tyndale, The Great, Genevan, Bishops' and Rhemes versions, King James (A.V.), American Standard Version, Revised Standard Version.]

History of the English Bible, 1521–1611

Anderson, C., *The Annals of the English Bible* (London, 1845, 1862).

Bruce, F. F., *The English Bible* (London, 1961).

Butterworth, C. C., *The Literary Lineage of the King James Bible, 1340–1611* (Philadelphia, 1941).

Carleton, J. G., *The Part of Rheims in the Making of the English Bible* (Oxford, 1902).

Cotton, H., *Editions of the Bible and Parts thereof in English, 1505–1850* (Oxford, 1852).

Daiches, D., *The King James Version of the English Bible...with special reference to the Hebrew Tradition* (Chicago, 1941).

Eadie, J., *The English Bible*, 2 vols. (London, 1876).

Fry, F., *Description of the Great Bible of 1539* (London, 1865).

Lovett, R. (ed.), *The English Bible in the John Rylands Library* (Manchester, 1899).

Mombert, J. I., *A Hand-book of the English Versions of the Bible* (New York, 1883).

Mombert, J. I., *English Versions of the Bible* (London, 1906).

Mozley, J. F., *William Tyndale* (London, 1937).

Mozley, J. F., *Coverdale and his Bibles* (London, 1953).

Pollard, A. W., *Records of the English Bible* (London, 1911).

Robinson, H. W. (ed.), *The Bible in its Ancient and English Versions* (Oxford, 1940), rev. ed. 1954, chaps. VI, VII (J. Isaacs).

Westcott, B. F., *A General View of the History of the English Bible* (London, 1868), 3rd ed. revised by W. A. Wright (1905).

Bibliography

CHAPTER V

General

Anderson, D., *The Bible in Seventeenth-century Scottish Life and Literature* (London, 1936).

Bush, D., *English Literature in the Earlier Seventeenth Century* (Oxford, 1945).

Cragg, G. R., *From Puritanism to the Age of Reason* (Cambridge, 1950).

Cragg, G. R., *Puritanism in the Period of the Great Persecution, 1660–1688* (Cambridge, 1957).

Grierson, H., *Cross Currents in English Literature of the Seventeenth Century* (London, 1929).

Haller, W., *The Rise of Puritanism* (New York, 1938).

Horton Davies, *The Worship of the English Puritans* (Westminster, 1948).

Miller, Perry, *The New England Mind: the Seventeenth Century* (New York, 1939).

More, P. E. and Cross, F. L., *Anglicanism* (London, 1935). [Especially chapters IV and V.]

Powicke, F. J., *The Cambridge Platonists* (London, 1926).

Tulloch, J., *Rational Theology and Christian Philosophy in England in the Seventeenth Century* (Edinburgh, 1872).

Willey, B., *The Seventeenth-century Background* (London, 1934).

On Milton's theology

Lewis, C. S., *A Preface to 'Paradise Lost'* (Oxford, 1942).

Sewell, W. A., *A Study of Milton's Christian Doctrine* (Oxford, 1939).

Tillyard, E. M. W., *Milton* (London, 1930).

Waldock, A. J. A., *'Paradise Lost' and its Critics* (Cambridge, 1947).

On Bunyan

Brown, J., *Bunyan, His Life, Times and Work* (revised by F. M. Harrison), (London, 1928).

Talon, H. A., *John Bunyan, The Man and His Work* (English transl.) (London, 1951).

For Europe in general, but especially Roman Catholicism:

Willaert, L., *Après le concile de Trente: La Restauration catholique.*

Préclin, E. and Jarry E., *Les luttes politiques et doctrinales aux XVIIe et XVIIIe siècles.*

[These are vols. 18 and 19 of *Histoire de l'Église*, ed. A. Fliche and V. Martin (Paris, 1960, 1955); they contain ample bibliographical references, particularly for France.]

For Germany

Aland, K., *Spener-Studien* (Berlin, 1943).

Bertram, O., *Geschichte der von Cansteinschen Bibelanstalt in Halle* (Halle, 1863).

Drummond, A. L., *German Protestantism since Luther* (London, 1951).

Jungst, J., *Pietisten* (Tübingen, 1906).

Mirbt, C., in Hauck-Herzog, *Realencyklopädie,* *s.v.* Pietismus, or in the *New Schaff-Herzog Encyclopaedia*, *s.v.* Pietism.
Ritschl, A., *Geschichte des Pietismus* (Bonn, 1884–6).
Schmidt, M. and Stallmann, M., in *Religion in Geschichte und Gegenwart*, ed. 3, *s.v.* Pietismus (1961). [Valuable references to recent periodical literature.]
Tholuck, A., *Der Geist der lutherischen Theologen Wittenbergs im Verlaufe des 17. Jahrhundertes* (Hamburg, 1852).
Tholuck, A., *Geschichte des Rationalismus* (Berlin, 1865).

CHAPTER VI

General

Sutcliffe, E. F., S.J., and Orchard, B., O.S.B., *The Catholic Commentary on Holy Scripture* (London, 1953).

Individual topics

Buzy, P., 'Le concordisme préhistorique', *Mélanges Podechard* (Lyons, 1945).
de Dominis, M. A., *De republica christiana* (Cologne, 1622). [The theory of inspiration is in Book VII.]
D'Elia, P., *Galileo in Cina* (Rome, 1947).
Deville, R., 'Richard Simon, Critique catholique du Pentateuque', *Nouvelle revue théologique*, LXXIII (1951), 723–39.
Giacchi, O., 'Considerazioni sui due Processi contro Galileo', *Nel Terzo Centenario della Morte di Galilei* (Milan, 1942), pp. 383–406.
Le Bachelet, S. J., *Bellarmin et la Bible Sixto-Clémentine* (Paris, 1911). [This was attacked by P. Baumgarten, but further research by C. A. Kneller, in *Zeitschrift für katholische Theologie*, LII (1928), 202–24, has confirmed its conclusions.]
Seynaeve, J., *Newman's Doctrine on Holy Scripture* (Louvain, 1953). [A thesis containing unpublished notes of Newman about inspiration, with some unfortunate errors of transcription.]
Stummer, F., *Die Bedeutung Richard Simons für die Pentateuchkritik* (Münster, 1912).
Veit, L. A. and Lenhart, D., *Kirche und Volksfrömmigkeit im Zeitalter des Barocks* (Freiburg, 1956).

Council of Trent

Jedin, H., *Geschichte des Konzils von Trient*, vol. II (Freiburg, 1957); English trans. E. Graf (Edinburgh, 1961).

Père Lagrange and Modernism

Cahiers de la Nouvelle Journée, XXVIII (1935).
Braun, F., O.P., *L'œuvre du Père Lagrange* (Fribourg, 1943).
Calès, J., *Le père Ferdinand Prat* (Paris, 1942).
Coppens, J., *Le chanoine A. van Hoonacker* (Bruges, 1935)
Vincent, H., O.P., *Revue biblique*, XLVII (1938), 321–54.

Bibliography

Decrees

Denzinger, H. (ed.), *Enchiridion Symbolorum et definitionum.* [Many editions with uniform numbering.]

Acta Apostolicae Sedis.

Works in progress

The Abbey of St Jerome in Rome has begun an edition of the Vulgate (eleven vols. published).

The Abbey of Beuron in Germany has begun an edition of the *Itala.*

CHAPTER VII

Bury, J. B., *History of Freedom of Thought* (Home Univ. Library, London, 1914).

Carpenter, J. E., *The Bible in the Nineteenth Century* (London, 1903).

Cheyne, T. K., *Founders of Old Testament Criticism* (London, 1893).

Conybeare, F. C., *History of New Testament Criticism* (London, 1910).

Dampier-Whetham, W. C. D., *A History of Science* (Cambridge, 1948).

Elliott-Binns, L., *Religion in the Victorian Era* (London, 1936).

Farrar, F. W., *History of Interpretation* (London, 1886).

Glover, W. B., *Evangelical Nonconformists and Higher Criticism in the Nineteenth Century* (London, 1954).

Grant, R. M., *The Bible in the Church* (New York, 1948).

Huxley, T. H., *Science and Hebrew Tradition* (London, 1901).

Moore, E. C., *An Outline of the History of Christian Thought since Kant* (London, 1912).

Pattison, M., 'Tendencies of Religious Thought in England 1688–1750', *Essays and Reviews* (1860).

Raven, C. E., *Natural Religion and Christian Theology* (Cambridge, 1953).

Raven, C. E., *Science, Religion and the Future* (Cambridge, 1943).

Robertson, J. M., *A History of Freethought* (London, 1936).

Schweitzer, A., *The Quest of the Historical Jesus* (London, 1910).

Simpson, J. Y., *Landmarks in the Struggle between Science and Religion* (London, 1925).

Stephen, Sir L., *History of English Thought in the Eighteenth Century* (London, 1902).

CHAPTER VIII

Butterfield, Herbert, *Man on his Past* (Cambridge, 1955).

Carpenter, J. Estlin, *The Bible in the Nineteenth Century* (London, 1903).

Cheyne, T. K., *Founders of Old Testament Criticism* (London, 1893).

Faber, Geoffrey, C., *Jowett, A Portrait with a Background*, chaps. XI and XII (London, 1957).

Forbes, Duncan, *The Liberal Anglican Idea of History* (Cambridge, 1952).

Garvie, A. E., *The Ritschlian Theology* (Edinburgh, 1899).

Hunter, A. M., *Interpreting the New Testament, 1900–1950* (London, 1951).

Knowling, R. J., 'Criticism' in Hastings's *Dictionary of Christ and the Gospels*, vol. I (Edinburgh, 1906), 383–94.

Lichtenberger, F., *History of German Theology in the Nineteenth Century*, English trans. (Edinburgh, 1889).

Peardon, T. P., *The Transition in English Historical Writing, 1760–1830* (New York, 1933).

Pfleiderer, Otto, *The Development of Theology in Germany since Kant and its Progress in Great Britain since 1825* (London, 1890).

Richardson, Alan, *The Bible in the Age of Science* (London, 1961).

Richardson, Alan, *History, Sacred and Profane* (London, 1963).

Robinson, J. M., *A New Quest of the Historical Jesus* (London, 1959).

Schweitzer, A., *The Quest of the Historical Jesus: A Critical Study of its Progress* English trans. (London, 1910).

Smart, J. D., *The Interpretation of Scripture* (New York, 1960; London, 1961).

Sykes, Norman, *Man as Churchman* (Cambridge, 1960).

CHAPTER IX

Schmid, Josef (ed.), 'A Survey of Modern Translations of the Bible into Many Languages', *Zeitschrift für katholische Theologie*, LXXXII (1960), 290–323.

German versions

Bertram, O., *Geschichte der von Cansteinschen Bibelanstalt in Halle* (Halle, 1863).

Leeman-van Elck, P., *Der Buchschmuck der Zürcher Bibel bis 1800* (Bern, 1938).

Mezger, J. J., *Geschichte der deutschen Bibelübersetzung in der schweizerisch-reformierten Kirche* (Basel, 1876).

Panzer, G. W., *Geschichte der Nürnbergischen Ausgaben der Bibel* (Nürnberg, 1791).

Centenary publications of the Bible Societies

Breest, E., *Die Preussische Hauptbibelgesellschaft* (Berlin, 1914).

Fries, W., *Die Cansteinsche Bibelanstalt* (Halle, 1910).

Risch, A., *Die Privilegierte Württembergische Bibelanstalt* (Stuttgart, 1912).

Zimmerman, W., *Die Bibelanstalt Altenburg* (Altenburg, 1952).

Die Bibel in der Welt (annual.).

Articles

Nestle, E., 'Bibelübersetzungen, deutsche', in the *Realenzyklopädie für protestantische Theologie und Kirche* (3rd ed., Leipzig, 1896–1913).

'Bibelwerke', 'Bibelgesellschaften', and 'von Canstein' in the *Realenzyklopädie*, and in the 2nd and 3rd editions of *Die Religion in Geschichte und Gegenwart* (Tübingen, 1928–32 and 1956); 'Die neueren deutschen Bibelübersetzungen' in *Gutachten der Ev. Luth. Landeskirchenrat* (München, 1956).

Catholic versions

Auer, W., *Katholische Bibelkunde* (Stuttgart, 1956).

Panzer, G. W., *Geschichte der römisch-katholischen deutschen Bibelübersetzung* (Nürnberg, 1781).

Schwegler, T., 'Die deutsche katholische Bibelübersetzung seit Luther', *Schweiz. Rundschau*, N.F. XLIX (1949), 503–8.

Religion in Geschichte und Gegenwart, 3rd ed. (Tübingen, 1957), *s.v.* Bibelübersetzungen IV *and* Ess, Leander van.

Italian versions

Cassuto, U., *Encyclopaedia Judaica*, X, cols. 1249–54.

Minocchi, S., *Dictionnaire de la Bible* (ed. Vigouroux), III (1903), cols. 1031–8.

Ricciotti, G., *Enciclopedia Cattolica* (Vatican City, 1949), II, cols. 1559–63.

Vaccari, A., 'Bibbie protestanti e Bibbia cattolica', *Civiltà Cattolica*, LXXIV (1923), 343–51.

Vaccari, A., *Enciclopedia Italiana*, VI, 902–3.

Dutch versions

Bruin, C. C. de, *De Statenbijbel en zijn voorgangers* (Leiden, 1937).

Kijne, J. J. and Visser, F., *De nieuwe Vertaling van het Nederlandsch Bijbelgenootschap* (Amsterdam, 1952).

French versions

See chapter III.

Scandinavian versions

See chapter III.

CHAPTER X

Bridges, R. and Weigle, L. A., *The Bible Word Book* (New York, 1960).

Chambers, T. W., *A Companion to the Revised Version* (London, 1885).

Cotton, Henry, *Editions of the Bible and Parts thereof in English* (2nd ed., Oxford, 1852).

Darlow, T. H. and Moule, H. T., *Historical Catalogue of the Printed Editions of Holy Scripture in the Library of the British and Foreign Bible Society*, 4 vols. (London, 1903–11).

Documentary History of the American Committee on Revision (New York, 1885).

Hemphill, Samuel, *A History of the Revised Version of the New Testament* (London, 1906).

Knox, R., *On Englishing the Bible* (London, 1949).

Metzger, Bruce M., *An Introduction to the Apocrypha* (New York, 1957).

Moulton, W. F., *The History of the English Bible* (5th ed., London, 1911).

Murray, J. H., *Mistranslated Passages in Our Bible* (London, 1881).

Plea for a New English Version of the Scriptures, by a Licentiate of the Church of Scotland (London, 1864).

Pope, Very Rev. Hugh, O.P., *English Versions of the Bible*, revised and amplified by Rev. Sebastian Bullough, O.P. (London, 1952).

Price, Ira M., *The Ancestry of Our English Bible* (2nd revised ed., New York, 1949).

Robertson, E. H., *The New Translations of the Bible* (London, 1959).

Robinson, H. Wheeler (ed.), *The Bible in Its Ancient and English Versions* (Oxford, 1940; revised ed. 1954).

Schaff, Philip, *A Companion to the Greek Testament and English Version* (4th ed., New York, 1894).

Scrivener, F. H. A. *The Authorized Edition of the English Bible (1611), its Subsequent Reprints and Modern Representatives* (Cambridge, 1884).

Weigle, L. A., *The English New Testament from Tyndale to the Revised Standard Version* (Nashville, 1949; Edinburgh, 1950).

Weigle, L. A., *Bible Words in Living Language* (Edinburgh, 1957).

Westcott, B. F., *A General View of the History of the English Bible*, 3rd ed., revised by W. A. Wright (London, 1905).

CHAPTER XI

Bible and the Missionary

Canton, W., *The History of the Bible Society (1804–1904)*, The British and Foreign Bible Society.

Chirgwin, A. M., *The Bible in World Evangelism* (Student Christian Movement Press, 1954).

Dobschütz, E. von, 'The Bible in the Church', article in the *Encyclopaedia of Religion and Ethics* (1909).

Kilgour, R., *The Gospel in Many Years* (A chronological list of the dates of the first publication of any portion of God's Word in 835 languages) (B.F.B.S., 1925).

Latourette, K. S., *The Expansion of Christianity*, vols. 4, 5, 6 (London, 1938).

North, Eric, *The Book of a Thousand Tongues* (American Bible Society, 1938).

CHAPTER XII

Catalogues

Darlow, T. H. and Moule, H. F., *Historical Catalogue of the Printed Editions of Holy Scripture in the Library of The British and Foreign Bible Society*, 2 vols. (London, 1903–11).

See also the catalogues of the principal national libraries, especially the British Museum and Bibliothèque Nationale. The general catalogue of the British Museum gives a volume to the Bible.

General

Faulmann, K., *Illustrirte Geschichte der Buchdruckerkunst* (Vienna, 1882). [Valuable for the nineteenth century, and conditions of service in the trade.]

Febvre, L. and Martin, H. J., *L'Apparition du livre* (Paris, 1958). [Excellent introduction, with very full bibliographies.]

Handover, P. M., *Printing in London* (London, 1960). [Especially valuable for the Bible trade in the sixteenth and seventeenth centuries.]

McKerrow, R. B., *Introduction to Bibliography* (Oxford, 1928).

Mumby, F. A., *Publishing and Bookselling* (4th ed., London, 1956).

Plant, Marjorie, *The English Book-Trade* (London, 1939).

Bibliography

Pollard, A. W., *Records of the English Bible* (Oxford, 1911).
Steinberg, S. H., *Five Hundred Years of Printing* (London, 1955).

Monographs

Armstrong, Elizabeth, *Robert Estienne, Royal Printer* (Cambridge, 1954).
Blagden, Cyprian, *The Stationers' Company* (London, 1960).
Davies, David W., *The World of the Elseviers, 1580–1712* (The Hague, 1954).
Haebler, K., *Handbuch der Inkunabelkunde* (Leipzig, 1925).
Johnson, John and Gibson, Strickland, *Print and Privilege at Oxford to the year 1700* (Oxford, 1946).
Leeman-van Elck, Paul, *Die Offizin Froschauer* (Zürich, 1940).
Roberts, S. C., *The Cambridge University Press, 1521–1921* (Cambridge, 1921).
Rooses, Max, *Christophe Plantin, Imprimeur Anversois* (Antwerp, 1882).
Ruppel, Aloys, *Johannes Gutenberg, sein Leben und sein Werk* (2nd ed., Berlin, 1947).
Scholderer, Victor, *Greek Printing Types 1465–1927* (London, 1927).
Simpson, Percy, *Proof-reading in the Sixteenth, Seventeenth and Eighteenth Centuries* (Oxford, 1935).
Strachan, James, *Early Bible Illustrations* (Cambridge, 1957).
Volz, Hans, *Hundert Jahre Wittenberger Bibeldruck, 1522–1626* (Göttingen, 1954).

Articles

Black, M. H., 'The Evolution of a Book-Form: The Octavo Bible from MS to the Geneva Version', *The Library*, March 1961.
De Clercq, C., 'Les éditions bibliques, liturgiques et canoniques de Plantin', *Gedenkboek der Plantin Dagen* (Antwerp, 1956).
De Clercq, C., 'La Bible française de René Benoist', *Gutenberg Jahrbuch* (1957).
Hart, H., 'Charles Earl Stanhope and the Oxford University Press', *Collectanea*, series III (Oxford, 1896).
Geldner, Ferdinand., 'Die Bibel im ältesten Buchdruck', *Schrift, Bild und Druck der Bibel* (Hamburg, 1955).
Vogel, P. H., 'Erstdrucke Dänischer Bibeln', *Schrift, Bild und Druck der Bibel* (Hamburg, 1955).
Vogel, P. H., 'Die Deutsche Bibel vor Luther', *Libri*, VII (1958), no. 4; 'Luthers deutsche Bibel sowie römisch-katholische deutsche Bibeldrucke im 16. Jahrhundert', *Libri*, VIII (1958), no. 1; 'Niederländische und englische Bibeldrucke des 15. und 16. Jahrhunderts', *Libri*, VIII (1958), no. 2; 'Romanische und skandinavische Bibeldrucke im 15. und 16. Jahrhundert', *Libri*, VIII (1958), no. 3–4.
Vogel, P. H., *Europäische Bibeldrucke des 15. und 16. Jahrhunderts in den Volkssprachen* (Baden-Baden, 1962).

Government publication

Report of the Select Committee on the Queen's Printer's Patent together with the proceedings of the committee, minutes of evidence, appendix and index (London, 1860).

NOTES ON THE PLATES

1 The 'Gutenberg', 'Mazarin' or 42-line Bible: the Cambridge University Library copy (? Mainz, ? J. Gutenberg, ? 1455, folio). The explicit at the foot of column 1 is inserted by hand, in red. The book-initial and page-head are also handwritten, and every capital letter has been touched with red ink. Note the square formal black-letter type, and the space between the columns. (Much reduced.)

2 The *editio princeps* of the German Bible, in the pre-Lutheran translation (Strassburg, J. Mentelin, 1466, folio). Compared with the 42-line Bible it is immediately plain that the smaller rounded informal type allows much more to be printed on the page. Again the editorial incipits and explicits are written by hand; so are the page-heads and initials. (Much reduced.)

3 The first printed Dutch Bible, printed by Jacobsoen and Yemantszoen of Middelborch and published at Delft in 1477. A simple two-column arrangement as in the first two plates; note the chapter break, in what was to become the traditional international arrangement, and the distinction in size between chapter and book initials. The incipits are here printed, in black. There is no page-head or folio number. (Reduced.)

4 The first printed portion of the French Bible is this New Testament in the old Bible *historiée* version, printed by Le Roy for B. Buyer at Lyons in 1476. It is in 'long lines' (single column) and very simple, even primitive, in its arrangement. (Slightly reduced.)

5 The *Glossa ordinaria*, the culmination of the tradition of medieval commentary, was often printed to meet a steady demand, not only from conservative scholars. This edition (printed by the brothers de Paganinis of Venice in 1495 in four volumes, folio) shows the elaborate typographical repertory called for, and the mastery of the compositor's art. Four sizes of type are used—the largest for the page-heads, the second for the text and catchwords in the notes, the third for the surrounding notes, the smallest for the interlinear gloss. Fourteen lines of text are commented on this page. (Greatly reduced. The page size is about 18 by 12 inches.)

6 The first octavo-printed bible; Froben's *fontibus ex grecis* edition of 1491. Note the use of a second size of type for the first line of the book (also used on the rectos for the page-head). Initial directors for the chapter and book-initials have been supplemented by written initials. Explicits and incipits

are printed, but written paragraph-marks are added (also to the chapter-numbers in the traditional position). Parallel passages are noted in the margins and the A B C D chapter-division is used. (Slightly reduced.)

7 The standard, or traditional black-letter layout: with printed chapter- but not book-initials, printed paragraph marks, and three sizes of type. The largest is used for page-head and folio, and the first line of books, the smallest for the marginal notes. The book-initial is still to be hand-done though an initial-director is supplied: a practice which survived until the mid-sixteenth century. (Langendorff and Froben, Basle, 1509, folio). (Reduced.)

8*a*. Hopyl's *Biblia exigue molis ac plures in partes divisibilis* (Paris, 8vo, 1510, 5 parts). As the title suggests, a small portable Bible in separate parts. Essentially it is a division of the traditional black-letter page into quarters printed successively instead of together. Note some shakily centred headings, and the arabic page number. (Slightly reduced.)

8*b* *Opus quatuor evangelistarum*, a gospel-book by Prevel of Paris (32 mo, 1522). Another attempt at a very small format. Note the spacing. (Slightly reduced.)

9 The Soncino Bible. A page of the first complete Hebrew Bible (O.T.) printed by Abraham ben Chaim dei Tintori at Soncino in 1488.

10 Erasmus's *Novum Instrumentum*, the opening of the Epistles. The bridge-shaped interlace in tawny red marks the introduction into Bible-printing of the influences of eastern book production. The roman type is Jensonian, the Greek Aldine. (Basle, Froben, 1516, folio.) (Reduced.)

11 The Aldine Greek Bible (containing the LXX and Erasmus's N.T.) printed by Aldus at Venice in 1518–19. The cursive Greek type with its many ligatures is based on the business hand of fifteenth-century Byzantine scribes. Compare the interlace headpiece (printed in red) with that in plate 10. (Reduced.)

12 The Compultensian Polyglot: a verso in one of the volumes of the O.T. The 'Transla. Chal.' is the Targum of Onkelos, accompanied by a Latin translation made for this edition. Note the pointing of the Hebrew text, which is unique in printing history. The N.T., which was printed first, used a fine formal Greek character in the Jensonian tradition. The Greek here is Aldine, and is combined with roman, black-letter and Hebrew. (Alcalá, Arnao Guillen de Brocar, six volumes, 1514–17, published 1522, folio.) (Greatly reduced.)

13 One of the very few Bibles in italic. This quarto, printed by Wolf at Basle in 1522, contains the Vulgate O.T. and Erasmus's N.T. Italic editions of the Erasmus Latin N.T. had a brief vogue, and like this Bible used the long line, decorative headpieces, engraved title-pages in the Holbein manner, woodcut inhabited book-initials and the 'Basle' titling capitals. The italic is modelled on Aldus's. (Slightly reduced.)

14 Luther's December Testament, the second impression printed by Melchior II Lotther for the publishers Cranach and Döring in December 1522 at Wittenberg. It is like the September Testament in all but minor respects. Though it is a folio, it uses long lines in the new 'humanist' style, though it also uses a round black-letter (the vehicle of the vernacular). The text is divided into paragraphs. (Reduced.)

15*a* Tyndale's New Testament, the edition of 1526 (Worms, Schoeffer, 8vo). Compare the general arrangement with Luther's: the use of long lines, the separate paragraphs, the small cut of the apostle, the chapter-heading.

15*b* Tyndale's New Testament: his corrected edition of 1534 (Antwerp, M. de Keyser, 8vo). The setting out of the genealogy of Christ in single-line entries had been first used by Luther. (Reduced.)

16 Van Liesveldt's Bible (Antwerp, folio, 1526). A text based on Luther's, with some Lutheran typographical features: principally the paragraph-divisions and centred chapter-headings (cf. plates 14, 15). (Reduced.)

17 Pagnini's new Latin version (? Lyons, Du Ry, 1528, 4to). The first Bible with printed verse-divisions, and one of the earliest complete Bibles in roman type; but the general appearance is clumsy and archaic. Note the transliteration of Hebrew names. (Reduced.)

18 The 'Antwerp Bible'; Lefèvre's complete French version (Antwerp, M. de Keyser, 1530, folio). (Much reduced.)

19 The 'Neuchâtel Bible': Olivetan's version (Neuchâtel, P. de Wingle, 1535, folio). (Much reduced.)

20 Brucioli's Bible (Venice, Lucantonio Giunti, folio, 1532). Only in Italy at this time was roman type considered the appropriate vehicle for the vernacular. The very long line and the absence of interlinear spacing make the book hard to read; but this kind of close texture was sought after by early printers. (Much reduced.)

21 Coverdale's Bible (? Soter and Cervicornus, Cologne, 1535, folio). An elegant version of the Lutheran format for the complete Bible. (Much reduced.)

22 Matthew's Bible—the first printed in England (London, Grafton and Whitchurch, 1537, folio). An attempt has been made to censor the notes. This was more effective originally than it seems now, for the water-based ink has faded to brown so that the oil-based printing ink shows through. (Reduced.)

23 Robert Estienne's folio Vulgate of 1532. Note the page- and book-headings in Garamond's *gros canon* roman, the long lines, the chapter-headings in the 'traditional' position. (Much reduced.)

24 Robert Estienne's octavo Vulgate of 1534, in small roman type. Again, note the page-head (a 'running-head'); the book opening, the chapter-headings: conversions into roman type of traditional features (cf. plates 6, 7). This format is the basis of the Genevan style (plates, 30, 33). (Slightly reduced.)

25 The *Bible de l'Epée* (Geneva, Girard, 1540, 4to). An early Genevan Bible, typographically archaic. (Reduced.)

26 Castellio's (Châteillon's) Bible (Basle, Hervage, 1555, folio). Note Estienne's running-heads and book-titles in a version of the now fashionable 'garamond'; the text is in an archaic face in the Jensonian tradition. The columns, not the pages, are numbered. The red lines round the columns are ruled by hand, a common survival (cf. plates 23 and, very faintly, 25). (Much reduced.)

27 Jean de Tournes's folio Latin Bible (Lyons, 1556, folio). Note the harmony of type and decoration. (Much reduced.)

28 Robert Estienne's Greek text in its third edition (1550, folio). This is the large size of Garamond's *Grec du roi*, based on the hand of the Cretan calligrapher Vergetios. Note the harmony of headpiece, initial and type, and the variant readings in the margin. (Reduced.)

29 Widmanstadt's Syriac N.T. (Vienna, Zimmermann, 4to, 1555). The text shows John xvii and xviii. The phrase at the head of ch. xviii shows that the following passage is the lection for the vigil of Good Friday.

30–1 An opening of the Plantin Polyglot (Antwerp, 1569–72, 8 volumes, folio). See pp. 54–5. (Much reduced.)

32 The Geneva Bible (Geneva, Rowland Hall, 1560, 4to). The first English Bible in roman type, with numbered verses. Note the characteristic 'argument' to the book, and the extensive annotation, swelling across the foot of the page. (Reduced.)

33 The first complete Spanish Bible; Reyna's version (Basle, 1569). (Reduced.)

34 Bishop Gudbrand's Icelandic Bible (Hólar, 1584, folio). An example of the Lutheran influence. Compare plate 14. (Much reduced.)

35 A correction in the Sixtine Bible (Rome, Vatican Press, 1590, folio). Near the bottom of the second column INDE has been inserted, on a pasted slip. Other corrections were made by pen. (Much reduced.)

36 Diodati's Italian version (Geneva, 1607, 4to). (Reduced.)

37 The 'Douay' New Testament (Douai, Laurence Kellam, 1609–10, 2 volumes, 4to). (Reduced.)

38 The 'King James' version (London, Barker, 1611, folio). Note that black-letter is still used. (Much reduced.)

39 The London 'Polyglot' (London, T. Roycroft, 1655–7, 6 volumes, folio). On the facing page, not shown, are the Massoretic Hebrew text, the LXX Greek, and their Latin translations. The Arabic version shown here is of the thirteenth century or later; the Samaritan text, in modified archaic Hebrew characters, became known to the West in 1616.

40 John Eliot's 'Indian' Bible; the first Bible printed in America. The Algonquin tongue is rendered in a Roman transliteration with some specially cast extra 'sorts'. (Cambridge, Mass., S. Green, 1663.)

41 The Mons New Testament (Amsterdam, Daniel Elsevier, for Gaspar Migeot of Mons, 1667, 12mo).

42 A Germantown Bible. The Bible in German for the immigrant German communities of Philadelphia (Germantown, Christoph Sauer, 2nd. ed. 1763, 4to). (Reduced.)

43 The Baskerville Bible. The greatest typographical achievement in the printing of the Bible in the eighteenth century. The type was designed by Baskerville himself. (Cambridge, 1763, folio.) (Much reduced.)

44 The Cambridge Stereotype Bible. The first Bible printed from stereotype plates. (Cambridge, 1806, 12mo.) (Slightly reduced.)

45 Charles Knight's Pictorial Bible (London, 1836). The engraving is after Rubens. (Reduced.)

46 A French edition of the Gospels (Paris, L. Curmer, 1836, 2 volumes) in the translation by the Abbé Dassance. It has a lithographed frontispiece, 12 copper- and 10 wood-engravings, and an ornamental border round each page of text. (Reduced.)

47 The Doves Press Bible, the first page of the text. The initial 'I' and the first line of large capitals were written by the great calligrapher Edward Johnston. The next three lines are in capitals (a sixteenth-century Italian practice). Note the paragraph-mark between verses (cf. plate 17) and the solidity of the text area (cf. plate 20). (Much reduced.)

48 Bruce Rogers's folio Bible (Oxford, 1935). The type is Rogers's own 'Centaur', a revival of a Jensonian roman. Compare the headlines with Estienne's (plates 23, 24), and in the traditional black-letter arrangement (plate 7); and the paragraph-mark verse-divisions with Pagnini's (plate 17). (Much reduced.)

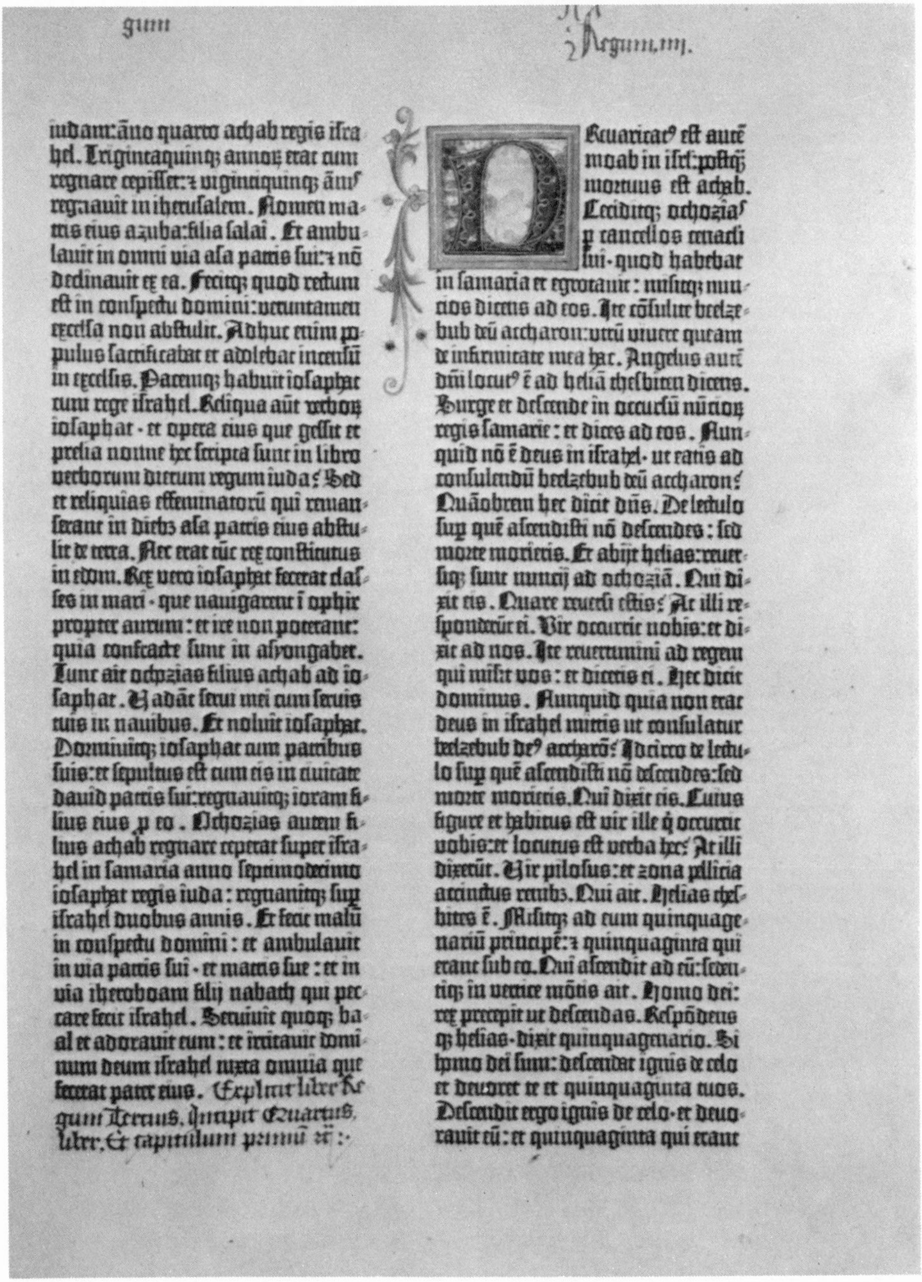

gum

Regum. iiij.

iudam: āno quarto achab regis israhel. Trigintaquinq; annoꝝ erat cum regnare cepisset: & viginiquinq; ānis regnauit in iherusalem. Nomen matris eius azuba: filia salai. Et ambulauit in omni via asa patris sui: & nō declinauit ex ea. Feciq; quod rectum est in conspectu domini: verumtamen excelsa non abstulit. Adhuc enim populus sacrificabat et adolebat incensū in excelsis. Pacemq; habuit iosaphat cum rege israhel. Reliqua aūt verboꝝ iosaphat · et opera eius que gessit et prelia nonne hec scripta sunt in libro verborum dierum regum iuda? Sed et reliquias effeminatorū qui remanserant in diebz asa patris eius abstulit de terra. Nec erat tūc rex constitutus in edom. Rex vero iosaphat fecerat classes in mari · que nauigarent i ophir propter aurum: et ire non potuerant: quia confracte sunt in asiongaber. Tunc ait ochozias filius achab ad iosaphat. Vadāt serui mei cum seruis tuis in nauibus. Et noluit iosaphat. Dormiuitq; iosaphat cum patribus suis: et sepultus est cum eis in ciuitate dauid patris sui: regnauitq; ioram filius eius ꝓ eo. Ochozias autem filius achab regnare ceperat super israhel in samaria anno septimodecimo iosaphat regis iuda: regnauitq; sup israhel duobus annis. Et fecit malū in conspectu domini: et ambulauit in via patris sui · et matris sue: et in via ieroboam filij nabath qui peccare fecit israhel. Seruiuit quoq; baal et adorauit eum: et irritauit dominum deum israhel iuxta omnia que fecerat pater eius. Explicit liber Regum Tercius. Incipit Quartus. Liber. Et capitulum primū.

Preuaricat' est autē moab in isrl: postq̄ mortuus est achab. Ceciditq; ochozias ꝑ cancellos cenaculi sui · quod habebat in samaria et egrotauit: misitq; nuncios dicens ad eos. Ite cōsulite beelzebub deū accharon: utrū uiuere queam de infirmitate mea hac. Angelus autē dñi locut' ē ad heliā thesbiten dicens. Surge et descende in occursū nūcioꝝ regis samarie: et dices ad eos. Nunquid nō ē deus in israhel · ut eatis ad consulendū beelzebub deū accharon? Quāobrem hec dicit dñs. De lectulo sup quē ascendisti nō descendes: sed morte morieris. Et abijt helias. Reuersiq; sunt nuncij ad ochoziā. Qui dixit eis. Quare reuersi estis? At illi responderūt ei. Vir occurrit nobis: et dixit ad nos. Ite reuertimini ad regem qui misit vos: et dicetis ei. Hec dicit dominus. Nunquid quia non erat deus in israhel mittis ut consulatur beelzebub de' accharō? Idcirco de lectulo sup quē ascendisti nō descendes: sed morte morieris. Qui dixit eis. Cuius figure et habitus est uir ille q̄ occurrit vobis: et locutus est verba hec? At illi dixerūt. Vir pilosus: et zona pellicia accinctus renibz. Qui ait. Helias thesbites ē. Misitq; ad eum quinquagenariū principē: & quinquaginta qui erant sub eo. Qui ascendit ad eū: sedentiq; in uertice mōtis ait. Homo dei: rex precepit ut descendas. Respōdens q; helias · dixit quinquagenario. Si homo dei sum: descendat ignis de celo et deuoret te et quinquaginta tuos. Descendit ergo ignis de celo · et deuorauit eū: et quinquaginta qui erant

1 THE 42-LINE BIBLE

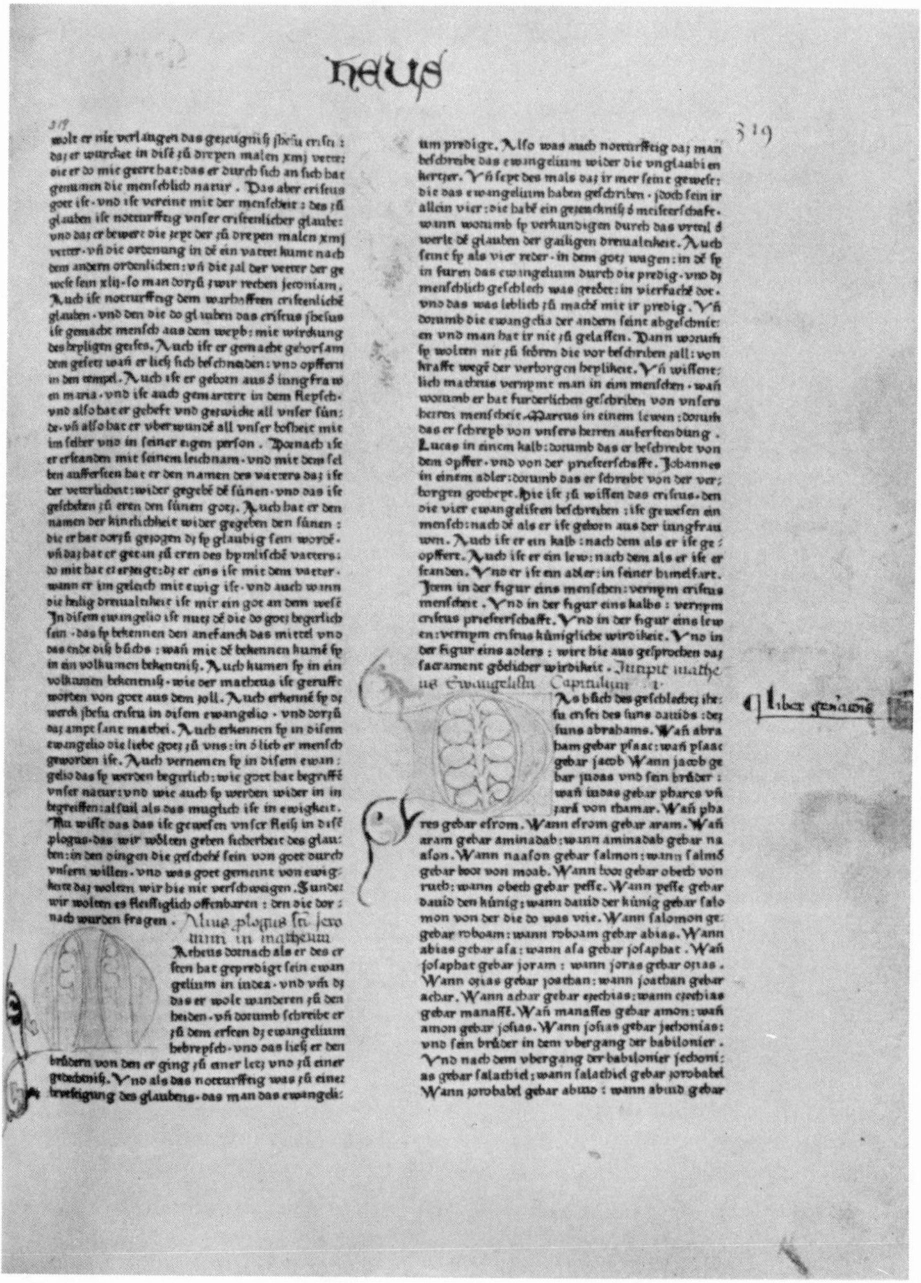
Mattheus

319

wolt er nit verlangen das gezeugniß jhesu cristi:
das er würchet in disē zů dreyen malen xiiij vetter:
die er do mit geert hat: das er durch sich an sich hat
genumen die menschlich natur. Das aber cristus
got ist. vnd ist vereint mit der menschheit: des zů
glauben ist notturfftig vnser cristenlicher glaube:
vnd das er bewert die zeyt der zů dreyen malen xiiij
vetter. vñ die ordenung in dē ein vatter kumt nach
dem andern ordenlichen: vñ die zal der vetter der ge
west sein xlij. so man dorzů zwir rechen jeroniam.
Auch ist notturfftig dem warhafften cristenlichē
glauben. vnd den die do glauben das cristus jhesus
ist gemacht mensch aus dem weyb: mit wirckung
des heyligen geistes. Auch ist er gemacht gehorsam
dem gesetz wañ er ließ sich beschneiden: vnd opffern
in den tempel. Auch ist er geborn aus d̄ iungfraw
en maria. vnd ist auch gemartert in dem fleysch.
vnd also hat er gehelt vnd getilckt all vnser sün:
de. vñ also hat er vberwundē all vnser boßheit mit
im selber vnd in seiner eigen person. Dornach ist
er erstanden mit seinem leichnam. vnd mit dem sel
ben aufferstent hat er den namen des vatters das ist
der vetterlichheit: wider gegebē dē sünen. vnd das ist
geschehen zů eren den sünen gots. Auch hat er den
namen der kindlichheit wider gegeben den sünen:
die er hat dorzů gezogen dz sy glaubig sein wordē.
vñ das hat er getan zů eren des hymlischē vatters:
do mit hat er erzeyget: dz er eins ist mit dem vatter.
wann er im geleich mit ewig ist. vnd auch wann
die heilig dreiualtikeit ist mit ein got an dem wesē
In disem ewangelio ist nutz dē die do gotz begerlich
sein. das sy bekennen den anefanck das mittel vnd
das ende diß bůchs: wañ mit dē bekennen kumē sy
in ein volkumen bekentniß. Auch kumen sy in ein
volkumen bekentniß. wie der matheus ist geruffet
worden von gott aus dem zoll. Auch erkennē sy dz
werck jhesu cristi in disem ewangelio. vnd dorzů
das ampt sant mathei. Auch erkennen sy in disem
ewangelio die liebe gotz zů vns: in d̄ lieb er mensch
geworden ist. Auch vernemen sy in disem ewan:
gelio das sy werden begirlich: wie gott hat begriffē
vnser natur: vnd wie auch sy werden wider in in
begreiffen: alsuil als das muglich ist in ewigkeit.
Nu wißt das das ist gewesen vnser fleiß in disē
plogus. das wir wölten geben sicherheit des glau:
ben: in den dingen die geschehē sein von gott durch
vnsern willen. vnd was gott gemeint von ewig:
keit das wolten wir hie nit verschweigen. Sunder
wir wolten es fleissiglich offenbaren: den die dor:
nach wurden fragen. Alius plogus sti jero
nimi in matheum
Mattheus dornach als er des er
sten hat gepredigt sein ewan
gelium in iudea. vnd vñ dz
das er wolt wanderen zů den
heiden. vñ dorumb schreibt er
zů dem ersten dz ewangelium
hebreysch. vnd das ließ er den
brüdern von den er ging zů einer letz vnd zů einer
gedechtniß. Vnd als das notturfftig was zů einer
bvestigung des glaubens. das man das ewangeli:
um predigt. Also was auch notturfftig das man
beschreibe das ewangelium wider die vnglaubi en
ketzer. Vñ seyt des mals das ir mer seint gewest:
die das ewangelium haben geschriben. jdoch sein ir
allein vier: die habē ein gezeucknis d̄ meisterschafft.
wann worumb sy verkundigen durch das vrteil d̄
werk dē glauben der heiligen dreiualtikeit. Auch
seint sy als vier reder. in dem gotz wagen: in dē sy
in furen das ewangelium durch die predig. vnd dz
menschlich geschlech was geedet: in vierfachē dot.
vnd das was leblich zů machē mit ir predig. Vñ
dorumb die ewangelia der andern seint abgeschnit:
en vnd man hat ir nit zů gelassen. Dann worumb
sy wolten nit zů stören die vor beschriben zall: von
krafft wegē der verborgen heylikeit. Vñ wissent:
lich matheus vernymt man in eim menschen. wañ
worumb er hat furderlichen geschriben von vnsers
herren menschheit. Marcus in einem lewen: dorumb
das er schreyb von vnsers herren auferstendung.
Lucas in einem kalb: dorumb das er beschreibt von
dem opffer. vnd von der priesterschafft. Johannes
in einem adler: dorumb das er schreibt von der ver:
borgen gotheyt. Hie ist zů wissen das cristus. den
die vier ewangelisten beschreiben: ist gewesen ein
mensch: nach dē als er ist geborn aus der iungfrau
wen. Auch ist er ein kalb: nach dem als er ist ge:
opffert. Auch ist er ein lew: nach dem als er ist er
standen. Vnd er ist ein adler: in seiner himelfart.
Item in der figur eins menschen: vernym cristus
menschheit. Vnd in der figur eins kalbs: vernym
cristus priesterschafft. Vnd in der figur eins lew
en: vernym cristus künigliche wirdikeit. Vnd in
der figur eins adlers: wirt hie aus gesprochen das
sacrament gödlicher wirdikeit. Incipit mathe
us ewangelista Capitulum 1.
Das bůch des geschlechtz ihe:
su cristi des suns dauids: des
suns abrahams. Wañ abra
ham gebar ysaac: wañ ysaac
gebar jacob Wann jacob ge
bar iudas vnd sein brůder:
wañ iudas gebar phares vñ
zarā von thamar. Wañ pha
res gebar esrom. Wann esrom gebar aram. Wañ
aram gebar aminadab: wann aminadab gebar na
ason. Wann naason gebar salmon: wann salmō
gebar boor von raab. Wann boor gebar obeth von
ruth: wann obeth gebar yesse. Wann yesse gebar
dauid den künig: wann dauid der künig gebar salo
mon von der die do was vrie. Wann salomon ge:
gebar roboam: wann roboam gebar abias. Wann
abias gebar asa: wann asa gebar josaphat. Wañ
josaphat gebar joram: wann joras gebar ozias.
Wann ozias gebar joathan: wann joathan gebar
achaz. Wann achaz gebar ezechias: wann ezechias
gebar manassē. Wañ manasses gebar amon: wañ
amon gebar josias. Wann josias gebar jechonias:
vnd sein brůder in dem vbergang der babilonier.
Vnd nach dem vbergang der babilonier jechoni:
as gebar salathiel: wann salathiel gebar zorobabel
Wann zorobabel gebar abiud: wann abiud gebar

Liber generationis

 THE FIRST PRINTED GERMAN BIBLE, 1466

hemels ſal ſijn dijn hulper. Sijn groot
heit loopt omtrēt die wolkē: ſijn wo-
ninghe is bouen: ende onder die ewe-
like armē. Hi ſal den viant verdriuē
van dinē aenſicht: ende hi ſal ſeggen
worde vertreden. Iſrahel ſal betrou-
welijc wonē eñ allene. Jacobs oge int
lāt des tarwē eñ des wijns: eñ die he-
melen ſullē verdonckeren vā douwe
Du biſte ſalich iſrahel. Wie is dijn
ghelijc volc. dattu behouden wordeſ-
te inden here? Dijn god is die ſchilt
dijnre hulpen: ende dat zwaert dijnre
glorien. Dijn ſullen lochenen dine viā
den: ende du ſultſte tredē hare halſen

Vandē campaengen Ca. xxxiiij
van moab ghinc moyſes opten
berch nebo indē top van phaſga iegēs
iericho: eñ die here thoende hē al dat
lant van galaad tot dan. ende al nepta
lim dat lant van effraym ende manaſ
ſes eñ al dat lant totter achterſter zee
ende die zuytzide ende die breetheit
des velts van iericho der ſtat vanden
palmen tot ſegor. Ende die here ſeide
tot hem. Dit is dat lant daer ic of ge
ſworen heb abraham yſaac ende iacob
ſegghende. Dinen ſade ſal ic et gheuen
Du hebſtet gheſien mit dinen oghē:
eñ du en ſults niet ouergaen tot daer
Dus is moyſes des herē knecht daer
doot int lant van moab na des heren
gebot: ende hi groeffen in eenre valey
en indē lande van moab tegē phogor:
eñ gheē mēſche en bekēde ſijn gracht
tot in deſen daghe toe. Ende moyſes
was hondert ende twintich iaer out
doe hij ſtarf. Sijn oghe en wort nye
verdonckert noch ſijn tanden en wor
den niet beruert. Ende die kinder
van iſrahel beweenden hem dertich
daghe inden campaengen van moab:
ende die daghen worden voldaē van
dē ghenen die moyſes beweendē. Eñ
ioſue nuns ſoen wort veruolt mit dē
gheeſt der wijſheit: want moyſes lei-
de ſijn handē op hem. Eñ die kinder
van iſrahel warē hem ghehoerſaem.
eñ ſi dedē alſo die here moyſen beuo-
len hadde Eñ voert ſo en vertees geē
propheet in iſrahel gelijc moyſes diē
die here bekēde van aenſichte te aenſichte in alle dē teykenē eñ wonderē.
die hi ſende mit hem dat hiſe doē ſou
de int lant van egiptē pharaoni ende
alle ſine knechten. eñ allen ſinen lan
de: eñ al die vrome hant ende die gro
te wonderē die moyſes dede voer al
iſrahel . Hier endt deutronomiū
twelc tleſte boec is van moyſes vijf
bokē Ende hier beghīt ioſue Ca. J

Ende het geſchiede
na moyſes ſheren
knechts doot. dat
die here ſprac tot
ioſue nuns ſoen
moyſes dienre: eñ
dat hi hē ſeide. Moyſes mijn knecht
is doot. Stant op ende gāc ouer die
iordane du eñ al tvolc metti: int lāt
dat ic den kinderē van iſrahel geuen
ſal. Ic ſal v leueren alle ſtat die de
voetſtap uwes voets treden ſal: alſo
ic moyſes ghesproken hebbe. Vāder
wildernisſen ende den libano eñ totter groter riuieren van eufraten: al-

3 THE FIRST PRINTED DUTCH BIBLE, 1477

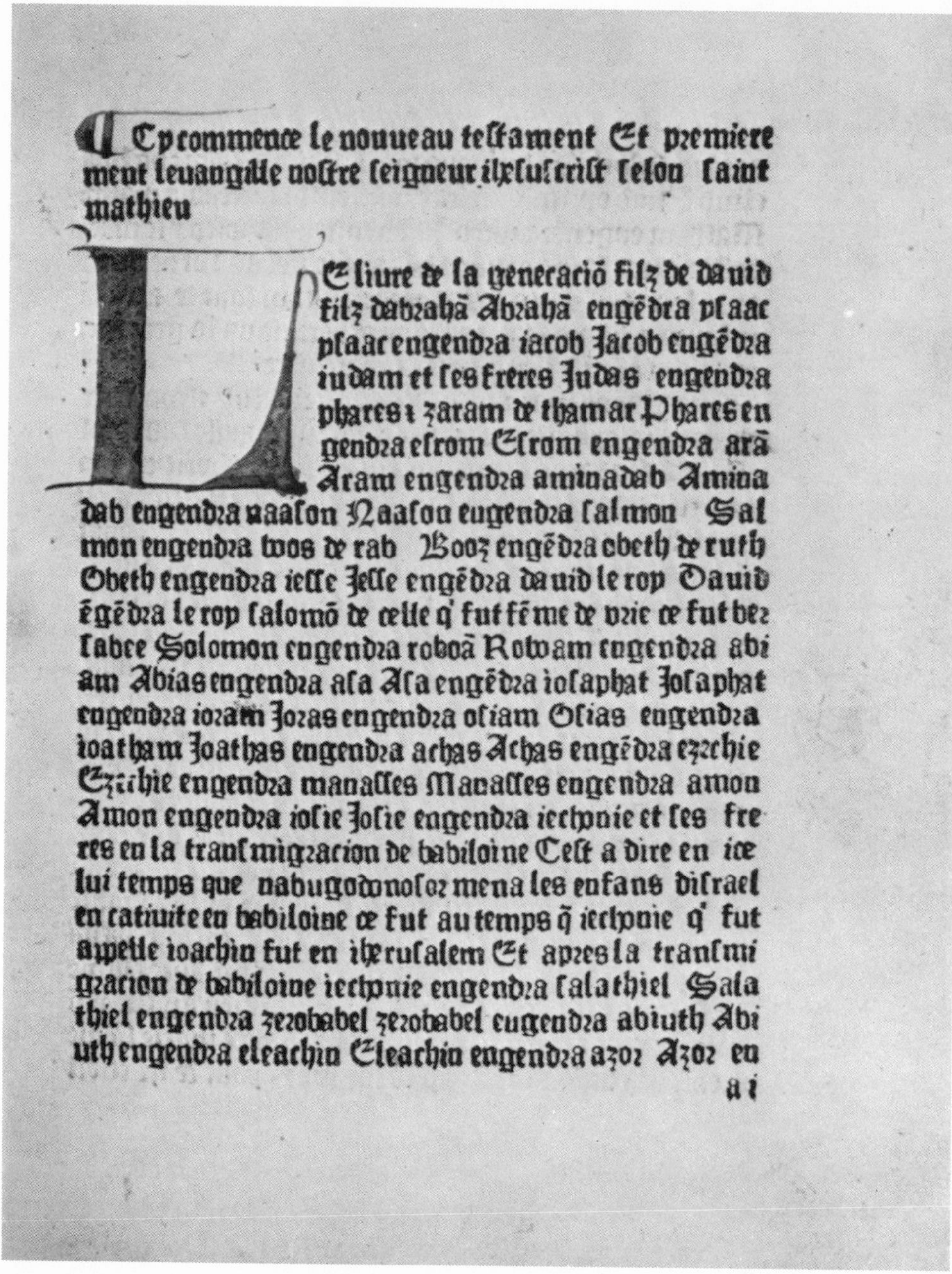
Cy commence le nouueau testament Et premiere
ment leuangille nostre seigneur ihesucrist selon saint
mathieu

Le liure de la generaciõ filz de dauid
filz dabrahã Abrahã engẽdra ysaac
ysaac engendra iacob Jacob engẽdra
iudam et ses freres Judas engendra
phares ⁊ zaram de thamar Phares en
gendra esrom Esrom engendra arã
Aram engendra aminadab Amina
dab engendra naason Naason engendra salmon Sal
mon engendra boos de rab Booz engẽdra obeth de ruth
Obeth engendra iesse Jesse engẽdra dauid le roy Dauid
ẽgẽdra le roy salomõ de celle q̃ fut fẽme de urie ce fut bez
sabee Solomon engendra roboã Roboam engendra abi
am Abias engendra asa Asa engẽdra iosaphat Josaphat
engendra ioram Joras engendra osiam Osias engendra
ioatham Joathas engendra achas Achas engẽdra ezechie
Ezechie engendra manasses Manasses engendra amon
Amon engendra iosie Josie engendra iechonie et ses fre
res en la transmigracion de babiloine Cest a dire en ice
lui temps que nabugodonosor mena les enfans disrael
en catiuite en babiloine ce fut au temps q̃ iechonie q̃ fut
appelle ioachin fut en iherusalem Et apres la transmi
gracion de babiloine iechonie engendra salathiel Sala
thiel engendra zorobabel zorobabel engendra abiuth Abi
uth engendra eleachin Eleachin engendra azor Azor en
a i

4 FRENCH NEW TESTAMENT, 1476

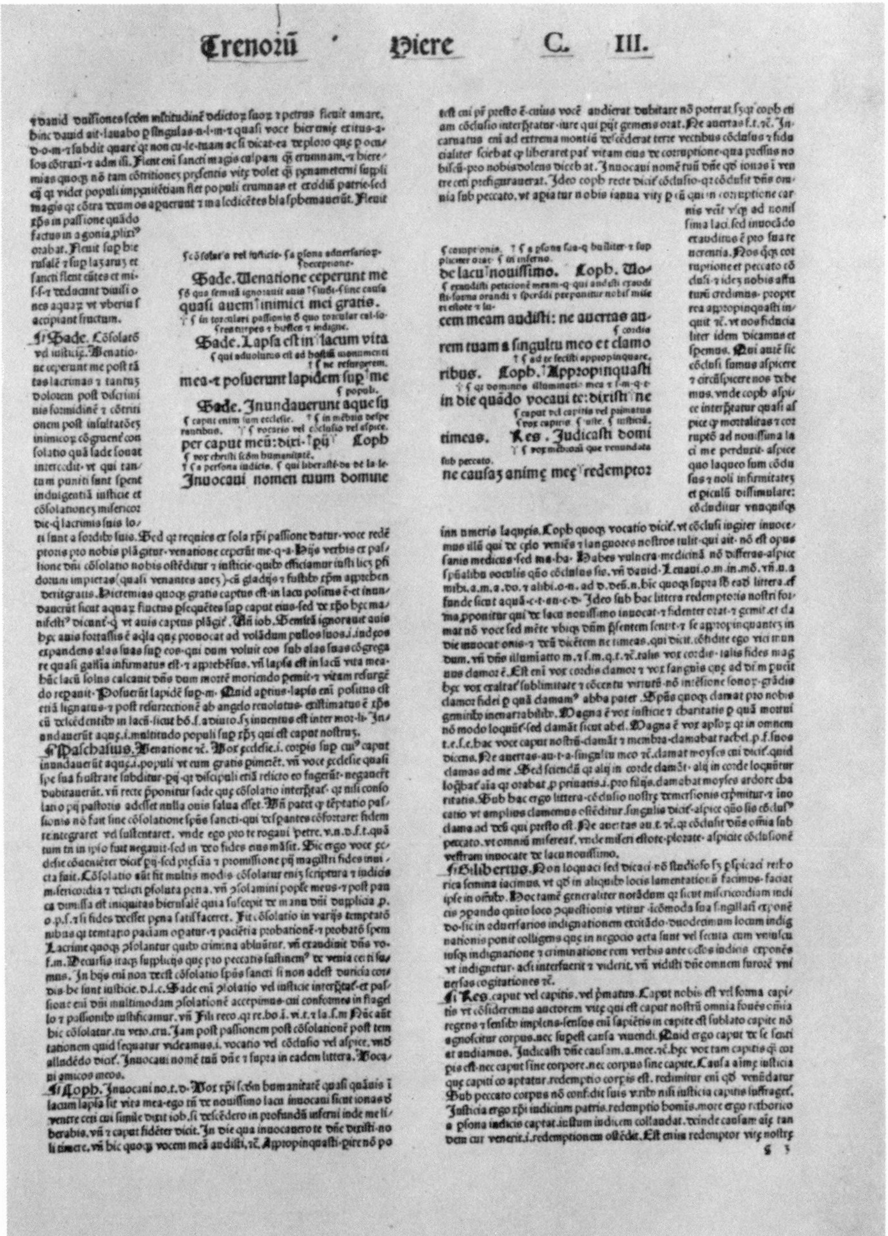
Trenorū Hiere C. III.

Sade. Uenatione ceperunt me quasi auem inimici mei gratis. Sade. Lapsa est in lacum vita mea et posuerunt lapidem sup me. Sade. Inundauerunt aque sup caput meū: dixi: pij Coph Inuocaui nomen tuum domine de lacu nouissimo. Coph. Uocem meam audisti: ne auertas aurem tuam a singultu meo et clamoribus. Coph. Appropinquasti in die quādo vocaui te: dixisti ne timeas. Res. Judicasti domine causaʒ anime meę redemptor

5 AN EDITION OF THE ‘GLOSSA ORDINARIA’

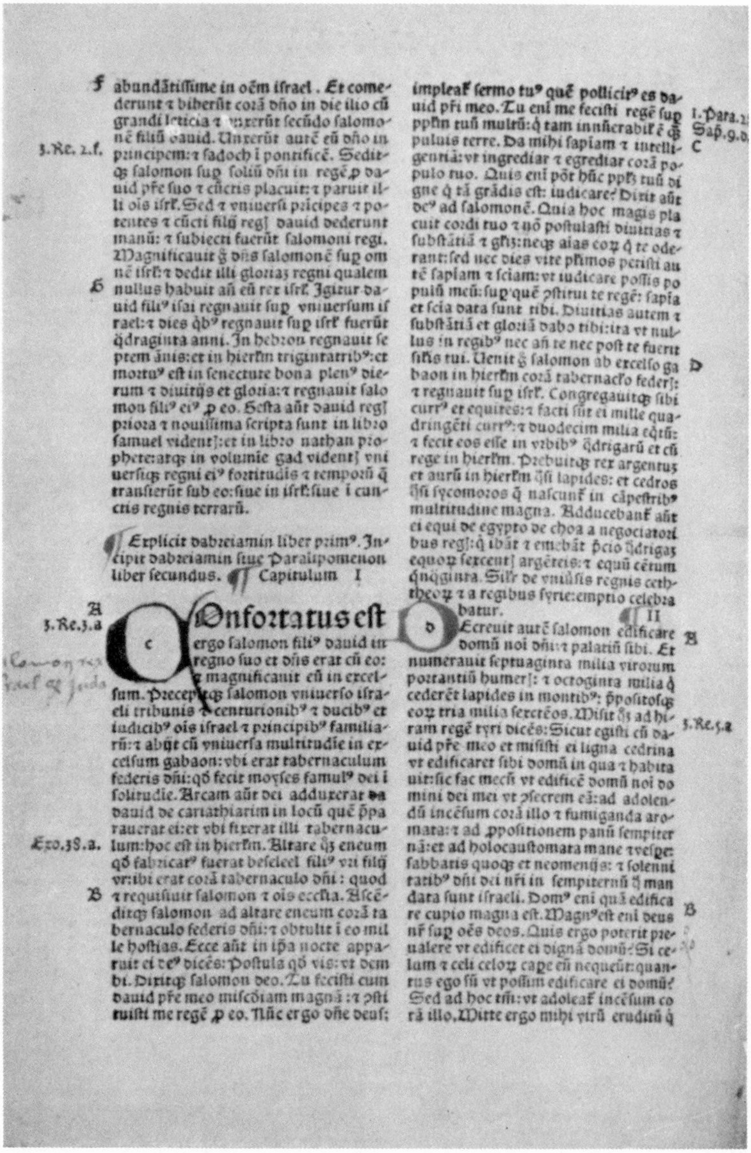

abundãtissime in oẽm israel. Et comederunt ⁊ biberũt corã dño in die illo cũ
grandi leticia ⁊ unxerũt secũdo salomonẽ filiũ dauid. Unxerũt autẽ eũ dño in
principem: ⁊ sadoch i pontificẽ. Sedit-
q; salomon sup soliũ dñi in regẽ p dauid pr̃e suo ⁊ cũctis placuit: ⁊ paruit illi oĩs isrł. Sed ⁊ vniuersi pricipes ⁊ potentes ⁊ cũcti filij reg dauid dederunt
manũ: ⁊ subiecti fuerũt salomoni regi.
Magnificauit ẽ dñs salomonẽ sup om
nẽ isrł: ⁊ dedit illi gloriã regni qualem
nullus habuit añ eũ rex isrł. Igitur dauid fili⁹ isai regnauit sup vniuersum is
rael: ⁊ dies qb⁹ regnauit sup isrł fuerũt
qdraginta anni. In hebron regnauit se
ptem ãnis: et in hierłm triginta trib⁹: et
mortu⁹ est in senectute bona plen⁹ dierum ⁊ diuitijs et gloria: ⁊ regnauit salo
mon fili⁹ ei⁹ p eo. Gesta aũt dauid reg
priora ⁊ nouissima scripta sunt in libro
samuel videntis: et in libro nathan prophete: atq; in volumie gad videntis vni
uersiq; regni ei⁹ fortitudis ⁊ tempoũ q
transierũt sub eo: siue in isrł: siue i cunctis regnis terrarũ.

¶ Explicit dabreiamin liber prim⁹. Incipit dabreiamin siue Paralipomenon
liber secundus. ¶ Capitulum I

Onfortatus est
ergo salomon fili⁹ dauid in
regno suo et dñs erat cũ eo:
⁊ magnificauit eũ in excel-
sum. Precepitq; salomon vniuerso israeli tribunis ⁊ centurionib⁹ ⁊ ducib⁹ et
iudicib⁹ oĩs israel ⁊ principib⁹ familiarũ: ⁊ abijt cũ vniuersa multitudie in ex-
celsum gabaon: vbi erat tabernaculum
federis dñi: qđ fecit moyses famul⁹ dei i
solitudie. Arcam aũt dei adduxerat da
dauid de cariathiarim in locũ quẽ ppa
rauerat ei: et vbi fixerat illi tabernaculum: hoc est in hierłm. Altare q; eneum
qđ fabricat⁹ fuerat beseleel fili⁹ vri filij
vr: ibi erat corã tabernaculo dñi: quod
⁊ requisiuit salomon ⁊ oĩs eccłia. Ascẽ-
ditq; salomon ad altare eneum corã ta
bernaculo federis dñi: ⁊ obtulit i eo mil
le hostias. Ecce aũt in ipa nocte apparuit ei de⁹ dicẽs: Postula qđ vis: vt dem
bi. Dixitq; salomon deo. Tu fecisti cum
dauid pr̃e meo misedĩam magnã: ⁊ csti
tuisti me regẽ p eo. Nũc ergo dñe deus:
impleaẽ sermo tu⁹ quẽ pollicit⁹ es dauid pr̃i meo. Tu eni me fecisti regẽ sup
ppłm tuũ multũ: q tam innũerabił ẽ q
puluis terre. Da mihi sapiam ⁊ intelli-
gentiã: vt ingrediar ⁊ egrediar corã po-
pulo tuo. Quis eni pőt hũc ppłm tuũ di
gne q tã grãdis est: iudicare? Dixit aũt
de⁹ ad salomonẽ. Quia hoc magis pla
cuit cordi tuo ⁊ nõ postulasti diuitias ⁊
substãtiã ⁊ głiã: neq; aias eoꝝ q te ode-
rant: sed nec dies vite plimos petisti au
tẽ sapiam ⁊ sciam: vt iudicare possis po
puiũ meũ: sup quẽ cstitui te regẽ: sapia
et scia data sunt tibi. Diuitias autem ⁊
substãtiã et gloriã dabo tibi: ita vt nullus in regib⁹ nec añ te nec post te fuerit
silis tui. Uenit ẽ salomon ab excelso ga
baon in hierłm corã tabernacło federis:
⁊ regnauit sup isrł. Congregauitq; sibi
curr⁹ et equites: ⁊ facti sũt ei mille qua-
dringẽti curr⁹: ⁊ duodecim milia eqtũ:
⁊ fecit eos esse in vrbib⁹ qdrigarũ et cũ
rege in hierłm. Prebuitq; rex argentũ
et aurũ in hierłm qsi lapides: et cedros
qsi sycomoros q nascunẽ in cãpestrib⁹
multitudine magna. Adducebanẽ aũt
ei equi de egypto de choa a negociatori
bus regis: q ibãt ⁊ emebãt pcio qdrigas
equoꝝ sexcentis argẽteis: ⁊ equũ cẽtum
qnqginta. Silr de vniũsis regnis ceth-
theoꝝ ⁊ a regibus syrie: emptio celebra
batur. ¶ II
Ecreuit autẽ salomon edificare
domũ noi dñi: ⁊ palatiũ sibi. Et
numerauit septuaginta milia virorum
portantiũ humeris: ⁊ octoginta milia q
cederẽt lapides in montib⁹: ppositosq;
eoꝝ tria milia sexcẽtos. Misit q; ad hi-
ram regẽ tyri dicẽs: Sicut egisti cũ dauid pr̃e meo et misisti ei ligna cedrina
vt edificaret sibi domũ in qua ⁊ habita
uit: sic fac mecũ vt edificẽ domũ noi do
mini dei mei vt csecrem eã: ad adolen-
dũ incẽsum corã illo ⁊ fumiganda aro-
mata: ⁊ ad ppositionem panũ sempiter
nã: et ad holocaustomata mane ⁊ vespe-
sabbatis quoq; et neomenijs: ⁊ solenni
tatib⁹ dñi dei nr̃i in sempiternũ q man
data sunt israeli. Dom⁹ eni quã edifica
re cupio magna est. Magn⁹ est eni deus
nr̃ sup oẽs deos. Quis ergo poterit pre-
ualere vt edificet ei dignã domũ? Si ce-
lum ⁊ celi celoꝝ cape eũ nequeũt: quan-
tus ego sũ vt possim edificare ei domũ?
Sed ad hoc tm̃: vt adoleaẽ incẽsum co
rã illo. Mitte ergo mihi virũ eruditũ q

6 FROBEN'S FIRST OCTAVO, 1491

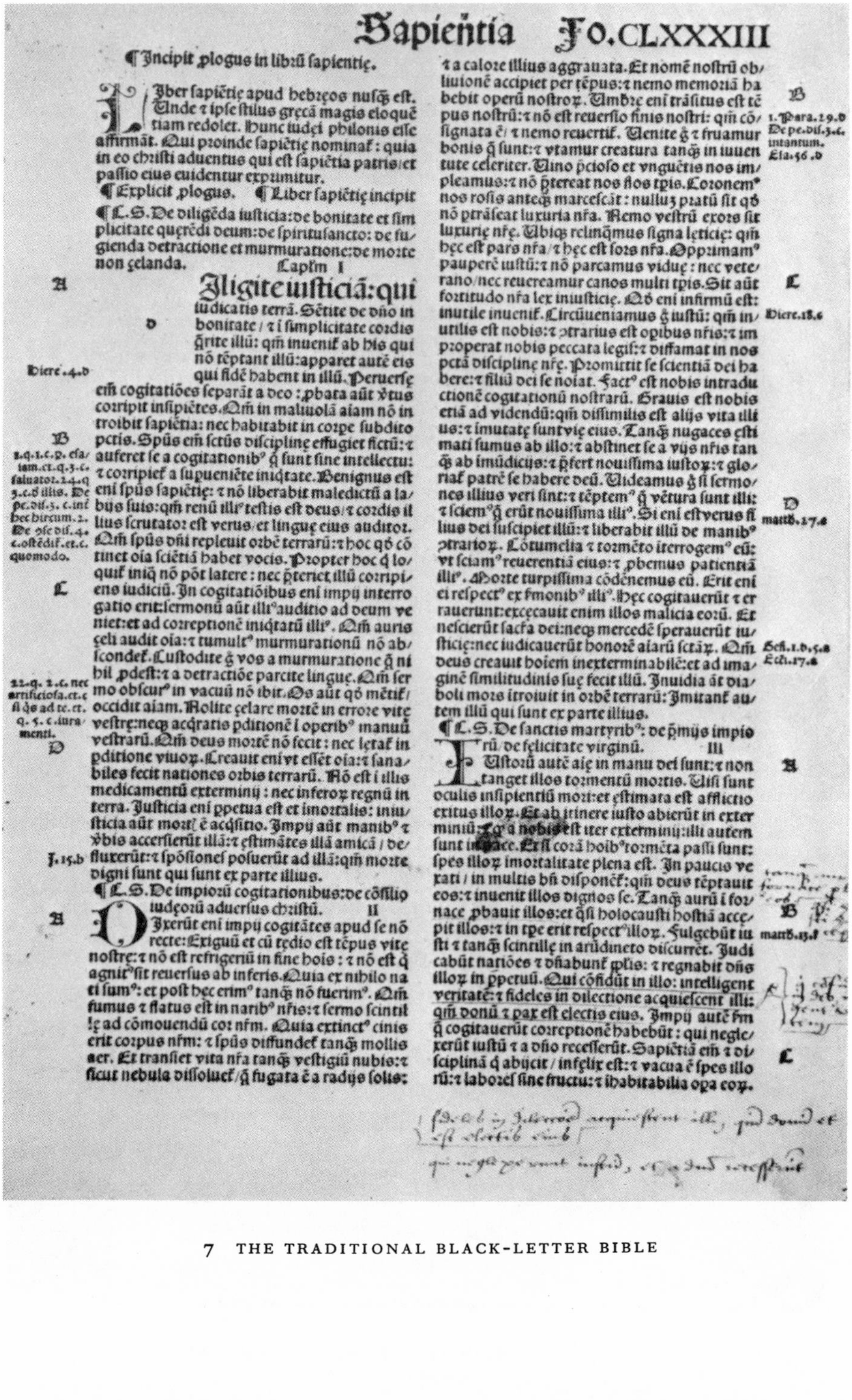

Sapientia Fo.CLXXXIII

¶ Incipit plogus in libru sapientie.

Liber sapiētie apud hebreos nusq̄ est. Unde ꝛ ipse stilus greca magis eloquētiam redolet. Hunc iudei philonis esse affirmāt. Qui proinde sapiētie nominat: quia in eo christi aduentus qui est sapiētia patris/et passio eius euidentur exprimitur.

¶ Explicit plogus. ¶ Liber sapiētie incipit

¶ C.S. De diligēda iusticia: de bonitate et simplicitate querēdi deum: de spiritusancto: de fugienda detractione et murmuratione: de morte non zelanda. Capl'm I

A Diligite iusticiā: qui iudicatis terrā. Sētite de dño in bonitate/ꝛ i simplicitate cordis q̄rite illū: q̄m inuenit ab his qui nō tēptant illū: apparet autē eis qui fidē habent in illū. Peruerse enī cogitatiōes separāt a deo: pbata aūt virtus corripit insipiētes. Q̄m in maliuolā aiam nō introibit sapiētia: nec habitabit in corpe subdito pctis. Spūs enī sctūs discipline effugiet fictū: ꝛ auferet se a cogitationib' q̄ sunt sine intellectu: ꝛ corripiet a superueniēte iniqtate. Benignus est enī spūs sapiētie: ꝛ nō liberabit maledictū a labiis suis: q̄m renū illi' testis est deus/ꝛ cordis illius scrutator est verus/et lingue eius auditor. Q̄m spūs dñi repleuit orbē terrarū: ꝛ hoc qd cōtinet oia sciētiā habet vocis. Propter hoc q̄ loquit iniq nō pōt latere: nec pteriet illū corripiens iudiciū. In cogitatiōibus enī impij interrogatio erit: sermonū aūt illi' auditio ad deum veniet: et ad correptionē iniqtatū illi'. Q̄m auris zeli audit oia: ꝛ tumult' murmurationū nō abscondet. Custodite ḡ vos a murmuratione q̄ nihil pdest: ꝛ a detractiōe parcite lingue. Q̄m sermo obscur' in vacuū nō ibit. Os aūt qd mētit occidit aiam. Nolite zelare mortē in errore vite vestre: neq̄ acqratis pditionē i operib' manuū vestrarū. Q̄m deus mortē nō fecit: nec letat in pditione viuoꝝ. Creauit enī vt essēt oia: ꝛ sanabiles fecit nationes orbis terrarū. Nō est i illis medicamentū exterminij: nec inferoꝝ regnū in terra. Justicia enī ppetua est et inmortalis: iniusticia aūt mors est acqsitio. Impij aūt manib' ꝛ vbis accersierūt illā: ꝛ estimātes illā amicā/defluxerūt: ꝛ spōsiones posuerūt ad illā: q̄m morte digni sunt qui sunt ex parte illius.

¶ C.S. De impiorū cogitationibus: de cōsilio iudeorū aduersus christū. II

A Dixerūt enī impij cogitātes apud se nō recte: Exiguū et cū tedio est tēpus vite nostre: ꝛ nō est refrigeriū in fine hois: ꝛ nō est q̄ agnit' sit reuersus ab inferis. Quia ex nihilo nati sum': et post hec erim' tanq̄ nō fuerim'. Q̄m fumus ꝛ flatus est in narib' nrīs: ꝛ sermo scintille ad cōmouendū cor nrm. Quia extinct' cinis erit corpus nrm: ꝛ spūs diffundet tanq̄ mollis aer. Et transiet vita nra tanq̄ vestigiū nubis: ꝛ sicut nebula dissoluet/q̄ fugata ē a radijs solis: ꝛ a calore illius aggrauata. Et nomē nostrū obliuionē accipiet per tēpus: ꝛ nemo memoriā habebit operū nostroꝝ. Umbre enī trāsitus est tēpus nostrū: ꝛ nō est reuersio finis nostri: q̄m cōsignata ē/ꝛ nemo reuertit. Uenite ḡ ꝛ fruamur bonis q̄ sunt: ꝛ vtamur creatura tanq̄ in iuuentute celeriter. Uino pcioso et vnguētis nos impleamus: ꝛ nō ptereat nos flos tpis. Coronem' nos rosis anteq̄ marcescāt: nullū pratū sit qd nō ptrāseat luxuria nra. Nemo vestrū exors sit luxurie nre. Ubiq̄ relinq̄mus signa leticie: q̄m hec est pars nra/ꝛ hec est sors nra. Opprimam' pauperē iustū: ꝛ nō parcamus vidue: nec veterano/nec reuereamur canos multi tpis. Sit aūt fortitudo nra lex iniusticie. Qd enī infirmū est: inutile inuenit. Circūueniamus ḡ iustū: q̄m inutilis est nobis: ꝛ ɔtrarius est opibus nrīs: ꝛ improperat nobis peccata legis: ꝛ diffamat in nos pctā discipline nre. Promittit se scientiā dei habere: ꝛ filiū dei se noiat. Fact' est nobis intraductionē cogitationū nostrarū. Grauis est nobis etiā ad videndū: q̄m dissimilis est alijs vita illius: ꝛ imutate sunt vie eius. Tanq̄ nugaces estimati sumus ab illo: ꝛ abstinet se a vijs nrīs tanq̄ ab imūdicijs: ꝛ pfert nouissima iustoꝝ: ꝛ gloriat patrē se habere deū. Uideamus ḡ si sermones illius veri sint: ꝛ tēptem' q̄ vētura sunt illi: ꝛ sciem' q̄ erūt nouissima illi'. Si enī est verus filius dei suscipiet illū: ꝛ liberabit illū de manib' ɔtrarioꝝ. Cōtumelia ꝛ tormēto iterrogem' eū: vt sciam' reuerentiā eius: ꝛ pbemus patientiā illi'. Morte turpissima cōdēnemus eū. Erit enī ei respect' ex smonib' illi'. Hec cogitauerūt ꝛ errauerunt: excecauit enim illos malicia eorū. Et nescierūt sacra dei: neq̄ mercedē sperauerūt iusticie: nec iudicauerūt honorē aiarū sctāꝝ. Q̄m deus creauit hoiem inexterminabilē: et ad imaginē similitudinis sue fecit illū. Inuidia āt diaboli mors itrouit in orbē terrarū: Imitant autem illū qui sunt ex parte illius.

¶ C.S. De sanctis martyrib': de pmijs impiorū: de felicitate virginū. III

Iustorū autē aie in manu dei sunt: ꝛ non tanget illos tormentū mortis. Uisi sunt oculis insipientiū mori: et estimata est afflictio exitus illoꝝ. Et ab itinere iusto abierūt in exterminiū: ꝛ q̄ a nobis est iter exterminij: illi autem sunt in pace. Et si corā hoib' tormēta passi sunt: spes illoꝝ imortalitate plena est. In paucis vexati/in multis bñ disponēt: q̄m deus tēptauit eos: ꝛ inuenit illos dignos se. Tanq̄ aurū i fornace pbauit illos: et q̄si holocausti hostiā accepit illos: ꝛ in tpe erit respect' illoꝝ. Fulgebūt iusti ꝛ tanq̄ scintille in arūdineto discurrēt. Iudicabūt natiōes ꝛ dñabunt pplis: ꝛ regnabit dñs illoꝝ in ppetuū. Qui cōfidūt in illo: intelligent veritatē: ꝛ fideles in dilectione acquiescent illi: q̄m donū ꝛ pax est electis eius. Impij autē fm q̄ cogitauerūt correptionē habebūt: qui neglexerūt iustū ꝛ a dño recesserūt. Sapiētiā enī ꝛ disciplinā q̄ abijcit/infelix est: ꝛ vacua ē spes illorū: ꝛ labores sine fructu: ꝛ ihabitabilia opa eoꝝ.

7 THE TRADITIONAL BLACK-LETTER BIBLE

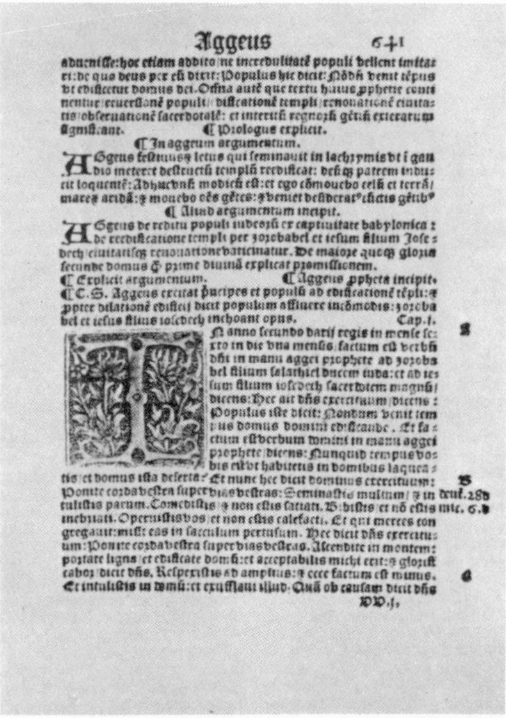

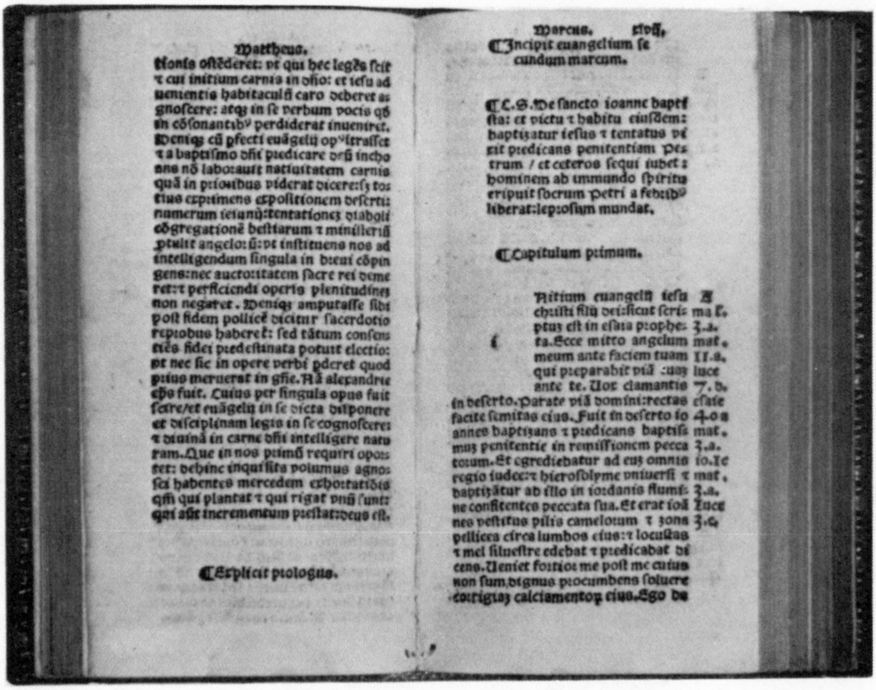

8 EARLY ATTEMPTS AT SMALL FORMATS

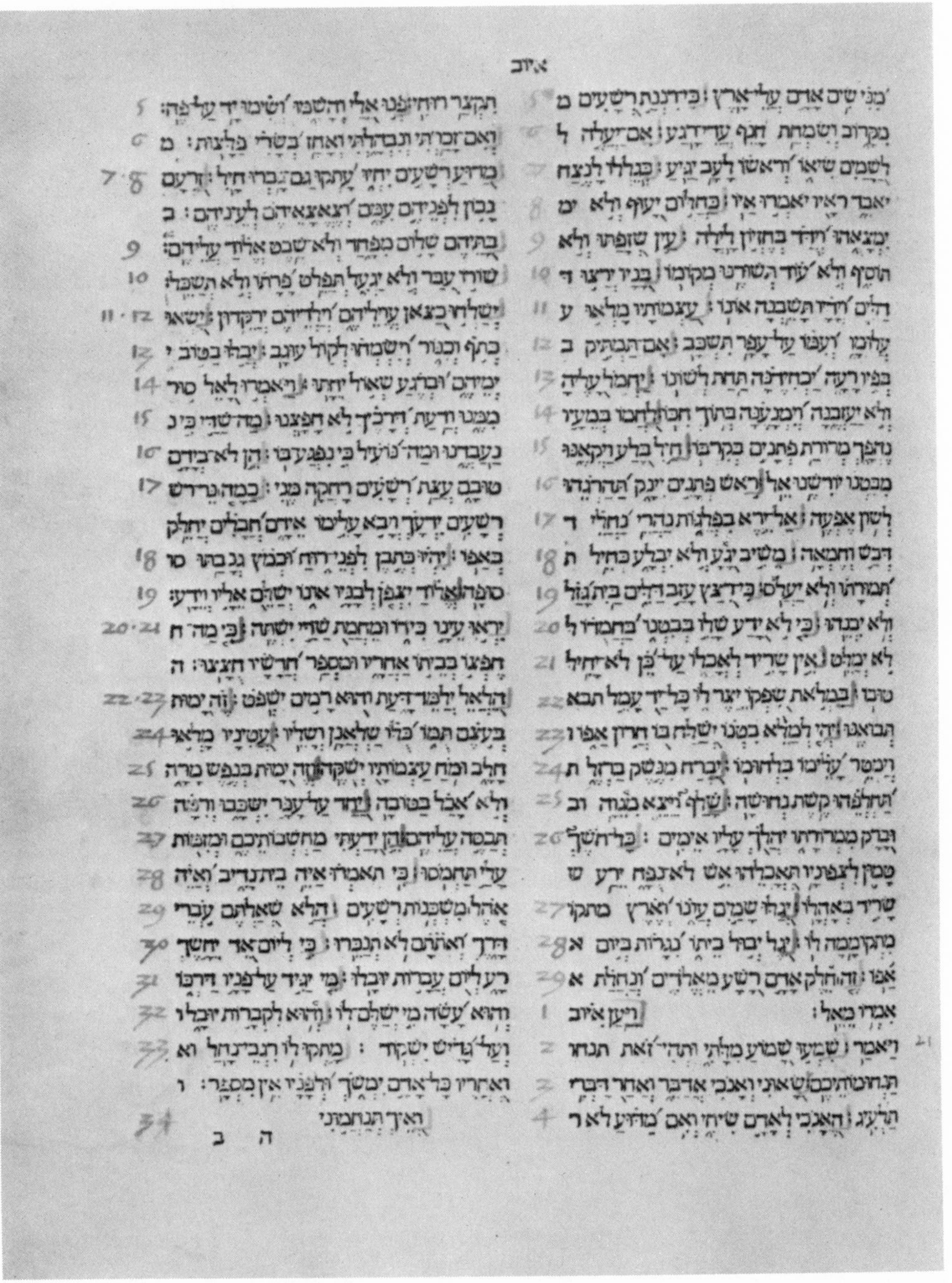

5 מני שים אדם עלי ארץ: כי רננת רשעים מ
6 מקרוב ושמחת חנף עדי רגע: אם יעלה ל
7 שמים שיאו וראשו לעב יגיע: כגללו לנצח
8 יאבד ראיו יאמרו איו: כחלום יעוף ולא ימ
9 צאהו וידד כחזיון לילה: עין שזפתו ולא
10 תוסיף ולא עוד תשורנו מקומו: בניו ירצו ד
11 לים וידיו תשבנה אונו: עצמותיו מלאו ע
12 לומו ועמו על עפר תשכב: אם תמתיק ב
13 פיו רעה יכחידנה תחת לשונו: יחמל עליה
14 ולא יעזבנה וימנענה בתוך חכו: לחמו במעיו
15 נהפך מרורת פתנים בקרבו: חיל בלע ויקאנו
16 מבטנו יורשנו אל: ראש פתנים יינק תהרגהו
17 לשון אפעה: אל ירא בפלגות נהרי נחלי ד
18 בש וחמאה: משיב יגע ולא יבלע כחיל ת
19 מורתו ולא יעלס: כי רצץ עזב דלים בית גזל
20 ולא יבנהו: כי לא ידע שלו בבטנו בחמודו ל
21 לא ימלט: אין שריד לאכלו על כן לא יחיל
22 טובו: במלאות שפקו יצר לו כל יד עמל תבוא
23 תבואנו: יהי למלא בטנו ישלח בו חרון אפו ו
24 ימטר עלימו בלחומו: יברח מנשק ברזל ת
25 תחלפהו קשת נחושה: שלף ויצא מגוה וב
26 רק ממררתו יהלך עליו אמים: כל חשך
טמון לצפוניו תאכלהו אש לא נפח ירע ש
27 שריד באהלו: יגלו שמים עונו וארץ מתקו
28 מתקוממה לו: יגל יבול ביתו נגרות ביום א
29 אפו: זה חלק אדם רשע מאלהים ונחלת א
1 אמרו מאל: ויען איוב
21 2 ויאמר: שמעו שמוע מלתי ותהי זאת תנחו
3 תנחומתיכם: שאוני ואנכי אדבר ואחר דברי
4 תלעיג: האנכי לאדם שיחי ואם מדוע לא ת

5 תקצר רוחי: פנו אלי והשמו ושימו יד על פה:
6 ואם זכרתי ונבהלתי ואחז בשרי פלצות: מ
7·8 דוע רשעים יחיו עתקו גם גברו חיל: זרעם
נכון לפניהם עמם וצאצאיהם לעיניהם: ב
9 בתיהם שלום מפחד ולא שבט אלוה עליהם:
10 שורו עבר ולא יגעל תפלט פרתו ולא תשכל:
11·12 ישלחו כצאן עויליהם וילדיהם ירקדון: ישאו
13 כתף וכנור וישמחו לקול עוגב: יבלו בטוב י
14 מיהם וברגע שאול יחתו: ויאמרו לאל סור
15 ממנו ודעת דרכיך לא חפצנו: מה שדי כי נ
16 עבדנו ומה נועיל כי נפגע בו: הן לא בידם
17 טובם עצת רשעים רחקה מני: כמה נר רש
רשעים ידעך ויבא עלימו אידם חבלים יחלק
18 באפו: יהיו כתבן לפני רוח וכמץ גנבתו סו
19 סופה: אלוה יצפן לבניו אונו ישלם אליו וידע:
20·21 יראו עינו כידו ומחמת שדי ישתה: כי מה ח
חפצו בביתו אחריו ומספר חדשיו חצצו: ה
22·23 הלאל ילמד דעת והוא רמים ישפוט: זה ימות
24 בעצם תמו כלו שלאנן ושליו: עטיניו מלאו
25 חלב ומח עצמותיו ישקה: וזה ימות בנפש מרה
26 ולא אכל בטובה: יחד על עפר ישכבו ורמה
27 תכסה עליהם: הן ידעתי מחשבותיכם ומזמות
28 עלי תחמסו: כי תאמרו איה בית נדיב ואיה
29 אהל משכנות רשעים: הלא שאלתם עוברי
30 דרך ואתתם לא תנכרו: כי ליום איד יחשך
31 רע ליום עברות יובלו: מי יגיד על פניו דרכו
32 והוא עשה מי ישלם לו: והוא לקברות יובל ו
33 ועל גדיש ישקוד: מתקו לו רגבי נחל וא
ואחריו כל אדם ימשוך ולפניו אין מספר: ו
34 ואיך תנחמוני

ה ב

9 THE SONCINO BIBLE, 1488

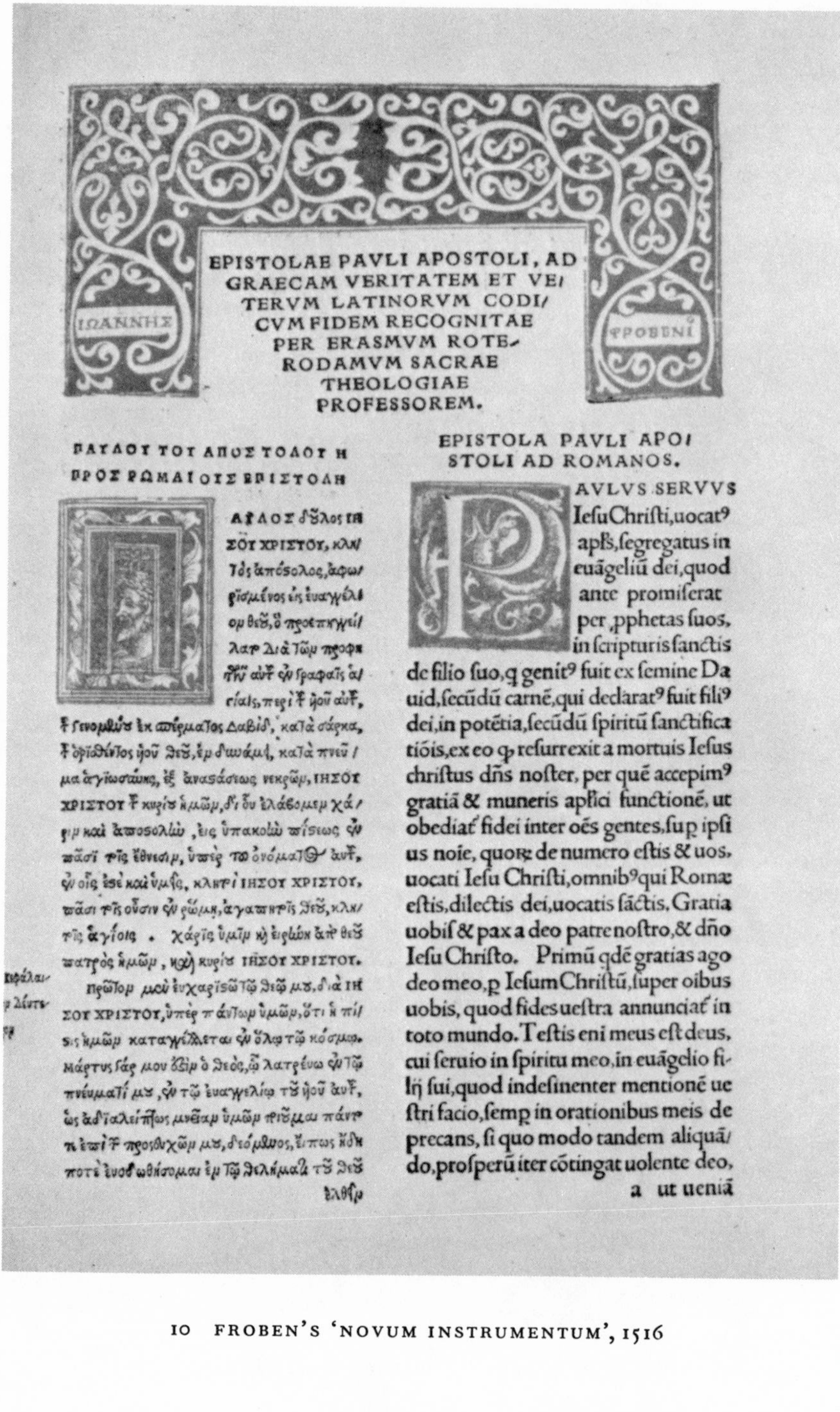
EPISTOLAE PAVLI APOSTOLI, AD GRAECAM VERITATEM ET VETERVM LATINORVM CODICVM FIDEM RECOGNITAE PER ERASMVM ROTERODAMVM SACRAE THEOLOGIAE PROFESSOREM.

ΙΩΑΝΝΗΣ ΦΡΟΒΕΝΙ

ΠΑΥΛΟΥ ΤΟΥ ΑΠΟΣΤΟΛΟΥ Η ΠΡΟΣ ΡΩΜΑΙΟΥΣ ΕΠΙΣΤΟΛΗ

ΠΑΥΛΟΣ δοῦλος ἸΗΣΟΥ ΧΡΙΣΤΟΥ, κλητὸς ἀπόστολος, ἀφωρισμένος εἰς εὐαγγέλιον θεοῦ, ὃ προεπηγγείλατο διὰ τῶν προφητῶν αὐτοῦ ἐν γραφαῖς ἁγίαις, περὶ τοῦ υἱοῦ αὐτοῦ, τοῦ γενομένου ἐκ σπέρματος Δαβίδ, κατὰ σάρκα, τοῦ ὁρισθέντος υἱοῦ θεοῦ, ἐν δυνάμει, κατὰ πνεῦμα ἁγιωσύνης, ἐξ ἀναστάσεως νεκρῶν, ΙΗΣΟΥ ΧΡΙΣΤΟΥ τοῦ κυρίου ἡμῶν, δι' οὗ ἐλάβομεν χάριν καὶ ἀποστολὴν, εἰς ὑπακοὴν πίστεως ἐν πᾶσι τοῖς ἔθνεσιν, ὑπὲρ τοῦ ὀνόματος αὐτοῦ, ἐν οἷς ἐστὲ καὶ ὑμεῖς, κλητοὶ ΙΗΣΟΥ ΧΡΙΣΤΟΥ, πᾶσι τοῖς οὖσιν ἐν ῥώμῃ, ἀγαπητοῖς θεοῦ, κλητοῖς ἁγίοις. χάρις ὑμῖν καὶ εἰρήνη ἀπὸ θεοῦ πατρὸς ἡμῶν, καὶ κυρίου ΙΗΣΟΥ ΧΡΙΣΤΟΥ. πρῶτον μὲν εὐχαριστῶ τῷ θεῷ μου, διὰ ΙΗΣΟΥ ΧΡΙΣΤΟΥ, ὑπὲρ πάντων ὑμῶν, ὅτι ἡ πίστις ὑμῶν καταγγέλλεται ἐν ὅλῳ τῷ κόσμῳ. μάρτυς γάρ μου ἐστὶν ὁ θεὸς, ᾧ λατρεύω ἐν τῷ πνεύματί μου, ἐν τῷ εὐαγγελίῳ τοῦ υἱοῦ αὐτοῦ, ὡς ἀδιαλείπτως μνείαν ὑμῶν ποιοῦμαι πάντοτε ἐπὶ τῶν προσευχῶν μου, δεόμενος, εἴπως ἤδη ποτὲ εὐοδωθήσομαι ἐν τῷ θελήματι τοῦ θεοῦ ἐλθεῖν

EPISTOLA PAVLI APOSTOLI AD ROMANOS.

PAVLVS SERVVS Iesu Christi, uocatus apostolus, segregatus in euangelium dei, quod ante promiserat per prophetas suos, in scripturis sanctis de filio suo, qui genitus fuit ex semine Dauid, secundum carnem, qui declaratus fuit filius dei, in potentia, secundum spiritum sanctificationis, ex eo quod resurrexit a mortuis Iesus christus dominus noster, per quem accepimus gratiam & muneris apostolici functionem, ut obediatur fidei inter omnes gentes, super ipsius nomine, quorum de numero estis & uos, uocati Iesu Christi, omnibus qui Romae estis, dilectis dei, uocatis sanctis. Gratia uobis & pax a deo patre nostro, & domino Iesu Christo. Primum quidem gratias ago deo meo, per Iesum Christum, super omnibus uobis, quod fides uestra annunciatur in toto mundo. Testis enim meus est deus, cui seruio in spiritu meo, in euangelio filii sui, quod indesinenter mentionem uestri facio, semper in orationibus meis deprecans, si quo modo tandem aliquando, prosperum iter contingat uolente deo,

a ut ueniam

10 FROBEN'S 'NOVUM INSTRUMENTUM', 1516

ΑΡΙΘΜΟΙ.

ΚΕΦ. Α. 1

Καὶ ἐλάλησε κύριος πρὸς μωϋσῆν ἐν τῇ ἐρήμῳ τῇ σινᾶ ἐν τῇ σκηνῇ τοῦ μαρτυρίου ἐν μιᾷ τοῦ μηνός. τοῦ δευτέρου ἔτους δευτέρου ἐξελθόντων αὐτῶν ἐκ γῆς αἰγύπτου λέγων. λάβετε ἀρχὴν πάσης συναγωγῆς υἱῶν ἰσραὴλ κατὰ συγγενείας αὐτῶν. κατ᾽ οἴκους πατριῶν αὐτῶν. κατὰ ἀριθμὸν ἐξ ὀνόματος αὐτῶν κατὰ κεφαλὴν αὐτῶν. πᾶς ἄρσην ἀπὸ εἰκοσαετοῦς καὶ ἐπάνω. πᾶς ὁ ἐκπορευόμενος ἐν δυνάμει ἰσραὴλ ἐπισκέψασθε αὐτοὺς σὺν δυνάμει αὐτῶν. σὺ καὶ ἀαρὼν ἐπισκέψασθε αὐτούς. καὶ μεθ᾽ ὑμῶν ἔσονται σὺν δυνάμει αὐτῶν ἕκαστος. ἕκαστος κατὰ φυλὴν. ἑκάστου ἀρχόντων κατ᾽ οἴκους πατριῶν ἔσονται. καὶ ταῦτα τὰ ὀνόματα τῶν ἀνδρῶν, οἵτινες παραστήσονται μεθ᾽ ὑμῶν. τῶν ῥουβὴν ἐλισοὺρ υἱὸς σεδιούρ. τῶν συμεὼν, σαλαμιὴλ υἱὸς σουρισαδαί. τῶν ἰούδα. ναασσὼν. υἱὸς ἀμιναδάμ. τῶν ἰσσάχαρ. ναθαναὴλ υἱὸς σωγάρ. τῶν ζαβουλὼν ἐλιὰμ υἱὸς χαιλών, τῶν υἱῶν ἰωσήφ. τῶν ἐφραὶμ ἐλισαμὰ υἱὸς σεμιούδ. τῶν μανασσῆ, γαμαλιὴλ υἱὸς φαδασσούρ. τῶν βενιαμὶν, ἀβιδὰν υἱὸς γαδεωνί. τῶν δάν. ἀχιέζερ υἱὸς ἀμισαδαί. τῶν ἀσήρ, φαγαιήλ. υἱὸς ἐχράν. τῶν γάδ, ἐλισὰφ υἱὸς ῥαγουήλ. τῶν νεφθαλείμ, ἀχιρὲ υἱὸς αἰνάν. οὗτοι ἐπίκλητοι τῆς συναγωγῆς ἄρχοντες τῶν φυλῶν κατὰ πατριὰς αὐτῶν χιλίαρχοι ἰσραὴλ εἰσι. καὶ ἔλαβε μωϋσῆς καὶ ἀαρὼν τοὺς ἄνδρας τούτους τοὺς ἀνακληθέντας ἐξ ὀνόματος, καὶ πᾶσαν τὴν συναγωγὴν, συνήγαγεν, ἐν μιᾷ τοῦ μηνὸς τοῦ δευτέρου ἔτους. καὶ ἐπεσκέπησαν κατὰ γενέσεις αὐτῶν, κατὰ πατριὰς αὐτῶν. κατὰ ἀριθμὸν ὀνομάτων αὐτῶν, ἀπὸ εἰκοσαετοῦς καὶ ἐπάνω. πᾶν ἀρσενικὸν κατὰ κεφαλὴν αὐτῶν. ὃν τρόπον συνέταξε κύριος τῷ μωϋσεῖ. καὶ ἐπεσκέπησαν αὐτοὶ ἐν τῇ ἐρήμῳ τῇ σινᾶ. καὶ ἐγένοντο υἱοὶ ῥουβὴν πρωτοτόκου ἰσραὴλ κατὰ συγγενείας αὐτῶν. κατὰ δήμους αὐτῶν. κατ᾽ οἴκους πατριῶν αὐτῶν, κατὰ ἀριθμὸν ὀνομάτων αὐτῶν, κατὰ κεφαλὴν αὐτῶν, πάντα ἀρσενικὰ ἀπὸ εἰκοσαετοῦς καὶ ἐπάνω, πᾶς ὁ ἐκπορευόμενος ἐν τῇ δυνάμει, ἡ ἐπίσκεψις αὐτῶν ἐκ τῆς φυλῆς ῥουβήν. ἓξ καὶ τεσσαράκοντα χιλιάδες καὶ πεντακόσιοι. καὶ τοῖς υἱοῖς συμεὼν κατὰ συγγενείας αὐτῶν, κατὰ δήμους αὐτῶν, κατ᾽ οἴκους πατριῶν αὐτῶν, κατὰ ἀριθμὸν ὀνομάτων αὐτῶν, κατὰ κεφαλὴν αὐτῶν. πᾶν ἀρσενικὸν ἀπὸ εἰκοσαετοῦς καὶ ἐπάνω. πᾶς ὁ ἐκπορευόμενος ἐν τῇ δυνάμει. ἡ ἐπίσκεψις αὐτῶν ἐκ τῆς φυλῆς συμεὼν, ἐννέα καὶ πεντήκοντα χιλιάδες καὶ τριακόσιοι. τοῖς υἱοῖς ἰούδα κατὰ συγγενείας αὐτῶν. κατὰ δήμους αὐτῶν. κατ᾽ οἴκους πατριῶν αὐτῶν, κατὰ ἀριθμὸν ὀνομάτων αὐτῶν. κατὰ κεφαλὴν αὐτῶν, πάντα ἀρσενικὰ, ἀπὸ εἰκοσαετοῦς καὶ ἐπάνω. πᾶς ὁ ἐκπορευόμενος ἐν τῇ δυνάμει, ἡ ἐπίσκεψις αὐτῶν. ἐκ τῆς φυλῆς ἰούδα τέσσαρες καὶ ἑβδομήκοντα χιλιάδες καὶ ἑξακόσιοι. τοῖς υἱοῖς ἰσσάχαρ κατὰ συγγενείας αὐτῶν, καὶ κατὰ δήμους αὐτῶν, κατ᾽ οἴκους πατριῶν αὐτῶν. κατὰ ἀριθμὸν ὀνομάτων αὐτῶν. κατὰ κεφαλὴν αὐτῶν, πάντα ἀρσενικὰ ἀπὸ εἰκοσαετοῦς καὶ ἐπάνω, πᾶς ὁ ἐκπορευόμενος, ἐν τῇ δυνάμει, ἡ ἐπίσκεψις αὐτῶν. ἐκ τῆς φυλῆς ἰσσάχαρ, τέσσαρες καὶ πεντήκοντα χιλιάδες καὶ τετρακόσιοι. τοῖς υἱοῖς ζαβουλὼν κατὰ συγγενείας, κατὰ δήμους αὐτῶν κατ᾽ οἴκους πατριῶν αὐτῶν, κατὰ ἀριθμὸν ὀνομάτων αὐτῶν, κατὰ κεφαλὴν αὐτῶν, πάντα ἀρσενικὰ ἀπὸ εἰκοσαετοῦς καὶ ἐπάνω, πᾶς ὁ ἐκπορευόμενος, ἐν τῇ δυνάμει. ἡ ἐπίσκεψις αὐτῶν, ἑπτὰ καὶ πεντήκοντα χιλιάδες καὶ τετρακόσιοι. τοῖς υἱοῖς ἰωσὴφ υἱοῖς ἐφραὶμ κατὰ συγγενείας αὐτῶν κατὰ δήμους αὐτῶν, κατ᾽ οἴκους πατριῶν αὐτῶν. κατὰ ἀριθμὸν ὀνομάτων αὐτῶν. κατὰ κεφαλὴν αὐτῶν. πάντα ἀρσενικὰ ἀπὸ εἰκοσαετοῦς καὶ ἐπάνω. πᾶς ὁ ἐκπορευόμενος, ἐν τῇ δυνάμει. ἡ ἐπίσκεψις αὐτῶν, ἐκ τῆς φυλῆς ἐφραὶμ, τεσσαράκοντα χιλιάδες καὶ πεντακόσιοι. τοῖς υἱοῖς μανασσῆ κατὰ συγγενείας αὐτῶν, κατὰ δήμους αὐτῶν, κατ᾽ οἴκους πατριῶν αὐτῶν, κατὰ ἀριθμὸν ὀνομάτων αὐτῶν, κατὰ κεφαλὴν αὐτῶν, πάντα ἀρσενικὰ, αὐτῶν ἀπὸ εἰκοσαετοῦς καὶ ἐπάνω, πᾶς ὁ ἐκπορευόμενος, ἐν τῇ δυνάμει. ἡ ἐπίσκεψις αὐτῶν, ἐκ τῆς φυλῆς μανασσῆ, δύο καὶ τριάκοντα χιλιάδες καὶ διακόσιοι. τοῖς υἱοῖς βενιαμὶν κατὰ συγγενείας αὐτῶν, κατὰ δήμους αὐτῶν, κατ᾽ οἴκους πατριῶν αὐτῶν, κατὰ ἀριθμὸν ὀνομάτων αὐτῶν. κατὰ κεφαλὴν αὐτῶν, πάντα ἀρσενικὰ αὐτῶν ἀπὸ εἰκοσαετοῦς καὶ ἐπάνω, πᾶς ὁ ἐκπορευόμενος, ἐν τῇ δυνάμει, ἡ ἐπίσκεψις αὐτῶν, ἐκ τῆς φυλῆς βενιαμὶν, πέντε καὶ τριάκοντα χιλιάδες καὶ τετρακόσιοι. τοῖς υἱοῖς γάδ, κατὰ συγγενείας αὐτῶν, κατὰ δήμους αὐτῶν, κατ᾽ οἴκους πατριῶν αὐτῶν, κατὰ ἀριθμὸν ὀνομάτων αὐτῶν, κατὰ κεφαλὴν αὐτῶν, πάντα ἀρσενικὰ αὐτῶν ἀπὸ εἰκοσαετοῦς καὶ ἐπάνω, πᾶς ὁ ἐκπορευόμενος ἐν τῇ δυνάμει, ἡ ἐπίσκεψις αὐτῶν, ἐκ τῆς φυλῆς γάδ. πέντε καὶ τεσσαράκοντα χιλιάδες, καὶ ἑξακόσιοι καὶ πεντήκοντα. τοῖς υἱοῖς δὰν κατὰ συγγενείας αὐτῶν, κατὰ δήμους αὐτῶν, κατ᾽ οἴκους πατριῶν αὐτῶν, κατὰ ἀριθμὸν ὀνομάτων αὐτῶν, κατὰ κεφαλὴν αὐτῶν, πάντα ἀρσενικὰ αὐτῶν ἀπὸ εἰκοσαετοῦς καὶ ἐπάνω, πᾶς ὁ ἐκπορευόμενος ἐν τῇ δυνάμει, ἡ ἐπίσκεψις αὐτῶν, ἐκ τῆς φυλῆς δάν. δύο καὶ ἑξήκοντα χιλιάδες, καὶ ἑπτακόσιοι. τοῖς υἱοῖς ἀσὴρ κατὰ συγγενείας αὐτῶν, κατὰ δήμους αὐτῶν, κατ᾽ οἴκους πατριῶν αὐτῶν, κατὰ ἀριθμὸν ὀνομάτων αὐτῶν, κατὰ κεφαλὴν αὐτῶν, πάντα ἀρ-

11 THE ALDINE GREEK BIBLE, 1518–19

Priitiua heb. Ter. Heb. Leui. Ca. i. Trāsla. B. Hiero. Trāsla. Gre. lxx. cū interp. latina

tabernaculū deferebat. pficiscebātur filii isrl' p turmas suas. Si pēde bat desup: manebāt i eo dē loco. Nubes qppe dñi incubebat per diē tabernaculo & ignis in nocte: videntibus cunctis populis israel per cunctas māsiones suas.

Explicit liber Exodi.

Incipit vaiechra. i. liber Leuiticus. Cap. i.

Vocauit aūt moysen & locutus ē ei dñs de tabernaculo testimonii: dicēs. Loqre filiis israel: & dices ad eos. Hō qui obtulerit ex vobis hostiam domino de pecoribus idest, de bobus & ouibus offerens victimas: si holocaustum fuerit eius oblatio ac de armēto: masculū immaculatū offeret ad ostiū tabernaculi testimonii ad placandum sibi dominum. Ponetq; sup caput hostie manus & acceptabilis erit: atq; in expiationē eius pficiēs. Immolabitq; vitulum coram domino: & offerent filii aaron sacerdotes sanguinem eius fundentes per altaris circuitum: quod est ante ostium tabernaculi. Detractaq; pelle hostie artus in frusta concident: & subiicient in altari ignem strue lignorum ante compositā: & membra que sunt cesa desuper ordinātes:

Priitiua chal. Interp. chal. Transla. Chal.

12 A PAGE OF THE COMPLUTENSIAN POLYGLOT

iubileum pretium, & dabit ille qui uouerat eum domino. In iubileo autem reuertetur ad priorem dominū qui uendiderat eum et habuerat in sortē possessionis suæ. Omnis æstimatio siclo sanctuarij ponderabitur. Siclus uiginti obolos habet. Primogenita quæ ad deum pertinent nemo sanctificare poterit & uouere. Siue bos sue ouis fuerit, domini sunt. Quod si immundum est animal, redimet qui obtulit iuxta æstimationem suam, & addet quintam partem pretij. Si redimere noluerit, uendetur alteri, quantumcunq; fuerit ante æstimatum. Omne quod domino consecratur siue homo fuerit siue animal siue ager, non ueniet nec redimi poterit. Quicquid semel fuerit consecratū, sanctum sanctorū erit domino. Et omnis cōsecratio quæ offertur ab homine nō redimetur, sed morte morietur. Omnes decimæ terræ siue de pomis arborum siue de frugibus, domini sunt, & illi sanctificantur. Siquis autem uoluerit redimere decimas suas, addet quintam partem earum. Omniū decimarum bouis & ouis & capræ, quæ sub pastoris uirga transeunt, quicquid decimum uenerit, sanctificabitur domino: nō eligetur nec bonū nec malū, nec altero cōmutabitur. Siquis mutauerit, & quod mutatū est, & pro quo mutatum est sanctificabitur domino, & non redimetur. Hæc sunt præcepta quæ mandauit dominus Moysi ad filios Israël in monte Sinai. FINIS.

Exodi. 30.
Nume. 3.
Ezech. 45.

De decimis.

LIBER NVME RI. HEBRAICE. Vaiedaber. CAP. I.

LOCVTVS QVE est dominus ad Moysen in deserto Sinai in tabernaculo fœderis, prima die mensis secundi, anno altero egressionis eorū ex Aegypto, dicens: Tollite summam uniuersæ cōgregationis filiorū Israël per cognatiōes & domos suas, et noīa singulorū, quicqd sexus est masculini à uicesimo anno & supra, omniū uirorū fortiū ex Israël: et numerabitis eos p turmas suas tu et Aarō: eruntq; uobiscū principes tribuū ac domorū in cognatiōibus suis, quorū ista sunt nomina. De tribu Rubē, Elisur filius Sedeur. De tribu Symeō, Salamihel filius Surisaddai. De tribu Iuda, Naasō filius Aminadab. De tribu Isachar, Nathanaël filius Suar, de tribu Zabulō, Heliab filius Helō. Filiorū aūt Ioseph de tribu Ephraim, Elisama filius Ammiud. De tribu Manasse, Gamaliel filius Phadassur.

Præcipit dominus numerari ad pugnam aptos.

Noīa pricipū.

13 AN ITALIC BIBLE

Das erste Capitel.

Gen. 1. M anfang war dz wort.
vnnd das wort war bey
Gott/vnnd Gott war das wort/da
sselb war ym anfang bey Gott / Alle ding sind durch dasselb gemacht/
vnnd on dasselb ist nichts gemacht
was gemacht ist / Jn yhm war das
leben/vnnd das leben war eyn liecht
der menschen / vnd das liecht schey-
net ynn die finsternis/ vnd die finster
nis habens nicht begriffen.

Matth. 3. Marci 1. Luce 3. Es wart eyn mensch / von Gott
gesand/der hies Johannes/der selb
kam zum zeugnis/das er von dem li-
echt zeugete/auff das sie alle durch yhn glewbten / Er war nicht das
liecht sondern dz er zeugete von dem liecht/Das war eyn warhafftigs
liecht/wilchs alle menschē erleucht/durch seyn zukunfft yñ dise welt/
Es war ynn der wellt/vnd die welt ist durch dasselb gemacht/vñ die
welt kandt es nicht.

Er kam ynn seyn eygenthum / vñ die seynen namen yhn nicht auff/
Wie viel yhn aber auffnamen / den gab er macht /Gottis kinder zu
werden/denen /die da an seynen namen glawben / wilche nicht von
dem geblut/noch von dem willen des fleyschis /noch von dem willen
eynes mannes/sondern von Gott geporen sindt.

Math. 1. Luce 2. Vnd das wort wart fleysch/vnd wonete vnter vns/vnd wyr sahen
seyne herlickeyt / eyn herlickeyt als des eyngepornen sons vom vatter/
voller gnade vnd warheyt.

Johannes zeuget von yhm/schreybt vnd spricht / Diser war es/ vō
dem ich gesagt habt/Nach myr wirt komen/der fur myr gewesen ist/
denn er war ehe denn ich/vñ von seyner fulle/haben wyr alle genom
men/gnade vmb gnade / denn das gesetz ist durch Mosen geben/die
gnade vnd warheyt ist durch Jhesum Christ worden/ Niemant hatt
Gott yhe gesehen/der eyngeporne son/der ynn des vatters schos ist/
der hats vns verkundiget.

(gnad vmb gnad) Unser gnad ist vns geben/ vmb Christus gnade/ die ym geben ist/das wyr durch yhn das gesetz erfullen vnnd den vatter erkennē/ da mit heuchley aufhore vnd wyr ware rechtschaffne menschen werden.

Vnd dis ist das zeugnis Johannis/da die Juden sandten vō Jerusalem priester vnd Leuiten / das sie yhn fragten / wer bistu? Vnnd
er bekandt vnd leugnet nicht/vnd er bekandt/ich byn nicht Christus/
vnd sie fragten yhn/was denn? Bistu Elias? Er sprach/ Jch byns
nicht. Bistu eyn Prophet? vnd er antwort/Neyn/Da sprachen sie zu
yhm / Was bistu denn /das wyr antwort geben denen / die vns ge
Math. 3. sand haben? Was sagistu vō dyr selbs? Er sprach/ich byn eyn ruffen
de stym ynn der wusten/ Richtet den weg des hern/ wie der Prophet
Jsaias gesagt hat.

Vnd die gesand waren/die waren/von den Phariseern/vnnd frag
ten yhn vnd sprachen zu yhm/warumb teuffestu denn / so du nit Chri-
L stus

The pistle off paul

Vnto the Hebrues.

The fyrst Chapter.

GOd in tyme past diversly and many wayes / spake vnto the fathers by prophetes: but in these last dayes he hath spoken vnto vs by hys sōne / whom he hath made heyre of all thyngs: by whom also he made the worlde. Which sonne beynge the brightnes of his glory / and very ymage off his substance / bearynge vppe all thyngs with the worde of his power / hath in his awne person pourged oure synnes / and is sytten on the right honde of the maiestie an hye / and is more excellent then the angels / in as moche as he hath by inheritaunce obteyned an excellēter name then have they.

For vnto which off the angels sayde he at eny tyme: Thou arte my sonne / this daye begate I the? And agayne: I will be his father / ād he shalbe my sonne. And agayne whē he bryngeth in the fyrst begotten sonne in the worlde / he sayth: And all the angels of god shall worshippe hym. And vnto the āgels he sayth: He maketh his angels spretes / and his ministers flammes of fyre. But vnto the sonne he sayth: God thy seate shal

The Gospell

Fo. i.

of S. Mathew.

¶ The first Chapter.

A This is the boke of the generacion of Jesus Christ the sonne of Dauid / the sonne also of Abraham.

Dauid and Abraham are first rehersed: because that Christ was specially promised vnto thē, to be of their seede

Abraham begat Isaac:
Isaac begat Jacob:
Jacob begat Judas and his brethren:
Judas begat Phares and zaram of Thamar: Genesis. xxxviii.g.
Phares begat Hesrom:
Hesrom begat Aram: i. Parali. ii.a.
Aram begat Aminadab: Rut. iiii.b.
Aminadab begat Naasson:
Naasson begat Salmon:
Salmon begat Boos of Rahab:
Boos begat Obed of Ruth:
Obed begat Jesse:
Jesse begat Dauid the kynge:
Dauid the kynge begat Salomon / of her that was the wyfe of Vry: ii. Regu. xii.f. i. Parali. iii.b.
Salomon begat Roboam:
Roboam begat Abia:
B Abia begat Asa:
Asa begat Josaphat:
Josaphat begat Joram:
Joram begat Osias:

A.ii. Osias

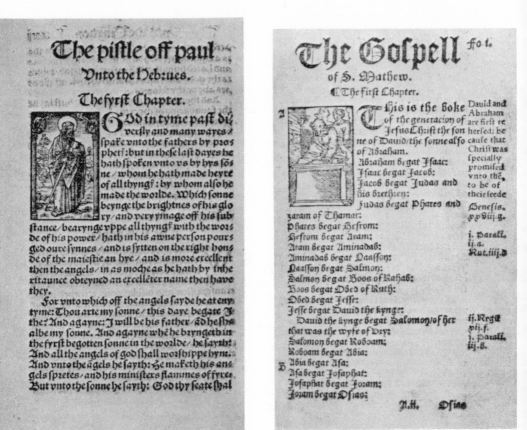

15 EARLY EDITIONS OF TYNDALE'S NEW TESTAMENT

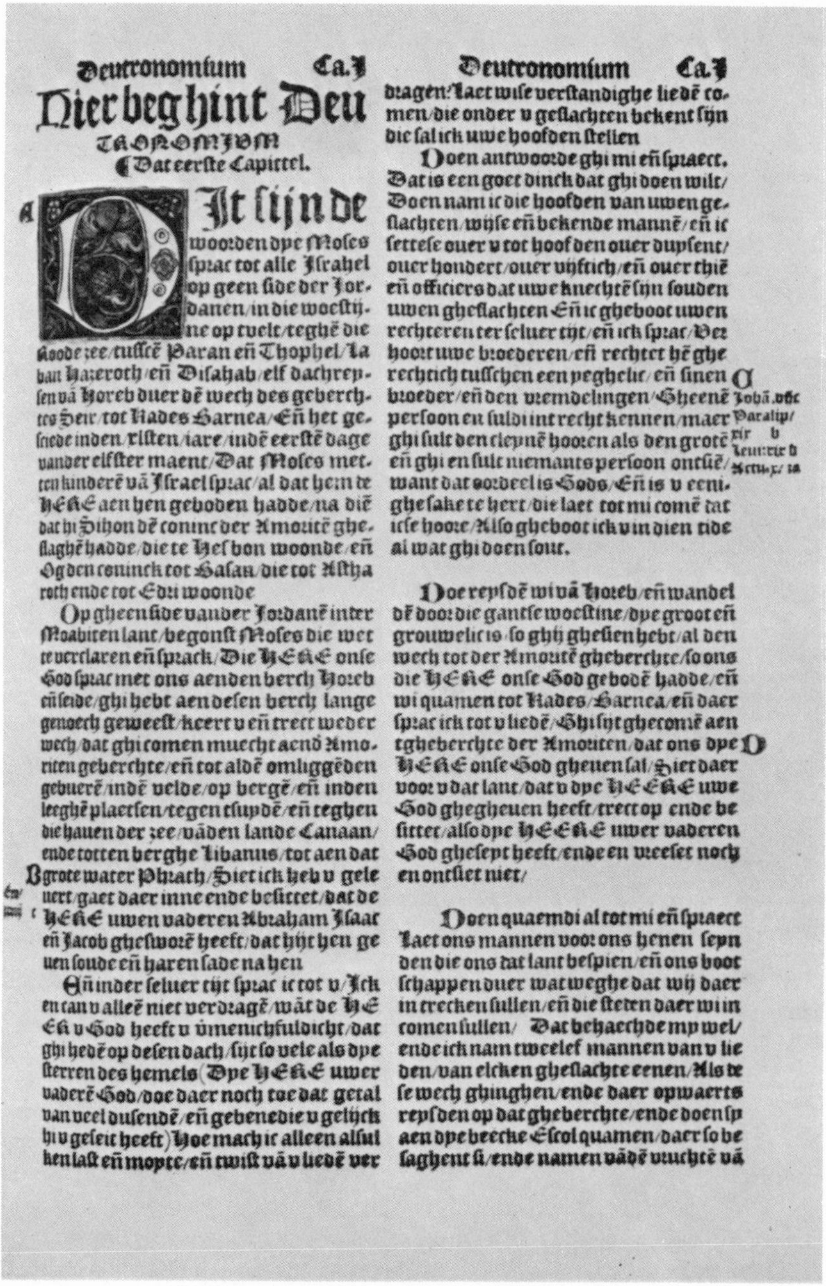

Deutronomium Ca. I

Hier beghint Deu TRONOMIUM

Dat eerste Capittel.

A Dit sijn de woorden dye Moses sprac tot alle Israhel op geen side der Jordanen/ in die woestijne op tvelt/ teghẽ die Roode zee/ tussc̃ Paran eñ Thophel/ Laban Hazeroth/ eñ Disahab/ elf dachreysen vã Horeb ouer dẽ wech des geberchtes Seir/ tot Kades Barnea/ Eñ het geschiede inden xlsten iare/ indẽ eerstẽ dage vander elfster maent/ Dat Moses metten kinderẽ vã Israel sprac/ al dat hem de HERE aen hen geboden hadde/ na diẽ dat hi Sihon dẽ coninc der Amoritẽ gheslaghẽ hadde/ die te Hesbon woonde/ eñ Og den coninck tot Basan/ die tot Astharoth ende tot Edri woonde

Op gheen side vander Jordanẽ inder Moabiten lant/ begonst Moses die wet te verclaren eñ sprack/ Die HERE onse God sprac met ons aenden berch Horeb eñ seide/ ghi hebt aen desen berch lange genoech geweest/ keert v eñ trect weder wech/ dat ghi comen muecht aend Amoriten geberchte/ eñ tot aldẽ omliggẽden gebuerẽ/ indẽ velde/ op bergẽ/ eñ inden leeghẽ plaetsen/ tegen tsuydẽ/ eñ teghen die hauen der zee/ vãden lande Canaan/ ende totten berghe Libanus/ tot aen dat

B grote water Phrath/ Siet ick heb v gheleuert/ gaet daer inne ende besittet/ dat de HERE uwen vaderen Abraham Isaac eñ Jacob ghesworẽ heeft/ dat hijt hen geuen soude eñ haren sade na hen

Eñ inder seluer tijt sprac ic tot v/ Ick en can v alleẽ niet verdragẽ/ wãt de HERE v God heeft v vmenichfuldicht/ dat ghi hedẽ op desen dach/ sijt so vele als dye sterren des hemels (Dye HERE uwer vaderẽ God/ doe daer noch toe dat getal van veel dusendẽ/ eñ gebenedie v gelijck hi v geseit heeft) Hoe mach ic alleen alsulken last eñ moyte/ eñ twist vã v liedẽ verdragen? Laet wise verstandighe liedẽ comen/ die onder v geslachten bekent sijn die sal ick uwe hoofden stellen

Doen antwoorde ghi mi eñ spraect. Dat is een goet dinck dat ghi doen wilt/ Doen nam ic die hoofden van uwen geslachten/ wijse eñ bekende mannẽ/ eñ ic settese ouer v tot hoofden ouer duysent/ ouer hondert/ ouer vijftich/ eñ ouer thiẽ eñ officiers dat uwe knechtẽ sijn souden uwen gheslachten Eñ ic gheboot uwen rechteren ter seluer tijt/ eñ ick sprac/ Verhoort uwe broederen/ eñ rechtet hẽ ghe

C rechtich tusschen een yeghelic/ eñ sinen broeder/ eñ den vremdelingen/ Gheenẽ persoon en suldi int recht kennen/ maer ghi sult den cleynẽ hooren als den grotẽ eñ ghi en sult niemants persoon ontsiẽ/ want dat oordeel is Gods/ Eñ is v eenighe sake te hert/ die laet tot mi comẽ dat icse hoore/ Also gheboot ick v in dien tide al wat ghi doen sout.

Johã. vii c
Paralip/ xix b
Leuiti xix b
Actuũ x/ iii a

Doe reysdẽ wi vã Horeb/ eñ wandeldẽ door die gantse woestine/ dye groot eñ grouwelic is/ so ghij ghesien hebt/ al den wech tot der Amoritẽ gheberchte/ so ons die HERE onse God gebodẽ hadde/ eñ wi quamen tot Kades Barnea/ eñ daer sprac ick tot v liedẽ/ Ghi sijt ghecomẽ aen

D tgheberchte der Amoriten/ dat ons dye HERE onse God gheuen sal/ Siet daer voor v dat lant/ dat v dye HEERE uwe God ghegheuen heeft/ trect op ende besittet/ also dye HEERE uwer vaderen God gheseyt heeft/ ende en vreeset noch en ontsiet niet/

Doen quaemdi al tot mi eñ spraect Laet ons mannen voor ons henen seyn den die ons dat lant bespien/ eñ ons bootschappen duer wat weghe dat wij daer in trecken sullen/ eñ die steden daer wi in comen sullen/ Dat behaechde my wel/ ende ick nam tweelef mannen van v lieden/ van elcken gheslachte eenen/ Als dese wech ghinghen/ ende daer opwaerts reysden op dat gheberchte/ ende doen sy aen dye beecke Escol quamen/ daer so besaghent si/ ende namen vãdẽ vruchtẽ vã

16 VAN LIESVELDT'S BIBLE, 1526

EVANGE

LIVM SECVNDVM MATTHAEVM IN TERPRETE SANCTE PAGNINO LVCENSI SACRAE THEOLOGI. DOCTORE.

Capitulum. I.

Liber genera-
1 tiõis Iesúah
Christi filij
Dauid, filij
2 Abrahám.
¶Abrahám
3 gẽnuit Ischác
¶Ischác ãt
genuit Iaha-
4 cób. ¶Iaha
cób autẽ ge-
nuit Iehudáh
& frẽs eius.
5 ¶Iehudáh aũt genuit Péres, & Zérach è Ta
6 már. ¶Péres aũt genuit Chesrón. ¶Ches
7 rón aũt genuit Arám. ¶Arám autẽ genuit
8 Hãminadáb. ¶Hãminadáb ãt genuit Nach
9 són. ¶Nachsón aũt genuit Salmón. ¶Sal
10 món aũt genuit Bóhaz. ¶Bóhaz aũt genuit
11 Hobéd. ¶Hobéd aũt genuit Isái, ¶Isái ãt
12 genuit Dauid regẽ. ¶Dauid ãt rex genuit
13 Selomóh ex ea quæ fuerat Vriiáh. ¶Selo-
14 móh ãt genuit Rechabhã. ¶Rechabhã aũt
15 gẽuit Abijáh. ¶Abijáh ãt gẽuit Asá. ¶Asá
16 ãt genuit Iehosaphath. ¶Iehosaphath ãt ge
17 nuit Iehorã. ¶Iehorã aũt genuit Huzziiáh
18 ¶Huzziiáh ãt genuit Iothã. ¶Iothã ãt ge
19 nuit Acház. ¶Acház autẽ genuit Chizchi-
20 iáh. ¶Chizchiiáh autem genuit Menasséh.
21 ¶Menasséh aũt genuit Amón. ¶Amón au
22 tẽ genuit Iosiiáh. ¶Iosiiáh ãt genuit Iecho
23 niáh, & fratres eius in trãsmigratiõe Babél.
24 ¶Post transmigrationẽ uero Babél Iecho-
25 niáh genuit Sealthiél. ¶Sealthiél ãt genuit
26 Zerubabél. ¶Zerubabél ãt genuit Abihúd
27 ¶Abihúd ãt genuit Eliachím. ¶Eliachím
28 ãt genuit Hazór. ¶Hazór ãt genuit Sadóc
29 ¶Sadóc aũt genuit Achím. ¶Achím aũt
30 genuit Elihúd. ¶Elihúd ãt genuit Elhazár.
31 ¶Elhazár aũt genuit Matthán. ¶Matthán
32 aũt genuit Iahacób. ¶Iahacób aũt genuit
33 Ioséph, uirũ Miriám, ex qua genit' est Iesúah
34 q dicitur Massiách (.i. Christ'.) ¶Oẽs igitur
35 generatiões ab Abrahám usq; ad Dauid gña
36 tiões quatuordecĩ, et à Dd' usq; ad trãsmigra
tionẽ Babél gñatiões quatuordecĩ, & à trãs
37 migratiõe Babél usq; ad Xpm gñatiões qua-
38 tuordecĩ. ¶Iesúah uero Xpi gñatio, sic erat.
39 ¶Desponsata eñi matre ei' Miriám Ioséph
40 añq; cõuenissent, repta est in utero habens è
41 spiritu sancto ¶Ioséph aũt uir ei', iust' exi-
42 stens, & nolens eã uituperare, uoluit clã di-
43 mittere eã. ¶Hæc aũt cũ aĩo cogitaret, ec-
44 ce angel' dñi ĩ somnis apparuit illi dicens.
45 ¶Ioséph fili Dauid ne timeas assumere Mi
riám uxorẽ tuã. Qđ eñi ĩ ea natũ est è spũ san
46 cto est. ¶Pariet aũt filiũ, & uocabis nomẽ
eius Iesúah. Ipse eñ saluũ faciet populũ suũ à
47 pctis eoꝝ. ¶Hoc aũt totũ factũ est, ut ĩple-
ret, qđ dictũ fuerat à dño p pphetã dicentẽ.
48 ¶Ecce uirgo ĩ utero habebit, & pariet filiũ
& uocabũt nomen ei' Himmanuel, qđ ẽ iter
49 pretatũ nobiscũ de'. ¶Excitat' aũt Ioséph
à somno fecit sicut mandauit sibi angel' dñi,
& assũpsit uxorẽ suã, & nõ cognouit eã, donec pepit filiũ suũ primogenitũ, & uocauit
nomen eius Iesúah.

Capitulum. 2.

1 Quum aũt nat' eẽt Iesúah ĩ Beth
léchem Iehudáh ĩ dieb' Herodis regis, ecce magi ab oriente
aduenerũt Ierusaláim dicẽtes:
Vbi est q nat' est rex Iehudæo-
rũ? Vidim' eñ illi' stellã in oriẽ
2 te, & uenim' ut adoremus eũ. ¶Cũ audisset
aũt Herodes rex turbat' ẽ, & tota Ierusaláim
cũ illo. Et cũ cõgregasset oẽs pricipes sacer-
dotũ, & scribas populi, percũctatus est eos
ubi Christ' nasceret. Illi ãt dixerũt ei: In Beth
léchem Iehudáh. Sic enim scriptũ est p pphe
3 tam. ¶Et tu Bethléchem terra Iehudáh, ne
quaq; minĩa es ĩter duces Iehudáh. Ex te eñ
mihi egrediet dux, q reget populũ meũ Isrl.
4 ¶Tũc Herodes clã cũ uocasset magos, dili
gẽter cognouit ab illis tẽp', quo appuit stel
la. Et cũ misisset eos ĩ Bethléchẽ, dixit: Profe
cti diligẽter cognoscite de puerulo. Vbi uero ĩueneritis, renũciate mihi, ut & ego pfe-
5 ctus adorẽ illũ. ¶Illi ãt cũ audissẽt regẽ, pfe
cti sũt, & ecce stella quã uiderũt ĩ oriẽte, pce
debat eos, donec progressa staret supra locũ
6 ubi erat puerul'. ¶Cũ aũt uidissent stellã,
gauisi sũt gaudio magno ualde, & igressi do
mũ, ĩuenerũt puerulũ cũ Miriám mře ei', &
pstrati adorauerũt illũ, et cũ aperuissẽt the
sauros suos obtulerũt ei munera, aurũ, thus,
& myrrhã. Et oraculo admoniti in somnis,
ne rediredirent ad Herodem, per aliã uiã re-
7 uersi sunt in regionẽ suam. ¶Digressis aũt
illis, ecce angelus dñi apparet ĩ sõnis Ioséph

a ij

17 PAGNINI'S VERSION, 1528

De Exode. Chapitre.xl. xxx viij

Aussy les filz de Israel offrirẽt les vestemẽs
desquelz les prestres ascauoir Aarõ & ses filz
vsent au saictuaire: ainsy q̃ le Seigne' auoit
cõmande. Et quãt Moyses eut veu toutes
les choses acomplies/ il les beneist.

Cõment le tabernacle fut dresse/ & la gloire du Seigne' se monstra/ par vne nuee couurãt le tabernacle.

Chapitre.xl.

A L E Seigneur parla a Moyses/
disant: Au premier mois/ le premier io' du mois/ tu dresseras le
tabernacle de tesmõgnage & met
teras larche ẽ cestuy/ & laisseras
pendre le voile deuãt elle: & apres q̃ la table
sera mise/ tu metteras sus icelle les choses q̃
sont ordinairemẽt cõmandees. Le chandelier
se tiendra debout auec ses lampes / & lautel
dor auq̃l est lencẽs offert/ deuãt larche du tes
mõgnage. Tu metteras la tẽte a lentree du
tabernacle: & deuãt icelle lautel de lholocauste. Le lauoir entre lautel & le tabernacle/ q̃
vo' emplirez deaue. Et enuirõneras lattre &
B son entree des tentes. Et quãt tu auras prin
se lhuyle de vnctiõ/ tu oindras le tabernacle
auec ses vasseaux/ affin q̃ lautel de lholocau
ste & to' ses vasseaux/ le lauoir auec son sou-
bassemẽt soiẽt sainctifiez. Tu cõsacreras tou
tes choses de lhuyle de vnctiõ/ affin q̃lz soiẽt
Exo.30.c les sainctz des sainctz. * Et feras venir Aaron & ses filz a lhuys du tabernacle de tesmõ
gnage: & apres q̃lz seront lauez deaue/ tu les
vestiras des sainctz vestemẽs / affin q̃lz me
seruent/ & q̃ lunctiõ diceulx poursuyue en pre
Nũ.7.a strise eternelle. * Moyses feist toutes les cho
ses q̃ le Seigne' auoit cõmande. Dõt au pre
mier mois de la seconde annee/ au premier io'
du mois fut colloque le tabernacle. Et Moy
ses le dressa/ & mist les tableaux & les soubas
C semens & les verroux/ & ordonna les colom-
nes/ & estẽdit le toict sus le tabernacle/ ẽ met
tant la couuerture par dessus/ ainsy q̃ le Sei
gneur auoit cõmande. Il mist aussy le tesmõ
gnage en larche/ apres q̃ les verroux furent
mis par dessoubz/ & le propiciatoire p dessus.
Et quãt il eut porte larche au tabernacle du
tesmõgnage/ il pendit deuãt elle le voile: affin q̃l acõplist le cõmandement du Seigneur
Il mist aussy la table au tabernacle du tesmongnage a la region septẽtrionale hors le
voile/ apres q̃l eut ordonne p auãt les pains
de proposition: ainsy q̃ le Seigneur auoit cõmande a Moyses. Il mist aussy le chãdelier
au tabernacle du tesmõgnage/ a lopposite de
la table/ en la partie de midy/ apres q̃ les lã-
pes furẽt mises par ordre selon le commande
ment du Seigneur. Il mist aussy lautel dor
soubz le toict du tesmõgnage/ cõtre le voile: &
offrit sus cestuy lencẽs des aromatz/ ainsy q̃
le Seigne' auoit cõmande a Moyses. Il mist
aussy la tente a lentree du tabernacle du tes-
mongnage/ & lautel de lholocauste a lentree
du tesmongnage/ offrant sus cestuy holocau
stes & sacrifices/ ainsy q̃ le Seigne' auoit cõ- D
mande. * Aussy ordõna le lauoir entre le ta- Exo.30.c
bernacle du tesmongnage & lautel/ le emplis
sant deaue. Et lauoient en cestuy Moyses &
Aaron & ses filz/ leurs mains & leurs piedz/
quãt il entroient au toict de laliance/ & quilz
approchoiẽt a lautel/ ainsy que le Seigneur
auoit cõmande a Moyses. Il dressa aussy la-
tre tout autour du tabernacle & de lautel/ a-
pres quil eut mise la tente a lentree diceluy.
* Et apres q̃ toutes les choses furẽt parfaic Nũ.9.c
tes: la nuee courit le tabernacle du tesmongnage: & la gloire du Seigne' le remplist. Et
ne pouoit Moyses entrer le toict de laliance
po' ce q̃ la nuee couuroit toutes choses/ & q̃ la
maieste du Seigne' resplendissoit: car la nuee
auoit couuert toutes les choses. Se aucunef-
fois la nuee laissoit le tabernacle / les filz de
Israel sen alloient selon leurs ordres: sy elle
pendoit par dessus/ ilz demouroiẽt au mesme
lieu. La nuee du Seigneur certainemẽt cou-
choit par iour sus le tabernacle / & le feu par
nuict / en la presence de to' les filz de Israel/
par toutes leurs mansions.

Le liure du Leuitique: en He-
brieu appelle Vaicra.

Lordonnance pour offrir les grosses bestes/ les trop-
peaux/ & les oyseaux.

Chapitre.j.

E T le Seigneur appella A
Moyses/ & parla a luy du taber
nacle de tesmõgnage/ disãt: Par
le aux filz de Israel / & le' diras.
Lhõe de vous q̃ aura offert au Seigne' hostie
des bestiaulx: cest adire/ des beuf & des brebis
celuy q̃ offre les oblatiõs/ se son offrãde est sa
crifice brusle/ & de la vacherie: il offrera vng
masle sãs macule/ a lhuys du tabernacle de
tesmõgnage/ po' pacifier le seigne' enuers soy.

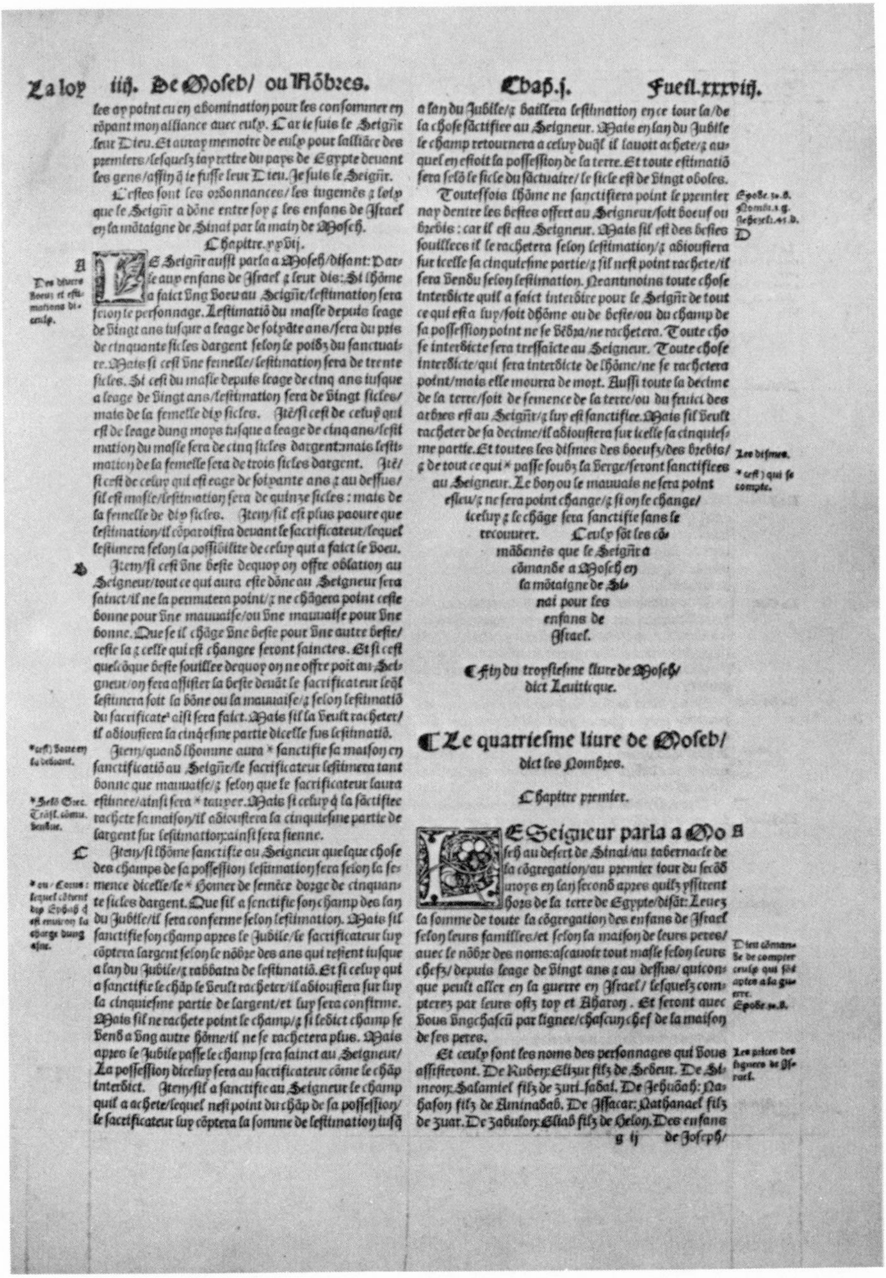

les ay point eu en abomination pour les consommer en rõpant mon alliance auec eulx. Car ie suis le Seignr leur Dieu. Et auray memoire de eulx pour lalliãce des premiers/lesquelz iay retire du pays de Egypte deuant les gens/affin q̃ ie fusse leur Dieu. Je suis le Seignr.

Cestes sont les ordonnances/les iugemẽs & loix que le Seignr a dõne entre soy & les enfans de Israel en la mõtaigne de Sinai par la main de Moseh.

Chapitre.xxvij.

A
Des veux et estimations diceulx.

LE Seignr aussi parla a Moseh/disant: Parle aux enfans de Israel & leur dis: Si lhõme a faict vng veu au Seignr/lestimation sera selon le personnage. Lestimatiõ du masle depuis leage de vingt ans iusque a leage de soixãte ans/sera du pris de cinquante sicles dargent selon le poidz du sanctuaire. Mais si cest vne femelle/lestimation sera de trente sicles. Si cest du masle depuis leage de cinq ans iusque a leage de vingt ans/lestimation sera de vingt sicles/mais de la femelle dix sicles. Jtẽ/si cest de celuy qui est de leage dung moys iusque a leage de cinq ans/lestimation du masle sera de cinq sicles dargent: mais lestimation de la femelle sera de trois sicles dargent. Jtẽ/si cest de celuy qui est eage de soixante ans & au dessus/sil est masle/lestimation sera de quinze sicles: mais de la femelle de dix sicles. Jtem/sil est plus paoure que lestimation/il cõparoistra deuant le sacrificateur/lequel lestimera selon la possibilite de celuy qui a faict le veu.

B Jtem/si cest vne beste dequoy on offre oblation au Seigneur/tout ce qui aura este dõne au Seigneur sera sainct/il ne la permutera point/& ne chãgera point ceste bonne pour vne mauuaise/ou vne mauuaise pour vne bonne. Que se il chãge vne beste pour vne autre beste/ceste la & celle qui est changee seront sainctes. Et si cest quelcõque beste souillee dequoy on ne offre poit au Seigneur/on fera assister la beste deuãt le sacrificateur leq̃l lestimera soit la bõne ou la mauuaise/& selon lestimatiõ du sacrificateur aisi sera faict. Mais sil la veult racheter/il adioustera la cinqesme partie dicelle sus lestimatiõ.

*cest) voue en la vouant.
*Selõ Grec. Trãsl. cõmu. vendue.

Jtem/quand lhomme aura * sanctifie sa maison en sanctificatiõ au Seignr/le sacrificateur lestimera tant bonne que mauuaise/& selon que le sacrificateur laura estimee/ainsi sera * tauxee. Mais si celuy q̃ la sãctifiee rachete sa maison/il adioustera la cinquiesme partie de largent sur lestimation: ainsi sera sienne.

C
*ou/Coros: lequel cõtient vng Ephah q̃ est enuiron la charge dung asne.

Jtem/si lhõme sanctifie au Seigneur quelque chose des champs de sa possession lestimation sera selon la semence dicelle/le * Homer de semẽce dorge de cinquante sicles dargent. Que sil a sanctifie son champ des lan du Jubile/il sera conferme selon lestimation. Mais sil sanctifie son champ apres le Jubile/le sacrificateur luy cõptera largent selon le nõbre des ans qui restent iusque a lan du Jubile/& rabbatra de lestimatiõ. Et si celuy qui a sanctifie le chãp le veult racheter/il adioustera sur luy la cinquiesme partie de largent/et luy sera confirme. Mais sil ne rachete point le champ/& si ledict champ se vend a vng autre hõme/il ne se rachetera plus. Mais apres le Jubile passe le champ sera sainct au Seigneur/La possession diceluy sera au sacrificateur cõme le chãp interdict. Jtem/sil a sanctifie au Seigneur le champ quil a achete/lequel nest point du chãp de sa possession/le sacrificateur luy cõptera la somme de lestimation iusq̃ a lan du Jubile/& baillera lestimation en ce iour la/de la chose sãctifiee au Seigneur. Mais en lan du Jubile le champ retournera a celuy duq̃l il lauoit achete/& auquel en estoit la possession de la terre. Et toute estimatiõ sera selõ le sicle du sãctuaire/le sicle est de vingt oboles.

Exode.xiii.b.
Nomb.iii.g.
Ezechi.xliiii.d.
D

Toutesfois lhõme ne sanctifiera point le premier nay dentre les bestes offert au Seigneur/soit boeuf ou brebis: car il est au Seigneur. Mais sil est des bestes souillees il le rachetera selon lestimation/& adioustera sur icelle sa cinquiesme partie/& sil nest point rachete/il sera vendu selon lestimation. Neantmoins toute chose interdicte quil a faict interdire pour le Seignr de tout ce qui est a luy/soit dhõme ou de beste/ou du champ de sa possession point ne se vẽdra/ne rachetera. Toute chose interdicte sera tressaincte au Seigneur. Toute chose interdicte/qui sera interdicte de lhõme/ne se rachetera point/mais elle mourra de mort. Aussi toute la decime de la terre/soit de semence de la terre/ou du fruict des arbres est au Seignr/& luy est sanctifiee. Mais sil veult racheter de sa decime/il adioustera sur icelle sa cinquiesme partie. Et toutes les dismes des boeufz/des brebis/& de tout ce qui * passe soubz la verge/seront sanctifiees au Seigneur. Le bon ou le mauuais ne sera point esleu/& ne sera point change/& si on le change/iceluy & le chãge sera sanctifie sans le recouurer. Ceulx sõt les cõmãdemẽs que le Seignr a cõmande a Moseh en la mõtaigne de Sinai pour les enfans de Israel.

Les dismes.
* cest) qui se compte.

Fin du troysiesme liure de Moseh/dict Leuitique.

Le quatriesme liure de Moseh/dict les Nombres.

Chapitre premier.

A

LE Seigneur parla a Moseh au desert de Sinai/au tabernacle de la cõgregation/au premier iour du secõd moys en lan second apres quilz yssirent hors de la terre de Egypte/disãt: Leuez la somme de toute la cõgregation des enfans de Israel selon leurs familles/et selon la maison de leurs peres/auec le nõbre des noms: ascauoir tout masle selon leurs chefz/depuis leage de vingt ans & au dessus/quiconque peult aller en la guerre en Israel/lesquelz compterez par leurs ostz toy et Aharon. Et seront auec vous vng chascũ par lignee/chascun chef de la maison de ses peres.

Dieu cõmande de compter ceulx qui sõt aptes a la guerre.
Exode.xxx.b.

Et ceulx sont les noms des personnages qui vous assisteront. De Ruben: Elizur filz de Sedeur. De Simeon: Salamiel filz de Zuri-sadai. De Jehudah: Nahason filz de Aminadab. De Issacar: Nathanael filz de Zuar. De Zabulon: Eliab filz de Helon. Des enfans

Les princes des lignees de Israel.

g ij de Joseph/

19 OLIVETAN'S NEUCHÂTEL BIBLE, 1535

D re,fra gli animali,non lo ſantifichera l'huomo,o bue,o pecora,è del Signore.Ma ſe ſia de gli animali
immondi,recuperera ſecondo la ſtima,& aggiugnera la quinta parte di quella ſopra quella,& ſe non
recuperera,vendaſi ſecondo la ſtima.Ma neſſuna ſcomunicatione,laquale ſara ſcomunicare l'huomo
al Signore,di tutte le coſe che gli ha,da l'huomo,& dal giumento,& dal campo de la ſua poſſeſſione
ſi vendera,& non ſi recuperera,ogni ſcomunicatione ſara ſantita di ſantita al Signore.Ogni ſcomunicatione che ſara ſcomunicata da l'huomo,non ſi recuperera,morendo morra.Et ogni decima de la
terra,del ſeme de la terra del frutto del l'arbore,è del Signore,ſantita al Signore.Ma ſe vorra recupera
re l'huomo da la decima ſua,gli aggiugnera ſopra,la qnta parte di quella.Et tutte le decime de buoi,
& de le pecore,& di tutte le coſe che trapaſſono ſotto la virga,il decimo ſara ſantita al Signore. Non
cerchi ſe buono,o cattiuo , & non permutera quello , & ſe permutera quello , & la permutatione di
quello ſara ſantita,non ſi recuperera. Queſti ſono i precetti che comandò il Signore à Moſe à figliuoli di Iſrael nel monte Sinai.

FINE DEL LEVITICO.

IL LIBRO DE NVMERI

CAP. I.

A ET parlò il Signore à Moſe nel diſerto di Sinai,nel padiglione de la con
gregatione,nel primo dì del meſe ſecondo,ne l'anno ſecondo , da che
vſcirno de la terra di Egytto,dicēdo.Pigliate la ſomma di tutta la congregatione de figliuoli di Iſrael,per le famiglie loro,per le caſe de padri
loro,ſecondo il numero de nomi, ogni maſchio per i capi loro , da la
eta di venti anni,& ſopra,ciaſcuno che eſce à la militia in Iſrael,nume-
rerete quegli per gli eſerciti loro,tu,& Aharon. Et conſeſſouoi ſaranno
vn huomo per tribu,& l'huomo ſara capo di caſa de padri ſuoi.Et queſti ſono i nomi de gli huomini che ſtaranno conſeſſouoi , di Ruben Elizur figliuolo di Sedeur,di Simeon,Selumiel figliuolo di Zuriſaddai,di
Iuda,Naheſon figliuolo di Hamminadab,di Iſſachar,Nethanel figli-
B uolo di Zuhar,di Zebulon,Eliab figliuolo di Helon.De figliuoli di Io-
ſeph,di Ephraim,Eliſamah figliuolo di Hammiud,di Menaſſeh,Gamliel figliuolo di Pedazur,di Be
niamin,Abidan figliuolo di Ghidoni,di Dan,Achihezer figliuoi di Hammiſaddai,di Aſer,Paghiel
figliuolo di Hochran,di Ghad,Eliaſaph figliuolo di Dehuel,di Nephtali,Achira figliuol di Henan.
Queſti ſono i nominati de la congregatione , principi de le tribu de padri loro, che erano capi de
le migliaia di Iſrael.Et preſe Moſe,& Aharon,queſti huomini che ſi ſono denominati per i nomi. Et
tutta la congregatione feciono congregare nel primo del meſe ſecondo,& dettono in nota le loro ge
neologie per le famiglie loro,per la caſa de padri loro,ſecondo il numero de nomi , da la eta di venti
anni,& ſopra,per i capi loro,come comãdo il Signore à Moſe,& numero quegli nel diſerto di Sinai.
Et furno i figliuoli di Ruben primogenito di Iſrael,per le generationi ſue,per le famiglie ſue,& per le
caſe de padri ſuoi,ſecondo il numero de nomi,per i capi ſuoi,ogni maſchio da la eta di venti anni,&
ſopra,ciaſcuno che vſciua à la militia. I numerati di quegli de la tribu di Ruben,quarantaſei mila,&
C cinquecento.De figliuoli di Simeon,per le generationi loro,per le famiglie loro,per la caſa de padri
loro,i numerati di quello,ſecondo il numero de nomi,per i capi loro,ogni maſchio da l'eta di venti
anni,& ſopra,ciaſcuno che vſciua à la militia. I numerati di quegli de la tribu di Simeon,cinquanta
noue mila trecento.De figliuoli di Ghad,per le generationi loro,per le famiglie loro,per la caſa de pa
dri loro,ſecondo il numero de nomi,da la eta di venti anni,& ſopra,ciaſcuno che vſciua à la militia.
I numerati di quegli,de la tribu di Ghad,quarantacinque mila,& ſecento cinquanta.De figliuoli di
Iuda,per le generationi loro,per le famiglie loro,per la caſa de padri loro , ſecondo il numero de nomi,da la eta di venti anni,& ſopra , caſcuno che vſciua à la militia. I numerati di quegli de la tribu
di Iuda,ſettantaquattro mila,& ſecento.De figliuoli di Iſſachar,per le generationi loro,per le famiglie loro,per la caſa de padri loro,ſecondo il numero de nomi,da la eta di venti anni,& ſopra,ciaſcu
no che vſciua à la militia. I numerati di quegli de la tribu di Iſſachar,cinquãtaquattro mila,& quat

The gospel of S. Mathew.

The first Chapter.

A Luc.3.d This is the boke of the
generacion of Jesus
Christ ỹ sonne of Da
uid, the sonne of Abra
Gen.21.a ham. Abrahã begat
Gen.25.c Isaac: Isaac begat
Gen.29.f Jacob: Jacob begat
Judas & his brethrẽ:
Gen.38.e Judas begat Phares & Zarã of Thamar:
Gen.46.b Phares begat Hesrom:
Ruth.4.d Hesrom begat Aram:
1.Par.2.a Aram begat Aminadab:
Num.1.a Aminadab begat Naasson:
Naasson begat Salmon:
Salmon begat Boos of Rahab:
Boos begat Obed of Ruth:
Obed begat Jesse:
1.Reg.16.a Jesse begat Dauid the kynge:
2.Re.12.c Dauid the kynge begat Salomon, of her
1.Par.3.b 3.Re.1.g that was the wyfe of Vry:
Salomon begat Roboam:
Roboam begat Abia:
Abia begat Asa:
Asa begat Josaphat:
B Josaphat begat Joram:
Joram begat Osias:
1.Par.26.d Osias begat Joatham:
2.Par.27.b Joatham begat Achas:
2.Par.28.d Achas begat Ezechias:
4.Re.20.c Ezechias begat Manasses:
4.Re.21.d Manasses begat Amon:
4.Re.21.c Amon begat Josias:
4.Re.23.f 24.25 Josias begat Jechonias and his brethren
aboute the tyme of the captiuyte of Ba-
bylon.
1.Par.3.c And after the captiuyte of Babylon, Je
Agg.1.a chonias begat Salathiel:
1.Esd.3.a Salathiel begat Zorobabel:

Zorobabel begat Abiud:
Abiud begat Eliachim:
Eliachim begat Azor:
Azor begat Sadoc:
Sadoc begat Achin:
Achin begat Eliud:
Eliud begat Eleasar:
Eleasar begat Matthan:
Matthan begat Jacob:
Jacob begat Joseph the hußbande of Ma
ry, of whõ was borne that Jesus, which is
called Christ.

All the generacions from Abrahã to Da
uid are fourtene generacions: From Dauid
vnto the captiuite of Babylon, are fourtene generacions. From the captiuite of Babylon vnto Christ, are also fourtene generacions.

The byrth of Christ was on thys wyse: C
When his mother Mary was maried to Jo Luc.1.b
seph * before they came together, she was
foũde with chylde by ỹ holy goost, But Jo Some rea de: before
seph her hußbande was a perfect man, and they sat
wolde not bringe her to shame, but was myn at home
ded to put her awaie secretely. Neuertheles together.
whyle he thus thought, beholde, the angell
of the LORDE appered vnto him in a dreame, saynge: Joseph thou sonne of Dauid, fea
re not to take vnto the Mary thy wyfe. For
that which is cõceaued in her, is of ỹ holy
goost. She shall brynge forth a sonne, and
thou shalt call his name Jesus. For he shall Phi.2.a
saue his people from their synnes. Act.4.a

All this was done, ỹ the thinge might
be fulfilled, which was spoken of the LORDE
by the Prophet, saynge: Beholde, a mayde
shall be with chylde, and shall brynge forth Esa.7.c
a sonne, and they shall call his name Emanuel, which is by interpretacion, God wt vs.

Now whan Joseph awoke out of slepe
he did as the angell of ỹ LORDE bade hym,
and toke his wyfe vnto hym, and knewe her
not, tyll she had brought forth hir fyrst bor Luc.2.a
ne sonne, and called his name Jesus.

The II. Chapter.

When Jesus was borne at Bethleẽ A
in Jury, in the tyme of Herode the
kynge, Beholde, there came wyse
men from the east to Jerusalẽ, saynge: Whe
re is the new borne kynge of the Jues? We
haue sene his starre in the east, and are come
to worship him.

When Herode ỹ kynge had herde thys,
he was troubled, & all Jerusalẽ with hym,
and he gathered all the hye Prestes and
Scribes of ỹ people, & axed of them, where Christ shulde be borne. And they sayde vn-

A A ij

21 COVERDALE'S BIBLE, 1535

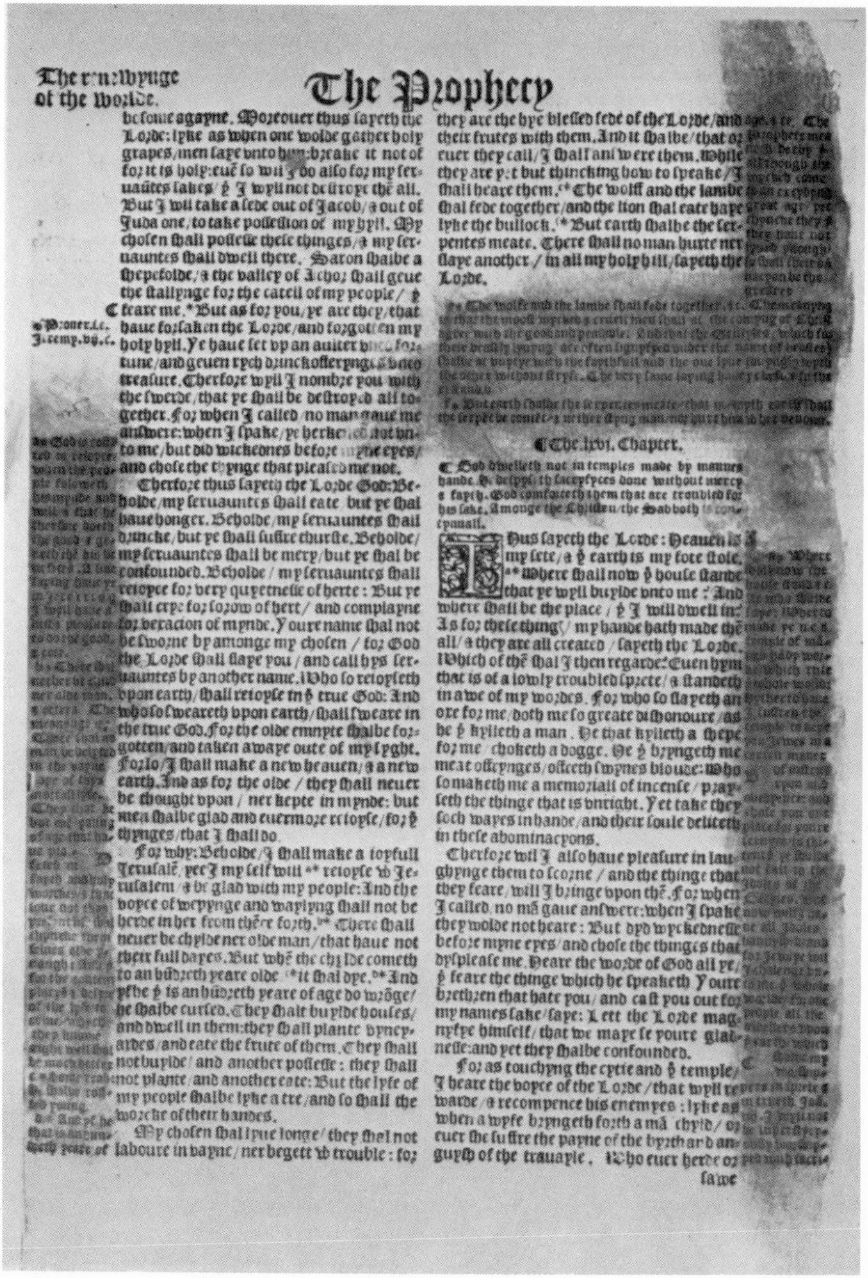

The renewynge of the worlde. **The Prophecy**

be founde agayne. Moreouer thus sayeth the Lorde: lyke as when one wolde gather holy grapes, men saye vnto hym: breake it not of for it is holy: euē so wil I do also for my seruaūtes sakes, ẏ I wyll not destroye thē all. But I wil take a sede out of Jacob, & out of Juda one, to take possession of my hyll. My chosen shall possesse these thinges, & my seruauntes shall dwell there. Saron shalbe a shepefolde, & the valley of Achor shall geue the stallynge for the catell of my people, ẏ feare me. *But as for you, ye are they, that haue forsaken the Lorde, and forgotten my holy hyll. Ye haue set vp an aulter vnto fortune, and geuen rych dryncke offerynges vnto treasure. Therfore wyll I nombre you with the swerde, that ye shall be destroyed all together. For when I called, no man gaue me answere: when I spake, ye herkened not vnto me, but did wickednes before myne eyes, and chose the thynge that pleased me not.

Therfore thus sayeth the Lorde God: Beholde, my seruauntes shall eate, but ye shal haue honger. Beholde, my seruauntes shall drincke, but ye shall suffre thurste. Beholde, my seruauntes shall be mery, but ye shal be confounded. Beholde, my seruauntes shall reioyce for very quyetnesse of herte: But ye shall crye for sorow of hert, and complayne for vexacion of mynde. Youre name shal not be sworne by amonge my chosen, for God the Lorde shall slaye you, and call hys seruauntes by another name. Who so reioyseth vpon earth, shall reioyse in ẏ true God: And who so sweareth vpon earth, shall sweare in the true God. For the olde enmyte shalbe forgotten, and taken awaye oute of my syght. For lo, I shall make a new heauen, & a new earth. And as for the olde, they shall neuer be thought vpon, ner kepte in mynde: but men shalbe glad and euermore reioyse, for ẏ thynges, that I shall do.

For why: Beholde, I shall make a ioyfull Jerusalē, yee I my self will *reioyse wt Jerusalem, & be glad with my people: And the voyce of wepynge and waylyng shall not be herde in her from thēce forth. *There shall neuer be chylde ner olde man, that haue not their full dayes. But whē the chylde cometh to an hūdreth yeare olde *it shal dye. *And yf he ẏ is an hūdreth yeare of age do wrōge, he shalbe cursed. They shall buylde houses, and dwell in them: they shall plante vyneyardes, and eate the frute of them. They shall not buylde, and another possesse: they shall not plante, and another eate: But the lyfe of my people shalbe lyke a tre, and so shall the worcke of their handes.

My chosen shal lyue longe, they shal not laboure in vayne, ner begett wt trouble: for they are the hye blessed sede of the Lorde, and their frutes with them. And it shalbe, that or euer they call, I shall answere them. While they are yet but thincking how to speake, I shall heare them. *The wolff and the lambe shal fede together, and the lion shal eate haye lyke the bullock. *But earth shalbe the serpentes meate. There shall no man hurte ner slaye another, in all my holy hill, sayeth the Lorde.

The wolfe and the lambe shall fede together. [illegible]

But earth shalbe the serpentes meate [illegible]

The .lxvi. Chapter.

God dwelleth not in temples made by mannes hande. He despyseth sacryfyces done without mercy & fayth. God comforteth them that are troubled for his sake. Amonge the Christen, the Sabboth is contynuall.

Thus sayeth the Lorde: Heauen is my sete, & ẏ earth is my fote stole. *Where shall now ẏ house stande that ye wyll buylde vnto me? And where shall be the place, ẏ I will dwell in? As for these thinges, my hande hath made thē all, & they are all created, sayeth the Lorde. Which of thē shal I then regarde? Euen hym that is of a lowly troubled sprete, & standeth in awe of my wordes. For who so slayeth an oxe for me, doth me so greate dishonoure, as he ẏ kylleth a man. He that kylleth a shepe for me, choketh a dogge. He ẏ bryngeth me meat offrynges, offereth swynes bloude: Who so maketh me a memoriall of incense, prayseth the thinge that is vnright. Yet take they soch wayes in hande, and their soule deliteth in these abominacyons.

Therfore wil I also haue pleasure in laughynge them to scorne, and the thinge that they feare, will I bringe vpon thē. For when I called, no mā gaue answere: when I spake they wolde not heare: But dyd wyckednesse before myne eyes, and chose the thinges that dyspleace me. Heare the worde of God all ye, ẏ feare the thinge which he speaketh. Youre brethren that hate you, and cast you out for my names sake, saye: Lett the Lorde magnyfye himselfe, that we maye se youre gladnesse: and yet they shalbe confounded.

For as touchyng the cytie and ẏ temple, I heare the voyce of the Lorde, that wyll rewarde, & recompence his enemyes: lyke as when a wyfe bryngeth forth a mā chyld, or euer she suffre the payne of the byrth and anguysh of the trauayle. Who euer herde or sawe

Prouer.i.c. Jeremy.vii.c.

22 THE 'MATTHEW' BIBLE, 1537

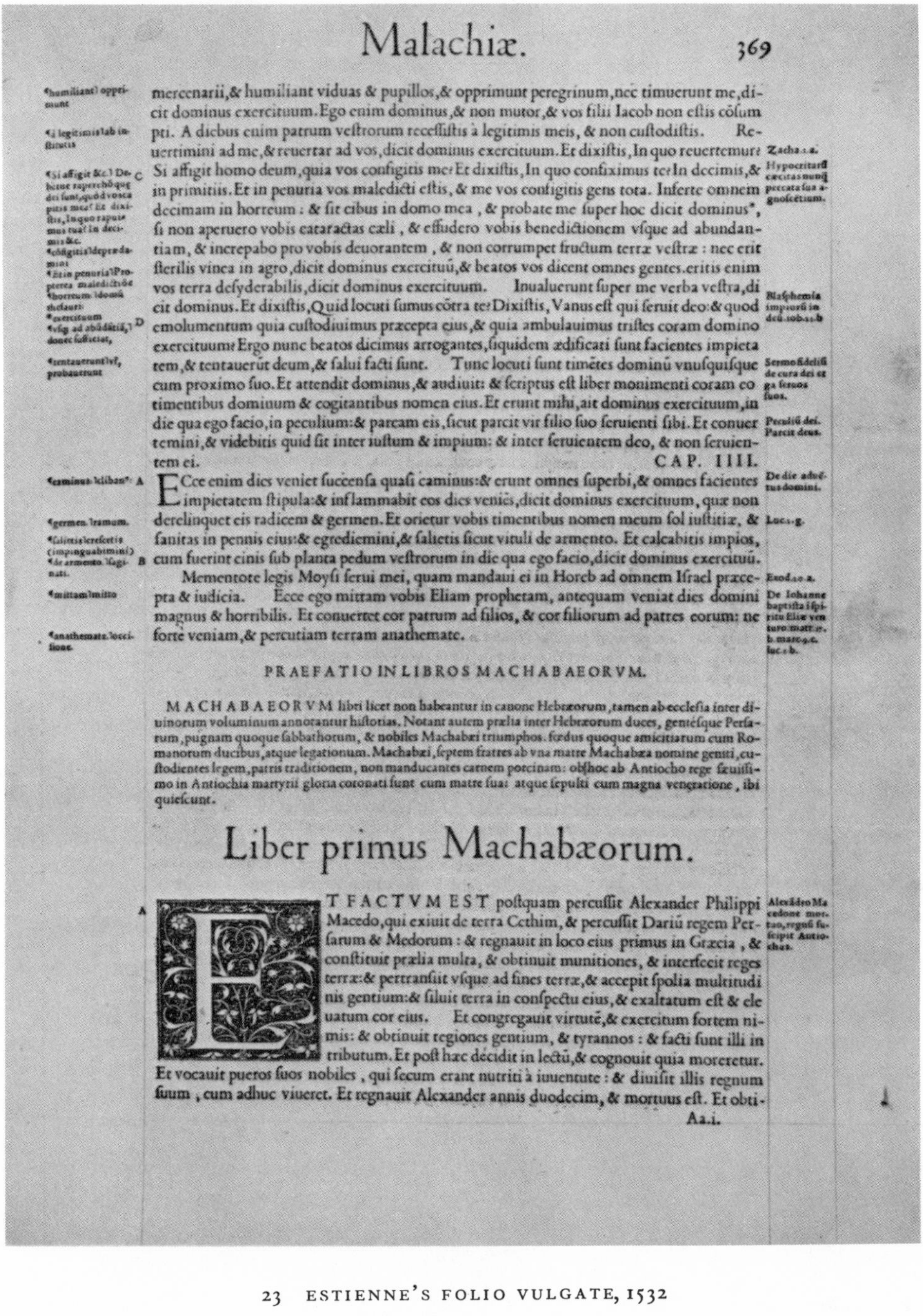

mercenarii,& humiliant viduas & pupillos,& opprimunt peregrinum,nec timuerunt me,dicit dominus exercituum. Ego enim dominus,& non mutor,& vos filii Iacob non estis cõsumpti. A diebus enim patrum vestrorum recessistis à legitimis meis, & non custodistis. Reuertimini ad me,& reuertar ad vos,dicit dominus exercituum. Et dixistis,In quo reuertemur? Si affigit homo deum,quia vos configitis me? Et dixistis,In quo confiximus te? In decimis,& in primitiis. Et in penuria vos maledicti estis, & me vos configitis gens tota. Inferte omnem decimam in horreum : & sit cibus in domo mea , & probate me super hoc dicit dominus*, si non aperuero vobis cataractas cæli , & effudero vobis benedictionem vsque ad abundantiam, & increpabo pro vobis deuorantem , & non corrumpet fructum terræ vestræ : nec erit sterilis vinea in agro,dicit dominus exercituũ,& beatos vos dicent omnes gentes.eritis enim vos terra desyderabilis,dicit dominus exercituum. Inualuerunt super me verba vestra,dicit dominus. Et dixistis,Quid locuti sumus cõtra te? Dixistis, Vanus est qui seruit deo:& quod emolumentum quia custodiuimus præcepta eius,& quia ambulauimus tristes coram domino exercituum? Ergo nunc beatos dicimus arrogantes,siquidem ædificati sunt facientes impietatem,& tentauerũt deum,& salui facti sunt. Tunc locuti sunt timẽtes dominũ vnusquisque cum proximo suo. Et attendit dominus,& audiuit: & scriptus est liber monimenti coram eo timentibus dominum & cogitantibus nomen eius. Et erunt mihi,ait dominus exercituum,in die qua ego facio,in peculium:& parcam eis,sicut parcit vir filio suo seruienti sibi. Et conuertemini,& videbitis quid sit inter iustum & impium: & inter seruientem deo, & non seruientem ei.

CAP. IIII.

ECce enim dies veniet succensa quasi caminus:& erunt omnes superbi,& omnes facientes impietatem stipula:& inflammabit eos dies veniẽs,dicit dominus exercituum, quæ non derelinquet eis radicem & germen. Et orietur vobis timentibus nomen meum sol iustitiæ, & sanitas in pennis eius:& egrediemini,& salietis sicut vituli de armento. Et calcabitis impios, cum fuerint cinis sub planta pedum vestrorum in die qua ego facio,dicit dominus exercituũ.

Mementote legis Moysi serui mei, quam mandaui ei in Horeb ad omnem Israel præcepta & iudicia. Ecce ego mittam vobis Eliam prophetam, antequam veniat dies domini magnus & horribilis. Et conuertet cor patrum ad filios, & cor filiorum ad patres eorum: ne forte veniam,& percutiam terram anathemate.

PRAEFATIO IN LIBROS MACHABAEORVM.

MACHABAEORVM libri licet non habeantur in canone Hebræorum,tamen ab ecclesia inter diuinorum voluminum annorantur historias. Notant autem prælia inter Hebræorum duces, gentésque Persarum,pugnam quoque sabbathorum, & nobiles Machabæi triumphos. fœdus quoque amicitiarum cum Romanorum ducibus,atque legationum. Machabæi,septem fratres ab vna matre Machabæa nomine geniti,custodientes legem,patris traditionem, non manducantes carnem porcinam: ob hoc ab Antiocho rege sæuissimo in Antiochia martyrii gloria coronati sunt cum matre sua: atque sepulti cum magna veneratione , ibi quiescunt.

Liber primus Machabæorum.

ET FACTVM EST postquam percussit Alexander Philippi Macedo,qui exiuit de terra Cethim,& percussit Dariũ regem Persarum & Medorum : & regnauit in loco eius primus in Græcia , & constituit prælia multa, & obtinuit munitiones, & interfecit reges terræ:& pertransiit vsque ad fines terræ,& accepit spolia multitudinis gentium:& siluit terra in conspectu eius,& exaltatum est & eleuatum cor eius. Et congregauit virtutẽ,& exercitum fortem nimis: & obtinuit regiones gentium, & tyrannos : & facti sunt illi in tributum. Et post hæc decidit in lectũ,& cognouit quia moreretur. Et vocauit pueros suos nobiles , qui secum erant nutriti à iuuentute : & diuisit illis regnum suum , cum adhuc viueret. Et regnauit Alexander annis duodecim, & mortuus est. Et obti-

Aa.i.

23 ESTIENNE'S FOLIO VULGATE, 1532

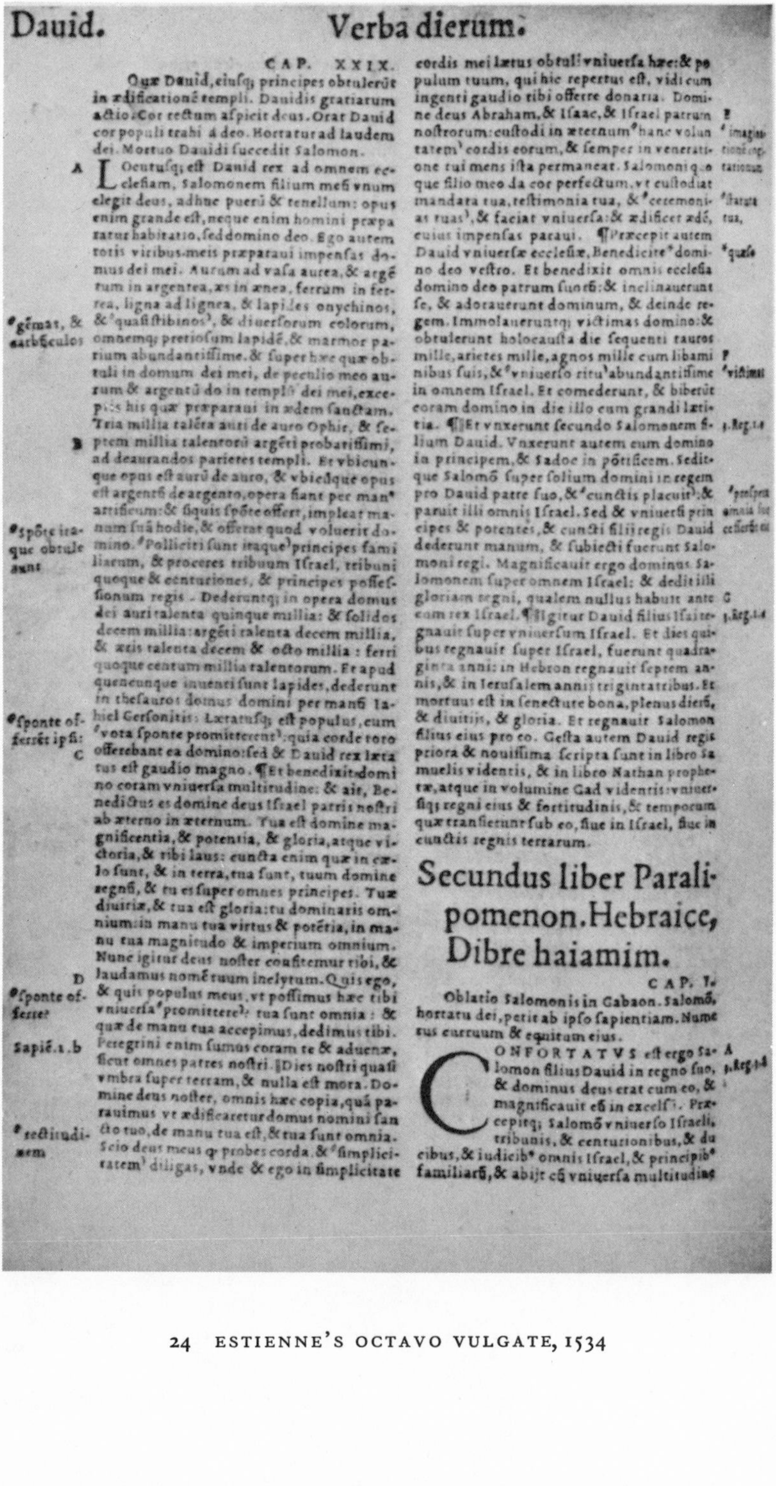

CAP. XXIX.

Quæ Dauid, eiusq; principes obtulerũt in ædificationẽ templi. Dauidis gratiarum actio. Cor rectum aspicit deus. Orat Dauid cor populi trahi à deo. Hortatur ad laudem dei. Mortuo Dauidi succedit Salomon.

A LOcutusq; est Dauid rex ad omnem ecclesiam, Salomonem filium meũ vnum elegit deus, adhuc pueri & tenellum: opus enim grande est, neque enim homini præparatur habitatio, sed domino deo. Ego autem totis viribus meis præparaui impensas domus dei mei. Aurum ad vasa aurea, & argẽtum in argentea, æs in ænea, ferrum in ferrea, ligna ad lignea, & lapides onychinos, & (quasi stibinos), & diuersorum colorum, omnemq; pretiosum lapidẽ, & marmor parium abundantissime. & super hæc quæ obtuli in domum dei mei, de peculio meo aurum & argentũ do in templũ dei mei, exceptis his quæ præparaui in ædem sanctam. Tria millia talẽta auri de auro Ophir, &

B septem millia talentorũ argẽti probatissimi, ad deaurandos parietes templi. Et vbicunque opus est aurũ de auro, & vbicũque opus est argentũ de argento, opera fiant per man⁹ artificum: & siquis spõte offert, impleat manum suã hodie, & offerat quod voluerit domino. (Polliciti sunt itaque) principes familiarum, & proceres tribuum Israel, tribuni quoque & centuriones, & principes possessionum regis. Dederuntq; in opera domus dei auri talenta quinque millia: & solidos decem millia: argẽti talenta decem millia, & æris talenta decem & octo millia: ferri quoque centum millia talentorum. Et apud quemcunque inuenti sunt lapides, dederunt in thesauros domus domini per manũ Iahiel Gersonitis. Lætatusq; est populus, cum (vota sponte promitterent): quia corde toto

C offerebant ea domino: sed & Dauid rex lætatus est gaudio magno. ¶Et benedixit domino coram vniuersa multitudine: & ait, Benedictus es domine deus Israel patris nostri ab æterno in æternum. Tua est domine magnificentia, & potentia, & gloria, atque victoria, & tibi laus: cuncta enim quæ in cælo sunt, & in terra, tua sunt, tuum domine regnũ, & tu es super omnes principes. Tuæ diuitiæ, & tua est gloria: tu dominaris omnium: in manu tua virtus & potẽtia, in manu tua magnitudo & imperium omnium. Nunc igitur deus noster confitemur tibi, &

D laudamus nomẽ tuum inclytum. Quis ego, & quis populus meus, vt possimus hæc tibi vniuersa (promittere)? tua sunt omnia: & quæ de manu tua accepimus, dedimus tibi. Peregrini enim sumus coram te & aduenæ, sicut omnes patres nostri. Dies nostri quasi vmbra super terram, & nulla est mora. Domine deus noster, omnis hæc copia, quã parauimus vt ædificaretur domus nomini sancto tuo, de manu tua est, & tua sunt omnia. Scio deus meus quod probes corda, & (simplicitatem) diligas, vnde & ego in simplicitate cordis mei lætus obtuli vniuersa hæc: & populum tuum, qui hic repertus est, vidi cum ingenti gaudio tibi offerre donaria. Domi-

E ne deus Abraham, & Isaac, & Israel patrum nostrorum: custodi in æternum (hanc voluntatem) cordis eorum, & semper in veneratione tui mens ista permaneat. Salomoni quoque filio meo da cor perfectum, vt custodiat mandata tua, testimonia tua, & (ceremonias tuas), & faciat vniuersa: & ædificet ædẽ, cuius impensas paraui. ¶Præcepit autem Dauid vniuersæ ecclesiæ, Benedicite (domino deo vestro). Et benedixit omnis ecclesia domino deo patrum suorũ: & inclinauerunt se, & adorauerunt dominum, & deinde regem. Immolaueruntq; victimas domino: & obtulerunt holocausta die sequenti tauros

F mille, arietes mille, agnos mille cum libaminibus suis, & (vniuerso ritu) abundantissime in omnem Israel. Et comederunt, & biberũt coram domino in die illo cum grandi lætitia. ¶Et vnxerunt secundo Salomonem filium Dauid. Vnxerunt autem eum domino in principem, & Sadoc in põtificem. Seditque Salomõ super solium domini in regem pro Dauid patre suo, & (cunctis placuit): & paruit illi omnis Israel. Sed & vniuersi principes & potentes, & cuncti filij regis Dauid dederunt manum, & subiecti fuerunt Salomoni regi. Magnificauit ergo dominus Salomonem super omnem Israel: & dedit illi

G gloriam regni, qualem nullus habuit ante eum rex Israel. ¶Igitur Dauid filius Isai regnauit super vniuersum Israel. Et dies quibus regnauit super Israel, fuerunt quadraginta anni: in Hebron regnauit septem annis, & in Ierusalem annis triginta tribus. Et mortuus est in senectute bona, plenus dierũ, & diuitijs, & gloria. Et regnauit Salomon filius eius pro eo. Gesta autem Dauid regis priora & nouissima scripta sunt in libro Samuelis videntis, & in libro Nathan prophetæ, atque in volumine Gad videntis: vniuersiq; regni eius & fortitudinis, & temporum quæ transierunt sub eo, siue in Israel, siue in cunctis regnis terrarum.

Marginal notes: gẽmas, & carbũculos — Spõte itaque obtulerunt — sponte offerrẽt ipsi: — sponte offerre — Sapiẽ. 1. b — rectitudinem — imaginationẽ cogitationum — statuta tua, — quæso — victimis — 3. Reg. 1. — prospera omnia successerunt — 3. Reg. 2.

Secundus liber Paralipomenon. Hebraice, Dibre haiamim.

CAP. I.

Oblatio Salomonis in Gabaon. Salomõ, hortatu dei, petit ab ipso sapientiam. Numerus curruum & equitum eius.

A CONFORTATVS est ergo Salomon filius Dauid in regno suo, & dominus deus erat cum eo, & magnificauit eũ in excelsũ. Præcepitq; Salomõ vniuerso Israeli, tribunis, & centurionibus, & ducibus, & iudicib⁹ omnis Israel, & principib⁹ familiarũ, & abijt cũ vniuersa multitudine

Marginal note: 3. Reg. 3.

sera sus la terre de froment & de vin.
Aussi son ciel distillera rousée. Tu és
bien heureux Israël: qui est comme toy ô
peuple qui és sauué par le Seigneur, bou-
clier de ton ayde, & glaiue de ta magnifi-
cence? Tés ennemys seront affoiblys vers
toy: & marcheras sur leurs haultesses.

CHAP. XXXIIII.

A LOrs Moyse, monta de la plaine de
Moab, en la montaigne de Nebo
au sommet de Phasgah, qui est con
tre Iericho. Et le Seigneur luy feit veoir
toute la terre de Galaad iusque à Dan: &
toute la terre de Nephthali, & toute la
terre d'Ephraim, & de Manassé: & toute
la terre de Iuda, iusque à la derniere mer.
Et le midy, & la plaine des prairies de
B Iericho cité dés palmes, iusq̃ à Zoar. Et
Gen. 12. b. 15. d. le Seigneur luy dist: * Ceste est la terre, de
laquelle i'ay iuré à Abraham, à Isaac, &
Iacob, en disant: Ie la donneray à ta semence: ie te l'ay faict veoir de tés yeux:
mais tu n'y passeras point. Et
Moyse seruiteur du Seigneur mourust là,
en la terre de Moab, selon la parolle du
Seigneur. Et on l'enseuelit en la vallée en
la terre de Moab, contre Beth-Pheor: &
si nul n'a congneu son sepulchre iusque
au iourdhuy. Ledict Moyse estoit eagé
C de cent & vingt ans quand il mourut: sa
veuë n'estoit point obscurcie, & sa vi-
gueur n'estoit point passée. Et lés enfans d'Israël plourerent Moyse trente
iours, en la plaine de Moab. Et ainsi furent accomplis lés iours du pleur & dueil
de Moyse. Lors Iosué filz de
Nun fut remply de l'esprit de sapience:
car Moyse auoit mis sa main sur luy. Et
lés enfans d'Israël luy obeyrent, & feirẽt
ainsi que le Seigneur auoit commandé à
Moyse: & depuis ne s'est leué prophete
D en Israël comme Moyse, lequel le Seigneur ayt congneu face à face, en tous
signes & miracles, pour lesquelz le Seigneur l'auoit enuoyé, affin qu'il lés feit
en la terre d'Egypte deuant Pharaoh &
tous sés seruiteurs & toute sa terre: en
toute ceste main forte, & toute vision grã
de, lesquelles Moyse a faict deuant lés
yeux de tout Israël.

La fin du Deuteronome: &
consequamment dés
cinq liures de
Moyse.

LE LIVRE DV PROPHETE Iosué.

CHAP. I.

OR aprés la mort de Moyse ser- A
uiteur du Seigneur: le Seigneur
parla à Iosué filz de Nun, mi-
nistre de Moyse, disant: Moyse
mon seruiteur est mort: or maintenant
leue toy, & passe outre ce Iordan, toy &
tout ce peuple, à la terre laquelle ie leur
donne: assauoir, aux enfans d'Israël. Ie
vous ay baillé comme i'ay dict à Moy-
se, * tout lieu que la plante de vostre pied Deu. 11. c.
aura marché. Voz fins seront, depuis le
desert & Liban icy iusque au grãd fleu-
ue Euphrates: toute la terre dés Hethéens
iusque à la grand mer, contre le soleil cou
chant. Nul ne pouurra resister deuant
toy, tant que tu viuras. Car comme i'ay
esté auec Moyse, ainsi seray-ie auec toy:
* ie ne te laisseray point, & ne t'abandon Ebr. 13. a
neray. Sois donc fort & robuste: car tu
diuiseras à ce peuple-cy en heritage la
terre, laquelle i'ay iuré à leurs peres de
leur donner. Seulement conforte toy &
sois vaillant tant que faire ce pourra, af- B
fin que tu garde & face selon toute la
loy, que Moyse mon seruiteur t'a commandé: tu ne declineras point d'icelle n'y
à dextre n'y à senestre, affin que tu te
gouuerne prudentement par tout ou tu
iras. Que le volume de ceste loy ne
bouge de ta bouche, ains mediteras en
iceluy iour et nuict, affin que tu garde &
face selon tout ce qui est escrit en iceluy.
Car lors feras prosperer ta voye, & lors
procederas prudentement. Ne t'ay-ie
point commãdé, que tu fusse fort & vaillant, & q̃ tu ne t'espouantasse point, et ne
craingnisse? Car le Seigneur ton Dieu est
auec toy par tout ou tu chemine. C

Iosué donc commanda aux preuostz
du peuple, disant: Passez par le milieu du
camp, & commandez au peuple, disant,
Preparez pour vous de la prouision, car
aprés troys iours vous passerez ce Iordan: affin que vous entriez & possediez
la terre, laquelle le Seigneur vostre Dieu
vous donne, pour la posseder. Iosué
aussi parla aux Rubenites & Gadites &
à la moytie de la lignée de Manassé, disant: Ayez souuenance de la parolle, que
vous commanda Moyse seruiteur du Seigneur, disant: Le Seigneur vostre Dieu
vous a mis en repos, & vous a donné ceste terre. Voz femmes voz enfans, & voz
1 5 bestes

25 THE 'BIBLE DE L'ÉPÉE', 1540

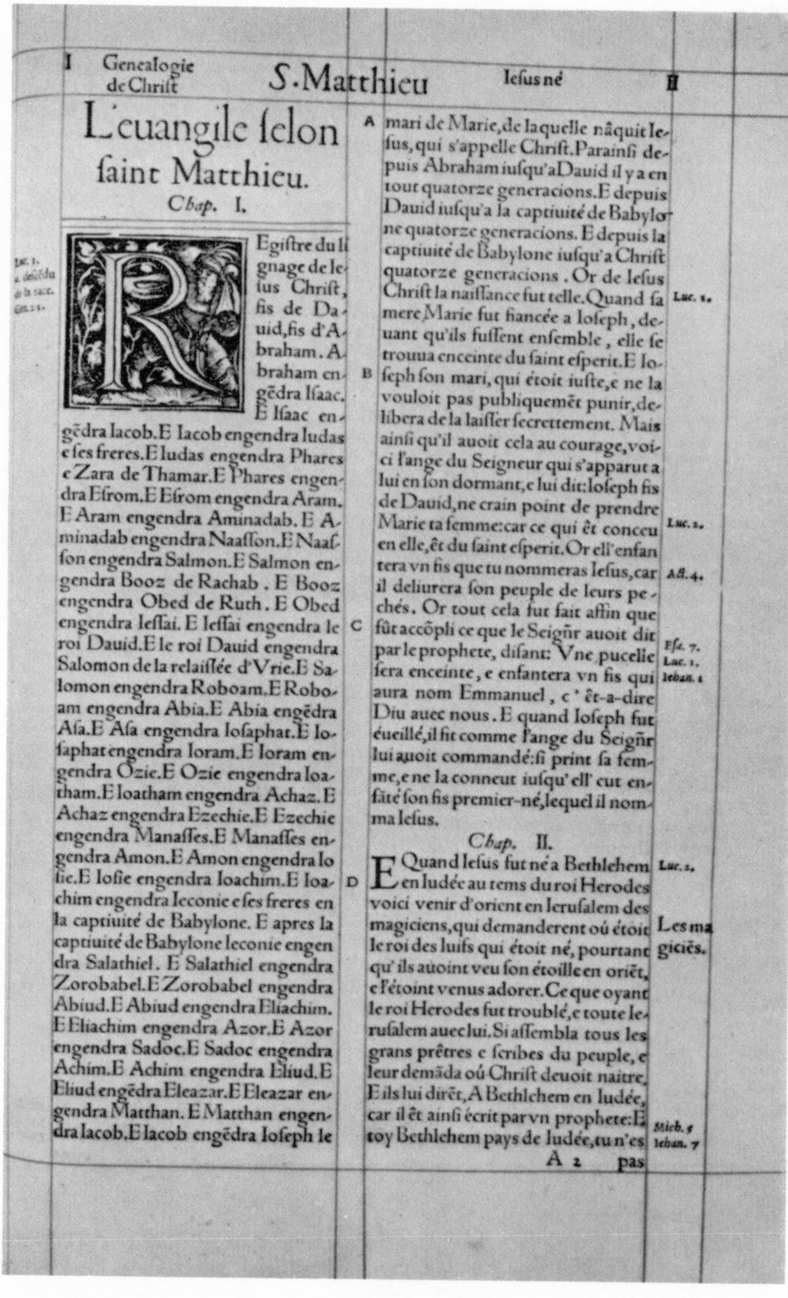

I Genealogie de Christ S. Matthieu Iesus né II

L'euangile selon saint Matthieu.

Chap. I.

Luc. 3. a. descēdu de la race. Gen. 21.

REgistre du li-
gnage de Ie-
sus Christ,
fis de Da-
uid, fis d'A-
braham. A-
braham en-
gēdra Isaac.
E Isaac en-
gēdra Iacob. E Iacob engendra Iudas
e ses freres. E Iudas engendra Phares
e Zara de Thamar. E Phares engendra Esrom. E Esrom engendra Aram.
E Aram engendra Aminadab. E A-
minadab engendra Naasson. E Naasson engendra Salmon. E Salmon engendra Booz de Rachab. E Booz
engendra Obed de Ruth. E Obed
engendra Iessai. E Iessai engendra le
roi Dauid. E le roi Dauid engendra
Salomon de la relaissée d'Vrie. E Salomon engendra Roboam. E Roboam engendra Abia. E Abia engēdra
Asa. E Asa engendra Iosaphat. E Iosaphat engendra Ioram. E Ioram engendra Ozie. E Ozie engendra Ioatham. E Ioatham engendra Achaz. E
Achaz engendra Ezechie. E Ezechie
engendra Manasses. E Manasses engendra Amon. E Amon engendra Io
sie. E Iosie engendra Ioachim. E Ioachim engendra Ieconie e ses freres en
la captiuité de Babylone. E apres la
captiuité de Babylone Ieconie engen
dra Salathiel. E Salathiel engendra
Zorobabel. E Zorobabel engendra
Abiud. E Abiud engendra Eliachim.
E Eliachim engendra Azor. E Azor
engendra Sadoc. E Sadoc engendra
Achim. E Achim engendra Eliud. E
Eliud engēdra Eleazar. E Eleazar engendra Matthan. E Matthan engendra Iacob. E Iacob engēdra Ioseph le

A mari de Marie, de laquelle nâquit Iesus, qui s'appelle Christ. Parainsi depuis Abraham iusqu'a Dauid il y a en
tout quatorze generacions. E depuis
Dauid iusqu'a la captiuité de Babylone quatorze generacions. E depuis la
captiuité de Babylone iusqu'a Christ
quatorze generacions. Or de Iesus
Christ la naissance fut telle. Quand sa Luc. 1.
mere Marie fut fiancée a Ioseph, deuant qu'ils fussent ensemble, elle se
trouua enceinte du saint esperit. E Io-
B seph son mari, qui étoit iuste, e ne la
vouloit pas publiquemēt punir, de-
libera de la laisser secrettement. Mais
ainsi qu'il auoit cela au courage, voici l'ange du Seigneur qui s'apparut a
lui en son dormant, e lui dit: Ioseph fis
de Dauid, ne crain point de prendre
Marie ta femme: car ce qui êt conceu Luc. 2.
en elle, êt du saint esperit. Or ell'enfan
tera vn fis que tu nommeras Iesus, car Act. 4.
il deliurera son peuple de leurs pe-
chés. Or tout cela fut fait affin que
C fût accōpli ce que le Seignr auoit dit
par le prophete, disant: Vne pucelle Esa. 7.
sera enceinte, e enfantera vn fis qui Luc. 1.
aura nom Emmanuel, c'êt-a-dire Iehan. 1
Diu auec nous. E quand Ioseph fut
éueillé, il fit comme l'ange du Seignr
lui auoit commandé: si print sa femme, e ne la conneut iusqu'ell'eut en-
fāté son fis premier-né, lequel il nom-
ma Iesus.

Chap. II.

EQuand Iesus fut né a Bethlehem Luc. 2.
D en Iudée au tems du roi Herodes
voici venir d'orient en Ierusalem des
magiciens, qui demanderent oú étoit Les magiciēs.
le roi des Iuifs qui étoit né, pourtant
qu'ils auoint veu son étoille en oriēt,
e l'étoint venus adorer. Ce que oyant
le roi Herodes fut troublé, e toute Ierusalem auec lui. Si assembla tous les
grans prêtres e scribes du peuple, e
leur demāda oú Christ deuoit naitre.
E ils lui dirēt, A Bethlehem en Iudée,
car il êt ainsi écrit par vn prophete: E Mich. 5
toy Bethlehem pays de Iudée, tu n'es Iehan. 7

A 2 pas

 CASTELLIO'S FRENCH VERSION, 1555

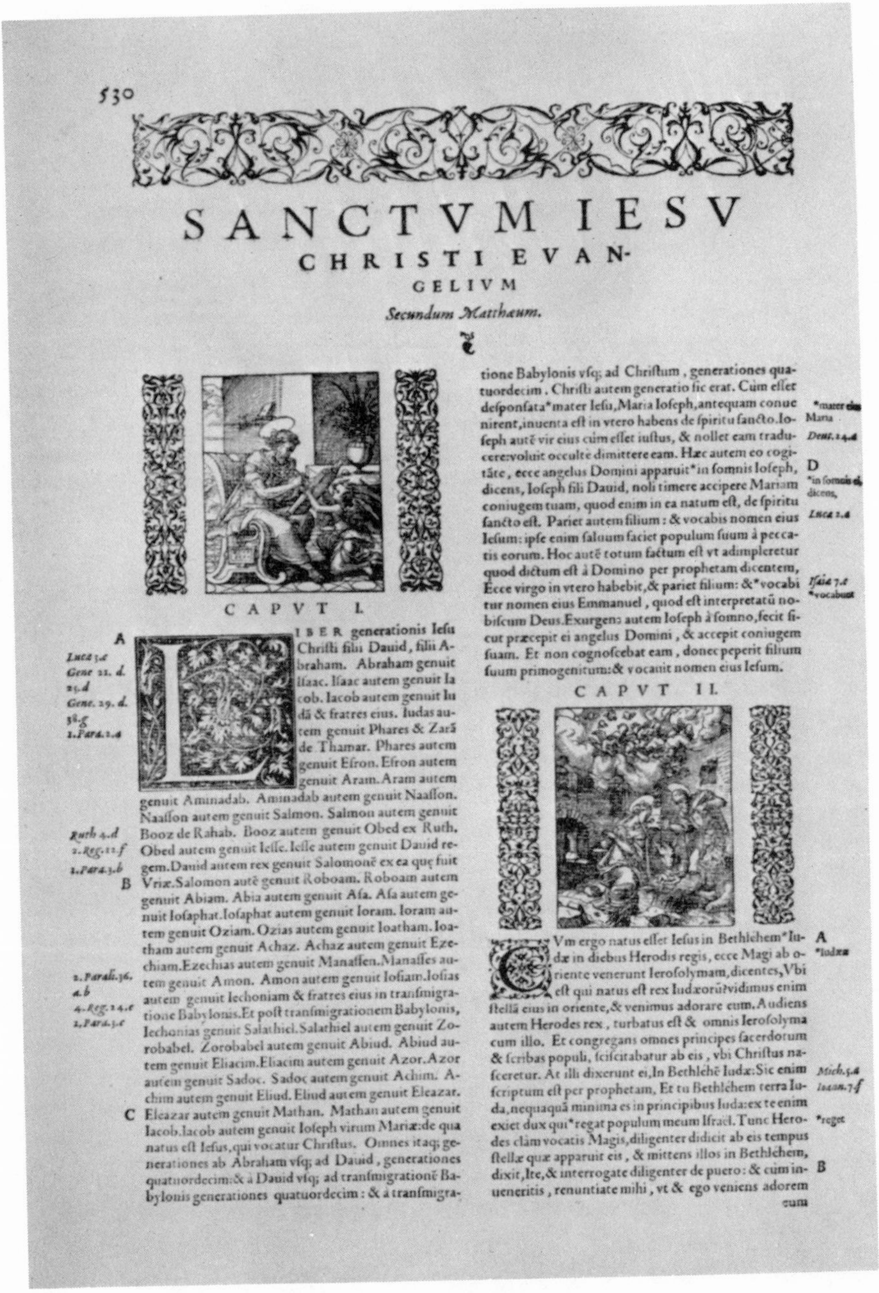

530

SANCTVM IESV CHRISTI EVANGELIVM

Secundum Matthæum.

CAPVT I.

A LIBER generationis Iesu
Luca 3.e Christi filii Dauid, filii A-
Gene 22. d. braham. Abraham genuit
21.d Isaac. Isaac autem genuit Ia
Gene. 29. d. cob. Iacob autem genuit Iu
38.g dã & fratres eius. Iudas au-
1.Para.2.a tem genuit Phares & Zarã
de Thamar. Phares autem
genuit Esron. Esron autem
genuit Aram. Aram autem
genuit Aminadab. Aminadab autem genuit Naasson.
Naasson autem genuit Salmon. Salmon autem genuit
Ruth 4.d Booz de Rahab. Booz autem genuit Obed ex Ruth.
1.Reg.22.f Obed autem genuit Iesse. Iesse autem genuit Dauid re-
1.Para.3.b gem. Dauid autem rex genuit Salomonẽ ex ea quę fuit
B Vriæ. Salomon autẽ genuit Roboam. Roboam autem
genuit Abiam. Abia autem genuit Asa. Asa autem ge-
nuit Iosaphat. Iosaphat autem genuit Ioram. Ioram au-
tem genuit Oziam. Ozias autem genuit Ioatham. Ioatham autem genuit Achaz. Achaz autem genuit Eze-
chiam. Ezechias autem genuit Manassen. Manasses au-
2.Parali.36. tem genuit Amon. Amon autem genuit Iosiam. Iosias
a.b autem genuit Iechoniam & fratres eius in transmigra-
4.Reg.24.e tione Babylonis. Et post transmigrationem Babylonis,
1.Para.3.e Iechonias genuit Salathiel. Salathiel autem genuit Zorobabel. Zorobabel autem genuit Abiud. Abiud au-
tem genuit Eliacim. Eliacim autem genuit Azor. Azor
autem genuit Sadoc. Sadoc autem genuit Achim. A-
chim autem genuit Eliud. Eliud autem genuit Eleazar.
C Eleazar autem genuit Mathan. Mathan autem genuit
Iacob. Iacob autem genuit Ioseph virum Mariæ: de qua
natus est Iesus, qui vocatur Christus. Omnes itaq; generationes ab Abraham vsq; ad Dauid, generationes
quatuordecim: & à Dauid vsq; ad transmigrationẽ Babylonis generationes quatuordecim: & à transmigra-
tione Babylonis vsq; ad Christum, generationes quatuordecim. Christi autem generatio sic erat. Cùm esset
desponsata *mater Iesu, Maria Ioseph, antequam conue *mater eius Maria
nirent, inuenta est in vtero habens de spiritu sancto. Ioseph autẽ vir eius cùm esset iustus, & nollet eam tradu- *Deut.24.a*
cere: voluit occultè dimittere eam. Hæc autem eo cogi-
tãte, ecce angelus Domini apparuit *in somnis Ioseph, D
dicens, Ioseph fili Dauid, noli timere accipere Mariam *in somnis ei, dicens,
coniugem tuam, quod enim in ea natum est, de spiritu
sancto est. Pariet autem filium: & vocabis nomen eius *Luca 2.a*
Iesum: ipse enim saluum faciet populum suum à pecca-
tis eorum. Hoc autẽ totum factum est vt adimpleretur
quod dictum est à Domino per prophetam dicentem,
Ecce virgo in vtero habebit, & pariet filium: & *vocabi *Isaia 7.c*
tur nomen eius Emmanuel, quod est interpretatũ no- *vocabunt
biscum Deus. Exurgens autem Ioseph à somno, fecit sicut præcepit ei angelus Domini, & accepit coniugem
suam. Et non cognoscebat eam, donec peperit filium
suum primogenitum: & vocauit nomen eius Iesum.

CAPVT II.

CVm ergo natus esset Iesus in Bethlẽhem *Iu- A
dæ in diebus Herodis regis, ecce Magi ab o- *Iudææ
riente venerunt Ierosolymam, dicentes, Vbi
est qui natus est rex Iudæorũ? vidimus enim
stellã eius in oriente, & venimus adorare eum. Audiens
autem Herodes rex, turbatus est & omnis Ierosolyma
cum illo. Et congregans omnes principes sacerdotum
& scribas populi, sciscitabatur ab eis, vbi Christus na-
sceretur. At illi dixerunt ei, In Bethlẽhẽ Iudæ: Sic enim *Mich.5.a*
scriptum est per prophetam, Et tu Bethlẽhem terra Iu- *Ioann.7.f*
da, nequaquã minima es in principibus Iuda: ex te enim
exiet dux qui *regat populum meum Israel. Tunc Hero- *reget
des clàm vocatis Magis, diligenter didicit ab eis tempus
stellæ quæ apparuit eis, & mittens illos in Bethlẽhem,
dixit, Ite, & interrogate diligenter de puero: & cùm in- B
ueneritis, renuntiate mihi, vt & ego veniens adorem
eum

27 DE TOURNES'S FOLIO VULGATE, 1556

ΤΟ ΚΑΤΑ ἸΩΑΝΝΗΝ ἉΓΙΟΝ ΕὐΑΓΓΕΛΙΟΝ.

ἘΝ ἀρχῇ ἦν ὁ λόγος, καὶ ὁ λόγος ἦν
πρὸς τὸν Θεόν, καὶ Θεὸς ἦν ὁ λόγος. οὗτος
ἦν ἐν ἀρχῇ πρὸς τὸν Θεόν. Πάντα δι᾽
αὐτοῦ ἐγένετο, καὶ χωρὶς αὐτοῦ ἐγένετο οὐδὲ ἕν, ὃ γέγονεν. ἐν αὐτῷ ζωὴ ἦν, καὶ
ἡ ζωὴ ἦν τὸ φῶς τῶν ἀνθρώπων, καὶ τὸ
φῶς ἐν τῇ σκοτίᾳ φαίνει, καὶ ἡ σκοτία αὐ-
τὸ οὐ κατέλαβεν. Ἐγένετο ἄνθρωπος ἀπεσταλμένος παρὰ
Θεοῦ, ὄνομα αὐτῷ Ἰωάννης. οὗτος ἦλθεν εἰς μαρτυρίαν, ἵνα μαρτυρήσῃ περὶ τοῦ φωτός, ἵνα πάντες πιστεύσωσι δι᾽ αὐτοῦ. οὐκ ἦν ἐ-
κεῖνος τὸ φῶς, ἀλλ᾽ ἵνα μαρτυρήσῃ περὶ τοῦ φωτός. Ἦν τὸ
φῶς τὸ ἀληθινόν, ὃ φωτίζει πάντα ἄνθρωπον ἐρχόμενον εἰς τὸν
κόσμον. ἐν τῷ κόσμῳ ἦν, καὶ ὁ κόσμος δι᾽ αὐτοῦ ἐγένετο, καὶ ὁ κό- B
σμος αὐτὸν οὐκ ἔγνω. Εἰς τὰ ἴδια ἦλθε, καὶ οἱ ἴδιοι αὐτὸν οὐ παρέ-
λαβον. ὅσοι δὲ ἔλαβον αὐτόν, ἔδωκεν αὐτοῖς ἐξουσίαν τέκνα
Θεοῦ γενέσθαι, τοῖς πιστεύουσιν εἰς τὸ ὄνομα αὐτοῦ, οἳ οὐκ ἐξ αἱμά-
των, οὐδὲ ἐκ θελήματος σαρκός, οὐδὲ ἐκ θελήματος ἀνδρός,
ἀλλ᾽ ἐκ Θεοῦ ἐγεννήθησαν. καὶ ὁ λόγος σὰρξ ἐγένετο, καὶ ἐσκή-
νωσεν ἐν ἡμῖν, (καὶ ἐθεασάμεθα τὴν δόξαν αὐτοῦ, δόξαν ὡς
μονογενοῦς παρὰ πατρός,) πλήρης χάριτος καὶ ἀληθείας. Ἰωάννης μαρτυρεῖ περὶ αὐτοῦ, καὶ κέκραγε, λέγων, Οὗτος ἦν ὃν εἶπον,
ὁ ὀπίσω μου ἐρχόμενος, ἔμπροσθέν μου γέγονεν· ὅτι πρῶτός
μου ἦν. καὶ ἐκ τοῦ πληρώματος αὐτοῦ ἡμεῖς πάντες ἐλάβομεν,
καὶ χάριν ἀντὶ χάριτος· ὅτι ὁ νόμος διὰ Μωσέως ἐδόθη, ἡ χά- Γ
ρις καὶ ἡ ἀλήθεια διὰ Ἰησοῦ Χριστοῦ ἐγένετο. Θεὸν οὐδεὶς ἑώρα-
κε πώποτε· ὁ μονογενὴς υἱός, ὁ ὢν εἰς τὸν κόλπον τοῦ πατρός, ἐκεῖ-
νος ἐξηγήσατο. Καὶ αὕτη ἐστὶν ἡ μαρτυρία τοῦ Ἰωάννου, ὅτε

l.i.

28 ESTIENNE'S FOLIO GREEK TEXT, 1550

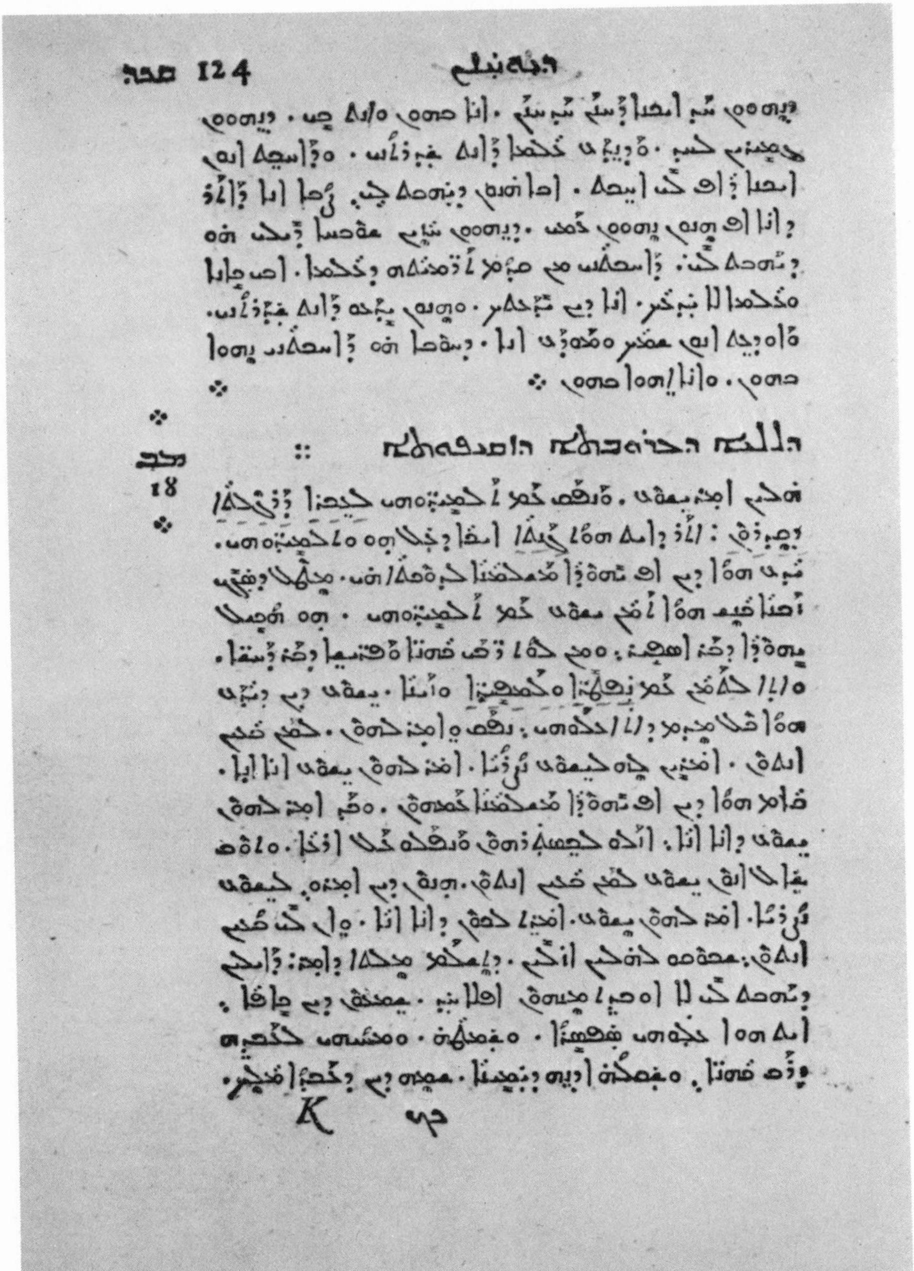

29 WIDMANSTADT'S SYRIAC NEW TESTAMENT, 1555

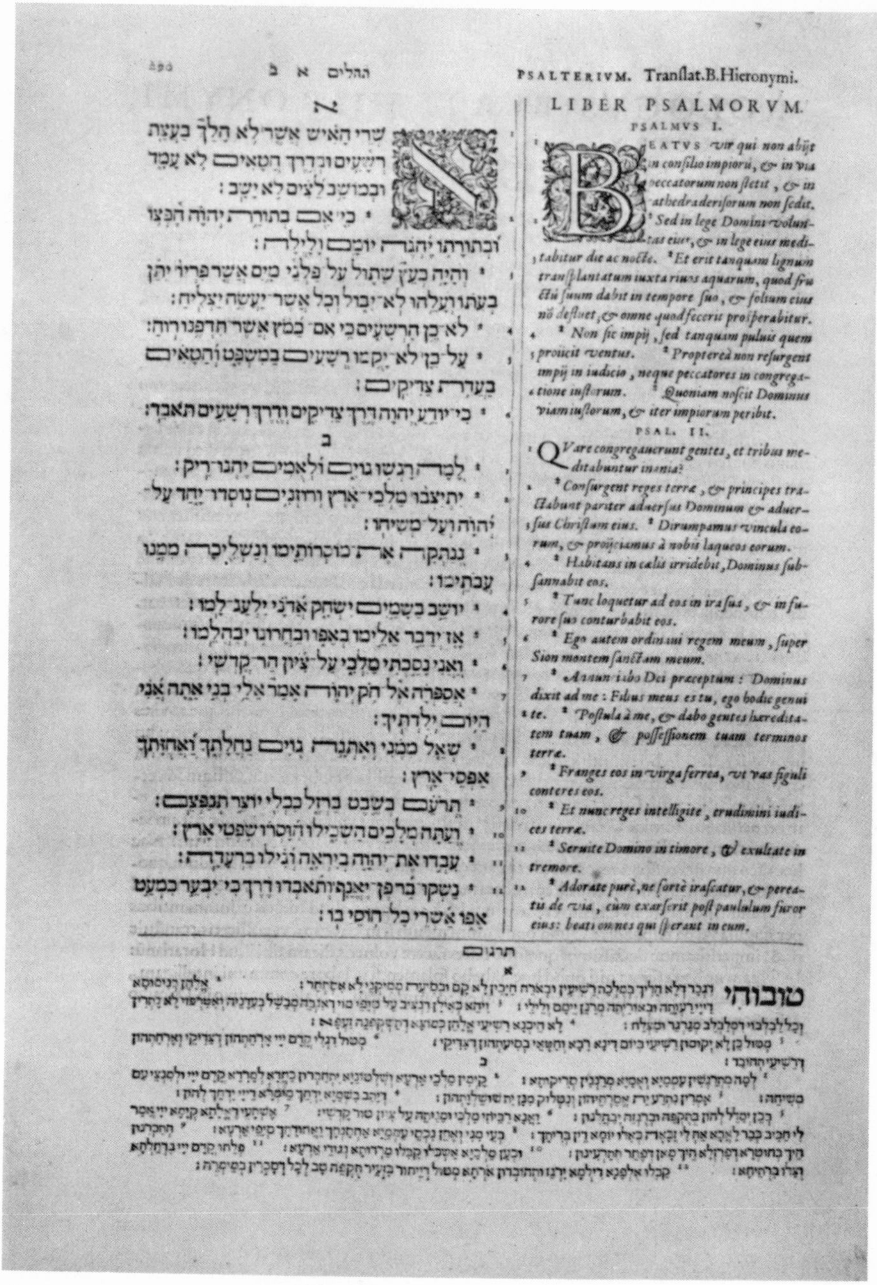
תהלים א ב
PSALTERIVM. Translat. B. Hieronymi.
א
1 אשרי האיש אשר לא הלך בעצת רשעים ובדרך חטאים לא עמד ובמושב לצים לא ישב:
2 כי אם בתורת יהוה חפצו ובתורתו יהגה יומם ולילה:
3 והיה כעץ שתול על פלגי מים אשר פריו יתן בעתו ועלהו לא יבול וכל אשר יעשה יצליח:
4 לא כן הרשעים כי אם כמץ אשר תדפנו רוח:
5 על כן לא יקמו רשעים במשפט וחטאים בעדת צדיקים:
6 כי יודע יהוה דרך צדיקים ודרך רשעים תאבד:
ב
1 למה רגשו גוים ולאמים יהגו ריק:
2 יתיצבו מלכי ארץ ורוזנים נוסדו יחד על יהוה ועל משיחו:
3 ננתקה את מוסרותימו ונשליכה ממנו עבתימו:
4 יושב בשמים ישחק אדני ילעג למו:
5 אז ידבר אלימו באפו ובחרונו יבהלמו:
6 ואני נסכתי מלכי על ציון הר קדשי:
7 אספרה אל חק יהוה אמר אלי בני אתה אני היום ילדתיך:
8 שאל ממני ואתנה גוים נחלתך ואחזתך אפסי ארץ:
9 תרעם בשבט ברזל ככלי יוצר תנפצם:
10 ועתה מלכים השכילו הוסרו שפטי ארץ:
11 עבדו את יהוה ביראה וגילו ברעדה:
12 נשקו בר פן יאנף ותאבדו דרך כי יבער כמעט אפו אשרי כל חוסי בו:
LIBER PSALMORVM.
PSALMVS I.
1 BEATVS vir qui non abiit in consilio impioru, & in via peccatorum non stetit, & in cathedra derisorum non sedit.
2 Sed in lege Domini voluntas eius, & in lege eius medi-
3 tabitur die ac nocte. Et erit tanquam lignum transplantatum iuxta riuos aquarum, quod fructu suum dabit in tempore suo, & folium eius nō defluet, & omne quod feceris prosperabitur.
4 Non sic impii, sed tanquam puluis quem
5 proiicit ventus. Propterea non resurgent impii in iudicio, neque peccatores in congrega-
6 tione iustorum. Quoniam nouit Dominus viam iustorum, & iter impiorum peribit.
PSAL. II.
1 QVare congregauerunt gentes, et tribus meditabuntur inania?
2 Consurgent reges terræ, & principes tractabunt pariter aduersus Dominum & aduer-
3 sus Christum eius. Dirumpamus vincula eorum, & proiiciamus à nobis laqueos eorum.
4 Habitans in cælis irridebit, Dominus subsannabit eos.
5 Tunc loquetur ad eos in ira sua, & in furore suo conturbabit eos.
6 Ego autem ordinaui regem meum, super Sion montem sanctum meum.
7 Annuntiabo Dei præceptum: Dominus dixit ad me: Filius meus es tu, ego hodie genui
8 te. Postula à me, & dabo gentes hereditatem tuam, & possessionem tuam terminos terræ.
9 Franges eos in virga ferrea, vt vas figuli conteres eos.
10 Et nunc reges intelligite, erudimini iudices terræ.
11 Seruite Domino in timore, & exultate in tremore.
12 Adorate purè, ne fortè irascatur, & pereatis de via, cùm exarserit post paululum furor eius: beati omnes qui sperant in eum.
תרגום
א
טובוהי

30–31 AN OPENING OF THE

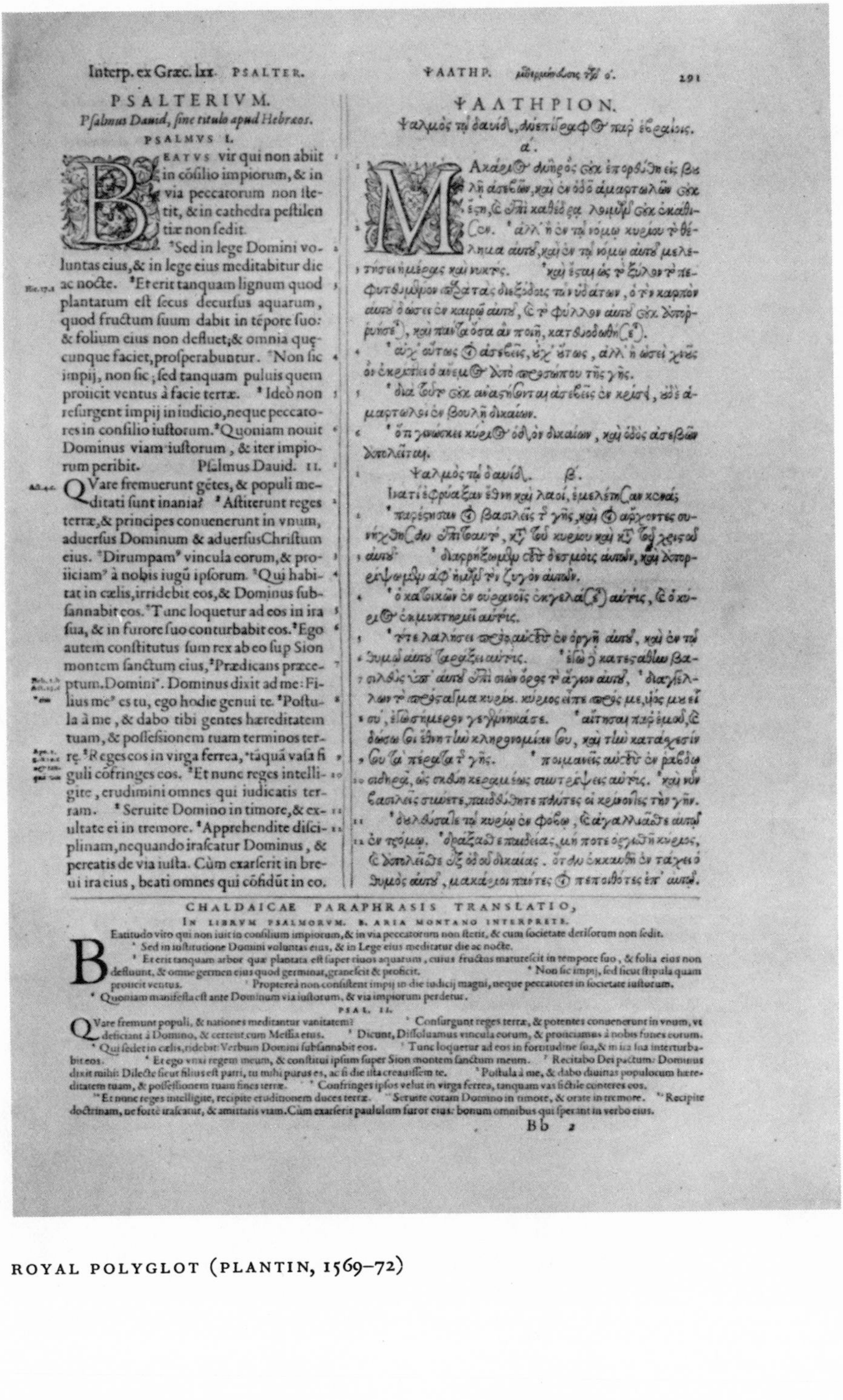
Interp. ex Græc. lxx PSALTER. ΨΑΛΤΗΡ. μεθηρμηνευμένος τῶν ό. 291

PSALTERIVM.

Psalmus Dauid, sine titulo apud Hebræos.

PSALMVS I.

BEATVS vir qui non abiit 1
in cõsilio impiorum, & in
via peccatorum non ste-
tit, & in cathedra pestilen
tiæ non sedit.
[2]Sed in lege Domini vo- 2
luntas eius, & in lege eius meditabitur die
Hie.17.a ac nocte. [3]Et erit tanquam lignum quod 3
plantatum est secus decursus aquarum,
quod fructum suum dabit in tẽpore suo:
& folium eius non defluet; & omnia quę-
cunque faciet, prosperabuntur. [4]Non sic 4
impij, non sic; sed tanquam puluis quem
proiicit ventus à facie terræ. [5]Ideò non 5
resurgent impij in iudicio, neque peccatores in consilio iustorum. [6]Quoniam nouit 6
Dominus viam iustorum, & iter impiorum peribit. Psalmus Dauid. II.
Act.4.c. QVare fremuerunt gẽtes, & populi me- 1
ditati sunt inania? [2]Astiterunt reges 2
terræ, & principes conuenerunt in vnum,
aduersus Dominum & aduersus Christum
eius. [3]Dirumpam[9] vincula eorum, & pro- 3
iiciam[9] à nobis iugũ ipsorum. [4]Qui habi- 4
tat in cælis, irridebit eos, & Dominus subsannabit eos. [5]Tunc loquetur ad eos in ira 5
sua, & in furore suo conturbabit eos. [6]Ego 6
autem constitutus sum rex ab eo sup Sion
montem sanctum eius, [7]Prædicans præce- 7
ptum Domini. Dominus dixit ad me: Filius me[9] es tu, ego hodie genui te. [8]Postu- 8
la à me, & dabo tibi gentes hæreditatem
tuam, & possessionem tuam terminos terræ. [9]Reges eos in virga ferrea, tãquã vasa fi- 9
guli cõfringes eos. [10]Et nunc reges intelli- 10
gite, erudimini omnes qui iudicatis terram. [11]Seruite Domino in timore, & ex- 11
ultate ei in tremore. [12]Apprehendite disci- 12
plinam, nequando irascatur Dominus, &
pereatis de via iusta. Cùm exarserit in bre-
ui ira eius, beati omnes qui cõfidũt in eo.

ΨΑΛΤΗΡΙΟΝ.

Ψαλμὸς τῷ δαυὶδ, ἀνεπίγραφος παρ' ἑβραίοις.

α.

1 ΜΑκάριος ἀνὴρ ὃς οὐκ ἐπορεύθη ἐν βουλῇ ἀσεβῶν, καὶ ἐν ὁδῷ ἁμαρτωλῶν οὐκ
ἔστη, καὶ ἐπὶ καθέδρᾳ λοιμῶν οὐκ ἐκάθι-
2 σεν. [2]ἀλλ' ἢ ἐν τῷ νόμῳ κυρίου τὸ θέ-
λημα αὐτοῦ, καὶ ἐν τῷ νόμῳ αὐτοῦ μελε-
3 τήσει ἡμέρας καὶ νυκτός. [3]καὶ ἔσται ὡς τὸ ξύλον τὸ πε-
φυτευμένον παρὰ τὰς διεξόδους τῶν ὑδάτων, ὃ τὸν καρπὸν
αὐτοῦ δώσει ἐν καιρῷ αὐτοῦ, καὶ τὸ φύλλον αὐτοῦ οὐκ ἀπορ-
ρυήσεται, καὶ πάντα ὅσα ἂν ποιῇ, κατευοδωθήσεται.
4 [4]οὐχ οὕτως οἱ ἀσεβεῖς, οὐχ οὕτως, ἀλλ' ἢ ὡσεὶ χνοῦς
ὃν ἐκρίπτει ὁ ἄνεμος ἀπὸ προσώπου τῆς γῆς.
5 [5]διὰ τοῦτο οὐκ ἀναστήσονται ἀσεβεῖς ἐν κρίσει, οὐδὲ ἁ-
μαρτωλοὶ ἐν βουλῇ δικαίων.
6 [6]ὅτι γινώσκει κύριος ὁδὸν δικαίων, καὶ ὁδὸς ἀσεβῶν
ἀπολεῖται.

1 Ψαλμὸς τῷ δαυίδ. β.

Ἱνατί ἐφρύαξαν ἔθνη καὶ λαοί, ἐμελέτησαν κενά;
2 [2]παρέστησαν οἱ βασιλεῖς τῆς γῆς, καὶ οἱ ἄρχοντες συ-
νήχθησαν ἐπὶ τὸ αὐτό, κατὰ τοῦ κυρίου καὶ κατὰ τοῦ χριστοῦ
3 αὐτοῦ· [3]διαρρήξωμεν τοὺς δεσμοὺς αὐτῶν, καὶ ἀπορ-
ρίψωμεν ἀφ' ἡμῶν τὸν ζυγὸν αὐτῶν.
4 [4]ὁ κατοικῶν ἐν οὐρανοῖς ἐκγελάσεται αὐτούς, καὶ ὁ κύριος ἐκμυκτηριεῖ αὐτούς.
5 [5]τότε λαλήσει πρὸς αὐτοὺς ἐν ὀργῇ αὐτοῦ, καὶ ἐν τῷ
6 θυμῷ αὐτοῦ ταράξει αὐτούς. [6]ἐγὼ δὲ κατεστάθην βα-
7 σιλεὺς ὑπ' αὐτοῦ ἐπὶ σιὼν ὄρος τὸ ἅγιον αὐτοῦ, [7]διαγγέλ-
λων τὸ πρόσταγμα κυρίου. κύριος εἶπε πρός με, υἱός μου εἶ
8 σύ, ἐγὼ σήμερον γεγέννηκά σε. [8]αἴτησαι παρ' ἐμοῦ, καὶ
δώσω σοι ἔθνη τὴν κληρονομίαν σου, καὶ τὴν κατάσχεσίν
9 σου τὰ πέρατα τῆς γῆς. [9]ποιμανεῖς αὐτοὺς ἐν ῥάβδῳ
10 σιδηρᾷ, ὡς σκεῦη κεραμέως συντρίψεις αὐτούς. [10]καὶ νῦν
βασιλεῖς συνίετε, παιδεύθητε πάντες οἱ κρίνοντες τὴν γῆν.
11 [11]δουλεύσατε τῷ κυρίῳ ἐν φόβῳ, καὶ ἀγαλλιᾶσθε αὐτῷ
12 ἐν τρόμῳ. [12]δράξασθε παιδείας, μή ποτε ὀργισθῇ κύριος,
καὶ ἀπολεῖσθε ἐξ ὁδοῦ δικαίας. ὅταν ἐκκαυθῇ ἐν τάχει ὁ
θυμὸς αὐτοῦ, μακάριοι πάντες οἱ πεποιθότες ἐπ' αὐτῷ.

CHALDAICAE PARAPHRASIS TRANSLATIO,

IN LIBRVM PSALMORVM. B. ARIA MONTANO INTERPRETE.

BEatitudo viro qui non iuit in consilium impiorum, & in via peccatorum non stetit, & cum societate derisorum non sedit. [2]Sed in institutione Domini voluntas eius, & in Lege eius meditatur die ac nocte. [3]Et erit tanquam arbor quæ plantata est super riuos aquarum, cuius fructus maturescit in tempore suo, & folia eius non defluunt, & omne germen eius quod germinat, grandescit & proficit. [4]Non sic impij, sed sicut stipula quam proiicit ventus. [5]Propterea non consistent impij in die iudicij magni, neque peccatores in societate iustorum. [6]Quoniam manifesta est ante Dominum via iustorum, & via impiorum perdetur.

PSAL. II.

QVare fremunt populi, & nationes meditantur vanitatem? [2]Consurgunt reges terræ, & potentes conuenerunt in vnum, vt deficiant à Domino, & certent cum Messia eius. [3]Dicunt, Dissoluamus vincula eorum, & proiciamus à nobis funes eorum. [4]Qui sedet in cælis, ridebit: Verbum Domini subsannabit eos. [5]Tunc loquetur ad eos in fortitudine sua, & in ira sua interturbabit eos. [6]Et ego vnxi regem meum, & constitui ipsum super Sion montem sanctum meum. [7]Recitabo Dei pactum: Dominus dixit mihi: Dilecte sicut filius est patri, tu mihi purus es, ac si die ista creauissem te. [8]Postula à me, & dabo diuitias populorum hæreditatem tuam, & possessionem tuam fines terræ. [9]Confringes ipsos velut in virga ferrea, tanquam vas fictile conteres eos. [10]Et nunc reges intelligite, recipite eruditionem duces terræ. [11]Seruite coram Domino in timore, & orate in tremore. [12]Recipite doctrinam, ne fortè irascatur, & amittatis viam. Cùm exarserit paululum furor eius: bonum omnibus qui sperant in verbo eius.

Bb 2

ROYAL POLYGLOT (PLANTIN, 1569–72)

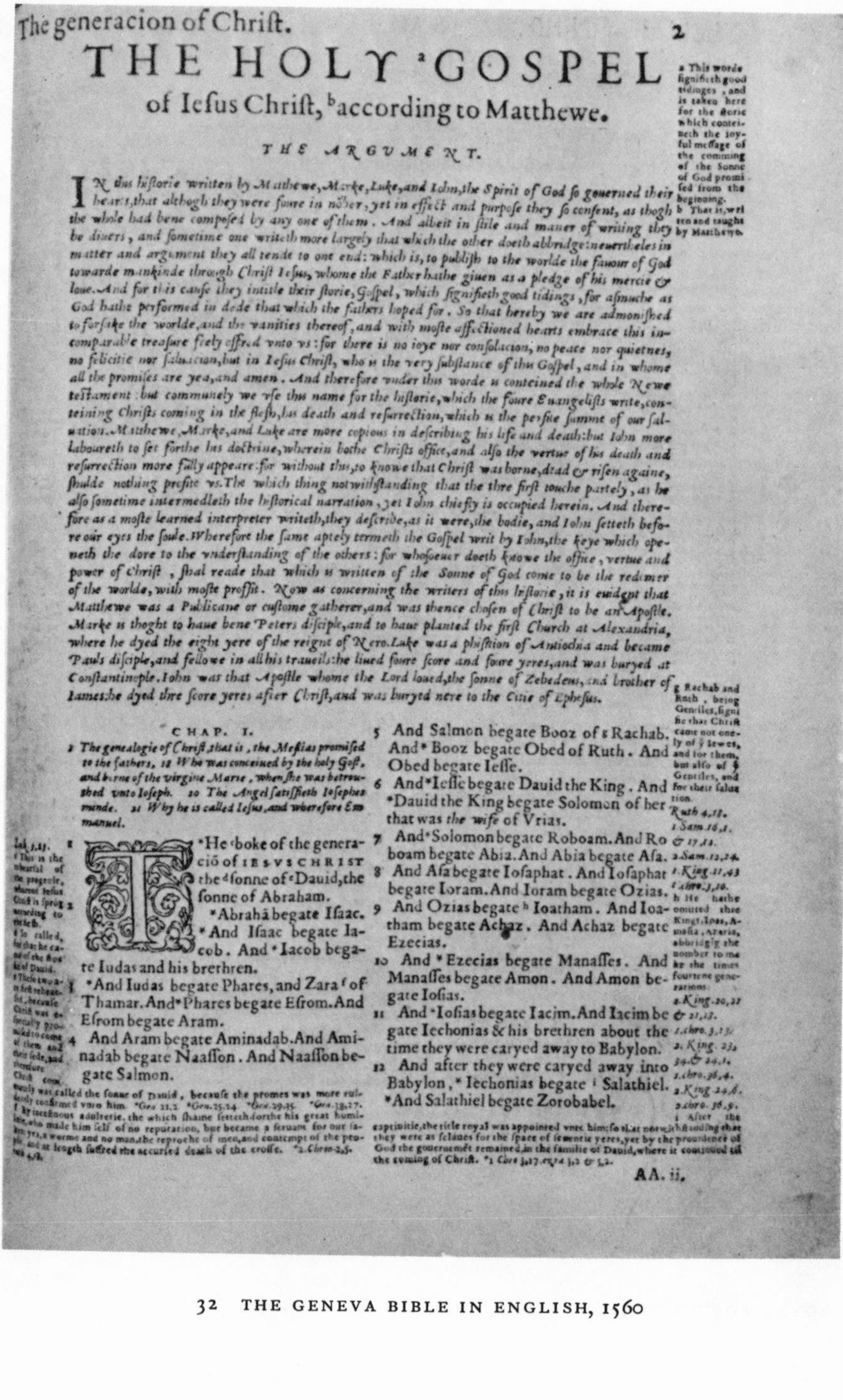

The generacion of Christ. 2

THE HOLY [a]GOSPEL of Iesus Christ, [b]according to Matthewe.

a This worde signifieth good tidinges, and is taken here for the storie which conteineth the ioyful message of the comming of the Sonne of God promised from the beginning.
b That is, writen and taught by Matthewe.

THE ARGUMENT.

IN this historie written by Matthewe, Marke, Luke, and Iohn, the Spirit of God so gouerned their hearts, that althogh they were foure in nōber, yet in effect and purpose they so consent, as thogh the whole had bene composed by any one of them. And albeit in stile and maner of writing they be diuers, and sometime one writeth more largely that which the other doeth abbridge: neuertheles in matter and argument they all tende to one end: which is, to publish to the worlde the fauour of God towarde mankinde through Christ Iesus, whome the Father hathe giuen as a pledge of his mercie & loue. And for this cause they intitle their storie, Gospel, which signifieth good tidings, for asmuche as God hathe performed in dede that which the fathers hoped for. So that hereby we are admonished to forsake the worlde, and the vanities thereof, and with moste affectioned hearts embrace this incomparable treasure frely offred vnto vs: for there is no ioye nor consolacion, no peace nor quietnes, no felicitie nor saluacion, but in Iesus Christ, who is the very substance of this Gospel, and in whome all the promises are yea, and amen. And therefore vnder this worde is conteined the whole Newe testament: but communely we vse this name for the historie, which the foure Euangelists write, conteining Christs coming in the flesh, his death and resurrection, which is the perfite summe of our saluation. Matthewe, Marke, and Luke are more copious in describing his life and death: but Iohn more laboureth to set forthe his doctrine, wherein bothe Christs office, and also the vertue of his death and resurrection more fully appeare: for without this, to knowe that Christ was borne, dead & risen againe, shulde nothing profite vs. The which thing notwithstanding that the thre first touche partely, as he also sometime intermedleth the historical narration, yet Iohn chiefly is occupied herein. And therefore as a moste learned interpreter writeth, they descride, as it were, the bodie, and Iohn setteth before our eyes the soule. Wherefore the same aptely termeth the Gospel writ by Iohn, the keye which openeth the dore to the vnderstanding of the others: for whosoeuer doeth knowe the office, vertue and power of Christ, shal reade that which is written of the Sonne of God come to be the redemer of the worlde, with moste proffit. Now as concerning the writers of this historie, it is euident that Matthewe was a Publicane or custome gatherer, and was thence chosen of Christ to be an Apostle. Marke is thoght to haue bene Peters disciple, and to haue planted the first Church at Alexandria, where he dyed the eight yere of the reigne of Nero. Luke was a phisition of Antiochia and became Pauls disciple, and fellowe in all his traueils: he liued foure score and foure yeres, and was buryed at Constantinople. Iohn was that Apostle whome the Lord loued, the sonne of Zebedeus, and brother of Iames: he dyed thre score yeres after Christ, and was buryed nere to the Citie of Ephesus.

CHAP. I.

1 The genealogie of Christ, that is, the Messias promised to the fathers, 18 Who was conceiued by the holy Gost, and borne of the virgine Marie, when she was betrouthed vnto Ioseph. 20 The Angel satisfieth Iosephes minde. 21 Why he is called Iesus, and wherefore Emmanuel.

1 THe [c]boke of the generaciō of IESVS CHRIST
the [d]sonne of [e]Dauid, the
sonne of Abraham.
2 *Abrahā begate Isaac.
*And Isaac begate Iacob. And *Iacob begate Iudas and his brethren.
3 *And Iudas begate Phares, and Zara [f]of
Thamar. And *Phares begate Esrom. And
Esrom begate Aram.
4 And Aram begate Aminadab. And Aminadab begate Naasson. And Naasson begate Salmon.
5 And Salmon begate Booz of [g]Rachab.
And *Booz begate Obed of Ruth. And
Obed begate Iesse.
6 And *Iesse begate Dauid the King. And
*Dauid the King begate Solomon of her
that was *the wife* of Vrias.
7 And *Solomon begate Roboam. And Roboam begate Abia. And Abia begate Asa.
8 And Asa begate Iosaphat. And Iosaphat
begate Ioram. And Ioram begate Ozias.
9 And Ozias begate [h]Ioatham. And Ioatham begate Achaz. And Achaz begate
Ezecias.
10 And *Ezecias begate Manasses. And
Manasses begate Amon. And Amon begate Iosias.
11 And *Iosias begate Iacim. And Iacim begate Iechonias & his brethren about the
time they were caryed away to Babylon.
12 And after they were caryed away into
Babylon, *Iechonias begate [i]Salathiel.
*And Salathiel begate Zorobabel.

Luk.3,23.
c This is the rehearsal of the progenie, whereof Iesus Christ is sprong according to the flesh.
d Is called, for that he came of the stocke of Dauid.
e These two are first rehearsed, because Christ was especially promised to come of them and their sede, and therefore Christ commonly was called the sonne of Dauid, because the promes was more euidently confirmed vnto him. *Gen.21,2. *Gen.25,24. *Gen.29,35. *Gen.38,27.
f By incestuous adulterie, the which shame setteth forthe his great humilitie, who made him self of no reputation, but became a seruant for our sakes, yea, a worme and no man, the reproche of men, and contempt of the people, and at length suffred the accursed death of the crosse. *1.Chron.2,5. Ruth 4,18.

g Rachab and Ruth, being Gentiles, signifie that Christ came not onely of ye Iewes, and for them, but also of ye Gentiles, and for their saluation.
Ruth 4,18.
1.Sam.16,1. & 17,12.
2.Sam.12,24.
1.King.11,43
1.chro.3,10.
h He hathe omitted thre Kings, Ioas, Amasia, Azaria, abbridgig the nomber to make the times fourtene generations.
2.King.20,21 & 21,18.
1.chro.3,15.
2.King.23,34.& 24,1.
2.chro.36,4.
2.King.24,6.
2.chro.36,9.
i After the captiuitie, the title royal was appointed vnto him: so that notwithstanding that they were as sclaues for the space of seuentie yeres, yet by the prouidence of God the gouernemēt remained in the familie of Dauid, where it continued til the coming of Christ. *1.Chro.3,17. ezra 3,2 & 5,2.

AA. ii.

20 Y mirando Areuna, vido àl Rey y à
ſus ſieruos que paſſauan a el: Y ſaliendo A-
reuna inclinoſe delante del Rey hazia
tierra.
21 Y dixo Areuna: Porque viene mi ſeñor el Rey à ſu ſieruo? y Dauid reſpondió:
para comprar deti eſta era para edificar *en*
ella altar à Iehoua, y que la mortádad ceſſe
del pueblo.
22 Y Areuna dixo à Dauid: Tome y ſacri-
fique mi ſeñor el Rey loque bien le pare-
ciere. He aqui bueyes para el holocauſto, y
trillos, y otros adereços de bueyes para
leña,
23 †Todo lo da el rey Areuna àl Rey. Y † Son pala-
dixo Areuna àl Rey: Iehoua tu Dios te ſea bras del
propicio. miſmo A-
24 Y el Rey dixo à Areuna: No, ſino por reuna que
precio télo compraré: porque no offrece- babla de ſi
ré à Iehoua mi Dios holocauſtos por nada. en tercera
Entonces Dauid compró la era y los bue- perſona.
yes por cincuenta ſiclos de plata. 1. Chron. 21,
25 Y edificó alli Dauid *vn* altar à Iehoua, 23.
y ſacrificó holocauſtos, y pacificos, y Iehoua ſe aplacó con la tierra, y ceſſó la plaga de
Iſrael.

FIN DEL SEGVNDO LIBRO
de Samuel.

El tercero libro de los reyes, y primero Segun los Ebreos.

CAPIT. I.

Refriado ya Dauid por la vejez, ſus criados le proueen de vna donzella virgen Abiſag, que duerma conél, y lo caliente y regâle con toda limpieza. II. Eſtando Adonias adereçando de leuantarſe con el Reyno es dado auiſo à Dauid, el qual haze luego proclamar Rey a Salomõ con toda ſolennidad à la peticion de Berſabee ſu madre y de Nathã propheta. III. Oyendolo Adonias ſe retrâe àl altar de miedo de Salomon, mas el lo perdona, y lo haze venir delante de ſi.

Omo el rey Dauid *ſe*
hizo viejo, y entrado
endias, cubrianlo de
veſtidos, mas no ſe
callentaua.
2 Y dixeron le ſus
ſieruos, Buſqué à mi
ſeñor el Rey vna mo-
ça virgen, que eſté delante del Rey, y lo ca-
a Heb. en ſu ſeno. liente, y duerma[a] à ſu lado, y callentará à
nueſtro ſeñor el Rey.
3 Y buſcaron vna moça hermoſa por todo
b Ioſ. 19, 18. el termino de Iſrael, y hallârõ à Abiſag [b] Su-
namita, y truxeronla àl Rey.
4 Y la moça *era* muy hermoſa, la qual ca-
lentaua àl Rey, y le ſeruia: mas el Rey nunca la conoció.
II. 5 ¶ Entonces Adonias hijo de Agith ſe
leuantó diziendo, Yo reynaré. Y hizoſe ha-
zer carros y gente de cauallo, y cincuenta
varones [c] que corrieſſen delante deel. c Para ſu
6 Y ſu padre [d] nunca lo entriſteció en to- guarda.
dos ſus dias para dezirle: Porque hazes an- d Nunca lo
ſi? Y tambien eſte era de hermoſo parecer: caſtigó de
y auialo engendrado deſpues de Abſalom. coſa q̃ mal
7 [e] Y tenia tratos con Ioab hijo de Sarui- hizieſſe.
as, y cõ Abiathar ſacerdote, los quales ayu- e Heb. Y ha-
dauan à Adonias. bló cõ Ioab &c.
8 Mas Sadoc ſacerdote, y Banaias hijo de
Ioiada, y Nathan propheta, y Semei, y Rei,
y todos los grandes de Dauid no ſeguian à
Adonias.
9 Y matando Adonias ouejas y vacas, y
animales engordados junto à la peña de Zo-
heleth, que *eſtá* cerca de la fuente de Rogel,
cõbidó a todos ſus hermanos los hijos del
Rey, y à todos los varones de Iuda ſieruos
del Rey.
10 Mas à Nathan propheta, ni à Banaias,
ni à los grandes, ni à Salomon ſu hermano,
no combidó.
11 Y habló Nathan à Berſabee madre de
Salomõ diziendo: No has oydo que [f] rey- f Es alçado
na Adonias hijo de Agith, ſin ſaberlo nueſ- por rey.
tro ſeñor Dauid?
12 Ven pues aora, y toma mi conſejo, pa-
raque guardes tu vida, y la vida de tu hijo
Salomon.

V iij

33 THE FIRST COMPLETE SPANISH VERSION, 1569

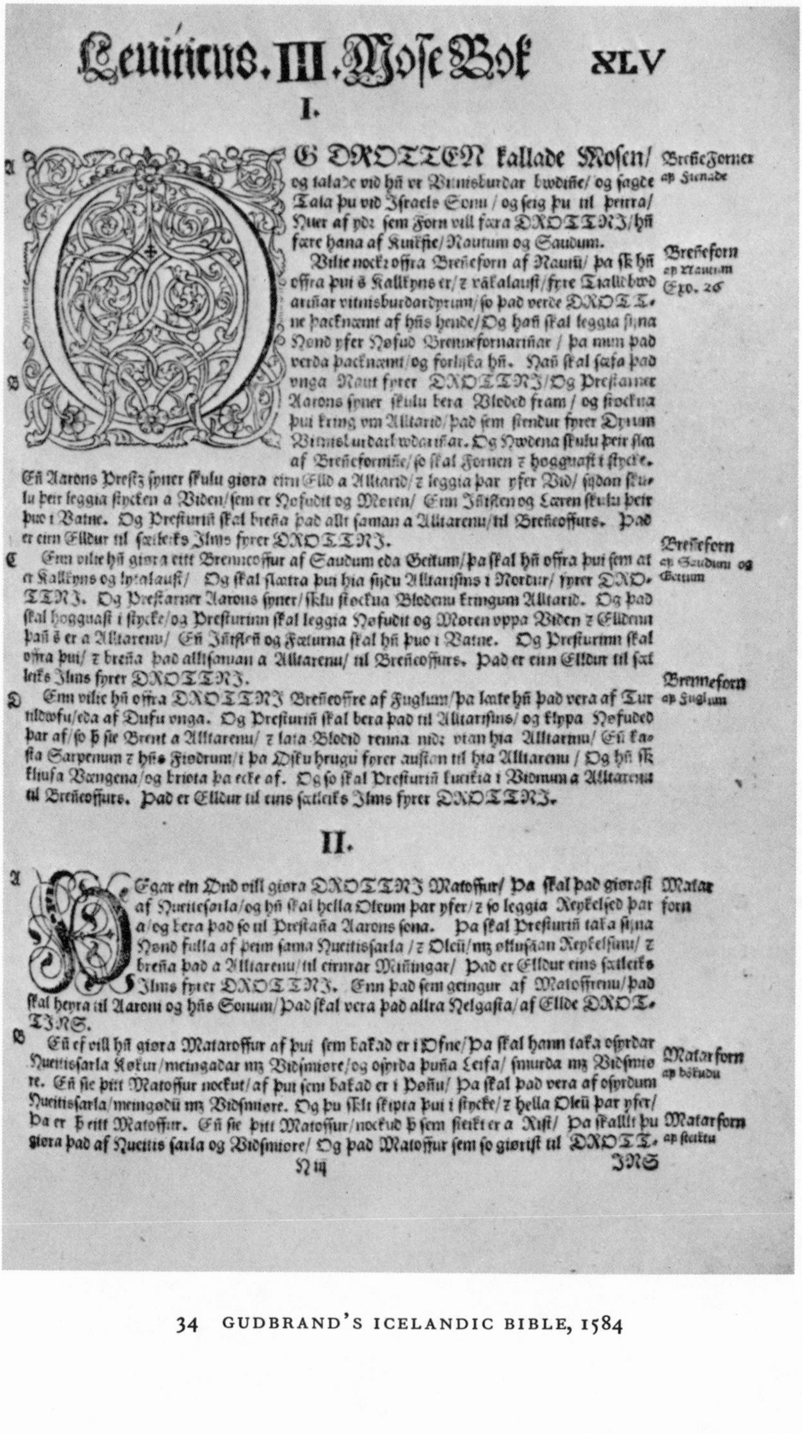

Leuiticus. III. Mose Bok XLV

I.

A OG DROTTEN kallade Mosen/ BrēñeFornet
og talade vid hn̄ vr Vitnisburdar budinne/ og sagde ap Jtenade
Tala þu vid Jsraels Sonu / og seig þu til þeirra/
Huer af ydr sem Forn vill færa DROTTNI/ hn̄
fære hana af Kuikfie/ Nautum og Saudum.
Vilie nockr offra Brēñeforn af Nautū/ þa sk hn̄ Brēñeforn
offra þui ꝫ Kallkyns er/ ⁊ vākalaust/ fyrer Tiallbud ap Nautum
arinnar vitnisburdardyrum/ so þad verde DROTT- Exo. 26
ne þacknæmt af hn̄s hende/ Og hañ skal leggia sijna
Hond yfer Hofud Brenneforarinnar / þa mun þad
verda þacknæmt/ og forlijka hn̄. Hañ skal slatra þad
B vnga Naut fyrer DROTTNI/ Og Prestarner
Aarons syner skulu bera Blodid fram / og stockua
þui kring vm Alltarid/ þad sem stendur fyrer Dyrum
Vitnisburdarbudarinnar. Og Hudena skulu þeir flea
af Brēñeforninne/ so skal Fornen ⁊ hogguast i stycke.
Eñ Aarons Prestz syner skulu giora eirn Elld a Alltarid/ ⁊ leggia þar yfer Vid/ sijdan skulu þeir leggia stycken a Viden/ sem er Hofudit og Moren/ Enn Jñyflen og Læren skulu þeir
þuo i Vatne. Og Presturiñ skal brēña þad allt saman a Alltarenu/ til Brēñeoffurs. Þad
er eirn Elldur til sætleiks Ilms fyrer DROTTNI. Brēñeforn
C Enn vilie hn̄ giora eitt Brenneoffur af Saudum eda Geitum/ þa skal hn̄ offra þui sem at ap Saudum og
er Kallkyns og lytalaust/ Og skal slatra þui hia sijdu Alltarisins i Nordur/ fyrer DRO- Geitum
TTNI. Og Prestarner Aarons syner/ skulu stockua Blodenu kringum Alltarid. Og þad
skal hogguast i stycke/ og Presturinn skal leggia Hofudit og Moren vppa Viden ⁊ Elldenn
þañ ꝫ er a Alltarenu/ Eñ Jñyflen og Fæturna skal hn̄ þuo i Vatne. Og Presturinn skal
offra þui/ ⁊ brēña þad allt saman a Alltarenu/ til Brēñeoffurs. Þad er eirn Elldur til sætleiks Ilms fyrer DROTTNI. Brenneforn
D Enn vilie hn̄ offra DROTTNI Brēñeoffre af Fuglum/ þa late hn̄ þad vera af Tur ap Fuglum
tildwfu/ eda af Dufu vnga. Og Presturiñ skal bera þad til Alltarisins/ og klypa Hofuded
þar af/ so þ sie Brent a Alltarenu/ ⁊ lata Blodid renna nidr vtan hia Alltarenu/ Eñ ka-
sta Sarpenum ⁊ hn̄s Fiodrum/ i þa Osku hrugu fyrer austan til hia Alltarenu / Og hn̄ sk
kliufa Vængena/ og briota þa ecke af. Og so skal Presturiñ kueikia i Vidnum a Alltarenu
til Brēñeoffurs. Þad er Elldur til eins sætleiks Ilms fyrer DROTTNI.

II.

A NEgar ein Ond vill giora DROTTNI Matoffur/ Þa skal þad giorast Matar
af Hueitiesarla/ og hn̄ skal hella Oleum þar yfer/ ⁊ so leggia Reykelsed þar forn
a/ og bera þad so til Prestaña Aarons sona. Þa skal Presturiñ taka sijna
Hond fulla af þeim sama Hueitissarla / ⁊ Oleū/ m̄ ollu saman Reykelsinu/ ⁊
brēña þad a Alltarenu/ til eirnrar Miñingar/ Þad er Elldur eins sætleiks
Ilms fyrer DROTTNI. Enn þad sem geingur af Matoffrenu/ þad
skal heyra til Aaron og hn̄s Sonum/ Þad skal vera þad allra Helgasta/ af Ellde DROT-
TINS.
B Eñ ef vill hn̄ giora Mataroffur af þui sem bakad er i Ofne/ Þa skal hann taka osyrdar
Hueitissarla Kokur/ meingadar m̄ Vidsmiore/ og osyrda þuña Leifa/ smurda m̄ Vidsmio- Matarforn
re. Eñ sie þitt Matoffur nockut/ af þui sem bakad er i Poñu/ Þa skal þad vera af osyrdum ap bökudu
Hueitissarla/ meingodū m̄ Vidsmiore. Og þu skalt skipta þui i stycke/ ⁊ hella Oleū þar yfer/
Þa er þ eitt Matoffur. Eñ sie þitt Matoffur/ nockud þ sem steikt er a Rist/ Þa skallt þu Matarforn
giora þad af Hueitis sarla og Vidsmiore/ Og þad Matoffur sem so giorist til DROTT- ap steiktu
H iij INS

34 GUDBRAND'S ICELANDIC BIBLE, 1584

tes cum illis. * Et confeſtim omnis popu- 13
lus videns Ieſum, ſtupefactus eſt, & expaue-
runt, & accurrentes ſalutabant eum. * Et 14
interrogauit eos: Quid inter vos conquiri-
tis? * Et reſpondens vnus de turba, dixit: 15
Magiſter attuli filium meum ad te habẽtem
ſpiritum mutum: qui vbicumque eum ap-
prehenderit, allidit illum, & ſpumat, & ſtri-
det dentibus, & areſcit: & dixi diſcipulis tuis
vt eijcerent illum, & non potuerunt. * Qui 16
reſpondens eis, dixit: O generatio incredu-
la, quamdiu apud vos ero? quamdiu vos pa-
tiar? afferte illum ad me. * Et attulerunt eũ. 17
Et cum vidiſſet eum, ſtatim ſpiritus contur-
bauit illum: & eliſus in terram, volutaba-
tur ſpumans. * Et interrogauit patrẽ eius: 18
Quantum temporis eſt ex quo ei hoc acci-
dit? Et ille ait: * Ab infantia: & frequẽter 19
eum in ignem, & in aquas miſit vt eum per-
deret. ſed ſi quid potes, adiuua nos, miſer-
tus noſtri. * Ieſus autem ait illi: Si potes cre- 20
dere, omnia poſſibilia ſunt credenti. * Et cõ- 21
tinuo exclamans pater pueri, cum lacrymis
aiebat: Credo Domine: adiuua incredulita-
tem meam. * Et cum videret Ieſus concur- 22
rentem turbam, comminatus eſt ſpiritui im-
mundo, dicens illi: Surde, & mute ſpiritus,
ego præcipio tibi, exi ab eo: & amplius ne
introeas in eũ. * Et exclamans, & multum 23
diſcerpens eum, exijt ab eo, & factus eſt ſicut
mortuus ita vt multi dicerẽt: Quia mortuus
eſt. * Ieſus autem tenens manum eius, eleua- 24
uit eum, & ſurrexit. * Et cũ introiſſet in do- 25
mũ, diſcipuli eius ſecreto interrogabant eũ:
Quare nos non potuimus eijcere eum? * Et 26
dixit illis: Hoc genus in nullo poteſt exire,
niſi in oratione, & ieiunio. * Et inde profecti 27
prætergrediebantur Galilæam: nec volebat
quemquam ſcire. * Docebat autem diſcipu- 28
los ſuos, & dicebat illis: Quoniam filius ho-
minis tradetur in manus hominum, & oc-
cident eũ, & occiſus tertia die reſurget. * At 29
illi ignorabant verbum: & timebant inter-
rogare eum. * Et venerunt Capharnaum. 30
Qui cũ domi eſſent, interrogabat eos: Quid
in via tractabatis? * At illi tacebant. ſiquidem 31
in via inter ſe diſputauerant quis eorum ma-
32 ior eſſet. * Et reſidens vocauit duodecim, &
ait illis: Si quis vult primus eſſe, erit omnium
33 nouiſſimus, & omnium miniſter. * Et ac-
cipiens puerum, ſtatuit eum in medio eorũ:
quem cum complexus eſſet, ait illis: Quiſquis
vnum ex huiuſmodi pueris receperit in nomine meo, me recipit: & quicumque me ſu-
ſceperit, non me ſuſcipit, ſed eum, qui miſit
34 me. * Reſpondit illi Ioannes, dicens: Magiſter vidimus quemdam in nomine tuo eij-
cientem dæmonia, qui non ſequitur nos, &
35 prohibuimus eum. * Ieſus autem ait: Nolite prohibere eum. nemo eſt enim, qui faciat virtutem in nomine meo, & poſſit cito
male loqui de me. qui enim non eſt aduer-
36 ſum vos, pro vobis eſt. * Quiſquis enim
potum dederit vobis calicem aquæ frigidæ
in nomine meo, quia Chriſti eſtis: amen di-
37 co vobis, non perdet mercedem ſuam. * Et
quiſquis ſcandalizauerit vnum ex his puſillis
credentibus in me: bonum eſt ei magis ſi
circumdaretur mola aſinaria collo eius, &
38 in mare mitteretur. * Et ſi ſcandalizauerit
te manus tua, abſcinde illam: bonum eſt
tibi debilem introire in vitam, quàm duas
manus habentem ire in gehennam, in ignẽ
inextinguibilem: vbi vermis eorum non
39 moritur, & ignis non extinguitur. * Et ſi
pes tuus te ſcandalizat, amputa illum: bonum eſt tibi claudum introire in vitã æter-
nam, quàm duos pedes habentem mitti in
gehennam ignis inextinguibilis: vbi vermis
eorum non moritur, & ignis non extingui-
40 tur. * Quòd ſi oculus tuus ſcandalizat te, eij-
ce eum: bonum eſt tibi luſcum introire in
regnum Dei, quàm duos oculos habentem
mitti in gehennam ignis: vbi vermis eorum
41 non moritur, & ignis nõ extinguitur. * Omnis enim igne ſalietur: & omnis victima ſale
42 ſalietur. * Bonum eſt ſal: quòd ſi ſal inſul-
ſum fuerit: in quo illud condietis? Habete
in vobis ſal, & pacem habete inter vos.

CAP. X.

1 ET INDE exurgens venit in fines
Iudææ vltra Iordanem: & conueniunt
iterum turbæ ad eum: & ſicut conſueue-
Kkkk 2 rat,

35 THE SIXTINE BIBLE CORRECTED, 1590

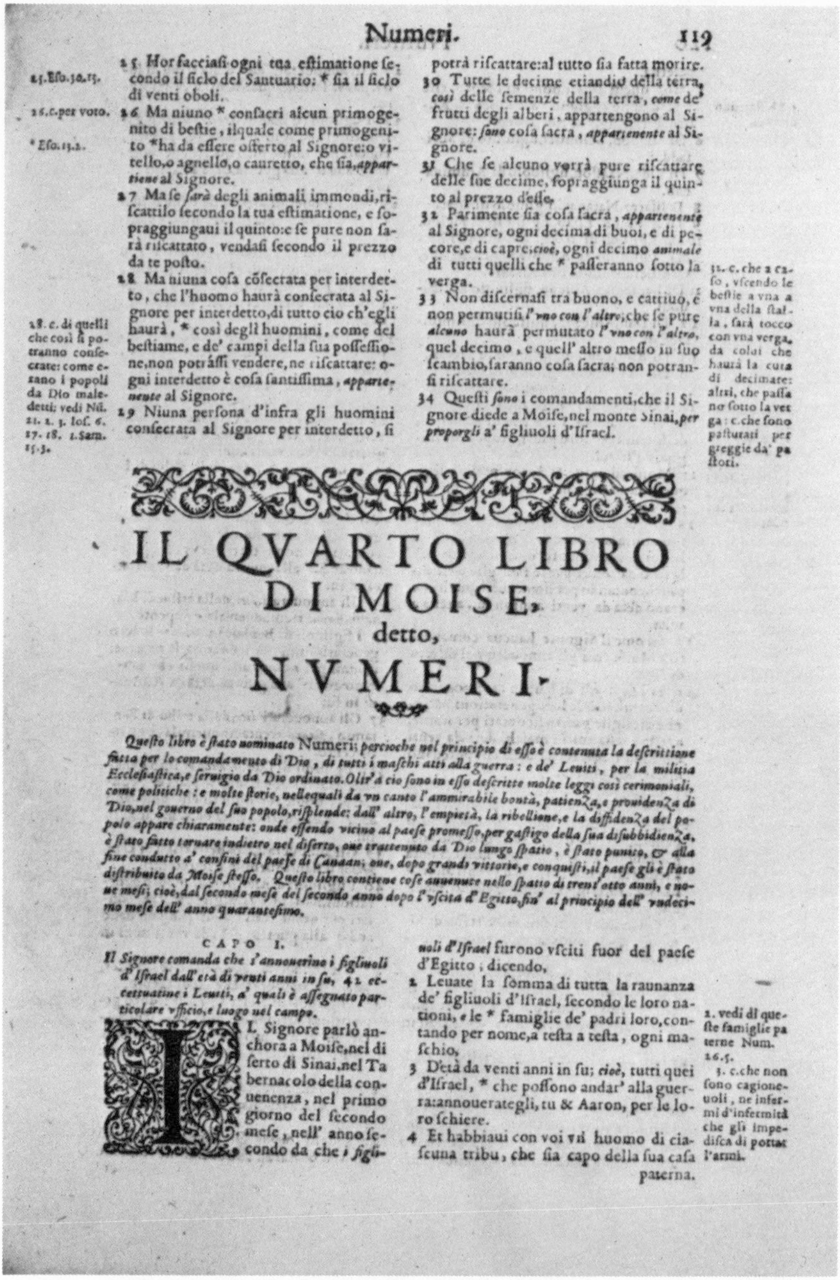

Numeri. 119

25 Hor facciasi ogni tua estimatione secondo il siclo del Santuario: * sia il siclo
di venti oboli.
26 Ma niuno * consacri alcun primogenito di bestie, ilquale come primogenito *ha da essere offerto al Signore: o vi-
tello, o agnello, o cauretto, che sia, *appar-*
tiene al Signore.
27 Ma se *sarà* degli animali immondi, ri-
scattilo secondo la tua estimatione, e so-
praggiungaui il quinto: e se pure non sarà riscattato, vendasi secondo il prezzo
da te posto.
28 Ma niuna cosa cõsecrata per interdetto, che l'huomo haurà consecrata al Signore per interdetto, di tutto cio ch'egli
haurà, * così degli huomini, come del
bestiame, e de' campi della sua possessio-
ne, non potrassi vendere, ne riscattare: o-
gni interdetto è cosa santissima, *apparte-*
nente al Signore.
29 Niuna persona d'infra gli huomini
consecrata al Signore per interdetto, si
potrà riscattare: al tutto sia fatta morire.
30 Tutte le decime etiandio della terra,
così delle semenze della terra, *come* de'
frutti degli alberi, appartengono al Signore: *sono* cosa sacra, *appartenente* al Signore.
31 Che se alcuno vorrà pure riscattare
delle sue decime, sopraggiunga il quinto al prezzo d'esse.
32 Parimente sia cosa sacra, *appartenente*
al Signore, ogni decima di buoi, e di pecore, e di capre, *cioè*, ogni decimo *animale*
di tutti quelli che * passeranno sotto la
verga.
33 Non discernasi tra buono, e cattiuo, e
non permutisi *l'vno con l'altro*; che se pure
alcuno haurà permutato *l'vno con l'altro*,
quel decimo, e quell' altro messo in suo
scambio, saranno cosa sacra; non potran-
si riscattare.
34 Questi *sono* i comandamenti, che il Signore diede a Moise, nel monte Sinai, *per*
proporgli a' figliuoli d'Israel.

25. Eso. 30. 13.
26. c. per voto.
* Eso. 13. 2.
28. c. di quelli che così si potranno consecrate: come erano i popoli da Dio maledetti: vedi Nû. 21. 2. 3. Ios. 6. 17. 18. 1. Sam. 15. 3.
32. c. che a caso, vscendo le bestie a vna a vna della stalla, sarà tocco con vna verga, da colui che haurà la cura di decimare: altri, che passano sotto la verga: c. che sono pasturati per greggie da' pastori.

IL QVARTO LIBRO DI MOISE, detto, NVMERI.

Questo libro è stato nominato Numeri: *percioche nel principio di esso è contenuta la descrittione fatta per lo comandamento di Dio, di tutti i maschi atti alla guerra: e de' Leuiti, per la militia Ecclesiastica, e seruigio da Dio ordinato. Oltr'a cio sono in esso descritte molte leggi così cerimoniali, come politiche: e molte storie, nellequali da vn canto l'ammirabile bontà, patienza, e prouidenza di Dio, nel gouerno del suo popolo, risplende: dall' altro, l'empietà, la ribellione, e la diffidenza del popolo appare chiaramente: onde essendo vicino al paese promesso, per gastigo della sua disubbidienza, è stato fatto tornare indietro nel diserto, oue trattenuto da Dio lungo spatio, è stato punito, & alla fine condutto a' confini del paese di Canaan; oue, dopo grandi vittorie, e conquisti, il paese gli è stato distribuito da Moise stesso. Questo libro contiene cose auuenute nello spatio di trent'otto anni, e noue mesi; cioè, dal secondo mese del secondo anno dopo l'vscita d'Egitto, fin' al principio dell' vndecimo mese dell' anno quarantesimo.*

CAPO I.

Il Signore comanda che s'annouerino i figliuoli d'Israel dall'età di venti anni in su, 42 eccettuatine i Leuiti, a' quali è assegnato particolare vfficio, e luogo nel campo.

IL Signore parlò an-
chora a Moise, nel di
serto di Sinai, nel Ta
bernacolo della con-
uenenza, nel primo
giorno del secondo
mese, nell' anno se-
condo da che i *figli-*
uoli d'Israel furono vsciti fuor del paese
d'Egitto; dicendo,
2 Leuate la somma di tutta la raunanza
de' figliuoli d'Israel, secondo le loro na-
tioni, *e* le * famiglie de' padri loro, con-
tando per nome, a testa a testa, ogni ma-
schio,
3 D'età da venti anni in su; *cioè*, tutti quei
d'Israel, * che possono andar' alla guerra: annouerategli, tu & Aaron, per le loro schiere.
4 Et habbiaui con voi vn huomo di cia-
scuna tribu, che sia capo della sua casa
paterna.

2. vedi di queste famiglie paterne Num. 26. 5.
3. c. che non sono cagioneuoli, ne infermi d'infermità che gli impedisca di portar l'armi.

 DIODATI'S VERSION, 1607

THE HOLY GOSPEL OF IESVS CHRIST ACCORDING TO IOHN.

CHAP. I.

The 1. parte: THE ACTES of Chriſt before his manifeſtation, whiles Iohn Baptiſt was yet baptizing.

The preface of the Euangeliſt, commending Chriſt (as being God the Sonne incarnate) to the Gentils, and ſetting out the blindnes of the Ievves in not receiuing him. 19 Then, the teſtimonies of Iohn Baptiſt, firſt to the ſolemne legacie of the Ievves: 29 ſecondly, vvhen he ſavv IESVS come to him: 35 thirdly, to his ovvne Diſciples alſo, putting them ouer from him ſelf to IESVS. Vvho made it plainer to them that he is Chriſt, 40 and ſo began he alſo to haue Diſciples.

The Goſpel at the third Maſſe vpō Chriſtmas day. And euery day at the end of Maſſe.

IN THE beginning " vvas the WORD, 1
and the WORD vvas " vvith God, and
" God vvas the WORD. † This vvas in 2
the beginning vvith God. † Al things 3
vvere made " by him: and vvithout him
vvas made ˋnothing. That vvhich vvas
made', † in him vvas life, and the life vvas 4
the light of men: † and the light ſhineth in darkeneſſe, and 5
the darkeneſſe did not comprehend it. † There vvas a man 6
ſent from God, vvhoſe name vvas Iohn. † This man came 7
for teſtimonie: to giue teſtimonie of the light, that al might
beleeue through him. † He vvas not the light, but to giue 8
teſtimonie of the light. † It vvas the true light, vvhich ligh- 9
teneth euery man that commeth into this vvorld. † He vvas 10
in the vvorld, and the vvorld vvas made by him, and the
vvorld knevv him not. † He came into his ovvne, and his 11
ovvne receiued him not. † But as many as receiued him, " he 12
gaue them povver to be made the ſonnes of God, to thoſe
that beleeue in his name. † Vvho, not of bloud, nor of the 13
vvil of fleſh, nor of the vvil of man, but of God are borne.
† AND " THE VVORD VVAS MADE FLESH, 14
and dvvelt in vs (and vve ſavv the glorie of him, glorie as it
vvere of the only-begotten of the Father) ful of grace and
veritie.

ˋ*nothing that was made.*

ET VERBVM CARO FACTVM EST.

37 THE 'DOUAY' NEW TESTAMENT, 1609

THE GOSPEL ACCORDING to S. Matthew.

CHAP. I.

1 The genealogie of Christ from Abraham to Ioseph. 18 Hee was conceiued by the holy Ghost, and borne of the Virgin Mary when she was espoused to Ioseph. 19 The Angel satisfieth the misdeeming thoughts of Ioseph, and interpreteth the names of Christ.

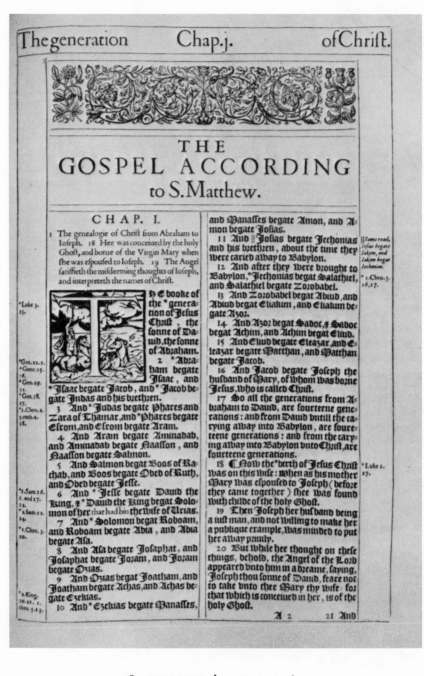

THE booke of
the *genera-
tion of Iesus
Christ, the
sonne of Da-
uid, the sonne
of Abraham.
2 *Abra-
ham begate
Isaac, and
*Isaac begate Iacob, and *Iacob be-
gate Iudas and his brethren.
3 And *Iudas begate Phares and
Zara of Thamar, and *Phares begate
Esrom, and Esrom begate Aram.
4 And Aram begate Aminadab,
and Aminadab begate Naasson, and
Naasson begate Salmon.
5 And Salmon begat Booz of Rachab, and Booz begate Obed of Ruth,
and Obed begate Iesse.
6 And *Iesse begate Dauid the
King, & *Dauid the King begat Solomon of her that had bin the wife of Urias.
7 And *Solomon begat Roboam,
and Roboam begate Abia, and Abia
begate Asa.
8 And Asa begate Iosaphat, and
Iosaphat begate Ioram, and Ioram
begate Ozias.
9 And Ozias begat Ioatham, and
Ioatham begate Achas, and Achas begate Ezekias.
10 And *Ezekias begate Manasses,
and Manasses begate Amon, and A-
mon begate Iosias.
11 And ‖Iosias begate Iechonias
and his brethren, about the time they
were caried away to Babylon.
12 And after they were brought to
Babylon, *Iechonias begat Salathiel,
and Salathiel begate Zorobabel.
13 And Zorobabel begat Abiud, and
Abiud begat Eliakim, and Eliakim begate Azor.
14 And Azor begat Sadoc, & Sadoc
begat Achim, and Achim begat Eliud.
15 And Eliud begate Eleazar, and E-
leazar begate Matthan, and Matthan
begate Iacob.
16 And Iacob begate Ioseph the
husband of Mary, of whom was borne
Iesus, who is called Christ.
17 So all the generations from A-
braham to Dauid, are fourteene generations: and from Dauid vntill the ca-
rying away into Babylon, are foure-
teene generations: and from the cary-
ing away into Babylon vnto Christ, are
fourteene generations.
18 ¶ Now the *birth of Iesus Christ
was on this wise: When as his mother
Mary was espoused to Ioseph (before
they came together) shee was found
with childe of the holy Ghost.
19 Then Ioseph her husband being
a iust man, and not willing to make her
a publique example, was minded to put
her away priuily.
20 But while hee thought on these
things, behold, the Angel of the Lord
appeared vnto him in a dreame, saying,
Ioseph thou sonne of Dauid, feare not
to take vnto thee Mary thy wife: for
that which is conceiued in her, is of the
holy Ghost.

*Luke 3. 23.
*Gen. 21. 2. *Gene. 25. 26. *Gen. 29. 35. *Gen. 38. 27. *1. Chro. 2. 5. ruth. 4. 18.
*1. Sam. 16. 1. and 17. 12. *2. Sam. 12. 24. *1. Chro. 3. 10.
*2. King. 20. 21. 1. chro. 3. 13.
‖Some read, Iosias begate Iakim, and Iakim begat Iechonias.
*1. Chro. 3. 16, 17.
*Luke 1. 27.

A 2 21 And

39 A PAGE OF THE LONDON POLYGLOT, 1655–7

Kesteoux muttaok Chap. 1. nequttatahshikqunne

NEGONNE OOSUKKUHWHONK *MOSES*

Ne asowetamuk

GENESIS

CHAP. I.

1 *The creation of heaven and earth &c.* 26 *Of man in the image of God,* 29 *The appointment of food.*

a Psal. 33.6. & 136. 5. Acts 14.15. & 17. 24. Heb. 11. 3. W Eske kutchissik a ayum Gon Kesuk & Ohke.
2 Kah Ohke mô-
matta kuhkenaaau-
nennkquttinnoo kah
monteagunninno, &
pohkenum woskeche
moonôi, kah wun
Nashauanittoomoh-
God popomshau wos-
keche nippekontu.
b 2 Cor. 5.6. 3 Onk noowau God, b Wequaiaj, kah
mô wequai.
4 Kah wunnaumun God wequai ne en
wunnegen: Kah wutchadchaube ponumun
God nôeu wequai kah nôeu pohkenum:
5 Kah wutussowetamun God wequai Kesukod, kah pohkenum wutussowetamun
Nukon: kah mô wannonkooouk kah mô
mohtompog negoone kesukod
6 Kah noowau God c Sepakehtamoudj
c Psal. 136.5. Jer. 10. 12. & 51.15. nôeu nippekontu, kah chadchapemooudj na-
shauweit nippe wutch nippekontu.
7 Kah ayimup God sepakehtamóonk, kah
wutchadchabeponumunnap nashaueu nippe
agwu, uttiyeu agwu sepakehtamóonk, kah
nashaueu nippekontu uttiyeu ongkouwe se-
pakehtamôonk, kah mónkô n nih.
8 Kah wuttissoweetamun God d sepakeh-
d Jer. 51. 15. tamóonk Kesukquash, kah mô wunnonkooook, kah mô mohtompog nahohtoeu kesukok
9 Kah noowau God moémooidj nippe ut
agwu kesukquash pasukqunnu, kah pah-
e Psal. 33.7. & 136.5 Job 38.8. kemoidj nanabpeu, kah mónkó n nih.
10 Kah wuttissoweetamun God nanabpi,
Ohke, kah moémoo nippe wuttissoweetamun
Kehtoh & wunnaumun God ne en wunnegen
11 Kah noowau God drannékej ohke moskeht, mosketh skannémunûook skannémunash
kah meechummué mehtugquash meechum-
muok meechummuonk nishnoh pasuk neane wuttinnussuonk, ubbuhkuminuook ut
woskeche ohke, kah mónkó n nih
12 Kah ohke drannegeuup moskeht, kah
mosket skannemunnêook skannemanash, nish
noh pasuk neane wuttinnussuonk, kah mah-
tug meechummuook, ubbubkumingoook
wuhhogkat nish noh pasuk neane wuttinnussuonk, kah wunnaumun God ne en wunnegen
13 Kah mo wunnonkooook, kah mo mohtompog shwekesukod
14 Kah noowau God, f Wequanantega-
nuohettitch ut wussepakehtamoonganit ke- f Deut. 4.19.
sukquash kah pohshehettich ut nashauwe ke- Psal.
sukod, kah ut nashauwe nukkonut, kah kuk- 136.7
kinneasuonganuhettich, kah uttoocheyeu-
hettich, kah kesukodtuoowuhhettich, kah
kodtummoowuhhettich.
15 Kah n nag wequanantéganwóhettich
ut sepaketamoowongane kesukqut wequa-
suméhettich ohke, onk mo n nih.
16 Kah ayum God neetunash missiyeuash
wequanantéganash, wequananteg mohsag na-
nanumumoo kesukod, wequananteg peasik
nananumoomoo nukon, kah anogqsog
17 Kah uttponuh God wussepakehtamoo-
ongauit kesukquash, woh wequasumwog
ohke.
18 Onk woh g wunnananumunneau kesuk-
od kah nukkon, kah pohshemoo nashaueu g Jer. 31.35.
wequai, kah nashaueu pohkenum, kah wunnaumun God ne en wunnegen
19 Kah mô wunnonkoouk kah mô mohtompog yaou-quinukok
20 Kah noowau God, Moonahettich nippekontu pomantamwae pomomotcheg, kah
puppinshaussog pumunahettich ongkouwe
ohket woskeche wussepakehtamoonganit
kesukquash.
21 Kah kezheau God matikkenunutcheh
Pootâopoh, kah nishnoh pomantamoe ôtas
noh pompâmayit uttiyeug moonacheg nip-
pekóntu, nishnoh pasuk neane wuttinnussuonk, kah nishnoh ounnuppohwhunin puppin-
shaash, nishnoh pasuk neane wuttinnussuonk,
kah wunnaumun God ne en wunnegan.
22 Kah oonanumoh nahhog God noowau, h Gen. 8.17. & 9.1.
Mshéneetuónittegk, h kah muttaanook, kah
numwapegk nippe ut kehtohhannit, kah
puppinshasog muttaanhettich ohket.
23 Kah mo wanonkooouk kah mo mohtompog napanna audtahshikquinukok,

24 Kah

 ELIOT'S INDIAN BIBLE, 1663

§. 7. *Demon rentrant. Rechûtes.*

43 Lorſque l'eſprit impur eſt ſorti d'un hom- *Luc 11.*
me il va dans des lieux arides cherchant du re- 24.
pos, & il n'en trouve point.

44 Alors il dit : Je retourneray dans ma maiſon d'où je ſuis ſorti : & revenant il la trouve
vuide, nettoyée, & parée.

45 En même temps il va prendre avec luy
ſept autres eſprits plus meſchans que luy ; & en-
trant *dans cette maiſon*, ils y habitent : & le der- 2. *Pier.* 2.
nier eſtat de cet homme devient pire que le pre- 20.
mier. C'eſt ce qui arrivera à cette race crimi-
nelle.

§. 8. *Mere & Freres de Jeſus Chriſt.*

46 Lorſqu'il parloit encore au peuple, ſa me- *Marc* 3.
re & ſes freres eſtoient dehors, qui demandoient 31.
à luy parler. *Luc* 8. 19.

47 Et quelqu'un luy dit : Voilà voſtre mere,
& vos freres qui ſont dehors, & qui vous de-
mandent.

48 Mais il répondit à cette perſonne : Qui eſt
ma mere, & qui ſont mes freres ?

49 Et étendant ſa main ſur ſes diſciples : Voicy, dit-il, ma mere, & voicy mes freres.

50 Car quiconque fait la volonté de mon pe-
re qui eſt dans le ciel, celuy là eſt mon frere, ma
ſœur, & ma mere ¶.

CHAPITRE XIII.

§. 1. *Parabole des ſemences. Cœurs aveuglez.*
Heureux l'œil qui voit.

1 CE même jour JESUS eſtant ſorti de
la maiſon s'aſſit auprés de la mer. *Marc* 4. 1.
2 Et une ſi grande multitude de perſonnes *Luc* 8. 4.

41 THE MONS NEW TESTAMENT, 1667

29. Wenn ihr aber wollt dem HERRN ein lobopfer thun, das für euch angenehm sey;
30. So sollt ihrs desselben tages essen, und sollt nichts übrig bis auf den morgen behalten: Denn Ich bin der HERR.
31. Darum * haltet meine gebote, und thut darnach: Denn Ich bin der HERR. * c. 18, 30.
32. Daß ihr meinen heiligen namen nicht entheiliget, und ich geheiliget werde unter den kindern Israel; Denn Ich bin der HErr, der euch heiliget;
33. Der euch aus Egyptenland geführet hat, daß ich euer GOtt wäre, Ich der HERR.

Das 23 Capitel.

Ordnung der vornehmsten feste.

UND der HERR redete mit Mose, und sprach:
2. Sage den kindern Israel, und sprich zu ihnen: Dis sind die feste des HERRN, die ihr heilig und meine feste heissen sollt, da ihr zusammen komt.
3. Sechs * tage solt du arbeiten; der siebende tag aber ist der grosse heilige sabbath, da ihr zusammen kommt: Keine arbeit sollt ihr drinnen thun: Denn es ist der sabbath des HERRN, in allen euren wohnungen. * 2 Mos. 20, 8. 9. &c.
4. Dis sind aber die feste des HERRN, die ihr heilige feste heissen sollt, da ihr zusammen kommt:
5. Am * vierzehenden tage des ersten monats zwischen † abend ist des HERRN passah. * 2 Mos. 12, 18. c. 23, 15. † 2 Mos. 12, 6.
6. Und am fünfzehenden desselben monats ist das fest der ungesäuerten brod des HERRN: Da sollt ihr * sieben tage ungesäuert brod essen. * 2 Mos. 12, 15.
7. Der erste tag soll heilig unter euch heissen, da ihr zusammen kommt: Da sollt ihr keine dienstarbeit thun.
8. Und dem HERRN opfern sieben tage. Der siebende tag soll auch heilig heissen, da ihr zusammen kommt: Da sollt ihr auch keine dienstarbeit thun.
9. Und der HERR redete mit Mose, und sprach:
10. Sage den kindern Israel und sprich zu ihnen: wenn ihr ins land kommt, das Ich euch geben werde, und werdets ernten: So sollt ihr eine garbe der erstlinge eurer ernte zu dem priester bringen.
¶ 11. Da soll die garbe gewebet werden vor dem HERRN, daß es von euch angenehm sey: Solches soll aber der priester thun des andern tages nach dem sabbath.
12. Und solt des tages, da eure garbe gewebet wird, ein brandopfer dem HERRN thun, von einem lamm, das ohne wandel und jährig sey,
13. Samt dem speisopfer, zwo zehenden semmelmehl mit öhl gemenget, zum opfer dem HERRN eines süssen geruchs; dazu das tranckopfer, ein viertheil Hin weins.
14. Und sollt kein neu brod, noch sangen, noch korn zuvor essen, bis auf den tag, da ihr eurem GOtt opfer bringet. Das * soll ein recht seyn euren nachkommen in allen euren wohnungen. * c. 6, 18. 2 Mos. 27, 21.
15. Darnach sollt ihr zehlen vom * andern tage des sabbaths, da ihr die webegarbe brachtet, sieben gantzer sabbath, * 5 Mos. 16, 9. 10.
16. Bis an den andern tag des siebenden sabbaths, nemlich fünfzig tage sollt ihr zehlen, und neu speisopfer dem HERRN opfern.
17. Und sollts aus allen euren wohnungen opfern, nemlich zwey webebrod von zwo zehenden semmelmehl, gesäuert und gebacken, zu erstlingen dem HERRN.
18. Und sollt herzubringen, neben eurem brod, sieben-jährige lämmer ohne wandel, und Einen jungen farren, und zween widder: Das soll des HERRN brandopfer, speisopfer und tranckopfer seyn, das ist ein opfer eines süssen geruchs dem HERRN.
19. Dazu sollt ihr machen Einen ziegenbock zum sündopfer, und zwey jährige lämmer zum danckopfer.
20. Und der priester solls weben samt dem brod der erstlinge vor dem HERRN, und den zweyen lämmern; und soll dem HERRN heilig, und des priesters seyn.
21. Und sollt diesen tag ausruffen, denn er soll unter euch heilig heissen, da ihr zusammen kommt, keine dienstarbeit sollt ihr thun. Ein ewiges recht soll das seyn bey euren nachkommen in allen euren wohnungen.
22. Wenn ihr aber * euer land erntet, sollt ihrs nicht gar auf dem felde einschneiden, auch nicht alles genau auflesen, sondern sollts den armen und fremdlingen lassen: Ich bin der HERR, euer GOtt. * c. 19, 9. &c.
23. Und der HERR redete mit Mose, und sprach:
24. Rede mit den kindern Israel, und sprich: Am ersten tag des siebenden monats sollt ihr den heiligen * sabbath des blasens zum gedächtniß halten, da ihr zusammen kommt; * 4 Mos. 29, 1.
25. Da solt ihr keine dienstarbeit thun, und sollt dem HERRN opfern.

P 2   26. Und

Z E C H A R I A H.

Before CHRIST cir. 520.

CHAP. I.

1 Zechariah exhorteth to repentance. 7 The viſion of the horſes. 12 At the prayer of the angel, comfortable promiſes are made to Jeruſalem. 18 The viſion of the four horns, and the four carpenters.

IN the eighth month, [a] in the ſecond year of Darius, came the word of the LORD [b] unto Zechariah, the ſon of Berechiah, the ſon of Iddo the prophet, ſaying,

2 The LORD hath been [*] ſore diſpleaſed with your fathers.

3 Therefore ſay thou unto them, Thus ſaith the LORD of hoſts; Turn [c] ye unto me, ſaith the LORD of hoſts, and I will turn unto you, ſaith the LORD of hoſts.

4 Be ye not as your fathers, unto whom the former prophets have cried, ſaying, Thus ſaith the LORD of hoſts; [d] Turn ye now from your evil ways, and *from* your evil doings: but they did not hear, nor hearken unto me, ſaith the LORD.

5 Your fathers, where *are* they? and the prophets, do they live for ever?

6 But my words and my ſtatutes, which I commanded my ſervants the prophets, did they not † take hold of your fathers? and they returned and ſaid, [e] Like as the LORD of hoſts thought to do unto us, according to our ways, and according to our doings, ſo hath he dealt with us.

cir. 519. 7 ¶ Upon the four and twentieth day of the eleventh month, which *is* the month Sebat, in the ſecond year of Darius, came the word of the LORD unto Zechariah, the ſon of Berechiah, the ſon of Iddo the prophet, ſaying,

8 I ſaw by night, and behold, [f] a man riding upon a red horſe, and he ſtood among the myrtle-trees that *were* in the bottom; and behind him *were there* [g] red horſes, ‡ ſpeckled, and white.

9 Then ſaid I, O my lord, what *are* theſe? And the angel that talked with me, ſaid unto me, I will ſhew thee what theſe be.

10 And the man that ſtood among the myrtle-trees anſwered, and ſaid, Theſe *are they* whom the LORD hath ſent to walk to and fro through the earth.

11 And they anſwered the angel of the LORD that ſtood among the myrtle-trees, and ſaid, We have walked to and fro through the earth, and behold, all the earth ſitteth ſtill, and is at reſt.

12 ¶ Then the angel of the LORD anſwered and ſaid, [h] O LORD of hoſts, how long wilt thou not have mercy on Jeruſalem, and on the cities of Judah, againſt which thou haſt had indignation [i] theſe threeſcore and ten years?

13 And the LORD anſwered the angel that talked with me, *with* good words, *and* comfortable words.

14 So the angel that communed with me, ſaid unto me, Cry thou, ſaying, Thus ſaith the LORD of hoſts; I am [k] jealous for Jeruſalem and for Zion with a great jealouſy.

15 And I am very ſore diſpleaſed with the heathen *that are* at eaſe: for [l] I was but a little diſpleaſed, and they helped forward the affliction.

16 Therefore thus ſaith the LORD; I am returned to Jeruſalem with mercies: my houſe ſhall be built in it, ſaith the LORD of hoſts, and a line ſhall be ſtretched forth upon Jeruſalem.

17 Cry yet, ſaying, Thus ſaith the LORD of hoſts; My cities through ‖ proſperity ſhall yet be ſpread abroad; and the LORD ſhall yet comfort Zion, and [m] ſhall yet chooſe Jeruſalem.

18 ¶ Then lifted I up mine eyes, and ſaw, and behold, four horns.

19 And I ſaid unto the angel that talked with me, What *be* theſe? And he anſwered me, [n] Theſe *are* the horns which have ſcattered Judah, Iſrael, and Jeruſalem.

20 And the LORD ſhewed me four carpenters.

21 Then ſaid I, What come theſe to do? And he ſpake, ſaying, Theſe *are* the horns which have ſcattered Judah, ſo that no man did lift up his head: but theſe are come to fray them, to caſt out the horns of the Gentiles, which lifted up *their* horn over the land of Judah to ſcatter it.

Before CHRIST cir. 519.

CHAP. II.

1 God, in the care of Jeruſalem, ſendeth to meaſure it. 6 The redemption of Zion. 10 The promiſe of God's preſence.

I Lifted up mine eyes again, and looked, and behold, [a] a man with a meaſuring-line in his hand. 519.

2 Then ſaid I, Whither goeſt thou? And he ſaid unto me, [b] To meaſure Jeruſalem, to ſee what *is* the breadth thereof, and what *is* the length thereof.

3 And behold, the angel that talked with me, went forth, and another angel went out to meet him,

4 And ſaid unto him, Run, ſpeak to this young man, ſaying, Jeruſalem ſhall be inhabited *as* towns without walls for the multitude of men and cattle therein.

5 For I, ſaith the LORD, will be unto her a wall of fire round about, [c] and will be the glory in the midſt of her.

6 ¶ Ho, ho, *come forth*, and flee [d] from the land of the north, ſaith the LORD: for I have ſpread you abroad as the four winds of the heaven, ſaith the LORD.

7 [e] Deliver thyſelf, O Zion, that dwelleſt *with* the daughter of Babylon.

8 For thus ſaith the LORD of hoſts; After the

[a] Ezra 4. 24. Hag. 1. 1. [b] Ezra 5. 1. [*] Heb. *with diſpleaſure.* [c] Jer. 25. 5. & 35. 15. Mic. 7. 19. Mal. 3. 7. [d] Iſa. 31. 6. Jer. 3. 12. & 18. 11. Ezek. 18. 30. Hoſ. 14. 1. † Or, *overtake.* [e] Lam. 1. 18. [f] Joſh. 5. 13. [g] ch. 6. 1—7. ‡ Or, *bay.* [h] Rev. 6. 10. [i] Dan. 9. 2. ch. 7. 5. [k] ch. 8. 2.

[l] Iſa. 47. 6. ‖ Heb. *good.* [m] Iſa. 14. 1. ch. 2. 12. [n] Ezra 4. 1, 4, 7. & 5. 3. [a] Ezek. 40. 3. [b] Rev. 11. 1. [c] Iſa. 60. 19. Rev. 21. 23. [d] Iſa. 48. 20. & 52. 11. Jer. 1. 14. & 50. 8. & 51. 6. 45. [e] Rev. 18. 4.

43 THE BASKERVILLE BIBLE, 1763

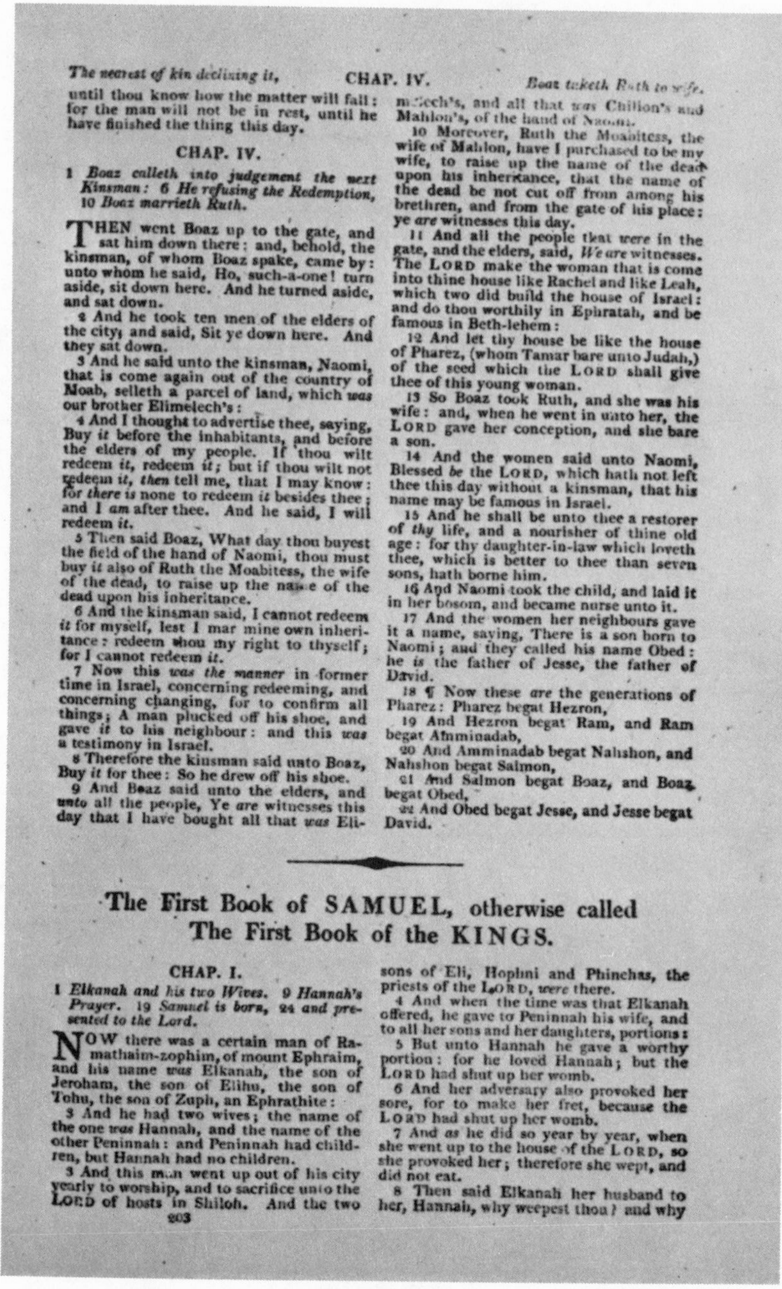

until thou know how the matter will fall: for the man will not be in rest, until he have finished the thing this day.

CHAP. IV.

1 *Boaz calleth into judgement the next Kinsman:* 6 *He refusing the Redemption,* 10 *Boaz marrieth Ruth.*

THEN went Boaz up to the gate, and sat him down there: and, behold, the kinsman, of whom Boaz spake, came by: unto whom he said, Ho, such-a-one! turn aside, sit down here. And he turned aside, and sat down.

2 And he took ten men of the elders of the city, and said, Sit ye down here. And they sat down.

3 And he said unto the kinsman, Naomi, that is come again out of the country of Moab, selleth a parcel of land, which *was* our brother Elimelech's:

4 And I thought to advertise thee, saying, Buy *it* before the inhabitants, and before the elders of my people. If thou wilt redeem *it*, redeem *it*; but if thou wilt not redeem *it*, *then* tell me, that I may know: for *there is* none to redeem *it* besides thee; and I *am* after thee. And he said, I will redeem *it*.

5 Then said Boaz, What day thou buyest the field of the hand of Naomi, thou must buy *it* also of Ruth the Moabitess, the wife of the dead, to raise up the name of the dead upon his inheritance.

6 And the kinsman said, I cannot redeem *it* for myself, lest I mar mine own inheritance: redeem thou my right to thyself; for I cannot redeem *it*.

7 Now this *was the manner* in former time in Israel, concerning redeeming, and concerning changing, for to confirm all things; A man plucked off his shoe, and gave *it* to his neighbour: and this *was* a testimony in Israel.

8 Therefore the kinsman said unto Boaz, Buy *it* for thee: So he drew off his shoe.

9 And Boaz said unto the elders, and *unto* all the people, Ye *are* witnesses this day that I have bought all that *was* Elimelech's, and all that *was* Chilion's and Mahlon's, of the hand of Naomi.

10 Moreover, Ruth the Moabitess, the wife of Mahlon, have I purchased to be my wife, to raise up the name of the dead upon his inheritance, that the name of the dead be not cut off from among his brethren, and from the gate of his place: ye *are* witnesses this day.

11 And all the people that *were* in the gate, and the elders, said, *We are* witnesses. The LORD make the woman that is come into thine house like Rachel and like Leah, which two did build the house of Israel: and do thou worthily in Ephratah, and be famous in Beth-lehem:

12 And let thy house be like the house of Pharez, (whom Tamar bare unto Judah,) of the seed which the LORD shall give thee of this young woman.

13 So Boaz took Ruth, and she was his wife: and, when he went in unto her, the LORD gave her conception, and she bare a son.

14 And the women said unto Naomi, Blessed *be* the LORD, which hath not left thee this day without a kinsman, that his name may be famous in Israel.

15 And he shall be unto thee a restorer of *thy* life, and a nourisher of thine old age: for thy daughter-in-law which loveth thee, which is better to thee than seven sons, hath borne him.

16 And Naomi took the child, and laid it in her bosom, and became nurse unto it.

17 And the women her neighbours gave it a name, saying, There is a son born to Naomi; and they called his name Obed: he *is* the father of Jesse, the father of David.

18 ¶ Now these *are* the generations of Pharez: Pharez begat Hezron,

19 And Hezron begat Ram, and Ram begat Amminadab,

20 And Amminadab begat Nahshon, and Nahshon begat Salmon,

21 And Salmon begat Boaz, and Boaz begat Obed,

22 And Obed begat Jesse, and Jesse begat David.

The First Book of SAMUEL, otherwise called The First Book of the KINGS.

CHAP. I.

1 *Elkanah and his two Wives.* 9 *Hannah's Prayer.* 19 *Samuel is born,* 24 *and presented to the Lord.*

NOW there was a certain man of Ramathaim-zophim, of mount Ephraim, and his name *was* Elkanah, the son of Jeroham, the son of Elihu, the son of Tohu, the son of Zuph, an Ephrathite:

2 And he had two wives; the name of the one *was* Hannah, and the name of the other Peninnah: and Peninnah had children, but Hannah had no children.

3 And this man went up out of his city yearly to worship, and to sacrifice unto the LORD of hosts in Shiloh. And the two sons of Eli, Hophni and Phinehas, the priests of the LORD, *were* there.

4 And when the time was that Elkanah offered, he gave to Peninnah his wife, and to all her sons and her daughters, portions:

5 But unto Hannah he gave a worthy portion: for he loved Hannah; but the LORD had shut up her womb.

6 And her adversary also provoked her sore, for to make her fret, because the LORD had shut up her womb.

7 And *as* he did so year by year, when she went up to the house of the LORD, so she provoked her; therefore she wept, and did not eat.

8 Then said Elkanah her husband to her, Hannah, why weepest thou? and why

44 THE CAMBRIDGE STEREOTYPE BIBLE, 1806

THE BRASEN SERPENT.—RUBENS.

us up out of Egypt to die in the wilderness?
for *there is* no bread, neither *is there any*
water; and [5]our soul loatheth this light
bread.
6 And [6]the LORD sent fiery serpents
among the people, and they bit the people;
and much people of Israel died.
7 ¶ Therefore the people came to Moses,
and said, We have sinned, for we have spoken
against the LORD, and against thee; pray
unto the LORD, that he take away the serpents from us. And Moses prayed for the
people.
8 And the LORD said unto Moses, Make
thee a fiery serpent, and set it upon a pole:
and it shall come to pass, that every one
that is bitten, when he looketh upon it, shall
live.
9 And [7]Moses made a serpent of brass,
and put it upon a pole, and it came to pass,
that if a serpent had bitten any man, when
he beheld the serpent of brass, he lived.
10 ¶ And the children of Israel set forward, and [8]pitched in Oboth.
11 And they journeyed from Oboth, and
pitched at [9]Ije-abarim, in the wilderness
which *is* before Moab, toward the sunrising.
12 ¶ From thence they removed, and
pitched in the valley of Zared.
13 From thence they removed, and pitched
on the other side of Arnon, which *is* in the
wilderness that cometh out of the coasts of
the Amorites: for Arnon *is* the border of
Moab, between Moab and the Amorites.
14 Wherefore it is said in the book of the
wars of the LORD, [10]What he did in the Red
sea, and in the brooks of Arnon,
15 And at the stream of the brooks that
goeth down to the dwelling of Ar, and [11]lieth
upon the border of Moab.

[5] Chap. 11. 6. [6] Wisd. 16. 1, 5. 1 Cor. 10. 9. [7] 2 Kings 18. 4. John 3. 14. [8] Chap. 33. 43. [9] Or, *heaps of Abarim.* [10] Or, *Vaheb in Suphah.* [11] Heb. *leaneth.*

45 CHARLES KNIGHT'S PICTORIAL BIBLE, 1836

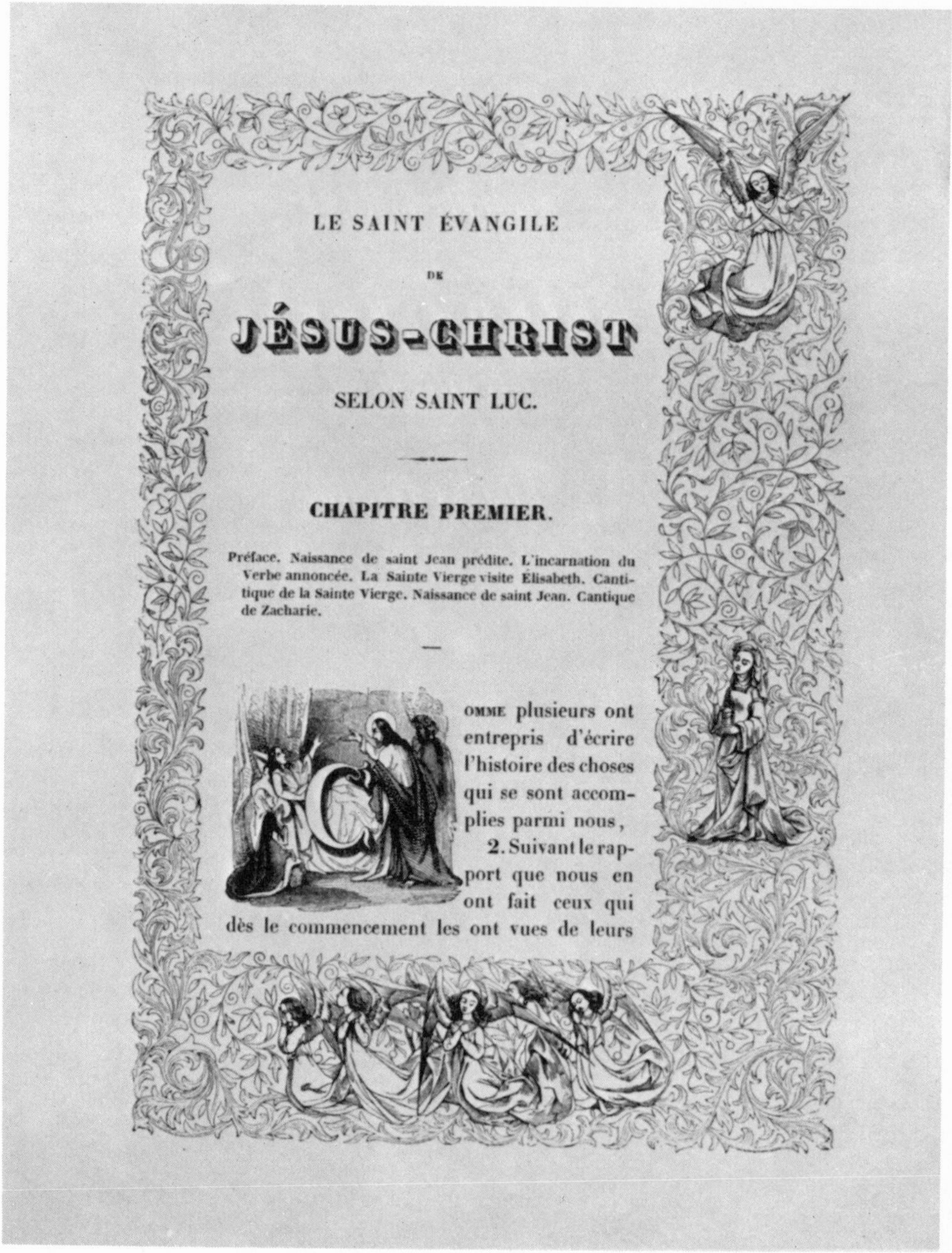

LE SAINT ÉVANGILE

DE

JÉSUS-CHRIST

SELON SAINT LUC.

CHAPITRE PREMIER.

Préface. Naissance de saint Jean prédite. L'incarnation du Verbe annoncée. La Sainte Vierge visite Élisabeth. Cantique de la Sainte Vierge. Naissance de saint Jean. Cantique de Zacharie.

Comme plusieurs ont entrepris d'écrire l'histoire des choses qui se sont accomplies parmi nous,

2. Suivant le rapport que nous en ont fait ceux qui dès le commencement les ont vues de leurs

46 A FRENCH ILLUSTRATED GOSPEL BOOK, 1836

IN THE BEGINNING GOD CREATED THE HEAVEN AND THE EARTH. ¶ AND THE EARTH WAS WITHOUT FORM, AND VOID; AND DARKNESS WAS UPON THE FACE OF THE DEEP, & THE SPIRIT OF GOD MOVED UPON THE FACE OF THE WATERS. ¶ And God said, Let there be light: & there was light. And God saw the light, that it was good: & God divided the light from the darkness. And God called the light Day, and the darkness he called Night. And the evening and the morning were the first day. ¶ And God said, Let there be a firmament in the midst of the waters, & let it divide the waters from the waters. And God made the firmament, and divided the waters which were under the firmament from the waters which were above the firmament: & it was so. And God called the firmament Heaven. And the evening & the morning were the second day. ¶ And God said, Let the waters under the heaven be gathered together unto one place, and let the dry land appear: and it was so. And God called the dry land Earth; and the gathering together of the waters called he Seas: and God saw that it was good. And God said, Let the earth bring forth grass, the herb yielding seed, and the fruit tree yielding fruit after his kind, whose seed is in itself, upon the earth: & it was so. And the earth brought forth grass, & herb yielding seed after his kind, & the tree yielding fruit, whose seed was in itself, after his kind: and God saw that it was good. And the evening & the morning were the third day. ¶ And God said, Let there be lights in the firmament of the heaven to divide the day from the night; and let them be for signs, and for seasons, and for days, & years: and let them be for lights in the firmament of the heaven to give light upon the earth: & it was so. And God made two great lights; the greater light to rule the day, and the lesser light to rule the night: he made the stars also. And God set them in the firmament of the heaven to give light upon the earth, and to rule over the day and over the night, & to divide the light from the darkness: and God saw that it was good. And the evening and the morning were the fourth day. ¶ And God said, Let the waters bring forth abundantly the moving creature that hath life, and fowl that may fly above the earth in the open firmament of heaven. And God created great whales, & every living creature that moveth, which the waters brought forth abundantly, after their kind, & every winged fowl after his kind: & God saw that it was good. And God blessed them, saying, Be fruitful, & multiply, and fill the waters in the seas, and let fowl multiply in the earth. And the evening & the morning were the fifth day. ¶ And God said, Let the earth bring forth the living creature after his kind, cattle, and creeping thing, and beast of the earth after his kind: and it was so. And God made the beast of the earth after his kind, and cattle after their kind, and every thing that creepeth upon the

27

47 THE DOVES PRESS BIBLE

say, Cast ye up, cast ye up, prepare the way,
take up the stumblingblock out of the way of
my people. ¶15 For thus saith the high and lofty
One that inhabiteth eternity, whose name is
Holy; I dwell in the high and holy place, with
him also that is of a contrite and humble spirit,
to revive the spirit of the humble, and to revive
the heart of the contrite ones. ¶16 For I will not
contend for ever, neither will I be always wroth:
for the spirit should fail before me, and the souls
which I have made. ¶17 For the iniquity of his
covetousness was I wroth, and smote him: I hid
me, and was wroth, and he went on frowardly
in the way of his heart. ¶18 I have seen his ways,
and will heal him: I will lead him also, and
restore comforts unto him and to his mourners.
¶19 I create the fruit of the lips; Peace, peace
to him that is far off, and to him that is near,
saith the LORD; and I will heal him. ¶20 But
the wicked are like the troubled sea, when it
cannot rest, whose waters cast up mire and dirt.
¶21 There is no peace, saith my God, to the
wicked.

CHAPTER 58

CRY aloud, spare not, lift up thy voice like
a trumpet, and shew my people their
transgression, and the house of Jacob their
sins. ¶2 Yet they seek me daily, and delight to
know my ways, as a nation that did righteousness, and forsook not the ordinance of their God:
they ask of me the ordinances of justice; they
take delight in approaching to God.

¶3 Wherefore have we fasted, say they, and
thou seest not? wherefore have we afflicted our
soul, and thou takest no knowledge? Behold, in
the day of your fast ye find pleasure, and exact
all your labours. ¶4 Behold, ye fast for strife
and debate, and to smite with the fist of wickedness: ye shall not fast as ye do this day, to make
your voice to be heard on high. ¶5 Is it such a
fast that I have chosen? a day for a man to afflict
his soul? is it to bow down his head as a bulrush,
and to spread sackcloth and ashes under him?
wilt thou call this a fast, and an acceptable day
to the LORD? ¶6 Is not this the fast that I have
chosen? to loose the bands of wickedness, to
undo the heavy burdens, and to let the oppressed
go free, and that ye break every yoke? ¶7 Is it
not to deal thy bread to the hungry, and that
thou bring the poor that are cast out to thy
house? when thou seest the naked, that thou
cover him; and that thou hide not thyself from
thine own flesh?

¶8 Then shall thy light break forth as the
morning, and thine health shall spring forth
speedily: and thy righteousness shall go before
thee; the glory of the LORD shall be thy rere-
ward. ¶9 Then shalt thou call, and the LORD
shall answer; thou shalt cry, and he shall say,
Here I am. If thou take away from the midst
of thee the yoke, the putting forth of the finger,
and speaking vanity; ¶10 And if thou draw out
thy soul to the hungry, and satisfy the afflicted
soul; then shall thy light rise in obscurity, and
thy darkness be as the noon day: ¶11 And the
LORD shall guide thee continually, and satisfy
thy soul in drought, and make fat thy bones:
and thou shalt be like a watered garden, and like
a spring of water, whose waters fail not. ¶12 And
they that shall be of thee shall build the old
waste places: thou shalt raise up the foundations
of many generations; and thou shalt be called,
The repairer of the breach, The restorer of paths
to dwell in.

¶13 If thou turn away thy foot from the
sabbath, from doing thy pleasure on my holy
day; and call the sabbath a delight, the holy of
the LORD, honourable; and shalt honour him,
not doing thine own ways, nor finding thine
own pleasure, nor speaking thine own words:
¶14 Then shalt thou delight thyself in the LORD;
and I will cause thee to ride upon the high places
of the earth, and feed thee with the heritage of
Jacob thy father: for the mouth of the LORD
hath spoken it.

CHAPTER 59

BEHOLD, the LORD's hand is not shortened,
that it cannot save; neither his ear heavy,
that it cannot hear: ¶2 But your iniquities
have separated between you and your God, and
your sins have hid his face from you, that he
will not hear. ¶3 For your hands are defiled with
blood, and your fingers with iniquity; your lips
have spoken lies, your tongue hath muttered per-
verseness. ¶4 None calleth for justice, nor any
pleadeth for truth: they trust in vanity, and speak
lies; they conceive mischief, and bring forth iniquity. ¶5 They hatch cockatrice' eggs, and weave

INDEXES

GENERAL INDEX

General Index

General Index

General Index

INDEX TO BIBLE REFERENCES

OLD TESTAMENT

APOCRYPHA

(*see also main Index*)

NEW TESTAMENT